The Transformation
of Palestine

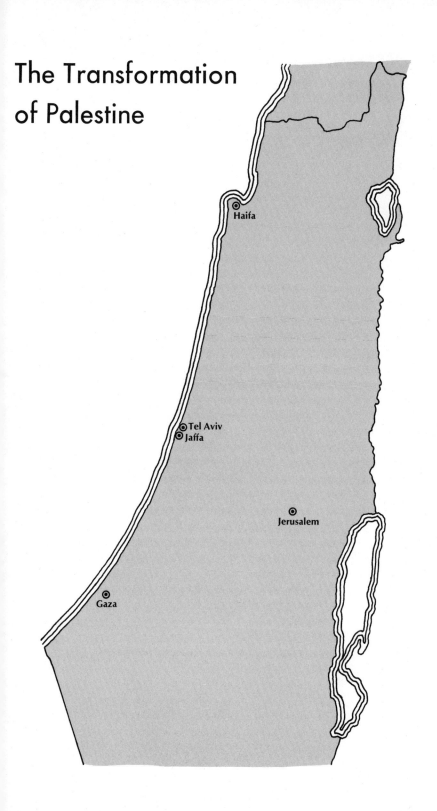

Haifa

Tel Aviv
Jaffa

Jerusalem

Gaza

The Transformation of Palestine

Essays on the Origin and Development of the Arab-Israeli Conflict

edited by Ibrahim Abu-Lughod

with a foreword by Arnold J. Toynbee

Northwestern University Press
Evanston 1971

Library of Congress Catalog Card Number: 71–137791
ISBN 0–8101–0345–1
Copyright © 1971 by Ibrahim Abu-Lughod
All rights reserved
Printed in the United States of America

Ibrahim Abu-Lughod is Professor of Political Science and
Associate Director of the Program of African Studies at
Northwestern University.
He is the author of *Arab Rediscovery of Europe* and edi-
tor of *The Arab-Israeli Confrontation of June 1967*.

Contents

Foreword

This book supports the Arab case in the conflict over Palestine. The presentation is nonpolemical and factual. It will be enlightening for readers who have assumed that Israeli claims are so obviously valid that they do not need arguing and who have been unaware, so far, that there is such a thing as a case for the Arabs.

Readers who start from this position will not find in the book anything that might incline them to discount it as being partisan propaganda. They will find in it facts that are well documented, and these facts are set out by scholars whose first concern is to ascertain and communicate the truth. If this is also the readers' first concern, the book may lead them to reconsider previous opinions that they may have formed without having verified the statements and assumptions on which these opinions have been based. If these readers are responsible-minded citizens of the "one world" in which we are all now living, they will go beyond revising their opinions; they will go on to change the political action that their former opinions have led them to take.

This, in turn, might change the course of public events. An uncritical sympathy and support for Israel has been very widespread. It has influenced the policy of the government of the United States, and the United States and the Soviet Union, between them, have in their hands the future of the Middle East. Since the publication of the Balfour Declaration in 1917, the situation in the Middle East has progressively worsened. This is a tragedy that cannot be kept confined within geographical limits. It is a tragedy for the Arabs today. By tomorrow it may have become a tragedy for the whole world. The Middle Eastern conflict carries in itself the seeds of world war.

One of the strangest features of the conflict over Palestine is that it should be necessary to demonstrate that the Arabs have a case. By now, there are more than one million Palestinian Arab refugees. Their ancestral homes are in Israeli hands, and so is the property of those of them whose homes are on the Israeli side of the armistice lines of 1949. If this treatment had been suffered by any people other than the Arabs, and if it had been inflicted by any other than the Israelis, the whole world would have recognized that an enormous wrong had been committed against victims who had done nothing to deserve it—this flagrant breach of human rights would have evoked not only indignation and remonstrance but effective action to undo the injustice.

The present generation of mankind is sensitive, in general, to human suffering anywhere in the world—in Nigeria, for instance, and in Vietnam. The Arabs' sufferings have been disregarded by the world as callously as the wrongs by which the sufferings have been caused. Yet there is no reason why the Arabs' case should be ignored or why the Israelis' conduct should be condoned. Right and wrong are the same in Palestine as anywhere else. What is peculiar about the Palestine conflict is that the world has listened to the party that has committed the offense and has turned a deaf ear to the victims.

The chapter on vision and intent in Zionist thought shows, by examining the successive stages of the Zionist movement until now, that the Zionists have ambitions that are unlimited though unavowed. The extent of these ambitions has been unfolding itself at each step in the movement's advance. No limit is set and no end is in sight. The history of the drafting of the Balfour Declaration shows that the British government that underwrote it was cognizant of the Zionists' ultimate aims. Its action was therefore more irresponsible than is apparent from the final wording of the repeatedly redrafted text. If British statesmen supposed that they would be able to keep Zionism, once given an opening, within the limits that they laid down for it, they were naïve. Insofar as they foresaw what the Balfour Declaration was going to lead to, they were more cynical and dishonest than they have confessed themselves to have been. In the light of the declaration's origins and sequel, British assurances to the Arabs ring hollow.

The second part of the book, on the land and demographic transformation of Palestine, is particularly revealing. Study the figures of the population and the ownership of land in the area on the Israeli side of the 1949 armistice lines on the eve of the war of 1948—the scale of the Zionist immigrants' spoliation of the Arab inhabitants is startling. The Arabs had been there for thirteen centuries—that is to say, for as long as the Jews during their first occupation of a patch of the country and for nearly twice as long as the Ten Tribes that constituted the ancient kingdom of Israel. The Palestinian Arabs did not leave their homes voluntarily or in obedience to instructions from the governments of the adjoining Arab states. They fled from fear of death. The terrorism, made convincing by local measures, to which the Israelis resorted in order to clear the Arabs out, is exposed, with chapter and verse, belying the legend that has been given currency by Israeli propaganda.

The facts presented in Part II are shocking; the international perspectives analyzed in Part V are alarming. If the conflict were confined to Palestine, the injustice and the suffering would be bad enough. But the immediate parties to the Palestinian conflict have become pawns in a worldwide power game. No doubt the United States and the Soviet Union do not intend to be drawn into war with one another over Palestine. Both superpowers have enough preoccupations in Eastern Asia to disincline them from deliberately involving themselves in any other theater. If they were wholehearted in their desire for peace in the Middle East, they could impose a settlement; and, though no settlement could now fully redress the wrongs that have been inflicted on the Palestinian Arabs within the last half century, their sufferings could be reduced and at least some reparations could be made. Unhappily, neither of the superpowers seems yet to have made up its mind whether its wish to avoid the risk of war with its rival is to have the priority in determining its policy, or whether it is prepared to face the ever-increasing risk of its being involved directly in the Middle Eastern war for the sake of jockeying for local advantages in its pursuit of the competition for world power. This ambiguity in the attitude of both superpowers threatens to enlarge the tragedy in the Middle East into a tragedy for all mankind.

There is a nemesis for condoning wrongs, as well as for committing them. The world has condoned the wrong that has been done to the Palestinian Arabs by Zionism. The Palestinian Arabs have been despoiled and evicted by force, and the force by which they have been coerced was first British before the Israelis built up the military strength to do their own fighting—with American supplies of arms and American economic and political support. The responsibility for the wrong done to the Palestinian Arabs is widespread: now nations and individuals alike must assume the imperative task of informing themselves of the nature of the conflict in the Middle East. That is why the present book is needed. It is a pity that it has come so late in the day.

ARNOLD J. TOYNBEE

Preface

In the wake of the bicommunal Palestinian war of 1947–48 and the Arab-Israeli hostilities of 1948, Palestine was politically transformed into Israel, an Egyptian-administered Gaza Strip, and a Jordanian West Bank. That political transformation had the apparent effect of transforming the original conflict between European and Arab in Palestine into one between nation states in which the protagonists are thought to be primarily Israel and the three adjacent Arab states. The "national" character of the conflict has been reinforced in the public mind not only by all writings on the conflict since 1948, irrespective of their source, but additionally by the periodic eruption of war, the perennial deliberations in the United Nations, which address themselves to sovereign states, and by the coverage of the conflict in the mass media.

The impact of these writings and deliberations has been toward designation of the conflict as the Arab-Israeli conflict, and projected solutions to the conflict hitherto have been decisively affected by that designation. Occasionally, intermittently, and differentially, a reminder is interjected to the effect that the conflict had its origin in Palestine and the people most adversely affected by its outcome should raise serious concern. That they have been designated as "refugees" had the effect in the public mind of removing them as an original party to the conflict and projecting them as a "problem" in search of a solution. In that context, the Palestinian people became a secondary factor in the Arab-Israeli conflict.

Such emphases as these do in some measure reflect an apparent reality in that the current actors on the stage are some Arab states and Israel. But that this was not always the case is quite evident; two events in recent history suffice to remind us that the conflict in the Middle East is one with a history which at different times in its evolution involved other actors with more pressing and perhaps more decisive claims. For two successive years, in December of 1969 and of 1970, the United Nations passed resolutions reaffirming "the inalienable rights of the Palestinian people," and thereby reminded all concerned that one of the two original parties to the conflict had been denied the exercise of those rights. It was not accidental that the United Nations passed these resolutions; since the June war of 1967 the Palestinian people have reasserted their initiative and pressed their claims to Palestine more forcefully than at any time since 1947–48. And by doing so they helped focus the attention of the world community on their deep and long-standing grievance and claims.

In this sense, the need for a volume that addresses itself more clearly and directly to the original and basic conflict that has set Israel against some Arab states is overdue. Its relevance was enhanced not only by the eruption of war in June, 1967, but more significantly by the postwar developments. For as the reader is fully aware, the Palestinian resistance, which the defeat of the three Arab states helped spark, has demonstrated not only its potential for considerable regional upheaval but the direct involvement of the superpowers in the defense of their respective allies has also generated tensions that transcend the territorial confines of the conflict. The recession of a potentially world-wide conflict, its eventual containment, and finally the successful solution of the original conflict cannot be effected without an understanding of the issues of contention among the protagonists—real and apparent. In that sense, the objective of this volume is two-fold: on the one hand it seeks to make an important contribution to the scholarly understanding of the underlying issues involved in the Arab-Israeli conflict and, on the other, by clarifying these issues it aims at the promotion of serious efforts that seek a solution to the conflict.

Accordingly the major thrust of the essays in this volume is toward the Palestine, rather than the more derivative Arab-Israeli, conflict. Collectively they not only analyze the vision and aspirations of the original protagonists but additionally highlight the major issues of contention among them set against their historic regional or European background. And while they clarify the original issues that set European against Arab in Palestine and analyze critically the process of its political transformation, they also address themselves to the eventual implications of that transformation.

The underlying rationale for undertaking the study in this particular form should be evident. Hitherto, the scholarship on the Palestine or the Arab-Israeli conflict reflects serious shortcomings. For one thing, most writings tend to reflect the predominant "national" or ethnic perspective of the writers; for another, the findings tend to confirm the assumption that the conflict is one between sovereign states. The current reader is therefore entitled to an appreciation of the history and evolution of the conflict from a scholarly perspective not prejudiced by the national commitments of the authors or their assumptions. This volume provides correctives for the imbalance in two ways: in the first place, the authors are specialists in disciplines combining professional concern with the cultures of the Middle East with personal familiarity with the region; in the second place, no author is an Arab or a Zionist. As is evident from the brief biographical notes, they have made significant scholarly contributions to Middle East studies.

Time may have failed to heal the wounds the Palestine conflict generated, and time may have obfuscated the original issues involved in it—but there should be no question about the timely relevance of the findings embodied in this volume.

IBRAHIM ABU-LUGHOD

Acknowledgments

The editor wishes to acknowledge his debt to and appreciation for the many whose help was instrumental in the publication of this volume. While many personal friends have been concerned with this work from its beginning, I wish to single out A. M. Kattan and S. Alami for special thanks. In revising the manuscript, the thoughtful, careful, and generous comments of Professors Charles J. Adams of McGill University and Robert A. Fernea of the University of Texas were most helpful.

In verification of data, tracking down sources, compiling and revising the bibliography, typing and retyping of the manuscript, and proof-reading, many of my students and friends gave generously of their time and talent. Vaughn Bishop, Sheila Levine, Claudia Horty, Barbara Teising, Michael Culhane, Donna Weaver, Gail Kaba, Dorothy Vines, William Longwell, and T. Khalidi have made especially significant contributions. The professional concern and critical judgment of the Northwestern University Press staff contributed considerably to the high quality of this publication. At all times in the preparation of this volume, Dr. Robert P. Armstrong, Director of the Press, gave wise counsel; Senior Editor Jack Putnam was ever ready with informed solutions to knotty problems; Ann Paden's perceptive judgment and editorial skills were generously placed and exploited; Elizabeth G. Stout skillfully coordinated design considerations. The greatest measure of appreciation is reserved for the authors, whose thoughtful and scholarly essays have more than rewarded the efforts of the many others who have been involved in the production of this book.

The authors and the editor wish to record their deep appreciation to Dr. Arnold J. Toynbee whose foreword honors this volume.

The Transformation
of Palestine

PART I

Palestine and
the Zionist Movement

That a discussion of the conflict over Palestine and, consequently, the origin of the Arab-Israeli conflict begins with an analysis of Zionist thought should require no comment. For it is certain that had Zionism failed to materialize, the world would not have witnessed the conflict over Palestine. Yet history and world conditions dictated otherwise; Zionism emerged and placed important demands on the world at large as well as on the specific environment in which it was to witness its partial fulfillment. Two immediate forces helped to produce what has come to pass. On the one hand, the particular and persistent Judaic theme of "return" provided the underpinning upon which Zionism was later to base its political aspiration. But more urgently, the explosive forces of European nationalism helped to produce a reaction among European people which was sometimes contradictory to, sometimes harmonious with, the vision of Europe, and which was frequently destructive. Zionism emerged in the European world of the nineteenth century; it articulated a political philosophy for European Jews who, like many of the other European people attracted by the idea of nationalism, then relied on it in pressing for the fulfillment of the Jewish identity by establishing a political community for Jews. But unlike other European people, the goal of the Zionists was to establish a state on non-European terrain. And when the Zionists eventually agreed that that state was to be in Palestine, the aspiration to possess Palestine became one of the principal factors of a conflict whose dimensions no one would have anticipated. In that context, the visions and inner ideas of Zionism become critical for an understanding of the possible happenings in Palestine.

Only a perceptive student of Zionist thought, fully apprehending the dynamics and fluidity of its philosophy, could provide the reader with an intimate appreciation of its origin and intent. Alan R. Taylor, Associate

3

Professor of History at the School of International Relations at the American University in Washington, has concerned himself with the thought and ideas presaging the political emergence of Israel. His book Prelude to Israel: An Analysis of Zionist Diplomacy, 1897–1947 *has often been quoted and acclaimed as a classic in that field. His equal concern with the Arab-Israeli conflict underlies another contribution of which he is co-editor:* Palestine: A Search for Truth. *His essay in this volume confines itself to an analysis of the inner forces of Zionist thought and of its territorial intent.*

Unlike Taylor, Richard P. Stevens, Professor and Chairman of the Department of Political Science at Lincoln University, is concerned with the pragmatic forces within, and to some extent external to, Europe which helped in the materialization of the Zionist vision in a particular terrain. It was quite evident from the beginning of the Zionist movement in Europe that the political community of Jews to be fashioned by Zionists in the territory of Palestine had to be accomplished within a certain framework and had to assume a specific form. Although Zionism was partially based on specifically Jewish inner forces, the European social and political milieu was of the greatest significance for the eventual attainment of statehood. Zionists, as Stevens and others have demonstrated, had to secure the support of a major power if they were to achieve their political objective. The great powers at the conclusion of the nineteenth century and in the first half of the twentieth were—as they are now—fiercely competitive. Zionists used that competitiveness to their advantage; they tried to induce the relevant power to extend the critically needed political, moral, and legal support. The competitiveness of the powers was related to their ambition for the domination and ultimate occupation of the Middle East, then still part of the political entity known to posterity as the Ottoman Empire. The aspiration of the Zionists to induce the Ottoman government to concede the political right of colonization of Palestine ultimately came to nought; hence the constant activity of Zionists in major capitals of the European world in the hope that the powers—those competing for the control, dismemberment, and eventual occupation of what was then euphemistically referred to as the "sick man of Europe"—would perceive the benefits to be derived from the support they could extend in realizing the Zionist dream.

That the Ottoman Empire was to be dismembered was evident. Its external weakness, manifest in its failure to withstand the steady and nagging encroachment of one or another European power, was symptomatic of its internal disorientation. The erosion of the military and political power of the Ottoman Empire was in no small measure related to the steady pressures exerted by its constituent communities for larger shares in its public affairs or, better still, for independent political communities. By the time the Zionists were pressing the major powers for recognition of the integrity and utility of their scheme for the colonization of Palestine (1897–1917), the Ottoman Empire had already relinquished control of Tunisia, Egypt, and Tripolitania to France, Great Britain, and Italy and was fighting a hopeless battle against the Arab nationalists of the Fertile Crescent. These too were anxiously seeking supportive allies who would assist them in their seemingly forlorn hope of constituting themselves into an Arab political community. The independent ambition of the European powers for the dismemberment of the Ottoman Empire was long contained by their mutual fears and suspicions of one another. Yet with the rise of independent nationalist movements within the empire actively seeking the same dismemberment but for a totally different objective, the subject assumed greater urgency.

The outbreak of the First World War provided creative opportunities for all parties concerned: for the Zionists, exigencies of war might provide the necessary leverage by which they could pressure one or another of the European powers to extend the recognition which had eluded them since 1897; for the Arab nationalists of the Fertile Crescent, an opportunity to obtain valuable assistance from the enemy of their common enemy by which they could concert their action to realize an independent status; for the powers, to confront once and for all the long-postponed question of dismemberment and to maximize their private holdings out of the wreckage of the Ottoman Empire. It was Great Britain that was finally to seize the initiative in recognizing the enormous possibilities inherent in the tangled conditions of war. Having reached an accord with the leadership of the Arab nationalist movement that was theoretically satisfactory for both, Great Britain proceeded toward the realization of its real objective by reaching a more satisfying accord with France—one that would allot to each particular territories in the Fertile Crescent. Instead of an eventually independent Arab state in the Fertile Crescent, the entire area was to be apportioned out, and new frontiers marking newer types of political jurisdiction and control by colonial powers were to be established.

A new political map was to be drawn in accordance with the Sykes-Picot Agreement of 1916, and entirely new self-definitions imposed by the colonial system were to emerge. Instead of an integral political community of the Arabs of the Fertile Crescent, the world was to be confronted with a fragmented territory, each part of which would assume a new name. It was within the context of that would-be divided area that mandated Palestine emerged, possessing a jurisdictional integrity conferred upon it by the European colonial system. And it was in the context of such frag-

mentation and in the presence of a new jurisdictional entity under the control of Great Britain that Zionist colonization of Palestine, even a political colonization, commended itself to Zionist as well as imperialist. For, as Professor Stevens clearly demonstrates, what happened in Palestine was neither unique nor incomprehensible. Placed against the background of European colonial expansion, a colonial settler regime might serve well an empire in search of vital bases and reliable terrain. A Zionist colonization of Palestine was to some extent perceived to fulfill those imperial needs that imperialists must protect.

That Israel is increasingly recognized as a settler regime is therefore not accidental but is rooted first in the empirical fact of colonization by Europeans and second in the circumstances of the acceptance of the legitimacy of the principle of colonization itself. Quite frequently scholars have looked at Palestine in a particularistic fashion and have failed to identify the process of colonization as one with universal dimensions. Professor Stevens, who has had a long interest in Africa and the Middle East, brings into his analysis that element missing in previous studies of the Palestine conflict. For he clearly illustrates in his essay the dynamics of political interaction between Zionists and Great Britain within the framework of the universal process of European expansion and colonialism. Professor Stevens appropriately has made two major previous contributions: with regard to Zionism and its relation to foreign policy, he wrote American Zionism and U.S. Foreign Policy, 1942–1947 *and with regard to the colonial experience,* Lesotho, Botswana and Swaziland: The Former High Commission Territories in Southern Africa. *A number of his essays address themselves to the specific contrasts and similarities of settler regimes in Africa and the Middle East.*

Thought and vision are important but not sufficient for a political triumph, as the Zionists long recognized. Conditions and an appropriate climate are imperative for the translation of thought and vision into an actuality, and the commitment of a power that has the means and seeming legitimacy to do so is imperative for realization in territorial terms of the political actuality. Eventually that commitment was made by Great Britain, whose independent ambition helped it focus on Palestine as a territory to be placed under British rather than French or Arab jurisdiction. As the war proceeded, Britain's ambitions were assured, and with British military forces in occupation of Palestine, the Zionists succeeded in obtaining the long-awaited legitimization of their political colonization of Palestine.

It will be evident in reading both Taylor's and Stevens' essays that the basic premise of the colonization of Palestine was to be a legal one; and that the Zionist immigrants to Palestine were to proceed with the clearly understood objective of the eventual establishment of a state rather than simply a settlement and fusion. As Herzl and the Basle Congress realized, the legal right to do so had to be internationally recognized. The twenty-year effort of the Zionists was finally crowned with success when the British government on November 2, 1917, issued a note in the name of its foreign secretary, Lord Balfour, which, irrespective of the conflicting interpretation of its content or dimensions, provided the needed "legal" premise for Zionist colonization of Palestine. Whether the British government undertook to facilitate the establishment of a Jewish state in the full sense of the term, whether it had the right to do so aside from the right of conquest, and whether it could derogate the rights of the people of Palestine by its unilateral note to the Zionists is not quite material at this point. It is sufficient to say that the Zionists concluded that the British government had undertaken a solemn commitment to facilitate Zionist colonization of Palestine, the objective of which was the establishment of a Jewish state. The Balfour Declaration has been used quite extensively to confirm the legal basis of Zionist colonization of Palestine. That it was in conflict with another equally solemn undertaking by His Majesty's government and that it implicitly equivocated on the right of self-determination of the Palestinians has also been noted. Professor W. T. Mallison, Jr., Professor of Law at George Washington University, has long concerned himself with the fate of Palestine, particularly insofar as questions of law are relevant. In his essay in this volume Professor Mallison, with precision and objectivity, recreates the context of the negotiations which eventuated in the final text that came to be known as the Balfour Declaration. This material elaborates and further documents the analyses by Taylor and Stevens and is thus of great interest to the historian of the period. Mallison makes an equally significant contribution to legal scholarship in his analysis of the meaning of the declaration and his discussion of the implications of, and limitations upon, the Balfour Declaration within the context of international law. Professor Mallison's previous publications include his frequently cited study The Legal Problems Concerning the Juridical Status and Political Activities of the Zionist Organization/Jewish Agency: A Study in International and United States Law.

1. Vision and Intent in Zionist Thought

Alan R. Taylor

When Winston Churchill referred to Soviet Russia as a "riddle wrapped in a mystery inside an enigma," he could also have been referring to modern Zionism and the state of Israel. For just as the inner realities of Soviet development and direction have been obscured by official articulation, the basic aims and nature of Zionism are blurred by rhetoric and misunderstanding.

The study of modernization is new and controversial. We are still confronted with such a vast body of unanalyzed data that it is difficult to establish universal laws of behavior. Nevertheless, there is sufficient evidence to posit two general principles. The first is that transforming societies tend to develop a subjective, ideological myth which explains the present in terms of a revered past and an anticipated future. Such a myth is necessary to alleviate the tension created by the departure from tradition and the thrust into an uncertain renaissance stimulated by the pressure of contemporary challenges. Its basic components are notions of vision and intent which generally assert the society's endowment with special, humanizing characteristics and a messianic vocation.

The second principle is that the institution of ideological myths usually involves a discrepancy between statement and design. This is because the protagonists need to articulate a creed for their own people and an explanation of it for foreigners. The society must be convinced that the myth is valid and become galvanized by its concepts. Its members must also agree to participate in the movement and accept its goals as sound and just. The related world outside must be persuaded that the myth is appropriate and that the intentions of the movement are in accord with other values and interests. The subjective and metaphysical nature of such dialectics stand in contrast to the immediacies of everyday life and therefore give rise to systematic apologetics in which statement of purpose and actual design can become far removed. This discrepancy becomes proportionately more pronounced as the content of the myth diverges from the fundamental values of the receiving audiences. This is one of the reasons why ours is an age of concealment and propaganda, of riddles wrapped in mysteries.

The purpose of this essay is to investigate the nature of vision and intent in the Zionist movement. This requires first an examination of the underlying myth and its theoretical elaboration, both for the Jews and for the world. Following this, we will concentrate on the political, social, and territorial aims of Zionism and their implementation. In both cases, the relationship between statement and design will be analyzed.

TRADITION AND MODERNISM IN THE DIASPORA

Contrary to the popular view, Zionism is not rooted in the history and culture of the Jews. It is a very recent movement, constituting a branch of the broader phenomenon of modern nationalism. And like many contemporary national movements, it represents an innovating tendency with regard to tradition. Not only, then, is Zionism unrepresentative of traditional attitudes but in certain respects it is in direct opposition to them.

The idea of a Jewish commonwealth in Palestine is a controversial subject in the annals of Jewish cultural history. Such a political entity existed from the eleventh to the sixth centuries B.C. and for about a century preceding the Roman occupation in 63 B.C. This is a relatively short period considering the totality of Jewish history, which covers over three millennia. Furthermore, there were divergent attitudes toward the state. Many of the prophets saw the political tradition as a worldly preoccupation which interfered with the spiritual vocation of ancient Israel. Indeed, Isaiah seemed to be advocating the exodus of Israel from itself, the termination of political and social confinement.

Following the Roman sieges of Jerusalem in A.D. 70 and 135, Judaism lost its center in Palestine. At this point begins the history of the Diaspora, during which the Jews lived in communities in many parts of the world. This phase of Jewish development remained until the Renaissance a politically quiet tradition. Palestine was revered, as it has always been in Judaism, but in a purely religious, not a political, sense. There were no programs of "return" and no political ideologies. Jews turned their attention primarily to constructing a system of piety in their dispersed communities and thought of Palestine only in terms of a future messianic age which would witness a "return" in connection with the reconstitution of the Jews as a holy people, a nation of priests.

Zionism is a product of the modern age. It represents the translation of diasporan religious orientation into a secular ideology inspired by the political thought of Gentile Europe. The political revolution which began in the Renaissance stressed a secular and pragmatic approach to politics and the construction of integrated national states. The impact of these concepts on the Jews was profound and confusing. They implied two alternate paths of Jewish development. On the one hand, they suggested a new social integration in Europe, involving the extensive participation of minorities in the political and cultural life of the Continent. On the other, they introduced the idea of nationalism as the appropriate order for all self-identified communities. Hence the door was opened at the same time to Jewish integration in the lands of the Diaspora and to a separatist Jewish movement.

There were a variety of reactions. One reaffirmed the cultural isolation of the Jews and adherence to tradition. Another sought to assert Jewish identity in terms of a national ethos and a "return" to Palestine under political auspices. A third school advocated the participation of the Jews in the social and cultural life of the West, while retaining a sense of separate identity.

The pattern of Jewish development which emerged reflected this tripartite paradigm of reactions. The traditionalists rejected the modernist formulas, including nationalism, finding them a source of innovation, compromise, and estrangement from God. A few traditionalist individuals and sects developed aspects of nationalist thought within a religious context, but these were a distinct minority, and their views were quite removed from the secular Zionism which was constructed in the nineteenth century.

Rabbi Liva of Prague (1520–1609) was perhaps the earliest Orthodox Jew in diasporan history to suggest a reestablishment of the Jews in Palestine as essential to their fulfillment as a people. In subsequent generations, other Orthodox rabbis tried to combine elements of tradition with the emerging doctrines of modern nationalism, but most of these remained isolated figures until the late nineteenth century.

A more important link between tradition and cosmopolitanism was the Hasidic movement, inaugurated in Eastern Europe in the eighteenth century by Baal Shem Tov (1700–60). Hasidism represents a reaction against the formalism and intellectual rigidity of Talmudic Judaism without a corresponding rejection of traditional values and observances. Inspired by Jewish mysticism, it injected a new communalism and messianic sense into Jewish thought. This included a renewed interest in the idea of "return," and thus, on the eve of the French Revolution, Hasidism gave birth to a kind of religious proto-Zionism. But this also remained very removed from the secular versions of Jewish nationalism which developed in the post-revolutionary era. In the nineteenth century, Orthodoxy and Hasidism became increasingly atypical of Jewish life, which had begun to move rapidly toward integration and cosmopolitanism.

In contrast to the developments in conservative circles was the advent of modernism in contemporary Jewish society. Initially this took the form of a cosmopolitan and integrationist movement. The life and work of Spinoza (1632–77) in the seventeenth century and of Moses Mendelssohn (1728–86) in the eighteenth established examples of Jewish social and intellectual participation in European thought and experience. The post-Napoleonic era witnessed the growth of cosmopolitanism among the Jews of Europe. But the transition from neo-classical to Romantic thought gradually effected an interpretive split. The Enlightenment of the eighteenth century had suggested a planned progression toward emancipation from the prejudices and injustices of existing institutions and the formation of a liberal and enlightened society. But the disappointments of the French Revolution and the disenchantment with rationalism as the ultimate solution to human problems stimulated the Romantic reaction, with its emphasis on emotion, a metaphysical approach to reality, particularist endeavor, and nonrational modes of evolution.

It was in this context that the Hegelian school, which dominated the intellectual climate of the nineteenth century, forwarded the idea of modern messianism. The "Absolute" was coming into its own in human history through the vehicle of unique and eventful peoples. The era of "Synthesis" had arrived, and the agents of cosmic evolution were called upon to achieve man's ultimate fulfillment in an hour of crisis. It was a time when the antagonistic forces of world history would be resolved in a final struggle and a blending of opposites. Earlier, Goethe had pictured the modern hero—Faust—as a man committed to a restless search for self-realization, less concerned with the ethic of love than with finding the way to existential becoming and fulfilling experience.

It was a restless age, one of intermittent revolution, messianic regimes, and war. Its ideas and political development had a profound impact on all men, including the Jews. Suddenly, the philosophy of enlightenment was confronted with another set of values and a new perspective. The current ideas were geared to visionary doctrines of becoming and evolution, to dynamic activity and dialectical prescriptions. The particular was elevated to a new importance, creating special roles and destinies for peoples and movements which had acquired a new sense of identity and purpose.

During the first half of the nineteenth century, Jewish modernism pursued for the most part the path of social integration. It was in this period that Jews emerged in large numbers as European cosmopolitans and that Reform Judaism was established as a Western-oriented system of religious observance. The second half of the century, however, witnessed the rise of Romantic social and political concepts in Jewish thought. Though a large body of Jews continued to cherish the idea of emancipation and integration, a new ideology, which was to become known as Zionism, began to be formulated. The adherents of this school were in conscious departure from the integrationist position, the premises of which they challenged.

The life and work of Moses Hess (1812–75) reflect the transition from integrationism to the Zionist revolution. As a young man Hess was borne by the strong secularizing currents of his native Germany. An admirer of Spinoza, he left Judaism and became associated with Marx in the socialist movement. Then a gradual change took place in his outlook as he turned from Marxism to a philo-Jewish idealism. In 1862 he published *Rome and Jerusalem,* in which his ideas are set forth systematically.

Essentially Hess's new philosophy is an adaptation of Hegelian dialectics to the Jewish question. Like Hegel, Hess conceived of history as a dialectical process, in which diametric opposites engage and gradually effect a synthesis of principles in an age of reconciliation. Also in conformity with Hegel, he thought that such an age was close at hand. But while Hegel thought the modern Germans were providing the synthetic example, Hess considered the Jews to possess this role.

The Jews were a history-making people and were destined to transform the world. This was because only they in their own national life had realized the principle of unity between the spiritual and material spheres. The Greeks had stressed diversity and mundane religion, while Christianity had overspiritualized the Judaic tradition. It remained for the Jews, then, to bring about the "Sabbath of History," an age of maturity and reconciliation in which all national types would fall into a harmonious organic relationship with regard to each other. In order to fulfill this mission, the Jews must reconstitute their national life in Palestine, thereby rediscovering themselves as a people and providing an example of synthetic orientation for the world. Hence the development of a Jewish national movement was the essential key to the future not only of the Jews but of all mankind.

Hess remained a relatively isolated thinker in the Jewish life of his time, but the metaphysical and ethnocentric concepts which he developed became the first systematic expression of the Zionist idea. The later generations of Jews who converted Zionism into a movement returned to his thought and made it a foundation of their new ideology.

POLITICAL, PRACTICAL, AND CULTURAL ZIONISM

Organized Zionism began as a visionary movement in Eastern Europe. The first Zionists were members of the young generation of the 1860s and 1870s who had become associated with the Russian revolutionary movement and were deeply influenced by the radical thought of the time. This generation formed the *Haskalah* (enlightenment) movement and looked to a new socialist era in which all minorities would be granted equal status and rights of autonomy.

Haskalah was related in outlook to the Jewish integrationism of Central and Western Europe. Though a sizable body of the *maskilim* (adherents of Haskalah) remained faithful to the original precepts and ultimately formed the League of Jewish Workingmen, or the Bund, others gradually established a more specifically Jewish movement. Finding Russian radicalism permeated with Slavophile undertones, they felt the need for a uniquely Jewish program of emancipation. It was in this context that Peretz Smolenskin (1842–85), Moshe Lilienblum (1843–1910), and others suggested a secular Jewish nationalism and colonization of Palestine as the keys to Jewish evolution in the modern age.

From this trend in Jewish radical thought emerged the *Choveve Zion,* or Lovers of Zion, movement, which came under the leadership of Leo Pinsker (1821–91) in the early 1880s. The young Lovers of Zion were inspired by the idea of "auto-emancipation" through emigration to Palestine and the founding of agricultural colonies there. Small groups actually made the journey and established the earliest Zionist settlements. Though the movement proved to be very limited in scope, it inaugurated an activist spirit and stimulated a variety of polemical speculation on the Zionist idea.

In the late 1880s and the 1890s, the ideology of Zionism was formulated by several schools, which shaped the vision of the nascent movement. Primary among these were practical, political, and cultural Zionism. The practical Zionists developed the tradition of Choveve Zion, stressing the emancipating effects of establishing agricultural collectives in Palestine. Aaron David Gordon (1856–1922), who constructed a religion of Jewish regeneration through labor in the Land of Israel and became the father of Mapai, was the dominant personality in this branch of early Zionism.

Political Zionism emphasized the importance of a politically independent Jewish state and was less insistent on Palestine as the site. The major premise of this school was that Jewish emancipation was illusory and that a political program leading to sovereign status was the only solution to a Judeophobia apparently native to Gentiles. The leaders of this movement were Leo Pinsker in Eastern Europe and the Hungarian Jew Theodor Herzl (1860–1904), who developed similar ideas outside the context of the Zionist movement in Russia.

Though Pinsker became the leader of Choveve Zion, he was initially opposed to formulating the Jewish national idea in terms of Palestine, which implied attachment to the traditional belief in a messianic redemption. Like the majority of Zionists, he was as concerned with the emancipation of Jews from archaic concepts as with the threat of anti-Semitism. Herzl was of like mind. A highly cosmopolitan journalist for a Viennese newspaper, Herzl's main concern was the "normalization of a people." He initially considered a program involving the mass conversion of Jewish youth to the Catholic Church, but subsequently abandoned this impractical scheme in favor of a Jewish national movement. Though he ultimately settled on Palestine as the site of the projected state, he regarded other locations, such as Argentina, Cyprus, Sinai, and Uganda as more feasible because of their relative underpopulation.

Cultural Zionism was also secular in orientation, but took a more metaphysical approach to the Zionist idea. The adherents of this school were deeply moved by the vision of a Jewish cultural renaissance. They were in search of a new and galvanizing sense of Jewish identity, freed from archaic tradition, diasporan customs, and alien influence. The Palestine project was not important as a political or economic program but as the basis of a cultural center which would give the Jews a quickening sense of their own *élan* and special role.

Ahad Ha'Am (1856–1927), a renowned Zionist essayist and the acknowledged leader of the cultural faction, interpreted the movement in Hegelian and populist terms. Palestine was the symbolic key to a Jewish future marked by new values and a new sense of mission. In an essay entitled "Judaism and Nietzsche," Ahad Ha'Am argued that the Jews were essentially a superior people. He agreed with Nietzsche that "the highest moral aim is not the advancement of the human race as a whole, but the realization of a more perfect human type in the chosen few," but rejected what he regarded as Nietzsche's "Aryan" orientation and attachment to relative values of physical strength and beauty. In another passage, he asserts that the Jews "have regarded their election as an end to which everything else was subordinate, not as a means to the happiness of the rest of humanity."[1]

In Ahad Ha'Am's view, the establishment of a Jewish center in Palestine would release the Jews from an unnatural bondage and allow them to realize that their "mission as a people is to be a super-nation in the moral sense." His vision of the historic role of the Jews was expressed in these terms:

1. *Essays, Letters, Memoirs,* trans. Leon Simon (Oxford: East and West Library, 1946), p. 81.

There must be one nation whose inherent characteristics make it better
fitted than others of moral development, and whose scheme of life is
governed by a moral law superior to the common type of morality, so
that it may provide the ideal conditions for the growth of the superman
we want. This idea opens up a wide prospect, in which Judaism appears
in a new and splendid light, and many of the alleged shortcomings, which
the world condemns and our own apologists are at pains to deny or
excuse, turn out to be actually evidence of its superiority.[2]

Though cultural Zionism later became known for its moderation and
sensitivity to the ethics of the Arab problem, it was initially stated as a populist philosophy with metaphysical overtones. Ahad Ha'Am, who was appropriately dubbed by Arthur Hertzberg the "agnostic rabbi," was absorbed
in the genius of a people. More deeply influenced by the prescriptions of
nineteenth-century European idealism than by Judaic tradition, he provided
an important dimension to the Zionist idea, to its secular orientation, and
to its modernist idolization of a folkish cult.

Numerous intellectual circles and less-organized groups gave further
definition to the movement. Worthy of mention are the Hebrew authors
Mica Berdychewski (1865–1921) and Saul Tchernichowsky (1875–
1943). Expressive of the early Zionist thought of the East European Haskalah movement, they became spokesmen of an emerging martial spirit
in the ideological evolution of Zionism. Berdychewski regarded the main
problem confronting the Jews to be the fact that they as a people had
become secondary to Judaism as a religion. Since "Israel precedes the
Torah," therefore "We must cease to be Jews by virtue of an abstract
Judaism and become Jews in our own right, as a living and developing
nationality."

An essential element in Berdychewski's program of Jewish regeneration
was an emphasis on physical assertiveness: "The book is no more than the
shade of life . . . the blade is the materialization of life in its boldest lines,
in its essential and substantial likeness." The poet Tchernichowsky expressed similar views in verse: "I kneel to life, to beauty, and to strength
. . . which the dead-in-life, the bloodless ones, the sick, have stifled in the
living God, the God of wonders of the wilderness, the God of gods, who
took Canaan with storm before they bound him in phylacteries." In another
poem he idolized the revival of warrior values among the Jews and adopted
a positive attitude toward war and militarism: "The groan of the slain is
music in my ears."

2. *Ibid.*, p. 80.

Such attitudes reflect more than revolt from the ghetto and defiance of anti-Semitism. They affirm force not only as a means but as an end in itself, an attribute of a higher type. The thought of Berdychewski and Tchernichowsky had a clear and far-from-minimal influence on the Zionist movement. They belonged to a generation which read and was profoundly swayed by the neo-idealism of Nietzsche, and their application of his views to Jewish life was neither uncommon nor ineffective. It was thus at an early stage that Zionism acquired an aura of aggressive activism which represents a marked departure from the pacific stance which Judaism had assumed for two millennia.

THE ZIONIST SYNTHESIS

The organized Zionism for which Theodor Herzl provided the institutional foundation in 1897 represents a mixture of these ideological roots, and was further defined by the traditions of leadership established by Herzl and by the patterns of operational development that the movement assumed. Vision and intent in Zionist thought stem from these varied influences. Most basic is the modernist approach to Jewish social and cultural evolution, an approach which the ideological founders formulated from different points of view.

Reduced to fundamentals, the philosophy of Jewish futurism which emerged from the Zionist synthesis envisioned a new Jewish *élan* geared to the pragmatic and metaphysical precepts of nineteenth-century European political thought. In one sense the projected society was to reflect the democratic and positivist ideals of the West. This view was forwarded by Herzl in his novel about the future Israel, *Altneuland,* published in 1902. The hero comments on the character of the country in these words:

> The New Society rests squarely on the ideas which are the common stock of the whole civilized world. . . . We made the New Society not because we were better than others, but simply because we were ordinary men with the ordinary human needs for air and light, health and honor, for the right to acquire property and security of possession.

There was also an idealist picture of the Jewish state to be. Its social and political dimensions were drawn from the works of Hess and Ahad Ha'Am, from the Hebraist poets and essayists, and from the Utopianism of Labor Zionism. The new Israel was to comprise a model society, to provide an example to the world. Its people were cast in a messianic role and were in a sense a law unto themselves. The ethical standard under which they operated placed the welfare of their state and the fulfillment of their ideological goals before other considerations. They were a history-making people through whom the dialectical conflicts of human develop-ment were to be resolved in what Hess had called the "Sabbath of History." For this reason they were not subject to the common morality of other men, for their self-realization was of ultimate importance to the world.

Though these two views are essentially contradictory, they were com-bined to form a composite political philosophy. This created a dualism of vision and intent and a corresponding dichotomy of statement and design which required a synthetic mechanism to blend components and coordinate the consequent incompatibilities of policy.

The dilemma was resolved by the political structure which organized Zionism assumed. At the outset, Herzl effected a unique combination of democratic and authoritarian principles within the movement. The Zionist Congress was established as a democratic forum in which the various schools of Zionist thought could find expression through a party system. At the same time, a directive leadership defined policy and designated opera-tional measures. As Herzl put it in his diaries, "I conduct the affairs of the Jews without their mandate, though I remain responsible to them for what I do."

The leadership institution, known first as the Family Council and then as the Inner Actions Committee and the Executive, remained responsive to the congress on broad issues of policy and goals but relegated to itself the conduct of affairs and the selection of methods. Herzl envisioned a hier-archical system in which graded echelons would participate in the plans and operations of the movement in descending order.

The functional structure that Herzl created was subsequently enlarged and elaborated, but remained essentially the same under the leadership of Dr. Chaim Weizmann (1874–1952) and following the establishment of the state. The only major change was a broadening of executive authority to encompass the expanding political facets of the movement. Once the immigration of Jews into Palestine had reached significant proportions and the campaign to indoctrinate the international Jewish community had be-come an intensive program, the leadership had to assume a less-confined focus. Following the formation of the state, the executive function became more complex and resided in the interlocking tripartite control of the Mapai Party, the Histadrut, and the Jewish Agency for Palestine, which constitutes the new form of the Zionist Organization.

At either stage, the leadership structure was concerned with conducting a *modus operandi* in the context of diverse opinion within the movement and in the world. The major issues were Jewish participation, international

approbation, and the problem of Arab resistance in relationship to territorial aims. The publicity aspect was resolved in part by means of an extensive propaganda campaign which enlisted Jewish and international support by capitalizing on the circumstances of German anti-Semitism and by
presenting the Zionist question in simplistic and generalized terms. In this
regard, Zionist vision and intent were concealed by an equivocation of
statement and design. The statement of purpose always conformed to
the morality of the world and the sympathies of each audience, while the
design often did not.

Despite the victory of Zionist publicity in Jewish and international
circles, the questions of Jewish identity and Arab displacement remained.
For the Jews the implications of the Zionist revolution stood as a perplexing
issue of direction and involvement. Though many Jews consider the movement valid and reflective of their own sense of direction, they cannot really
answer to its call and its message. The Jew in the world essentially affirms
the Diaspora and progressively discovers new avenues of relationship with
the non-Jewish community in which he lives. He is also confronted with the
departure from Jewish tradition which the Zionist experiment has institutionalized in the form of a secular Jewish state.

The Arab question, which poses the most basic issues of moral interpretation and international law, underlies the broader questions of vision and
intent and of statement and design. Once Palestine was established as the
projected site of the Jewish state, the Arab problem came into being. It
was a matter of land and people.

LAND AND PEOPLE

The territorial aim of organized Zionism is elusive and enigmatic. This
is because there has never been any definitive statement as to territorial
design and because Zionists have always taken a pragmatic approach to the
geographical question. Officially, Zionist leaders have agreed to very limited
borders, such as those proposed by the Peel Commission in 1937 and the
U.N. partition plan of 1947. In practice, they have sought to expand
these delimitations by force or cunning. Weizmann accepted the partition
suggested by the Peel Commission, but considered the exclusion of the
Negev from the projected Jewish state as a reversible condition. Commenting on his position to critics, he pointed out that in any event the
Negev "would not run away," implying that it could later be incorporated.
Hence, at quite an early date, Weizmann anticipated an initially small but
subsequently expansionist Jewish state. The later U.N. partition plan was
more widely accepted in Zionist circles, but when the war situation evolved,

the Israeli military campaign sought the acquisition of all of mandate Palestine. The campaign of 1956 tried to establish control of Gaza and parts of Sinai, while that of 1967 resulted in Israeli occupation of the West Bank, the Golan Heights, Gaza, and all of Sinai.

If Zionist expansionism is not a clearly defined policy, expansion has, in fact, been the result of each Arab-Israeli war. Withdrawal has not taken place except under considerable American pressure, and then only in 1957. The more recent occupation of Jordanian, Egyptian, and Syrian territory in 1967 has been explained by Israel as a temporary situation pending the conclusion of a general peace. But in the interim, the old city of Jerusalem has been incorporated, Arab homes and villages have been destroyed, and Israeli settlements have been established in various parts of the occupied territory. Furthermore, Israel's initial encouragement of Arab evacuation of the West Bank, the increasingly frequent intimations later that the new borders might become permanent, and hesitancy with regard to the U.S. peace initiative raise further questions as to statement and design.

There is no way to prove or disprove the existence of a long-range Israeli policy of expansion, but there is enough circumstantial evidence to suggest a strong tendency in this direction. More indicative even than the gradual enlargement of territory beyond the boundaries of the U.N. partition plan and the discrepancy between statement and design in Zionist policy are the statements on the scope of *Eretz Israel* made quite openly during the earlier stages of the movement.

What is most striking in these anticipations is that the Land of Israel was conceived in proportions considerably larger than what became mandate Palestine (see map 1). The Israel of Herzl's *Altneuland* extended to the Euphrates and included Beirut and the Lebanon range. Similar boundaries were suggested in a publication of the youth movement of the Zionist Organization of America in 1917. Entitled *A Zionist Primer,* its purpose was to indoctrinate new Zionists in the principles of Zionism, including the question of territory. One of the essays is called "No, You Do Not Know the Land," and makes very explicit reference to the full scope of Eretz Israel, with an accompanying map, in these words:

> There in our own land, we the Hebrews of long standing and you the Hebrews to come, will unitedly lay our hands on every spot which once belonged to us: from Sidon to Sukkoth, from Tadmor to Ur-Kasdim, from the Mediterranean to the Red Sea, from the mighty Euphrates to the far-stretching Desert.

Though this is the view of the author of the essay, it is implicit in the title of the book that the positions taken in all the essays were to be considered representative of a broad segment of Zionist opinion.

Further definition of the territorial question was made by the Zionist delegation to the Paris Peace Conference in 1919. Addressing the conference, Dr. Weizmann and other members of the delegation called for recognition of the historic title of the Jews to Palestine but endorsed an interim British mandate in an area which included Transjordan, southern Lebanon, and Mount Hermon in addition to Palestine proper.

Later, the Zionists were more careful to conceal the full extent of their territorial ambitions, though many continued to cherish the idea of a Jewish state in greater Palestine. It is known, for example, that Weizmann and many other Zionists took strong exception to the Churchill White Paper of 1922 which prohibited Jewish settlement in Transjordan. Subsequently, both Weizmann and Ben Gurion expressed the hope that Zionist colonization would become operative in that area. In a speech at Jerusalem in 1926, Weizmann suggested a pacific infiltration of Jews into the region: "The road to Allenby Bridge, along which we will cross over to Transjordan, will not be paved by soldiers, but by Jewish labor and the Jewish plough."

Addressing the Seventeenth Zionist Congress in 1931, Ben Gurion expressed a similar interest in the Transjordanian region:

> In eastern Palestine, there are broader and emptier acres, and Jordan is not necessarily the perpetual limit of our immigration and settlement. . . . Without amending the Mandate, we are entitled to ask the right to enter and settle in Transjordan; its closure in our faces neither accords with the Mandate as it stands, nor considers the crying economic needs of a fertile but underpopulated and impecunious region.

Also relevant to the issue of territory is the policy of "gradualism" first developed by Weizmann and inherited by subsequent leaders. In accepting the Balfour Declaration, the Churchill White Paper, and the partition plan of the Peel Commission, Weizmann did not really agree to their terms or intend to abide by them. Throughout his tenure as the recognized leader of organized Zionism, he tried ceaselessly to circumvent the restrictions of official British policy without openly challenging their legality. And in most cases the limitations he sought to overcome were directly or indirectly related to the scope of the projected state.

That such attitudes continue to exist is borne out by the attempts in 1956 and 1967 to expand the borders established by the armistice agreements and by the policies of the more aggressive parties and political figures, which have had increasing voice since the June war (see map 2). This is not to say that all Zionists and Israelis are expansionists but to point out that the concept of Eretz Israel is a living idea. Its diminution in practical policy does not reflect discarded interest but a sensitivity to world opinion.

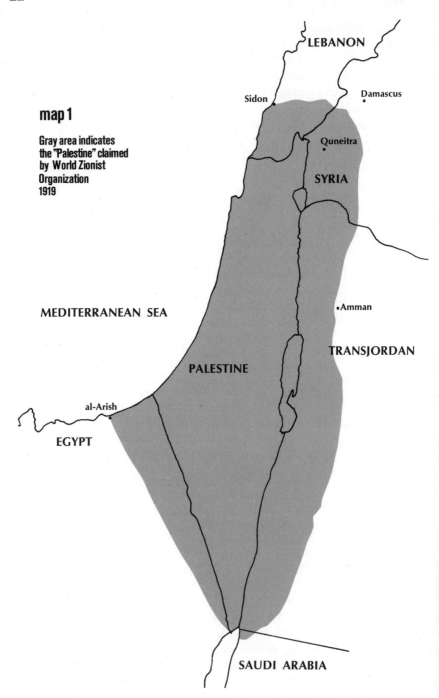

map 1

Gray area indicates
the "Palestine" claimed
by World Zionist
Organization
1919

LEBANON

Sidon

Damascus

Quneitra

SYRIA

MEDITERRANEAN SEA

Amman

TRANSJORDAN

PALESTINE

al-Arish

EGYPT

SAUDI ARABIA

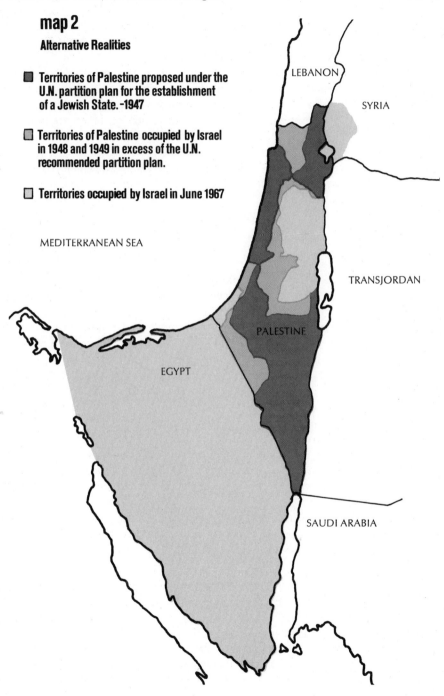

map 2

Alternative Realities

▮ Territories of Palestine proposed under the
   U.N. partition plan for the establishment
   of a Jewish State. -1947

▧ Territories of Palestine occupied by Israel
   in 1948 and 1949 in excess of the U.N.
   recommended partition plan.

☐ Territories occupied by Israel in June 1967

LEBANON

SYRIA

MEDITERRANEAN SEA

TRANSJORDAN

PALESTINE

EGYPT

SAUDI ARABIA

The commitments of the greater powers since 1948 have been geared to the maintenance of the territorial *status quo,* consigning Israeli revisionism to an awkward position. Futhermore, the matter of incorporating new territories creates fresh problems of opposition and integration, which Israel's occupation of the West Bank in 1967 has clearly demonstrated. Therefore, the realities of the Israeli position on expansion today can be determined only by weighing the relative influence of inherited policies and more recent deterrent factors. It is an elusive question, but one which is subject to analytical conjecture.

The other side of the Arab problem in Zionist vision and intent concerns the Arabs themselves, the people in whose midst and on whose land the Jewish state was established. The issue of Arab displacement was recognized at an early stage in the history of the movement. This was one of the reasons why Herzl, Pinsker, Israel Zangwill (1864–1926), and others had reservations about Palestine as the site of the projected state. But once Zionism became an organized movement, the insistence on Palestine by the sizable East European contingent established a Palestinian focus. This raised the question of the indigenous population, which had begun to participate in the new Arab nationalism.

The early Zionists realized that their own movement ran directly counter to Arab aspirations and sought to find a way out of the dilemma. A variety of Arab policies were formulated, ranging from the hard to the soft line. Herzl felt that the only solution was to manipulate the situation by cunning and prowess, an inconsistency with respect to the image of Arab-Jewish cordiality portrayed in *Altneuland.* In his diaries, he anticipates extensive land purchase from the gentry by offering exorbitant prices, and a corresponding program "to spirit the penniless population across the border by procuring employment for it in the transit countries, while denying it employment in our own country." He adds that "the process of expropriation and removal of the poor must be carried out discreetly and circumspectly."

Vladimir Jabotinsky (1880–1940), who became the leader of the more extreme revisionist faction in Zionism, also endorsed the plan of gradual and systematic expropriation and suggested an induced migration of the Arab masses in Palestine to Iraq. A. D. Gordon, the father of Labor Zionism, took a more moderate position, but regarded Arab evacuation as essential. He commented on the issue in these words:

> If mastery of the land implies political mastery, then the Arabs long ago have forfeited their title. Turks ruled the country for centuries and now the British are its rulers. If we bar the right acquired through living on the land and working it, the Arabs, like ourselves, have no

other than a historic claim to the land, except that our claim beyond question is the stronger; it cannot therefore be said that we are taking the land from the Arabs. As for rights accruing from occupation and from work upon the land, we, too, live and work upon it. Between us and the Arabs the real difference is based on numbers, not on the character of our claim.[3]

Though Gordon also specified that infringement on Arab rights should be avoided, the program he envisioned was clearly one of rationalized expropriation. In accordance with the general tenor of Zionist outlook, he regarded the moral issues of the Arab problem as subordinate to the establishment of a modern Jewish commonwealth in Palestine.

The adherents of cultural Zionism later became very sensitive to the ethical implications of Arab expulsion. In the 1920s, Ahad Ha'Am spoke out in opposition to Jewish terrorism against the Arabs. Reflecting on the mission of Zionism, he questioned: "Are we really doing it only to add in an Oriental corner a small people of new Levantines who vie with other Levantines in shedding blood, in desire for vengeance, and in angry violence? If this be the 'Messiah,' then I do not wish to see his coming."[4]

Judah Magnes (1877–1948) commented in a similar vein:

> The time has come for the Jews to take into account the Arab factor as the most important facing us. If we have a just cause, so have they. If promises were made to us, so were they to the Arabs. If we love the land and have a historical connection with it, so too the Arabs. Even more realistic than the ugly realities of imperialism is the fact that the Arabs live here and in this part of the world, and will probably live here long after the collapse of one imperialism and the rise of another. If we, too, wish to live in this living space, we must live with the Arabs.[5]

Ultimately the compassionate Zionism of Judah Magnes was reduced to the status of a curious anomaly. The more militant approach prevailed and became the criterion of the Israeli attitude toward the Arabs. The Arabophobic tendency was expressed succinctly and graphically by the commander of the Palmach in his commentary on an operation which was designed to expel the Arabs from Galilee in 1948:

3. *Selected Essays,* trans. Frances Burnce (New York, 1938), p. 25.

4. Hans Kohn, "Zion and the Jewish National Idea," *Palestine: A Search for Truth,* ed. Alan R. Taylor and Richard N. Tetlie (Washington, D.C., 1970), p. 46.

5. From a speech by Judah L. Magnes quoted in Taylor and Tetlie, *Palestine: A Search for Truth,* p. 68.

We saw a need to clean the inner Galilee and to create a Jewish territorial succession in the entire area of upper Galilee. . . . We therefore looked for means which did not force us into employing force, in order to cause tens of thousands of sulky Arabs who remained in Galilee to flee. . . . We tried to use a tactic which took advantage of the impression created by the fall of Safed and the [Arab] defeat in the area which was cleaned by Operation Metateh—a tactic which worked miraculously well.

I gathered all of the Jewish Mukhtars, who have contact with the Arabs in different villages, and asked them to whisper in the ears of some Arabs that a great Jewish reinforcement has arrived in Galilee and that it is going to burn all the villages of the Huleh. They should suggest to these Arabs, as their friends, to escape while there is still time. And the rumor spread in all the areas of the Huleh that it is time to flee. The flight numbered myraids. The tactic reached its goal completely.[6]

Zionism is representative of many modern movements. Though its adherents consider it unique, it remains an institutional response of contemporary Jewry to the impact of modernization. Its vision of "return" and regeneration is characteristic of a host of modernizing ideologies which have employed an archaic myth to galvanize a society into futuristic endeavor. Similarly, its program of intent is caught between the Scylla of a dream and the Charybdis of reality. For the ideal of a permanent Jewish state in the Middle East cannot be realized without the establishment of cordial relations in the immediate area.

An equally disturbing problem is the discrepancy between statement and design. In the long run, such a dichotomy leads to a way of life based on equivocation and duplicity. It ultimately destroys the capacity to conduct normal relations and results in a distortion based on double standards. Hence, Zionism is above all faced with its own problem of subjective interpretation, which the objective world outside will perceive with increasing clarity in the course of time. And the most perceptive of all will be the Jewish people themselves, who were the first to articulate those values which modern Zionism must ultimately confront.

6. Walid Khalidi, "Plan Dalet," *The Arab World* (October–November, 1969); quoted from a passage by Yigael Alon in *Ha sepher ha Palmach* [The book of the Palmach], II, 286.

2. Zionism as a Phase
of Western Imperialism

Richard P. Stevens

Notwithstanding the theological attachments of some Orthodox Jews to Palestine over the centuries and the occasional efforts of Jewish communities to settle in Palestine with the approval of the Ottoman authorities, the crucial advantage eventually achieved by Zionism in that region resulted from the identification of the movement with the historical phenomenon of Western imperialism as it expanded and consolidated its dominance over the Afro-Asian world during the course of the late nineteenth and early twentieth centuries. In its early phase, Western imperialism—whether manifested in a French, British, Russian, or German presence—endeavored to direct or influence Middle Eastern governments not only through military and civilian advisers but through consular authorities, each of which successfully claimed some rights of protection over specified religious minorities. But in the wake of the First World War, archaic imperialistic practices such as extra-territorial privilege and rights of religious-national protection increasingly gave way to legal enactments which, in theory at least, guaranteed a common criteria of justice and administration under Western-patterned constitutional forms. However, while these constitutional arrangements superficially acknowledged the rising tide of nationalism touched off by Napoleon's incursion at the opening of the nineteenth century, they essentially reflected the capacity of such imperialistic powers as Britain and France to adapt themselves to the new mode of "enlightened liberalism" and Wilsonian idealism without abandoning traditional colonial objectives.

The mandatory regimes established under the authority of the League of Nations did not fail to reflect the continued primacy of Western interests under the facade of international legality. Whether it was the French mandates over Syria and Lebanon, the British over Palestine, Transjordan

27

and Iraq, or the South African mandate over South-West Africa, the traditional power interests of Western states were attained. In like manner the
Balfour Declaration, eventually translated into a virtual article of international "law," demonstrated anew the capacity of a Western power to
define the test of legality without regard for the wishes of those concerned
and without their consent. In each case it was for the "natives" to abide
by Western-imposed legal and constitutional structures. Resistance was
not only treasonable and illegal but violated the canons of international
morality.

EARLY JEWISH SETTLEMENTS AND
THE ADVENT OF ZIONISM: 1840–1897

It was in the context of imperialistic enterprise and psychology that
Zionism successively defined itself and established political goals that
coincided with the power realities, if not the interests, of the Western world.
Prior to the birth of political Zionism in the late nineteenth century, Jewish
communities in Russia and Poland were as likely to find refuge from
Eastern anti-Semitism in Palestine and other parts of the Ottoman Empire
as in the urban centers of Western Europe. Messianic revivals and the
impulse of piety also led occasional scholars and people of means to the
Holy Land. By the end of the eighteenth century, rival Hassidic factions
and their opponents saw some advantage in terms of theological purity in
settling in Palestine. Always, except in time of outside threat or internal
pressures from minority Christian communities,

> Jewish subjects of the Sultan moved freely in and out of Palestine from
> other parts of the far-flung Empire, from North Africa to the Balkans—as
> did Moslems and Christians. . . . But the Jewish immigrants and residents
> were drawn to Constantinople, Damascus, or Cairo, where economic and
> political conditions were far more favorable, rather than to Palestine.[1]

Of those who settled in the Holy Land, only a small part were supported
by the local economy as tradesmen, artisans, or farmers. Leaders of such
Jewish groups as the Ashkenazim and the Sephardic opposed ill-considered
immigration because of financial and other difficulties. Both of these
communities endeavored to enlist financial support for their own cause
among Jews in Europe and in the United States as well. It was, however,

1. Ben Halpern, *The Idea of the Jewish State* (Cambridge, Mass., 1961), p. 105.

Sir Moses Montefiore, reputedly a personal friend of Muhammad Ali, vice-roy of Egypt, who most benefited the Palestine Jewish settlements in the nineteenth century. From the early 1840s until his death in 1885, Montefiore labored to improve their condition. By his numerous visits to Palestine he also aroused greater interest in Western Europe in the small Jewish settlements.[2] Still, Montefiore was not alone, since "the growing influence of the West in Near Eastern affairs caused the Western Jewish communities to play an increasingly important role in the Holy Land as well as in other parts of the crumbling Ottoman Empire."[3]

But as Western influence in the area developed, it altered substantially the conditions of the Jewish community and elicited new responses. First and foremost, an increase in Western influence meant an increase in the Jewish population. By 1856 the Jewish population of Palestine was 10,600. Twenty years later, in 1876, it was reported to be 13,920.[4] The population increase, as Ben Halpern notes, could not be attributed to improved economic conditions or other general factors benefiting the country as a whole but rather to the fact that "from 1840 on, European consuls were stationed in Jerusalem, and they, together with the ambassadors of the Western powers in Constantinople, extended their protection to non-Ottoman Jewish pilgrims and settlers who come to the Holy Land." Larger numbers of settlers without an accompanying expansion of economic activities now required "political means to solve a problem that could no longer be ignored." The problem, as Halpern observes, was the growing dependence "upon Western Jews for both financial and political assistance." But while Western Jews had assumed major responsibility for settlement in Palestine they were unable to accept continued "economic and political dependency as a basis of communal existence."[5]

After 1840 Western Jewry—British, French, German, Austrian, and American—turned its attention to the rights of Jews in the Ottoman Empire and its various autonomous entities. This interest and involvement was "a natural consequence of the special position European powers began to occupy in Ottoman affairs."[6] But it was Britain which systematically began to extend its mantle of protection over the Jewish community in Palestine, including Russian Jewish settlers who, in 1847–49, the Russians "agreed to release to British protection." Palmerston's decision in 1839 to

2. James Parkes, *A History of Palestine from 135* A.D. *to Modern Times* (New York, 1949), p. 263.

3. Halpern, *Jewish State*, p. 107.

4. *Ibid.*, p. 108.

5. *Ibid.*, pp. 108–9.

6. *Ibid.*, p. 109.

protect Jews generally in Palestine was due to the influence of Lord
Shaftesbury,

> who had become convinced that a Jewish resettlement of Palestine would
> be advantageous not only for the Jewish people, but also for the sultan,
> who could count on the loyalty of new subjects who would, at the same
> time, restore a desolate province to prosperity. At the time when the
> powers were decided to compel Mehmet Ali to abandon Syria, but were
> still uncertain of its future, the project was mooted of creating a Jewish
> commonwealth in the southern half of the country—i.e., in the area of
> Biblical Palestine. That nothing came of these projects was in some meas-
> ure due to the fact that Western European Jewry was primarily engaged
> in the struggle for its emancipation and its consequent assimilation, and
> saw no point in the political re-establishment of a Jewish nation.[7]

The very extension of European influence into the Ottoman Empire
was "itself a major indirect cause of unrest in the area." Not only did it
produce difficulties for Jews and other minorities but it stimulated further
Western intervention. In some instances Jews were treated as actual or
potential allies of the enemy intruder. This assumption, as the Algerian case
revealed, was not without foundation; there the effect of the French conquest and French Jewish influence was the attainment by the local Algerian
Jewish community of the privileged status of French citizenship.

Western Jewish support for Palestinian Jewish communities necessarily
meant a rejection of the latter's traditional methods of problem solving.
In the first instance the new approach became increasingly political in
character as Western Jews endeavored both to secure a special status for
Jews in Palestine and for potential immigrants and to press ahead with
plans for indigenous economic development. Under the direction of the
Ailliance Israélite Universelle, founded in 1860 in conjunction with the
French branch of the house of Rothschild, hospitals, workshops, and
schools were established wherever the resources and the influence of various
Western governments could reach. Education along utilitarian Western
lines, although in strong contrast to the traditional religious orientation of
Jewish settlers, was destined to provide the practical foundation for an
expansive Jewish community. Following the Crimean War there was generally a renewed interest in extending French influence in the Levant, and
various political writers championed not only the protection of an autonomous Christian province of Lebanon but an autonomous Jewish province
of Palestine.

7. Parkes, *History of Palestine*, p. 266.

But it was not until the appearance of political Zionism in the 1880s that the modern period of Jewish immigration and colonization of Palestine truly began. After 1881 Russian anti-Semitism spawned numerous writings and efforts calling for emigration. Leo Pinsker's rousing pamphlet *Auto-Emancipation* (1882) led to the founding of societies of Choveve Zion (Lovers of Zion) which took root throughout Russia, Western Europe, and America. In 1882 three Zionist-inspired groups arrived in Palestine from Rumania and Poland.[8] Immediately there developed a conflict between Zionist ideology and the Western Jewish-sponsored operation. The French-language medium used in the Alliance schools was assailed for its "assimilationist" assumptions, and Hebrew was enjoined as necessary for building a new social-political community. In the sphere of economics, however, the Western Jews, such as Sir Moses Montefiore, the traditionalists, and the Zionists were in full agreement on the necessity for economic self-sufficiency.

Although Western Jews and political Zionists came to terms on some issues relating to the strengthening, expansion, and development of Jewish settlements in Palestine, serious, if not bitter, divisions developed in other areas. While the philosophy of Montefiore and the Rothschilds might have been predisposed in favor of Jewish settlement in Palestine, they and other Western Jews were also willing to see Jewish settlement in various other countries as a concrete solution to particular problems of anti-Semitism. Jewish statehood was not envisaged. For most Zionists, however, a philosophy of settlement or colonization which did not lead to statehood was just as unacceptable in the early 1900s as it was to be during the period of Nazi persecution. Another general cleavage between Zionists and Western Jews related to the relative priority of rehabilitating long-time residents or of providing for the new settlers, the bulk of whom after 1880 were brought in on a wave of Zionist impulse. Ultimately, however, Zionist philosophy was to pressure, assimilate, or convert Western Jews to its philosophy and plan of action. Thus, by the 1890s there were already strong indications that "the use of Zionist immigration coincided with, or brought about, a greater, more complex, and more institutional involvement of Western Jewry with the Palestine community and with the problems of immigration to Palestine."[9]

Between 1840 and 1880 the number of Jewish settlers in Palestine reached 25,000 and during the next thirty-five years it would reach 60,000.

8. *Ibid.,* p. 212.
9. Halpern, *Jewish State,* p. 120.

The political motives and the objective political effects of the new immigration had a historic bearing that did not escape contemporaries. From the 1880s on, the Turks, who until then had fluctuated between benevolence and negligent obstruction in their attitude towards Jewish immigrants, now became set in their opposition—though they were far from being perfectly efficient in preventing the growth of the community, and quite capable of being persuaded to relax their bans when suitably pressed or courted.[10]

For the first time in history Jews were subjected by the Ottoman authorities to an ordinance permitting them to visit Palestine on pilgrimage but absolutely prohibiting them from acquiring land or taking up permanent residence.[11]

But even when the Ottoman government had seen fit to permit Jewish immigration into Syria and Palestine, the local authorities and inhabitants "remained as ill-disposed to Jewish as to Christian settlers."[12] After 1880 European intercession on behalf of non-Muslim Ottoman subjects or consular protection for persons long resident in the Empire met hardening resistance. British occupation of Cyprus in 1878 and of Egypt in 1882, followed by the Congress of Berlin in 1884–85, showed in clear and naked terms Europe's resolve to preserve the balance of power at the expense of the Ottoman Empire. Britain and Russia were thereafter almost equally feared in Constantinople. Henceforth the sultan preferred Arab Palestinian cultivators and Lebanese investors to Western-protected Russian or Rumanian Jews, "with their ideas of an autonomous or sovereign Jewish status."[13] The result was, as Halpern noted, that

Western Jews had to deal with a new political problem in their traditional constructive work in Palestine. Instead of a country in which the ruling power willingly recognized certain Western privileges and responsibilities, Palestine had become an area in which Turkey resisted not only Russian, but also British and French influence. Moreover, instead of working with a settled population alone, Western Jews found themselves involved with the political problems of facilitating immigration to Palestine, and of cooperating with immigrants with a Zionist ideology. It was a considerable ideological concession for the Western Jews to adopt emigration at all

10. *Ibid.*, p. 212.
11. Parkes, *History of Palestine*, p. 269.
12. Halpern, *Jewish State*, p. 122.
13. *Ibid.*, p. 123.

as a method for solving the Jewish problem. To do so meant conceding that in Rumania and Russia, or in Persia and Morocco, the solution of the Jewish problem by emancipation could not yet be achieved, and it was necessary, in defeat, to remove the Jews to more hospitable lands.[14]

The Young Turk "coup" of 1908 considerably improved the opportunities for Zionist development in Palestine. Writing at the time, Professor Richard Gottheil, for seven years president of the American branch of the Zionist Organization, affirmed, however, Zionist respect for Ottoman suzerainty over Palestine:

Among the Jews, none rejoice with fuller heart than do the Zionists [over the Young Turk "coup"]. The cornerstone of Theodor Herzl's policy in his various dealings with the Sultan was a frank concession of the suzerain rights of the Padishah to the territories under his scepter, and the wish to make the accomplishment of Zionist ideals a source of material gain and of intellectual progress to the Turkish Empire. This was the keynote of his presentments to the Sultan and of his pronouncements at the Zionist congresses.[15]

Far from implying Jewish sovereignty, Professor Gottheil saw in the Young Turk philosophy a lesson in government for all:

In fact, the Young Turks may teach Europe a second lesson no less momentous than the first, that a state is far better served when it allows the widest range to the national and racial aspirations of its coherent parts than when it seeks to stifle these aspirations and to produce sores which fester for all time to come.[16]

While Western Jews discovered numerous reasons for collaborating with Eastern European Zionists, the latter had even more reason to seek Western cooperation. With uncertain legal status and the always present threat of Czarist repression, the Eastern Zionists addressed themselves to those organizations which had concerned themselves with Palestine over the previous decades. Dr. Pinsker and Theodor Herzl both sought Western political and financial support. In those early days of Zionist activity, however, the only Western Jew to give himself completely to the idea of

14. *Ibid.*
15. "The New Turkey and Zionism," *Independent*, LXV (October 15, 1908), 894.
16. *Ibid.*, p. 895.

Palestinian settlement was Baron Edmond de Rothschild, and he worked along independent but parallel lines. But even the Baron was soon criticized by Zionists for his paternalistic administration of Jewish colonies and for permitting the development of a Jewish planter class dependent upon the labor of Arab farm workers.

> The French schooling of the planters' sons, on the one hand, and the predominance of Arab village culture in the area of Jewish settlements, on the other, seemed to doom the hope of an indigenous Jewish culture; and these conditions certainly gave no grounds for confidence that the hope of Jewish sovereignty . . . was being significantly advanced.[17]

ZIONISM AND THE WESTERN POWERS: 1897–1914

Despite numerous differences of opinion over practical policy and general philosophy, both Western Jews and Zionists tacitly agreed to be silent on the question of Jewish sovereignty itself and of the political means to achieve it.

> The urgent task in the 1880s and 90s was one which fell far short of the Zionist ideal and yet was fundamental to the activities of both the Eastern Zionists and the Western Jews: merely to keep the doors of Palestine open to Jewish immigrants and procure the right to buy land and settle it. All were agreed in their willingness to adopt any legal or semilegal arrangement or subterfuge that would accomplish these ends in the Ottoman Empire.[18]

The publication of Theodor Herzl's *Der Judenstaat* [The Jewish state] in 1896 had both a polarizing and a mobilizing effect upon the world Jewish community. Not only did it threaten to bolster the credibility of anti-Semitic attacks because of its postulate that Jews could not assimilate, but primary emphasis upon statehood—hopefully in Palestine, or, if necessary, in some region able to be granted or sold by an imperial power—seemed to open a Pandora's box of possible misfortunes for Jews. On the other hand, by 1897 Herzl's influence had also opened a new phase in Zionism. Previously an Eastern European movement, Zionism now embraced the Eastern Jews, Westerners of Herzl's persuasion, and Palestinian settlers. Within this merger the "practicals" and the "politicals" favored

17. Halpern, *Jewish State,* p. 127.
18. *Ibid.*

direct diplomatic intervention with the sultan so as to secure "an open agreement by which an autonomous Jewish colonization of Palestine on a large scale might take place."[19] Ultimately both factions would be synthesized under the leadership of Chaim Weizmann. In either approach, however, the fact was ignored that Arabs, like other national groups within the Ottoman Empire, were already challenging the very basis of Constantinople's claim to rule over and direct the fortunes of its various national components.

Intent first upon enlisting imperial German and Russian support, Herzl confessed that in terms of strategy "the most suitable person would be the German Kaiser."[20] On being elected president of the World Zionist Organization by the First Zionist Congress meeting at Basle in August, 1897, Herzl's ideas emerged in a carefully worded resolution calling for a "publicly recognized, legally secured homeland in Palestine." By October, 1898, Herzl was clearly anticipating German support:

> To live under the protection of strong, great, moral, splendidly governed and thoroughly organized Germany is certain to have most salutary effects upon the national character of the Jews. Also, at one stroke we should obtain a completely legalized internal and external status. The suzerainty of the Porte and the protectorate under Germany surely ought to be adequate legal under-pinning.[21]

At a time when Germany was drawing close to the Ottoman Empire, the likelihood of successful German influence with Constantinople seemed most encouraging. Following the kaiser's visit to Constantinople in mid-October, 1898, where he met with Herzl, Wilhelm II went on to Palestine. Although the trip was ostensibly undertaken as a religious pilgrimage, it turned into a political demonstration in tune with German strategy to penetrate the Near East. Although Herzl accompanied the royal party and entertained high hopes of German support, it soon became apparent that Herzl's plans for Palestine were beyond German capability.

While Germany lacked the will or the power to carry off a political scheme in Palestine, the same was not to be the case with Great Britain. When an outbreak of Jewish pogroms in Russia at the turn of the century

---

19. Parkes, *History of Palestine*, p. 271; cf. Alan R. Taylor, "both groups were adherents of political Zionism, the only difference being that one accentuated legalization and the other stressed colonization of Palestine and an historico-cultural Romanticism" (*Prelude to Israel: An Analysis of Zionist Diplomacy 1897–1947* [New York, 1959], p. 8).

20. *Diaries*, ed. and trans. Marvin Lowenthal (New York, 1956), p. 105.

21. *Ibid.*, p. 252.

brought a flood of refugees into England, with their presumed threat to the English standard of living, the British government, presided over by Prime Minister Arthur James Balfour, appointed a royal commission to examine the question of alien immigration. As popular demand mounted to impose restrictions, Herzl's friends persuaded the royal commission to hear him as an expert witness—a request granted in 1902 despite the vigorous objections of Lord Rothschild, the foremost Western Jewish patron of Palestinian settlement but a strong opponent of political Zionism. Herzl's testimony not only struck a responsive chord among English politicians seeking a diminution of Jewish immigration but led to a revealing exchange with Rothschild. On July 12, 1902, Herzl confessed to Rothschild in a private and confidential letter that

> In addition to this human interest, I have a political motive. A great Jewish settlement in the East Mediterranean [Cyprus or Sinai] would strengthen our own efforts for Palestine.[22]

A few days later Herzl would again stress the connection between Zionism and British imperial interests and the personal advantage such a course offered:

> So far, you still have elbow room. Nay, you may claim high credit from your government if you strengthen British influences in the Near East by a substantial colonization of our people at the strategic point where Egyptian and Indo-Persian interests converge. How long do you imagine that these advantages, now to be seized [the establishment of a Land and Trade Company], will remain unnoticed?[23]

Although Lord Rothschild was not convinced by Herzl's argument, Joseph Chamberlain, the colonial secretary, well known for his anti-Semitic feelings but one of the most influential figures in the Cabinet, impressed Herzl as being even more important for the Zionist cause. Herzl informed an intermediary that he "should like to gain Mr. Chamberlain's support for a Jewish settlement on a considerable scale within the British dominions,"[24] preferably in Cyprus or the Egyptian Sinai Peninsula. Herzl did reach Chamberlain, and the colonial secretary indicated that only Cyprus fell within the jurisdiction of the Colonial Office since Egypt was the concern

22. *Ibid.*, p. 370.
23. *Ibid.*
24. *Ibid.*, p. 373.

of the Foreign Office. The secretary's response to Herzl's request for Cyprus dramatically revealed the direction of Zionist strategy and the philosophy of British imperialism. "As to Cyprus," Herzl reported, "[Chamberlain said] the island was inhabited by Greeks and Moslems, whom he could not evict for the sake of newcomers." Still, "he was willing, however, to help if he could: he liked the Zionist idea. If I could show him a spot among the British possessions which was not yet inhabited by *white* settlers, then we could talk."[25]

To this objection Herzl replied that "not everything in politics is disclosed to the public—but only results, or what can be serviceable in a controversy." He then unfolded his plan, which contemplated the creation of a favorable current of opinion in Cyprus. He suggested that once Jews had been invited into the country and had made a large capital investment, "the Moslems would leave, and the Greeks would gladly sell their lands at a good price and migrate to Athens or Crete."[26]

To Lord Lansdowne, minister for foreign affairs, Herzl suggested that the Sinai would provide "an assemblage center for the Jewish people in the neighborhood of Palestine." In return, said Herzl, Britain "would gain an increase of her power and the gratitude of ten million Jews." "When we are under the Union Jack at El Arish," said Herzl to Chamberlain, "then Palestine too will fall into 'the British sphere of influence.' " Although a Sinai colony was to be but a stepping-stone to Palestine, Herzl informed Chamberlain, in a subsequent conversation, that the Zionists could place themselves only under British rule, not Egyptian, to which the colonial secretary remarked that

> we shall not leave Egypt. Originally that was our intention. I am able to tell you this for I was in the Government. But we were obliged to sink so much money in the country, and now have so many interests there, that we can no longer pull out. Thus you and your settlement will be sharing the futures of that British possession.[27]

Although both the foreign secretary and the colonial secretary had indicated their interest in the Zionist project, Cyprus and Egypt presented difficulties. In the latter case, Lord Cromer, British consul-general and *"de facto"* viceroy of Egypt, was not receptive to Herzl's plan. But Chamberlain advanced another territory for Jewish colonization, one which was

25. *Ibid.,* p. 375 (italics added).
26. *Ibid.*
27. *Ibid.,* p. 376.

without white settlers. On April 23, 1903, Chamberlain proposed Uganda, which, while "hot on the coast," had a climate in the interior considered "excellent for Europeans." (He was speaking of areas of present-day Kenya, then part of a larger territory called Uganda.) To this proposal Herzl replied that the Zionist base "must be in or near Palestine. Later on we could also settle Uganda, for we have great masses of human beings ready to emigrate."[28]

While Cyprus, Sinai, and Uganda were clearly conceived by Herzl as colonial bases for the ultimate attainment of Palestine, the Russian Kishinev massacre of April, 1903, stirred Herzl to accept "territorial" Zionism as a legitimate end without reference to Palestine. Even before that event Herzl, like Pinsker, had accepted the pragmatic case for large-scale territorial colonization wherever possible. Although he had committed himself to Palestine through the Zionist Organization, Herzl was amenable to other suggestions. His plan was to win over outstanding Western leaders, Jewish and Gentile, to the general project of planned Jewish settlement. Only with such Western support could "public, international arrangements, formally establishing adequate legal rights in a suitable territory as well as suitable understandings concerning the transfer of emigrants and their property" be attained.[29]

At the Sixth Zionist Congress, August 22–28, 1903, at Basle, Herzl accepted and endorsed a proposal advanced by the British government for Jewish colonization of Uganda. The British proposal, formulated on instructions from Herzl's Zionist colleagues by David Lloyd George, M.P., was dispatched to Herzl on August 14, 1903. At the time Herzl was in Russia securing the endorsement of Vyacheslav Phehve, minister of interior (and responsible for the Kishinev massacre), for Russian Jewish emigration to Palestine. The proposal from the Foreign Office, involving "a considerable area of land" and entailing local autonomy under a Jewish governor,[30] seriously divided the Zionist Congress when a vote was taken to investigate the offer. Herzl stressed that while East Africa was not Palestine, but only "an auxiliary colonization," it could still provide "a national and state foundation."[31] "I do not believe," said Herzl, "that for the sake of a beautiful dream or a legitimist flag we ought to withhold relief from the unfortunate."[32]

28. *Ibid.*, p. 383.

29. Halpern, *Jewish State*, p. 129.

30. Herzl, *Diaries*, p. 407.

31. *Ibid.* White settler reaction to the Uganda proposal was so hostile that the British government withdrew the settlement proposal. (See Robert G. Weisbord, *African Zion* [Philadelphia, 1968], pp. 81–97).

32. Cited in Halpern, *Jewish State*, p. 154.

The Uganda proposal split the Zionist movement and induced those who would accept an alternative to Palestine to form the Jewish Territorial Organization (ITO) under the leadership of Israel Zangwill. Zangwill contended that present conditions, not historic attachments, should determine the proper location of the Jewish homeland. Supported by outstanding non-nationalist Jews such as Lucien Wolf (British), Oscar S. Straus, Daniel Guggenheim, and Judge Mayer Sulzberger (Americans), and James Simon and Paul Nathan (Germans), Zangwill explored anew the feasibility of settlements in East Africa and Portuguese Angola. Although the 1908 reforms under the Young Turks induced Zangwill to believe that conditions in Palestine might permit total concentration of Zionist efforts on that territory, he made clear his belief that the possession of some territory was an absolute necessity. Whether the Jewish nation be planted in North Africa (Tripoli), a possibility then being investigated, or in Palestine, it must meet not only the needs of Russian refugees but also those of English and American Jews. Lord Rothschild, he complained, "did great good to England" when he bought the Suez Canal bonds "but none at all for the Jews as a people." In America Zangwill found many instances of discrimination, and he expressed the belief that since "matters of this sort are growing worse instead of better" the Zionists could "expect to draw many from the two millions of Jews now in America."[33]

The outbreak of war in 1914 ended all hope that settlements in Africa could be effected but opened entirely new possibilities with regard to Palestine. With the Ottoman Empire opposed by the Allied Powers, Zionist associations with the expected victors offered the most realistic avenue to the acquisition of Palestine. The Jewish Territorial Organization thus lots its reason to exist, and the movement died.

In Palestine, meanwhile, the old settlers, who were largely dependent upon such benefactors as Lord Rothschild, "viewed political Zionism with suspicion and disfavour, and feared that a large influx of Jewish immigrants with political pretensions would endanger their good-neighbourly relations with the Arabs." Thus, with the publication of the Uganda proposal at Basle, "the Jews in Palestine itself, with a very few exceptions, were fanatical 'Ugandists.' "[34]

Within the Zionist Organization the contest between "practicals" and

---

33. "Zionism of Today," *Independent*, LXV (October 15, 1908), 893. Zangwill informed an American audience in 1904 that "Palestine proper was already inhabited. . . . The alternatives open to the Zionists bent on having Palestine were to drive out the inhabitants by the sword or to grapple with the problem of a large alien population, mostly hostile Moslems" (cited in Weisbord, *African Zion*, p. 227).

34. Arthur Koestler, *Promise and Fulfillment: Palestine 1917–1949* (New York, 1949), pp. 36–37.

"politicals" led to the victory of the former. Thus, even in the absence of legal permission, the practicals, drawing upon assistance of the World Zionist Organization, opened the Anglo-Palestine Bank in 1903; the Jewish National Fund began purchasing land in 1905; and in 1908 the Palestine Office was opened in Jaffa. The Palestine Land Development Fund was founded in 1908 to make land ready for settlement for buyers still abroad. With these and other sources of financial assistance provided by the Palestine Jewish Colonization Association (P.I.C.A.), the number of Zionist settlers reached 12,000 by 1914, out of an estimated Jewish population of about 60,000. Jews owned 2 per cent of the land. In the same year, the Arab population was 644,000, of which 70,000 were Christian and 574,000 Muslim. The whole Zionist enterprise, in keeping with the prevailing political philosophy, was seen as self-justifying in its results. As the Zionist historian Rufus Learsi saw it,

> The Jews, by race and origin an eastern people and by experience and skills a part of the west, were exceptionally qualified to bring the stagnant east into the orbit of western civilization. . . . Zionism was introducing a dynamic impulse into Palestine which promised to infuse new life into the entire Near East.[35]

Following Herzl's death in 1904, the Seventh Zionist Congress, which met that year, refused to consider an alternative to Palestine. As the movement expanded its activities into Britain and the United States these countries developed as the main power centers of Zionist activity. In both instances the political structures lent themselves admirably to a systematic direction of organized and mobilized opinion toward those responsible for formulating foreign policy.

After 1912 Supreme Court Justice Louis D. Brandeis became the most commanding American authority in the movement. A close confidant of President Wilson and highly respected in liberal circles, Justice Brandeis called out to educated American Jews to reject assimilation as "national suicide" and to strive for a Palestine "where the Jewish life may be naturally led."[36] Among those Jewish Americans who opposed Brandeis, none was more eloquent in addressing himself to the imperialistic philosophy embedded in Zionism than Mayer Sulzberger, former president of the Court of Common Pleas of the state of Pennsylvania. Sulzberger based his opposition to Zionism on the ground that it denied democracy to those who lived in Palestine:

35. *Fulfillment: The Epic Story of Zionism* (Cleveland, 1951), p. 172.
36. *Ibid.,* p. 181.

Democracy means that those who live in a country shall select their rulers and shall preserve their powers. Given these principles a Convention of Zionists looking to the government of people who are in Palestine would be in contravention of the plainest principle of democracy. It can have no practical meaning unless its intent is to overslaugh the people who are in Palestine and to deprive them of the right of self-government by substituting the will of persons outside, who may or may not ever see Palestine.[37]

In Britain the mantle of Zionist leadership fell upon Dr. Chaim Weizmann. Born in Russia and involved in Zionist activities as a student in the universities of Berlin and Geneva, he had opposed Herzl's efforts to secure legal permission from the sultan before endeavoring to build a Zionist colony in Palestine. As a "practical" he urged the promotion of modest projects which would lead to a buildup of the Jewish community in Palestine. Weizmann went to England on the conviction that the British were the most promising potential sympathizers with Zionism. From 1903 he taught chemistry in the University of Manchester where his scientific attainments would play their part in his diplomatic success. According to Weizmann, it was only in 1907, after he had embarked on a program of establishing rapport with British politicians, that he learned from the director of the Anglo-Palestine Bank "of the nascent Arab national movement."[38] By 1914 Weizmann had been converted to the role of a "political."

Weizmann methodically proceeded to build up a group of influential Jews and non-Jews who could obtain support in government circles. Among the more prominent of these were Herbert Samuel, who became secretary of state for home affairs in 1916; Lord Lionel Walter Rothschild; James Rothschild, son of Edmond Rothschild of Paris, the patron of Jewish colonization in Palestine; Norman Bentwick, jurist; Major Ormsby-Gore; and the editors of the *Manchester Guardian* and London *Times*.[39]

---

37. Cited in J. M. N. Jeffries, *Palestine: The Reality* (London, 1939), p. 153.

38. Cited in Moshe Menuhin, *The Decadence of Judaism in Our Time* (New York, 1965), p. 50; cf. Taylor, *Prelude to Israel,* p. 9.

39. Weizmann wrote to C. P. Scott, editor of the *Manchester Guardian,* in November, 1914 (before meeting with Samuel and Lloyd George), that "we can reasonably say that should Palestine fall within the British sphere of influence and should Britain encourage Jewish settlement there, as a British dependency, we could have in twenty to thirty years a million Jews out there, perhaps more; they would develop the country, bring back civilization to it and form a very effective guard for the Suez Canal" (cited in Taylor, *Prelude to Israel,* p. 12).

ZIONISM AND THE WESTERN ALLIES: 1914–1918

It was the outbreak of war in November, 1914, that gave the Zionist Organization its moment of historical opportunity. Initially, however, the war had a traumatic effect upon the Zionist Organization. Not only was the world headquarters in Berlin but Zionists in Russia had no sympathy with Czarist war efforts and hoped for Russian defeat. The Zionist policy-making body established a bureau in Copenhagen to stress the Organization's neutrality, and some efforts were made to discourage Weizmann's outspoken support for the Allied cause.

Weizmann, however, correctly perceived the likely course of events and successfully worked to bring about the development of autonomous Zionist units after the dismantling of the Berlin headquarters. Joined by several outstanding continental Zionists, headed by Sokolow and Tschlenow, who arrived in Britain in November, 1914, Weizmann was instrumental in establishing close contact with American Zionists.[40]

American Zionist support was crucial for the survival of the Palestinian Zionist communities now deprived, as they were, of European funds. "It became clear that America alone must not only save the Yishuv but keep the Zionist Movement alive."[41] The raising of $10 million between November, 1914, and December, 1917, by the American Jewish Joint Distribution Committee gave some idea of the potential power and influence of the American Zionists.[42]

In both the United States and Britain, Zionists bent their efforts toward obtaining a guarantee from the Allies that, in the event of Ottoman defeat, Palestine would be recognized as a Jewish commonwealth open to unrestricted immigration. During the first two years of the war, Zionist efforts to influence the British government bore no visible fruit. In April, 1916, the Allies negotiated a secret pact, the Sykes-Picot Agreement, dividing the area among themselves. No direct reference to Zionist aspirations was made. In this agreement an Arab confederation under the joint protection of France and Britain was delimited. The region of Palestine was to be under an international regime with Jews accorded "political, religious, and civil equality," but no more.[43]

By 1917, however, patient and persistent Zionist efforts began to show signs of success. Victory with the British Cabinet was due in no small part

40. George Lenczowski, ed., *The Middle East in World Affairs* (Ithaca, N. Y., 1956), pp. 77–78.
41. Learsi, *Fulfillment*, p. 178.
42. *Ibid.*, p. 184.
43. *Ibid.*, p. 189.

to the role played by Herbert Samuel, who, as early as November 9, 1914, had put the case to Lord Grey for the founding of a Jewish state with the help of Britain and the United States, "the most progressive of the countries in which the Jews find themselves." The same day he also met Lloyd George whose backing later proved decisive. In January, 1915, he sent Prime Minister Asquith a draft Cabinet memorandum, "the first formulation, at top level, of an actual plan. It proposed annexation and a Protectorate within the British Empire." The protectorate, he argued, would "enable England to fulfill in yet another sphere her historic part of the civiliser of the backward countries."[44]

Although Samuel's first proposal was greeted with mirth, if not contempt, by Asquith, Samuel advanced a revised memorandum in March, 1915. This document, according to Samuel's biographer, "marked a turning point in the history of the Middle East and of the world."[45] Here Samuel set forth five possibilities for the future of Palestine in the event of the breakup of the Turkish Empire. First, Palestine might be annexed by France and thus constitute a menacing threat to British lines of communication. Second, it might be returned to Turkey to fall once more into squalor. A third alternative would be internationalization, but this could well prove "a steppingstone to a German protectorate." The last two alternatives, the early establishment of a Jewish state or the establishment of a British protectorate proved decisive (as subsequent events revealed) in the formulation of British policy. The "immediate" establishment in Palestine of an autonomous Jewish state was rejected by Samuel as too costly and dangerous for the Zionist movement:

> Whatever be the merits or the demerits of that proposal, it is certain that the time is not ripe for it. Such increase of population as there has been in Palestine in recent years has been composed, indeed, mostly of Jewish immigrants; the new Jewish agricultural colonies already number about 15,000 souls; in Jerusalem itself two-thirds of the inhabitants are Jews; but in the country, as a whole, they still probably do not number more than about one-sixth of the population.

> If the attempt were made to place the 500,000 or 600,000 Mahommedans of Arab race under a Government which rested upon the support of 90,000 or 100,000 Jewish inhabitants, there can be no assurance that such a Government, even if established by the authority of the Powers, would be able to command obedience. The dream of a Jewish State, prosperous, progressive, and the home of a brilliant civilisation, might

44. John Bowle, *Viscount Samuel* (London, 1957), p. 170.
45. *Ibid.*, p. 172.

vanish in a series of squalid conflicts with the Arab population. And even if a State so constituted did succeed in avoiding or repressing internal disorder, it is doubtful whether it would be strong enough to protect itself from external aggression on the part of the turbulent elements around it. To attempt to realise the aspiration of a Jewish State one century too soon might throw back its actual realisation for many centuries more. These considerations are fully recognised by the leaders of the Zionist movement.

The only feasible alternative, Samuel concluded, was the establishment of a British protectorate. It is worth quoting at length:

Its establishment would be a safeguard to Egypt. It is true that Palestine in British hands would itself be open to attack, and the acquisition would bring with it extended military responsibilities. But the mountainous character of the country would make its occupation by an enemy difficult, and, while this outpost was being contested, time would be given to allow the garrison of Egypt to be increased and the defences to be strengthened. . . .

A British protectorate, according to the Egyptian Intelligence Department report already quoted, would be welcomed by a large proportion of the present population. There have been many previous indications of the same feeling. I am assured, both by Zionists and non-Zionists, that it is the solution of the question of Palestine which would be by far the most welcome to the Jews throughout the world.

It is hoped that under British rule facilities would be given to Jewish organisations to purchase land, to found colonies, to establish educational and religious institutions, and to co-operate in the economic development of the country, and that Jewish immigration, carefully regulated, would be given preference, so that in course of time the Jewish inhabitants, grown into a majority and settled in the land, may be conceded such degree of self-government as the conditions of that day might justify. . . .

The course which is advocated would win for England the gratitude of the Jews throughout the world. In the United States, where they number about 2,000,000, and in all the other lands where they are scattered, they would form a body of opinion whose bias, where the interest of the country of which they were citizens was not involved, would be favourable to the British Empire. Just as the wise policy of England towards Greece in the early part of the nineteenth century, and towards Italy in the middle of the nineteenth century, has secured for this country the goodwill of Greeks and Italians, wherever they may be, ever since, so help given now towards the attainment of the ideal which great numbers of Jews have never ceased to cherish through so many centuries of suffering cannot fail to secure, into a far-distant future, the gratitude of a whole race, whose goodwill, in time to come, may not be without its value.

The British Empire, with its present vastness and prosperity, has little addition to its greatness left to win. But Palestine, small as it is in area, bulks so large in the world's imagination, that no Empire is so great but its prestige would be raised by its possession. The inclusion of Palestine within the British Empire would add a lustre even to the British Crown. It would make a most powerful appeal to the people of the United Kingdom and the Dominions, particularly if it were avowedly a means of aiding the Jews to reoccupy the country. Widespread and deep-rooted in the Protestant world is a sympathy with the idea of restoring the Hebrew people to the land which was to be their inheritance, an intense interest in the fulfilment of the prophecies which have foretold it. The redemption also of the Christian Holy Places from the vulgarisation to which they are now subject and the opening of the Holy Land, more easily than hitherto, to the visits of Christian travellers, would add to the appeal which this policy would make to the British peoples. There is probably no outcome of the war which would give greater satisfaction to powerful sections of British opinion.

The importance that would be attached by British opinion to this annexation would help to facilitate a wise settlement of another of the problems which will result from the war. Although Great Britain did not enter the conflict with any purpose of territorial expansion, being in it and having made immense sacrifices, there would be profound disappointment in the country if the outcome were to be the securing of great advantages by our Allies and none by ourselves. But to strip Germany of her colonies for the benefit of England would leave a permanent feeling of such intense bitterness among the German people as to render such a course impolitic. We have to live in the same world with 70,000,000 Germans, and we should take care to give as little justification as we can for the hatching, ten, twenty, or thirty years hence, of a German war of revenge. Certain of the German colonies must no doubt be retained for strategic reasons or on account of the interests of our Dominions. But if Great Britain can obtain the compensations, which public opinion will demand, in Mesopotamia and Palestine, and not in German East Africa and West Africa, there is more likelihood of a lasting peace.[46]

Although this cogent document most clearly articulated the advantages which might accrue to the British Empire by extending a protectorate over

46. Cited in *ibid.*, pp. 173–77.

Palestine, Asquith was not impressed. "Curiously enough," the prime minister recorded, "the only other partisan of this proposal is Lloyd George, who, I need not say, does not care a damn for the Jews or their past or their future, but thinks it will be an outrage to let the Holy Places pass into the possession or under the protectorate of 'agnostic, aesthetic France.' "[47]

Samuel's proposal fell on more receptive ears when, in December, 1916, Lloyd George became prime minster and Arthur Balfour, foreign secretary. Whatever Lloyd George's feelings were toward Jews generally, as chairman of the War Munitions Board he was grateful to Dr. Weizmann for his discovery in the early days of the war of a new process for the large-scale production of acetone, a substance essential in the manufacture of explosives.

Balfour, even more than Lloyd George, was sympathetic to Zionist goals. His association with Zionism went back at least a decade, roughly to that period when his opinion was also vital in another area of European settlement, namely, South Africa. Balfour's basic philosophy had then been revealed in debates on the proposed Union of South Africa. Although that prospect was greeted with the greatest enthusiasm as a testament to the liberal English tradition, it would also set the stage for the legal subjugation of the African majority. Balfour's defense of the proposed Union was undoubtedly rooted in the same creed which later dictated his approach to an analogous situation in Palestine. With regard to South Africa he had argued thus:

> If the races of Europe have really conquered, by centuries of difficulty and travail, great rights and privileges for themselves, they have given some of those rights and some of those privileges to men quite incapable, by themselves, of fighting for them at all, or obtaining them at all. That is the plain, historic truth of the situation, which it is perfect folly for us to attempt to forget. It is this very fact of the inequality of the races which makes the difficulty.[48]

Balfour, like the new colonial secretary, Lord Milner, found Samuel's proposal attractive. Immediately, arrangements were made to modify the Sykes-Picot Agreement. Sir Mark Sykes, himself a keen Zionist since 1916,[49] thus secured permission to repudiate that part of the agreement

47. Cited in *ibid.*, p. 178.
48. Cited in Leonard M. Thompson, *The Unification of South Africa, 1902–1910* (London, 1960), p. 427.
49. Elizabeth Monroe, *Britain's Moment in the Middle East, 1914–1956* (Baltimore, 1963), p. 38.

which provided for the internationalization of Palestine. The fact that in March, 1917, Russia collapsed, thus making France more amenable to modifications, facilitated the Zionist task, as did the entry of the United States into the war the following month. Thereafter President Wilson's attitude on this and all other questions became crucially important.

In America, under the leadership of Brandeis, the Zionist Organization cooperated closely with Zionist efforts in London. In 1914, after Brandeis became head of the Zionist Provisional Committee, and with the support of Rabbi Stephen Wise and Dr. Gottheil, Zionist hopes and claims were submitted to Wilson whose sympathy for the cause was strengthened by his respect for Brandeis.

> As the war years dragged on the conviction grew in the minds of American Zionists that Herzl's dream was on the verge of fulfillment, and after April 6, 1917, when America entered the war, it was clear that American influence might prove decisive. Brandeis and his associates were kept informed of the negotiations that were proceeding in London, and in May he had a "satisfactory talk" with President Wilson and with Balfour, who had come to America on a war mission. Among other Americans whose good will was cultivated were Secretary of State Robert Lansing and Colonel Edward M. House, Wilson's principal adviser.[50]

Other converts to the Zionist cause included William Jennings Bryan; Newton D. Baker, secretary of war; and Josephus Daniels, secretary of the Navy.[51]

The Zionist's aim in the United States was to secure a public statement from President Wilson in support of the Zionist formula then being discussed in London. Since the United States was not at war with Turkey, Wilson first declined to make a statement. However, by July, 1917, Zionist conversations with the British government had reached an advanced stage over a proposed declaration which would commit Britain to Jewish settlement, if not a Jewish state, in Palestine. According to Learsi, given the strong anti-Zionist feelings of prominent Jewish leaders in Britain, such as Sir Edwin S. Montagu, it was the work of Brandeis that made the vital difference:

> What finally tipped the scales in its favor was a message which President Wilson, at the request of Brandeis, addressed to Prime Minister Lloyd George, approving the pronouncement. The final version was laid before the Zionist leaders as well as a number of prominent anti-Zionists. The

50. Learsi, *Fulfillment*, p. 191.
51. Lenczowski, *Middle East*, p. 80.

latter rejected it; the former, although it fell short of their expectations, accepted it.[52]

By November, 1917, Weizmann and Sokolow had, with the support of Sykes, Samuel, and Rothschild, secured the endorsement of Lloyd George, Churchill, Balfour, Lord Milner, Lord Cecil, and General Smuts of South Africa, to a declaration of support. The result was that on November 2, 1917, Lord Balfour, on behalf of the Cabinet, addressed the following letter to Lord Rothschild:

> I have much pleasure in conveying to you, on behalf of His Majesty's Government, the following declaration of sympathy with Jewish Zionist aspirations, which has been submitted to and approved by the Cabinet: "His Majesty's Government view with favour the establishment in Palestine of a national home for the Jewish people, and will use their best endeavours to facilitate the achievement of this object, it being clearly understood that nothing shall be done which may prejudice the civil and religious rights of existing non-Jewish communities in Palestine, or the rights and political status enjoyed by Jews in any other country."
>
> I should be grateful if you would bring this Declaration to the knowledge of the Zionist Federation.[53]

That Britain had not formally committed itself to the establishment of a Jewish state was patently clear; that such a state might eventually emerge seemed only logical. Of the Jewish state, Samuel wrote, "at some future time it might come about . . . but so long as the great majority of the inhabitants are Arabs, it is out of the question."[54] The ambiguity in the declaration was not only a concession to anti-Zionist Jewish sentiment but was also intended to overcome Arab protests likely to arise in view of British commitments to an Arab state made to Sharif Husayn in 1915. Allusion to the Arab 92 per cent of the population as the "non-Jewish communities" perhaps indicated the government's primary concern for the expected immigrants. Although the declaration fell short of the wishes of Zionist militants, it was generally greeted by Jews as the beginning of a new era, the preliminary to statehood. As Herbert Adams Gibbons, writing in 1919, observed, from the day of the declaration's appearance,

---

52. *Fulfillment,* p. 192.

53. J. C. Hurewitz, ed., *Diplomacy in the Near and Middle East* (Princeton, 1956), II, 26.

54. Cited by Bowle, *Viscount Samuel,* p. 179.

the Zionists . . . looked upon the letter of Mr. Balfour to Lord Rothschild as official British sanction to the establishment of a Jewish state in Palestine by means of wholesale immigration and buying up of the land.[55]

With their task in Britain accomplished, it remained to give the declaration the sanction of international recognition. France and Italy approved the declaration in February, 1918, and Wilson approved it in October. Thereafter the Zionists were closely linked to the Allies and became an unofficial partner in the Allied cause.

The Foreign Office went so far as to grant them the privilege of British diplomatic pouch. In return the Zionists were expected to render valuable assistance in the prosecution of the war. The extent to which they contributed to the Allied victory is, obviously, hard to determine, but it may be helpful to quote Britain's wartime prime minister, David Lloyd George, who made the following statement before the Palestine Royal Commission in 1936: "The Zionist leaders gave us a definite promise that, if the Allies committed themselves to giving facilities for the establishment of a national home for the Jews in Palestine, they would do their best to rally Jewish sentiment and support throughout the world to the Allied cause. They kept their word." Amplifying this statement in the House of Commons in 1937, Lloyd George declared that the Zionists "were helpful in America and in Russia, which at that moment was just walking out and leaving us alone."[56]

With Allied endorsement it was henceforth assumed that the "legal" right of the Jews to build a "national home" in Palestine had been established, an argument which thereafter would be employed to win over a larger segment of world public opinion to the Zionist cause. In the words of Bernard Rosenblatt, a leading figure at the 1918 Zionist Conference in Pittsburgh, Zionists could feel that

after convincing the powerful governments of Great Britain, France, and Italy, and after securing endorsement . . . from the President of the United States, we feel that we have won our case before the world, and that it is altogether unnecessary to expend valuable energy in order to convert a negligible opposition. The Jewish Commonwealth of Palestine is a fact and we are now fixing the boundaries of the state.[57]

55. "Zionism and the World Peace," *Century*, XCVII (January, 1919), 369.
56. Lenczowski, *Middle East*, pp. 81–82.
57. "Zionism at the Peace Conference," *Public*, XXII (February 1, 1919), 112.

ZIONISM AND THE ADMINISTRATION
OF PALESTINE: 1918–1922

General Edmund Allenby's force had scarcely crossed into Palestine
from Egypt when word of the Balfour Declaration arrived from London.
On November 9, 1917, while the Third Battle of Gaza raged, Allenby
was informed of the declaration. Such was the general's concern over
the possible impact of the document that he forbade its publication in
Palestine.[58] Thanks both to Allenby's immediate action and the generally
poor state of communications, the full effect on Arab opinion of the Balfour Declaration was not to be felt for some months. Allenby's determined
refusal to accord any Jewish privileges on the strength of that document
until the fate of the country had been clearly settled by the Peace Conference also had a calming effect, although it quickly provoked criticism in
London from militant Zionists and from some few of the general's own
staff. Among the local populace, both Jewish and Arab, however, there
remained a fair degree of trust and goodwill,[59] and Allenby was enabled
to pursue the enemy without hindrance, until on September 18, 1918, the
Turkish army in Palestine surrendered.

The occupation of Jerusalem in early December, 1917, confronted
Allenby with an ever growing number of political and military problems.
The impossibility of reconciling British undertakings in the Sykes-Picot
Agreement with the Balfour Declaration and with promises made to
Sharif Husayn all pressed upon the commander in chief, and his deputy,
Lt. Gen. Louis Bols. Although Allenby's staff and advisers such as Wavell,
Storrs, and Lawrence emphatically pressed for greater attention to Arab
interests, both on moral and strategic grounds, Allenby's political officer,
Meinertzhagen, soon informed the Foreign Office that the general was not
ruling Palestine in accordance with the Balfour Declaration. Allenby also
came into collision with the French political representative, Georges Picot,
since Picot apparently thought that an Anglo-French administration might
yet be set up in Jerusalem. Not only did Allenby dismiss the suggestion
out-of-hand,[60] but he thereafter strongly advised both the British government and the Paris Peace Conference against imposing the French upon
an unwilling Syria.[61] Jealousies and disputes between various Christian
sects further complicated the problems of administration. Allenby refused
to yield to any of these pressures and insisted that Palestine must be

---

58. Brian Gardner, *Allenby of Arabia* (New York, 1965), p. 168.
59. *Ibid.,* p. 216.
60. Archibald Wavell, *Allenby—A Study in Greatness* (New York, 1941), p. 236.
61. Gardner, *Allenby of Arabia,* p. 219.

administered as occupied enemy territory and that the principles laid down by international law, which prescribed as little change as possible in existing methods of government, must be strictly followed. His administrators, General Clayton and Maj. Gen. Sir Arthur Money, would have a free hand in terms of Allenby's general philosophy of government.

During the two and a half years of British military rule, from December, 1917, to July, 1920, General Allenby made strenuous efforts to live up to his promise to protect the rights of all the inhabitants and to restore the country to normality. At the war's outset European consulates were closed, and most European educators and missionaries left the country. Leaders of indigenous Christian communities were deported, and the Jewish community was reduced through deportation or disease to about 56,000 in 1918.[62] Severe as the effects of Turkish repression were upon both the Jewish and Christian communities, it took an even heavier toll of Arab nationalists—Muslim and Christian. Many prominent Arabs were executed and thousands of Arab peasants were conscripted. Food and livestock were commandeered, and by the time of Allenby's arrival the country was on the brink of starvation and total collapse.

Shortly after the occupation of Jerusalem a Zionist Commission established its headquarters at Tel Aviv and another office in Jerusalem. The commission was appointed by the Zionist Organization as the representative in Palestine of both Palestinian Jewry and world Jewry. Under the chairmanship of Dr. Weizmann, its function was to mediate with the British administration. In March, 1918, Dr. Weizmann visited Palestine accompanied by several Zionist leaders and Major Ormsby-Gore, a pro-Zionist British liaison officer. The presence of this Zionist Commission brought adverse comments from both Palestinian Arabs and Allenby's staff, a foreshadowing of difficulties to come. At a public gathering Weizmann expressed, in vain, deep interest "in the struggle for freedom which the ancient Arab race is now waging against Turkey." The mufti and other Muslim notables withdrew from the room in protest. So unanimous was Palestinian Arab opinion that the French censor permitted in the Arab newspaper of Paris, *Al Moustaqbal,* a Jerusalem protest stating that "moslems will never allow Jews to control Palestine."[63] Few Arabs ventured to meet with the Zionist leader. An offer of an agricultural bank was refused, and Weizmann was told that there could be no agreement "except between the element already settled in Palestine." Gibbons' analysis in 1919 of Weizmann's failure to relate to the Arabs and of the consequences

62. Oscar I. Janowsky, *Foundations of Israel* (Princeton, 1959), p. 14
63. August 30, 1918; cited in Gibbons, "Zionism," p. 373.

of the probable course of events at the Peace Conference were to prove
prophetic and must be quoted in full:

> Under the influence of the dazzling victories of the autumn of 1918, the
> Internationalist Zionist Commission is probably able to report a "working
> agreement," which will be cited to prove the groundlessness of my state-
> ments and my fears. Resignation is the cardinal virtue of Islam, we are
> assured. But we must not be deceived by appearances. History proves
> the Mohammedan acceptance of the inevitable, cheerful and definite
> acceptance. But history proves also the unwisdom—no; more, the im-
> possibility—of changing the political and social nature of a Mohammedan
> country by forced European immigration. Colonists, products of another
> civilization, backed in agricultural and commercial competition with in-
> digenous elements by large grants of money and protected by diplomacy
> behind which stood armies and battleships, have failed to take root or
> have been massacred. Zionists should study the failure of France in
> Tunis, the pitiful shipwreck of Italian ambitions in Tripoli, and the
> disastrous results of Greek attempts to increase colonization along the
> Sea of Marmora and the Aegean coast of Asia Minor. The resignation
> of Mohammedans is an article of faith; but their inability to accept
> political domination in their own country of non-Moslem elements is
> also an article of faith. Oil does not mix with water. It is a sad mistake
> to attribute the comparative failure of earlier Zionist attempts at coloniza-
> tion in Palestine to the corruption of the Turkish rule. Arabs are far more
> Mohammedan than are Turks. Their fanaticism is more to be feared.
>
> If the peace conference decides to restore the Jews to Palestine, immi-
> gration into and development of the country can be assured only by the
> presence of a considerable army for an indefinite period. Not only the
> half million Moslems living in Palestine, but the millions in surrounding
> countries, will have to be cowed into submission by the constant show
> and the occasional use of force.
>
> But how can we reconcile such a policy in Palestine with the principles
> for the *world-wide* maintenance of which we have announced that we
> are fighting? Is the peace conference to give with one hand and take
> away with the other? We have made the issues of this conflict the triumph
> of right over force and the liberation of small nations from the yoke of
> the foreigner. Each race is to be consulted in regard to its own destinies.
> If we consult the Palestinian Arabs, Christian as well as Moslem, we
> shall find them *unanimous* in their desire, their determination, not to
> have Zionism foisted upon them. They comprise over eighty per cent
> of the population of Palestine. Even in the Jewish minority there is
> strong anti-Zionist element, for Jewry is no more united than are
> Christendom and Islam. The Sephardim, who understand the spirit of the
> Orient better than Occidental and Northern Jews and who are in large

majority among the indigenous Palestine Jews, do not sympathize with the Zionist program.

. . . In the Near East, as in the Far East, arrogance, insolence, indifference to the political *and social* rights of "natives" *in their own countries* will have to go the way of ante-bellum diplomacy. If we do not change radically our attitude toward *all* Asiatic races, the present war is nothing to what is coming, and in the twentieth century, too.[64]

In 1919 Palestine received the attention of the King-Crane Commission, the Peace Conference at Versailles, and Justice Brandeis. In the first instance, the King-Crane Commission grew out of President Wilson's second thoughts on the policies of the Allies. Having made numerous concessions contrary to his idealistic proposals, Wilson decided that the right of self-determination should be applied to the Ottoman Near East. He thus refused to recognize the Anglo-French wartime commitments and requested in March that an international commission on mandates in Turkey be sent out to ascertain the wishes of the various peoples. The prospect of such a commission alarmed both the Zionists and the French. On May 8, 1919, Felix Frankfurter wrote the president of the "deepest disquietude to the representatives of the Jewry of the world" caused by the appointment of the Inter-Allied Syrian Commission.[65] The French declined to participate knowing full well the hatred felt toward them by the Syrians, and Britain withdrew its representatives. Rather than delay any longer, Wilson sent the American section, popularly known as the King-Crane Commission, to the Near East in June, 1919.

After spending fifteen days in Palestine the commission concluded that only the Zionist Jews, about one-tenth of the total population, favored the establishment of a Jewish national home. In its final report the Commission advised "serious modification of the extreme Zionist program" of unlimited immigration. There was nothing on which the population of Palestine was more united, said the report, than its hatred of the entire Zionist program. "To subject a people so minded to unlimited Jewish immigration, and to steady financial and social pressure to surrender the land, would be a gross violation of the principle just quoted [free acceptance], and of the people's rights, though it kept within the forms of law."[66]

The King-Crane Commission delivered its report to Wilson in the autumn of 1919. Meanwhile, the Covenant of the League of Nations, approved by the Paris Peace Conference on April 28, 1919, was incorporated

64. *Ibid.*, pp. 374–76.
65. Cited in Harry N. Howard, *The King-Crane Commission* (Beirut, 1963), p. 73.
66. *Ibid.*, pp. 224–25.

into the Treaty of Versailles, signed on June 28, 1919. Article 22 of the Covenant provided for the mandates system under the supervision of the League. Paragraph 4 of article 22 pertained to the Near East provinces of the Ottoman Empire and gave the Arabs stronger reason to believe that their expectations would be fulfilled:

> Certain communities formerly belonging to the Turkish Empire have reached a stage of development where their existence as independent nations can be provisionally recognized subject to the rendering of administrative advice and assistance by a Mandatory until such time as they are able to stand alone. The wishes of these communities must be a principle consideration in the selection of the Mandatory.[67]

But Arab hopes, based on article 22 and the 1915 British promises to Husayn, proved unfounded in view of the pressures mounting at Paris in support of the Zionist cause.

The Supreme Council heard the Zionist case on February 27, 1919. Many of the suggestions contained in the Zionist memorandum would eventually find their way into the mandatory instrument approved by the League. Of no little interest in terms of events fifty years later, the Zionist delegation proposed boundaries which went considerably beyond the ultimate limits of mandate Palestine. Parts of Lebanon, Syria, Egypt, and Transjordan, as far east as the Hejaz Railway, were requested.[68]

Although the Zionists carefully refrained from mentioning a Jewish state, the call for unlimited immigration, powers of local government, and other privileges, left little doubt of the ultimate object. Zionist writers of the period graphically set forth the methods to be employed in securing that end, and their description of the indigenous population, both as to culture and disposition, are remarkable testaments to the prevailing psychology. Elsie Weil, for example, concluded that "friction between the two races, arose not . . . on racial grounds so much as economic ones. . . . The Arab is as likely to gain as to lose by Jewish occupation of the country."[69] Bernard Rosenblatt, President of the Zion Commonwealth, Inc., noted that in buying land

> there is no reason why we should pour wealth into the hands of those who happen to hold title to the land of Palestine, when the increased

67. Hurewitz, *Diplomacy*, p. 62.
68. *Ibid.*, p. 46.
69. "The Jewish Commonwealth," *Asia*, February, 1919.

value will be due, not to labor on the part of landlords, but to the new government which Great Britain and the Zionists will have established. . . . the land values should be taxed for the benefits received from the conquest of Great Britain and the Jewish mass immigration.[70]

As for the Arab population, Albert Hyamson, an English Zionist later appointed to the Palestine administration, concluded that

> there will be a new incentive, and strong one, for a Moslem Arab emigration from Palestine. Close at hand there is to be a Moslem Arab State, organized under its own rulers. . . . This State should of itself be a magnet to the Moslem Arabs settled in other lands. . . . It should be unnecessary to say that no Arab will be dispossessed or forced by any means to leave his home. If he does so, it will be of his own free will; and his removal will leave no cause for bitterness.[71]

In a more realistic vein, however, Israel Zangwill, president of the Jewish Territorial Organization, spoke pointedly of the only alternative if a Jewish state were to be established:

> The whole planet is in the grip of Allied Might and it needs but Allied Right to reshape all racial boundaries and international relations. . . . But a Hebrew Palestine, if it is to exist at all must be a reality, not a sham. . . . The power in every country . . . always remains in the land-owning classes. Yet over 30,000 Arab landlords and some 600,000 fellahin are to continue in possession of the Holy soil. . . . And hence we must suppose that this new system of creative politics . . . will be carried out in Palestine as elsewhere. Thus the Arabs would gradually be settled in the new and vast Arabian Kingdom. . . . Only thus can Palestine become a "Jewish National Home." . . . Only with a Jewish majority (not of course a Jewish totality), only with the land nationalized—and Jewish as well as Arab land must be expropriated with reasonable compensation—can Israel enter upon the task of building up that model State, the construction of which American Zionism, in its trustful acceptance of the [Balfour] Declaration, has already outlined. And it is now or never.[72]

70. Mary Fels and Bernard A. Rosenblatt, "The Palestine Land Program," *Public,* XXII (May 24, 1919), 542.

71. "Problems of the New Palestine," *Quarterly Review,* XXIII (April, 1919), 324.

72. "Before the Peace Conference," *Asia,* February, 1919.

The first serious interference by the Zionists in the administration of
the country occurred during the July, 1919, visit of Justice Brandeis. On
his arrival in Jerusalem, Brandeis visited British Military Headquarters
and told Gen. Louis Bols, the chief administrator, that "ordinances of the
military authorities should be submitted first to the Zionist Commission."
When reply was made by the military authorities that such action would
derogate the position of the government, Brandeis warned that "the British
Government is committed to the support of the Zionist cause."[73] Bols complained to London that

> every department of my Administration is claimed or impinged upon
> by the Zionist Commission and I am of the opinion that this state of
> affairs cannot continue without grave danger to the public peace. . . .
> It is no use saying to the Moslem and Christian elements of the popula-
> tion that our declaration as to the maintenance of the "status quo" on
> our entry into Jerusalem has been observed. Facts witness otherwise. . . .
> It is manifestly impossible to please partisans who officially claim nothing
> more than a "National Home" but in reality will be satisfied with nothing
> less than a Jewish state and all that it politically implies.[74]

Upon his return to London Brandeis complained about the attitude of
the military. On August 4, 1919, Balfour wrote the military commander
in Jerusalem to impress upon him that the Jewish national-home policy
was a *"chose jugée,"* and urged him to discourage Arab "agitation against
it."[75]

The final Zionist victory came on April 24, 1920, when the Allied
Supreme Council, meeting at San Remo, allotted Palestine, Transjordan,
and Iraq to Great Britain, while France was given Syria. Although Britain
did not submit the draft of the mandate for Palestine to the League until
July 24, 1922, to be formally accepted on September 23, 1922, it was
understood that the Balfour Declaration would provide the framework
of British rule. The fate of the country was now decided. Wilson had been
forced to admit that there was an irreconcilable conflict between his belief
that the Jews must be helped and his belief in self-government and self-
determination. The decisions at San Remo accorded neither with the wishes
of the inhabitants nor with the purported objects of the war. Under the
noble-sounding title of "mandate," Britain tried to reconcile its conscience
with the facts of imperial and political interest. The word, by contrast,

73. Cited in Jeffries, *Palestine*, pp. 237–38.
74. Cited in Nevill Barbour, *Nisi Dominus* (London, 1946), p. 97.
75. Learsi, *Fulfillment*, p. 219.

struck dismay into Arab hearts and became the very embodiment of Western hypocrisy. Not only had it turned Palestine over to a Jewish minority but the Arab heartland had been callously divided among the Allied Powers.

The San Remo decision was greeted throughout the Jewish world with even more jubilation than the Balfour Declaration. In less than three months Britain showed its determination to meet Zionist expectations by replacing, on July 1, 1920, the military regime with a civilian administration. If further proof of British intent were needed, it came with the announcement that the first high commissioner would be Herbert Samuel, a "father" to the Balfour Declaration; other Zionist notables, such as Norman Bentwich, appointed attorney general and chief legislator, and Albert Hyamson, appointed director of immigration, were also named to the administration.

ARAB RESPONSE: WARNINGS UNHEEDED

Portentously, however, for the future of Palestine, the prospect that the Arab cause was lost, at least in terms of Western decision-making, precipitated the April, 1920, anti-Jewish riots in Jerusalem and Jaffa. Had the Arabs possessed meaningful power to uphold their demands, the outcome might have been different, but power was clearly not in Arab hands. Rather than read the violence of April, 1920, as a sign of events to come, Britain chose to interpret them as "disturbances" which it was hoped would not be repeated. Zionists professed to see the violence as the work of a small group of agitators inspired by "the upper circles in the Arab countries."[76] When clashes occurred between Jews and Arabs, they were perceived to be "not the result of national antagonism, but rather of a zest for plunder which harked back to remote times."[77] With the arrival of the high commissioner, "the Arabs, it was believed, would now accept the inevitable, and in place of the obstructive and unimaginative army officers" the new administration would enable the foundation of a Jewish state to be laid.[78]

The cry of "Palestine for the Palestinians" was interpreted, however, by the Arabic press as arising precisely from "economic and national consideration[s]." A Palestinian conference protested on December 27, 1919:

76. *Ibid.,* p. 212.
77. *Ibid.,* p. 171.
78. *Ibid.,* p. 222.

If it is possible for France to establish Alsace-Lorraine as French land, when it had been annexed by the French for only two hundred years, before which it was German, how can it be possible to obliterate our sovereignty over this land, which has lasted for 1,200 years, and while its sons are still masters of it. How can the Zionists go back in history two thousand years to prove that by their short sojourn in Palestine they have now a right to claim it and to return to it as a Jewish home, thus crushing the nationalism of a million Arabs?[79]

Ironically, it was in 1920 that Ahad Ha'Am, the Russian Zionist patriarch, wrote:

The Arab people regarded by us as non-existent since the beginning of the colonization of Palestine, heard and believed that the Jews were coming to drive them from their soil and deal with them at their own will. . . . For [Arabs] too, the country is a national home, and they have a right to develop national forces to the extent of their ability.[80]

Many voices were raised pleading the case of the Palestinians at this crucial juncture in history. Lord Sydenham of Comb noted that

a veil has since fallen between the British people and the rightful owners of Palestine, for whose welfare they have become responsible. The Moslem-Christian League has been reduced to silence. Local disturbances still apparently occur; but we do not hear of them. A Jew has been made Chief of the Judicial Branch; another is Assistant-Governor of Jerusalem, and Zionists are evidently winning their way into the administration. They have already succeeded in imposing Hebrew as a third official language upon this little country, with objects that are evident. Neither Moslems nor Christians are likely to learn a dead language, and the result will be to create a number of posts which can be held only by Jews. Jewish children are being forced into schools where Hebrew is taught, and as textbooks of modern science cannot well be rendered in the language of the Talmud, education—complications apart—will receive a setback. The resignations of experienced British officers is an even more serious matter. In Palestine it is privately given out that the purpose of the Government is to allow the country to be filled up by Jewish immigrants and then to hand it over to a Zionist administration. As this plan appears to conflict violently with some official assurances,

---

79. "Syrian Protests Against Zionism," *Literary Digest*, LXVI (July 3, 1920), 31.
80. Cited in Menuhin, *Decadence of Judaism*, pp. 65–66.

it is easy to understand that an honourable man may feel strong con-
scientious objections to participating in a policy which has not been
openly avowed.[81]

Anstruther MacKay, writing in *Atlantic,* noted that "the whole population
will resist the Zionist Commission's plan of wholesale immigration of
Jews." To fulfill their aspirations, he noted, "the Zionists must obtain the
armed assistance of one of the European powers, presumably Great Britain,
or the United States of America." Even more prophetic of events which
now, some fifty years later, seem closer to realization, MacKay concluded
that

> the theory that the Jews are to come into Palestine and oust the Moslem
> cultivators by "equitable purchase" or other means is in violation of
> principles of sound policy, and would, if accepted, arouse violent out-
> breaks against the Jewish minority. It would, moreover, arouse fierce
> Moslem hostility and fanaticism against the Western powers that per-
> mitted it. The effect of this hostility would be felt all through the Middle
> East, and would cause trouble in Syria, Mesopotamia, Egypt, and India.
> To this might be ascribed by future historians the outbreak of a great
> war between the white and the brown races, a war into which America
> would without doubt be drawn.[82]

81. "Palestine and the Mandate," *Nineteenth Century and After,* LXXXIX
(April, 1921), 625.
82. "Zionist Aspirations in Palestine," *Atlantic,* CXXVI (July, 1920), 123–25.

Foreign Office,
November 2nd, 1917.

Dear Lord Rothschild,

I have much pleasure in conveying to you, on
behalf of His Majesty's Government, the following
declaration of sympathy with Jewish Zionist aspirations
which has been submitted to, and approved by, the Cabinet

"His Majesty's Government view with favour the
establishment in Palestine of a national home for the
Jewish people, and will use their best endeavours to
facilitate the achievement of this object, it being
clearly understood that nothing shall be done which
may prejudice the civil and religious rights of
existing non-Jewish communities in Palestine, or the
rights and political status enjoyed by Jews in any
other country"

I should be grateful if you would bring this
declaration to the knowledge of the Zionist Federation.

3. The Balfour Declaration: An Appraisal in International Law

W. T. Mallison, Jr.

> This right ["of the Jewish people to national rebirth in its own country"] was recognised in the Balfour Declaration of the 2nd November, 1917, and re-affirmed in the Mandate of the League of Nations which, in particular, gave international sanction to the historic connection between the Jewish people and Eretz-Israel and to the right of the Jewish people to rebuild its National Home.
>
> —The Declaration of the Establishment
> of the State of Israel (1948)[1]

The central legal issues of this study may be set forth briefly. Is the Balfour Declaration valid in public international law? If so, what is its juridical meaning? Is the declaration consistent with the pre-eminent international law principle of the self-determination of peoples? As illustrated by the quoted portion of the Declaration of the Establishment of the State of Israel, the Zionists claim that it is valid and provides international authority for the Zionist State in Palestine.

It is important at the outset to recognize that Zionism is both a political ideology and a blueprint for action for "Jewish" nationalism.[2] Although

The author expresses appreciation to his wife, Sally Vynne Mallison, and to Anis F. Kassim, Graduate Fellow in Law, The George Washington University, for assistance in the preparation of this study.

1. Israel, Laws, Statutes, etc., *Laws of the State of Israel* (authorized trans.), I ([Tel Aviv], 1948), 3; the quoted paragraph is the fifth; the wording in brackets is from the fourth paragraph.

2. Theodor Herzl, *Der Judenstaat* (Leipzig, 1896); an English translation is *The Jewish State: An Attempt at a Modern Solution of the Jewish Question*, trans. Sylvie D'Avigdor and Israel Cohen (New York, 1943). Further Zionist writings combining ideology and action are collected in *The Zionist Idea: A Historical Analysis and Reader*, ed. Arthur Hertzberg (1959; New York, 1969).

some Zionists profess to be adherents of Judaism, it is clear that many Jews reject Zionism and regard it as an exploitation of their religion for political purposes.[3] Jews who have been aware of Zionist objectives have frequently taken different, and indeed inconsistent, positions from the Zionist ones on basic moral and juridical issues. This is illustrated by the negotiations leading to the Balfour Declaration where the Jews and the Zionists were the principal antagonists.[4]

HISTORICAL BACKGROUND OF THE
CENTRAL ZIONIST OBJECTIVES

The principal juridical objectives of the First Zionist Congress which met in Basle in 1897 have been summarized as follows:

The First Zionist Congress was called by Dr. Theodor Herzl to provide political and juridical implementation for his basic assumption of ineradicable anti-Semitism and the consequent necessity of a "Jewish" state. In the opening address Herzl stated the object of the meeting: "We are here to lay the foundation stone of the house which is to shelter the Jewish nation." The Congress then proceeded to constitute the Zionist Organization, and concluded with the adoption of a statement of Zionist purpose known as the Basle Program. The key provision stated: "The aim of Zionism is to create for the Jewish people a home in Palestine secured by public law." Four means were formulated to obtain this objective: (1) the promotion of Zionist (termed "Jewish") immigration to Palestine; (2) the "organization and binding together of the whole of Jewry" through appropriate means; (3) "strengthening and fostering of Jewish national sentiment and consciousness"; (4) taking steps toward "obtaining government consent" for the objectives of Zionism.[5]

The present study analyzes the basic objective of the Basle Program, "to create for the Jewish people a home in Palestine secured by public law." Dr. Herzl, as the first president of the Zionist Organization, took ener-

3. See, for example, Morris R. Cohen, *The Faith of a Liberal: Selected Essays* (New York [1946]), chap. 39, "Zionism: Tribalism or Liberalism"; Elmer Berger, *Judaism or Jewish Nationalism: The Alternative to Zionism* (New York, 1957).

4. See below, "Analysis of the Negotiations Leading to the Declaration."

5. W. T. Mallison, Jr., "The Zionist-Israel Juridical Claims to Constitute 'The Jewish People' Nationality Entity and to Confer Membership in It: Appraisal in Public International Law," *George Washington Law Review*, XXXII (June, 1964), 983.

getic diplomatic steps to obtain public law authority for the Zionist national home enterprise in Palestine. During 1898 he met with Kaiser Wilhelm II who was visiting the Ottoman Empire. He suggested, as a first step, the creation of a land development company which would be operated under German protection in Palestine.[6] Herzl expected that the German government would make appropriate arrangements to effectuate this enterprise with the Ottoman government. As stated in a pro-Zionist historical study, the kaiser's initial enthusiasm for the project was motivated, at least in part, by anti-Semitic considerations.[7] The kaiser, nevertheless, shortly thereafter rejected the proposal.[8]

In 1901 Herzl attempted direct negotiations with the sultan of Turkey. He proposed Zionist immigration to Palestine accompanied with the attractive offer of financial assistance for the development of the natural resources of the Ottoman Empire.[9] Humanitarian motives have been ascribed to the sultan in allowing the immigration of Jewish refugees.[10] It was simultaneously made clear that the "national aspects" of immigration were to be rejected.[11]

In 1902 Herzl and his associates in the Zionist Executive entered into negotiations with the British government to obtain the legal right to Zionist settlement in portions of the Sinai Peninsula. These negotiations came to nothing, although diplomatic contacts with the British government were maintained.[12] The efforts bore fruit in 1903 when the British government offered the Zionists the right to colonize a portion of East Africa, then called Uganda.[13] While Herzl favored the Uganda offer, Dr. Chaim Weizmann, an able scientist and a brilliant politician of Russian origin, opposed it vehemently.[14] Because of the bitter conflict within the Zionist Organization, no practical steps were taken to implement the British offer and the Uganda proposal was dropped following Herzl's death in 1904.[15] This proposal, however, was significant in two respects. Its serious con-

6. Esco Foundation for Palestine, *Palestine: A Study of Jewish, Arab, and British Policies*, 2 vols. (New Haven, 1947), I, 43.

7. *Ibid.*

8. *Ibid.*

9. *Ibid.*, p. 44.

10. *Ibid.*

11. *Ibid.*

12. A. R. Taylor, *Prelude to Israel: An Analysis of Zionist Diplomacy, 1897–1947* (New York, 1959), p. 7.

13. Esco, *Palestine* I, 48; Taylor, *Prelude to Israel*, p. 7.

14. *Trial and Error: The Autobiography of Chaim Weizmann* (East and West Library, illus. ed.; London, 1950), pp. 110–17.

15. *Ibid.*, p. 117.

sideration by the Zionists as a substitute for Palestine provided indication of the secular character of the movement. It was also revealing in demonstarting British imperial sympathy and support for the territorial objectives of Zionist nationalism.

In 1904 Dr. Weizmann moved to England because of his conviction that, among the great powers, Great Britain was most likely to provide effective support for Zionism.[16] During the ensuing decade he and his associates painstakingly laid the foundations for what they hoped would be public international law authority for Zionist territorial objectives in Palestine.[17] British imperialists were readily interested in these objectives.[18] At the same time, the Zionist leaders were aware that no meaningful action could be taken until their friends came to political power.

PUBLIC LAW SOURCES AND
CRITERIA OF THE PRESENT STUDY

There is no doubt concerning the centrality of the Balfour Declaration in the Zionist-Israel juridical claims.[19] The issue of its accurate juridical interpretation is, therefore, one of very substantial importance. In view of these considerations, it is necessary to use the most reliable evidence, the primary public law source materials, for interpretational purposes. Among these sources, the negotiating history of the declaration including the various negotiating positions, as well as the final official text, are essential. Dr. Weizmann's autobiography[20] is of particular value in reflecting the successive positions of the Zionist negotiators and their interpretations. Mr. Leonard Stein, an English lawyer and leading Zionist, has provided a careful history of the negotiations leading to the declaration.[21] His interpretations should be recognized as reflecting an authoritative Zionist perspective and be given thorough consideration.

The Balfour Declaration, originally a unilateral public law announcement of the British Cabinet, has been accorded the multilateral agreement of the member states of the League of Nations and the assent of the United

---

16. *Ibid.*, pp. 123–24.

17. *Ibid.*, especially chaps. 7, 8, 12–15.

18. *Ibid.*

19. The primary authority for the textual statement is the continuing use of the declaration as a juridical claim before and after the establishment of the state of Israel in 1948. In addition to the examples provided in the present study, see the numerous examples in Mallison, " 'The Jewish People' " Study.

20. *Trial and Error.*

21. *The Balfour Declaration* (New York, 1961).

States.[22] It must, accordingly, be interpreted under the same juridical criteria which are applicable to any other multilateral international agreement. The context of conditions which usually afford insight into the most accurate possible meaning which can be attributed to an international agreement or treaty is the negotiations. Elihu Root, a distinguished former secretary of state of the United States, in a statement made when he was serving as a member of the United States Senate, emphasized the importance of negotiations. He stated with particular reference to the Hay-Pauncefote Treaty:

> If you would be sure of what a treaty means, if there be any doubt, if there are two interpretations suggested, learn out of what conflicting public policies the words of the treaty had their birth; what arguments were made for one side or the other, what concessions were yielded in the making of a treaty. Always, with rare exceptions, the birth and development of every important clause may be traced by the authentic records of the negotiators and of the countries which are reconciling their differences.[23]

There is a high degree of unanimity among the international law authorities concerning the basic importance of the negotiating history in ascertaining the most accurate interpretation of an international agreement.[24] It should be recognized that these authorities refer to a serious interpretive problem such as that involved in the Balfour Declaration. The suggestion is sometimes made that "the plain meaning rule" must be employed if the words under interpretation in a particular questioned agreement are "in themselves clear and free from ambiguity."[25] For the purpose of complete-

22. See below, "Multilateral International Agreement to the Balfour Declaration."

23. Green Haywood Hackworth, *Digest of International Law,* V (Washington, D. C., 1943), 259.

24. Myres S. McDougal, Harold D. Lasswell, and James C. Miller, *The Interpretation of Agreements and World Public Order* (New Haven, 1967), chap. 4; Arnold D. McNair, *The Law of Treaties* (London, 1961), chaps. 20–23; Harvard Research in International Law, "Draft Convention on the Law of Treaties," *American Journal of International Law,* XXIX, Supplement (1935), 947.
American Law Institute, *Restatement of the Foreign Relations Law of the United States* (Philadelphia, 1965), §147, includes the context of the negotiations but accords it insufficient importance.

25. The quoted words appear in the majority opinion in the case entitled *Interpretation of the 1919 Convention Concerning the Employment of Women During the Night,* Permanent Court of International Justice, Ser. A/B, No. 50 (1922), p. 373. Article 31 of the Vienna Convention on the Law of Treaties reveals extraordinary faith in "the ordinary meaning" and then attempts to establish a rigid hierarchy of supplementary factors (American Society of International Law, *International Legal Materials,* VIII [Washington, D.C., 1969], 691–92).

ness, therefore, this "rule" will be considered in interpreting the Balfour Declaration after it has been analyzed in the context of its negotiations.[26]

ANALYSIS OF THE NEGOTIATIONS
LEADING TO THE DECLARATION

The negotiations took place over a period of three years,[27] and the last months prior to the issuance of the declaration involved careful examination of two preliminary drafts and four substantive ones as well as the final text itself.

Negotiating Objectives

There were three direct participants in the negotiations. First, the British government was actually or ostensibly concerned with advancing its national self-interest and in order to do this it had to serve as an arbitrator between the conflicting interests represented by the Jews and the Zionists. The second participant was the Zionist group, represented by the most important Zionist leaders living in Great Britain during the World War, Dr. Weizmann, the president of the English Zionist Federation, and Mr. Nahum Sokolow, a member of the Executive of the World Zionist Organization and consequently Weizmann's senior in the Zionist hierarchy. The third participating group was composed of British Jews. Edwin Montagu, the secretary of state for India in the British government at the time of the issuance of the declaration was the pre-eminent Jewish leader. Mr. Claude Montefiore, a private citizen, was another eminent leader of the Jewish cause. At the beginning of the negotiations the Jews were deeply suspicious concerning Zionist political objectives. After the Zionist drafts of the declaration were revealed, they became committed to an unequivocal anti-Zionist position in order to preserve basic Jewish values as well as the legal rights of the Palestinians.[28]

The Palestinians themselves constituted a group of major importance who could not be ignored in spite of the Zionist desire to do so.[29] Both the Jews and the British government were aware that it was essential to recog-

26. See below, "The Declaration in 'Plain Meaning' Interpretation."

27. Stein, *Balfour Declaration*, p. 514; see also the Weizmann-Rothschild memorandum quoted below, *The Milner-Amery Draft*.

28. The textual paragraph is based upon Stein, *Balfour Declaration;* Weizmann, *Trial and Error;* and Taylor, *Prelude to Israel*.

29. See below, "The Safeguard Clauses in Context."

nize the existence of the Muslim and Christian Palestinians.[30] In 1918 there were approximately 700,000 Palestinians, and only 56,000 of them were of Jewish religious identification.[31]

British Objectives. The British government had two principal political objectives during the period of the negotiations. The first was to win the war, and the second was to maximize the British power position through the ensuing peace settlement.[32] In view of the increasing success of the German submarine war in 1917, the British government was desperately searching for support from all sources. Dr. Weizmann, Mr. Sokolow, and their fellow Zionists offered the assistance of their claimed constituency of "the Jewish people" in return for a British public law declaration of support for Zionist nationalism including, they hoped, the territorial objective in Palestine.[33]

The two principal proponents of a pro-Zionist declaration in the British government were Prime Minister Lloyd George and Foreign Secretary Balfour. Mr. Stein introduces Balfour's attitudes this way: "If Balfour became an ardent pro-Zionist it was not simply out of a sentimental tenderness for Jews."[34] Then, after pointing out that Balfour regarded the Jews as possessing admirable qualities,[35] he proceeds to record Balfour's anti-Semitism. Balfour and Weizmann met briefly and discussed Zionism in 1906,[36] and they became friendly during the First World War. In 1914 Balfour told Weizmann that he shared certain "anti-Semitic postulates."[37] Early in 1917 when British Jews appealed to him as foreign secretary for

---

30. See below, *Jewish Objectives.*

31. Henry Cattan, *Palestine, The Arabs and Israel: The Search for Justice* (London, 1969), p. 21.

32. See below, *Zionist Objectives,* for documentation of Weizmann's awareness of the realities.

33. "That [the Balfour Declaration] is in purpose a definite contract between the British Government and Jewry represented by the Zionists is beyond question. In spirit it is a pledge that in return for services to be rendered by Jewry the British Government would 'use their best endeavours' to secure the execution of a certain definite policy in Palestine" (*A History of the Peace Conference of Paris,* ed. Harold W. V. Temperley, VI [London, 1924], 173–74).

"It is, on the face of it, nonsensical to imagine that the Declaration was handed to [Weizmann] as a kind of good conduct prize. We shall see later how closely the case for the Declaration was considered before being finally approved by the War Cabinet as a deliberate act of policy" (Stein, *Balfour Declaration,* p. 120).

Stein indicates the Zionist offer of "Jewish" political support in return for a public law declaration.

34. *Ibid.,* pp. 163–64.

35. *Ibid.,* p. 165.

36. Weizmann, *Trial and Error,* pp. 142–45.

37. Stein, *Balfour Declaration,* pp. 154, 163.

humanitarian assistance, he refused to intercede diplomatically with the Russian government on behalf of the Jewish victims of persecution. While admitting the "abominable" treatment of Jews in Russia, he stated that "the persecutors had a case of their own."[38] The "case" was particularized by him as including Jews belonging to "a distinct race" and having a separate religion which was in Russia "an object of inherited hatred."[39]

Balfour's role as prime minister prior to the First World War in supporting legislation which reduced Jewish immigration to Great Britain is also revealing concerning his attitudes. In explaining the basis for his opposition to the immigration of Jews, he stated in the House of Commons:

> A state of things could easily be imagined in which it would not be to the advantage of the civilisation of this country that there should be an immense body of persons who, however patriotic, able and industrious, however much they threw themselves into the national life, remained a people apart, and not merely held a religion differing from the vast majority of their fellow-country-men, but only intermarried among themselves.[40]

Stein introduces Lloyd George's perspectives in this way:

> Like some other eminent pro-Zionists, Lloyd George had mixed feelings about Jews. In some of his speeches on the South African War and its aftermath there can be discerned a streak of ordinary vulgar anti-Semitism.[41]

So that there can be no ambiguity, specific examples of the anti-Semitic statements are provided. Stein recounts that Lloyd George stated in the House of Commons at the time of the Uganda offer: "There were a good many Jews they could well spare."[42] He was also much impressed, it is added, by biblical history including "the prophecies which foretold the restoration of the Jews to the Holy Land."[43] The reassuring statement is provided that Lloyd George "was sensitive to the Jewish mystique."[44]

38. *Ibid.*, p. 164.
39. *Ibid.*
40. *Ibid.*
41. *Ibid.*, p. 143.
42. *Ibid.*
43. *Ibid.*
44. *Ibid.* Stein describes varying kinds of anti-Semitic support for Zionism. For example, Wickham Steed of the *Times* (London) illustrated "the civilised type of anti-semitism" (*ibid.*, p. 324).

These facts, as documented by Mr. Stein, are significant in further explaining the objectives of some British Cabinet members during the negotiations. It is not possible to avoid the conclusion that anti-Semitism was an objective of considerable importance along with the expressed concern for British national interests.

Zionist Objectives. The consistent Zionist objectives before and during the negotiations were to obtain public law authority for their territorial ambitions. In the words of Dr. Herzl, writing in 1896 in *The Jewish State*: "Let the sovereignty be granted us over a portion of the globe large enough to satisfy the rightful requirements of a nation; the rest we shall manage for ourselves."[45] In the following year at the First Zionist Congress the territorial objective was reformulated as "a home in Palestine secured by public law."[46] The purpose of the change in terminology was to avoid antagonizing those Jews who had a religious or cultural attachment to Palestine but who opposed the concept of "Jewish" nationality and a Zionist state.[47] Herzl recognized, nevertheless, that the Zionists would continue to interpret it as meaning a "Jewish State."[48]

The Zionists entered the negotiations with the expectations of obtaining their full territorial demands.[49] These expectations, however, were necessarily limited by two objective factors. The first was that the number of Jews in Palestine during the World War was only a small fraction of the entire population of the country.[50] The second was that the Zionists could not expect anything from the British government which did not accord with its actual or supposed imperial interests. Mr. Stein has summarized the situation in this way:

> The Declaration [sought by the Zionists] itself presupposed that the Jewish people counted for something in the world and that the ideas bound up with the connection between the Jews and Palestine had not lost their potency. But the war years were not a time for sentimental gestures. The British Government's business was to win the War and to safeguard British interests in the post-war settlement. Fully realising that these must in the end be the decisive tests, Weizmann was never under the illusion that the Zionists could rely on an appeal *ad misericordiam*. Zionist as-

---

45. P. 39.
46. See above, "Historical Background of the Central Zionist Objectives"; Esco, *Palestine*, I, 41.
47. Taylor, *Prelude to Israel*, pp. 5–6.
48. *Ibid.*, p. 6; Esco, *Palestine*, I, 41.
49. Taylor, *Prelude to Israel*, pp. 18–20; Esco, *Palestine*, I, 87–92.
50. See above, "Negotiating Objectives."

pirations must be shown to accord with British strategic and political interests.[51]

In seeking the territorial objective in Palestine, the Zionist negotiators regarded two points as crucial to their cause. First, the Zionist national home enterprise must be "reconstituted" in order to give a semblance of reality to the Zionist claim of a historic title to Palestine.[52] Second, it was regarded as essential that the British government make an unequivocal commitment to carry out the Zionist territorial objective in Palestine.[53] In seeking these objectives, the Zionists deliberately ignored the existence of the Palestinians.[54]

Jewish Objectives. The Jewish objectives manifested in the negotiations were humanitarian. Montagu and his associates were, however, realists who recognized that humanitarian ends required juridical means. The immediate objective was to protect the existing equality of rights, including the religious freedom of Jews in Great Britain. Zionism threatened the political rights of such Jews through their involuntary inclusion in the claimed "Jewish people" nationality constituency.[55] The leading British Jews, however, recognized that Zionist nationalism was directed not only at British Jews but at all Jews. One of their central objectives, consequently, was to maintain the existing legal rights of Jews in other states in addition to Great Britain. In their view, the victories won in obtaining emancipation and individual equality in many states could not be surrendered in return for the creation of a Zionist ghetto in Palestine.[56]

The Jews, in direct opposition to the Zionists, sought to maintain the existing rights of the Palestinians. Because of their full awareness of the historic persecution suffered by Jews, they believed it essential to protect Palestinians in the enjoyment of their rights. The Zionist position that the Palestinians were either a non-people or had no rights worthy of consideration imposed a moral obligation upon the Jews to attempt to protect these people, an obligation which they readily accepted.[57]

51. *Balfour Declaration*, p. 126.
52. See below, *The Zionist Draft.*
53. Stein, *Balfour Declaration*, p. 552.
54. See below, *The First Safeguard.*
55. See Mallison, " 'The Jewish People' " Study.
56. The textual paragraph is based, in part, upon Weizmann *Trial and Error*, pp. 199–208; Esco, *Palestine*, I, 104–5; Taylor, *Prelude to Israel*, pp. 22–23. For Montagu's use of the word "ghetto," see below, *The Milner Draft.*
57. The Jews' objectives are further particularized in the ensuing text describing their role in the negotiations.

The British government became willing to acknowledge the rights of the Palestinians because in addition to the moral factors there were basic military ones involved. In 1917 the British forces under General Allenby were seeking a major victory in Palestine against the Turkish armies. Arab military participation and civilian cooperation were essential for this military objective. The British could not expect to be welcomed as liberators unless they recognized the basic human rights of the inhabitants of the country.[58]

The Six Drafts and the Final Text

The Foreign Office Preliminary Draft (June or July, 1917). The key words, when drafting began at the Foreign Office, were "asylum" and "refuge."[59] The conception was that the British government was to declare itself in favor of establishing in Palestine "a sanctuary for Jewish victims of persecution."[60] The late Sir Harold Nicolson wrote many years later with reference to the preliminary drafting: "We believed that we were founding a refuge for the disabled and did not foresee that it would become a nest of hornets."[61] This indicates that the working-level personnel in the Foreign Office knew very little about the Zionist objectives. Mr. Sokolow protested that the language referred to "would by no means meet the case,"[62] and the Zionists then prepared a preliminary draft of their own.

The Zionist Preliminary Draft (July 12, 1917). This draft, reflecting the work of Sokolow and others, included the central point that the British government

accepts the principle of recognising Palestine as the National Home of the Jewish people and the right of the Jewish people to build up its national life in Palestine under a protection to be established at the conclusion of peace following upon the successful issue of the War.[63]

It also referred to "the grant of internal autonomy to the Jewish nationality in Palestine, [and] freedom of immigration for Jews."[64]

58. British military objectives are described in Esco, *Palestine* I, 117–18.
59. Stein, *Balfour Declaration*, p. 468.
60. *Ibid.;* earlier informal Zionist drafting is described in *ibid.*, pp. 466–67.
61. *Ibid.*, p. 468, n. 24.
62. *Ibid.*, p. 468.
63. *Ibid.*, pp. 468–69.
64. *Ibid.*, p. 469.

Both Sokolow and Balfour found some objections to this draft, and it was not submitted officially. Sokolow, in a letter of explanation to Lord Rothschild, stated that there should be two basic principles set forth in order to meet Zionist objectives: "(1) the recognition of Palestine as the national home of the Jewish people, (2) the recognition of the Zionist Organisation."[65]

The Zionist Draft (July 18, 1917). Sokolow's statement of basic principles was closely followed in the revised draft.

1. His Majesty's Government accepts the principle that Palestine should be reconstituted as the national home of the Jewish people.

2. His Majesty's Government will use its best endeavours to secure the achievement of this object and will discuss the necessary methods and means with the Zionist Organisation.[66]

This draft was accompanied by a letter from Lord Rothschild which asked for a message indicating formal governmental approval. Both were sent to Balfour about a month after he had invited the submission of an authoritative Zionist draft of a declaration.[67]

This draft contains the central objective that the Zionist enterprise in Palestine be "reconstituted." The word "reconstituted" was of particular importance to the Zionists since it implies establishment as a matter of legal right.[68] It is also important that the principle proposed for acceptance by His Majesty's government would apply to Palestine as a whole since no limitations are included which specify only a part of Palestine. The reference to "the Jewish people" involved the related claim of the transnational nationality entity alleged to comprise all Jews.

By the second paragraph the British government would be obligated to employ "its best endeavours" to achieve the Zionist territorial objective. The reference to discussions with the Zionist Organization to achieve the objective would probably amount to British recognition of the Zionist Organization as a public body, at least *de facto*.

The Balfour Draft (August, 1917). It is not surprising that the resultant Balfour draft accepted the Zionist objectives, without qualifications or

---

65. *Ibid.*
66. *Ibid.*, p. 470.
67. *Ibid.*
68. See below, "The League of Nations Mandate For Palestine."

limitations, since Balfour was a Zionist in the functional sense of supporting their juridical objectives.

> His Majesty's Government accept the principle that Palestine should be
> reconstituted as the national home of the Jewish people and will use
> their best endeavours to secure the achievement of this object and will be
> ready to consider any suggestions on the subject which the Zionist Organi-
> sation may desire to lay before them.[69]

It is apparent that some of the key words in this draft are taken directly
from the Zionist draft, and Mr. Stein accurately characterizes it as a
"slightly amended version of the Zionist draft."[70] Since it was prepared by
the foreign secretary, it was an official approval of the substance of the
Zionist draft of July 18, 1917, subject only to the approval of the Cabinet.
There can be no doubt but that the governmental Zionists, including the
prime minister himself, approved it. It represented, in summary, a very
important tentative governmental acceptance of Zionist objectives, including the comprehensive territorial objective of Palestine.

The Milner Draft (August, 1917). The contingent acceptance of Zionist
aims in the Balfour draft was not, however, even submitted to the Cabinet.
Apparently this draft was thought likely to be rejected. The Milner governmental draft was prepared in its place, and it provided:

> His Majesty's Government accepts the principle that every opportunity
> should be afforded for the establishment of a home for the Jewish people
> in Palestine and will use its best endeavours to facilitate the achievement
> of this object and will be ready to consider any suggestions on the subject
> which the Zionist organisations may desire to lay before them.[71]

This draft involved a substantial retreat from the acceptance of Zionist
objectives. Apparently this was quite intentional since the new draft was
designed to obtain the support of the Cabinet as a whole. In the changed
draft it was now "a home" rather than "the national home." There was
only expressed acceptance of "the principle that every opportunity should
be afforded" for the creation of this home. Further, this "opportunity"
would be afforded "in" Palestine, and thus there was no implication that

69. Stein, *Balfour Declaration*, p. 664.
70. *Ibid.*, p. 520.
71. *Ibid.*, p. 664.

Palestine belonged to the Zionists or their claimed constituency of "the Jewish people." The wording "best endeavours" was repeated, but it now referred to a reduced set of objectives. The precatory wording concerning Zionist "suggestions" was repeated with minor variations. Stein accurately summarizes the new situation by referring to the Milner draft as "a considerably watered down version of Balfour's [August] formula."[72] Even though this represented a marked retreat from the Zionist objectives, it was not as dangerous to them as subsequent developments. Specifically, it contained no direct statements that there were interests other than Zionist ones involved in Palestine.

In spite of the retreat from Zionist objectives manifested by the Milner draft, the Jews were not prepared to accept it. Mr. Edwin Montagu, an eminent Jew and Englishman, was appointed to the Cabinet as secretary of state for India, and this was announced publicly on July 18, 1917.[73] He regarded Zionism as a repudiation of Judaism and as a nationalism designed to promote anti-Semitism. Stein states concerning the appointment: "thus, the question of a pro-Zionist declaration reached the War Cabinet at a time when the only Jew with direct access to the inner circle was an implacable anti-Zionist."[74]

Montagu was also disturbed concerning the Zionist impact upon his goal of obtaining reforms in the British administration in India. As the Zionist historian reports Montagu's concern on this point: "nor could anything better be calculated to prejudice his work in India, than a British declaration which, as he saw it, would imply that he belonged, as a Jew, to a people apart, with its home—the real focus of its loyalties—in Palestine."[75]

With characteristic directness, Montagu prepared a careful memorandum entitled "The Anti-Semitism of the Present Government"[76] and circulated it to his fellow Cabinet ministers. This remarkable document contains a concise but powerful statement of the Jewish case against Zionism. It was written in the face of tentative governmental approval of Zionist objectives and stated in the first paragraph, "I wish to place on record my view that the policy of His Majesty's Government is anti-Semitic in result and will prove a rallying ground for Anti-Semites in every country in the world."[77]

As to the objective of "the national home of the Jewish people" set forth in the draft of July 18, 1917, he stated with a manifestation of prescient

72. *Ibid.,* p. 521.
73. *Ibid.,* p. 496, n. 46.
74. *Ibid.,* p. 484.
75. *Ibid.,* pp. 498–99.
76. Great Britain, Public Records Office, Cab. No. 24/24 (August 23, 1917).
77. *Ibid.*

insight into Zionist plans, "I assume that it means that Mohammedans and Christians are to make way for the Jews, and that the Jews should be put in all positions of preference and should be peculiarly associated with Palestine in the same way that England is with the English."[78] He added that "you will find a population in Palestine driving out its present inhabitants, taking all the best in the country."[79]

Some of his comments, written decades before the Law of Return was enacted by the Knesset of Israel,[80] point with uncanny accuracy to this discriminatory basic law of the state of Israel. He stated, "perhaps also citizenship must be granted only as a result of a religious test."[81] His own appraisal of such a test was unequivocal: "a religious test of citizenship seems to me to be only admitted by those who take a bigoted and narrow view of one particular epoch of the history of Palestine, and claim for the Jews a position to which they are not entitled."[82] In classic summary, Montagu stated: "Palestine will become the world's Ghetto."[83] His memorandum indicated that the Zionist and Balfour drafts were not acceptable to the Jews. In addition, there was no reason to believe that the Milner draft, although a blow to the Zionists, would satisfy him and the other Jews.

Mr. Montagu expanded on his memorandum orally at a War Cabinet meeting on September 3.[84] Although not a member of the War Cabinet (or inner Cabinet), he had been specifically invited to be present to state his views.[85] He was the only Jewish member of the Cabinet, and it is not surprising that the result of his presentation was that no action was taken by the War Cabinet to support Zionist objectives.[86] Such an action would have been of limited consequence in any event since the actions of the War Cabinet were subject to the approval of the Cabinet as a whole.

Montagu also had a far more formidable alternative course of action available to him than merely presenting the Jewish case to the Cabinet: he could resign from the Cabinet, of which he had so recently become a

78. *Ibid.*
79. *Ibid.*
80. Israel, *Laws of the State of Israel* (authorized trans.), IV (1950), 114. This statute is an immigration law for Jews only.
81. Great Britain, Public Records Office, Cab. No. 24/24 (August 23, 1917).
82. *Ibid.*
83. *Ibid.*
84. Stein, *Balfour Declaration,* pp. 502–3.
85. *Ibid.,* p. 502.
86. *Ibid.,* p. 503.

member, on the stated grounds of its anti-Semitism.[87] It would have been impossible for even such committed Zionists as Lloyd George and Balfour to represent a declaration as having pro-Jewish aspects following the resignation of the only Jewish member of the Cabinet in protest.

The Zionists, although deeply discouraged, were not yet prepared to accept defeat. Weizmann, who was fully aware of the situation at the time, later wrote that he "did not feel as desperate as Lord Rothschild."[88]

In planning their counteroffensive, Weizmann and Mark Sykes, the pro-Zionist secretary of the War Cabinet, collaborated on a memorandum which was circulated to the Cabinet before the issues involved in a declaration were considered again. In their view it was essential to set forth exactly what the Zionists were asking for as well as what they were not asking for. This is the way their memorandum of about September 22, 1917, put it:

> What the Zionists do not want is:
>
> I. To have any special political hold on the old city of Jerusalem itself or any control over the Christian or Moslem Holy Places.
>
> II. To set up a Jewish Republic or other form of State in Palestine or any part of Palestine.
>
> III. To enjoy any special rights not enjoyed by other inhabitants of Palestine.
>
> On the other hand, the Zionists do want:
>
> I. Recognition of the Jewish inhabitants of Palestine as a national unit, federated with [? other] national units in Palestine.
>
> II. The recognition of [the] right of bona fide Jewish settlers to be included in the Jewish national unit in Palestine.[89]

The retreat from the original Zionist objectives is striking. This not only renounced "a Jewish Republic," but also any "other form of State in Palestine or any part of Palestine." It expressly claimed the desire of "recognition" as "a national unit" to be federated with other such units

---

87. The near certainty of resignation, in the event of a Zionist victory, was implicit in his basic position. Dr. Weizmann has recognized "the implacability of his opposition" (*Trial and Error*, p. 259).

88. *Ibid.*, p. 257.

89. Stein, *Balfour Declaration*, p. 512 (material in brackets supplied by Stein); quoted here by permission of Sir Richard Sykes, Bart.

within Palestine. The reference to "bona fide Jewish settlers" suggests that Jews were to come to Palestine as individuals rather than as units of a Zionist-organized and -directed political entity designed to infiltrate Palestine and to supplant the mandatory government with a Zionist one.[90] These drastic changes in the stated juridical objectives would most certainly facilitate the British government in agreeing to some kind of a declaration, but they could not ensure that the remaining Zionist objectives would not be abandoned in the process. If the purpose of the memorandum was to reassure Montagu and the other Jews so that they would accept a pro-Zionist declaration, it was a complete failure.

The Milner-Amery Draft (October 4, 1917). Dr. Weizmann and Lord Rothschild, the actual and nominal heads of the Zionist movement in the United Kingdom, were increasingly concerned about the impact which Montagu made upon the British government and the inability of the pro-Zionist members of that government to overcome his objections. Weizmann and Rothschild, consequently, prepared a further memorandum which they sent to Balfour on October 3 for transmission to the government. It began with a deferential reference to Montagu as "a prominent Englishman of the Jewish faith" and stated, in part:

> We must respectfully point out that in submitting our resolution [sic] we entrusted our national and Zionist destiny to the Foreign Office and the Imperial War Cabinet in the hope that the problem would be considered in the light of Imperial interests and the principles for which the Entente stands. We are reluctant to believe that the War Cabinet would allow the divergence of views on Zionism existing in Jewry to be presented to them in a strikingly one-sided manner. . . . We have submitted it after three years of negotiations and conversations with prominent representatives of the British nation. We therefore humbly pray that this declaration may be granted to us.[91]

90. The facts concerning the Zionist infiltration are set forth in the Anglo-American Committee of Inquiry, *Report to the United States Government and His Majesty's Government in the United Kingdom:* "There thus exists a virtual Jewish nonterritorial State [through the Jewish Agency] with its own executive and legislative organs, parallel in many respects to the Mandatory Administration, and serving as the concrete symbol of the Jewish National Home. This Jewish shadow Government has ceased to cooperate with the Administration in the maintenance of law and order, and in the suppression of terrorism" (U.S. Department of State Publication No. 2536 [Washington, D.C., 1946], p. 39). See also Herzl, *The Jewish State;* Weizmann, *Trial and Error;* Howard M. Sachar, *The Course of Modern Jewish History* (New York, 1963), pp. 460–88; Institute for Special Research, *Conquest Through Immigration: How Zionism Turned Palestine into a Jewish State,* ed. G. W. Robnett (Pasadena, 1968).

91. Stein, *Balfour Declaration,* p. 514.

This was a basic change in strategy from presenting demands to a respect-fully worded petition for help from British imperialism. It may be ap-praised as an indication of the position of weakness in which they had been placed by Montagu.

Leopold Amery, an assistant secretary of the Cabinet, has written that just before the War Cabinet meeting of October 4, he was asked by Lord Milner, a member of the Cabinet, to draft "something which would go a reasonable distance to meeting the objections, both Jewish and pro-Arab, without impairing the substance of the proposed Declaration."[92] The directions were obviously inconsistent because by meeting the Jewish and Arab objections the outcome would be further impairment of the substance of the Balfour draft even as it had been diluted in the Milner draft. The text of the Milner-Amery draft demonstrates a further diminu-tion of the Zionist substance and the failure of the Weizmann-Rothschild petition.

> His Majesty's Government views with favour the establishment in Pales-tine of a national home for the Jewish race and will use its best en-deavours to facilitate the achievement of this object, it being clearly understood that nothing shall be done which may prejudice the civil and religious rights of existing non-Jewish communities in Palestine or the rights and political status enjoyed in any other country by such Jews who are fully contented with their existing nationality and citizenship.[93]

Mr. Stein states that in the Milner-Amery draft "the main substance of the British undertaking, as expressed in Milner's August draft, remained unchanged."[94] He adds that Amery made "his main contribution" to the draft by adding "the two limiting provisos,"[95] that is, the safeguard clauses, and also that

> the progressive watering down of the formula submitted by Rothschild in July, and in substance accepted at the time by Balfour, was clearly a response, not only to the pressure of the Jewish anti-Zionists, but also to reminders that in dealing with the Palestine question there were other claims and interests to be considered besides those of the Jews.[96]

92. *Ibid.*, p. 520.
93. *Ibid.*, p. 521; the last two words in the text of the draft were added two days later (*ibid.*, pp. 524, 525 n. 31).
94. *Ibid.*, p. 521.
95. *Ibid.*, p. 522.
96. *Ibid.*

Dr. Weizmann's appraisal of the Milner-Amery draft recognized the existence of a "compromise formula":

> Certain it was that Montagu's opposition, coupled with the sustained attacks which the tiny anti-Zionist group had been conducting for months—their letters to the press, the pamphlets, some of them written pseudonymously by Lucien Wolf, their feverish interviews with Government officials—was responsible for the compromise formula which the War Cabinet submitted to us a few days later.[97]

In a juridical analysis, it is significant that "the principle" which had been set forth in various forms in earlier drafts to meet the objectives of Zionist nationalism was now eliminated. It was replaced with nothing more than the vague statement that the government viewed the Zionist national home enterprise "with favour" and "will use its best endeavours to facilitate" this object. This draft clause, in short, obligates the British government to do nothing. Even if a very loose interpretation could somehow conclude that it was a kind of a political commitment, it was at most a very restricted one, and it was further limited by being expressly subordinated to the safeguard clauses.

The safeguard clauses set forth in the Milner-Amery draft frustrated the Zionist negotiating objectives in the most direct manner. The first of these two clauses protected the existing rights of the overwhelming majority of the population of Palestine, that is, the Muslim and Christian Arabs. The second protected the rights of Jews in other countries than Palestine from inclusion within the Zionist claimed constituency of "the Jewish people." Both safeguards are given express priority over the favor clause.

The October 4 draft was sent by the Cabinet, with an invitation for comments upon it as a proposed declaration, "from Zionist leaders and from representative British Jews."[98] When it became apparent that the Cabinet was inviting the views of the Jews as well as the Zionists, Weizmann regarded this as an additional concession to Montagu and "did not conceal his indignation."[99] Weizmann, nevertheless, proceeded with great caution in expressing the Zionist position and apparently asked for nothing more than a change from "establishment" to "re-establishment" so that "the historical connection with the ancient tradition would be indicated."[100]

97. *Trial and Error*, p. 259.
98. Stein, *Balfour Declaration*, p. 524.
99. *Ibid.*, p. 518.
100. *Trial and Error*, p. 261; see also *The Zionist Draft*, above.

Dr. Weizmann wrote in description of the retrenched Zionist position:

> We, on our part, examined and re-examined the formula, comparing the old text with the new. We saw the differences only too clearly, but we did not dare to occasion further delay by pressing for the original formula, which represented not only our wishes, but the attitude of the [Zionist] members of the Government.[101]

Mr. Stein states that Claude Montefiore "was an important and impressive figure in Anglo-Jewish life and was recognized by the Zionists themselves as an opponent worthy of respect."[102] Montefiore expressed the Jewish views as follows:

> The phrase "a national home for the Jewish race" appears to assume and imply that Jews generally constitute a nationality. Such an implication is extremely prejudicial to Jewish interests, as it is intensely obnoxious to an enormous number of Jews. . . . emancipation and liberty in the countries of the world are a thousand times more important than a "home." . . . It is very significant that anti-Semites are always very sympathetic to Zionism.[103]

The essential situation, however, was that since the safeguards and the "watered-down" favor clause met Mr. Montagu's requirements, they were also acceptable to the other Jews. Even those who would have preferred no declaration at all were willing to accept one which met Montagu's juridical objectives.[104]

Weizmann was sufficiently resigned to the Milner-Amery draft to telegraph it to Justice Brandeis in the United States for his approval.[105] Brandeis and his friends objected to it in two respects. They proposed eliminating the part of the second safeguard clause which read "by such Jews who are fully contented with their existing nationality and citizenship," and substituting for it "the rights and civil political status enjoyed by Jews in any other country."[106] Brandeis also apparently proposed the

---

101. *Trial and Error*, p. 261.
102. *Balfour Declaration*, p. 175.
103. *Ibid.*, p. 525; quoted here by permission of Mr. Alan Montefiore.
104. Montagu's power position and his confidence in maintaining the substantive gains of the Milner-Amery draft in the final declaration were reflected by his plans to depart for India. He left for India on Oct. 18, 1917 (*ibid.*, p. 500).
105. *Ibid.*, p. 530.
106. *Ibid.*, p. 531.

change of "Jewish race" to "Jewish people."[107] In both respects the final
Balfour Declaration appeared to reflect his recommended changes.

Dr. Weizmann has provided an instructive comparison between the
Milner-Amery draft and the Balfour draft, characterizing the former as
"a painful recession." His analysis states:

> A comparison of the two texts—the one approved by the Foreign Office
> and the Prime Minister, and the one adopted on October 4, after
> Montagu's attack—shows a painful recession from what the Government
> itself was prepared to offer. The first [the Balfour Draft] declares that
> "Palestine should be reconstituted as the National Home of the Jewish
> people." The second [the Milner-Amery Draft] speaks of "the establish-
> ment in Palestine of a National Home for the Jewish people." The first
> adds only that the "Government will use its best endeavours to secure
> the achievement of this object and will discuss the necessary methods
> with the Zionist Organization"; the second introduces the subject of the
> "civil and religious rights of the existing non-Jewish communities" in
> such a fashion as to impute possible oppressive intentions to the Jews,
> and can be interpreted to mean such limitations on our work as com-
> pletely to cripple it.[108]

The Weizmann appraisal of the scope and breadth of the first safeguard
clause is particularly candid and significant.[109]

The Final Text (October 31, 1917; issued November 2, 1917). As Dr.
Weizmann expressly recognized, the Milner-Amery draft could be interpreted to frustrate, or "cripple," their central political objectives. This draft
of October 4 also demonstrated that the Zionist-proclaimed limitations in
the Weizmann-Sykes memorandum were being taken seriously in the sense
of being acted upon, although they had not been effective in disarming the
opposition and in producing a declaration consistent with the Zionist
objectives.

With considerable understatement, Mr. Stein refers to "the War Cabinet's
sensitiveness to the protests of the anti-Zionists."[110] The ensuing actions
taken by Weizmann and his associates demonstrate their deep concern
that the Milner-Amery Draft, without substantial changes and retaining
the safeguards, would become the final official declaration. Their reaction

107. *Ibid.*
108. *Trial and Error*, p. 260.
109. It is also atypical since most Zionist analyses ignore the first safeguard.
110. *Balfour Declaration*, p. 519.

was to shift their case from the negotiating forum to the political one. On October 11, the Council of the English Zionist Federation, with Dr. Weizmann presiding, decided on pressure group tactics to produce resolutions on behalf of "the Jewish people." Stein reports that "resolutions in these terms were passed, on October 21st, by some three hundred Zionist and other Jewish bodies all over the country and forwarded to the Foreign Office."[111]

Weizmann's other technique was to attempt an informal approach to the anti-Zionist Jews:

> So concerned was Weizmann about the situation which seemed to be developing that he considered the possibility of some understanding behind the scenes which would avert a head-on collision with the anti-Zionists.[112]

Stein reports that Weizmann's attempt to reach such an "understanding" came to nothing.[113] The inference which an observer may draw is that the Jews were confident that they could maintain their victory reflected in the Milner-Amery draft and, consequently, were not interested in participating in such discussions.

Dr. Weizmann has described the Zionist dilemma:

> It is one of the "ifs" of history whether we should have been intransigent, and stood by our guns. Should we then have obtained a better statement? . . . Our judgment was to accept, to press for ratification.[114]

He thus concedes, after all attempts to change the substance of the Milner-Amery draft—or at least to remove or soften the safeguards—had been defeated, that it was decided to accept it as better than any alternative the Zionists had the power to obtain.

It is significant that the letter from Balfour containing the declaration was sent to Lord Rothschild rather than to Weizmann or Sokolow. This

111. *Ibid.*, p. 520.

112. *Ibid.* It is perhaps significant that the attempt was made in a letter to Herbert Samuel of Oct. 18, 1917, the day Montagu sailed for India. Weizmann referred to Sir Philip Magnus (an anti-Zionist) and Sir Stuart Samuel (equivocal concerning Zionism) as those with whom "a satisfactory arrangement" could be made *(ibid.).*

113. *Ibid.* Even if such an understanding could have been achieved, it would have had no significance to the Cabinet without Montagu's concurrence in it.

114. *Trial and Error,* p. 261.

had the advantage of associating the declaration with the prestige of the Rothschild name even though the Rothschild family was bitterly divided on the subject of Zionism.[115] The use of the Rothschild name was likely to promote the propaganda aspects of the declaration in obtaining Jewish support, in addition to that of the Zionists, for the British government.[116] The text was preceded by a short introductory sentence describing the declaration as one "of sympathy with Jewish Zionist aspirations which has been submitted to, and approved by, the Cabinet." The statement of "sympathy," in contrast to any suggestion of a principle or a commitment, leads to a further diminution of the already "watered down" favor clause of the declaration. It seems more accurate to view the first substantive clause of the text of the declaration as merely a "favour" clause rather than as a political "promise" clause since it promised nothing.[117]

The final text of the declaration retained each of the substantive elements of the Milner-Amery draft, including the safeguard clauses which made it so objectionable to the Zionists:

> His Majesty's Government view with favour the establishment in Palestine of a national home for the Jewish people and will use their best endeavours to facilitate the achievement of this object, it being clearly understood that nothing shall be done which may prejudice the civil and religious rights of existing non-Jewish communities in Palestine or the rights and political status enjoyed by Jews in any other country.[118]

INTERPRETATION OF THE
MEANING OF THE DECLARATION

The most accurate interpretation of the meaning of each clause of the declaration requires an analysis in its context.

The Favor Clause in Context

The Zionist Interpretation. Mr. Stein provides this introduction to the Zionist interpretation:

115. Leopold de Rothschild and his wife were "furiously anti-Zionist" (*ibid.,* p. 205).

116. The propaganda aspects are considered in Harold Lasswell, *Propaganda Technique in the World War* (New York, 1927), p. 176.

117. The term "political promise clause," but with appropriate emphasis upon its narrow scope, appears in Mallison, " 'The Jewish People' " Study, pp. 1016–18.

118. The quoted text is taken from the facsimile of the declaration which appears at the opening of this chapter.

> What, then, were the Zionists being promised? The language of the
> Declaration was studiously vague, and neither on the British nor on the
> Zionist side was there any disposition, at the time, to probe deeply into
> its meaning—still less was there any agreed interpretation.[119]

This description is typical of many Zionist interpretations since it ignores
the safeguards and treats the declaration as consisting only of the favor
clause. There can be no reasonable doubt concerning the "studiously
vague" character of this clause. It must be interpreted as even more vague
when compared with the precise wording of the safeguards. It is interesting
that Stein states that neither "the British" nor the Zionists wished to probe
deeply into the meaning. This is eminently correct concerning the Zionists,
since any probing would reveal the declaration to be a repudiation of their
negotiating objectives. If by "the British" he refers to the Cabinet which
issued the declaration, he commits a profound error. The Cabinet, after
careful consideration of six drafts and both Jewish and Zionist memoranda,
issued a declaration which met Jewish objectives, including the protection
of the Palestinians, and repudiated Zionist ones.[120] This indicates that
the Cabinet, probing far too deeply from the Zionist standpoint, rejected
the Zionist juridical objectives with deliberation and precision.

The Zionist historian concedes that the declaration also failed to provide direct British government assumption of responsibility for the establishment of the Zionist national home enterprise in Palestine, although
Weizmann and his associates "had from the start regarded [this] as
fundamental."[121] Stein continues his analysis by stating:

> What the British Government did undertake was to use its best endeavours
> to "facilitate" (no more) "the establishment in Palestine of a national
> home for the Jewish people"—not, as it had been put in the Zionist draft
> and as Balfour would, apparently, have been prepared to concede, the
> reconstitution of Palestine as the national home of the Jews.[122]

119. *Balfour Declaration*, p. 552.

120. The Zionists and the British government, nevertheless, received some propaganda benefits from the declaration. These are emphasized in David Lloyd George,
The Truth About the Peace Treaties, II (London, 1938), p. 1118.

121. Stein, *Balfour Declaration*, p. 552; see the report of the American ambassador
in London, n. 142 below.

122. *Balfour Declaration*, pp. 552–53 (note omitted). Howard M. Sachar, a Zionist
historian, states that "Montagu had done his work better than he knew" (*Modern
Jewish History*, p. 375).

Some of the words in the introductory paragraph of Balfour's letter to Rothschild were interpreted by the Zionist Organization/Jewish Agency in 1947:

> The phrase "Jewish Zionist aspirations" in the first paragraph of the Document referred to the age-old hope of Jews the world over that Palestine shall be restored to its ancient role as the "Land of Israel." These aspirations were formulated as a concrete aim at the first World Zionist Congress at Basle, Switzerland, in 1897, under the leadership of Dr. Theodore Herzl, in these words: "Zionism aims to create a publicly secured, legally assured home for the Jewish people in Palestine."[123]

The same Zionist source provides an interpretation of the words "national home for the Jewish people":

> The phrase "the establishment in Palestine of a National Home for the Jewish people" was intended and understood by all concerned to mean at the time of the Balfour Declaration that Palestine would ultimately become a "Jewish Commonwealth" or a "Jewish State," if only Jews came and settled there in sufficient numbers.[124]

The inaccuracy of the statement that this alleged meaning of an ultimate "Jewish state" was "intended and understood by all concerned" is obvious. Such an understanding could not be attributed accurately to the Jews, including Montagu, and to the British Cabinet which issued the final text of the declaration. In the same way, if the Palestinians may be regarded as "concerned" with a declaration pertaining to Palestine, it is ridiculous to attempt to attribute this meaning to them.

Dr. Weizmann's views on the declaration, expressed ten years after the event, are of particular importance because of his role as the pre-eminent Zionist negotiator.

> The Balfour Declaration of 1917 was built on air, and a foundation had to be laid for it through years of exacting work; every day and every hour of these last ten years, when opening the newspapers, I thought: Whence will the next blow come? I trembled lest the British Government would call me and ask: "Tell us, what is this Zionist Organisation? Where are

123. Jewish Agency for Palestine, *Book of Documents Submitted to the General Assembly of the United Nations,* ed. Abraham Tulin, (New York, 1947) p. 1.
124. *Ibid.,* p. 5.

they, your Zionists?" For these people think in terms different from ours. The Jews, they knew, were against us.[125]

The "foundation," which had to be laid after the event, included attempted drastic changes in the meaning of the favor clause combined with a virtual elimination of the safeguards.[126] These are, of course, the same objectives which were rejected in the negotiations and the declaration.

Consideration should also be given to Dr. Weizmann's contemporaneous reaction which he recounts in his autobiography:

> While the cabinet was in session, approving the final text, I was waiting outside, this time within call. Sykes brought the document out to me with the exclamation: "Dr. Weizmann, it's a boy!"
>
> Well—I did not like the boy at first. He was not the one I had expected.[127]

In spite of his disappointment at that time, Dr. Weizmann later developed a method of interpretation which satisfied the Zionists: "It would mean exactly what we would make it mean—neither more nor less."[128]

The Juridical Interpretation. In a juridical interpretation it is necessary to consider the views of the humanitarian Jews who supported the final text of the Balfour Declaration. This support was, of course, extremely welcome to the Zionists at the time since it tended to identify them with the Jews. Later it became highly embarrassing because of the basic divergences in interpretations which arose. Justice Brandeis supported the Balfour Declaration and suggested words to strengthen the second safeguard.[129] Thereafter, "irreconcilable differences on questions of principle" developed between Brandeis and Weizmann which led "to an open breach."[130] The essential difference between the two was that Brandeis insisted upon interpreting the declaration as the end of the political work of Zionism. Dr. Weizmann wrote of the situation:

---

125. "Address at Czernowitz, Roumania" (December 12, 1927), in *Chaim Weizmann: A Tribute on his Seventieth Birthday,* ed. Paul Goodman (London, 1945), p. 199.

126. See the text of the present section.

127. *Trial and Error,* p. 262.

128. *Ibid.,* p. 302.

129. See above, *The Milner-Amery Draft.*

130. Stein, *Balfour Declaration,* p. 581. See Berger, "Disenchantment of a Zionist," concerning Brandeis' disillusionment with Zionism (*Middle East Forum,* Vol. XXXVIII, No. 4 [1962], 21).

What struck me as curious was that the American Zionists, under Justice Brandeis, though fully aware of what was going on in England and in Palestine, nonetheless shared the illusions of our Continental friends; they too assumed that all political problems had been settled once and for all [by the Balfour Declaration], and that the only important task before Zionists was the economic upbuilding of the Jewish National Home.[131]

Ahad Ha'Am [Asher Ginsberg] provided considerable discomfiture to the Zionists. Ahad Ha'Am lived in Palestine during the early years of the British mandate and increasingly recognized Zionism as a repudiation of the ethical values of Judaism.[132] He was the leader of a humanitarian and religious movement usually termed "spiritual" or "cultural" Zionism. This movement valued, and sought to achieve, individual rights and human dignity for all Palestinians including the Muslims and Christians.[133] Ahad Ha'Am supported the final text of the declaration but interpreted it very differently from the Zionists. He emphasized that the Zionist objectives sought by Weizmann and Sokolow were frustrated and the declaration protected the interests of the Muslim and Christian Palestinians and stated:

This position, then, makes Palestine common ground for different peoples, each of which tries to establish its national home there; and in this position it is impossible for the national home of either of them to be complete and to embrace all that is involved in the conception of a "national home." If you build your house not on untenanted ground, but in a place where there are other inhabited houses, you are sole master only as far as your front gate. Within you may arrange your effects as you please, but beyond the gate all the inhabitants are partners, and the general administration must be ordered in conformity with the good of all of them.[134]

The favor clause, as "watered down," was also a part of a bargain between the Zionists and the British government. In return for this admittedly vague clause, the Zionists promised to deliver the political support of their worldwide alleged constituency of Jews ("the Jewish people") to

131. *Trial and Error*, p. 301.

132. Hans Kohn, "Zion and the Jewish National Idea," *Menorah Journal*, XLVI (Autumn–Winter, 1958), 17; reprinted in *Palestine: A Search for Truth*, ed. Alan R. Taylor and Richard N. Tetlie (Washington, D.C., 1970).

133. *Selected Essays of Ahad Ha'am*, trans. Leon Simon (Cleveland, 1962).

134. *Ten Essays on Zionism and Judaism*, trans. Leon Simon (London, 1922), pp. xvi–xx.

the British government during and after the war. Next to Balfour, Prime
Minister Lloyd George was the pre-eminent governmental Zionist. He described the *quid pro quo* in this way:

> The Zionist leaders gave us a definite promise that, if the Allies com-
> mitted themselves to giving facilities for the establishment of a National
> Home for the Jews in Palestine, they would do their best to rally to the
> Allied cause Jewish sentiment and support throughout the world. They
> kept their word in the letter and the spirit.[135]

The British interest in the bargain also reflected concern with the power
position following the war. A pro-Zionist study has stated: "The essential
reason, accounts agree, was strategic and had to do with the need of
strengthening Great Britain's lifeline to the East."[136] The same source adds:
"Through the Balfour Declaration Great Britain ultimately strengthened
and extended her position in the whole Near East."[137]

It was, of course, essential that the bargain involved not be reflected
in the text of the declaration. The danger for both the official Zionists,
including Weizmann and Sokolow, and the British functional Zionists in
the government was that Jews, citizens of their respective national states,
would have expressly repudiated the Zionist leaders' claim to act for them
and to deliver their loyalties. In addition to obviating this danger, the
innocuous favor clause, when combined with the second safeguard clause
to protect existing Jewish rights, would be juridically interpreted as a
humanitarian measure in behalf of refugee Jews which should merit the
support of men of good will. Thus the Zionists in and out of the government were in a position to obtain credit for a humanitarian document,[138]
and the Jews could support this interpretation of the favor clause as restricted by the safeguards. In consequence, a persuasive juridical interpretation of the favor clause is that it is a humanitarian measure to allow
Jewish refugees to emigrate to Palestine.

The interpretation just summarized is more reasonable than an alternative
interpretation which contends that the favor clause was designed for the
benefit of the Zionists rather than of refugee Jews.[139] Even though the

135. Lloyd George, *Peace Treaties*, p. 1139.
136. Esco, *Palestine*, I, 117.
137. *Ibid.*, p. 118.
138. The propaganda aspects are mentioned above, *The Final Text*.
139. This interpretation is set forth, as a possible alternative, in Mallison, " 'The
Jewish People' " Study, pp. 1026–29.

Zionist alleged constituency of "the Jewish people" is referred to in the favor clause, the purpose of the second safeguard is to prevent the involuntary inclusion of Jews in this claimed constituency. If the limited "Jewish people" of the declaration had been frankly described as "Zionists," a humanitarian interpretation of the declaration would not have been possible, and Montagu and the other Jews were prepared to accept only a declaration that had humanitarian objectives rather than political ones. For this reason, the favor clause must be given a humanitarian interpretation. A further and even more compelling reason is that this is consistent with the first safeguard clause. Any interpretation which accorded legal authority for Zionist, as opposed to Jewish, immigration to Palestine could be understood to permit a direct attack upon the safeguarded rights which would far exceed mere "prejudice" to them.

In early 1918 an official of the British government removed any doubts concerning the purpose of Jewish immigration to Palestine by informing the sharif of Mecca that "Jewish settlement in Palestine would only be allowed insofar as would be consistent with the political and economic freedom of the Arab population."[140] The result was that the sharif, as Professor Taylor has described it, "welcomed the Jews to the Arab lands on the understanding that a Jewish state in Palestine would not be in the offing."[141] This action was, of course, consistent with the humanitarian interpretation of the favor clause of the Balfour Declaration which has just been described.

A contemporaneous Zionist writer concurred in upholding this view of the favor clause by ruling out the possibility of a "Jewish State." Writing in the author's introduction to his semi-official history of Zionism, Sokolow stated:

> It has been said, and is still being obstinately repeated by anti-Zionists again and again that Zionism aims at the creation of an independent "Jewish State." But this is wholly fallacious. The "Jewish State" was never a part of the Zionist programme.[142]

140. Taylor, *Prelude to Israel,* p. 32.

141. *Ibid.*

142. *History of Zionism,* I (London, 1919), xxiv–xxv. In reporting by telegram upon the British official position concerning Palestine to the secretary of state, the American ambassador in London stated on December 21, 1917: "No Discrimination shall be made against [the Jews]. This is as far as the British Government has yet gone" (U.S. Department of State, *Papers Relating to the Foreign Relations of the United States* [1917], I [Washington, D.C., 1933], suppl. 2, 483).

The Safeguard Clauses in Context

The First Safeguard: Palestinian Rights. In considering the Zionist interpretation of the first safeguard, it is necessary to examine briefly their attitude concerning the Palestinians. The Zionist slogan, "give the land without a people to the people without a land,"[143] reflected the basic policy of studied indifference to the existence of the Palestinians. When their existence had, on occasion, to be recognized, the situation did not represent much of an improvement from a human-rights standpoint. Leonard Stein wrote in 1923: "The fact has to be faced that so far as the great mass of the population [of Palestine] is concerned, the Arabs are immature and irresponsible to the point of childishness."[144] The consistency in the Zionist basic policy is reflected in the official statement of Mr. Galili, the minister of information of the government of Israel in 1969: "We do not consider the Arabs of the land an ethnic group nor a people with a distinct nationalistic character."[145]

Dr. Frankenstein, a Zionist lawyer, provides a narrow analysis of the first safeguard clause:

> It confines the protection of non-Jews to their civil and religious rights, omitting political status, while the immediately following words explicitly protect "the rights and political status enjoyed by Jews in any other country." There is a deliberate differentiation between the protection of the non-Jews in Palestine and of the Jews abroad.[146]

The purpose of this analysis, since the Zionists failed to have this safeguard removed from the declaration, is to interpret it in such a restrictive manner as to frustrate its protective purpose. It will be recalled that both the anti-Zionist Jews and the British government believed it essential to protect the existing rights of the Palestinians. The more accurate interpretation, therefore, is that the wording "civil and religious rights" was intended to describe and protect the existing rights then possessed by the Palestinians.

143. The slogan is widely attributed to Zangwill.

144. "The Problem of Self-Government," in *Awakening Palestine,* ed. Leon Simon and Leonard Stein (London, 1923), p. 235.

145. J. L. Talmon, "An Open Letter to Y. Galili," *Arab World,* Vol. XV, No. 9 (1969), p. 3; Professor Talmon, an Israeli historian, provides strong criticism of the quoted words. Uri Avnery demonstrates the inconsistencies between Zionist objectives and Israeli national interests in *Israel Without Zionists: A Plea for Peace in the Middle East* (New York, 1968).

146. "The Meaning of the Term 'National Home for the Jewish People,'" *Jewish Yearbook of International Law* (Jerusalem, 1948), pp. 29–30.

A somewhat different, but equally narrow and restrictive interpretation is offered by Stein who states:

> It is not quite clear whether the rather curious expression "existing non-Jewish communities in Palestine" was meant to refer to the Arabs or whether this part of the proposed declaration was directed primarily to the position of the various Christian communities, whose traditional rights were of special concern to the French and Italian Governments and to the Roman Catholic and Orthodox Churches.[147]

This supposed choice between alternatives is quite inconsistent with the purposes of the first safeguard which was introduced in the Milner-Amery draft. It will be recalled that the draft safeguard was written to meet "pro-Arab objections." There is not a scintilla of evidence to suggest that the existing rights of non-Jewish communities belonged only to Muslim or only to Christian Palestinians. Such a false alternative would frustrate the comprehensive protective purpose by arbitrarily excluding some of the protected "non-Jewish communities" without warrant in either the negotiations or the final text of the safeguard.

There is persuasive judicial authority concerning the interpretation of an agreement in which the beneficiaries, like the Palestinians in the Balfour Declaration, have no direct negotiating or decisional role. In the famous *Cayuga Indians Case* (Great Britain v. United States)[148] the fact situation involved an agreement or covenant in which the covenantees, the Indian claimants, had no effective role. The tribunal referred to "universally admitted principles of justice and right dealing"[149] as being the applicable criteria in interpreting the covenant in favor of the Indians. The opinion emphasized the undesirable alternative method of applying "the harsh operation of the legal terminology of a covenant which the covenantees had no part in framing."[150] In applying these juridical criteria, it should be recognized that the purpose of the declaration including the first safeguard was protective rather than "harsh." It follows, a fortiori, that the entire document must be effectuated according to the "universally admitted principles" of elementary justice. If the Zionist interpretation were accepted, the document would then be one of "harsh operation."

147. *Balfour Declaration*, p. 522 (note omitted).
148. Fred K. Nielsen, *Report of the Case Decided Under the Special Agreement Between the United States and Great Britain of August 18, 1910* (Washington, D.C., 1926), pp. 203, 307.
149. *Ibid.*, p. 320.
150. *Ibid.*

In a juridical interpretation of the first safeguard protecting the "civil and religious rights" of the Palestinians, it must be recognized that it was inserted by the British Cabinet over the express objections of the Zionist negotiators. In this context, it appears that subsequent Zionist attempts to narrow the content of "civil and religious rights" are not very persuasive. The most reasonable interpretation is that the clause protected the rights which were possessed and exercised by the Palestinians when Palestine was a part of the Ottoman Empire. In addition to freedom of religion, such rights included a measure of local political autonomy, the rights to livelihood, to own land, and to have an individual home as well as to maintain the integrity of the Palestinian community as a political entity.[151]

In view of the subsequent systematic Zionist violation of the first safeguard clause, a consideration of the full measure of the rights protected by it may appear to be rather theoretical. Even if these rights should be construed in a narrow and restrictive manner, for the purpose of legal analysis only, it remains clear that they have been violated by the Zionist Organization/Jewish Agency and its associated terror groups as well as by the government of Israel.[152]

Professors Oppenheim and Lauterpacht, while recognizing that "many treaties stipulating immoral obligations have been concluded and executed," emphasize that "this does not alter the fact that such treaties were legally

---

151. Cattan demonstrates that Palestinians, of whatever religion, enjoyed equality with other Turkish subjects in religious, civil, and political rights including local autonomy (*Palestine, the Arabs and Israel,* pp. 4–9). Arnold Toynbee describes the Ottoman millet-system of communal autonomy which included all the inhabitants of the Empire (*A Study of History,* VIII [Galaxy ed; New York, 1963], 184–86. He summarizes it as "a far-reaching communal autonomy" (*ibid.,* p. 184). George E. Kirk states concerning the higher posts in the Empire: "While the bulk of senior officials were Turks, Syrian and Palestinian townsmen gained by their innate keenness of intellect an appreciable number of senior posts" *A Short History of the Middle East,* 7th ed. rev. [New York, 1964], pp. 59–60).
At least implicit recognition of elementary Palestinian rights appears in Stein, *Balfour Declaration,* chap. 41 entitled "The Arab Question," pp. 621–51. Palestine under Ottoman rule is described unsympathetically but with the admission of local autonomy in Esco, *Palestine,* I, 297–98, 436–37.

152. English-language accounts of the Zionist terror directed against Palestinians and the mandatory government include: Menahem Begin, *The Revolt: Story of the Irgun,* trans. Samuel Katz (New York, 1951); Avner Gruszow [Avner], *Memoirs of an Assassin: Confessions of a Stern Gang Killer,* trans. Burgo Partridge (New York, 1959); Meir Mardor, *Haganah,* ed. D. R. Elston, trans. H. A. G. Schmuckler (New York, 1964). Don Peretz describes the mass murder of Palestinian civilians in the village of Kafr Qasim in 1956 (*Israel and the Palestine Arabs* [Washington, D. C., 1958], p. 107). Sabri Jiryis documents systematic violations of the first safeguard clause, including the use of terror (*The Arabs in Israel 1948–1966,* trans. Meric Dobson [Beirut, 1968]).

not binding upon the contracting parties."[153] The same scholars enunciate the doctrine applicable to "immoral obligations" in these unequivocal terms:

> It is a customarily recognised rule of the Law of Nations that immoral obligations cannot be the object of an international treaty. Thus, an alliance for the purpose of attacking a third State without provocation is, from the beginning, not binding.[154]

It must be obvious that the principal feature of the declaration as interpreted by the Zionists is its immoral character in violating, *inter alia,* the rights protected by the first safeguard. There may be some borderline situations in which the legal scholars could properly engage in disputation as to whether or not a particular obligation is immoral. The Zionist interpretation of the Balfour Declaration does not put it in such a category. For this further reason the declaration, if thus interpreted, would be invalid.

The Second Safeguard: Jewish Rights. This safeguard protected "the rights and political status enjoyed by Jews in any other country" than Palestine. It is appropriate to recall that it also was placed in the declaration over the strong objections of the Zionist negotiators. In particular, the Jews sought protection from the prejudice and injury to their existing political status which would be caused by their inclusion in the claimed "Jewish people" nationality entity.[155] There is no evidence which suggests that the word "political" was employed in the second safeguard to reduce the Palestinian rights which were protected in the first.

The differences between the wording of the second safeguard in the Milner-Amery draft and that in the final declaration have been considered. The important juridical consequence is a substantial strengthening of the protection afforded to the Jews. Rather than having the scope of the clause determined by the subjective test of ascertaining which individuals were "fully contented with their existing nationality," as the Milner-Amery draft provided, the second safeguard was made broadly applicable to "Jews in any other country" than Palestine.

Many Zionist interpreters of the declaration have simply ignored the

---

153. Lassa Oppenheim, *International Law,* ed. H. Lauterpacht, 8th ed. (New York, 1955) I, *Peace,* 896.

154. *Ibid.*

155. The Zionist nationality claims are appraised in Mallison, "'The Jewish People'" Study.

second safeguard. In striking contrast, Professor Feinberg of the Law Faculty of the Hebrew University of Jerusalem has attempted a direct analysis. His highly original interpretation attempts to demonstrate that the second safeguard is intended to protect Zionist Jews in carrying out Zionist political objectives. In his words, it was necessary

> that the grant of the National Home, and the ensuing right of all Jews to take part in the upbuilding of that home, did not in any way affect their status and allegiance as citizens of the countries to which they belonged.[156]

The Feinberg fallacy and the elaborate argument supporting it have been criticized in detail elsewhere.[157] It is sufficient, for present purposes, to point out that this interpretation of the second safeguard clause is completely inconsistent with the negotiating history of the declaration, including the unsuccessful Zionist attempts to eliminate the safeguards.

It should be mentioned that any juridical interpretation of the declaration must recognize that each of its three clauses is an integral part of the negotiated compromise. Even if there were no clear wording stressing the pre-eminence of the safeguards, they would have to be accorded priority over the favor clause since they protected existing rights which the British government had no legal authority to change, or even to "prejudice," as provided in the declaration.

The Declaration in "Plain-Meaning" Interpretation

Although the availability of the negotiating context affords an exceptionally high degree of accuracy in interpreting the Balfour Declaration, completeness in analysis requires that the "plain-meaning" approach should also be considered. At the outset it is useful to recognize that this so-called rule is, in the thoughtful words of Lord McNair,

> merely a starting-point, a prima facie guide, and cannot be allowed to obstruct the essential quest in the application of treaties, namely to search for the real intention of the contracting parties in using the language employed by them.[158]

---

156. Nathan Feinberg, "The Recognition of the Jewish People in International Law," *Jewish Yearbook of International Law* (Jerusalem, 1948), p. 18.

157. Mallison, " 'The Jewish People' " Study, pp. 1021–26.

158. *The Law of Treaties*, p. 366.

Assuming, for purposes of analysis, either that there is no negotiating history of the declaration or that this history is unknown, it would then be necessary to use "a prima facie guide" to the interpretation of the final text of the declaration as it would stand alone.

Such a textualistic interpretation would note that the British government view "with favour" the national home enterprise, which is restricted by the words "in Palestine," and that the government "will use their best endeavours" to facilitate its achievement. In most usual legal usage such terms as "favour" and "best endeavours" are precatory or wishful words. They may be most obviously recognized as being in contrast to words of legal obligation or commitment which do not appear in the favor clause. It is clear that the favor clause, even if considered without the safeguards, specifies no legal obligation whatsoever, as is evidenced by the absence of words such as "rights" or "obligations" or terms of similar meaning.

The first safeguard clause refers to the civil and religious "rights" of the Palestinians. In the same way, the second safeguard refers to the "rights and political status" of Jews in any other country than Palestine. The word "rights," set forth in each of the safeguards, specifies a clear juridical obligation concerning the stated rights. The particular rights enunciated in the safeguard clauses are, consistent with the "ordinary" meaning of the words used, the then existing rights of both Palestinians and Jews. This conclusion is further supported by the fact that the words in the text make no reference to some indeterminate or unspecified possible type of theoretical rights.

Without consideration of other words which are in the text of the declaration, it is clear that the safeguard clauses are of a highly specific character and protect the stated "rights." When the safeguards are compared with the favor clause, the absence of any legal obligation in the favor clause becomes even more obvious. This leads to the conclusion that the safeguards set forth a legal requirement which must be given juridical priority over the favor clause since the latter lacks obligatory character.

It is not necessary, however, to rest the conclusion just stated upon the analysis made thus far because there are further words in the declaration which compel the same conclusion. The safeguards are preceded by the unequivocal words which state "it being clearly understood that nothing shall be done which may prejudice" the safeguarded rights. The conclusion, therefore, must also be reached because of the specific priority accorded to the safeguards by the quoted words that introduce them. In addition, it is desirable to note that the pre-eminence of the safeguarded "rights" is not written in terms of prevention of injury to or violation of them. The words of the declaration, with striking and clear choice of

terminology, provide that nothing shall be done which would even "prejudice" the safeguarded rights.

Dr. Weizmann's expressed disappointment with the final text of the declaration upon its issuance has been described. It is interesting that the "plain
meaning" of the words of the declaration has presented an interpretive
problem for him. He has written that "in spite of the phrasing, the intent
was clear."[159] When Dr. Weizmann states that the "intent" was "clear,"
although inconsistent with, or "in spite of," "the phrasing," it is apparent
that he is referring only to the Zionist intent. This intent, as analyzed above,
has always been inconsistent with both the wording and the meaning of the
declaration.

MULTILATERAL INTERNATIONAL AGREEMENT
TO THE BALFOUR DECLARATION

At the time of its issuance, the Balfour Declaration was only multilateral
in the narrow sense that three distinct parties with different interests, the
Jews, the Zionists, and the British government, were participants in the
negotiations. For this reason it is accurate to describe the declaration as
multipartite in terms of participants, but in form it was a unilateral declaration of the British government. The legal authority of the British government to make any changes in the juridical status of Palestine and the Palestinians would have been open to the gravest doubts if such changes had
been attempted.[160] The actual declaration of the British government, however, containing safeguards protecting existing Palestinian and Jewish rights,
stands upon a much more solid juridical basis. It must be accurately construed, consequently, as a solemn promise by the British government to
recognize and support these existing rights.

In order to establish the three clauses of the declaration as binding international law, it was necessary to obtain multilateral assent from other national states. This was accomplished mainly through the mandate system
provided for in the League of Nations Covenant.

*The League of Nations
Mandate for Palestine (1922)*

The central objectives of the mandate system are articulated in the
League of Nations Covenant.

159. *Trial and Error*, p. 265.
160. The applicable limitations of international law are considered below, "International Law Limitations upon the Declaration."

To those colonies and territories which as a consequence of the late war have ceased to be under the sovereignty of the States which formerly governed them and which are inhabited by peoples not yet able to stand by themselves under the strenuous conditions of the modern world, there should be applied the principle that the well-being and development of such peoples form a sacred trust of civilisation and that securities for the performance of this trust should be embodied in this Covenant.[161]

This basic principle of the covenant indicates that the "sacred trust of civilisation" is to be exercised for the benefit of the peoples inhabiting the particular territories. The principle applies, prima facie, to the then existing inhabitants of Palestine of Muslim, Christian, and Jewish religious identifications. It would constitute a flagrant violation of this "sacred trust" to take Palestine from the Palestinians and allot it to the Zionists. The basic inconsistency involved is recognized by J. Stoyanovsky, a Zionist legal authority, who has written:

The peculiarity of the national home policy seems to be the extension of this principle [protecting existing inhabitants] so as to include the Jewish people in the category of the above peoples.[162]

The League of Nations Covenant also recognized provisionally the independence of the territories formerly belonging to the Turkish Empire including, of course, Palestine. The applicable provision stated:

Certain communities formerly belonging to the Turkish Empire have reached a stage of development where their existence as independent nations can be provisionally recognised subject to the rendering of administrative advice and assistance by a Mandatory until such time as they are able to stand alone. The wishes of these communities must be a principal consideration in the selection of the Mandatory.[163]

Great Britain was designated by the League of Nations as the mandatory power for Palestine, and the Palestine mandate became effective on September 29, 1923.[164] The second paragraph of the preamble to the mandate for Palestine incorporated the Balfour Declaration with some changes in

---

161. Article 22, section 1.

162. *The Mandate for Palestine: A Contribution to the Theory and Practice of International Mandates* (London, 1928), p. 43.

163. Article 22, section 4.

164. Manley O. Hudson, ed., *International Legislation* (Washington, D.C., 1931), I, 109.

wording. It shortened the favor clause by omitting the wording concerning "best endeavours to facilitate the achievement of this object." Only one word in the phrase introducing the safeguards was changed: the term "which might prejudice" was substituted for "which may prejudice." The safeguard clauses remained unchanged.[165]

In view of the frustration of the Zionist objectives in the final text of the Balfour Declaration, Dr. Weizmann attempted to have an unequivocal Zionist right to Palestine recognized in the preamble to the mandate. He has written, "Zionists wanted to have it read: 'recognizing the historic rights of the Jews to Palestine.' "[166] Curzon had, however, replaced Balfour as the British foreign secretary, and this provided no encouragement for the Zionists. It is apparent that both safeguard clauses of the Balfour Declaration as well as the "rights and political status" enjoyed by British Jews under British municipal law required Curzon to reject the claim of the alleged Zionist "rights," and he did so.[167] The third paragraph of the preamble to the mandate provided:

Whereas recognition has thereby [through the Balfour Declaration] been given to the historical connection of the Jewish people and to the grounds for reconstituting their national home in that country.[168]

It will be recalled that Weizmann attempted unsuccessfully to change the word "establishment" in the Milner-Amery draft to "re-establishment."[169] Perhaps he found some solace in the word "reconstituting" quoted above. In view of the rejection of the Zionist claim of legal rights by Curzon combined with the retention of the safeguards in the mandate for Palestine, it is not possible to interpret the declaration as changed in meaning. The Zionists, of course, interpreted the Balfour Declaration as it was incorporated in the League of Nations mandate the same way that they interpreted the orignal declaration. Dr. Stoyanovsky, for example, wrote:

165. The text of the Palestine mandate used herein is the official one taken from the Convention Between the United States and Great Britain Concerning Palestine of December 3, 1924 (effectuated December 5, 1925) (U.S. *Statutes at Large*, XLIV [December, 1925–March, 1927], part 3 [Washington, D.C.], 2184–92). This Convention incorporated the entire Palestine mandate including the Balfour Declaration with the changes described. Other texts of the Palestine mandate are in Stoyanovsky, *Mandate for Palestine*, p. 355, and J. C. Hurewitz, ed., *Diplomacy in the Near and Middle East*, II (Princeton, 1956), p. 106.

166. *Trial and Error*, p. 348.

167. *Ibid.*

168. U.S. *Statutes at Large*, XLIV, 2184.

169. See above, *The Milner-Amery Draft.*

> There can hardly be any question now whether Jews constitute a distinct national entity in the eyes of international law. This seems to have been laid down, on the one hand, by the various treaties containing what is known as minority clauses, and on the other, by the mandate for Palestine providing for the establishment in that country of a *national* home for the Jewish people.[170]

Such interpretations are fallacious because, *inter alia,* they involve a violation of both safeguard clauses.

The mandate for Palestine was, under the primary authority of the League of Nations Covenant, the basic constitutional document for the interim government of Palestine agreed to by the League of Nations.[171] Its provisions, therefore, are of particular importance in implementing the juridical limitations imposed by the Balfour Declaration as an integral part of the mandate. It is fundamental that no part of the Palestine mandate could be valid if it were in violation of any provisions of the League of Nations Covenant. The covenant was the pre-eminent constitutional instrument of the organized world community of the time, and the Palestine mandate was authorized by it and subject to its limitations.[172] For example, the provisional granting of independence to Palestine by the covenant could not be withdrawn or limited by the Palestine mandate. In the same way, the mandate was juridically limited by "the sacred trust of civilisation" for the benefit of the inhabitants of the mandated territory.

Article 2 of the mandate makes the mandatory government responsible for placing the country under such conditions "as will secure the establishment of the Jewish national home, as laid down in the preamble."[173] The word "the" in reference to the national-home enterprise is not significant juridically since it is specifically limited by the terms "as laid down in the preamble" which refer to "a" national home. It is of particular importance that this article makes the mandatory responsible for "the development of self-governing institutions" for the existing inhabitants of Palestine.[174] This basic provision appears to be both reasonable and necessary to implement the Palestinian independence provisionally recognized in the League Covenant. Article 2 also obligates the mandatory, consistent with the safe-

170. *Mandate for Palestine,* p. 55.

171. The British government's Palestine Order in Council of Aug. 10, 1922, sometimes known as the "Palestine Constitution," sets forth the municipal governmental structure under the Palestine mandate. It is in *ibid.,* p. 363.

172. Article 20, section 1 prohibited past or future agreements by its members which were inconsistent with the covenant.

173. U.S. *Statutes at Large,* XLIV, 2185.

174. *Ibid.*

guards of the Balfour Declaration, to protect "the civil and religious rights of all the inhabitants of Palestine, irrespective of race and religion."[175]

Article 4 recognizes the Zionist Organization/Jewish Agency "as a public body" and specifies that it is "subject always to the control of the administration, to assist and take part in the development of the country."[176] This public-body status of the Zionist Organization was, of course, subject to each of the further express limitations of the covenant and the mandate.[177]

Article 5 is of particular relevance to ensuring the territorial integrity of Palestine and states in full:

> The Mandatory shall be responsible for seeing that no Palestine territory shall be ceded or leased to, or in any way placed under the control of, the Government of any foreign power.[178]

Article 6 considers "Jewish" immigration and, in relevant part, provides:

> The Administration of Palestine, while ensuring that the rights and position of other sections of the population are not prejudiced, shall facilitate Jewish immigration under suitable conditions.[179]

Such facilitation of Jewish immigration is consistent with the humanitarian interpretation of the favor clause of the Balfour Declaration. In addition, the facilitation is limited by the requirement that the rights of other sections of the population are not "prejudiced." This provision, with some of its wording taken from the safeguards of the declaration, is consistent with both the declaration and the covenant. Only if Zionist national immigration were to be facilitated in violation of the expressly protected Palestinian rights would there be a violation of article 6.[180]

The first paragraph of article 15 is of particular importance and provides:

---

175. *Ibid.*

176. *Ibid.*

177. This subject is examined in W. T. Mallison, Jr., "The Legal Problems Concerning the Juridical Status and Political Activities of the Zionist Organization/Jewish Agency: A Study in International and United States Law," *William and Mary Law Review,* IX (Spring, 1968), 556–629; this study was republished as Monograph No. 14 by the Institute for Palestine Studies (Beirut, 1968).

178. U.S. *Statutes at Large,* XLIV, 2185.

179. *Ibid.*

180. Subsequent illegal Zionist immigration is described in Taylor, *Prelude to Israel,* pp. 66–67; Esco, *Palestine,* II, 942–55.

The Mandatory shall see that complete freedom of conscience and the free exercise of all forms of worship, subject only to the maintenance of public order and morals, are ensured to all. No discrimination of any kind shall be made between the inhabitants of Palestine on the ground of race, religion or language. No person shall be excluded from Palestine on the sole ground of his religious belief.[181]

This is consistent with article 6 concerning immigration, and the two articles interpreted together permit the immigration of Jews, as well as adherents of other religions, on a basis of individual equality. The second sentence, which flatly prohibits "discrimination of any kind" between Palestinians, is, of course, entirely consistent with the first safeguard of the declaration.

In summary, the Zionist "national home" enterprise referred to in the preamble of the mandate was limited by the inclusion of both safeguards. The Zionist enterprise was also limited by each of the specific provisions of the mandate for Palestine which has been considered. The mandate is juridically significant because it involved the multilateral approval and agreement of the League of Nations to the provisions of the Balfour Declaration. It does not change the juridical interpretation of the declaration, including the lack of legal obligation in the favor clause and the comprehensive and explicit character of the safeguard clauses.

The Anglo-American Convention on Palestine (1924)

The entire League of Nations mandate for Palestine, including the Balfour Declaration and its safeguards, was set forth in the preamble to the Anglo-American Convention on Palestine.[182] The full scope of United States agreement is enunciated in the first article of the convention which expressly provides that the United States "consents" or agrees to the British administration of Palestine pursuant to the terms of the mandate.[183] The United States thus added its authority to the existing agreement to the mandate and thereby became a party to the Balfour Declaration as it was established as a multilateral agreement through the Palestine mandate.

An additional purpose of this convention was to put United States nationals in the same position as nationals of member states of the League of Nations in their business and other activities in Palestine. Article 7 of the

---

181. U.S. *Statutes at Large*, XLIV, 2187.
182. U.S. *Statutes at Large*, XLIV, 2184–85.
183. *Ibid.*, p. 2191.

convention provided that no part of the convention could "be affected by any modification which may be made in the terms of" the Palestine mandate without the assent of the United States.[184]

Customary International Law
Agreement to the Declaration

The United Nations General Assembly resolution of November 29, 1947, recommended the partition of Palestine into an Arab state and a "Jewish" state.[185] As to both proposed states, the resolution provided: "The State shall be bound by all the international agreements and conventions, both general and special, to which Palestine has become a party."[186] It is the position of the government of Israel, however, that it is not bound by the limiting provisions of the Palestine partition resolution.[187] In addition, the same government has enunciated the view that it is not a successor to the Palestine mandatory government in terms of being obligated by the international agreements which were applicable to the Palestine mandate under the League of Nations. In 1949 this view was set forth in a memorandum prepared by the government of Israel Foreign Ministry and sent to the United States government. In relevant part it stated:

> It is the view of the Government of Israel that, generally speaking, treaties to which Palestine was a party, or which the Mandatory Government had applied to Palestine, are not in force in relation to the Government of Israel.[188]

It should be noted that this is formulated as a general and not an invariable rule. Thus the government of Israel may, as an exception to the generalization, continue to rely upon the Balfour Declaration for claimed juridical authority for, *inter alia,* the Zionist territorial claims to Palestine.[189]

184. *Ibid.,* p. 2192.

185. United Nations, General Assembly, 2d Session (A/519) 1947, pp. 131–50.

186. *Ibid.,* p. 138.

187. This is illustrated by its seizure of territory in excess of that contemplated in the resolution (see map 5 in this volume).

188. Marjorie Whiteman, *Digest of International Law,* II (Washington, D.C., 1963), 972.

189. Other examples of the use of the Balfour Declaration as alleged authority for Zionist juridical claims before and after 1948 are provided in Mallison, " 'The Jewish People' " Study.

It is widely accepted that both the League of Nations mandate for Palestine and the Anglo-American Convention on Palestine were terminated at the end of the British mandate. There is no record, however, of any protest by the states that were parties to the Palestine mandate and to the Anglo-American Convention concerning the Zionist-Israel claims which rely upon the continuing validity of the Balfour Declaration. In particular, neither the United States nor Great Britain has protested.[190] The declaration is thereby established as international law through the recognized customary law-making processes of the implicit agreement of states expressed by toleration, acquiescence, and silence.[191]

There is no doubt that the proponents of the Zionist-Israel claims are no more interested in effectuating the safeguards in recent years than they have been at any earlier time.[192] The result, however, of the establishment of the Balfour Declaration as customary international law is its acceptance as a whole. This undoubtedly creates a very difficult situation for the state of Israel and its juridically linked Zionist Organization,[193] because of the systematic and continuing character of the violation of both of the safeguard clauses.[194]

190. Such protests would not be expected because of the protective purposes of the declaration.

191. American Law Institute, *Restatement of the Foreign Relations Law of the United States* emphasizes the law-making importance of failure of a state to object (p. 3). Other authorities and examples concerning customary law-making appear in Mallison, " 'The Jewish People' " Study, pp. 1061–65.

192. Jiryis documents systematic violations of the first safeguard (*The Arabs in Israel*). In response to complaints of Americans of Jewish religious faith concerning violations of the second safeguard, Assistant Secretary of State Talbot in a letter to Rabbi Elmer Berger of March 14, 1964, stated that "the Department of State does not regard the [Zionist] 'Jewish people' concept as a concept of international law" (Whiteman, *Digest of International Law*, VIII, (1967), 35.

193. The juridical linking and subordination of the Zionist Organization as a political instrument of the government of Israel is done through the Zionist Organization/Jewish Agency Status Law (*Laws of the State of Israel*, VII [1952], 3) and the Covenant Between the Government of Israel and the Zionist Executive (1954); both are set forth and appraised in Mallison, "Zionist Organization/Jewish Agency." The covenant has been in the file of the Zionist registrant (No. 208) in the Registration Section of the U.S. Department of Justice since Aug. 28, 1969, as required by the Foreign Agents Registration Act of 1938 as Amended (U.S. *Statutes at Large*, LII [Washington, D.C., 1938], 63; U.S. *Code*, XXII [Washington, D.C., 1964], 611).

194. See Begin, *The Revolt;* Avner, *Memoirs of an Assassin;* Mardor, *Haganah;* Peretz, *Israel and the Palestine Arabs;* Jiryis, *The Arabs in Israel*. The enforcement of international law is mentioned below, "International Law Limitations upon the Declaration."

INTERNATIONAL LAW LIMITATIONS
UPON THE DECLARATION

The Balfour Declaration, agreed to by the League of Nations and the United States and established in customary law, must be interpreted consistently with the basic limitations of public international law which apply to any international agreement. Professors McDougal, Lasswell, and Miller, with appropriate recognition of the necessity of according pre-eminence to the fundamental doctrines of international law over the subsidiary ones, have written: "The public order takes priority over particular agreements that contravene its fundamental values and institutions."[195] Unless this principle is implemented the result could be the frustration of the fundamental values of the international public order by a plethora of destructive subsidiary agreements. This is merely a recognition in the international community of the same principle of constitutional priority which is established in the municipal order systems.

The twelfth of President Woodrow Wilson's fourteen points dealt specifically with the non-Turkish portions of the Ottoman Empire and provided:

> The other [non-Turkish] nationalities which are now under Turkish rule should be assured an undoubted security of life and an absolutely unmolested opportunity of autonomous development.[196]

It need only be mentioned that Palestine was in no way excepted from this principle.

On February 11, 1918, President Wilson delivered a detailed address concerning the ultimate peace to be obtained to a Joint Session of the Congress. Of the four norms enunciated by the president, two have direct application to Palestine:

> Second, that peoples and provinces are not to be bartered about from sovereignty to sovereignty as if they were mere chattels and pawns in a game, even the great game, now forever discredited, of the balance of power; but that

> Third, every territorial settlement involved in this war must be made in the interest and for the benefit of the populations concerned, and not

---

195. *Interpretation of Agreements*, p. 261.

196. U.S. Department of State, *Papers Relating to the Foreign Relations of the United States* [1918], I (Washington, D.C., 1933), suppl. 1, 16.

as a part of any mere adjustment or compromise of claims amongst rival states.[197]

The Balfour Declaration may only be upheld as valid under these criteria if the favor clause is interpreted as a humanitarian provision for refugee Jews. In the same way, the first safeguard must be given a sufficiently broad interpretation to make it consistent with "the benefit of the populations concerned."

President Wilson spelled out the juridical concept of self-determination of peoples with particularity in the same statement:

> Peoples are not to be handed about from one sovereignty to another by an international conference or an understanding between rivals and antagonists. National aspirations must be respected; peoples may now be dominated and governed only by their own consent. "Self-determination" is not a mere phrase. It is an imperative principle of action, which statesmen will henceforth ignore at their peril. We cannot have general peace for the asking, or by the mere arrangements of a peace conference. It cannot be pieced together out of individual understandings between powerful states.[198]

It would be difficult indeed, even with the advantage of the knowledge of Zionist objectives and practices revealed during the past five decades, to enunciate an "imperative principle" which would be more inconsistent with the territorial objectives of Zionism in Palestine.

The principles of the peace settlement promulgated by President Wilson and reflected in the League of Nations Covenant have been applied to Palestine by the King-Crane Commission. This commission was sent to Palestine and the Near East by President Wilson to ascertain the facts and to make recommendations. Its recommendations are based upon a careful study and analysis of the relevant evidence.[199] The report of the commission refers particularly to the recognition of the provisional independence of "certain communities formerly belonging to the Turkish

197. *Ibid.,* p. 112.
198. *Ibid.,* p. 110.
199. The authoritative study and evaluation of the importance of the King-Crane Commission is Harry Howard, *The King-Crane Commission* (Beirut, 1963); Professor Howard appraises the recommendations made concerning Palestine as fair and involving a limited Jewish "national home" consistent with Palestinian rights (pp. 320–21).

Empire" by the Covenant of the League of Nations.[200] The report states:

> In his address of July 4, 1918, President Wilson laid down the following principle as one of the four great "ends for which the associated peoples of the world were fighting": "The settlement of every question, whether of territory, of sovereignty, of economic arrangement, or of political relationship upon the basis of the free acceptance of that settlement by the people immediately concerned, and not upon the basis of the material interest or advantage of any other nation or people which may desire a different settlement for the sake of its own exterior influence or mastery." If that principle is to rule, and so the wishes of Palestine's population are to be decisive as to what is to be done with Palestine, then it is to be remembered that the non-Jewish population of Palestine—nearly nine-tenths of the whole—are emphatically against the entire Zionist program. The tables show that there was no one thing upon which the population of Palestine were more agreed than upon this. To subject a people so minded to unlimited Jewish immigration, and to steady financial and social pressure to surrender the land, would be a gross violation of the principle just quoted, and of the peoples' rights, though it kept within the forms of law.[201]

The commission then quoted the relevant resolutions of the "General Syrian [including Palestinian] Congress" adopted on July 6, 1919, as an authentic manifestation of the views of the people.

> 7. We oppose the pretensions of the Zionists to create a Jewish commonwealth in the southern part of Syria, known as Palestine, and oppose Zionist migration to any part of our country; for we do not acknowledge their title, but consider them a grave peril to our people from the national, economical, and political points of view. Our Jewish compatriots shall enjoy our common rights and assume the common responsibilities.

> 8. We ask that there should be no separation of the southern part of Syria known as Palestine nor of the littoral western zone which includes Lebanon from the Syrian country. We desire that the unity of the country should be guaranteed against partition under whatever circumstances. . . .

---

200. U.S. Department of State, *Papers Relative to the Foreign Relations of the United States* [1919], XII (Washington, D.C., 1947) 784.
201. *Ibid.*, p. 793 (note omitted).

10. The fundamental principles laid down by President Wilson in condemnation of secret treaties impel us to protest most emphatically against any treaty that stipulates the partition of our Syrian country and against any private engagement aiming at the establishment of Zionism in the southern part of Syria; therefore we ask the complete annulment of these conventions and agreements.[202]

The recommendations of the commission concerning Palestine include the following:

We recommend, in the fifth place, serious modification of the extreme Zionist Program for Palestine of unlimited immigration of Jews, looking finally to making Palestine distinctly a Jewish State.

(1) The Commissioners began their study of Zionism with minds predisposed in its favor, but the actual facts in Palestine, coupled with the force of the general principles proclaimed by the Allies and accepted by the Syrians have driven them to the recommendation here made.

(3) The Commission recognized also that definite encouragement had been given to the Zionists by the Allies in Mr. Balfour's often quoted statement, in its approval by other representatives of the Allies. If, however, the strict terms of the Balfour Statement are adhered to—favoring "the establishment in Palestine of a national home for the Jewish people," "it being clearly understood that nothing shall be done which may prejudice the civil and religious rights of existing non-Jewish communities in Palestine"—it can hardly be doubted that the extreme Zionist Program must be greatly modified. For "a national home for the Jewish people" is not equivalent to making Palestine into a Jewish State; nor can the erection of such a Jewish State be accomplished without the gravest trespass upon the "civil and religious rights of existing non-Jewish communities in Palestine." The fact came out repeatedly in the Commission's conference with Jewish representatives, that the Zionists look forward to a practically complete dispossession of the present non-Jewish inhabitants of Palestine, by various forms of purchase.[203]

This analysis is, in the substance of its interpretation, the same as the one adopted in the present study.

The commissioners also stated:

202. *Ibid.*
203. *Ibid.*, p. 792.

The Peace Conference should not shut its eyes to the fact that the anti-Zionist feeling in Palestine and Syria is intense and not lightly to be flouted. No British officer, consulted by the Commissioners, believed that the Zionist program could be carried out except by force of arms. The officers generally thought that a force of not less than fifty thousand soldiers would be required even to initiate the program. That of itself is evidence of a strong sense of the injustice of the Zionist program, on the part of the non-Jewish populations of Palestine and Syria. Decisions, requiring armies to carry out, are sometimes necessary, but they are surely not gratuitously to be taken in the interests of a serious injustice. For the initial claim, often submitted by Zionist representatives, that they have a "right" to Palestine, based on an occupation of two thousand years ago, can hardly be seriously considered.[204]

The fundamental inconsistencies between the Zionist territorial objectives in Palestine and both the Balfour Declaration and the League of Nations Covenant are among the major conclusions of the present study. It is not, however, necessary to rely on this analysis alone. Mr. Balfour, in a memorandum of August 11, 1919, to the British government (intended for official use only) stated in relevant part:

The contradiction between the letter of the Covenant and the policy of the Allies is even more flagrant in the case of the "independent nation" of Palestine than in that of the "independent nation" of Syria. For in Palestine we do not propose even to go through the form of consulting the wishes of the present inhabitants of the country, though the American [King-Crane] Commission has been going through the form of asking what they are. The four Great Powers are committed to Zionism. And Zionism, be it right or wrong, good or bad, is rooted in age-long traditions, in present needs, in future hopes, of far profounder import than the desires and prejudices of the 700,000 Arabs who now inhabit that ancient land.

In my opinion that is right. What I have never been able to understand is how it can be harmonised with the declaration, the Covenant, or the instructions to the Commission of Enquiry.

. . . In short, so far as Palestine is concerned, the Powers have made no statement of fact which is not admittedly wrong, and no declaration

204. *Ibid.*, p. 794. In the actual event, the Zionist conquest of Palestine was accomplished by military force including the use of terror (see above; *The First Safeguard*). Concerning the Zionist alleged historic right to Palestine it is significant that an Israeli legal writer, Yehuda Blum, does not even mention it in a book dealing with historic titles: *Historic Titles in International Law* (The Hague, 1965).

of policy which, at least in the letter, they have not always intended to violate.[205]

It is well known that one of the basic purposes of the United Nations, set forth in the first article of its charter, is "the principle of equal rights and self-determination of peoples."[206] The charter also provides that member states of the United Nations which have responsibility for the administration of territories which were not yet self-governing

accept as a sacred trust the obligation to promote to the utmost, within the system of international peace and security established by the present Charter, the well-being of the inhabitants of these territories . . . to develop self-government to take due account of the political aspirations of the peoples, and to assist them in the progressive development of their free political institutions, according to the particular circumstances of each territory and its peoples and their varying states of advancement.[207]

Even though the provisions just set forth include Palestine, where the League of Nations mandate was still in effect when the Charter of the United Nations was written in 1945, there is another, more specific provision which applies to Palestine. The charter provides, without prejudice to the content of individual trusteeship agreements which may be entered into under the requirements of the charter, that

nothing in this Chapter shall be construed in or of itself to alter in any manner the rights whatsoever of any states or any peoples or the terms of existing international instruments to which Members of the United Nations may respectively be parties.[208]

Among the "rights" of "peoples" thus protected are the rights of the Palestinian people protected by the first safeguard clause of the Balfour Declaration as embodied in the Palestine mandate and customary international law.

205. *Documents on British Foreign Policy 1919–1939*, ed. E. L. Woodward and Rohan Butler, first series, IV (London, 1952), 345.
206. Article 1, section 2.
207. Article 73.
208. Article 80. Article 103 is a "supremacy clause" analogous to that for the Covenant of the League of Nations (Article 20, section 1).

On December 14, 1960, the General Assembly adopted a resolution entitled "Declaration on the Granting of Independence to Colonial Countries and Peoples." Among its provisions which are most obviously applicable to the Palestinian people and country are the following:

2. All peoples have the right to self-determination; by virtue of that right they freely determine their political status and freely pursue their economic, social and cultural development. . . .

6. Any attempt aimed at the partial or total disruption of the national unity and the territorial integrity of a country is incompatible with the purposes and principles of the Charter of the United Nations.[209]

Paragraph 2 is set forth in unqualified terms. Without attempting to determine the outer limits of the doctrine of self-determination, it is applicable to the people of Palestine under the United Nations Charter as it was under the League of Nations Covenant. A contrary conclusion would be based upon the false assumption that the Charter was intended to revoke the provisional independence granted to Palestine by the covenant.

Paragraph 6 states a basic principle concerning the disruption of "the territorial integrity of a country" with which the United Nations General Assembly Palestine Partition Resolution of November 29, 1947, is entirely inconsistent.[210] Although a detailed consideration of the Palestine Partition Resolution is beyond the scope of the present study, it should be apparent that any partition of a country contrary to the will of its inhabitants is a violation of the charter provisions which have been considered as well as a violation of the quoted paragraphs of the General Assembly resolution concerning decolonization.[211]

On December 10, 1969, the United Nations General Assembly adopted a resolution by more than the two-thirds majority required by the charter for "important questions."[212] It recognized "that the problem of the Pal-

209. United Nations, General Assembly, Res. 1514, Suppl. 16 (A/4684), XV, 1960, p. 67.

210. United Nations, General Assembly, 2d Session (A/519), 1947, pp. 131–50.

211. The following analysis concludes that the Partition Resolution is illegal: *Colloque de Juristes Arabes sur la Palestine, La Question Palestinienne* (Algiers, 1968), pp. 72–104; [*Seminar of Arab Jurists on Palestine, The Palestine Question,* trans. Edward Rizk (Beirut, 1968) pp. 73–91]; the French-language edition of the book is reviewed briefly in *American Journal of International Law,* LXIII (1969), 357.

212. United Nations, General Assembly, Resolution 2535B, December 10, 1969.

estine Arab refugees has arisen from the denial of their inalienable rights under the Charter of the United Nations and the Universal Declaration of Human Rights" and reaffirmed "the inalienable rights of the people of Palestine."[213] The General Assembly, the same organ which adopted the ill-fated Palestine Partition Resolution of 1947, has thus recognized that the Palestinians are a people who are entitled to the same inalienable human rights as other peoples. The implementation of this resolution would be a significant step toward the establishment of a peace based upon justice in the Middle East. Such a settlement would enable all Palestinians, Muslim, Christian, and Jewish, to live together on a basis of individual equality.[214]

Scholars and others who value human dignity and equal rights for all must address themselves to the task of enforcing the Balfour Declaration as now established in customary law and as interpreted consistently with the governing requirements of international law. This involves, first, a widespread educational process to include an understanding of the facts and the law concerning Palestine.[215] It involves, second, the development and application of an adequate sanctioning process by the organized world community to compel compliance with the law.[216]

213. *Ibid.*

214. The Palestinian proposal of a democratic, secular state is detailed in Yusif Sayigh, *Towards Peace in Palestine* (Beirut, 1970).

215. The lack of balance and fairness in press reports in the United States concerning the June, 1967, coercion situation is considered in American Institute for Political Communication, *Domestic Communications Aspects of the Middle East Crisis* (Washington, D.C., July, 1967). Censorship by the media is considered in Jerome A. Barron, "An Emerging First Amendment Right of Access to the Media?" *George Washington Law Review,* XXXVII (March, 1969), 487–509.

216. Adequate sanctions must involve a comprehensive process rather than isolated acts (Myres McDougal and Florentino Feliciano, *Law and Minimum World Public Order* [New Haven, 1961] pp. 261–383).

PART II

Land and People

The Balfour Declaration and the commitment it implied for Zionist colonization of Palestine was confirmed by the mandatory regime imposed upon Palestine by the European League of Nations in the wake of the Peace Conference. In pursuance thereof, the British government, now in full control of Palestine with definite frontiers imposed by imperial arrangements and convenience, had to undertake policies calculated to facilitate "the establishment in Palestine of a national home for the Jewish people." When all things are said and done, whether we are speaking in terms of ideas or in terms of declarations of universal processes of colonialism and settlements, both depend ultimately on two major spokes: land and people. The phrase "the land without a people to the people without a land" is as arresting as it is false; it disguises the fact that the people in question had been on lands for centuries but that it was their exit from those lands that was valued. On the other hand, the land that was "without a people" had been providing food and shelter to a people who had produced cities and a culture there and whose exit was also sought by externals. Yet the phrase is apt—to establish a state or a political community, land and people are needed first; the type and character of the polity and state can be determined next.

The Zionists had obtained the promise of settlement, and however ambiguously the mandatory regime acted in its efforts to facilitate the Jewish national-home principle, it had, as a matter of course, to facilitate land transfer to would-be settlers, and it had to permit, like any other organized government, immigration into the land over which it exercised jurisdiction. Had Palestine been without a people, the British government would have found no obstacle in carrying out its commitment to the Zionists. But Palestine had about three-quarters of a million people at the

*onset of the mandate who had been on the land since time immemorial.
Many of them owned their own lands; others had legal title to most of it.
Some were small landholders, others large. Some had worked and tilled
the land for as long as historical memory can validate, and others lived
in what might be termed urban settlements. Only a few were nomadic with
no specific abode which they could call their own. Some land was held
privately, some in common, and some was in state domain—the most
common form of landholding in the Islamic polity in which land was held
collectively by the people for whose benefit the state was to develop the
land.*

*Zionists recognized quite early that the land held by the Palestinian
people would have to be alienated so that settlement on the land and development by European would-be immigrants could eventually establish
the necessary basis for statehood. A slow process of land alienation from
Palestinians to European Jews and Zionist land companies characterized
the brief history of Palestine from 1921 to 1948. Though small and really
minor—when the state of Israel was proclaimed, no more than 8 per cent
of the land of Palestine was owned by Jewish-Zionist individuals and concerns—the political and strategic implications of the process were clear
to Arab and European alike. John Ruedy, Associate Professor of History
at Georgetown University, analyzes this process against the background of
Palestine itself, dealing with it in relation to the land-tenure system
then prevailing. His essay gives us a glimpse of the effects of the land
transfer within the broader context of the political aspects and significance
of the process. Professor Ruedy's examination of the alienation of land
in Palestine can be viewed as an extension of his concern with the dynamics
and fate of colonial settlement; he has contributed to our understanding
of a similar process of land alienation in another colonial/settler area in
his previous work* Land Policy in Colonial Algeria.

*Though the process of land alienation was slow and continued to be
a major problem for the European settlers of Palestine, the process of
immigration was relatively easier and in the end proved more significant
in affecting the destiny of Palestine. What the Zionists had failed to buy,
they eventually expropriated when they announced the establishment of
the state of Israel. The settlement of people was steady, though it proceeded at an uneven rate and pace, subject as it was to the pressures of
push-pull. In the absence of any major political pressure, European Jews,
from whom the Zionists hoped to draw the greatest number of settlers,
opted to stay where they were or, in the pursuit of their individual welfare,
to migrate to other Western countries. Palestine was the territory of the
politically or messianically inspired European Jew. Although the pace and
rate of migration were both facilitated and hindered by specific area pres-*

sures, in Palestine or elsewhere, over time a gradual alteration in the ratio of the population did occur. By how much the ratio of European to Arab, or Jew to Muslim and Christian, in Palestine was altered has always been a subject of controversy. For if we abandon the postulate that Palestine had no inhabitants either at the time of the Zionist Congress of 1897 or at the time of the 1917 Balfour Declaration as self-evidently ludicrous, it becomes of historical importance to determine the number of people who would be eventually affected by a large-scale migration of Europeans to Palestine. It also is a matter of historical importance to determine where the new migrants settled.

Yet students of Palestine and the Arab-Israeli conflict have been bedeviled by conflicting population figures, which predate the emergence of the "refugee" question. The conflicting claims are in part politically inspired but, as is evident from the population essay, may in part be results of faulty evidence and unscientific reasoning. Accustomed as we are to attribute certain shortcomings to the "developing" countries of the world in terms of the generation and analysis of census data, it is hard to explain the failure of the British government when in authority over Palestine to maintain reliable records of population change. In the entire history of mandated Palestine, only two censuses were undertaken—one in 1922 and another in 1931. The endemic troubles of Palestine itself may have accounted for the unwillingness of the British government to maintain an enumeration of population in the interwar period, and by 1941 the war in Europe was a more important priority than the undertaking of a head count in Palestine. The combined pressures of Arabs and Europeans— Jews, Christians, and Muslims—in the immediate postwar period may also have acted as a deterrent.

Whatever the actual reasons, everyone who has dealt with the population figures for Palestine either to ascertain the actual numbers involved or to estimate the number of eventual refugees had to work with the only documents available irrespective of their quality—and they were two in number. Writings on the subject which approximate scientific validity have the two British censuses as a base; others are subjective estimates made in the pursuit of a political objective. Yet the question of the demographic transformation of Palestine has not until now been analyzed scientifically and with precision. Mrs. Janet L. Abu-Lughod, Associate Professor of Sociology at Northwestern University, is a demographer-urbanist who has long concerned herself with migration patterns, urban forms, and population growth in the United States and North Africa. Her previous contributions deal with both areas. She is the co-author of Housing Choices and is the author of Cairo: 1001 Years of the City Victorious. Her essays on demographic change and migration patterns have appeared in various socio-

logical journals. In the present essay she depicts the process of population growth and the gradual alteration of the ethnic/religious ratio of the population of mandated Palestine. The reader is given, for the first time, an estimate derived by standard demographic techniques and based upon projections of the Palestinian population of 1946 of the displaced Palestinians of 1948–49. While the essay concerns itself principally with the Palestinian population up to 1949, the additional displacement of approximately 400,000 persons in consequence of the June war of 1967 necessitated a further discussion of the total Palestinian Arab population of today.

The world, particularly the Western world, increasingly began to view the Palestinian people as "refugees." If refugee means simply one who is, against his will, in a territory other than that he calls his own, then there is some justice in the term. Perhaps the majority of the Palestinian people are to be found in areas outside the boundaries of mandated Palestine. While the numbers question has arisen frequently, no writing on the Arab-Israeli conflict has been free of an attempt to settle an obvious question: How did these Palestinians become "refugees"? That bicommunal wars inevitably produce victims is obvious; various pressures—sometimes political, sometimes legal, and sometimes economic—have historically combined to produce human dislocations, the victims of which are categorized and subsumed under the terms "refugees." But it is rare for concerned people to attribute another causation to the emergence of such human problems. In the case of Palestine, had the world not been confronted with a familiar yet bizarre interpretation—that which attempts to demonstrate the culpability of Arab leadership in the removal of Palestinians from their homes as well as the individual responsibility of the Palestinians for being refugees—it would be sufficient to call the attention of the student to the fact that a bicommunal war occurred and that, as in all such wars, some people were dislocated as a result. But this curious picture has been drawn, and thus an essay dealing with the process by which Palestinians were transformed into refugees is called for.

It is not accidental that Erskine B. Childers, well-known Irish journalist and specialist not only on Middle East affairs but also on the course of imperialism generally, particularly that of the British, should address himself to this question. His concern with the Palestinians stemmed from a position paper which he was asked to prepare for an annual convention of the National Student Association early in the 1950s when he was studying in the United States on a Fulbright-Hays award. Prior to that he had no special interest in the Middle East or Palestine, but by the time he completed the research and prepared the requested paper he had come to appreciate the significant role that European colonialism played in pro-

*ducing the conflict in the Middle East. From that time onward he has con-
centrated his energies on studies of the anti-imperialist drive of the Arab
people and of their efforts to generate social and economic development,
and has continued to write on the conflict between European colonialism
and the Arab people. His essays are numerous, and his two well-known
books are* Common Sense About the Arab World *and* The Road to Suez.
*The essay which is included in this volume addressed itself, when it was
initially published in mimeographed form in 1965, specifically to the
process of dislocation in 1948–49. The June war of 1967 did not inspire
the kind of rationalization which is being analyzed in Childers' essay.
Unlike the 1948–49 war, the process of population excision in 1967 was
accomplished under the watchful eyes of the United Nations and other
international agencies. The systematic use of coercion was immediately
noted and documented, and thus obvious facts could not be denied.
It is abundantly clear from Mr. Childers' meticulous analysis that coercion
in 1948–49 was similarly employed in the pursuit of a policy long contemplated by Zionists to accomplish their purpose of settlement of a
people on "a land without a people."*

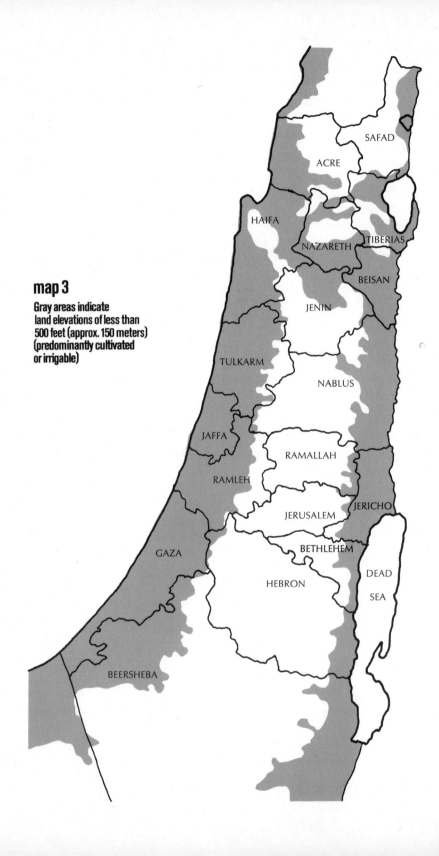

map 3

Gray areas indicate
land elevations of less than
500 feet (approx. 150 meters)
(predominantly cultivated
or irrigable)

SAFAD

ACRE

HAIFA

NAZARETH

TIBERIAS

BEISAN

JENIN

TULKARM

NABLUS

JAFFA

RAMALLAH

RAMLEH

JERUSALEM

JERICHO

GAZA

BETHLEHEM

DEAD

HEBRON

SEA

BEERSHEBA

4. Dynamics of Land Alienation

John Ruedy

The portion of geographic Syria today thought of as Palestine received its rather arbitrary boundaries between 1920 and 1922 as a result of negotiations among Great Britain, France, and the Permanent Mandates Commission of the League of Nations. These boundaries circumscribe a total land area of about 26,320 square kilometers. The heartland of the country consists of a central mass of hills running from northern Galilee to southern Judea. While these are often steep and rocky, their very highest peaks reach an altitude of only 800 to 1,000 meters. On either side of the hills lie lowlands—the Maritime Plain to the west and the Jordan Valley to the east. On the south sprawls the desert district of Beersheba, now commonly known as the Negev. Bisecting the hills on a northwest to southeast axis are the contiguous valleys of Esdraelon and Jezreel, which separate Samaria from Galilee.

The hill country of Palestine covers approximately 8,064,000 metric dunums, of which about 2.5 million are the largely uninhabited hill wilderness.[1] While the inhabited portion possesses scattered valleys of exceptional fertility, the steepness, the high limestone base, the many rock outcroppings, and the dependence upon unpredictable rainfall give it a general agricultural rating ranging from mediocre to incredibly poor. Much of it is uncultivable. This poverty has been partially attenuated through the exploitation of occasional springs or streams in the valleys and through

---

1. The metric *dunum* was established in 1928. It equals 1/10 hectare; 1,000 dunums, or 100 hectares, equal one square kilometer; 2.471 acres equal one hectare; .2471 acres equal one dunum. Areas in this section, which are rounded and approximate, are drawn from Great Britain, Colonial Office, Palestine, *Report on Immigration, Land Settlement and Development,* 2 vols., Parliamentary Papers, Cmd. 3686–87; London, 1930) [Hope Simpson Report], I, 12–23.

centuries of painstaking terracing of hillsides. Principal crops of the region during the early years of this century were grains, olives, vines, and deciduous fruits.

There are five principal plains surrounding the hills. Beginning with the largest and most important, these include the Maritime Plain from Rafah to Mount Carmel, the northern portion of which includes the Plain of Sharon. Figuring from the coast to the 150 meter contour on the east, the plain covers approximately 3.25 million dunums, of which two-thirds or more are irrigable. The light sandy soils of many of its districts, combined with the mild lowland winters make this an excellent citrus-growing country. The Plain of Acre covers 550,000 dunums lying along the coast north of Haifa. Heavy alluvial soils and a great deal of water from springs and streams make Acre suitable for very intensive cultivation of a wide variety of vegetables, fodders, and deciduous fruits. The 400,000 dunums of the Plain of Esdraelon are composed largely of alluvial clay, suitable for both cereal and fruit culture. This valley was viewed traditionally by Palestinians as the most fertile and productive region of their homeland. In the extreme northeast corner of Palestine is the Huleh Plain containing a great variety of alluvial soils. In the south this plain abuts on Lake Huleh, which is formed at the point where a basalt ridge, cutting across the Jordan Valley backs up the river. The northern shore of the lake historically scaled down into insalubrious marshes covering perhaps one-fifth of the soil. Lastly, there is the Valley of the Jordan to which, by appending the Jezreel Valley—richer even in some ways than the Esdraelon —an area of 1,065,000 dunums is ascribed. Where Jordan water is tapped, the valleys are extremely productive.

The mostly desert region south of Beersheba, which constituted in mandate times the subdistrict of Beersheba, extended over 12,576,000 dunums, or about 48 per cent of the entire country. Some of its soils would prove fertile if water from the northern reaches of the country could be provided.

LAND TENURE AND RURAL SOCIETY

At the turn of the twentieth century, Palestinian society was overwhelmingly rural and peasant. According to the first modern census, conducted late in 1922 by the mandatory government, about 65 per cent of Arab Muslims lived in essentially rural areas.[2] There is reason to believe that early in the nineteenth century the proportion of rural to urban inhabitants had been even greater. It would appear, especially after the Anglo-Ottoman

2. Census figures cited in *ibid.,* p. 24.

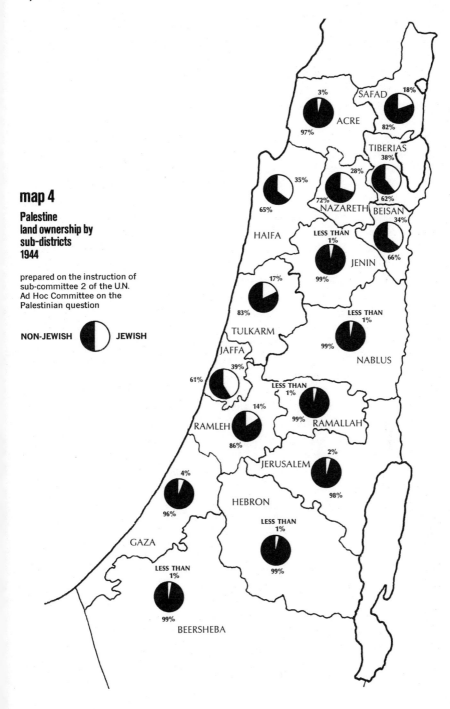

map 4

**Palestine
land ownership by
sub-districts
1944**

prepared on the instruction of
sub-committee 2 of the U.N.
Ad Hoc Committee on the
Palestinian question

NON-JEWISH   JEWISH

SAFAD

ACRE   3%   97%

18%   82%

TIBERIAS   38%   62%

NAZARETH   28%   72%

BEISAN   34%   66%

HAIFA   35%   65%

JENIN   LESS THAN 1%   99%

TULKARM   17%   83%

NABLUS   LESS THAN 1%   99%

JAFFA   39%   61%

RAMLEH   14%   86%

RAMALLAH   LESS THAN 1%   99%

JERUSALEM   2%   98%

HEBRON

GAZA   4%   96%

LESS THAN 1%   99%

BEERSHEBA   LESS THAN 1%   99%

Trade Agreement of 1838, that the combined pressures of competition upon village manufactures and of market agricultural production had produced a certain urbanizing trend. In addition to these pressures, the dramatically increased efficiency and security of Mediterranean travel over the century tended to increase the number and size of Christian, and to a lesser extent Jewish, colonies in the country; a perceptible rise in the pilgrim and tourist trade from overseas also seems to have occurred. These two factors probably combined to increase the opportunities for livelihood in certain towns.

The heart of rural society was the village, which from time immemorial has served to formalize and institutionalize that most important of all human adaptations, the reciprocal relationship between man and land. The majority of Palestinians were gathered into somewhat more than one thousand villages of varying size and fortune.[3] After the extended family, the village was the most important unit in the *fallah's* life. Its functions were not only social and economic but, in the broadest sense, political as well. As the organization, security, and communications of the high Ottoman period declined during the seventeenth century, the village, always self-contained, became even more so, standing as best it could— sometimes in concert with a neighboring community or two — for the preservation of members' lives, property, and honor against the exactions of venal tax farmers, provincial military bands, or marauding Bedouin.[4]

Most rural land in the Ottoman Empire was not "owned" in the Western sense of the term but was held hereditarily on a usufruct basis known as *miri*. Tenure could in theory be terminated for a number of reasons, including, principally, failure to cultivate or nonpayment of taxes. The ultimate owner, as elsewhere in Islam, was deemed to be the *umma muhammadiyya*, as personified in this case by the sultan. The government also owned a considerable amount of land, *jiflik*, which it rented as landlord on long-term or short-term leases to the cultivators directly or through the intermediary of larger private landlords. Some of the long-term leases in fact accorded rights which, except in the details of succession, were scarcely distinguishable from *miri* rights.

In a pattern which can be viewed as stemming either from nomadic attitudes or, and perhaps with more authority, from the ascendancy of the

---

3. See especially Government of Palestine, *Village Statistics, 1945* (Jerusalem, 1946) and table compiled by Sami Hadawi, *Palestine: Loss of a Heritage* (San Antonio, 1963), p. 138.

4. The best overall discussion of peasant and village life in the Levant is that of Jacques Weulersse, *Paysans de Syrie et du Proche-Orient* (Paris, 1946); see also briefer discussion in William R. Polk, David H. Stamler, and Edmund Asfour, *Backdrop to Tragedy: the Struggle for Palestine* (Boston, 1957), pp. 47–49, 227–38.

village group in the mind of the peasant and the necessity for its preservation, title to the land's use was vested in the collectivity. The individual's rights were always expressed as a fraction of the whole. In most villages, each constituent kinship group had become entitled to a fixed proportion of soil of each quality represented in the holding. The individual family within the kinship group was entitled to its share at a periodic redivision of his group's portion, a redivision which as often as not took place biannually.[5]

This system, called *masha'a,* was seen by British and Zionist observers as economically unsound, for the reason that with only temporary possession of a given plot families had little incentive to invest in permanent improvements or even in fertilizers. From a social and psychological point of view, however, and as a reflection of the dependence of the individual upon the group for every security during a disorganized period of history, *masha'a* represents an appropriate adaptation.

Rights to grazing lands were held by all villagers in common, as were traditional rights to wood, gathering, water, and other resources, which were frequently available on nearby state lands, or *mawat.* From the seventeenth century onward many villages had become increasingly autarkic, developing within themselves a great variety of manufacturing skills, whose practice frequently meant the difference between survival and extinction whenever demographic increase or loss of holdings cut the individual land shares to sizes below the threshold of economicity.[6]

In 1856, inaugurating the second installment of *tanzimat,* the imperial government at Constantinople issued the famous rescript known as the Hatt-i Humayun, which among other things tendered the state's pledge to hold inviolable from arbitrary *atteinte* the life, honor, and property of every subject. In implementation of the policy of guaranteeing property, the Ottoman Land Code of 1858 provided for the eventual registration and issuance pursuant thereto of title deeds on every piece of privately held land in the Empire. As progressive as these provisions sound, they were

5. Doreen Warriner, "Land-Tenure Problems in the Fertile Crescent in the Nineteenth and Twentieth Centuries," *The Economic History of the Middle East, 1800–1914: A Book of Readings,* ed. Charles Issawi (Chicago, 1966), pp. 71–78; each succeeding report of the British authorities during the mandate period also dealt with land-tenure questions; especially Hope Simpson Report, I, 29–34; Great Britain, Foreign Office, Palestine, *Report of the Palestine Commission* (Parliamentary Papers, Cmd. 5479; London, 1937) [Peel Commission Report], p. 219 ff.; Government of Palestine, *Survey of Palestine: Prepared in December 1945 and January 1946 for the Information of the Anglo-American Committee of Inquiry,* 2 vols. (Jerusalem, 1946), I, 233 ff.

6. Polk, Stamler, and Asfour, *Backdrop to Tragedy:* Hope Simpson Report, I, 140–44.

to have in the long run starkly disadvantageous effects upon Palestine's villagers.

The process of modernization always seems to entail substantive change in institutions, social relationships, and economic functions as well as the consolidation of power and authority necessary before such substantive changes can be imposed. The *fallahin* of Palestine, however dimly or intuitively, sensed only the latter task. Rightly fearing that the tax collector and army recruiter would make effective use of the new registers and hardly understanding the enormous importance of the new records and deeds to their own future, when the implementing regulations of the code began to be applied, they evaded massively and stubbornly. The least harmful course a peasant could take was to register the land in the name of a fictitious or long-dead individual.[7] This approach merely confused the records and successions, making his subsequent tenure insecure. More dangerously, he did nothing, allowing local town merchants, frequently the tax farmers, to file whole strings of villages in their own names. In other cases the peasant positively encouraged the city magnates to take title. The growing value of cash crops in the late nineteenth century encouraged the urban bourgeoisie of Beirut, Damascus, and Jerusalem to take advantage of the windfall.[8] Most often the lands they acquired were in the plains and valleys, soils suitable for producing the large harvests from which fortunes were to be compounded. Since the Ottoman Land Code of 1858 made no provisions at all for mediating the relationship between landlord and tenant, thousands of peasants from the 1870s onward found themselves in fact deprived of the most minimal rights of tenure as they became increasingly under the control of the owner, who might be landlord, tax collector, and moneylender combined. William R. Polk, concerning the code, observes that "long before the Balfour Declaration, which is often seen as the fount of all contention over Palestine, the inarticulate but ancient peasantry had slipped a rung on the ladder which was to lead them down into the refugee camps in 1948."[9]

JEWISH LAND ACQUISITIONS

Jewish holdings of land in Palestine prior to the 1880s were infinitesimal. As a matter of fact, they were still very small eleven months before the

---

7. Warriner "Land-Tenure Problems," p. 76; *Survey of Palestine,* I, 237–38.

8. The most frequently discussed beneficiaries of this process were the Sursuk family of tax farmers in Beirut, who gathered in, among other properties, an enormous tract in the lush Esdraelon Plain in 1872.

9. *Backdrop to Tragedy,* p. 236.

partition resolution of 1947, amounting in freehold and leases to about 7 per cent of the total land surface of the country.[10] During the mid-nineteenth century Western philanthropists assisted in the development of two small agricultural colonies at Safad and Tiberias, composed largely of indigenous Jews. The considerable Jewish minority of Jerusalem, whose concerns were principally religious, were overwhelmingly urban in residence and outlook.[11] It was the brutal Russian pogroms engineered by the government of Alexander III and Pobydonestev which accounted for the first important Jewish land acquisitions in Palestine. Driven forward by the intolerance of official Russia and the unconcern of even liberal Russia about that intolerance, a few young Jews rallied to the banners of Hibat Zion. The Hibat Zion movement, commonly subsumed under the label of "cultural Zionism," had only implicit or poorly articulated notions concerning the objective significance of landed settlement in Palestine. For them immigration to the Holy Land would bring personal emancipation, the possibility of physical and spiritual redemption upon the soil hallowed by their Scriptures and by the deeds of cultural forebears who had departed the land eighteen centuries earlier. A group of fifteen Kharkov students toured southwest Russia enlisting human and financial support for the founding of Rishon le Zion, southeast of Jaffa, the first Zionist settlement in modern Palestine. In time the movement acquired the interest of the Jewish Colonization Association of the Baron de Hirsch, which concerned itself primarily with Jewish settlement in South America, and, more importantly, of the Baron Edmond de Rothschild. The final result was the foundation, largely with the support of Rothschild money, of the important Palestine Jewish Colonization Association (P.I.C.A.).[12]

While other organizations and individuals became involved as well, the P.I.C.A. was the most important body devoted to Jewish acquisition of Palestinian land before the Great War and down into the 1920s. By 1930, according to figures in the John Hope Simpson Report, it held 454,840 dunums.[13] The P.I.C.A. in time discovered that few Jews possessed the

---

10. *Survey of Palestine,* I, 244; and *Supplement: Notes Compiled for the Information of the United Nations Special Committee on Palestine* (Jerusalem, 1947), p. 30; see also Avraham Granott, *Agrarian Reform and the Record of Israel* (Mystic, Conn., 1956), p. 28; Granott was an Israeli authority whose figures seem to be only fractionally higher than the official British figures. For further discussion of this subject, see below.

11. *Ibid.,* p. 24. Granott claims that Jews at Jerusalem were the majority in 1900. For the Safad and Tiberias settlements, see also Polk, Stamler, and Asfour, *Backdrop to Tragedy,* p. 50.

12. Hope Simpson Report, I, 38–39; Granott; *Agrarian Reform,* p. 27; Christopher Sykes, *Cross Roads to Israel: Palestine from Balfour to Bevin* (London, 1965), p. 147.

13. I, 49.

farming skills to make the proliferating colonies much more than objects of continuing Western philanthropy. When Rothschild insisted the farms become self-supporting, the settlers began to engage Western Christian agronomists and to employ large amounts of Arab labor.[14] At the same time it came to be association policy, once farms were established, to sell off land on easy fifty-year terms to enterprising Jewish families.[15] To the horror of postwar, socialistically minded Zionists, these privately owned farms often were quite substantial in size.[16]

Since for fifty years prior to the British occupation, Ottoman law officially forbade land acquisitions by foreigners, the P.I.C.A. and other Jewish buyers of the Hibat Zion period resorted to subterfuges in registration.[17] Because disappearance of, or irregularities in, Ottoman registers left the new British military administration hopelessly confused about real property matters, all land transactions were suspended between November, 1918, and September, 1920.[18] The opening of British registers at the latter date soon revealed total Jewish land acquisitions prior to 1920 of an estimated 650,000 dunums,[19] some small part of which may have represented illegal transfers during the twenty-two month moratorium.

While most of the property acquired by the P.I.C.A. and similar groups in the years after 1882 was located in potentially valuable plain areas, the buyers, finding themselves in a sellers' market, frequently were reduced to taking substandard, poorly developed or undeveloped tracts of marsh, swamp, or sand dune, which landlords were happy to sell at elevated prices to eager Jewish brokers.[20] As often as not, relationships with Pales-

14. *Ibid.*, p. 50; Polk, Stamler, and Asfour, *Backdrop to Tragedy*, p. 51.

15. Hope Simpson Report, I, 36.

16. See, for instance, Polk, Stamler, and Asfour, *Backdrop to Tragedy*, pp. 171–72; Granott, *Agrarian Reform*, p. 30.

17. Polk, Stamler, and Asfour, *Backdrop to Tragedy*, pp. 71, 76.

18. *Ibid.*, p. 71.

19. *Survey of Palestine*, I, 244.

20. Granott makes this point, as have many Zionist authorities (*Agrarian Reform*, p. 29). It was always to the Zionist advantage to stress the barrenness of the Palestine they came to settle. While it is true that, owing to low technological achievement, insufficiency of capital, destructive forms of land tenure among Arabs, and a differing concept of economic values, there were considerable stretches of land not exploited to levels Westerners might realize, the picture often conveyed in Zionist apologetics of a sparsely settled, largely desert-like land abused or unused by the native population is seriously overdrawn. Examples abound. One is the Esdraelon, which Sir Herbert Samuel depicted as largely desert and unexploited prior to Jewish settlement there in the early 1920s (Hope Simpson Report, I, 16–17). This was the same land which in 1887 Lawrence Oliphant described as "a huge green lake of waving wheat, with its village-crowned mounds rising from it like islands; and it presents one of the most striking pictures of luxuriant fertility which it is possible to conceive" (*Haifa, or Life in Modern Palestine* [London, 1887], p. 60).

tinians were satisfactory, as many settlements contributed markedly to the economies of their neighborhoods. The modest scope and generally un-threatening form of Jewish colonization of the Hibat Zion period seems to have occasioned some alarm among Ottoman authorities but relatively little among Palestinians themselves. A deeper study of Palestinian responses during this period would be useful.

The real trouble over Jewish acquisition of land began only after the issuance of the Balfour Declaration. Zionists knew that *Heimstätte* was a circumlocution for *Judenstaat;*[21] so did the War Cabinet of 1917;[22] so did the Arabs. More than anything else it was the ultimate political content of Zionist land acquisitions that drove the Palestinian Arab leadership to oppose these purchases. While immediate economic and human problems played their part in the rising resistance movement of the native leadership, that leadership correctly saw the keys to Palestinian survival or the seeds of its destruction in the twin issues of immigration and land. These were precisely the issues upon which the Zionists were also the most intransigent. Physical possession of, and intimate relationship to, the land by Jewish colonists were seen by them as the only certain method of possessing Palestine. Theoretically, Jews could of course have achieved their necessary majority by settling primarily in cities, thereby creating a Jewish-dom-inated industrial and commercial complement to Palestinian agriculture— a task for which they were eminently suited by virtue of their urban European backgrounds. As a matter of fact most Jewish colonists in the long run *did* settle in the cities. At no point during the "upbuilding" did the percentage of Jews on the land exceed 19.3 per cent of the total Jewish population in Palestine.[23]

The conditioning of Jews in Europe (a conditioning covering a far longer span than that of their ancestors in Biblical Palestine) had taught them that dignity and honor flowed from land, land from which European Christian society for a millennium and a half had systematically excluded the Jew. Forced into the urban ghetto and confined exclusively to city occupations, the Zionist Jew came to see himself and his culture as dis-torted, warped, lacking in balance; nor, of course, had his considerable urban and village accomplishments over the centuries ever permitted him to own any country. Cultural accomplishments were politically ephemeral, but land ownership had an aura of permanence.[24]

---

21. Sykes quotes Max Nordau, Weizmann's closest collaborator and inventor of the term *Heimstätte,* to this effect (*Cross Roads,* p. 24).

22. See, for instance, David Lloyd George's testimony before the Peel Commis-sion, quoted in Peel Commission Report, p. 24.

23. Granott, *Agrarian Reform,* p. 26.

24. *Ibid.*

While political Zionism is generally viewed — and properly so — as primarily a manifestation of nationalism, it borrowed heavily from the religious symbols of its adherents. The core mystique of the movement became the mutual redemption of land and people. The Jew would "return" to the land seized nineteen centuries ago by the interloper who had never known how to love it, to care for it, or to nurture it properly. In redeeming the land promised by God to his fathers, he would redeem himself, in the process restoring balance and wholeness to his people as well. Political Zionism was largely irrational but so are religion and nationalism. In spite of the fact that more than 80 per cent of immigrating Jews went directly from European cities to Palestinian cities, the kibbutzim and the minority living on them remain to this day at the emotional center of Zionism. But the possession of the countryside, to which the Jew aspired, would mean the destruction of precisely that which was most characteristic of Palestinian society. Against this threat the native population fought and lost.

In 1901, pursuant to an earlier resolution of the First Zionist Congress, the Jewish National Fund (J.N.F.) was organized.[25] The J.N.F.'s mandate was to purchase, develop, and settle lands as the inalienable property of the whole Jewish people. Strongly influenced by the revolutionary currents swirling across the autocratic Russia from whence so many of them came, political Zionists emphasized collective ownership and "self-labor" as keys to their land-acquisition and -development policy. Some settlements became collectives, others colonies of small freeholders, all with long-term leases. In neither case did title to the land itself escape from the J.N.F.[26]

In 1911 the Palestine Land Development Co., Ltd. was formed for the purpose of acting as buyer for Jews who had a penchant for private ownership.[27] Later this organization became the principal purchasing agent for J.N.F., which became the holder and settler of the lands under the general supervision of the Colonisation Department of the Jewish Agency for Palestine.[28] Individual brokers by the scores, and, in the 1930s, by the hundreds, were also in the business of purchasing for J.N.F. as well as for other organizations and for individuals. The J.N.F., however, as it grew more skilled and powerful eventually came into possession of 90 per cent of all lands newly acquired by Jewish buyers.[29]

25. *Ibid.*, p. 27.
26. *Ibid.*
27. Hope Simpson Report, I, 38–39.
28. *Ibid.;* Granott, *Agrarian Reform,* p. 31.
29. Granott, *Agrarian Reform,* p. 30.

There had been little plan or coherence to the land-settlement pattern of the prewar Zionists. The J.N.F., as it grew in experience and financial resources after 1920, gradually led in the development and implementation in the interwar years of what Avraham Granott did not hesitate to call "a national land policy."[30] Basic elements of this policy were (1) the suitability of the tract in question for sizable and economic colonization and (2) "above all its place in the upbuilding and attainment of a Jewish majority."[31] If an Arab nation were to be supplanted by a Jewish nation, this would best be accomplished by the systematic carving out and progressive extension of solid blocks of Jewish-held territory, thus building the national home district by district. Additional elements were (3) the avoidance of isolated settlements subject to attacks by the increasingly bitter Arab populace and (4) as the international climate made attainment of all or even part of the Jewish state questionable, the acquisition of land for political purposes in order to confront the great powers and international organizations with established Jewish presence in areas susceptible to loss in possible negotiations. Such "political" acquisitions included moves into Beisan and an eleventh-hour purchasing dash to Revivim in the Negev.[32]

RESPONSE TO LAND ALIENATION

During the mandate period, one of the factors that contributed to the increasing violence of Palestinian response to Zionist colonization was the escalating problem of landlessness—the growing misery in the villages and the effluence of the peasantry toward the cities, often to unemployment or underemployment. Such individuals needed little persuasion from their leaders to take up the standard against the outlander.

Before various governmental commissions of inquiry, Jewish Agency witnesses always staunchly denied that they had anything to do with displacing *fallahin* from the land. They argued that, on the contrary, Jewish settlements had contributed manifold benefits to the peasantry. In proof they would point to several P.I.C.A. settlements where Arab labor was considerable and where Arab-Jewish relationships were frequently cordial.[33] The deceptiveness of these statements is evident from the fact that

---

30. *Ibid.*, p. 32.
31. *Ibid.*
32. *Ibid.*, pp. 34–35.
33. "It is . . . very noticeable, in travelling through the P.I.C.A. villages, to see the friendliness of the relations which exist between Jew and Arab. It is quite a common sight to see an Arab sitting in the verandah of a Jewish house" (Hope Simpson Report, I, pp. 50–51).

the Jewish Agency itself categorically rejected in its own settlements the heterogeneous, interreligious organization of the P.I.C.A. colonies.

Almost four years before such things became common in Central Europe, the Jewish Agency Constitution of 1929 enjoined the following exclusivist policies in article 3:

> (d) Land is to be acquired as Jewish property and subject to the pro-visions of Article 10 of this Agreement, the title to the lands acquired is to be taken in the name of the Jewish National Fund, to the end that the same shall be held as the inalienable property of the Jewish people.
>
> (e) The Agency shall promote agricultural colonisation based on Jewish labour, and in all works or undertakings carried out or furthered by the Agency, it shall be deemed to be a matter of principle that Jewish labour shall be employed.[34]

The leases signed by J.N.F. lessees prescribed fines for, and eventual eviction of, farmers breaking a rule against employing non-Jewish labor. In his intensive report on the background to the 1929 disturbances, Sir John Hope Simpson observed that

> the result of the purchase of land in Palestine by the Jewish National Fund has been that land has been extra-territorialised. It ceases to be land from which the Arab can gain any advantage now or in the future. Not only can he never hope to lease or to cultivate it, but by the stringent provisions of the lease of the Jewish National Fund, he is deprived for ever from employment on that land. The land is in mort-main and in-alienable. It is for this reason that Arabs discount the professions of friendship and good will on the part of the Zionists in view of the policy which the Zionist Organisation deliberately adopted.[35]

The first important J.N.F. purchase under the mandate had been of seven Arab villages in the Jezreel Valley. The fears engendered by the project in some of the Arab population were judged to be a factor in the 1921 riots and led the government to amend its Land Transfer Ordinance to require that a tenant evicted from lands because of sale must retain sufficient land elsewhere to permit support of himself and his family.[36] While it is true that a considerable amount of land acquired by Jews

34. As cited in *ibid.,* p. 53.
35. *Ibid.,* p. 54.
36. *Ibid.,* pp. 34–35.

between the wars was not previously cultivated (Kabbara Swamp, Huleh Marshes, coastal sand dunes, etc.), it is also true that even more of it was inhabited and cultivated. Enormous J.N.F. purchases in the Esdraelon and elsewhere evicted thousands.[37] Evading the 1921 amendment was a simple matter. Jewish brokers made it clear to the seller that they would not accept transfer of the tract until it was clear of all tenants. The landlord, frequently the tenants' major creditor or possessed of other important influence, had little difficulty inducing them to leave without availing themselves of little-understood protections afforded by foreigners' laws.[38]

From 1929 to 1933 the government experimented with compensation for displacement.[39] Faced in the latter year with the potentially explosive pressures of economic depression, worsening land-man ratios, and vastly increased Jewish immigration, it issued a new Cultivators (Protection) Ordinance forbidding the eviction of *any* tenant who could prove one year's statutory tenure. No sale need be involved. Landlords evaded the new law by granting subsequently leases of only nine or ten months.[40]

By 1930 Sir John Hope Simpson observed that

> it has been shown that while an area of at least 180 dunums is required to maintain a fallah family in a decent standard of life in the unirrigated tracts, the whole of the cultivable land not already in the hands of the Jews would not afford an average lot in excess of 90 dunums. . . . It also appears that of the 86,980 rural Arab families in the villages, 29.4 per cent are landless.[41]

It is not the contention of this essay that Jewish immigration was the sole reason for growing Palestinian misery, landlessness, and unemployment during the mandate period. Natural increase ascribable principally to a falling death rate drove Arab population up 60 per cent between the time of Hope Simpson's report and the partition recommendation. In the same years Jewish population quadrupled for the most part as a result of immigration. The withdrawal of 180,000 hectares from the native rural economy at a time when all resources were needed to meet a crisis of gigantic proportions compounded the suffering needlessly.

---

37. *Ibid.,* p. 17; *Survey of Palestine,* I, 299 ff.; Polk, Stamler, and Asfour, *Backdrop to Tragedy,* pp. 236–39.

38. *Survey of Palestine,* I, 289.

39. Hope Simpson Report, I, 35–36.

40. *Survey of Palestine,* I, 290–91.

41. Hope Simpson Report, I, 142–43.

During the decade of the 1920s annual Zionist land purchases fluctuated from as few as 17,493 dunums in 1923 to as many as 176,124 dunums in 1926.[42] As a result of the riots of August, 1929, Sir Walter Shaw and Sir John Hope Simpson chaired on behalf of the government successive inquiries into causes and possible cures for the disturbances. Hope Simpson concluded in 1930 that parcelization of Arab land had already proceeded to a dangerous point, that Jewish land acquisition was compressing the population further, and that if all remaining lands were divided among the indigenous population, the latter still would not have enough to provide themselves with acceptable standards of living. He recommended a concentrated development program to increase land potential; while awaiting the outcome of these development schemes all Jewish immigration to rural areas should be suspended.[43] The Colonial Office accepted this report and issued the so-called Passfield White Paper announcing its intentions. The Zionist outcry at what they considered an attempt to crystallize the national home was immediate and effective. In London pressures were exerted from all sides. In a superb illustration of what Erskine Childers calls the "broken triangle,"[44] Ramsay MacDonald in February, 1931, retreated from what knowledgeable experts in the field knew must be done if tragedy were to be averted.[45]

The inclusion of "non-Zionist" Jews in the governing bodies of the Jewish Agency after 1929, as illusory as it proved to be in genuinely broadening the opinion base of the movement, had the immensely practical effect of channeling new sources of funds into the enterprise.[46] This new solvency and the vastly increased immigration triggered by Hitler's rise combined to place new and greater pressures upon the landed resources— pressures which finally led to open civil war. Rapid Jewish immigration threw far more buyers into the market; speculative activity multiplied as Jew bid against Jew for available parcels, and land values exploded upward.[47] Acquisitions of 18,893 dunums in 1932 doubled to 36,991 in 1933, and nearly doubled again to 67,114 by 1935.[48] The J.N.F. was

---

42. *Survey of Palestine,* I, 244.

43. Hope Simpson Report, I, 220.

44. Erskine B. Childers, "Palestine: The Broken Triangle," *Modernization of the Arab World,* ed. Jack H. Thompson and Robert D. Reischauer (Princeton, 1966), pp. 150–65.

45. Peel Commission Report, pp. 72–78.

46. Sykes, *Cross Roads,* pp. 130–33.

47. Avraham Granott, *Land Policy in Palestine* (New York, 1940), pp. 8–9; see also tables of transactions in *Survey of Palestine,* I, 242. Ad valorem tax receipts on land transactions rose from £ P 97,876 in 1932 to £ P 455,146 in 1935.

48. *Survey of Palestine,* I, 242.

securing in these years not only properties it saw immediate use for but reserves to assure future settlement in case of adverse decisions at the political level.[49] Throughout the whole mandate period, moreover, the Jewish Agency and its predecessor organization had pressed the mandatory government to turn over enormous tracts of state domain for their use. The fact that these lands frequently were occupied by securely settled tenants of long-term tenure did not preclude the agency's qualifying such lands as vacant and subject therefore under terms of the mandate to Jewish colonization. While the British resisted much of this pressure, by 1947 approximately 195,000 dunums of state domain had been conceded or leased to Jewish settlers.[50]

The Arab Higher Committee throughout the 1930s had demanded immediate and total cessation of immigration and of land sales to Jews. The McDonald White Paper of May, 1939, foresaw a gradual tapering off of both. In implementation of the new property rules, the Jerusalem government in February, 1940, issued new transfer regulations. The provisions divided the country into three zones. Within Zone A, which included general areas of little Jewish settlement, Zionist acquisitions were prohibited, except through judicial proceedings. In Zone B, the Esdraelon and Jezreel, eastern Galilee, part of Sharon, the region northeast of Gaza and the southern Negev, acquisitions were permitted only for consolidation purposes or for projects deemed by the high commissioner to be of general public interest. A free zone covered the greater part of the coastal plain, Haifa Bay, an area south of Jaffa, and the City Planning District of Jerusalem.[51]

Between exploiting loopholes in the law and purchasing within the approved guidelines at rapidly inflating prices, Zionist holdings increased at a steady, if considerably reduced, pace after 1940 (see map 2 for Jewish holdings in 1944). There were rumors as well of evasions of the law itself. Arab sentiment against the continuation of purchases led to the organization of an Umma Fund to purchase lands for the Arab nation. At Jaffa an Arab broker accused of selling to Jews was murdered. Nevertheless, attractive price levels inflated by war conditions and by the 1940 regulations continued to draw properties into the market.[52] During the years between the imposition of the 1940 regulations and the beginning of 1947, total Jewish land purchases amounted to 144,867 dunums.[53]

49. Granott, *Agrarian Reform*, p. 31.
50. *Survey of Palestine*, I, 258.
51. *Ibid.*, pp. 260–65.
52. *Ibid.*, pp. 268–71.
53. *Ibid.*, pp. 262–65, and *Supplement*, p. 31.

By the end of 1946, British authorities placed global Jewish ownership of land in Palestine at 1,624,000 dunums.[54] Granott places the figure for 1947 at 1,734,000.[55] To these figures in either case might well be added the 195,000 dunums of state land held on various tenancies by Jews at the time. The one million dunums acquired in freehold between 1920 and 1947 had cost the then enormous sum of £ P 10 million,[56] equal to £ P 10 per dunum or £ P 100 per hectare. That many Arab owners in the face of such prices consulted their pecuniary interests rather than those of a Palestinian nation just becoming self-aware is more than obvious. Responsible in large measure for this circumstance was the fact that since the 1870s legal title to tremendous sections of the plains and lesser areas elsewhere had been vested in urban landlords, many of whom were not even Palestinians after the demarcation of boundaries in 1920. The land expert representing the Jewish Agency before the Shaw Commission in 1929 claimed that 90 per cent of lands bought up to that time came from absentee landlords. During the 1930s the proportion fell to 80 per cent. In the last decade of the mandate they were about 73 per cent.[57]

While these figures make it clear that some Arabs, especially the so-called feudalists, are directly and personally responsible for the alienation of the Palestinian patrimony, the analyst should not ignore the fact that the overwhelming majority of Arabs did not sell their land. Even many large holders, for example, the al-Husaynis, maintained their properties intact until the end.

THE STATE OF ISRAEL

Total Jewish holdings, leased and owned, by the end of the mandate were somewhat more than 180,000 hectares, representing around 7 per cent of total land surface. In terms of cultivable land the percentages vary according to the definition of "cultivable." Motivated partly by idealism, partly by political considerations, Zionists always insisted the cultivable land was more extensive than the British claimed. Using British figures, Jewish holdings amounted to about 12 per cent of the arable land; using Zionist figures, they amounted to about 9 per cent. Put another way, on the eve of the proclamation of the state of Israel, 88 to 91 per cent of

54. *Survey of Palestine*, I, 244, and *Supplement*, p. 30.

55. *Agrarian Reform*, p. 28.

56. Estimated in Polk, Stamler, and Asfour, *Backdrop to Tragedy*, on the basis of figures developed by the Jewish Agency in 1946 (p. 334).

57. For a discussion of this question see *ibid.*, p. 236, n. 11.

the cultivable soil was neither owned nor leased by Jews. What was not vacant or publicly dedicated state domain was Arab under one form of right or another.

The mandatory government had designated soils of Palestine according to broad type classifications of "good," "medium," and "poor." When the general armistice agreements of 1948–49 had all been signed, Israel was left in occupation of 20,850 square kilometers, or 77.4 per cent, of the land and water surface of the former mandate. The Israeli region encompassed more than 95 per cent of the "good" soil, 64 per cent of the "medium," and, excluding the Negev, less than 39 per cent of the "poor."[58] While the new state controlled these lands, Israelis in 1948 did not own them. The Conciliation Commission for Palestine estimated that more than 80 per cent of the territory ruled by Israel represented land owned or otherwise held by Arab refugees, of which somewhat more than 4,574,000 dunums were cultivable.[59] Since a minute 1¼ per cent of Jewish-owned land fell to Egypt and Jordan in the armistice settlements, the Jews were left with almost all of their pre-independence purchases or holdings, which were, of course, overwhelmingly cultivable. Of the roughly 6,400,000 cultivable dunums then held by Jews in Israel, 72 per cent were Arab owned before statehood.[60]

As Israeli forces in 1948 surrounded and overwhelmed one Arab district after another, most Palestinians fled beyond the enemy lines. Before the spectacle of untold millions of pounds value in vacated property,

---

58. See map in *ibid.,* p. 313; table in Hadawi, *Palestine,* p. 137.

59. United Nations, General Assembly, *Progress Report of the United Nations Conciliation Commission for Palestine,* Suppl. 18, December 11, 1949–October 23, 1950, pp. 5–6, 12–15.

60. These figures were disputed by Israeli authorities and by Granott. The CCP arrived at its results by using the government of Palestine's *Village Statistics, 1945* and subtracting from its finding those lands controlled by Jordan or Egypt, those owned in 1947 by Jews, and those still cultivated by Arabs inside Israel. The Israeli government claimed it had taken over as "abandoned land" only 4,183,669 dunums; of this area, their Development Authority reported, only 2.5 million dunums were cultivable (these figures are taken from Don Peretz, *Israel and the Palestine Arabs* [Washington, D.C., 1958], p. 165, n. 16). Avraham Granott of Hebrew University says there were 5.8 million dunums "abandoned," of which about 3 million were cultivable (*Agrarian Reform,* p. 89). Neither of these Zionist sources seeks to account for or justify its computations. It is clear, however, that before independence the highest figure set by Zionists for the total surface *owned* by Jews was 1,734,000 dunums (Granott, *Agrarian Reform,* p. 28). The mandate government claimed absolute or presumed title to domain lands amounting to only 1,560,000 dunums in all of Palestine, including those let to Jewish and Arab groups and individuals (*Survey of Palestine,* I, 258). It therefore seems indisputable that the area of land acquired by Israel over which Arabs held, in 1947, one right of tenure or another was much closer to the CCP figure than to either set of Zionist figures.

several kinds of things happened. The authorities appealed for order and temperance. Military units occupied properties and subsequently turned them over to local Jewish authorities or to leaders of settlements. Squatters moved in to occupy homes, businesses, and villages. Often not realizing the owners would never return, Jewish settlers raided neighboring villages and farms for everything movable, including such "movables" as irrigation pipe and equipment; vandals destroyed trees, buildings, and equipment. Deprived of water and care, many Arab citrus and fruit holdings deteriorated beyond repair. Remaining Arabs in some cases were escorted out of their villages in "security" zones by Israeli forces, never to return.[61]

This was roughly the *de facto* situation at the moment the United Nations General Assembly passed its first resolution requiring Israel to allow refugees the choice of returning to live at home in peace or of compensations for what they left behind. By that time also Israeli ports had been flung open to the displaced and brutalized remnants of European Jewry. People by the tens of thousands were backing up in the reception camps and spilling uncontrollably into empty Arab quarters in Jaffa, Haifa, and the villages. In three and one-half years after May, 1948, the Jewish population increased by a spectacular 108 per cent. Despite massive infusions of capital from Diaspora Jews, American grants, and German reparations, the Zionist state hovered on the brink of bankruptcy for several years.

It has been claimed that security was the primary consideration in Israel's refusal to repatriate the indigenous population, that a fifth column of vengeful Arabs within its borders could have destroyed the state.[62] This is the position Israeli officials have always taken publicly. Yet the reality seems to be—committed as they were to unlimited ingathering, to the most precipitous possible establishment of a dominant Jewish presence in Palestine—that the overwhelming imperative in fact was economic. Without the capital windfall represented by the Arabs' 80 per cent share of the land and their uncalculated millions in movable property, homes, and businesses, this burgeoning Israel would have collapsed.

Probably fearing adverse international reaction, Israeli authorities have preferred not to be overly lucid concerning the land transactions and confiscations of the years after 1948. Minutes of official deliberations and decisions are shrouded in secrecy. Most information on the subject is developed from the reports of the Conciliation Commission for Palestine and from the excellent monographs of Don Peretz and Sami Hadawi.[63]

61. Peretz, *Israel and the Palestine Arabs*, pp. 148–53.

62. *Ibid.*, p. 141.

63. Peretz, *Israel and the Palestine Arabs;* Hadawi, *Palestine*. It is difficult to find fault with most of Hadawi's extensive tables; I have, however, taken issue with some of his interpretations.

The first ordinance of the provisional government affecting Arab land was taken as early as June, 1948, and declared any property surrendered to, or conquered by, Israeli forces or deserted by all or part of the inhabitants to be an "abandoned" area thereafter under the control of the minister of finance. In July a "custodian of abandoned property" dependent upon the Finance Ministry was named legal holder of the lands, and in October the minister of agriculture was empowered to lease properties to cultivators, most of whom had already arrived on the vacant lands.

The Absentee Property Regulations of December, 1948, conferred enormous powers upon the custodian, from whose decisions there was no appeal. Specifically, he was given administrative authority to declare any property vacant whose owner (1) was a citizen of Yemen, Iraq, Jordan, Saudi Arabia, Egypt, Syria, or Lebanon; (2) was in any part of Palestine outside Israeli-held lines; (3) who, even though within Israeli lines, had removed himself at any time since November 29, 1947, from his habitual place of residence. This last rule meant that even an Arab citizen of Israel who had never left the territory but who during the fighting or at any other time had moved a few yards or a few miles was classified as an absentee. Such an extraordinary measure is probably best understood as an effort to legalize the *de facto*. Israeli forces and settlers, with the exception of those who personally drove Arabs away, usually had no notion as to whether an absent Arab was permanently or temporarily gone, whether he was within Israel or without, nor, it can be conjectured, did most of them care. Those who wished to occupy holdings had done so. For political and economic reasons, the state was not inclined to evict Jews in favor of Arabs. Invoking a concept of collective responsibility also used in similar circumstances elsewhere in the world, all peasants of a village were liable to eviction, even if only a few families had fled during the fighting.

Peretz has estimated that 40 per cent of the properties held by Arab citizens of Israel were thus confiscated.[64] The census of 1949–50 showed that Israeli Arabs in 121 villages were then cultivating under every form of tenure only 533,851 dunums.[65]

Throughout the first years of statehood persistent Conciliation Commission requests for information concerning the status of absentee property were evaded by the Israeli authorities. The Israelis also refused to join an Arab-Israeli working group under Conciliation Commission leadership organized for the purpose of devising methods to identify, evaluate, administer, and preserve refugee holdings.[66] A typical answer when ques-

---

64. *Israel and the Palestine Arabs,* p. 142.
65. Cited in Granott, *Agrarian Reform,* p. 115.
66. Peretz, *Israel and the Palestine Arabs,* pp. 157–58.

tioned about the effect of the Absentee Property Law of 1950 was that the law was designed to bring order out of a chaotic situation emerging in the wake of the war. Such responses are reminiscent of the claims of French authorities in Algeria, where each successive ordinance promulgated after 1830 on behalf of "order" seemed to legalize and rationalize further the essentially extralegal land seizures by *colons*. Another answer was that lands were being held against eventual indemnity due by Arabs for launching the "illegal" Palestine war of 1947–48.

The Absentee Property Law of 1950 collected into a single piece of legislation the several *ad hoc* measures of the preceding years. While the law did institute the first procedures for judicial appeal, its principal innovation was to empower the custodian of absentee property to sell Arab lands which previously he could only lease. Under terms of the act a Development Authority was subsequently created with power to buy lands from the custodian. By 1953 the Development Authority had purchased lands from the custodian amounting in area to 2,373,677 dunums, which it in turn sold to the Jewish National Fund. The J.N.F. in its turn "leased" the properties to groups and individuals who in most cases had already been there for years. By this legal fiction the state avoided among other things the censure which might have accrued on direct confiscation.[67] During the 1950s two separate laws further pared the land holdings of Israeli Arabs. One permitted expropriation at 1950 prices of lands desired for Jewish settlement, while the other forced consolidation of Palestinian holdings, often with net losses in acreage or value to the owners.

All attempts at dialogue between the Conciliation Commission for Palestine and the government of Israel on the subject of Palestinian lands failed, though efforts were continued into the 1960s.[68] Compensation was never paid; the three quarters of a million refugees never came home to contest the possession of the custodian or of the J.N.F. after him. The Conciliation Commission for Palestine set an initial value on the confiscated land alone at £ P 100 million; the Arab League claimed it was worth £ P 2 billion. At any rate the *fallahin* and other Palestinians contributed more handsomely than any other group to the success of the greatest wave of the ingathering. That "close settlement upon the land" enjoined by the League mandate of 1922 had been achieved by the mid 1950s in nearly 80 per cent of Palestine. Since 1967 new Jewish settlements have begun to spring up in the hills and on the Golan Heights, and in Gaza. It is too early to predict the impact of these redemptions.

67. *Ibid.*, p. 180.
68. Hadawi, *Palestine*, pp. 86, 106 ff.

5. The Demographic Transformation of Palestine

Janet L. Abu-Lughod

Except for the extermination of the Tasmanians, modern history recognizes no cases in which the virtually complete supplanting of the indigenous population of a country by an alien stock has been achieved in as little as two generations. Yet this, in fact, is what has been attempted in Palestine since the beginning of the twentieth century. Herein lies the nub of the crisis in the Middle East—at once its greatest tragedy and its most perplexing but inescapable problem. Our natural tendency to assume that what exists today has always been, may afford us psychic peace but only at the terrible cost of denying reality. And once historic reality has been denied, our capacity to understand and react meaningfully to the present is similarly destroyed.

The purpose of this article is to present a factual account, based upon the most authoritative and unbiased statistical sources available,[1] of the process whereby the country of Palestine (known to the world prior to 1948 by that name but now completely occupied by Israel) was transformed from one inhabited by a settled Arabic-speaking community (mostly Muslim, but containing small minorities of indigenous Christians and Jews who were linguistically and culturally assimilated to the majority)

---

1. As a demographer I assume that no statistical sources are free from bias, whether intentional or inadvertent; all hard facts are to some extent "soft." In the case of a country which, from the inception of data collection in the modern sense, has been an object of contention among conflicting parties, distortions are endemic. Believing that "official" figures are a closer approximation to reality than contender-generated numbers, I have confined my research almost exclusively to official British records. Only to establish the absolute maximum for a figure one side wishes to inflate or, conversely, to determine the absolute minimum of a figure a contender wishes to minimize have I used the appropriate Arab or Jewish sources.

to one now inhabited overwhelmingly by Jews drawn from the continents of Europe, Asia, and Africa. This radical and still continuing replacement of population, over the opposition of the indigenous inhabitants, created a grievance which present proposed solutions to the Middle East crisis tend to relegate to the background. Yet what may appear to outside observers to be a peripheral issue is, to the Palestinians, the central and most basic issue from which all others follow. To understand *this* reality, one must become more fully aware both of the magnitude of the demographic transformation and, more importantly, of its startling recency.

It is neither feasible nor necessary to trace the demographic composition of Palestine back into dim history; a reasonably firm bench mark need (and, indeed, can) be established no earlier than the nineteenth century. From Turkish sources it can be estimated that by the middle of the nineteenth century more than one-half million persons lived in those provinces of the Ottoman Empire which later coalesced into the state of Palestine. Of these, more than 80 per cent were Muslims, about 10 per cent were Arabs whose families had remained Christian despite the massive conversion of the population to Islam between the seventh and tenth centuries, and perhaps 5 to 7 per cent were Jews, mostly those whose forebears had resisted the even earlier conversion to Christianity. While differing in religious beliefs, the three "communities of the book" enjoyed much in common linguistically and culturally. Under Ottoman law each community retained internal autonomy in matters of personal status, but all were under the jurisdiction of the state in other matters.

Since Israel bases its claim to Palestine in part upon an argument of continuous Jewish residence in that country, it is necessary to examine in some detail the size and distribution of the nineteenth-century Jewish community. In 1822, as reported by Israeli sources,[2] there were no more than 24,000 Jews in the general area of Palestine. Although toward the end of that century the number had almost doubled, the increase was due not to an excess of births over deaths but to the first wave of European migration, which came chiefly from Russia. By 1900, some 50,000 Jews inhabited Palestine, *virtually all* concentrated as minorities in the urban areas of Jerusalem and Jaffa where they neither tilled the soil nor had claim to the land.

---

2. The figures following are taken from the official *Israeli Yearbook, 1950/51* (Jerusalem), p. 81 n. The source is not given, nor are the boundaries defined within which the figures apply. I have assumed that since Israeli interests lie in maximizing rather than minimizing the presence of Jews in Palestine during the early periods, the true figure is probably no larger than this and may actually be smaller.

PHASE I: 1900–1922

The opening decades of the twentieth century altered the political framework of the region drastically and initiated what can now be recognized as the first phase of the demographic transformation of Palestine. In 1914, according to the results of a Turkish census summarized in the *Census of Palestine, 1922,* the population of that country totaled some 689,272 persons, of whom no more (and perhaps less) than 60,000 were Jews. During the dislocations of World War I, the overall population, particularly in the hill and southern regions, seems to have decreased slightly. This decline, however, was minimal in comparison with the drastic reduction in the size of the Jewish population, which was essentially halved by the deportation as "enemy aliens" of the immigrant Russian nationals.[3]

With the defeat of Turkey, however, came the postwar dismemberment of its territory and the division of these spoils chiefly between Great Britain and France. British control over Palestine and over the western edge of Transjordan was later formalized into mandate status, and under this administration restrictions upon Jewish immigration were relaxed and deported persons were permitted to return. As soon as adequate control over the country had been achieved, the British conducted the first modern census of Palestine as of December 31, 1922. Despite its flaws, this census constitutes a critical bench mark for any student of Palestine's population.[4]

---

3. These figures are taken from the introductory chapter to the official *Census of Palestine, 1922* (Jerusalem). According to the Turkish census of 1914, there were 398,362 residents in the southern province (including Jaffa, Jerusalem, and southward; evidently Bedouins were not counted); 153,749 inhabitants in the province of Samaria (including Nablus and the hills); and 137,164 persons in the northern province of Acre. The British estimate for 1920, perhaps an underestimate, gave a total population for the country of 673,193, of whom 385,101 were in the southern province, 138,364 in Samaria, and 149,728 in the northern province. Whether this figure should be accepted is dubious, for the British population estimate of 1921 yielded a total population of 761,796, while the official census figure of 1922 was 757,182, excluding Bedouins. Either the 1920 figure is ridiculously low or recovery was phenomenal. The estimate of the 1914 Jewish population is that of Arthur Ruppin, a not uninvolved scholar. It is reprinted in the *Census of Palestine, 1922.* Actually, he suggested a range, the lower limit being 57,000, the upper limit 62,000. Since his commitment dictated an upper rather than a lower error, we may accept this as the absolute maximum; the true figure may have been considerably less. Ruppin is also the source of the estimate of Turkish deportations, amounting, he claims, to 26,605 from the Jerusalem district and 6,309 from the Jaffa community. Accurate figures, however, are scarcely to be expected. How many of those deported remained in Egypt after the war and how many re-entered Palestine is not known with exactitude.

4. All figures in this section, unless otherwise noted, are taken from the *Census of Palestine, 1922.*

Far from substantiating Zionist claims that the region they sought for a
Jewish national home was virtually unpopulated, this first official census
enumerated more than three-quarters of a million inhabitants; furthermore,
most analysts agree that the enumeration of 757,182 souls erred significantly in the direction of undercount.[5] The official census figures indicated that, of the total, some 590,890 (78 per cent) were Muslim;
73,024 (9.6 per cent) were Christian, mostly Arab although some British
and other Europeans were included; less than 10,000 (1 per cent) were
"Other"; and 83,794 (11 per cent) were Jewish. Of the latter, perhaps
two-thirds were European immigrants and their offspring — some having
arrived late in the nineteenth century, others since the inception of
British rule.

Not much change in the geographic distribution of the Jewish minority
was discernible by this date. Most Jews were still located in a few urban
areas. The subdistrict of urban Jerusalem, for example, accounted for
fully 34,431 of the 83,794 Jews in the country. Of these, some 28,000
lived in the new quarters of the city growing up outside the walls of the
historic town, another 5,639 lived in the old city itself, and only a handful,
460, lived in rural settlements nearby. The other area of maximum concentration was the subdistrict of Jaffa which contained the newly established and exclusively Jewish suburb of Tel Aviv. There were some
15,000 Jews in Tel Aviv and another 5,000 (chiefly Arabic speaking and
indigenous) in the adjacent city of Jaffa; the remaining 4,000 were located
in smaller settlements nearby. Thus, with 34,431 Jews in Jerusalem and
some 24,000 Jews in the Jaffa–Tel Aviv district, it is apparent that fully
three-fourths of the total Jewish population of the country was concentrated
in the central urbanized belt of Palestine, i.e., the Jerusalem-Jaffa district
delineated in the 1922 census.

5. It should be noted that practically all censuses, even those conducted in highly
advanced countries such as the United States, undercount population by at least 5 per
cent, with undercounts most likely in rural areas. Official figures are usually adjusted
upward to compensate for this. There was apparently no such adjustment in the 1922
census of Palestine. Several additional factors contributed to an undercount in this
census. The occupying power had still not gained full command of the country, nor
was it intimately acquainted with all parts of it; some sections were undoubtedly
missed in the enumeration. Furthermore, the census was not only relatively unprecedented but was also the object of suspicion. While the Arab boycott of the
census was only semiorganized, many inhabitants, out of fear, were less than candid
in their returns. When one examines the age-sex breakdowns for the Arab population, one finds a consistent deficiency in the enumeration of males in the productive
ages of life. While some may have been out of the country temporarily, working
elsewhere or still undischarged from military service, others were evidently reluctant
to be enumerated for fear of conscription. The total figure of 757,000 excludes the
population living east of the Jordan River and does not include the 10,000 Arabs who
were added to the Palestinian state through a land transfer from French-mandated
Syria in 1923.

If in these small urban zones Jews were beginning to constitute a sizable minority of the population, there remained vast regions where virtually no Jews had settled. In the extremely large hill region of Samaria and in the even more extensive southern zone comprised of Gaza and Beersheba, Jews constituted considerably less than 1 per cent of the population (850 and 750 Jews respectively).

In the northern region of the country, however, some change had already begun to occur, for this was the area which received maximum attention in the Zionist land schemes. By 1922 some 20,000 Jews were settled in the north, where they constituted about 12 per cent of the population. Even there, despite the fact that the ideology stressed agricultural development, most Jews still resided in cities. More than 6,000 lived in the port city of Haifa, where they made up one-fourth of the population. Another 4,400 lived in the rapidly growing town of Tiberias, where they constituted two-thirds of the total inhabitants. Some 3,000 lived in Safad, where they accounted for a third of that town's residents. Thus, about 70 per cent of the 19,672 Jewish inhabitants of the northern district were urban, despite the fact that, except for Haifa, there were virtually no cities of any size there.

It is important, then, to recapitulate the demographic character of Palestine at the end of 1922, less than twenty-six years before the establishment of a Jewish state in the lion's share of that country and only some forty-five years before the conquest by Israel of the final vestiges of Palestine. As recently as the third decade of the twentieth century, Palestine was still overwhelmingly an Arab-Muslim country of stably settled agriculturists and town dwellers, supplemented by an Arab-Christian minority of equally long standing, and by a small, linguistically and culturally assimilated Jewish community which had been joined within the preceding generation by a larger, ethnically foreign group of settlers drawn chiefly from Eastern Europe. The Jewish communities, combined, constituted no more than 11 per cent of the total population of the country (possibly less if undercounting of the Arab rural population was as great as we have reason to believe). This Jewish population had settled, for the most part, in a handful of cities and towns located within an extremely limited geographical area. How Zionists could have advanced a serious claim to the country, as they did in London at that time, is one of those incredible facts which would appear merely ludicrous had it not resulted in tragedy.

PHASE II: 1923–1932

The situation as it developed during the second phase of the demographic transformation was, in large measure, a gradual extension of the trends which had already been established by 1922. Between 1923 and

1932 the population of Palestine continued to grow through natural increase and through sporadic immigration, but, despite some periods of
relatively heavy Jewish migration permitted by the British, by the end
of the period the relative representations of the various ethnic communities
had been only slightly altered. On December 31, 1931, the British conducted a second census in the country, the results of which were published
in the two volumes of the *Census of Palestine, 1931.*[6] This census was,
unfortunately, the last official enumeration in a country where numbers
became increasingly important and were the object of contention. Because
all later estimates take off in different directions as extrapolations from
the 1931 base, a detailed analysis of its findings must be presented here.

By the end of 1931, when the specter of Hitler had not yet shadowed
Europe, there were somewhat more than one million persons living in
Palestine, restless under a mandate they never sought and still aspiring
to the independence they had been promised during World War I. Most
of the population increase that had occurred during the nine-year intercensal period had come from natural increase. Despite the unrest and
tensions, health conditions had been improving, and a decline in mortality
rates was already evident as a result. Migration, although becoming a more
significant contributor to population growth, accounted for only a small
part of the total intercensal increase of 279,000. Of the 1,035,821 officially
enumerated inhabitants of the country, the overwhelming majority were
still Arab: 759,712 Muslims; 91,398 Christians (more than 90 per cent
of whom were Arabs); and 10,101 "Others," again mostly Arab. By this
time, however, the number of Jews in the country had doubled to 174,006,
chiefly due to immigration, and they constituted a powerful minority of
16 per cent of the population.

Before examining the geographic distribution of this minority, we might
look more closely at the demographic changes that had occurred in the
intercensal period, since by 1931 the dynamics of a contrast that has
continued to the present were already firmly established. The growth of
the Arab population of Palestine was almost entirely due to the forces of
natural increase while that of the Jewish population of Palestine was due
overwhelmingly to immigration from abroad. It was this fact that accounted
for the interesting anomaly revealed by the 1931 census, namely, that
although Jews constituted about 16 per cent of the total population, they
accounted for little more than 11 per cent of the citizens (even including
those who had applied for, but had not yet been granted, naturalization)

---

6. Figures in this section, unless otherwise noted, have been taken from the
Census of Palestine, 1931 (Jerusalem). Any computations going beyond the published figures are duly distinguished and supported.

and only 8 per cent of the native-born population. On the other hand, they constituted 77 per cent of all the foreign-born residents.[7]

The major changes between 1922 and the end of 1931 were summarized as follows in the *Census of Palestine, 1931.*

TABLE 1. Changes in Population in Palestine between December 31, 1922 and December 31, 1931 by Source of Growth

	Total Change	Change by Source	Notes
Total Population, 1922	757,000		
Total Population, 1931	1,036,000		
Net Change in nine years:	+279,000		
Of which			
a) Recorded Excess of Births over Deaths		+176,000	Largely Arab
b) Unrecorded Excess of Birth/Deaths (est.)		+ 20,000	Mostly Arab
c) Territorial Transfer from Syria in 1923		+ 10,000	Arab
d) Net Migration (Excess of Arrivals over Departures)		+ 57,000	Jewish
e) British Army Personnel		3,000	Foreign
f) Persons Illegally in the Country (est.)		9,000	Mostly Jewish
g) Unknown or Unidentified Increase		4,000	May have resulted from undercount of Arabs in 1922

Source: *Census of Palestine, 1931,* I, 45. All estimates in the table are from the source itself.

As noted above, the increase in the Arab population was largely attributable to an excess of births over deaths, since some 98 per cent of

7. These figures have been derived from *Census of Palestine, 1931,* which presents data by nationality (I, 77). According to my computations from these tables, among all citizens of Palestine as well as persons who had applied for naturalization, 87.7 per cent identified themselves as Arabs, some 11.5 per cent identified themselves as Jews, and 0.8 per cent identified themselves by some other designation. The figures on native and immigrant status are derived from *ibid.,* I, 74. Further amplification appears in Table 2 below.

the Muslim population and 80 per cent of the Christians (including British army personnel and other foreigners) were native born. The high rate of natural increase recorded was somewhat unusual at the time, although demographers are now familiar with even higher rates in countries beginning their demographic transitions. Palestine seems to have been one of the first of the non-Western countries to experience a marked drop in its death rate without a significant change in its birth rate. For example, the computed crude birth rate for Muslims in Palestine in 1931 was 53.2/1000 (not inconsistent with its extremely young age-structure and early marriage patterns), while the crude death rate was only 26/1000. This yielded a natural increase rate of 27/1000, or a growth rate of 2.7 per cent per annum.[8] The rate of natural increase was destined to rise even higher in the decades that followed, reaching 40/1000 (4 per cent per year) after the mid-1940s, when the death rate was further reduced by the introduction of D.D.T. and antibiotics. Among the Christian and Jewish communities of Palestine, fairly high rates of natural increase were also the rule. In 1931, each of these communities recorded a natural increase rate of 22/1000. (Intrinsically low Jewish fertility was temporarily masked in the crude birth rate of 20/1000 by the presence of large numbers of Jewish immigrants concentrated in the childbearing ages.)

If natural increase accounted for Arab population growth, migration was largely responsible for Jewish increase. The exact figures for net Jewish migration are difficult to establish, due to some indeterminate amount of illegal or unregistered migration. Israeli sources tend to inflate the net gain by including only in-migrants and failing to subtract out-migrants.[9] Figures upon which to base a more realistic estimate, however, are not lacking. The total net migration between 1923 and 1932 as given in the 1931 census was 57,000. Even if there had been some net out-migration of Arabs during that period, net Jewish in-migration could not have been much more than 60,000, since, of the total intercensal Jewish increase of 90,000, about one-third must have come from natural increase (see preceding paragraph). Summing official British figures on immigration and emigration between January, 1923, and December, 1931, one obtains a total of almost 87,000 Jewish immigrants and more than 25,000 Jewish emigrants, indicating a net in-migration of about 61,500.[10] This immigration did not follow a smooth trend. It mounted in 1924 and peaked in

8. Vital statistics for each community are presented in *Census of Palestine, 1931,* I, 142–43, 158.

9. For example, the *Israeli Yearbook, 1950/51* gives annual immigration between 1922 and 1931 which, if the numbers are summed, yields a total of almost 90,000.

10. Royal Institute of International Affairs, *Great Britain and Palestine, 1915–1945,* Information Paper No. 20 (London, 1946), p. 63; cumulation mine from raw annual figures.

1925 when some 34,000 Jews were admitted; after that, somewhat greater restrictions were imposed in response to unrest, and immigration fell off. The curve of out-migration followed slightly behind that of in-migration, since the years of maximal emigration began in 1926, indicating perhaps that at least some of the immigrants had become disillusioned enough to relocate.

An indirect measure of the significance of immigration for Jewish population growth can be obtained by comparing the places of birth of members of each religious community, as shown in Table 2. Of the approximately 174,000 Jews living in Palestine in 1931, only some 73,000 (or 42 per cent) had actually been born there; this native-born population included a substantial number of children born to recent immigrants. Four out of five Jewish immigrants (and thus almost half of the entire Jewish population of Palestine) had been born in Europe.

Given the increasingly alien character of the Jewish population and the ideologically supported policy of apartheid followed by Zionist organizations, it is not surprising that geographic specialization and concentration persisted into this period (see map 5 for the relative size and distribution of the Jewish population). It will be recalled that in 1922 some 75 per cent of the then-smaller Jewish population was found in the Jaffa-Jerusalem belt; by 1931 over 68 per cent of the Jews in Palestine were still concentrated in these two urban centers and their suburbs. Some 65,000 (or roughly one-third of the entire Jewish population) were living in the Jaffa–Tel Aviv urban complex, where they constituted almost one-half of the total population. In the urbanized area of Jerusalem, which by then had a total population of about 133,000, there were approximately 55,000 Jewish residents, mostly in the newer extramural section of the city; Jews made up about 41 per cent of the population of that area.

On the other hand, in other parts of the country Jews remained a negligible proportion of the population. No Jewish settlers were to be found in the subdistricts of Beersheba, Ramallah, Jenin, or Nablus. Well under 1 per cent of the populations of the subdistricts of Gaza (0.4 per cent), Hebron (0.2 per cent), Bethlehem (0.1 per cent), Tulkarm (0.14 per cent), and Acre (0.7 per cent) were Jewish.

Only in a few subdistricts in the north — those noted in 1922 — did Jews constitute a noticeable minority, and even there they were concentrated in urban areas. Thus, in the subdistrict of Haifa about 25 per cent of the population was Jewish (the same proportion as in 1922); in the subdistrict of Tiberias the figure was about 28 per cent. Minor communities were also found in Ramle (where 12 per cent of the population was Jewish), Nazareth (11 per cent), Beisan (13 per cent), and Safad (9 per cent).

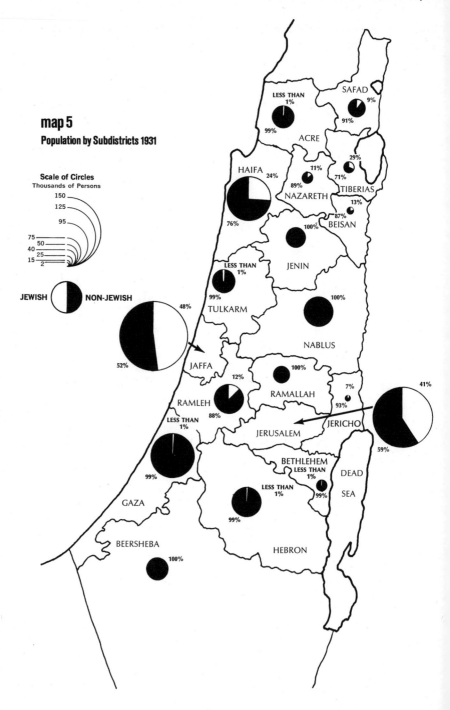

map 5
Population by Subdistricts 1931

Scale of Circles
Thousands of Persons
150
125
95
75
50
40
25
15
2

JEWISH   NON-JEWISH

TABLE 2. Population of Palestine in 1931 by Place of Birth for Each Religious Community.

Place of Birth	Muslim No.	Muslim %	Christian No.	Christian %	Jewish No.	Jewish %
			Religious Affiliation			
TOTAL NATIVE	**747,206**	**98.4**	**73,564**	**80.4**	**73,195**	**42.1**
Born in Palestine	680,653	89.6	73,564	80.4	73,195	42.1
De Jure Palestinians (Bedouins)*	66,553	8.8	0	0.0	0	0.0
TOTAL FOREIGN BORN	**12,506**	**1.6**	**17,834**	**19.4**	**100,811**	**57.9**
European-Born**	0	0.0	7,807***	8.5	80,347	46.2
Non-European	12,506	1.6	10,027	10.9	20,464	11.7
Sinai, Syria, and Jordan	8,364		3,011		0****	
Egypt, Ethiopia	2,316		856		0****	
Turkey, Hijaz	700		3,544		2,238	
Yemen, Iraq	0****		0****		9,113	
Persia	0		0		2,840	
Central Asia	0		213		0	
Miscellaneous	1,126		2,403		6,273	
TOTAL POPULA-TION (of known birthplace)	**759,712**	**100.0**	**91,398**	**100.0**	**174,006**	**100.0**

Source: Compiled from data presented in the *Census of Palestine, 1931,* I, 60–61; II, 166–67.

Notes:

*In 1922 an estimated 66,553 Bedouins, who were considered *de jure* residents of Palestine, were added to the *de facto* population. Evidently, no subsequent attempt was made to reestimate Bedouins, and each later census or official estimate simply carried over this figure, as if no natural increase were taking place. It is discomforting to find this same fictive number of Bedouins carried over into the first Israeli Census of November, 1948, especially when the number accounts for one-half of all Arabs in Israel in that year.

**Excludes Turkey.

***This figure includes 4,120 Englishmen, presumably those engaged in pacification, administration, and business.

****A figure of zero in this table indicates that the number of persons born in this area was negligible and was therefore included under miscellaneous, not that no persons were born in the particular country.

In short, one is struck primarily with the rather unrevolutionary nature of the immigration and the stability of its geographical distribution, even after a virtual doubling of the numerically still insignificant Jewish population. The threat of population displacement appeared distant indeed, but even in nascent form this potential threat seems to have been perceived and reacted against sharply, as evidenced by the increasingly vocal and organized protests of the indigenous population. Perhaps the latter sensed that the situation would be drastically altered in only a short time, even though the cause of that alteration — which Jews were to experience directly and Arabs indirectly — had not yet appeared. As it was, 1932 marked the end of the second phase of the demographic transformation of Palestine and the commencement of a third, more intense, phase.

PHASE III: 1932–1947

Had German politics gone differently in the early 1930s, there might have been no "Palestine Problem" in the 1940s and no Arab-Israeli conflict today. By the late 1920s, Jewish immigration to Palestine had tapered off to a minor net flow of a few thousand each year and would possibly have remained at such modest levels had normal conditions prevailed. But the early escape of the prescient, the lucky, and the wealthy from Germany, which began in 1932, brought a stream of refugees to England, to the United States and Canada — and to Palestine. Between the beginning of 1932 and the end of 1936, close to 174,000 Jews immigrated to Palestine. During the same period some 3,000 to 4,000 Jews emigrated from Palestine,[11] which meant that to the original 174,000 Jews living in Palestine in 1931 had been added over 170,000 immigrants. This radical change, occurring in the brief span of only five years, must certainly be recognized as an important underlying cause of the Arab rebellion of 1936.

The exact size of the Jewish population by the end of 1936 is not known. The Peel Commission, sent out in that year to investigate the "sources" of Arab dissatisfaction, estimated 370,000 Jews in Palestine in 1936.[12] Reestimates that suggest a total Jewish population of 384,000 by the end of 1936 appear later, this new figure having been provided by the

11. *Ibid;* this can only be approximate because figures on emigration by ethnicity are not available for three of the five years in question.
12. *Ibid.*

not disinterested Jewish Agency.[13] My own computations, based solely upon natural increase and net recorded immigration, yield a figure in agreement with that of the Peel Commission.[14] About 171,500 of the additional 200,000 Jews in the country can be accounted for by net in-migration; the remainder, some 26,000, is attributable to an excess of births over deaths (including births to new immigrants). The difference of 14,000 between the high (Jewish Agency) and low (Peel Commission) figures for total Jewish population is due to understandably unreliable assumptions as to the amount of illegal immigration that occurred during these years. (Such immigration could not have been less than 0 nor more than 14,000; the true figure lies somewhere between the two.) But regardless of which figure one accepts, the general conclusion is the same: within five years the Jewish population doubled, almost exclusively as a direct or indirect result of mass migration. By the end of 1936, Jews constituted some 28 per cent of the total population, as compared with the scant 16 to 17 per cent reported in the census that had been taken at the end of 1931.

It was therefore not surprising that the Arab population should have become alarmed at the rapid rate at which the demographic composition of their country was being altered, without their consent and against their will, especially since self-determination was becoming an increasingly distant prospect. What may seem surprising was that they were able to mount so determined and organized an opposition that the mandate government finally agreed to restrict immigration somewhat. (British documents of the period continued to claim that while the Jewish community had "structure" and therefore could be dealt with as a unit, the

13. All figures in this and the following section, unless otherwise noted, are taken from the Government of Palestine, Department of Statistics, *General Monthly Bulletin of Current Statistics*, XII (1947). In the December, 1947, issue, retrospective population estimates are presented, giving the total population of Palestine on December 31, 1936, as 1,366,692, of which 384,078 were Jews. This table carries a footnote to the effect that the revised figures for the Jewish population were suggested by the Jewish Agency (p. 686). Whether the entire discrepancy can be accounted for by illegal migration, as it was estimated by the Jewish Agency, is not clear. Certainly, in other sections of the *Monthly Bulletin* over the years, Jewish totals were consistently revised upward in footnotes citing the Jewish Agency as the source. No upward revisions, however, were ever appended to compensate for the possible under-enumeration of the Arab population.

14. My method was a simple one. Beginning with the population as given in the 1931 census, the annual increments to the Jewish population were derived by adding the natural increase of that year's base population (assumed to be 22/1000, or an average of the increase rates recorded for that period) and the net legal (recorded) migration. These were computed cumulatively, so that each year's increment plus the base served as the basis for computing the next annual natural increase.

Arabs were without organization and their wishes could therefore not be consulted. Could the protests coordinated in 1936 really have arisen in a community without "structure"?)

Perhaps as a result of the restrictions introduced and perhaps as a result of closer German supervision of the escape routes, Jewish immigration, at least of the legal variety, declined after 1939 to a level commensurate with the low years of the late 1920s, that is, about 3,000 to 4,000 per year. Some decline had already begun by 1937 when net migration dropped to under 10,000, and during 1938 and 1939 at least 2,000 Jews emigrated, mostly to the United States. Thus, between 1937 and the end of 1943, the recorded net immigration was only 53,268 for the entire period, although there were mounting numbers of illegal immigrants.

By the end of 1943, the Palestine Government Department of Statistics estimated the total population of the country at 1,676,571,[15] of whom about 500,000 were Jewish. Thus, only five years before the independent state of Israel was unilaterally declared and its effective control then expanded by force to most of the area contained within the former country of Palestine, the Jewish population still constituted a minority of less than one-third.

Nor were basic changes effected during the five years following 1943. While Jewish immigration picked up from the preceding low, it never reached anywhere near the peaks of the early 1930s. The natural increase of the Arab population, then growing at one of the highest rates in the world, reached the point where it literally compensated for relative Jewish gains. This was the result of sustained birth rates of between 50 and 53/1000, a very young age-structure, and improvements in health conditions that brought death rates down to between 15 and 18/1000. By 1945, the estimated total population had risen to 1,810,037, of which 67 per cent were Muslim, 3 per cent Christian and "Others," and 30 per cent Jewish.[16] Government estimates for the end of 1946 were little

15. The fiction of an unchanging *de jure* (as of 1922) Bedouin population is included here (see Table 2 above); despite the fact that informal estimates suggested a Bedouin population more on the order of 85,000, the figure continually carried over was 66,553. An adjustment of this figure would not change the relative distribution of population much. Probably more important than the non-enumeration of Bedouins was the cumulative deficiency in the estimation of the total Arab population which derived from the initial census under-enumerations of 1922 and 1931.

16. *General Monthly Bulletin,* XII (December, 1947), Table I, 686. The difference between official and Jewish Agency figures, presented as *de facto* revisions, by this time runs about 25,000. Certainly no one would deny that *de facto* estimates are probably more accurate than those arrived at by simple projection. However, no revised *de facto* estimates are presented for the majority of the population; thus, Jewish figures are continually corrected upward, whereas totals and Arab figures are not. Even if the Jewish Agency figure is accepted and even if undercounting of the Arab population is not compensated for, the difference is not great. The overall proportions at the end of 1945 still remain 31.5 per cent Jewish and 68.5 per cent Arab.

changed. Of a total estimated population of 1,887,214, the 583,327 Jews constituted 31 per cent.

Estimates of the regional distribution of the population in 1946 were also made by the government (with the aid of the Jewish Agency), and it is interesting to compare these with the distributions noted in the censuses of 1922 and 1931.[17] The Jewish population, which incidentally was still about 70 per cent urban, was concentrated as before in and around the three major urban centers: in new Jerusalem, with about 100,000 Jewish inhabitants; in the Jaffa–Tel Aviv complex, which contained 213,000 Jews in the twin cities and another 82,000 in surrounding settlements; and in Haifa, where about 74,000 Jews lived in the city and another 45,000 resided in surrounding communities. Even if the Jewish Agency revised total of 608,230 (some 25,000 higher than the official estimates) is accepted, these three areas of greatest concentration accounted for 516,700 Jews, or close to 85 per cent of all the Jewish residents of Palestine. The remaining 15 per cent were scattered in a few isolated sections of the north (7,000 in Safad; 3,000 in Acre; almost 14,000 in Tiberias; 7,600 in Beisan; and almost 8,000 in Nazareth) and in the single centrally located district of Ramle, with under 32,000. In the vast southern districts of Gaza and Beersheba there were a total of 4,000 Jewish residents who constituted an infinitesimal proportion of the population; in the rest of the country they did not constitute even that, since the hill regions of Nablus, Jenin, and Ramallah contained almost no Jews.

Thus, by the end of 1946, according to figures prepared jointly by the Department of Statistics and the Jewish Agency, Jews constituted a numerical majority in only one small subdistrict of Palestine. That was in the twin-city area of Jaffa–Tel Aviv (the former overwhelmingly Arab, the latter exclusively Jewish), where Jews constituted some 70 per cent of the total population. It is interesting to consider this fact soberly, for had the partition plan respected majority rule or had it been put to a plebiscite, the infant state of Israel would have been justified, if at all, only in this single subdistrict of the country. Even so, majority status there was achieved only because four out of every ten Jews in Palestine lived in that enclave.

PHASE IV: 1947–1948

This, then, was the state of the country as it entered the next and most

17. The breakdown of population by ethnicity and by geographic region is somewhat distorted by the fact that for this particular set of data (*General Monthly Bulletin*, XII [May, 1947], Table I, p. 240) the total population excludes the 66,553 unchanging number of Bedouins but accepts the Jewish Agency reestimate of Jewish population of 608,230 *in lieu* of its own estimate of 583,327. This tends to modify all figures slightly, but not enough to alter our basic conclusions.

violent stage of its demographic transformation. Here, numbers begin to break down (as did order), and the scholar is on dim, often consciously obfuscated terrain. In the following section I have used standard demographic techniques of projection, interpolation, and cross-checks between data sources and types, in order to arrive at reasonable range estimates of the enormous changes that occurred.

In the late fall of 1947, just after the partition plan had been recommended by the U.N. General Assembly, skirmishes between the Jewish and Arab populations broke out, presaging a civil war. Hostilities erupted first in Jaffa–Tel Aviv and in Jerusalem, the two areas of maximum Jewish concentration, but were carried well beyond these confines in the months that followed. The minority town of Jaffa surrendered to Jewish forces two days before the official termination of the British mandate at midnight, May 14, 1948. On May 15 an independent state of Israel was declared which laid claim to the territories recommended by the partition plan. However, fighting continued for several more months, despite the establishment of cease-fire agreements in June and July. Not until 1949 was an armistice ready for signature. The armistice recognized Israel's *de facto* control over the territories it had occupied as of then, territories that far exceeded the boundaries recommended in the partition plan and that encompassed areas where previously not even token numbers of Jews had lived. Except for a small number of Arabs who were later permitted repatriation, none of the population displaced during the civil war was allowed to return home. Thus, force of arms accomplished within little more than a year what decades of migration had decisively failed to do, namely, to effect a complete demographic transformation in the lion's share of Palestine.

So many wild estimates of the number of "Arab Refugees" from the 1948 war have appeared in print without adequate presentation of the methods used in reaching them that students of the problem have tended to abandon hope of discriminating among the conflicting numbers. Rather, they have, often unconsciously, selected those figures which best fit their interests, with Israeli supporters seeking to minimize the population displacement and UNRWA supporters seeking to maximize it. Actually, I do not believe that any accurate figures on "refugees" can be agreed upon since the definition has been so varied. However, I do believe that a reasonable estimate of the number of persons *displaced* during the war can be arrived at. The technical aspects of making such an estimate are relatively simple (far simpler, indeed, than many other estimates which demographers are called upon to make on the basis of far less trustworthy evidence), and I shall present in detail both the raw figures on which my estimates are based and the steps I have followed in establishing the final parameters.

Very simply, had there been no displacement of population during the war or had all displaced persons returned to their original homes by the end of 1948, how many Arabs would have been living in the state set up within Israeli-held territory in that year? The difference between *this* number and the *actual* number of Arabs enumerated in the Israeli census conducted in November of 1948 can be taken as a reasonable measure of population displacement. It is this figure that we shall try to determine.

While the figures used are merely estimates, the period for which we shall make projections is relatively short. The total population of Palestine, as of March 31, 1947, had been officially estimated and published by the Statistics Department of the Government of Palestine just before the war. The distribution of the population by region and religion had been officially estimated as of December 31, 1946. Using these figures as a basis for computation, we must estimate two parameters: first, the probable number of Arabs who would have been living in all of Palestine by December, 1948, had no population displacement occurred; and second, the probable number of Arabs who would have been residing by that date within the 20,700 square kilometers in Israel's possession, again assuming no population displacement. (Two assumptions must be made because there is no way to avoid them. First, we assume in our analysis that no major net immigration or emigration of Arabs would have occurred between March of 1947 and December of 1948, had the war not taken place. Second, we assume that, had hostilities not begun, there would have been only insubstantial internal movement of Arabs between subdistricts in Palestine. Given the fact that the Arab population had been relatively immobile and had in the past consistently grown almost exclusively from natural increase, these assumptions are not unreasonable.)

Our point of departure is the estimate of the total population of Palestine as of March 31, 1947, the last officially released figure.[18] According to the *General Monthly Bulletin* of December, 1947, the total settled population was 1,908,775, of whom 1,157,423 were Muslim; 589,341 were Jewish;[19] 146,162 were Christian; and 15,849 were "Other." We may project the non-Jewish portion of this estimate to December 31, 1948, by taking each of the recorded natural-increase rates for Muslims, Christians, and "Others" and applying them to the appropriate population bases for the next one year and nine months. During the calendar year 1946 (the last for which we have records), Muslims had an annual natural increase of 38/1000; Christians grew by natural increase at the rate of 24.2/1000 per year;

18. These last estimates as of March 31, 1947, are presented in the *General Monthly Bulletin,* XII (December, 1947), Table I, p. 686.
19. Footnoted in the table is the Jewish Agency figure in excess of 600,000.

and "Others" increased by 30/1000. Projecting these growth rates for the one-year-and-nine-month period, I arrive at an estimate of 1,235,645 Muslims; 152,394 Christians; and 16,691 "Others." *The total non-Jewish population of Palestine,* in the absence of any dislocations and net migration, then, *would have been* in excess of *1,400,000* by *the end of 1948.* This figure assumes that the natural-increase rates were no higher than 1946 (probably untrue, for death rates tended to decrease) and includes the fictive 66,553 Bedouins that had been estimated in 1922 and then never reestimated.

The second estimate we are called upon to make is the distribution of this non-Jewish population in various parts of Palestine, so that the number of Arabs who would normally have resided in the territories held by Israel at the end of 1948 can be compared with the actual number of Arabs enumerated by the Israeli census conducted toward the end of that year. This is a somewhat more difficult operation. Of the sixteen administrative districts of Palestine for which separate religious breakdowns can be obtained from the 1946 government of Palestine regional estimates cited above, nine districts were within the 1949 armistice lines of Israel; two were entirely in Arab-held territory; and five districts had been subdivided as a result of the war.

There is little technical difficulty in assigning Arab population to the undivided districts, whether Israeli or Arab held. In the nine Israeli-held districts of Safad, Tiberias, Acre, Nazareth, Beisan, Haifa, Jaffa, Beersheba, and Ramle, as of December 31, 1946, there had been 530,563 Muslims; 85,900 Christians; and 15,070 "Others." Projecting each of these separate groups by applying the natural-increase rate observed for each religious community in 1946 over the two-year period in question, one arrives at an estimated population by December 31, 1948, of approximately 677,713 non-Jews, of whom 571,652 would have been Muslim; 90,073 would have been Christian; and 15,988, "Other."

Similarly, a projection of the non-Jewish populations in the districts of Nablus and Ramallah, which were retained in their entirety by the Arabs, yields an estimated total as of December 31, 1948, of 157,673, of whom 146,975 would have been Muslim; 10,454 would have been Christian; and 244, "Other."

To recapitulate, of the estimated 1,400,000 (as projected from March 31, 1947) non-Jews who would have been living in Palestine at the end of 1948, some 677,713 would have been living in districts that were totally occupied by Israel by that time, and another 157,673 would have been living in districts that were totally in Arab control. Thus, approximately 835,400 of the non-Jewish Palestinians, as projected to the end of 1948, have been accounted for thus far in our analysis. The remainder of the projected total may be presumed to have resided in the five districts that were subdivided. Our difficult task will be to "assign" them to either side of the armistice line. This is an extremely difficult operation, and only a rough estimate can be made. Hence, all subsequent figures will be given in ranges.

Two major sources of data have been used to arrive at the following estimates. First, in 1944 an Anglo-American Committee of Inquiry prepared a large-scale map showing the locations of Jews, Christians, and Muslims in Palestine as of that date (see map 6 based upon it). Second, somewhat more detailed breakdowns of regional location by religion were available for 1946, again in the official reports of the Department of Statistics. By judiciously combining data from these sources, some estimates can be made. The five subdivided districts in question are Jenin, Tulkarm, Hebron, Jerusalem, and Gaza. According to the government estimates of the settled population in 1946, these contained a combined non-Jewish population of over 525,700.[20] Projected to December 31, 1948, the total would have been in excess of 560,000. What would have been their approximate division? Each district will be discussed separately.

Of all five districts, Jenin suffered the least territorial loss, only the fertile western and northern portions having been annexed by Israel. However, these were the portions that were most heavily populated, according to the 1944 Anglo-American Committee data. About one-fourth of the Arab population of the Jenin district (61,210 in 1946 and including no Jews, projected to about 66,000 by the end of 1948) lived in the region on the Israeli side of the armistice lines. Thus, had no displacement occurred, about 16,500 Arabs would have been living in Israeli-held portions of Jenin at the end of 1948.

The district of Tulkarm was roughly bisected by the armistice line. The western portion, which included the entire Jewish population of the district, went to Israel; the exclusively Arab eastern portion, including the Arab town of Tulkarm with about 9,000 inhabitants, was not annexed. However,

20. A discrepancy in figures should be noted here. At the end of 1946, according to the *General Monthly Bulletin* (May, 1947), Table I, p. 240, the number of non-Jews in Palestine was already 1,237,330, plus the fictive Bedouin population of 66,553, thus totaling 1,303,883. If this latter total is projected a full year and a quarter to March 31, 1947, the figure exceeds that given by the Department of Statistics for that date, which indicates that our overall projection to December 31, 1948, may be too low and certainly is not too high. In the five districts later subdivided there were 525,740 non-Jews at the end of 1946 which, when projected two years, would have yielded no less than 560,000 and possibly more. There appears to be no clear way to deal with these discrepancies except to note that since each is merely an estimate, either one is as believable as the other. The difference is still not large enough to substantially alter the conclusions.

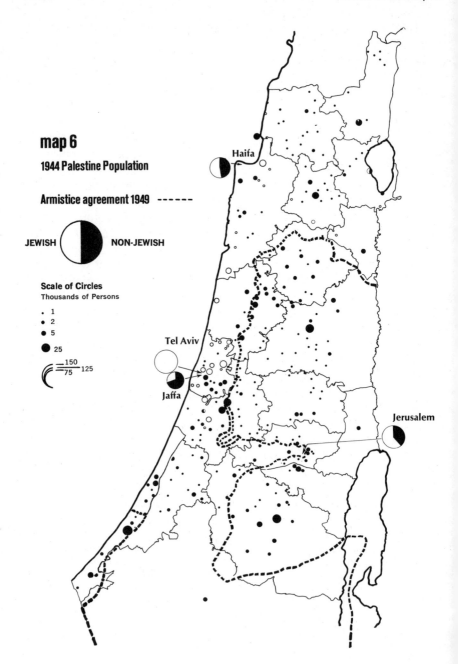

map 6

1944 Palestine Population

Armistice agreement 1949 - - - - - -

JEWISH   NON-JEWISH

Scale of Circles
Thousands of Persons

. 1
· 2
● 5
⬤ 25

Haifa

Tel Aviv

Jaffa

Jerusalem

two fairly large Arab settlements as well as numerous smaller villages were within the Israeli-held part of the Tulkarm district. In all, we would estimate that between 16,000 and 17,000 of the non-Jewish population that would normally have resided in the district by the end of 1948 would have been living in Israel if there had been no population displacement.

The district of Hebron was similarly split between the contending parties, although the dividing line was somewhat less regular. The central zone, containing the largest proportion of the population and including the sizable town of Hebron, became part of Arab-held Palestine. However, there were at least a dozen good-sized Arab villages and a multitude of smaller settlements of Arabs in the portion of the district occupied by Israel. This latter population—Arabs in Israeli-held portions of Hebron by the end of 1948—would have been in the neighborhood of about 30,000 ± 5,000.

Within the large district of Jerusalem, population was concentrated either in the old and new portions of the city itself or in the hundred or more towns and villages north, south, and west of the urban complex. Only a very small population normally resided in the zone east of Jerusalem city, for the terrain becomes increasingly desolate as the Jordan River is approached. After the war, only the old quarter of Jerusalem and the easternmost string of villages due north and south of it remained in Arab hands. While in terms of territory, Israeli-held western Jerusalem was quite small, because it contained the most heavily populated sections, we estimate a probable non-Jewish population of as many as 80,000 by 1948.

The district of Gaza presents the greatest discrepancies in estimates of the number of Palestinians displaced by the war. Since the so-called Gaza Strip was not annexed by Israel, it is frequently assumed that the Gaza population, although classified as refugees by UNRWA under the supplementary definition of "people deprived of their livelihoods," was not substantially displaced. My computations suggest that in the major towns of Gaza and Khan Yunis and in the handful of villages south of Gaza city —which became the Arab-controlled Gaza Strip—there would have been a normal population of about 80,000 Arabs by the end of 1948. However, almost as many residents of the Gaza district would normally have been residing in the northern portion of the district which was annexed to Israel.

The foregoing estimates have been summarized in Table 3. As can be seen from that summary, by the end of 1948 there were approximately 1.4 million Arab Palestinians. Had no displacement taken place, somewhere between 494,000 and 508,000 of them would have been living in their usual places of residence which were located on the Arab-held side of the armistice line. The remainder, between 890,000 and 904,000, would have been living in territories held by Israel, and would therefore have been counted as Israeli residents when the first postwar Israeli census was taken near the end of 1948. How many of them were actually within Israel?

According to the Israeli census taken in November, 1948, there were a total of between 120,000[21] and 130,000[22] non-Jews in all of Israel. These

TABLE 3. Estimated Number of Arabs Who Would Have Been Residing on Either Side of the 1949 Armistice Line by December 1948, Had No Population Displacement Taken Place or Had All Been Returned to Their Original Homes.

Number of Arabs Expected as of December, 1948
(as Projected from 1946)

Districts of	In Arab-held Territory according to Armistice	In Israeli-held Territory according to Armistice	Estimated Total of Arabs at end of 1948
Safad Tiberias Acre Nazareth Beisan Haifa Jaffa Ramle Beersheba		677,713 (includes 66,553 Bedouins)	677,713
Nablus Ramallah	157,673		157,673
Jenin*	49,500	16,500	66,000
Tulkarm	61,000 to 60,000	16,000 to 17,000	77,000
Jerusalem	84,000	80,000	164,000
Hebron	74,000 to 64,000	25,000 to 35,000	99,000
Gaza	81,700 to 78,700	75,000 to 78,000	156,700
Subtotal for subdivided districts			562,700
Minimum	336,200	212,500	
Maximum	350,200	226,500	
TOTAL PALESTINE AS DIVIDED:			1,398,000 (as projected from 1946)
Minimum	493,900	890,200	1,398,000
Maximum	507,900	904,200	(as calculated)

21. This figure is presented as an estimate by the Israeli Ministry of Foreign Affairs, Information Division, *Facts About Israel, 1963* (Jerusalem), p. 48. The same source indicates that by 1962 there were only 252,401 non-Jews in Israel, a figure which presumably would include not only the Arab minorities but foreign Christian residents as well.

22. Actually, the figure given in the *Israeli Yearbook, 1950/51* is 69,000 non-Jews (mostly Arab) as of the census of November, 1948 (p. 81). Elsewhere, the estimate is given as 130,000, indicating that the total was reached by adding in an estimated number of Bedouins equal to their *de jure* number in 1922!

figures included 66,000 Bedouins (of census lore), which means that in fact only some 60,000 to 64,000 Arabs were actually counted by the census takers. Our preceding analysis has indicated, however, that by that date there should have been some 900,000 non-Jews living in the territories held by Israel. The difference between these two figures, then, must be taken as a rough but reasonable estimate of the total number of Palestinians who were displaced persons at the time of the armistice, namely, about 770,000 to 780,000.

In order to estimate the refugees, one must add to the number of displaced persons those individuals who, while living in their own homes, had been deprived of their livelihoods. About 80,000 residents of the Gaza Strip were so classified, as were about half that many residents in border villages of the West Bank who lost their lands and livelihoods without actually being removed from their homes. Therefore, the UNRWA estimates of that period, which placed the number of Palestinians refugees as of the armistice date at slightly under 900,000, would not seem unreasonable.

While the above figures are "only estimates," they have been checked both for internal consistency and for external validity with figures reached by international bodies of inquiry and the British demographers of the Department of Statistics of the former government of Palestine. The margin of error is no more than $\pm$ 50,000 for the total and much less for the various subtotals. Even in the roundest terms, it is clear that the war of 1948 effected the dislocation of more than half of the original Arab inhabitants of Palestine, deprived some 60 per cent of their livelihoods, and drastically changed the lives of all.

PHASE V: 1949–1970

Between the wars of 1948 and 1967, a few tens of thousands of Palestinians were permitted repatriation under an arrangement facilitating the reunion of broken families. Their number was more than matched by the expulsion of Bedouins (who by 1962 numbered no more than 27,000 in Israel), and by the tens of thousands of Arabs who left Israel either permanently or temporarily. During this period, however, the Palestinian Arab population increased dramatically on both sides of the armistice lines, since natural increase had, of course, not terminated with the war. In the nineteen years between the 1948 war and the renewal of the conflict in June, 1967, the Palestinian Arab population almost doubled through natural increase. Including those Arab Palestinians who had remained in Israel after 1948, there would have been no less than 2,700,000 Arabs of Palestinian birth or descent by June of 1967. What has been their fate since Israel occupied the last remnants of Palestine during the most recent war?

It is still premature to obtain a firm answer to the above question. Since the war, all parties concerned have been reluctant to release *any* official figures—either those based upon enumerations or upon considered estimates—that would permit us to evaluate the effects of the June, 1967, war upon the further displacement of the Arabs of Palestine. The most recent bench-mark figures available are those dating from the censuses taken in Israel and Jordan in 1961. From these it is possible to estimate the distribution of Palestinian Arabs who were still within the geographic limits of Palestine on the eve of the June war. This picture can be completed through UNRWA figures on the number of Palestinian Arabs in the Gaza Strip. (Only very rough estimates can be made of the number of Palestinians who, at the time of the war, were already residing outside the borders of Palestine since, except for those still carrying ration cards, they cannot otherwise be distinguished from other residents of the countries in which they settled.)

According to my calculations, by June, 1967, there were 2,700,000 persons of Palestinian Arab origin, of whom approximately 1,700,000 were still residing within the geographical limits of British-mandated Palestine either in territories that had been occupied by Israel as of 1949 or in the remaining portions of the country conquered during the June, 1967, conflict. Of these, about 300,000 were within the armistice limits of Israel itself.[23] Another 975,000 to 1,000,000 were living in the districts of Jerusalem, Hebron, and Nablus (including Jenin), that is, on the so-called West Bank which until June had been under the jurisdiction of Jordan.[24] And finally, there were an additional 400,000 living in the Gaza

23. In the census of Israel taken in mid-1961, there were slightly under 244,000 Arabs (including Bedouins) living within Israel as delineated by the armistice lines. Projecting this figure to the end of May, 1967, according to a low estimate of natural increase (35/1000 per year compounded, based on an average of Israeli vital statistics rates for the various groups of non-Jews), one reaches an estimate of 292,000 Arabs in Israel. The figure may have been somewhat higher than this. Actually, several Israeli sources reveal disagreements in the original base figure for 1961, but these discrepancies might be accounted for by differences in the date to which the figure applies, whether mid-year population or end-of-year population. See *Statistical Abstract of Israel, 1961*, no. 12 (Jerusalem); and Ministry of Foreign Affairs, *Facts About Israel, 1963* (Jerusalem), unnumbered table on p. 48, which gives estimates of non-Jews in Israel between 1948 and the end of 1961. There is, of course, a slight difference between the number of Arabs in Israel and the number of non-Jews in Israel. Part of the above discrepancy may be due to this noncomparability.

24. The census of Jordan taken November 18, 1961, revealed that 805,450 persons were residing in the West Bank provinces on that date. Projecting this total according to an estimated rate of natural increase of only 35/1000 per year compounded (the recorded natural-increase rate according to Jordanian vital statistics records was actually 41/1000 in 1961), one arrives at a minimum of 975,000 residents by June, 1967. The actual number may have been higher. Figures have been derived from Department of Statistics, *Jordan, 1962*, (Amman), Table 7, p. 7.

Strip, according to UNRWA estimates of that date. The remaining 1,000,000 Arabs of Palestinian descent were distributed outside Palestine, most of them on the so-called East Bank of Jordan.

The war of 1967 initiated a fifth phase of their displacement from Palestine. During and directly after the war, some 400,000 residents of the West Bank sought refuge across the Jordan River, and the population of Gaza was reduced by at least 50,000 persons, either through flight or mortality. By August-September of 1967, according to unofficial Israeli estimates, there were slightly under 600,000 Arabs left on the West Bank and about 350,000 Arabs in the Gaza Strip. Since that date, the Israeli estimated figures have been going down, indicating that depopulation continues. Most of the displaced persons moved eastward toward Amman, although smaller numbers found their way into Lebanon, Syria, and Egypt.

What is the current distribution of the indigenous Arab population of Palestine, and what does the future hold in store for them? Here our estimates are more tentative than earlier ones and our predictions less reliable, for they turn upon the larger political indeterminancies of a solution to the entire problem of the Middle East. However, some rough estimates can be suggested. Within the past three years (June, 1967 to June, 1970), the Arab Palestinian population grew by natural increase to an estimated total of 3,000,000 persons. Between 1,350,000 and 1,400,000 of them are now within territories controlled by Israel, that is, in Palestine proper, somewhat under 400,000 having the status of Israeli citizens, the remaining 1,000,000 bearing the uncomfortable status of a conquered people. The rest of the Palestinian Arabs are scattered in various parts of the world. Jordan houses some 800,000 to 850,000 Palestinians; Lebanon and Syria combined contain about 600,000 more; and another 200,000 are distributed in other Arab countries or abroad.

The demographic dilemma of Palestine is, if anything, even more insoluble today than it was earlier. Despite the enormous tragedy of the displacements that have already occurred, Palestine still contains as many Arabs as inhabited the country in 1948 when the state of Israel was declared. An even larger number of Arab Palestinians live just beyond the borders of the homeland to which they have never relinquished their right to return. The occupying power maintains its avowed policy goal to make Israel "as Jewish as England is English." To achieve this end and also to expand territorially (i.e., to retain any of the occupied areas), it must, therefore, work to further displace the remnants of the Palestinian Arab population. The Palestinians, on the other hand, have resisted this displacement for two generations and there is every indication that they will continue to do so. Will the sixth phase of the demographic transformation reverse the process and bring peace?

6. The Wordless Wish: From Citizens to Refugees

Erskine B. Childers

One cannot help feeling ... that in their heart of
hearts, the white Rhodesians bear a wordless wish ...
that the Africans would disappear.

Patrick Keatley

They [Zionists] wax angry towards those who remind
them that there is still another people in Eretz
Israel that has been living there and does not
intend at all to leave.

Ahad Ha'Am, 1914

The psychopathology of the "wordless wish" in Euro-
pean settlers in Africa has been the subject of considerable attention, and
such enforced geographical segregation of the indigenous majority peoples
as these settler minorities achieved has been fully identified. It is an
integral and important part of the international history of Palestine in the
twentieth century that no remotely comparable attention has been paid
to Zionist motivations—and actions—as regards the indigenous Palestine
Arab majority. The prevailing received view in the Western world is, as
David Ben-Gurion asserted, that in 1948 "the Arabs fled the country,
and it was virtually emptied of its former owners. Pre-State Zionism could
not even have conceived of such a thing."[1] A minority Western impression
accepts that perhaps the Arabs were here and there "encouraged" by the
Zionists to "flee" but that this was merely a consequence of war and of

1. *Israeli Yearbook, 1952* (Jerusalem), p. 38.

Arab hostility toward the Zionists, not of any design, least of all any basic Zionist aim or motivation.

A detailed study of Zionist documents, and of other non-Arab sources, indicates an entirely different picture, and some important distinctions from the psychopathology of settlers in the African continent. Common to both groups was, of course, an underlying cultural distaste and racist antagonism. In 1891, the famous European Jewish writer Ahad Ha'Am published a report of his personal observations of the behavior of new Zionist settlers in Palestine:

> They treat the Arabs with hostility and cruelty, deprive them of their rights, offend them without cause, and even boast of these deeds; and nobody among us opposes this despicable inclination.[2]

The Zionist leadership, even more than the (far less organized and far less brilliant) leaders of white settlers in Africa, also faced the problem of needing continuous political and financial support from distant imperial or other great powers. But whereas settler groups in Africa did not begin to try to win over—or at least neutralize—liberals in the West until much later in the twentieth century, Zionist leaders positively set out to achieve liberal support from the outset, as well as support from all other points on the Western political spectrum.[3] One important result is notable in Zionist documents from the turn of the century onward: a not-unsympathetic British writer has recently called it the Zionist "habit to speak not only in two but in several voices, to run several lines of persuasion at the same time, [producing] a not-undeserved reputation in the world for chronic mendacity."[4]

THE SEVERAL VOICES

This "habit" was to have crucial effect in the story of the indigenous Palestine Arab majority in this century, and the effect can be traced from

2. "The Truth From Palestine," in *Nationalism and the Jewish Ethic*, ed. Hans Kohn (New York, 1962).

3. In a long-unknown diary entry, Herzl, outlining an extraordinary plan to get European statesmen to make anti-Semitic pronouncements so that the Jews "will come running to us barefoot," described "the public opinion of the world" whose support he would secure as "liberals, socialists, anti-semites" *Complete Diaries*, ed. Raphael Patai, trans. Harry Zohn, 5 vols. [New York, 1960], I, 88.

4. Christopher Sykes, *Cross Roads to Israel* (London, 1965), p. 26; see also Alan R. Taylor for examples of multiple "voices" (*Prelude to Israel: An Analysis of Zionist Diplomacy, 1897–1947* [New York, 1959], p. 23).

Theodor Herzl, the founder of the Zionist movement, onward. After Herzl's death in 1904, his private diaries were held by the Zionist movement, and until 1960 only edited versions were released in English. Among the long-suppressed diary entries is one, penned in 1895, setting down his ideas for "when we occupy the country." Writing that the Zionists must "gently expropriate private property," Herzl continued:

> We shall try to spirit the penniless population across the border by procuring employment for it in the transit countries, while denying it any employment in our own country.

> Both the process of expropriation and the removal of the poor must be carried out discreetly and circumspectly.

> Let the owners of immovable property believe that they are cheating us, selling things for more than they are worth. But we are not going to sell them anything back.[5]

Only four years later, however, we find Herzl answering a worried letter from a Jerusalem Arab notable:

> You see another difficulty, Excellency, in the existence of the non-Jewish population in Palestine. But who would think of sending them away? It is their well-being, their individual wealth, which we will increase by bringing in our own.[6]

By 1901, Herzl and his fellow-leaders had established the Jewish National Fund, in whose regulations his diary plan ("we are not going to sell them anything back") was given force by a prohibition on the resale or leasing of any Zionist-purchased land to non-Jews.[7] In 1902, Herzl published his famous novel, *Altneuland,* written for European consumption, in which happy Arabs, fully *in situ* in a future Jewish state speak to puzzled visitors with warm feelings toward the Zionists.[8] But in

5. *Diaries,* I, 88.
6. Herzl to Youssuf Zia Alkhaldy, March 19, 1899; cf. United Nations, *UNSCOP Report,* Annexes, 1947, p. 64.
7. This racist permanent "alienation" clause was later written into the Constitution of the Jewish Agency in Palestine, article 3(d).
8. The fictional Rashid Bey, replying to the visiting Christian, Mr. Kingscourt, who had asked "Don't you look upon the Jews as intruders?" was made by Herzl to say, "The Jews have enriched us, why should we be angry with them? They live with us like brothers. Why should we not love them?" Herzl's novel had a wide success in Europe.

the same year, when he turned to London and British Colonial Secretary Chamberlain with a plan to secure Cyprus and the al-'Arish area of the Sinai Desert as an "assemblage center" near Palestine, the other, "private-voice" Zionism may be heard. Chamberlain told him that Britain could do nothing against the will of the indigenous population of Cyprus. To this Herzl replied, according to his diary entry of the next day,

> that not everything in politics is disclosed to the public—but only results, or what can be serviceable in a controversy. I then unfolded my plan . . . . We must be invited to come into the country. I would lay the ground for this through half a dozen emissaries. And when we had founded the Jewish Eastern Company, with five million pounds capital, for settling Sinai and El Arish, the Cypriots would be anxious to divert some of that golden rain to their islands. The Moslems would leave, and the Greeks would gladly sell their lands at a good price and migrate to Athens or Crete.[9]

The similarity with Herzl's earlier diary plan for property owners and "penniless population" will be evident. The pattern of two voices continues from these early years onward through the decades. Before the First World War, one of the famous European orators of Zionism, Max Nordau, coined the slogan *Das Land ohne Volk: Das Volk ohne Land*—"The Land without People: the People without a Land." He and all Zionist leaders knew, of course, that Palestine was not only not "without people" but was in fact well populated in all but its marginal and unusable tracts of rocky hills and desert.[10]

At the turn of the century the process of removing the "penniless population" by "denying it any employment" had already begun in one newly acquired Zionist settlement after another, and by 1907 an organized racist boycott of Arab labor on such new Zionist farms was under way. At one settlement where forcible eviction of Arabs took place, Sejera in lower Galilee, a young Zionist immigrant named David Ben-Gurion declared to a friend that "force and force alone will win respect,"[11] and there began the organizing of the first armed Zionist force, the Hashomer, forerunner of the secret Zionist army of British mandate years, the Haganah. Gentler,

9. *Diaries,* entry of October 23, 1902.

10. Nordau had also coined the ambiguous term *Heimstätte* at the First Zionist Congress in 1897: "It was equivocal, but we all understood what it meant"; see Sykes, *Cross Roads,* pp. 24–25; see also Nevill Barbour, *Nisi Dominus* (London, 1946). Ahad Ha'Am had pleaded with Zionists to recognize and admit that Palestine was not empty as early as 1891.

11. Cited by Robert St. John, *Ben-Gurion* (New York, 1959), pp. 31–32.

more spiritual Zionists like Ahad Ha'Am continued to protest. Wiser and more liberal settlers in Palestine tried to oppose the increasingly institutionalized boycott of Arab labor and the parallel evictions of Arab tenants and workers. But by November of 1913, Ahad Ha'Am was writing to one such settler in Palestine, Moshe Smilansky, about the boycott of Arab labor, "if this be the 'Messiah,' I do not wish to see his coming."[12]

The non-Zionist student of Zionist history frequently confronts individual puzzles as to real motivation and real intention among Zionist leaders; reliable guidance cannot be obtained from most of their contemporaries' memoirs or other documents, since it can be so difficult to determine who had convinced whom of which "voice," the public or the private. An example that occurs at this point is Dr. Arthur Ruppin, a key figure in Palestine itself. At the 1913 Zionist Congress, we find him admonishing the delegates that Zionists must not merely assure the Arabs "that we are coming into the country as their friends. We must prove this by our deeds."[13] Yet the same Dr. Ruppin, at the same 1913 Congress, stated that the Zionist objective was "a closed Jewish economy" in which "producers, consumers and middlemen shall all be Jewish."[14] Had the overall demographic aim been one of strictly limited Jewish immigration, it might be possible to argue that there was no necessary inconsistency, that Zionists could operate their own closed, exclusivist economy within a Palestine still inhabited by Arabs. But the Zionist aim was one of *massive* immigration, into a country which they intended to make a Jewish state.

Whatever inconsistencies, inner conflicts, or sheer postponements of decision there may have been among some Zionist leaders, the fundamental posture of the movement toward the indigenous Arab majority was already clear before the Balfour Declaration. It was in these years, for example, that future Zionist leaders were being schooled at the elite Herzlia Gymnasia in Palestine. One of the students, Moshe Menuhin, later the father of a world-famous violinist, has recently recalled that "It was drummed into our young hearts that the fatherland must become ours, 'goyim rein' (clear of Gentiles—Arabs)."[15]

In the same years, Ahad Ha'Am was observing that the new Zionists, who had "regarded the Arabs as non-existent ever since the beginning of the colonization of Palestine,"[16] intensely disliked anyone reminding them

12. Letter of November 18, 1913, cited in Hans Kohn, "Zion and the Jewish National Idea," *Menorah Journal*, XLVI (Autumn–Winter, 1958), 34.

13. *Three Decades of Palestine* (Jerusalem, 1936), p. 35.

14. *Ibid.*, p. 62.

15. *The Decadence of Judaism* (New York, 1965), p. 52; the definition is Mr. Menuhin's in the text.

16. See Introduction to his *At the Crossroads* (Philadelphia, 1912).

that the Arabs did in fact exist and "do not intend at all to leave."[17] But until the Balfour Declaration, and the ensuing British mandate, the movement "stood before a blank wall" in all basic strategic respects—a wall which, according to the new leader of Zionism, Dr. Chaim Weizmann, "was impossible for us to surmount by ordinary political means."[18]

In Zionist documentation now available to the student, it is quite clear that the public protestations of 1917 and afterward as to the limited objective of the "national home," and its professed partnership with the Arabs, were more "circumlocutions"[19] to cover goals that could not be disclosed to the public.[20] But most of the historiography of the declaration has concentrated on its real substance in terms of Jewish statehood or less, and what the British Cabinet did or did not understand beside what the Zionists did or did not understand about the statehood issue. I was long curious whether in the secret negotiations for the declaration, and even in certain phrases in the short text, there lay understandings about removal of the Palestine Arabs. The particularly relevant clause in the declaration is the proviso that "nothing shall be done which may prejudice the civil and religious rights of existing non-Jewish communities in Palestine." Close examination of these words, within the full declaration text, suggests that they are most particularly the result of much redrafting and quite minute adjustment. The use of the brutally euphemistic term, "non-Jewish," to describe the huge indigenous Arab (Muslim and Christian) majority is not really a curiosity, nor is the culturally obliterative use of "communities," in the plural form.[21] Zionists had begun using the term, "non-Jewish," for obvious purposes, as far back as the time of Herzl.[22]

17. Cited in Kohn, "Jewish National Idea."

18. Recalling 1914 in a speech to the 1921 Zionist Congress.

19. Max Nordau's own term for the device of Heimstätte; see Sykes, *Cross Roads*, p. 24.

20. Weizmann to C. P. Scott, 1915: "The Jews take over the country" after a ten or fifteen-year British protectorate. Weizmann to Lord Robert Cecil in April, 1917, spoke of "a Jewish Palestine under a British Protectorate" by which "it would be easily understood that Great Britain [was] keeping the country in trust for the Jews"; Weizmann to a Zionist meeting, May, 1917: "the time is not yet ripe for the setting up of a State" (see Weizmann's memoirs, *Trial and Error* [Philadelphia, 1949]; and Leonard Stein's valuable study *The Balfour Declaration* [New York, 1961]).

21. It is not generally known that the Zionists faced not only an Arab population of over 650,000 but a majority of the *Jewish* population who were non-Zionist. Of the 60,000 Jews in Palestine in 1914, *two-thirds,* according to the Zionist writer, Arthur Ruppin, "still belonged to the old Orthodox type and only one-third to the new, national, progressive section" (*The Jews in the Modern World* [London, 1934], p. 389).

22. For example, Herzl to Youssuf Zia Alkhaldy, March 19, 1899, cited above.

But "existing"—and "existing" without the definite article, which would come naturally to any drafter of such a clause who knew full well that so many hundreds of thousands of Arabs did indeed exist—this is a distinct curiosity. The fact that the Arabs were to be assured only of civil and religious, not political, rights, has of course often been noted.

Repeated contemplation of this extraordinary wording, against the known background of Zionist "wordless wishes," compelled me toward one question. Had the word "existing" been inserted to cover a future time when, these unidentified "communities" having no *political* rights in British-occupied Palestine, might simply be *removed?* It could easily be verified from available documentation that the Zionists were not responsible for the inclusion of the so-called "Arab safeguard clause." It was in none of their draft versions of the declaration; it was inserted by British Foreign Office drafters, for very significantly admitted purposes;[23] and Weizmann and his colleagues in fact disliked it, for equally significantly worded reasons.[24]

There are also documentary indexes as to how the Zionist leadership then decided to interpret this unwanted clause about the unnamed Arabs of Palestine.[25] But the question whether there was any Zionist-British understanding about *removing* the Arabs remained unanswerable, given official British documentary withholdings, until the "Boothby bombshell." Lord Boothby is a highly independent (Americans would say "maverick") politician and a long-time supporter of Zionism. In a 1964 BBC program commemorating Chaim Weizmann, who was a close friend of Boothby, the always blunt peer stated that "the original Balfour Declaration had made provisions for the Arabs to be moved elsewhere, more or less." At once, there was uproar in London, with angry Zionist denials.

The entire uproar must be read by scholars in its originals.[26] Suffice it here to say that, within weeks, the widow of Chaim Weizmann wrote to

23. Leopold S. Amery, who drafted it "to go a reasonable distance to meeting the objections both Jewish and pro-Arab *without impairing the substance of the proposed declaration*" (Amery, *My Political Life,* 3 vols. [London, 1953], II, 116 [italics added]). The question then is, what was the undisturbed "substance"?

24. Weizmann wrote that they disliked the intimation of oppressive intentions, but that the clause could also "cripple our work" (*Trial and Error,* pp. 260–62). Again, what work?

25. The American Zionist co-drafter, Jacob de Haas, emphasized that "we draw a distinction between Jewish rights and Arab claims. . . . The term *'Political Rights'* does not appear in the Balfour Declaration"; see *The History of Palestine* (New York, 1934).

26. See, *Jewish Chronicle* (London), January 3, 17, 24, 1964; February 28, 1964; and note 29 below.

Lord Boothby confirming that he was correct. And most particularly, a senior staff officer of the Weizmann Archives in Israel wrote that

> Serious substantiation can be found for Lord Boothby's contention as to the original meaning of the Balfour Declaration prior to its final version. . . . The First [Zionist] draft defined "The principle that Palestine should be reconstituted as the National Home of the Jewish People," and contained neither the Arab clause [nor] the reservation about "The rights and political status enjoyed by Jews in any other country . . . ."
>
> The Arabs were never mentioned in the original draft and, by way of omission, the possibility of a transfer became plausible. . . .
>
> Regardless of whether or not the actual draft contained the "transfer" point in letter, it is the spirit and the logical consequence which count.[27]

Fortified (and somewhat provoked by heavy Zionist pressure upon him),[28] Lord Boothby then wrote to the *Jewish Observer* that "I am well aware that the present Zionist 'party line' is to maintain that a transfer of Arab population in the Middle East was never at any time contemplated, but I believe this to be quite untrue." Boothby then repeated his contention, writing that he based himself "on the memory of numerous conversations with Dr. Weizmann" and then reproducing an excerpt from a previously unpublished letter from Weizmann to James Marshall, as follows:

> There can be no doubt that the picture in the minds of those who drafted the Balfour Declaration and the mandate was that of a Jewish Commonwealth in Palestine. Palestine was to be a Jewish State, in which the Arab would enjoy the fullest civil and cultural rights; but for the expression of their own national individuality in terms of statehood, they were to turn to the surrounding Arab countries.[29]

There can be no doubt whatever that, in this newly published 1930 letter from Weizmann, the Zionist leader meant "turn to the surrounding Arab countries" in the full physical, geographical sense of Arabs leaving Palestine. Dr. Weizmann's invocation of Arab "civil and cultural rights"

27. *Jewish Chronicle* (London), March 6, 1964.

28. Lord Boothby to the present writer, June 15, 1964.

29. See Boothby's letter to the *Jewish Observer* and *Middle East Review*, February 28, 1964, in which he also disclosed that Mrs. Weizmann had told him he was correct.

in a Jewish state is also one of the most overt definitions of that peculiar definition of rights in the Balfour Declaration, and explains much that could hitherto only be surmised.

There is, however, more in the record for these crucial first years when the Zionist movement hoped to have the unqualified and executive patronage of a British occupying authority. In his memoirs, Sir Alec Kirkbride, one of the first British officials assigned to Palestine and then Transjordan after the 1918 armistice, wrote that the undeveloped areas east of the Jordan River

> were intended to serve as a reserve of land for use in the resettlement of Arabs once the National Home for the Jews in Palestine, which [the British government] were pledged to support, became an accomplished fact. There was no intention at that stage of forming the territory east of the river Jordan into an independent Arab state.[30]

No official documentation has been released on this, though this is not surprising, given the political dynamite involved even today. But corroborative evidence of Sir Alec's firm recollection [31] may be seen in such references as those by the avidly pro-Zionist British political officer especially nominated by Weizmann, Colonel Richard Meinertzhagen. In his memoirs, Meinertzhagen has described a 1922 exchange with Winston Churchill and T. E. Lawrence after they had arranged for Amir Abdullah to have an emirate in "Transjordan":

> I reverted to Transjordan and urged that Abdullah's tenure should cease; that eventually the Jews would attain sovereignty in Palestine and I did not wish them to be surrounded on all sides by hostile Arabs; moreover, as the Jewish population increased, they would require more land.

> At the expense of the Arab," said Lawrence.

> "No," I said. "There are thousands of acres in Transjordan lying fallow and unoccupied owing to Arab laziness."[32]

Meinertzhagen, who was privy to much of the thinking of the inner Zionist councils, did not get his way. Transjordan ceased to be an im-

---

30. *A Crackle of Thorns* (London, 1956), pp. 19–20.
31. Kirkbride to the present writer, March 1, 1964, reiterating the clarity of his memory of numerous discussions in official circles.
32. *Middle East Diary 1917–1956* (London, 1959), p. 118.

mediate possibility for any Zionist purpose. Weizmann could only confide
to the 1921 Zionist Congress that a way would have to be "forced" into
Transjordan.[33] At the same Congress, another leader, Ussishkin, said that
"if we keep on going to Palestine, in tens, in hundreds, in thousands, in
hundreds of thousands, the Arab question will solve itself."

But the documentary record continues, down the mandate years, both
with regard to deliberate Zionist efforts to obtain a British-executed removal of the Arabs and to a steady application of the original Herzlian
formula of denial of employment, combined with strategically planned
land acquisition.[34] Sanctioned by the British government, the Zionist Jewish
Agency had its racist land-alienation rule. Article 3(e) of the Jewish
Agency Constitution stressed Jewish labor. The Jewish National Fund
lease-form rules openly stipulated "only Jewish labour" (article 23).
Zionist settlers taking loans from the Palestine Foundation Fund had to
agree to "hire Jewish workmen only" (article 7). Methods of enforcement
of this boycott, especially against older settlers who resisted it, included
forcible picketing of them and the erection of new "labour colonies"
around them. The racist boycott of Arab labor was extended to Arab
produce, and a key Zionist-Israeli banking official has acknowledged that
"in order that the Jewish farmers might be able to sell their products it
was necessary to initiate a campaign of persuasion—and sometimes even
use force—to make the urban population buy the dearer Jewish agricultural products."[35]

By 1929, tension was such that the then Labour Government in Great
Britain sent out yet another commission. The Shaw Commission Report
declared that "the position is now acute. There is no alternative land to

33. 1921 Congress, *Minutes;* the way was to be forced by overwhelming immigration.

34. In a little-known article, one of Israel's chief 1948-war strategists, Yigael Alon,
has described how land acquisition aimed at ensuring "that an ever-increasing area
was brought under the ultimate authority of the Jewish People." Other lands were
earmarked for their strategic military location astride roads and surrounding major
Arab towns, often far from main settlement areas. In each new settlement, Alon
writes, the precise location of the buildings, etc., was decided by a secret staff unit of
the, itself then secret, Zionist army, Haganah, in order to ensure the best "offensive
and defensive" structure (in *Siege in the Hills of Hebron,* ed. Dov Knohl [New
York, 1958]).

35. A. S. Hoffien, Chairman of Israel Bank Leumi, annual address, 1953, cited in
Alexander Rubner, *The Economy of Israel* (London, 1960), p. 99; see also Barbour,
Nisi Dominus, pp. 135–36; Great Britain, Colonial Office, Palestine, *Report on Immigration, Land Settlement and Development* (Parliamentary Papers, Cmd. 3686–
3687; London, 1930) [Hope Simpson Report], I, giving an example in Ness-Zion
village; also, Esco Foundation for Palestine, *Palestine: A Study of Jewish, Arab and
British Policies,* 2 vols. (New Haven, 1947).

which persons evicted can remove. In consequence a landless and discontented class is being created." Soon, another British expert, Sir John Hope Simpson, was dispatched to examine the economic and land problems further. His report only elaborated the evidence, and bluntly noted that "the provisions included in legal documents binding on every settler in a Zionist colony are not compatible with [the] lofty sentiments ventilated at public meetings and in Zionist propaganda."

How Zionists were viewing a resolution of these injuries to the Arabs could be seen in a letter which the British socialist leader, Harold Laski, a close friend of Weizmann, wrote to Justice Felix Frankfurter in 1931. Palestine's "economic problem," Laski observed, seemed insoluble *"unless the British Government uses Transjordan for Arab settlement."*[36] In 1933, we read of Weizmann and Meinertzhagen attending a Zionist banquet in London and listening to Herbert Samuel asking for Zionist-Arab partnership. "At this point," Meinertzhagen recorded in his diary, "Weizmann winked at me. One might as well expect a ferret to cooperate with a rabbit."[37]

Chaim Weizmann is generally regarded as moderate, and as sensitive, among the pantheon of Zionist leaders, on the "Arab question." His public speeches to Zionist Congresses and to general Western audiences contain numerous expressions of earnest wish to reassure the Arabs that the Zionists were not going to drive them out of Palestine.

In 1937 yet another British commission submitted its report, this time following the 1936 national Arab rebellion in Palestine. The Peel Commission could see no way out of Britain's apparently conflicting obligations to Zionists and Arabs, save to partition Palestine. If the partition outlined was to be effective, the report stated, there would have to be not only an exchange of lands but, as far as possible, "an exchange of population".[38] The 1937 Zionist Congress, in Zurich, went into extraordinary secret session to debate the partition proposal.

On August 13, 1937, the *Jewish Chronicle* published a very detailed account of this secret session, including reproduction of a document initialed by Weizmann recording his secret discussions with the British colonial secretary, Ormsby-Gore. Weizmann's note of record of what he said to Ormsby-Gore includes

---

36. Cited in Kingsley Martin, *Harold Laski* (London, 1954), p. 210 (italics added).

37. Meinertzhagen, *Middle East Diary,* p. 148.

38. Great Britain, Colonial Office, Palestine, *Report of the Palestine Royal Commission* (Parliamentary Papers, Cmd. 5479; London, 1937) [Peel Commission Report], chap. XXII, including "compulsory" transfer in last resort.

Transfer of the Arab population. I said that the whole success of the
[partition] scheme depended upon whether the Government genuinely did
or did not wish to carry out this recommendation. The transfer could only
be carried out by the British Government and not by the Jews. I explained the reason why we considered the proposal of such importance.[39]

In 1949, Weizmann recorded in his memoirs profound distress over the
1944 British Labour Party proposal that the Arabs be encouraged "to move
out" of Palestine "as the Jews move in." Like Ben-Gurion, as quoted
above, Weizmann asserted that "we had never contemplated the removal
of the Arabs."[40] It is perhaps legitimate to observe that, in Weizmann no
less than in other Zionist leaders, the "two voices" may be detected.

The Peel Commission proposal came to nothing, but Ormsby-Gore did
take it, necessarily, to the League of Nations. He was instructed by the
British Cabinet, by then alarmed over German and Italian approaches to
the Arab states, to make clear to the League Mandates Commission that
Britain would never enforce a transfer of Arabs. But Ormsby-Gore was
therefore asked, by the commission, how his government envisaged the
Arabs moving out. He replied, in terms familiar since 1948, "it is quite
possible that the Arabs will trek voluntarily." To this, the commission
chairman made a comment—one that cannot seem other than poignant
today—that he was an old man, but never in his life had he heard of
people, especially peasants, voluntarily emigrating from the richest parts
of their country to the poorest parts.

Now the Second World War intervened. To prepare Western public
opinion for the historic Biltmore Resolution of 1942, Weizmann wrote a
long article for the quarterly *Foreign Affairs*. Promising full rights for
Arabs in a Jewish state, Weizmann went on, however, to say, "but if any
Arabs do not wish to remain in a Jewish state, every facility will be given
to them to transfer to one of the many and vast Arab countries."[41] In 1945,
Hannah Arendt noted that the 1942 and 1945 Zionist resolutions "leave
practically no choice for the Arabs but minority status in Palestine or

39. Note dated July 19, 1937, in *Jewish Chronicle* (London), August 13, 1937. The
authenticity of this Weizmann note has never been denied; the Zionist named as
furnishing it to the *Chronicle* was suspended by the Zionist Actions Committee.

40. *Trial and Error*, p. 535; Weizmann's denial, in memoirs written for Western
consumption, may also be judged in light of his widow's letter to Lord Boothby,
cited above.

41. "Palestine's Role in the Solution of the Jewish Problem," *Foreign Affairs*, XX
(January, 1942), 337–38; in thirteen pages Weizmann managed to range over the
whole modern history of Palestine without once hinting at the actual size of the
Arab population.

voluntary emigration." Miss Arendt asserted that a transfer of all Palestine Arabs, openly demanded by Zionist Revisionists, "was earnestly discussed a few years ago in general Zionist circles as well." And in a passage clearly worded with care, she observed of the narrowed choice left by Zionism to the Arabs that "it is obvious that in this question, too, the Revisionist principle, *if not yet the Revisionist methods,* has won a decisive victory."[42]

The conclusions of a not-unsympathetic writer on Zionism, a decade before the 1948 exodus, once again indicate the "wordless wish." T. R. Feiwel wrote in 1938:

> The history of Zionist policy towards the Arabs is that of this illusion, but an illusion fanatically upheld, [that] the Palestine Arabs *do not exist,* at least not as a separate nation with its own aims for national survival which would have to be reckoned with. . . .
>
> Increase in wealth, numbers, economic and social possibilities, has helped the Zionists to reach an astonishing degree of autarchy, to ignore their Arab neighbours even in mixed cities like Haifa or Jerusalem, and to prolong the illusion of an empty country.[43]

INSIDE THE ARENA

Ten years later, in the words of Israel's first premier, David Ben-Gurion, Palestine was "virtually emptied of its former owners." Against the documentary record, no elaborate comment is needed on Mr. Ben-Gurion's additional comment that "pre-State Zionism could not even have conceived of such a thing." It had been conceived throughout fifty years and more. It had been attempted, between 1917 and 1947, but a politically expedient time or method had never been found. By the beginning of 1948, the Zionist movement had fully decided that "the international calendar will not synchronize itself to ours."[44] Before the U.N. General Assembly had voted on the partition issue, Ben-Gurion ordered secret mobilization of all

42. "Zionism Reconsidered," *Menorah Journal,* XXXIII (Autumn, 1945), 167 (italics added); Miss Arendt's article is possibly one of the most incisive on Zionism, and highly pointed. Of the 1942 Biltmore Program she observed that "the Jewish minority had granted minority rights to the Arab majority."

43. *No Ease in Zion* (London, 1938), pp. 22, 250.

44. David Ben-Gurion to the Elected Assembly, October 2, 1947; see his *Rebirth and Destiny of Israel,* trans. Mordekhai Nurock (New York, 1954), p. 211.

Jewish manpower in Palestine and sent fresh missions to Europe to purchase massive quantities of arms.[45]

The strategic masterplans for Zionist forces were ready, including mapped and catalogued details of every Arab village in the whole of Palestine.[46] That the plan was for the military conquest of the whole of Palestine is no longer in doubt: the details have been amply provided by Zionist officials, albeit in documents studied only by specialists. Ten years earlier, Ben-Gurion had declared, during the Zionist debate of the Peel Commission's proposal, "no Zionist can forgo the smallest portion of the Land of Israel. The debate has concerned which of two routes would lead quicker to the common goal."[47] Although it is, of course, official Zionist-Israeli history that the movement was still ready to accept a partition ten years later, a growing volume of overwhelming evidence from Israeli and Zionist sources indicates that here too it was a matter of "voices."

Close study of this evidence further indicates that, of all the minority-settler communities of the twentieth century, the Zionists show a capacity for detailed long-term planning that sets them on an altogether different plane from settlers in Africa. "The entire country" that was to be "liberated" extended from the Litani River in Lebanon (and the Hauran Plateau in southwestern Syria up to the gates of Damascus), down along the banks of the River Jordan, and to the Suez Canal.[48] In the secret strategy of the Haganah during British mandate years, this ultimate objective was a priority, settlement by new settlement, in the precise location of Zionist settler manpower. The strategic-military planning of ostensibly civilian

45. Jon Kimche and David Kimche, *Both Sides of the Hill* (London, 1960), pp. 67–68, 75; see also Netanel Lorch, *The Edge of the Sword* (New York, 1961), pp. 79–80.

46. Haganah operations chief Yigael Yadin mentions "a map in which the strategic character of every Arab village, and the quality of its inhabitants, were indicated" (cited in Harry Sacher, *Israel: The Establishment of a State* (London, 1952), p. 217.

47. Speech at the Twentieth Zionist Congress, Zurich, August 15, 1937.

48. In 1964, for example, Ben-Gurion told the Israeli journal *Ha-Boker* (March) that if Moshe Dayan had been chief of staff in 1948, "the borders of the State might be different today." This provoked a brief and bitter public debate between 1948 leaders. Yigael Alon declared that Ben-Gurion had ordered the army to halt for political reasons just when "we had been on the crest of victory [from] the Litani River in the north to the Sinai Desert in the southwest. A few more days ... would have enabled us [to] liberate the entire country" (*Times* [London], March 9, 1964; *Jewish Chronicle,* March 13, 1964). In a war history publicly endorsed by Ben-Gurion, Jon Kimche and David Kimche have given details of one of the planned final-stage thrusts, "Operation Shin-Tav-Shin," to occupy "the whole of central Palestine as far as the Jordan" (*Both Sides,* p. 267). In the midst of the 1948 war, Ben-Gurion spoke of how the army had reached "our goal ... in a State made larger and Jewish by the Haganah" (*Rebirth,* p. 292).

and agricultural settlements has already been mentioned. In moving toward the climax of the story of most of the indigenous Palestine Arab population in 1948, it becomes important to elaborate this background.

It is in fact extraordinary how frank senior executors of these plans have become in recent years—in writings and statements inside Israel as well as in articles and books published in the West but not likely to be read widely. Some observers of Palestine in late 1947 and early 1948 were puzzled that the Zionist leadership did not withdraw its scattered outlying settlers from densely Arab-populated areas supposed to be included in the Arab-state U.N. partition area. The 1948 Palmach leader, Yigael Alon, has given the explanation:

> The strategic considerations which had underlain the plan of Zionist settlement decided, in large measure, the fate of many regions of the country, including areas largely or entirely settled by Arabs, such as Tiberias, Tsemah, Beit Shi'an, Acre, Haifa, and Jaffa, all of which were surrounded by Jewish villages.
>
> Those areas of Jewish settlement further inland, in the heart of Arab-controlled territory, constituted *forward bases* whose main function was to hold out at all costs until the advance of the main body of troops could extricate them.[49]

The Palmach commander went on to cite, as the second-stage aim of maintaining "isolated outposts in enemy territory," the mounting of an offensive to unite with those settlements. The Israeli military historian Colonel Lorch has also described the outlying settlements as "defensive barriers and potential offensive bases of the state which was about to be established."[50] We also learn from Lorch how Ben-Gurion, in June of 1948, during a State Council discussion as to whether the Zionists had "the military force required for the capture of the Old City" of Jerusalem, observed that "those who returned to Zion in our generation did not provide for a territorial link, consisting of settlements, with the capital. . . . We now pay the penalty for that sin, and we have to correct in war what we omitted in peace."[51]

To reconstruct the Arab exodus of 1948 in the context of these long-developed Zionist plans, we must examine how the leadership saw the coming war at the end of 1947. By mid-December, 1947, the Zionists had a

49. In Knohl, *Siege in the Hills,* p. 376 (italics added).
50. *Edge of the Sword,* p. 58.
51. Cited in *ibid.,* pp. 279–80.

fairly comprehensive picture of the relationship of U.N. involvement, British withdrawal, and their own manpower mobilization and arms imports to any likely Arab moves. The British had announced that they would terminate the mandate by May 15, and all British forces would be evacuated. In the mid-December British statement, a further extremely important factor had been added: contrary to their previous announced plans to progressively hand over authority to the two provisional governments of the partition scheme, the British were now going to retain mandate authority over the whole of Palestine until May 15.

Palestine was going to be like an arena, its gates juridically guarded by the British until mid-May, its interior progressively evacuated by British forces—their instructions from the British government being not to impose partition on the Arabs, but beyond that no clear orders are known. As early as October, 1947, Ben-Gurion had made one crucial estimate from all this: "It seemed unlikely that the neighbouring Arab States would march to the attack so long as the British remained at least in nominal control of the country."[52]

Inside the arena during this period, there was a crucial point of timing for the Zionists. Their historians have now disclosed that the earliest date at which they estimated being able to have total Zionist manpower mobilization trained and ready; the earliest date by which the final huge arms procurement Ben-Gurion ordered in October, 1947, would be landed and made ready; and the earliest date at which they could estimate British withdrawals to be sufficient for major action—all these factors were estimated for April, 1948.[53]

For the pre-April phase of the war, therefore, Zionist action must be restricted to holding operations—defined in their "Plan C" as securing all Zionist areas and keeping open communications between all Zionist settlements.[54] Colonel Lorch has been quite frank about the factors that would bring about a transition from this holding "Plan C" to the now-famous "Plan D," or *"Plan Dalet"*:

> Zero hour for Plan D was to arrive when British evacuation had reached a point where the Haganah would be reasonably safe from British intervention, and when mobilisation had progressed to a point where the implementation of a large-scale plan would be feasible.[55]

The metaphor of an arena for Palestine in 1948 is perhaps not quite complete. Inside it, the mandated custodians had introduced over thirty

52. In his reconstruction for October, 1947, (*Rebirth,* p. 31).
53. See Lorch, *Edge of the Sword,* p. 88; also, Kimche and Kimche, *Both Sides.*
54. Action planned against civilian Arabs for this phase is discussed below.
55. *Edge of the Sword,* p. 87; also, Kimche and Kimche, *Both Sides,* pp. 91–94.

years a fanatically and brilliantly led settled minority with a large element of technology and had judiciously closed their eyes to the secret arming and training of those zealots while forcefully prohibiting the indigenous majority from arming themselves and while breaking up the political leadership of that majority.[56] Starting from scratch in late 1947, volunteers from neighboring Arab countries began training in the Arab Liberation Army. But according to Zionists' own acknowledgments, the volunteers numbered at maximum only 4,000 men, of whom only 2,000 ever received even rudimentary training.[57] Inside the arena, at least until the middle of May, the Palestine Arabs and their newly formed Arab Higher Committee faced the most carefully organized, long-planned, and well-trained settler army of technically superior Europeans that has emerged anywhere in the era of colonial settler penetration.

In the last few years, since the origins of the Arab exodus of 1948 have been exposed to some open analysis and debate in the West,[58] a number of Zionist, non-Zionist-Israeli, and other writers have asserted that there was no evident intention to drive out the Arabs *before April*. The commonly agreed facts are that between December and April only about 30,000 Palestinians left the country—these, overwhelmingly, the more well-to-do middle- and upper-class families who had moved to places like Beirut in the 1936 Arab rebellion as well. Some official and para-official Israeli accounts claim that the exodus of these Palestinians lowered general Arab morale and progessively contributed to the mass exodus that followed. The available evidence controverts even this: most of these departing families were regarded as traitorous; the official Palestine Arab leadership repeatedly exhorted the people, by radio, by leaflet, and through the local committees, to stay in their homes and not listen to panic-mongers; and it issued orders in March to stop even this limited exodus.[59] The

56. See Meinertzhagen for his account of 1922 discussions between Weizmann, Lloyd George, Balfour, and Churchill agreeing to secret Zionist gunrunning ("don't speak about it," said Churchill) (*Middle East Diary*, p. 104). The pattern continued throughout the mandate, with British army officers like Orde Wingate covertly training Zionist commandos (see Leonard O. Mosley's biography, *Gideon Goes to War* [New York, 1956]. Key Palestine Arab leaders had been deported and kept in exile ever since the 1936 rebellion.

57. See Lorch, *Edge of the Sword*, p. 264.

58. See the long debate in the *Spectator* (London), May 12, 1961, which began with the writer's special article, "The Other Exodus."

59. Complete daily broadcast monitoring records of all radio transmissions in and around Palestine in 1948 may be studied at the British Museum in London for BBC monitorings, and at Princeton University for separate CIA monitorings. Throughout, Arab stations were exhorting the people to stay calm, in their homes and jobs. The leadership also sent letters in March to all neighboring Arab countries opposing admission of Palestinians. See documents in *The Arab States and the Arab League*, ed. Muhammad Khalil, 2 vols. (Beirut, 1962), II, 553, doc. no. 246; see also American University Beirut, *Middle East Forum* (December, 1959).

incontrovertible fact is that, although these wealthier families began moving out as early as December, the vast mass of Palestine Arabs stood firm in their homes for long and anxious months thereafter.

The contrast between official Palestine Arab measures against any evacuation and what Zionist authorities were doing in this pre-April first phase is equally marked. Official Israeli history is that, for this period as for later periods, Zionist authorities were actively appealing to the Palestine Arabs to stay and become partners. Making due allowances for spontaneous reaction to Arab guerrilla attacks, a distinct pattern of limited but powerful intimidation and preparatory terrorization emerges from the evidence. Monitoring records of Zionist radio broadcasts in the period show repeated psychological warfare designed to break Arab confidence in their own leadership, to spread panic about imminent dangers of epidemic diseases, and to relay stories of terrified Arab communities.[60] At the same time, both Haganah and Palmach units—the "official" Zionist military units—were engaged in palpable and now-acknowledged, intimidatory raids on Arab villages, significantly including raids announced as reprisals for Arab violent reactions to *"unofficial"* (Stern Gang and Irgun) Zionist attacks on civilian Arabs.[61]

One of the techniques that was to become increasingly familiar was the night raid on an Arab village, in which Haganah men would first silently place explosive charges around the stone houses and drench the wooden window and door frames in petrol, and then open fire, simultaneously dynamiting and burning the sleeping inhabitants to death.[62] Among the difficulties Zionist historians have in dealing with this period is that while some say the Haganah policy was not to attack Arab areas "that had remained quiet hitherto,"[63] others openly describe "deep-penetration" raids against completely "quiet" Arab villages "to impress and intimidate the Arab villagers by demonstrating to them that the Haganah's long arm could reach out even into the remotest Arab districts and hit back."[64]

60. Namely, Haganah Radio, February 19, 1948, 1700 hours, telling Arabs they would be ignored in the conflict of ambitions between Arab leaders; March 10, 1948, 1800 hours, reporting that the Arab states were conspiring with Britain against the Palestinians; February 18, 1948, saying that Arab Liberation volunteers "have brought smallpox with them"; February 27, 1948, saying that Palestinian doctors were fleeing; March 14, 1948, 1800 hours, reporting that "the people of Jaffa are so frightened they are remaining indoors."
61. For example, the raid on Balad al-Shaikh after the Haifa Refinery incident.
62. See, for example, Major R. D. Wilson's *Cordon and Search* (New York, 1952).
63. Lorch, *Edge of the Sword.*
64. Kimche and Kimche, *Both Sides,* p. 83.

These raids did precipitate a limited exodus, still within Palestine but away from areas lying near to Zionist settlers.[65]

On March 19, thousands of miles away in the U.N. Security Council, another kind of bombshell burst, with now-known impact on the Zionist leadership. The United States announced that it was not only not prepared to implement a partition by force but that it would propose instead a temporary U.N. trusteeship. The Zionists were not yet ready for *Plan Dalet*. Instead of the international political and jurisprudential vacuum which they had expected from Arab refusal to accept partition and British refusal to implement it, there was now a whole new prospect of U.N. intervention backed by the United States. And inside Palestine, it was proving extremely difficult to keep open those all-important communications to the defensive-offensive settlements throughout the territory. As Colonel Lorch describes the moment: "the Ides of March had come" upon the Zionists, with "political retreat at the United Nations, military failures on the roads." Toward the end of March, the Haganah operations chief instructed that "the only solution is to take the initiative into our hands, to try to achieve a military decision by going over to the offensive"; each offensive operation was to begin as soon as the British had evacuated a given area.[66] Ben-Gurion ordered attack throughout the whole of Palestine and outside it "wherever the enemy is found."[67] *Plan Dalet* had begun.

On March 27, at 1930 hours, the Zionist Free Hebrew Radio began a significant broadcast, in Arabic:

Do you know that it is a sacred duty to inoculate yourselves hastily against cholera, typhus and similar diseases, as it is expected that such diseases will break out heavily in April and May among Arabs in urban agglomerations?[68]

THE ARAB EXODUS

From April onward, the exodus of Palestine Arabs progressively increased until it reached cataclysmic proportions. In 1961, I published some results of detailed research into the official Israeli and Zionist assertions that these hundreds upon thousands of civilians left "on their own

65. Jon Kimche, *Seven Fallen Pillars* (London, 1950), p. 226.
66. Cited in Lorch, *Edge of the Sword*, pp. 84, 89.
67. Stated in *Rebirth,* giving the date of the attack order as April 6, 1948 (p. 39).
68. See BBC Monitoring Records, British Museum.

leaders' orders" and that the Zionist movement implored them not to leave.[69] These assertions, coupled with periodic categorical denials that any Arabs were expelled by Zionist-Israeli forces,[70] are supported by a series of standard quotations which, on detailed and precise investigation back to their sources, prove specious. Where appropriate and feasible within the confines of this essay, reference will be made to such quotations. What follows, however, is an attempt to set down what actual eyewitness and documentary evidence discloses as to the special causes of the massive Arab exodus.

Nathan Chofshi arrived in Palestine in 1908, dedicated not only to the land he loved as a Jew but to peace with the Arabs of that land. He was one of the founders of *Brith Shalom,* the movement led by Dr. Judah Magnes. In 1959, Mr. Chofshi wrote from Israel to the *Jewish Newsletter* to protest the version of the Arab exodus given in an article by Rabbi Mordecai Kaplan, saying that Rabbi Kaplan had "taken all his information from the official Israeli government sources." The only place, Mr. Chofshi wrote, where the Arabs were asked to remain was the city of Haifa. He continued:

> If Rabbi Kaplan really wanted to know what happened, we old Jewish settlers in Palestine who witnessed the flight could tell him how and in what manner we, Jews, forced the Arabs to leave cities and villages which they did not want to leave of their own free will. Some of them were driven out by force of arms; others were made to leave by deceit, lying, and false promises. It is enough to cite the cities of Jaffa, Lydda, Ramle, Beersheba, Acre, from among numberless others. Particularly shameful were the circumstances of the flight from the villages of Bar-am, Rebatsia, Bitbath, and Migdal-Gad.[71]

U.N. mediator Count Bernadotte, in his report published just before he was assassinated, gave two descriptions:

> The exodus of the Palestinian Arabs resulted from panic created by fighting in their communities, by rumors concerning real or alleged acts of terrorism, or expulsion.

> Almost the whole of the Arab population fled or was expelled from the area under Jewish occupation.[72]

69. "The Other Exodus."

70. For example, "not a single Arab was expelled by the Government since the establishment of the State" (Ben-Gurion to the Knesset, May 17, 1961).

71. "The Bitter Truth About the Arab Refugees," *Jewish Newsletter* (New York), February 9, 1959.

72. U.N. Progress Report, September 16, 1948, part one, paragraph 6; part three, paragraph 1.

Israeli editor Uri Avneri, who fought in the 1948 war, has given the following two accounts:

> The reorientation of Zionist policy would seem to have intervened in the second phase of events. It is possible that one of the Zionist leaders became convinced that the massive exodus of the Arabs could be a positive phenomenon. At that moment, no uniform policy had been established. Certain cases are known in which the local Jewish leaders tried to persuade the Arabs to remain in the conquered towns — for example, Haifa. But, as a general rule, they encouraged the Arabs to evacuate their towns and villages.
>
> I believe that during the third and last phase of the war, the evacuation of Arab civilians had become a war aim.[73]

The British military historian Major Edgar O'Ballance states that Palestine Arab resistance plans were based on the supposition that the civilian Arab population would stay put and act as the natural cover for resistance units. O'Ballance notes that, early in the war, some local Arab leaders ordered some villages near "mixed areas" to evacuate, but he does not say this meant to move out of Palestine. O'Ballance then goes on to give the following description of Zionist policy: "It was the Jewish policy to encourage the Arabs to quit their homes, and they used psychological warfare extensively in urging them to do so."[74]

Some of the psychological-warfare techniques acknowledged even by Zionist writers have been mentioned for the pre-April first phase. The single most devastating psychological blow to civilian Arabs was the massacre of some 250 old men, women, and children in the nonbelligerent village of Deir Yassin. The mutilation of corpses, the parading of Arabs not killed on open lorries through nearby Jerusalem to be spat upon, and the deliberate press conference called to announce the deed were the work of a unit of the "unofficial" Zionist Irgun Zvai Leumi.[75] The massacre was at once strongly and publicly condemned by the official Zionist leadership. A Zionist writer has stated, discussing operational relationships between the Irgun and the official Haganah, that "the (Israeli) Government does not think the time yet come to tell its story fully and

---

73. *Le Monde*, May 9, 1964. Avneri defines the third phase as after May 15, 1948.

74. *The Arab-Israeli War, 1948* (London, 1956), p. 63.

75. For accounts of Deir Yassin, see Jacques de Reynier, *A Jerusalem un drapeau* (Paris, 1950), pp. 72, 213; R. M. Graves, *Experiment in Anarchy* (London, 1949), p. 179; Menahem Begin, *The Revolt: Story of the Irgun*, trans. Samuel Katz (New York, 1951), pp. 162–65; Arthur Koestler, *Promise and Fulfillment: Palestine, 1917–1949* (New York, 1949), p. 160; Kimche, *Seven Fallen Pillars*, p. 227; *Daily Telegraph* (London), April 12, 1948; *New York Times*, April 10, 1948; and *Herald Tribune*, April 10, 1948.

frankly."[76] In the 1945–47 Zionist attacks on British installations in Palestine, it is now generally admitted that there was a secret Haganah-Irgun agreement whereby the Irgun would carry out jointly planned, especially devastating and shocking types of attacks, and the Jewish Agency would then publicly denounce these and dissociate itself from them. Although knowledgeable Israelis have stated that Irgun in 1948 was already operating under regional Haganah commanders, although it is a fact that a Haganah unit first occupied Deir Yassin and then handed it over to the Irgun squad, and although there is much circumstantial eivdence, it is not possible to make any conclusive judgment as to whether the Deir Yassin massacre was carried out with the approval of Haganah and the official Zionist leadership.[77]

What can not seriously be held in doubt is that, after their public denunciation of the massacre, official, no less than unofficial, Zionist forces proceeded to exploit the terror of Deir Yassin to the utmost. The International Red Cross official in Palestine at the time, Jacques de Reynier, reported that the news of Deir Yassin promoted "a widespread terror which the Jews always skillfully maintained." Major O'Ballance writes that "at the time [Deir Yassin] was roundly condemned but later the Jews did not scorn to make capital of it." The Irgun leader, Menahem Begin, openly boasted about the titanic psychological impact of Deir Yassin on civilian Arabs all over Palestine. In Jerusalem in later weeks, a Christian medical missionary, Bertha Spafford Vester, heard Haganah loudspeaker vans calling out, in Arabic, "unless you leave your homes, the fate of Deir Yassin will be your fate."[78]

In the second phase of the war, between April and May 15, it is apparent that extensive and special use was made of psychological and terror-warfare techniques against civilian Arab communities. Overall, while the Arab radio stations continued repeatedly to broadcast appeals to Palestine Arabs to stay in their homes, not to panic, and not to heed rumormongers,[79]

76. Sacher, *Israel,* pp. 192–93; see also Begin, *The Revolt,* pp. 341–47.

77. See Sacher, *Israel,* and Avneri in *Le Monde,* May 9, 1964. Begin, the Irgun commander, reproduces an alleged Haganah order (*The Revolt,* p. 163); press reports of February 3, 1948, on a Haganah-Irgun coordination agreement; and U.N. Security Council debate, December 28, 1948.

78. "Une terreur généralisée que les Juifs se sont toujours habilement arrangés a entretenir" (de Reynier, *A Jerusalem,* p. 46, n. 87); it should be noted, please, that I do not, myself, ever use the term *Jews* in discussing Zionists and Israelis); see also O'Ballance, *Arab-Israeli War,* p. 58; Begin, *The Revolt,* pp. 164–65; Vester, *Our Jerusalem,* special supplement printed in Beirut, 1962, because her original publisher deleted these pages from her book (p. 19).

79. Damascus Radio, April 4, 1948, 2050 hours; Sharq al-Adna, April 4, 1948; Al-Inqaz Radio, April 24, 1948, 1200 hours, warning against panic and flights; April 25, 1948, Jerusalem; May 4, 1948, 1900 hours, Beirut; May 15, 1948, Jerusalem.

the Zionist radio stations continued highly psychological broadcasts, in Arabic.[80] Another instrument was the Haganah's special "Arab Section," staffed by Zionists speaking fluent Arabic, chosen for their "Arab" features, dressing as Arabs, and moving through Arab communities both spreading rumors and picking up useful intelligence, including facts which could then quickly be broadcast by radio in Arabic, givng the Arabs the feeling they were surrounded by spies.

Within these identifiable overall methods, the official Zionist forces used special, localized terror-warfare techniques as each succeeding Arab city or town or densely populated rural area was attacked. One widely employed device was the Zionist-made mortar shell, nicknamed by them the *Davidka,* which hurled 60 pounds of high explosive about 300 yards, very inaccurately but with devastating psychological impact.[81] A more highly refined weapon was the "barrel-bomb," especially designed for the numerous Arab towns and city quarters which were densely packed onto the slopes of Palestine hills. In an article entiled "All's Fair . . .," written for the U.S. Marine Corps professional magazine to tell Marines about techniques developed by the Zionists, an Israeli army-reserve officer who fought in the 1948 war has given precise details of these bombs. They were barrels, casks, and metal drums, filled with a mixture of explosives and petrol, and fitted with two old rubber tires containing the detonating fuse. These devices were then rolled down the sharply sloping alleys and steplanes of Arab urban quarters and provincial towns until they crashed into walls and doorways, making "an inferno of raging flames and endless explosions."[82]

Arthur Koestler has also described "ruthless dynamiting of block after block in the rabbit-warren of bazaars and blind alleys until the panic had reached sufficient dimensions to end all resistance."[83] Koestler and other Zionist writers describe how, using these instruments, the Zionists began to make the civilian Arabs believe that "the Jews are dropping atomic bombs." Koestler also alluded, somewhat mysteriously, to Zionists using the modern equivalent of the "Trumpets of Jericho" to break civilian Arab nerve.[84] Until recently, it was not entirely clear what this meant. But the

80. Voice of the Jewish Defender, April 22, 1948, in Arabic about Arabs leaving; Haganah Radio, April 28, 1948, 1800 hours, in Arabic describing Arab panic in Jaffa; Haganah Radio, May 5, 1948, 1800 hours, in Arabic reporting Arabs fleeing from Beit Dagan; Haganah Radio, May 7, 1948, 1800 hours, in Arabic announcing that 150,000 Arabs had gone but no Jewish village had been evacuated; and Kol Israel, May 18, 22, 28, in Arabic about Arab "panic" and Arab evacuation of villages "in terror and fear."

81. See Lorch, *Edge of the Sword,* p. 103; Sacher, *Israel.*

82. Leo Heiman, in *Marine Corps Gazette* (June, 1964).

83. *Promise and Fulfillment,* p. 233.

84. Heiman, "All's Fair . . ."; Koestler, *Promise and Fulfillment,* p. 215.

Israeli army reserve officer, in his article for the U.S. Marine Corps has
provided the likely answer. It appears that the Haganah loudspeaker jeeps
and vans, used in almost every attack on Arab centers, were equipped
with especially ingenious materials. The Israeli writes that, amid barrel-
bombs,

> as uncontrolled panic spread through all Arab quarters, the Israelis
> brought up jeeps with loudspeakers which broadcast recorded "horror
> sounds." These included shrieks, wails, and anguished moans of Arab
> women, the wail of sirens and the clang of fire-alarm bells, interrupted
> by a sepulchral voice calling out in Arabic: "Save your souls, all ye
> faithful! Flee for your lives! The Jews are using poison gas and atomic
> weapons. Run for your lives in the name of Allah!"[85]

"Horror recordings" of this kind take some time—some deliberate fore-
thought as to objective and audience—to prepare and duplicate. The
student of Palestine history, who has read Israeli professional military
accounts like this, is struck by official Israeli government pamphlets distributed in Western countries which report that loudspeakers were used to
appeal to the Palestine Arabs to *stay*.[86]

In the second phase of the war, the port city of Haifa was one of the
first major centers to be emptied of its Arabs. It is perhaps of special
historical interest, in view of the common assertion that the city's Jewish
mayor in this case appealed to the Arab population to stay. It is true that
Shabetai Levi made just such an appeal, with tears of anguish streaming
down his cheeks. The question is *when* he made the appeal, relative to the
physical and psychological condition of the Arabs and to what the Zionist
military forces attacking Haifa were doing. To raise this question is in no
way to derogate the late Mr. Lèvi's motives—only to place the numerous
invocations of his appeal as proving some general official Zionist policy
in more correct perspective.

On April 21, the British commander in Haifa began withdrawing his
troops. He advised in advance the joint Haganah-Irgun command which
was poised to attack the Arab quarters of Haifa of his plans; he did not
advise Haifa's Arab leaders of his impending withdrawal.[87] The Zionist

85. Any researcher who has interviewed large numbers of Palestine Arab "refugees" has heard them describe the pandemonium, the sheer volume of *noise,* on the
night when they had to flee from a given city or town. I always assumed this was
retrospective exaggeration until reading Mr. Heiman's very professional, detailed
explanation "All's Fair . . .".
86. See, for example, Government of Israel, *Topics,* no. 3, 1961, p. 4.
87. For full evidence, see American University Beirut, *Middle East Forum* (December, 1959).

attack then began, not only to seize key Arab buildings but to launch what Zionist historians have called "a psychological blitz."[88] We may also turn to Arthur Koestler:

> Haganah was using not only its radio station but its loudspeaker vans, which blared their sinister news from the vicinity of the Arab suqs. They warned the Arab population to keep clear of the billets of the foreign mercenaries who had infiltrated the town, warned them to send their women and children away before any new contingents of savage Iraqis arrived, promised them safe conducts and escorts to Arab territory, and hinted at terrible consequences if their warnings were disregarded.[89]

At sundown that first day, the Zionists launched their full attack— the Davidka mortars lobbed indiscriminately from the Hadar ha-Carmel heights down into the packed Arab residential area; the barrel-bombs rolled down the alleys; machine-gun and rifle fire, loudspeaker "news," and horror-recordings rent the air—on an Arab population who had seen the British withdrawing their troops and who had only rudimentary volunteer defenses of their own.

> The Arab nerve broke shortly after dark, and the flight from the town assumed panic proportions even before general fighting had started. . . .

> The Arabs had left in great panic: I walked later through the suq and saw the state of disorder in which they had left their homes, often not bothering to pick up silver and valuables.[90]

The Irgun leader has written that Arabs fled actually crying out "Deir Yassin!" which had happened only twelve days earlier.[91] They could only flee in one direction: as the Zionist *Jerusalem Post* openly reported the next day about the exodus, it was an offensive "forcing them to flee by the only open escape route—the sea."[92] The flight to the harbor down the narrow

---

88. Kimche, *Seven Fallen Pillars*, p. 219.

89. Koestler, *Promise and Fulfillment*, p. 207; note here a well-known technique to create civilian distrust of defending troops: in this instance, Iraqi volunteer resistance fighters.

90. Kimche, *Seven Fallen Pillars*, p. 229; see also Sacher, *Israel*, p. 243; O'Ballance, *Arab–Israeli War*, p. 52.

91. Begin, *The Revolt*, p. 165.

92. April 23, 1948.

lanes, with children and older people being trampled to death and drowning in overloaded boats, was accompanied by clearly directed Zionist firing on them.[93]

The Arab Committee of Haifa asked to meet with the British commander, who refused until the following morning when he told them that he would assist with a truce, only to return ten minutes later with a printed copy of Zionist *surrender* terms.[94] At a meeting that second afternoon, the Zionist military delegates insisted on unconditional surrender; the British general, Stockwell, warned the Arabs to accept it, saying he would not be responsible for the likely hundreds more Arab deaths. It was *then* that Mayor Levi made his anguished appeal to the Arabs to stay—some 20 hours after the Arab panic exodus had already begun, 22 hours after surrounding Zionist forces had begun their "blitz." It may be seen that this is somewhat different from the common suggestion that the Arabs of Haifa were asked to stay but "left under their own leaders' orders."[95]

Jaffa was the next big Arab city to fall and be emptied, and it too has been the subject of special Israeli government quotations to advance the claim that the Palestinians left on their own leaders' orders. The standard quotation for Jaffa, printed in official Israeli literature, consists of the following sentence:

> When the Arab municipal leaders of Jaffa asked the Syrian Minister of Defence for arms, they received a negative reply, coupled with strong advice to leave the town, and definite assurances that it would soon be liberated by the Arab armies.[96]

Printed by itself, as one of a series of such quotations under an introductory paragraph asserting the "Arab orders" explanation of the exodus, a quotation like this does appear to be convincing, especially when attributed to an Arab. The words, and the preceding and subsequent brief quotations, all seem to reinforce the editorial assertion that the Arabs need not have evacuated—that Zionist leaders pleaded with them to stay,

93. Wilson, *Cordon and Search,* p. 193.

94. He refused to mediate; full details can be found in American University Beirut, *Middle East Forum* (December, 1959).

95. Later that day, having submitted to surrender, the Arab Committee asked the British for ambulances and for cover against Zionist gunfire to facilitate the mass exodus already begun. This request is also frequently made over by Israeli tracts into an "Arab evacuation order." By April 24, between 50,000 and 70,000 Haifa Arabs had fled to Acre and Lebanon.

96. See Government of Israel, *Topics,* no. 3, 1961.

but that, without Zionist pressure upon them, they fled when ordered to by their own leaders.

Reference to the source of the above quotation, *Shikreyat Suhugi Mudtahad* by Hashim al-Saba, discloses that the following is what the author *actually* wrote:

> When we visited the Syrian Minister of Defence, Ahmad Bey Sharabati, at his home, he began to explain to us with all frankness the hopelessness and impossibility of defending Jaffa militarily, as it was surrounded by Jews on all sides and keeping it would require a big army and a safe line of communication. Therefore, he would advise the population of Jaffa to leave their city as its fall had become imminent.

Jaffa had been attacked on April 25, first by units of the Irgun (the force that had moved into Deir Yassin two weeks earlier) which were then joined by units of the official Haganah. When the Arab municipal delegation asked Syria for arms, it was *following* this Zionist attack, the character of which has been described quite fully by a Zionist historian:

> The great bombardment of Jaffa was started with 3-inch mortars which the Irgun had "captured" a few weeks earlier in a raid on a British camp. . . . This bombardment started a panic among the Jaffa Arabs. . . .

> The Irgun activities in Jaffa also extended to yet another field. For the first time in the still undeclared war a Jewish force commenced to loot in wholesale fashion. . . . Everything that was movable was carried from Jaffa [and] what could not be taken away was smashed.[97]

Psychological warfare was employed against Jaffa's civilian Arab population, as against other Arab cities and towns—barrel-bombs; panic incitement by radio; loudspeaker vans;[98] and, as after Deir Yassin, the parading of Arab prisoners before Jewish crowds.[99] Arab villages surrounding Jaffa were seized, their inhabitants expelled, and the villages destroyed.[100] The same Zionist historian who described Irgun conduct at Jaffa has added,

97. Kimche, *Seven Fallen Pillars,* p. 233.

98. Heiman explictly names Jaffa as one of the cities where the barrel-bomb technique was used and mentions the "horror sounds" ("All's Fair . . .").

99. Haganah Radio, April 28, 1948, 1800 hours reported that "The Jaffa population is alarmed and is deserting . . . the general situation is chaotic"; the prisoners were blindfolded, according to Kimche (*Seven Fallen Pillars,* p. 233).

100. Avneri, *Le Monde,* May 9, 1964.

it was perhaps natural, though it was certainly detestable, that before
long the rest of the Jewish soldiers, of the Haganah and the Palmach,
should join in the orgy of looting and wanton destruction which hangs
like a black pall over almost all the Jewish military successes.[101]

It was after an attack such as this that Hashim al-Saba described the
Arab delegation being advised by the Syrian minister to evacuate the city
"as its fall had become imminent." The Arab garrison in Jaffa hung on
for three weeks, until surrender of the city became inevitable on May 12.
By that date, only 3,000 out of Jaffa's normal Arab population of over
70,000 remained in the city, which was in the proposed Arab-, not Jewish-,
state area of the partition.

Two days after the attack on Jaffa began, Zionist forces launched an
assault on the ancient fortress city of Acre, also supposed to be in the
Arab-state partition area. Acre was packed with thousands of refugees from
Haifa; over 80,000 civilians were jammed like sardines inside the fortress
walls. The attack was begun by heavy mortar-shelling into this mass of
civilians; the Zionist commander then demanded surrender. Acre is named
by both Nathan Chofshi and Major O'Ballance as one of the cities that
experienced Zionist expulsion methods. On May 17, the city was occupied
by the Zionists, with only 2,000 Arabs, mostly old men and children, left
out of over 80,000. Acre is also the subject of a standard official Israeli
quotation worked along the same lines as that for Jaffa.

The exodus from eastern Galilee began with the seizure and emptying
of Tiberias, again using barrel-bombs and loudspeakers with "horror
sounds."[102] On April 28, when British troops were pulled out of Safad,
Palmach units started up the road from Tiberias, seizing and physically
destroying all Arab villages along the way—the operation being code-
named *Matateh* (broom).[103] Safad was then attacked with barrel-bombs,
Davidka mortars, house-to-house dynamiting, and the atom-bomb loudspeaker message.[104] From these beginnings, the Palmach commander has
since written, "we saw a need to clean the inner Galilee," as economically
as possible, "to cause the tens of thousands of sulky Arabs who remained
in Galilee to flee." He then describes how he arranged this:

101. Kimche, *Seven Fallen Pillars,* pp. 233–34.
102. Heiman, "All's Fair."
103. Lorch, *Edge of the Sword,* p. 103.
104. See Heiman, "All's Fair . . ."; Sacher, *Israel;* Lorch, *Edge of the Sword.*
Koestler writes that Safad's Arabs left everything behind, "the last cup of coffee
half drunk in the tiny china cup" (*Promise and Fulfillment,* p. 215).

I gathered all of the Jewish Mukhtars, who have contact with Arabs in different villages, and asked them to whisper in the ears of some Arabs that a great Jewish reinforcement had arrived in Galilee and that it was going to burn all the villages of the Huleh. They should suggest to these Arabs, as their friends, to escape while there is still time. And the rumor spread in all the areas of the Huleh that it was time to flee. The flight numbered myriads.[105]

From Safad and from the "finger of Galilee," some 50,000 more Arabs thus became "refugees" by the time the crucial moment of the end of British authority arrived. On May 15, 1948, the official Israel Proclamation of Independence included a call to "the sons of the Arab people dwelling in Israel to keep the peace and to play their part in the development of the State, with full and equal citizenship." Citing this call, official Israeli literature asserts that appeals of this kind were broadcast to the Palestinians "through every available means of communication (radio, handbills, sound trucks)." On May 15, however, in Jerusalem, the Jewish writer Harry Levin wrote down in his diary what he heard the Zionist sound trucks calling:

Nearby a loudspeaker burst out in Arabic: Haganah, broadcasting to Arabs urging them to leave the district before 5:15 A.M. "Take pity on your wives and children and get out of this bloodbath. . . . Get out by the Jericho road, that is still open to you. If you stay, you invite disaster."[106]

As of May 15, and the entrance into Palestine of the Arab states' forces, the third major phase of the 1948 war began. There were already over 300,000 Palestine Arab "refugees" in the Jordan Valley, in Lebanon, and in Syria. Now, according to some frank Zionist accounts, there was indeed "encouragement" of flight by the Zionist forces. (It will have been noted that the methods used by the Zionists to obtain mass flight in the pre-May 15 second phase above, where not so obvious as to attract indisputable international notice.) Major O'Ballance, the British war historian, has described the new phase as follows:

105. Yigael Alon, *Ha sepher ha Palmach* [The book of the Palmach], II, 286; this revealing Hebrew war history includes a map showing the actual routes of flight of the civilian Arabs into Lebanon and Syria.
106. *Jerusalem Embattled* (London, 1950), p. 160.

No longer was there any "reasonable persuasion." Bluntly, the Arab inhabitants were ejected and forced to flee into Arab territory, as at Ramleh, Lydda, and other places. Wherever the Israeli troops advanced into Arab country, the Arab population was bulldozed out in front of them.[107]

On July 11, 1948, Moshe Dayan led a jeep commando column into the town of Lydda "with rifles, Stens, and sub-machine guns blazing. It coursed through the main streets, blasting at everything that moved . . . the corpses of Arab men, women, and even children were strewn about the streets in the wake of this ruthlessly brilliant charge."[108] Next day, the adjoining town of Ramle was seized. All Arab men of military age were rounded up and penned into special enclosures. Israeli loudspeaker vans then toured the two towns announcing that neither food nor water would be provided and that the Arabs had 48 hours to get out to Transjordan. Israeli troops then began sacking both towns.[109] On July 13, the loudspeakers gave final orders, naming the Kubah and the Hindas bridges as the exodus routes for Ramle and Lydda respectively.

There were between 75,000 and 100,000 civilian Palestine Arabs involved (no one can know precise figures: both towns' combined population of 65,000 was swollen with refugees from other Arab areas already seized and emptied). As they began their exodus out of the twin towns across the prescribed bridges, in the words of the London *Economist,* "the Arab refugees were systematically stripped of all their belongings before they were sent on their trek to the frontier. Household belongings, stores, clothing, all had to be left behind."[110]

As the long lines began their walk, Israeli troops fired bursts at and over them. According to Major O'Ballance, "some Israeli mortars opened up, to help them on their way."[111] The temperature was a hundred degrees in the shade. The Arabs had had neither water nor food for three days: if any had food left, it too was taken from them at the bridges.[112] Small Israeli planes buzzed the long files of expellees as they trudged up into the hills. Countless children died outright of thirst.[113] Eventually, most reached the Judaean

107. *Arab-Israeli War,* pp. 171–72.

108. Kenneth Bilby, *New Star in the Near East* (New York, 1950), p. 43; Bilby (New York *Herald Tribune* correspondent) entered Lydda the second day.

109. Kimche and Kimche, *Both Sides of the Hill,* p. 228.

110. August 21, 1948.

111. *Arab-Israeli War,* p. 147.

112. Detailed accounts to the writer by survivors of the march.

113. For eyewitness descriptions of mothers dropping dead babies in the bushes, see Sir John Glubb, *A Soldier with the Arabs* (London, 1957), p. 162.

Heights, the Jordan Valley, or the hills of Transjordan, where they have been ever since.

Further south, in the Falouja "pocket," a serving officer of the Israel Army Engineering Corps has given me his eyewitness account of what happened to that area's Arabs. Falouja town was taken after the Egyptian forces there surrendered. The Arab inhabitants were asked whether they wished to leave or to stay. They said they would stay. Thereupon, several of their houses were dynamited, and they were warned that the main Israeli force coming would treat them much more roughly. The Arabs then "changed their minds," and were transported out of the area to Transjordan.

In wide areas of their occupation, the Zionist forces acted quickly to create a *fait accompli*—either by putting new settlers into Arab houses and farms or by destroying the houses entirely.[114] By the end of 1948, Herzl's terse outline plan for removing the "penniless population" by "denying it any employment" had been given new meaning in policy officially enunciated by the state of Israel. In a letter dated August 1, 1948, to U.N. mediator Count Bernadotte, Israel's Foreign Minister Shertok denied the Arabs any right of return. He naturally pleaded issues of security. But he significantly added to these reasons, the following:

> On the economic side, the reintegration of the returning Arabs into normal life, and even their mere sustenance, would present an insuperable problem. The difficulties of accommodation, employment, and ordinary livelihood would be insuperable.[115]

There was, of course, no reason why there should be any such insuperable difficulty—assuming that the land, homes, businesses, and jobs of the expelled Arabs were returned to them. They owned or had inhabited roughly 80 per cent of the entire Zionist-occupied land area of Palestine (as of the end of 1948). The Arabs had raised, and owned, over 50 per cent of all the citrus orchards of the area the Zionists had occupied; over 90 per cent of the olive groves; 10,000 shops, stores, and other firms; and dwellings which, as late as 1954, were housing more than one-third of the Israeli population.[116]

Mr. Shertok's letter was drafted within two weeks of the bayonet-point expulsion of the 75,000 to 100,000 Palestine Arabs in the Lydda-Ramle

---

114. Bilby, *New Star*, p. 231; Harold A. Lehrman, *Israel: The Beginning and Tomorrow* (New York, 1952); and the *Economist* (London), August 21, 1948.

115. United Nations, Security Council, *Official Records*, Suppl. 108 (S/949), August, 1948, pp. 106–9.

116. Don Peretz, *Israel and the Palestine Arabs* (Washington, D.C., 1958).

area. The non-Zionist student of Palestine may therefore be excused from assuming that Shertok's all-encompassing economic projections of difficulty in reintegrating Palestine's Arabs had been made long before. Equally, it is difficult to accept the adjective in Chaim Weizmann's statement in 1949, to the new U.S. ambassador to Israel, that the Arab exodus had provided "a miraculous simplification of Israel's tasks."[117]

A NEW MYTHOLOGY

In 1895, Herzl had foreseen the necessity to remove the penniless population "discreetly and circumspectly." The 1948 efforts of his successors were not very discreet, nor were they circumspect, not even in the pre-April first phase. But it is notable and significant that Western reportage on the Arab exodus in 1948 was very sparing as to its organized causes: I have talked to many correspondents who were in Palestine in 1948 and who say that they reported some of the Zionist methods, "but these parts never seemed to get past the sub-editor back home." Far more significant, however, is the organized effort by the Israeli government, since 1949, to "cover" what was done to the Arabs by assertions, the quality of which is quite astonishingly mendacious when tested to the source.

Some examples of the official Israeli "evidence" of alleged Arab "evacuation orders" have already been cited. One of the earliest, which quite clearly influenced a group of distinguished Americans who presented a memorandum to the U.N. on the refugees in late 1951,[118] was a quotation from the Greek-Catholic archbishop of Galilee. From 1951 onward, the archbishop appears in virtually every official Israeli tract, in most of the annual Israeli statements to the United Nations on the Palestine refugees, and in countless books circulating throughout the world. The quotation of his so widely used is as follows, from a small Lebanese journal, *Sada al-Janub,* on August 16, 1948:

> The refugees had been confident that their absence from Palestine would not last long; that they would return within a few days—within a week or two. Their leaders had promised them that the Arab armies would crush the Zionist gangs very quickly and that there would be no need for panic or fear of a long exile.

It will be noted that this statement does not, in fact, allege that the Arab leaders ordered Palestine civilians to evacuate. But when used immediately

117. Cited in James G. McDonald, *My Mission to Israel, 1948–1951* (New York, 1951).

118. Signatories included Dr. Reinhold Niebuhr, Archibald Macleish, and other famous public figures; see the *Nation,* CLXXIII (December 29, 1951), 563–66; *New York Times,* December 20, 1951.

after an editorial assertion of such orders, after such bridging phrases as "contemporary statements fully confirm this appraisal,"[119] the effect of the words of the archbishop is almost subliminal—he does seem to be saying that there were official Arab evacuation orders.

I wrote directly to the same archbishop in Israel in 1958 asking for whatever primary and documentary evidence His Grace could provide for the official Arab evacuation orders which he was so widely quoted as confirming. The archbishop's reply, on official Archbishopric letterhead from Haifa, dated December 4, 1958, was as follows:

> There is nothing in this statement to justify the construction which many propagandists had put on it, namely, that it established the allegation widely disseminated by partisan sources that the Arab leaders had urged the Arab inhabitants of Palestine to flee.
>
> So far as I can recollect, the aforesaid statement was intended to voice the strong feeling of resentment and revulsion felt by the refugees. They were convinced by what they had heard and read that the defeat of the Jewish armed forces, the re-establishment of peace and order throughout the country, and the institution of Arab rule, would be achieved within a short time. Instead of such achievements the Arab States had twice agreed to a truce, and the Arab armies were inactive. Hence the strong feeling of disappointment and frustration among the file and rank of the refugees.
>
> At no time did I state that the flight of the refugees was due to the orders, explicit or implicit, of their leaders, military or political, to leave the country and seek shelter in the adjacent Arab territories. On the contrary, no such orders were ever made by the military commanders, or by the Higher Arab Committee, or, indeed, by the Arab League or Arab States. I have not the least doubt that any such allegations are sheer concoctions and falsifications.
>
> The truth is that the flight was primarily due to the terror with which the Arab population of Palestine were struck in consequence of atrocities committed by the Jews, i.e. the Deir Yassin massacre, the brutal throwing of bombs at a large group of innocent Arab workmen assembled at the outer gates of the Refineries near Haifa, the dastardly night attack on Balad Al-Sheik village in the vicinity of Haifa and other similar onslaughts. These brutalities were the cause of the flight of the inhabitants of Haifa, Jaffa, and Jerusalem.
>
> But as soon as hostilities began between Israel and the Arab States, it became the settled policy of the Government to drive away the Arabs

---

119. Israel's Abba-Eban, introducing the quote to U.N. Special Political Committee, November 27, 1957.

of the localities which its forces occupied, notably, Ramleh and Lydda and all the villages around them.

> Yours faithfully,
> [signed] G. Hakim
> Archibishop of Galilee

Another quotation used perennially by official Israeli spokesmen, and in virtually all official publications, is a statement attributed to Mr. Emile Ghoury. Again, the method of presenting this quotation as evidence, indeed Arab admission, of Arab evacuation orders has been to state that "an even more candid avowal came on 15 September 1948 from Mr. Emile Ghoury, who had been the Secretary of the Arab Higher Committee at the time of the invasion of Israel":[120]

> I do not want to impugn anyone but only to help the refugees. The fact that there are these refugees is the direct consequence of the action of the Arab States in opposing partition and the Jewish State. The Arab States agreed upon this policy unanimously and they must share in the solution of the problem.

The quotation not only appears—again, when suitably introduced—to confess Arab evacuation orders, it also appears to blame the Arab states in that they opposed partition at all, and it is consistently used by official Israeli spokesmen further to suggest that many Palestine Arab leaders want a "solution of the problem" in *resettlement,* in other Arab countries.

Study of the full, original text of Mr. Ghoury's statement indicates diametrically opposite and plain meaning in his words.[121] Nowhere in a long and very detailed statement did he so much as intimate that there had been official Arab evacuation orders. On the contrary, large parts of his statement which Israeli authorities do not choose to quote contain such descriptions as "the furnace of the Irgun, Stern, and Haganah" and, again, "their savage, bestial acts of which there are a thousand proofs." Specifically, the blunt intention of his statement was to lay responsibility upon the Arab states *for failing to protect the Palestine Arabs from being dispossessed.* The very next sentence in Mr. Ghoury's statement, after that used by Israel as quoted above, reads:

> The problem can never be solved practically and finally except by liberating those Palestine areas occupied by the Jews, so that the refugees can return to them.

120. *Ibid.*
121. The full text is in the Beirut newspaper *Telegraph,* August 6, 1948.

An exhaustive analysis, back to source, where source exists,[122] of all the "evidence" offered by the Israeli government as to Arab responsibility for the Arab exodus of 1948 reveals only more of this methodology. Again and again a slender quotation of one or two sentences attributed to some Arab source reveals blunt, yet skillful, use of "scissors and paste." Often, the original source also ironically provides more description of what really made the Arabs flee. For example, another standard official Israeli quote is from a book about the events of 1948 by Nimr al-Khatib, *Min Athar al-Nakba* [In the wake of the disaster]. It is illustrative to set down the Israeli quotation beside the original statement. As in the internationally used "Jaffa quote" and the "Acre quote" (as the student soon begins to call these standard items in the Israeli lexicon), this "Tira quote" demonstrates a deliberate effort to cite alleged official Arab evacuation orders to civilians who were not threatened in any way.

Israeli Quote	*Original Text*
One day there appeared in the village of Tira an Arab Legion [Jordan Army] officer representing the Legion's unit which was stationed 3 kilometres from the village. . . . The officer declared that he had come to supervise their [the villagers'] evacuation.	About 3 kilometres from the village an Arab Legion unit was stationed. While the villagers were engaged in a continuous struggle against the enemy, the officer of the unit with some of his men came to the village. Their presence raised the hopes and morale of the villagers as they thought they had come to help them or give them arms; they were, however, flabbergasted when the officer asked them to leave with an Arab Legion convoy. This conversation with the Jordanian officer had a most devastating effect on some of the villagers who panicked and joined the Arab Legion convoy. Yet others refused to accept the request and decided to remain in the village and fight to the death (p. 321).

122. In a number of instances, quotations offered from Arab newspapers are found not to exist at all, not even for suitable "reworking." An example is a much-used quote from *Falastin* for February 19, 1949; that was a Monday. *Falastin* was never printed on Mondays, and no such statement could be found anywhere in the paper on proximate other dates.

Tira village (sometimes *Tireh)* had *already* been repeatedly attacked by Zionist forces—the Israeli quotation carefully scissors away Nimr al-Khatib's reference to such prior "continuous struggle with the enemy." His actual description of what happened, as quoted above, is authentic and human. In many besieged places in Palestine, Arab military officers judged resistance hopeless, while Palestine civilians expected better of them. Nimr al-Khatib, on the same page from which the Israeli "Tira quote" has been scissored, describes the village being shelled, bombed, and machine-gunned. He also describes a night attack in which Zionist forces dynamited and petrol-incinerated the men, women, and children to death.[123]

If once the task of investigating all such Israeli quotations is undertaken, the impression evolves overwhelmingly that officials in Israel have searched Arab books and speeches for almost any single sentence which could be scissored out of context and presented as "Arab statements . . . avowals . . . admissions . . . confirmation." The well-known writer Edward Atiyah discussed the origins of the Arab exodus in some frank detail in his book, *The Arabs.*[124] In 1961 Professor Leo Kohn of Hebrew University, an official adviser to the Israeli Foreign Office, wrote an article in the London *Spectator* seeking to rebut my presentation of the researched causes of the exodus. Dr. Kohn stated, "there is also a wealth of evidence from Arab sources to show that the Arab League at an early stage of the campaign adopted a policy of evacuating the Arab population to the neighbouring countries."[125] What Dr. Kohn then immediately quoted thereunder from Mr. Atiyah's book is the sentence in italic type below. The preceding and following sentences of Mr. Atiyah clearly did not seem very suitable to Dr. Kohn's purpose:

"Seven or eight hundred thousand of the total Arab population of Palestine (of one-and-a-quarter millions) fled from the country or were driven out into Jordan, Lebanon, Syria and Egypt. *This wholesale exodus was partly due to the belief of the Arabs, encouraged by the boastings of an unrealistic Arabic press and the irresponsible utterances of some of the Arab leaders, that it could only be a matter of weeks before the Jews were defeated by the armies of the Arab states and the Palestinian Arabs enabled to re-enter and retake possession of their country.* But it was also, and in many parts of the country, largely due to a policy of deliberate terrorism and eviction followed by the Jewish commanders

123. The quotation may be found in Government of Israel, *The Arab Refugees—Arab Statements and the Facts* (Jerusalem, 1961).

124. (London, 1955).

125. June 16, 1961.

in the areas they occupied, and reaching its peak of brutality in the massacre of Deir Yassin.[126]

One interesting further feature of Israeli material may be mentioned. As was clearly hoped, over time in the years since 1949 many Western writers and even institutions have accepted the Israeli explanation of the exodus and have published it as their own assessment. In more recent years, official Israeli use of such ostensibly detached Western analysis of the causes of the exodus can be discerned—a kind of "closed-circuit" technique, giving undoubted further acceptability to the mythology of Arab "evacuation orders" and Zionist appeals to the Arabs to stay.[127]

It has not been the purpose of this essay to make projections into the future of Palestine or of its Arab population. Israeli expulsions of Arabs from Israeli-controlled territory have continued since the 1949 armistices, and up to 1959 numbered some further 10,000 people according to detailed U.N. Mixed Armistice Commission and Truce Supervision Organization reports.[128] Set against the documentary record going back to Theodor Herzl, however, the frank revelations of Jon and David Kimche writing in *Both Sides of the Hill* in 1960 cannot but seem prophetic. Mention has already been made of their description, in a book publicly endorsed by Mr. Ben-Gurion, of one of the last planned Zionist military operations for the 1948 war—"Operation Shin-Tav-Shin," to seize the whole of eastern Palestine to the banks of the River Jordan.

The Kimches relate that Shin-Tav-Shin was called off in 1948. In their discussion of the circumstances, a clause concerning what might apparently have been involved for the civilian Palestine Arabs of the eastern triangle stands out in bold relief. This is how the Kimches describe the cancellation of Shin-Tav-Shin, or perhaps postponement is a better term:

However, as the preparations for the offensive reached their climax, there were some serious second thoughts among the Israeli political and

126. Pp. 182–83.

127. For example Israeli use of the *1957 Bulletin* of the Research Group for European Migration as "a recent survey by an international authority." Analysis of the *Bulletin* study shows very clearly that its authors, who admit that the study is "based on literature research, not on field work," relied heavily on Israeli sources. Naturally, the key quotation is that of the Greek-Catholic archbishop of Galilee. See also Israeli use of *Regional Development for Regional Peace* (Washington, D.C., 1958); the Arab-refugee section of this publication contains almost all the stock Israeli quotations.

128. U.N. documents S/1797, S/2388, S/1907, S/3343, S/2300, S/PV/635, S/2084, S/2111, S/2157, S/2185, S/2213, S/2234, S/2389, S/2833.

military leaders: perhaps, it occurred to them, they might be tempting
fate once too often. They had been extremely fortunate after the October
offensive, and again after the December attack. They had enjoyed both
military successes and a favourable world opinion—a novel and refresh-
ing experience for them. Why risk this happy state on the uncertainties
of yet another military operation, *which would greatly intensify the
Arab refugee problem?*

"Shin-Tav-Shin" was cancelled. . . . But this unfinished battle has haunted
the Palestine situation ever since. It has returned to the international
scene time and again, but it has never been decided. "Shin-Tav-Shin" was
the last element in the first round; it remained the unsolved element of
the second round. It had not been removed by Israel's Sinai operation.[129]

129. Pp. 267–68, 272 (italics added); the reference to the Sinai campaign is not
that of 1948–49, but that of 1956.

PART III

Palestinian Resistance under the Mandate

The troubles impending for the British colonial administration of Palestine, like those of the French in Syria and Lebanon, were not unanticipated. Whatever may have been the particular configurations of the trouble in Palestine proper, it was recognized from 1919 onward, if not earlier, that the impending fragmentation of the Fertile Crescent into those countries that became known as Iraq, Syria, Lebanon, Transjordan, and Palestine and the containment of the Arab nationalist movement that sought political independence in that area would inevitably produce a relationship of hostility between the occupiers and the occupied. Having successfully denied the people of the Fertile Crescent countries the right of self-determination and independence, the two powers, Britain and France, delimited the areas that they wished to control, obtained a general European sanction for that control under a mandate system, and governed each as a more or less self-contained unit. It is within that context that we could properly speak of a specific geographic-political unit as mandated Palestine.

The reaction to the military occupation and the imposition of the mandate system was as to be expected: resistance that had to be crushed by military force, whether by the French in Syria-Lebanon or by the British in Iraq and Palestine. But unlike previous periods, the resistance had acquired a particular territorial, "national" form. Hence one speaks of the Syrian, Lebanese, Iraqi, or Palestinian nationalist resistance. Each, while not giving up the hope of an ultimate reintegration of the units, sought the independence from colonial control of its newly defined administrative area. But Palestine, unlike the other units which waged struggles only against colonial administrations, had to contend with a colonial power that was committed to a program of foreign settlement *on the land. The Palestinians therefore had to articulate their aspirations and concert their action in terms of the twin threat which they perceived to their national existence. Again unlike the other nationalist movements, the Palestinian nationalist resistance has not received the attention of scholars. This is, of course, surprising. If for no other reason save that armed resistance was much fiercer in Palestine than elsewhere, scholars should have been alerted to the disastrous implications of the events in Palestine beginning with 1921 when the Palestinian population reacted forcefully against the British colonial administration. Even today there is no serious, comprehensive study of the rise and fall of the Palestinian resistance during the mandate period. There are comments, hints, and an occasional narration, but a study of the totality of the Palestinian resistance—the way by which the national energy of the Palestinians was harnessed and the methods employed in handling it by the British colonial administration—awaits a competent scholar able to analyze it against the specific background of Palestine itself and in its wider context. Such a work would of course have to rely on the extensive and still extant, but undigested, Arabic sources. What follows in this section are studies of two important aspects of that resistance and of one method utilized by the mandatory power in dealing with it.*

David Waines, Fellow of the Institute of Islamic Studies at McGill University and author of The Unholy War: Israel and Palestine, *critically analyzes the resistance to British occupation of, and Zionist aspiration for, Palestine and assesses the factors that combined to defeat that resistance throughout the period of the mandate. Not only does he demonstrate the clearly anticolonial thrust of the Palestinian resistance but he analyzes the slow process of national cohesion obtained among the Palestinians as colonial repression gradually intensified. The internal fissures of the Palestinian nationalist movement, so evident in the 1930s, and the divergence, which contributed significantly to the success of the colonial effort, between a basically conservative leadership led by the mufti of Jerusalem and a more militant mass base are analyzed against the background of increasing regionalization and internationalization of the conflict in Palestine.*

Whereas Waines's essay deals with the major events during the entire period, Miss Barbara Kalkas, a Social Change Fellow at Northwestern University whose concern with political sociology has led her to an examination of the alteration of the class system in twentieth-century Egypt, addresses herself to a major revolt of the Palestinians, specifically to the six-month general strike and coordinated civil disobedience of the Palestinians in 1936. Her case study demonstrates the coincidence of interest that occurred at this time between the leadership and the masses and reveals in exacting detail the strategies employed in suppressing the rebellion. With the conclusion of the 1936 strike and revolt, Palestinian armed resistance to the British colonial administration and to Zionism effectively came to an end, although that was not so perceived at the time: the entire leadership of the Palestinian people was imprisoned or exiled, the organized and semiorganized political parties were outlawed, and the very stiff "defense" regulations promulgated by the British administration became fully operational.

Both essays capture the essence of the dramatic change in Palestine which occurred as a consequence of the forceful handling of the organized Palestinian resistance. The gradual mediation of the semi-independent Arab states prompted by their British patrons enabled them to play a more dominant, but negative, role in Palestinian affairs. The increasing strength of the Zionists in Palestine—epitomized by the increasing population, settlements, institutions, and an infrastructure—projected them by the late 1930s onto the Palestinian scene as a primary protagonist of the Palestinians. Thus by the late 1930s the conflict in Palestine began to appear as one increasingly between the two communities with the British administration playing the role of the maligned umpire, impelled by its own contradictory judgments and policies to use repression differentially against both communities.

Suppression cannot work forever; some kind of accommodation, compromise, and minimal satisfaction of grievances had to be tried. That was true in Palestine as elsewhere. The British fully appreciated, though were unable to act on that knowledge, that the Palestinians would not acquiesce to the fates envisaged for them by either the mandate administration or the Zionists. As in modern America, when the explosion finally occurs responsible governments hasten to appoint commissions to investigate the "causes" of the outbreak and to offer remedies—which most frequently are ignored. Confronted with perennial upheavals in Palestine that required large outlays of funds and the deployment of British military forces for their suppression and that caused considerable disruption to civilian life, and mindful of international pressures, responsibilities, and exertions of other powers, Britain appointed and dispatched "commissions of inquiry" to investigate what was referred to euphemistically as the "disturbances" that were endemic to the Palestine scene.

These commissions put forth their appreciation of the real, as well as the imaginary, causes of these "disturbances." Often they identified the underlying motives of the "disturbers" of peace whether in terms of the persistent effort of the mandate administration in denying the Palestinians' right to self-determination, or the mandate's facilitation of the establishment of the Jewish national home, or the increasing economic dislocations suffered by the Palestinians. Sometimes, by their emphasis, they implied that the Palestinian "disturbances" reflected the basic incompatibilities of two nationalisms whose aspirations had to be satisfied, but separately. They also offered constructive suggestions that, had they been implemented, would have resolved to some extent the sources of the conflict in Palestine. While these commissions were a result of British concern for "law and order" in Palestine, subsequent to the Second World War an expansion in the national orientation of these commissions occurred in response to the growing concern of other powers with the events in Palestine. Richard N. Verdery, Assistant Professor of History at the Institute of Islamic Studies at McGill University, is a historian of the modern Middle East whose previous contributions have appeared in the Journal of the American Oriental Society. *In his essay he chronicles, analyzes, and summarizes the findings of the British commissions of inquiry, paying particular attention to their background, the circumstances of their assessments, and the eventual disregard of their conclusions.*

7. The Failure of the Nationalist Resistance

David Waines

The six explosive days of June, 1967, altered more than the political map of Israel. The war unleashed political forces in the area on a scale which most observers had not foreseen and which even now are impossible to assess in terms of their impact upon future events. The rapid development of the Palestinian resistance movement marks a new stage in the reemergence of the Palestinians within the broader Arab-Israeli conflict. In the popular Palestinian view, the current guerrilla campaigns are the direct continuation of their struggle for national liberation waged during the years of the British mandate (1920–48), although it would be more accurate to say they mark the resumption of that struggle.

For nearly a decade after the war of 1948, the Palestinian people demonstrated an understandable, albeit uncharacteristic, passivity toward their fate; military defeat and the destruction of the fabric of their society forced Palestinians to adjust either to varying degrees and forms of statelessness or to citizenship in the new Israeli state. The Palestinian leaders, in defeat and disgrace, were content to seek the protection of individual Arab governments, or the collective patronage of the Arab League through which the Palestinian cause continued to be sponsored on the international scene.

The Suez crisis of 1956 ignited a spark of activism among Palestinian Arabs, and in the aftermath of that war, the nucleus of the Fatah movement was created. Nationalist pressure in Jordan mounted against King Husayn during the troubled months of 1957, led largely by Palestinians who constituted the majority of the kingdom's population. Later, in 1964, Palestinian activism was inadvertently reinforced by the Arab League's establishment of the Palestine Liberation Organization.[1] Meanwhile, in

1. Malcolm Kerr, *The Arab Cold War, 1958–1967: A Study of Ideology in Politics* (2d ed; New York, 1967), p. 151.

Israel itself, the Palestinian minority was rapidly becoming politicized. Israeli-Arab literati shifted their emphasis from dialogue and cooperation with their Jewish compatriots toward the confrontation between Zionism and Arab nationalism, while the poets expressed their community's growing sense of alienation from the Israeli government and from the country as a whole.[2] The years between Suez and the June war have, in fact, emphatically confirmed the observation made by Albert Hourani in 1958 that the most urgent problem of Palestine is "that of a whole community which wishes to go on living as a community."[3] The popular image of the continuing struggle for the liberation of their colonized and conquered land is thus a vivid reflection of the Palestinians' vision of their common fate and destiny.

The image, moreover, focuses on the fact that the mandate period was one of almost uninterrupted effort by Palestinians to establish a sovereign and independent state. The true character of this effort has, however, unfortunately been obscured by much subsequent historiography dealing with the period. The confusion over the nature of the nationalist movement in Palestine derives from the failure to identify precisely the nature of the forces operating within the total power profile, the dynamics of which produced what was, undoubtedly, a situation unique in the annals of colonialism and imperialism.

The source of this confusion may be illustrated by an example drawn from each of two different perspectives on the mandate years. While few writers have denied outright the presence of a genuine Arab nationalist movement in Palestine,[4] more frequent is the implicit denial that it was anti colonialist. This will depend upon the point of view adopted toward Zionism. Thus, one scholar has recently noted that "during the past seventy-five years an Israeli nation has been forged in the fires of struggle *no different* from that of nations all over Afro-Asia."[5] Although the writer is silent concerning the existence of a Palestinian nationalist movement, he also removes the ideological and politico-economic aspects of Zionism from the European colonial imperial context of which it was an integral

---

2. Jacob Landau, *Arabs in Israel: A Political Study* (London, 1969), pp. 57–58.
3. "The Middle East and the Crisis of 1956," in *St. Antony's Papers,* no. 4, Middle Eastern Affairs, no. 1 (London, 1958), p. 35.
4. In his *Communism and Nationalism in the Middle East* (New York, 1956), Walter Laqueur quotes with approval (p. 96) the observation of John Marlowe, that the outbreak in Palestine in 1936 "was not a national movement in the sense that it commanded the active support of the majority of the Arabs in Palestine" (*Rebellion in Palestine* [London, 1946]); Marlowe's view, however, is somewhat modified in his more recent work, *The Seat of Pilate: An Account of the Palestine Mandate* (London, 1959), p. 132.
5. Michael Brecher, *The New States of Asia* (London, 1963), p. 123 (italics added).

part and from which it drew much early inspiration.[6] Similarly, the nature of the conflict between the Palestinians and the British was obscured by Whitehall's policy of a dual obligation, incumbent upon the mandatory regime, whereby both the Arab and the nascent Jewish communities would receive equal and impartial treatment. This frequently has resulted in an interpretation of the political history of the mandate as simply the struggle between two irreconcilable nationalisms, Arab and Jewish, the burden of responsibility for the course and ultimate failure of the mandate being adroitly moved from the shoulders of the mandatory power onto the backs of the two contending parties.[7] The crucial factor which this interpretation ignores is, of course, the imperial relationship between Britain and the Arabs of Palestine.[8]

6. Israeli writers are particularly sensitive to the "accusation" of the colonialist nature of Zionism, as for example, Y. Harkabi, who states "considerer le sionisme comme un avatar colonialiste est evidement une falsification" (*Le Conflit Israélo Arabe*, ed. Jean-Paul Sartre [Paris, 1967], p. 498). For a contrary and often brilliant analysis, see Nathan Weinstock, *Le Sionisme contre Israel* (Paris, 1969), p. 97 ff. It is worth recalling that in the early stages of the movement, Zionists frankly referred to their efforts as colonial. Explaining Zionism to a committee at the Paris Peace Conference, Chaim Weizmann cited the outstanding success of the French in Tunisia and said, "What the French could do in Tunisia, we could do in Palestine with Jewish will, Jewish money, Jewish power and Jewish enthusiasm" (*Trial and Error* [Philadelphia, 1949], p. 244).

7. The source of this interpretation may be traced to the reports of the various royal commissions to Palestine. The report of the Shaw Commission reduces the disturbances of August, 1929, to "racial animosity" between Jews and Arabs, while the outbreak "neither was nor was intended to be a revolt against British authority" (Great Britain, Colonial Office, Palestine, Commission on the Palestine Disturbances of August, 1929, *Report of the Commission* [Parliamentary Papers, Cmd. 3530; London, 1930], p. 149). The Peel Commission reported that the "disturbances" which commenced in April, 1936, were the outcome of "two nations warring within the bosom of a single state" and that the conflict was one fundamentally of right versus right (Great Britain, Colonial Office, Palestine, *Report of the Palestine Royal Commission* [Parliamentary Papers, Cmd. 5479; London, 1937], p. 2). Recent studies in which this interpretation is advanced include Christopher Sykes, *Cross Roads to Israel* (London, 1965) and Walter Laqueur, *The Road to War: The Origin of the Arab-Israeli Conflict, 1967–68* (London, 1969), pp. 18–19.

8. Albert Hourani has observed that from the creation of the mandate system in the Middle East "there sprang a new moral relationship between the West and the Arab peoples." The imposition of an alien rule upon an unwilling people is called imperialism, and "the essence of imperialism is to be found in a moral relationship—that of power and powerlessness—and any material consequences which spring from it are not enough to change it" ("The Decline of the West in the Middle East" in *The Modern Middle East,* ed. Richard Nolte [New York, 1963], pp. 39, 41). Imperialism is a much-used, and often abused, word; however, Hourani's definition reflects the usage of a then contemporary anti-imperialist, Herbert Spencer, who held that imperialism was the relationship of captive and the free which must therefore always depend upon the successful assertion of power which, Spencer believed, was a threat to the English liberal tradition (A. P. Thornton, *The Imperial Idea and its Enemies* [New York, 1968], p. 85).

"The moving finger writes, and having writ moves on" was an English-man's brilliant paraphrase of a Persian's poetic genius. Time may not be reversed, yet as long as the past pervades the present conflict over Palestine, an understanding of that conflict is ill-served either by neglect of its true origins or by distortion of the real nature of the competing forces within the power profile.

ZIONIST COLONIALISM

The pattern of conflict was taking shape in Palestine even as the clouds of war gathered over Europe in 1914. By contrast, bitter enmity in the land of three faiths would have seemed as farfetched a generation earlier as world war itself. Indeed, Zionism, except in the abstract, had nothing to do initially with either the Arabs or the Middle East. Zionists were pre-occupied with the menace of continental anti-Semitism which had reached virulent proportions during the final quarter of the last century. It was true that European colonialism/imperialism was, on the other hand, a painful reality to many peoples of the Arab world. France was firmly en-trenched in North Africa, and Great Britain had "temporarily" occupied Egypt in 1882 to secure the Suez Canal, the vital artery of the imperial lifeline joining Britain to Gibralter, Malta, Cyprus, Aden, and thence to India. Palestine, however, assumed little prominence in Britain's overseas concerns beyond a few rather fitful activities in the spheres of religion and education.[9] Nevertheless, by the end of the Great War, a bond had been forged between the Zionists and the strategists of British imperial policy; the attention of each was focused on Palestine, and the bond which linked their common purpose was the Balfour Declaration.

The intricate series of events leading to the Balfour Declaration of November, 1917, and culminating in the drafting of the mandate for Palestine has been recounted elsewhere in great wealth of detail.[10] It will be necessary here only to sketch briefly certain developments which shaped the power profile and determined the response of the Palestinians to Zionism and British domination.

Zionism had emerged in response to the "Jewish problem" in the medieval ghetto communities of Central and Eastern Europe, where ideals such as had affected Jewish emancipation in post-revolutionary France had

9. A. L. Tibawi, *British Interests in Palestine, 1800–1901* (London, 1961).

10. See especially, Leonard Stein, *The Balfour Declaration* (New York, 1961); and Esco Foundation for Palestine, *Palestine: A Study of Jewish, Arab and British Policies*, 2 vols. (New Haven, 1947), I, 55–118.

failed to take root. The first coherent Zionist statement of the Jewish problem and its proposed solution appeared in 1882 when a small pamphlet entitled *Auto-Emancipation* was published anonymously by Leo Pinsker.[11] The violent pogroms in Russia the previous year drove Pinsker to argue (as Arthur Hertzberg has phrased it) that "anti-Semitism had made the status of a minority untenable for the Jew anywhere and that, in order to save himself, any land suitable for a national establishment would do."[12] The destiny of the Jewish people must, in other words, be molded within a Jewish nation-state dependent upon nought but its own will for survival.

Independently of Pinsker, Theodor Herzl, the founder and first president of the World Zionist Organization, set forth a more elaborate and audacious solution for the Jewish problem. In his now classic pamphlet, *The Jewish State,* written in 1895, Herzl was inspired by the conviction that anti-Semitism anywhere in any form was an immutable force which Jews could learn to use to their advantage.[13] Zionism was the quest for a kingdom on this earth, and as such it was a secular solution to the age-long confrontation between the Jew and the world, specifically the Gentile world, which, as Herzl shrewdly perceived, held the keys to that kingdom. Thus, the imperative of majority status in some land of their own and the need of great-power support in attaining this end were ever present in the Zionists' political program.[14]

Just how intimately these two ideas were linked in Herzl's mind is revealed in *The Jewish State.* Jewish sovereignty (that is, the attainment of majority status) was bound to the need to secure international recognition of the Jews' right to colonize some "neutral piece of land."[15] Colonization requires immigrants and the acquisition of land. A process of gradual immigration, however, is a fruitless pursuit, "for there comes the inevitable moment when the government in question, under pressure of the native populace — which feels itself threatened — puts a stop to further influx of Jews. Immigration, therefore, is futile unless it is based

11. The text of this pamphlet will be found in Arthur Hertzberg's excellent anthology of Zionist writings, *The Zionist Idea: A Historical Analysis and Reader* 1959; New York: Meridian, 1960), pp. 181–98.

12. *Ibid.,* p. 180.

13. *Ibid.,* p. 46; the text of Herzl's work is to be found on pp. 204–26.

14. The aim of the Zionist movement, as expressed in the resolution of the First World Zionist Organization conference in Basle, Switzerland (1897), was "to create for the Jewish people a home in Palestine secured by public law." At the time it was clearly understood by dedicated Zionists like Herzl, that the word *home* was synonymous with *state* (see Alan R. Taylor, *Prelude to Israel: An Analysis of Zionist Diplomacy, 1897–1947* [New York, 1959], pp. 5–6).

15. In the *The Zionist Idea,* p. 222.

upon our guaranteed autonomy."[16] In this passage Herzl at once anticipates and yet apparently ignores the one obstacle of paramount political importance to the future of his scheme. He is aware that his "neutral" piece of land possesses an indigenous populace which would oppose the mass immigration of Jews. This is the only reference in the whole work to a "native" population. Nevertheless it is important, for at this point Herzl was no longer groping with the question of Jew and anti-Semite alone. A third party, unobtrusively, had become involved. At the very time of his writing of *The Jewish State,* Herzl pondered this problem and confided in his diary that should Palestine one day become the Jewish state it would be necessary to "spirit the penniless population across the border by . . . denying it any employment."[17] The harshness of this sentiment may be related to Herzl's notion of reality which Hanna Arendt has described as "an eternal, unchanging, hostile structure—all *goyim* everlastingly against all Jews—[which] made the identification of hard-boiledness with realism plausible because it rendered any empirical analysis of actual political factors seemingly superfluous."[18]

Herzl's world view was shared in large part by his successors, particularly by the diplomats such as Weizmann and the activist ideologues such as Ben-Gurion. In practice this involved the a priori assumption (whether consciously held or not) that the Arabs of Palestine, too, were part of a hostile environment and hence cooperation and understanding between Arab and Jew in Palestine would be impossible or, at best, exceedingly difficult.[19] It is true, as Neville Mandel has admirably demonstrated, that prior to the outbreak of war in Europe, there were attempts to bring about

16. *Ibid.* The phrase "guaranteed autonomy" refers to the guarantee sought by the Zionists from the European powers. Translated into a reality this was to be the Balfour Declaration and the mandate document. The official Zionist translation of Herzl's *The Jewish State* rendered into English by Sylvie d'Avigdor (2d ed.; London, 1943) contains the expression "guaranteed supremacy." I have not seen the German original to be able to judge which phrase is the more apt.

17. *Complete Diaries,* ed. Raphael Patai, 5 vols. (New York, 1960), I, 88.

18. Quoted by Hans Kohn in "Zion and the Jewish National Idea," *Menorah Journal* (Autumn–Winter, 1958), p. 27. Nathan Weinstock argues that the concept of alienation from Gentile society drove Zionists to a form of racist thinking; he writes, "Démarche sioniste et raisonnement antisemite sont symétriques" (*Le Sionisme,* p. 56).

19. In a speech in New York (1915), David Ben-Gurion drew an interesting parallel between the pioneering activities of the Zionists in Palestine and the efforts of the early American settlers. The Zionists' American counterpart had to bear "fierce fights with wild nature and wilder redskins" (*Rebirth and Destiny of Israel,* trans. Mordekhai Nurock [New York, 1954], pp. 5–6). Was Ben-Gurion unconsciously linking the Palestinian with the American Indian? In the same work Ben-Gurion notes that he regarded the Arab as "the enemy" (pp. 15–16).

an entente between Zionist and Arab nationalist.[20] The basic reason for the failure of these attempts was that the Zionists could not compromise on the two issues on which the Arabs demanded reassurance, namely, immigration and land purchase.[21] If the Jewish national home were to be anything more than an idle dream, the Zionists quite naturally could not accept restrictions imposed upon the level of immigration or the extent of land acquisition.

The conquest of the land and the conquest of labor were the two ethical ideals upon which the "Jewish revolution" was based.[22] Zionist colonialism is, therefore, not to be confused with, or placed alongside, the ventures of classical colonialism such as the French in North Africa or the Dutch in the East Indies whose advocates proclaimed and practiced domination and exploitation of the native population. On the contrary, the construction of the Jewish national home made the *exclusion* of the Palestinian Arab implicit in theory and explicit in practice. The Zionists' view of the Arab contained a kind of self-fulfilling prophecy. If the Arab were the enemy, implacably determined to destroy the cherished ideals for which Zionism stood, then he had to be resisted at every step. When the Arab finally turned violently against those who sought to exclude him, possibly even to eliminate his community, the original assumption was proven correct and the "prophecy" fulfilled. When Zionists attempted to transform their ideals into reality their actions appeared to the Arab to give the lie to the genuineness of those very ideals. In his *Road to Jerusalem,* historian Barnet Litvinoff has described this Zionist attitude well. Theirs, he writes, was

> a ruthless doctrine, calling for monastic self-discipline and cold detachment from environment. The Jews who gloried in the name of socialist worker interpreted brotherhood on a strictly nationalist, or racial basis, for they meant brotherhood with Jew, not with Arab. As they insisted on working the soil with their own hands, since exploitation of others was anathema to them, they excluded the Arabs from their regime. . . . They believed in equality, but for themselves. They lived on Jewish bread raised on Jewish soil that was protected by a Jewish rifle.[23]

20. "Attempts at an Arab-Zionist Entente: 1913–1914," *Middle Eastern Studies,* I (1964), pp. 236–67. For Arab-Jewish relations prior to the First World War see Mandel, "Turks, Arabs and Jewish Immigration into Palestine, 1882–1914," in *St. Antony's Papers,* no. 17, Middle Eastern Affairs, no. 4 (1965), ed. A. Hourani, pp. 77–108.

21. Mandel, "Arab-Zionist Entente," p. 262.

22. See the later account (1944) by Ben-Gurion entitled "The Imperatives of the Jewish Revolution," in Hertzberg, *The Zionist Idea,* pp. 606–19.

23. (London, 1966), p. 132.

The attitude of isolation from the Arab was a conscious necessity. In *Thieves in the Night,* a chronicle of Jewish settlement in the late 1930s, Arthur Koestler has kibbutznik Bauman tell the recent and innocent immigrant Joseph, "We cannot afford to see the Arab's point of view."[24]

BRITISH COLONIALISM

The prewar Zionist attitudes and policies were sanctioned and reinforced by the terms of the mandate for Palestine which envisaged the parallel, but quite separate, development of the Arab (Muslim and Christian) and Jewish communities. The mandate provided the *legal* means whereby a Jewish subnational government could emerge with complete internal autonomy. The ultimate goal of the enterprise, however, was, in the words of Dr. Eder giving evidence before the Haycraft Commission in 1921, that there should be but "one National Home in Palestine, and that a Jewish one, and no equality in the partnership between Jews and Arabs, but a Jewish predominance as soon as the numbers of that race are sufficiently increased."[25] To the Palestinians it was evident that the political domination of the British was to be replaced gradually by that of another alien people. Zionists argued that there need be no conflict of interests between Arab and Jew,[26] and that Jewish investment and colonization would benefit all the inhabitants of Palestine.[27] In their own way Zionists saw themselves

24. (New York, 1946), p. 38.

25. Great Britain, Foreign Office, Palestine, *Disturbances in May 1921, Reports of the Commission of Inquiry with Correspondence Relating Thereto* (Parliamentary Papers, Cmd. 1540; London, 1921) [Haycraft Commission Report], p. 57. Dr. Eder was, at the time, the acting chairman of the Zionist Commission.

26. Zionism was, and is today, a complex phenomenon; indeed, one of its great strengths was that it could be different things to different people. Its two major trends comprised "cultural" Zionists and "political" Zionists, and the line between the two was not always clearly drawn. Chaim Weizmann could, without being inconsistent, address an assembly of Arab notables in Jerusalem and emphasize that the inner meaning of Zionist aspirations was the longing for a moral and spiritual center to bind the Jewish tradition of the past with the future, while to a group of Zionists he could state that the Jewish community must develop its institutions and colonies for the day when they shall be able to take over the administration of the country from the British (Esco, *Palestine,* I, 129–31). Palestinians saw Zionism as a purely political movement, and they would have understood the words of the Zionist theoretician Jacob Klatzkin, who had written that "in longing for our land we do not desire to create in Palestine a base for the spiritual values of Judaism. To regain our land is for us an end in itself" (in Hertzberg, *The Zionist Idea,* p. 65).

27. In a memorandum placed before the British Foreign Office in October, 1916, the Zionists asked for preferential powers to be granted them in Palestine (such as control of immigration, right of pre-emption of crown land, and the acquisition of

bearing a *mission civilisatrice* to the lands of Asia as a bridge between East and West. Although this was a rationalization common to all European colonial and imperial ventures (even the Covenant of the League of Nations referred euphemistically to the imperialist ambitions underlying the mandate system as a "sacred trust of civilization"), Zionist colonialism was unlike its European predecessors inasmuch as it stemmed from no "mother country" to which the material benefits of exploitation would accrue. Nor was a European Jewish minority to rule the native masses through sustained coercion which the relationship of force requires. Zionism was radical and absolute. Logically, it demanded the creation of a national life for the Jewish people by means of the conquest of the national life of the Palestinians and hence the emasculation of the Arab identity and character of the country. In this regard, Zionist colonialism as the instrument of Jewish nationalism was a unique phenomenon in European colonial-imperial history.[28]

Zionist political goals would have remained hypothetical had Britain and France fulfilled their pledges made to the Arabs during the course of the war. The two Allies fed the Arabs' expectations for their postwar destiny with such phrases as "liberation," "unity," and "consent of the governed."[29] Instead of granting them independence, however, the parties gathered at the Paris Peace Conference decided that the Arab peoples were "not yet able to stand by themselves under the strenuous conditions of the modern world."[30] Britain and France had already (May, 1916) secretly determined upon the partition of the eastern provinces of the Ottoman Empire. The rival claims had not been completely resolved, however, for the wartime Cabinet of Lloyd George was unhappy with the proposed international regime for Palestine, and its support for the Jewish national home was in part an attempt to frustrate French ambitions there.[31] In 1917, British

---

concessions) on the grounds that the Arab population was "too small, too poor, and too little trained to make rapid progress; [it] requires the introduction of a new and progressive element in the population, desirous of devoting all its energies and capital to the work of colonizing on modern lines" (Esco, *Palestine*, I, 88–89).

28. This, I think, follows from the unique nature of Jewish nationalism which Hertzberg has described as the "maverick in the history of modern nationalism" (*The Zionist Idea*, p. 15). Zionism was set apart from its European counterparts inasmuch as it lacked a national land and a language.

29. The texts of the various pledges made to the Arabs may be found in George Antonius, *The Arab Awakening* (1938; New York, 1946), appendixes.

30. From the Covenant of the League of Nations.

31. Thus the judicious view of H. F. Frischwasser-Ra'anan that "the decision to replace international government by British rule over Palestine was the mainspring behind the policy leading to the Balfour Declaration" (*Frontiers of a Nation* [London, 1955], p. 80).

forces under the command of General Allenby drove the Turk from Palestine, and Whitehall had acquired the lease to another "inn on the road to India."[32] The Zionists were to be installed as its most trustworthy tenants, not by gratuitous choice, but because the Zionist leadership had perceived the means whereby their movement could serve Britain's imperial policy. At the beginning of the war, Chaim Weizmann had written to his friend C. P. Scott, editor of the influential *Manchester Guardian,* that "should Palestine fall within the British sphere of influence . . . and should they encourage Jewish settlement there . . . [we could] develop the country, bring back civilization to it, *and form a very effective guard for the Suez Canal."*[33] Once the common bond was forged, the Zionists had acquired, in addition to international recognition of the concept of a Jewish national home, indirect access to an essential instrument of coercion in the form of the British military presence in Palestine.

Palestine was virtually declared a political *tabula rasa.* Arthur Balfour admitted privately that "in the case of Palestine we deliberately and rightly decline to accept the principle of self-determination."[34] Zionism, he once wrote, was of far profounder import than the "desires and prejudices" of the Arab inhabitants of the Holy Land.[35] In a similar vein, Zionists had put abroad the plea to "give us, a people without a land, a land without people." Palestine would be fashioned into any shape desired; and the shape of things to be was spelled out in the mandate document, which, like the Balfour Declaration, was the product of the close and active collaboration between the European conferees.[36]

Britain was pledged to place "the country under such political, administrative and economic conditions as will secure the establishment of the Jewish National Home."[37] This involved facilitating Jewish immigration into Palestine and "close settlement by the Jews on the land." An arm of the World Zionist Organization, the Jewish Agency, was recognized in

---

32. Thornton, *The Imperial Idea,* p. 175. The phrase originated during the heated controversy in England over whether Britain should acquire more overseas territory. Opponents of acquisition argued that for the empire to remain intact, it was not necessary to take a lease on all the inns on the road to India.

33. Cited in Taylor, *Prelude to Israel,* p. 12 (italics added).

34. Cited in A. L. Tibawi, *A Modern History of Syria* (London, 1969), p. 294.

35. "Memorandum by Mr. Balfour respecting Syria, Palestine and Mesopotamia," *Documents on British Foreign Policy, 1919–1939,* ed. Sir Llewellyn Woodward and Rohan Butler, First Series (London, 1956), IV, 345, document no. 242.

36. For the details, see Esco, *Palestine,* I, 55–178.

37. The mandate for Palestine, article 2; see also articles 4 and 6. The entire document is reprinted in *The Israel-Arab Reader: A Documentary History of the Middle East Conflict,* ed. Walter Laqueur (New York, 1969), pp. 34–42.

an advisory capacity and was to cooperate with the British administration in Palestine on all matters pertaining to the national home. On the other hand, the mandatory regime was responsible for safeguarding the civil and religious rights of the "non-Jewish" inhabitants, a phrase continually used to refer to the Christian and Muslim communities which constituted 90 per cent of the total population.

These provisions formed the basis for the official British policy that the mandate involved a dual or equal obligation to the Jewish and Arab communities. The "dual obligation policy" was, in fact, an illusion, for it rested upon an unrealistic premise. It assumed that in return for a pledge to safeguard their civil and religious rights (no mention of *political* rights was ever made in any document relating to the Palestinians),[38] the Palestinians as a people would submit, without opportunity to question or discuss, to a scheme which they had no part in conceiving — that they would, moreover, acquiesce in a plan which would fundamentally alter the political character of their society, as though that scheme in no way concerned them. British policy makers (and the Zionists) viewed the two "obligations" as entirely unrelated to each other. But if, as events were to prove, the fulfillment of the one resulted in the impossibility of fulfilling the second, then one obligation was indeed intimately connected with the other. It is here that the very nature of the mandate regime is revealed as coercive; Britain had the means to impose and sustain the regime by force and was prepared to do so while the Zionists held the "legal" privilege sanctioned by the League of Nations which made opposition to the Jewish national home "illegal" and therefore made suppression of such opposition justifiable. Such was the nature of the power profile in light of which Palestinian resistance must be understood.

THE NATIONALIST RESPONSE

At the turn of the century, Palestine lay entirely within the Ottoman Empire; politically, socially, and economically it was part of the adjacent territories which now constitute modern Syria and Lebanon. For the mass of the population, identity was established by the family or clan into which one was born and by the town or village in which one was raised.[39] Loyal-

---

38. One explanation for this curious omission is given in J. M. N. Jeffries, *Palestine: The Reality* (London, 1939), pp. 181–82. The point is that the Zionists, while claiming political rights for themselves in Palestine, dismissed them as unimportant for the Palestinians.

39. For details on the social structure of Palestine, see J. C. Hurewitz, *The Struggle for Palestine* (New York, 1950), chaps. 2, 4; and Esco, *Palestine*, I, 461–73, 500–16.

ties were, at best, regional. The political life of the country was likewise atomized, and vertical lines of alliance were its most common feature. Thus, the head of a *hamula* in a small village would align himself with a larger and more influential clan in the same district, and this in turn might be linked to one of the powerful landowning families which formed part of the urban upper classes. Political alliances, therefore, rather resembled factions centering around the chief personalities of one or another of these major landed families. Political rivalry on the "national" level could only rarely be based upon differences of program or ideology; it was based rather upon a conflict of interest between rival families or loose confederations of several leading families. The object of political rivalry was the acquisition of power and, thereby, the dispensation of patronage by which means power could be maintained.

A second, or class, division of Palestinian society roughly reflected the rural versus the urban sections of the populace, the former constituting by far the majority. Palestine was an agricultural society and approximately 80 per cent of the population consisted of peasants (*fallahin*) and agricultural laborers. While there did exist an urban proletariat of artisans, porters, boatmen, and unskilled laborers, the socioeconomic (and hence political) influence in the country lay in the hands of the urban upper class of large landowners, religious dignitaries, and professionals combined with an emerging middle class of merchants and shopkeepers.

The divisiveness of the Palestinian social structure was bound to weaken the response to postwar circumstances, yet countervailing forces were present to give that response a coherent and cohesive, and therefore national, character.

First was the fact that Zionist colonization affected Palestinian life from its very roots upward, beginning with the peasantry. Arab landowners and moneylenders, to whom many peasants were indebted, sold their land at the attractively high prices which Zionist organizations were willing to pay but at the expense of the peasant who was given no consideration and who was frequently evicted from his holdings. The *fallahin* harbored grudges against the foreign settler, and attacks on Jewish colonies occurred on and off in the years before the mandate, particularly in the more heavily populated northern regions of the country.[40] In those colonies where Arab labor was hired rather than excluded, Arab-Jewish relations were tolerable, although this pattern of colonization, given time, would develop along the lines of classical colonialist exploitation.[41] Altogether, there was sufficient indication before the establishment of the mandate that peasants throughout the country were actively concerned about the burgeoning Zionist colonies. Yusuf al-Khalidi foresaw the possibility of popular resistance

40. Mandel, "Turks, Arabs and Jewish Immigration," p. 85.
41. Weinstock, *Le Sionisme,* pp. 79–80.

to the Jewish settlers, and Nasif al-Khalidi had cautioned Dr. Thom of
the Zionist office in Jaffa that "governments are transient and fluctuate;
the people are the constant factor, and one must come to agreement with
the people."[42] Concern was expressed not only from below, but also from
the largely Christian middle class of tradesmen and professionals which
was apprehensive about the consequences of economic competition following upon the influx of Jewish capital and colonists. Even the landowners could sell only so much land before their economic welfare and
social prestige were adversely affected. Moreover, those who sold land
to the Zionists were pilloried in the Arabic press as betrayers of the
peasantry and the national patrimony.

The challenge of Zionism as a nationalist-colonialist movement, therefore, drew a like response from the Palestinians on a "national" basis, a
response which cut across regional and class lines. This was clearly recognized by the Haycraft Commission which investigated the outbreak of
violence in Palestine in May, 1921:

> A good deal has been alleged by Jewish witnesses about the instigation
> of the Arab mob to violence by their leaders. If this means no more
> than that while educated people talk and write, the mob acts, then there
> is truth in the allegation. But if it means that had it not been for incite-
> ment by the notables, effendis and sheikhs, there would have been no
> riots, the allegation cannot be substantiated. . . . All that can be truly
> said in favour of the Jewish view is that the leaders of Arab opinion not
> only make no secret of what they think, but carry on a political campaign.
> In this campaign, however, the people participate with the leaders, be-
> cause they feel that their political and material interests are identical.[43]

While the nationalist thrust was well established by this time in Greater
Syria, Zionism and British domination brought the nationalist drive to a
focus in Palestine. Zionism and British domination provided the
immediate stimulus to the Palestinian national movement, and events in
neighboring Arab countries furnished continued reinforcement to the
Palestinian cause.[44] The struggle against the mandate system was every-

42. Cited in Mandel, "Turks, Arabs and Jewish Immigration," pp. 90, 105.

43. Haycraft Commission Report, p. 45.

44. Until the end of 1920, Palestinian "nationalism" should be regarded as a
projection of Syrian nationalism. Palestinian delegates, for example, attended the
two Syrian General Congresses of July, 1919, and March, 1920. Moreover, an all-
Arab Palestine Congress which assembled in Jerusalem during January, 1919, cabled
resolutions to the Paris Peace Conference, one of which demanded union with an
independent Syria. The establishment of the mandate in Palestine and the expulsion of King Faysal from Syria by the French forced the Palestinian leaders
to formulate a new line of policy.

where the same inasmuch as it was directed at enforced European tutelage, and Palestinians could not view their own demands for independence except within the broader perspective of developments in Iraq, Syria, Lebanon, and Egypt. When, for example, other mandated territories gradually acquired self-governing institutions, Palestinians naturally claimed the right to a corresponding advance in their own status.[45] Acts of violence against other mandatory powers were also carefully followed by Palestinians who came to regard force as a legitimate option in the bid to govern their own destiny. In common with the nationalist movements of other Arab countries during this same period (1918–45), Palestinian nationalism was essentially nihilist in the sense that it contained no concept of the shape of future society but was concerned first and foremost with the destruction of European hegemony.[46] However, the termination of the Jewish national-home scheme (implying the end of the mandate as conceived by the British and Zionists) was, to the Palestinians, the *sine qua non* of their very existence, for it was their constant fear that "the intention to create the Jewish National Home is to cause the disappearance or subordination of the Arabic population, culture and language."[47]

THE ARAB EXECUTIVE

During the administrations of the first two high commissioners, Sir Herbert Samuel (1920–25) and Lord Plumer (1925–28), the politically articulate elements of the Palestinian Arab community worked for one immediate goal, namely, British repudiation of the promise to the Jews of a national home. The agency of the Palestinian leadership was the Arab Executive, a 24-member body (later enlarged) which grew out of the Palestine Arab Congress held in Haifa in December, 1920. The congress claimed to represent "all classes and creeds of the Arab people of Palestine,"[48] and regarded itself as a lawfully constituted body with which the British ought to deal.

45. In spite of the fact that Palestine was an "A" class mandate, it resembled a "B" class mandate in the provision that all powers of legislation and administration were invested in the mandatory power. Palestine differed from the mandates of Syria and Iraq in that it was placed on the level of a British colony.

46. I owe this idea to Professor Ibrahim Abu-Lughod who elaborated it during an address to the Canadian-Arab Federation meeting in Montreal, May, 1969.

47. Contained in the Arab delegation's reply to the Churchill White Paper of 1922 (Great Britain, Colonial Office, Palestine, *Correspondence with the Palestine Arab Delegation and the Zionist Organization* [Parliamentary Papers, Cmd. 1700; London, 1922], pp. 22–28).

48. Matiel E. T. Mogannam, *The Arab Woman and the Palestine Problem* (London, 1937), p. 125.

The congress did bring together all current factions, including the Nashashibi and Husayni, two families of great wealth and influence whose rivalry extended back to the mid-nineteenth century. Each family had its Christian supporters, Roman Catholics tending toward the Husaynis and Greek Orthodox toward the Nashashibis. The core of the congress was the Muslim-Christian Associations which had sprung up in towns and villages throughout the country immediately after World War I. These associations were inspired by the Husayni faction, and the Arab Executive was presided over by a former mayor of Jerusalem, Musa Kazem al-Husayni, a venerated patriarch of moderate views and disposition. The Husayni hold on the nationalist movement was further strengthened when al-Hajj Amin al-Husayni was made head of the Supreme Muslim Council and mufti of Jerusalem; the prestige of religious office was thereby added to the leadership of the Arab Congress. When the opportunity presented itself, however, Raghib al-Nashashibi (head of the Nashashibi faction and Musa Kazem's successor as mayor of Jerusalem) formed the National Muslim Societies which were the nucleus of his national party and a counterpoise to the Husayni-dominated Arab Executive. Each faction was able to reach down to the grass-roots level of society for support; thus the Peasant Parties,[49] which the Nashashibis helped set up in a number of rural districts (1923–24), counteracted support from the south where the Husayni influence was greatest. Factionalism in this way touched even the lower classes, and there does appear to have been more concern at that level for the practical matters of economics such as the reduction of taxes and the demand for government agricultural loans. Therefore, while a Nashashibi-backed peasant group might attack the tactics of the Arab Executive, it would also equally direct its barbs of criticism at the rigidly conservative policies of the British administration.[50]

Provisionally, the Palestine Arab Congress and the Arab Executive were able to command the support of all segments and factions of the population. The executive's program may be summed up in three points: (1) condemnation of the mandatory's Zionist policy of supporting the Jewish national home based upon the Balfour Declaration; (2) rejection of the principle of mass Jewish immigration; (3) establishment of a national representative government for Palestine.

The executive based its attack on the mandate on moral and legal considerations and on the nonfulfillment of pledges made to the Arabs in the Husayn-McMahon correspondence and other wartime declarations. It was further argued that the structure of the mandate was inconsistent

---

49. On the Peasant Parties, see Esco, *Palestine,* I, 483 ff.
50. *Ibid.,* p. 485.

with article 22 of the Covenant of the League of Nations which stipulated that "certain communities formerly belonging to the Turkish Empire have reached a stage of development where their existence as independent nations can be provisionally recognized, subject to the rendering of administrative advice and assistance by a Mandatory." The Balfour Declaration, moreover, was not in harmony with the spirit of the provision in the same article that "the wishes of these communities must be a principal consideration in the selection of a mandatory." The legal arguments may have seemed sound enough, but they only underlined the actual weakness of the Palestinian position within the total power profile. Under conditions of colonial rule, demands made peacefully by the governed upon legal or moral grounds pose no threat to the power of the established authority, and concessions can be safely refused. Britain offered "concessions," but in a manner which left the Palestinians only one peaceful option—that of debating the details of their gradual subordination and perpetual submission.

The Arab Executive's first attempt to persuade the British government to alter its policy was when Colonial Secretary Winston Churchill visited Palestine in March, 1921. Churchill not only rejected the executive's demands but also left the Arabs with the impression that representative institutions would not come to Palestine before the Jews had attained majority status.[51]

A delegation was then dispatched to London to plead the Palestinian case at Whitehall. The central question for the Arabs concerned the locus of power: in whose hands would the legislative and executive powers ultimately lie? The Palestinian answer was to urge the immediate creation of a representative Legislative Council to replace the high commissioner's Advisory Council on which sat ten appointed British officials. The problem was duly considered by the Colonial Office and a draft constitution prepared. It provided for a Legislative Council comprising, in addition to the high commissioner, ten official and twelve non-official members. The officials were to be appointed by the high commissioner and would be exclusively British. The non-official members would be elected, eight from the Muslim community, two from the Christian, and two from the Jewish.

---

51. Churchill argued that Jewish immigration could not be halted nor could the Balfour Declaration be revoked. At the same time, he tried to reassure the Palestinians that it was not the intention of the British government to create a Jewish government (a stand which he later renounced) which would dominate the Arabs. What concerned the Palestinians was his statement that "step by step we shall develop representative institutions leading to full self-government, but our children's children will have passed away before that is completed" (*Times* [London], April 2, 1921).

The draft constitution was received with bitter disappointment by the Palestinians, for the structure of the proposed council revealed that the mandate administration would enjoy an absolute majority (ten British officials plus the two elected Jewish members) of the twenty-two seats, by which it could enforce the national-home policy against the wishes of the representatives of the majority of Palestinians. The high commissioner could veto any legislation, and no ordinance could be passed which was "in any way repugnant to or inconsistent with the provisions of the Mandate." On the crucial question of immigration, real control was intended to remain with the British director of immigration and the Jewish Agency.[52] Colonial Secretary Churchill made it clear to the Palestinian delegation that the national-home policy was not susceptible to change nor was it subject to discussion between the delegation and the government. The proper topic of negotiation was the best method of safeguarding the Arabs' "civil and religious rights," and the secretary regarded the proposed constitution as adequate. Churchill further argued that he could not negotiate *officially* with a delegation which only "claimed" to represent the wishes of the people, and he urged acceptance of the draft constitution since its object was to provide Palestinians with a "constitutional channel for the expression of their opinions and wishes."[53] Confronted with this coercion, the Palestinians rejected both the draft constitution and the White Paper which stemmed from their discussions with the Colonial Office. No positive or practical proposals existed on paper that would genuinely protect the Arab position.[54]

For the moment, the question of self-governing institutions was left in abeyance, and Palestine continued to be governed by the high commissioner and his advisers as a beneficent autocracy. British policy was incomprehensible to the very people it was intended to convince, the Palestinians, and the gulf between ruler and the ruled grew daily wider. The Arab Executive's failure to wring political concessions from the British caused the Nashashibi faction to question the policy of noncooperation with the mandatory. Rather than deny the justice and validity of the mandate as a whole, the new National Party, for tactical reasons, was prepared to work

52. Fannie Fern Andrews, *The Holy Land under Mandate,* 2 vols. (Boston, 1931), II, 146, n. 1; the Arabs could only "advise" on immigration.

53. *Ibid.,* p. 86.

54. In October, 1923, the Palestine government proposed an Arab Agency for the Arab community which would be "exactly analogous" to the Jewish Agency. The proposal was rejected for the simple reason that the analogy did not exist. For example, the members of the Jewish Agency were elected by the whole Jewish community, while the members of the Arab Agency would be appointed by the high commissioner, who could maintain direct control over Palestinians' affairs.

within the system to attain the same ends as its opponents in the Executive. Despite this fissure in the nationalist ranks, the Arab Executive sustained its attack on the mandatory administration, now shifting to a detailed criticism of the government's economic and financial policies. The Fifth and Sixth Palestine Arab Congresses (August, 1922, and October, 1924) dealt with a wide range of economic problems; the sale of land to the Zionists; protest against the Rutenberg Concession which granted a Zionist corporation the monopoly in exploiting Palestine's chief water resources for electricity and irrigation; the establishment of a national bank; the failure of the government to encourage credit cooperatives; and the lack of cheap loans to Arab agriculturists. A Palestine Arab Economic Congress which met in Jerusalem (February, 1923) demanded protection of the small peasantry against expropriation along the lines of the Egyptian Five Faddan Law and the establishment of agricultural colleges and an agricultural bank. The Palestine government, however, was more concerned with security matters (which, in the 1930's consumed as much as 35 per cent of the budget) than with social services. It was intent on amassing a surplus to repay Palestine's portion of the Ottoman public debt, and it strove to make Palestine self-supporting and hence less of a burden on the ill-tempered British taxpayer.

PEASANT GRIEVANCES

Economic and political grievances fed the Palestinian frustration with the British mandate; both areas of grievance were dramatized by the single question of Jewish immigration, the political consequences of which had long been evident. In the mid-1920s, the economic consequences were viewed with equal alarm. In 1925, Jewish immigration had reached record level as nearly 34,000 souls entered Palestine. The Churchill White Paper of 1922 had set up the formula that "immigration cannot be so great in volume as to exceed whatever may be the economic capacity of the country at the time to absorb new arrivals."[55] The principle of "absorptive capacity" was variously interpreted, and to the extent that such factors as adverse soil and climatic conditions, existing social institutions and the population's low standard of living were ignored,[56] immigration became a function of political pressures rather than economic common sense.[57] The result was described

55. For the text of this document, see Laqueur, *Israel-Arab Reader,* pp. 45–50.

56. Doreen Warriner, *Land and Poverty in the Middle East* (London, 1948), chap. 4.

57. See Nevill Barbour, *Nisi Dominus* (London, 1946), chap. 11 on "economic absorptive capacity."

by Dr. Leo Wolman, one of a team of experts employed by the Zionist Organization in 1928 to study the growth potential of the country:

> Such rapid growth of population as characterized the expansion of Palestine in the years after 1922 is, under almost any circumstances, bound to produce dislocations that require time and planning to adjust. Much of the unemployment in the country during 1926 and 1927 was, in fact, the consequence of this hasty and unbalanced flow of Jewish immigration.[58]

Even in years of general prosperity, immigration had its attendant problems such as the increased infusion of capital via the new settlers. This was especially noteworthy in the years between 1932 and 1936 when over 20 per cent of the Jewish immigrants and their dependents fell into the capitalist class. Most of these were Germans escaping the menacing shadow of Nazism.[59] The capital infusion from this source alone was equal to about one-tenth of the total expenditure of the Palestine government for the same period.[60] By 1936, the nucleus of the Jewish national home was unquestionably a brilliant technical and social achievement, but economically, its very success had ensured a permanent gap between the Jewish and Arab communities. In that year the average income per capita of Arab rural population was about £7, and for the Jew it was about £34. Evidently, the technical success of the Jewish national home was due, in large measure, to the vast investment capital upon which it could draw (plus, of course, the European expertise), while, at the same time, the higher standard of living enjoyed in the Jewish settlements was of only indirect benefit to the Arab community.[61]

By 1928 the various competing nationalist factions were once again able to unite. The Seventh Arab Congress was convened in Jerusalem in June of that year. Several of the congress' resolutions—such as those with regard to abolition of tithes, reform of taxation, increased public expendi-

---

58. Cited in *ibid.,* p. 156. Unemployment in the Jewish community alone was put at 8,400, a level requiring extensive government relief assistance; at the same time Arab unemployment was around the 50,000 mark (Mogannam, *Arab Woman,* p. 161).

59. Sa'id Himadeh, ed., *Economic Organization of Palestine* (Beirut, 1938), pp. 22–23.

60. The fraction of one-tenth is a conservative one based upon the minimum amount of capital each immigrant in this category required, which was £1000. Weinstock gives the figure of £30 million of imported capital during this same period (*Le Sionisme,* p. 175), a figure which would represent 50 per cent *more* than the entire government expenditure for the whole country.

61. Warriner, *Land and Poverty,* pp. 69, 72.

ture on education, and social welfare for the Arab worker—dealt with economic problems. These resolutions reflected the serious state of tension which had built up over the preceding years among the Palestinian masses. A potentially explosive situation had been created, a situation, however, to which the high commissioner, Lord Plumer, paid no heed and which apparently escaped critical analysis by the Arab leadership and even the Communist Party.[62] The major resolution of the congress showed the leadership's abiding concern for the important, but purely *political* question of the locus of power. The resolution read, in part:

> The people of Palestine cannot and will not tolerate the present absolute colonial system of Government, and urgently insist upon and demand the establishment of a representative body to lay its own Constitution and guarantee the formation of a democratic parliamentary Government.[63]

The resolutions were presented to the new high commissioner, Sir John Chancellor, who promised to discuss them with the Colonial Office during his leave in the summer of 1929. But by then, events had swiftly overtaken both the Palestine government and the Arab leadership, and riots erupted throughout the country in August, 1929.

The proximate cause of the outbreak of violence was religious, involving the status of the Wailing Wall in Jerusalem.[64] Riots occurred in Hebron and Safad and other isolated settlements, and the death toll of Jews and Arabs was heavy. Although Jews appeared to be the sole target of Arab wrath, the violence constituted an unorganized and incoherent expression of pent-up frustration of the Palestinian masses against the mandate policy as a whole. In places like Hebron, where over 60 Jews were killed, the peasants' fury was particularly savage. In Nablus, a large, threatening crowd attempted, unsuccessfully, to raid the police barracks for arms. Everywhere the British military was able to restore order, but owing to the tension being generated from below, the country remained potentially explosive for some weeks. The 1929 riots were a significant portent of the future course of events.

For the first time, the revolutionary potential of the Palestinian masses became apparent. The position of the Arab peasant and worker had become

62. Laqueur, *Communism*, p. 82 ff.

63. League of Nations, Permanent Mandates Commission, *Minutes of the 14th Session,* October–November, 1928, annex 9, p. 246.

64. For a detailed account of the riots and events leading up to them, see Andrews, *The Holy Land,* II, 223–89.

intolerable; it was made worse by the fact that economic development plans were inescapably subject to political considerations involving the Jewish national home. In Palestine, highly productive agricultural land was scarce, and the rural Arab population was rapidly increasing. By 1930, when Sir John Hope Simpson investigated the development potential of the country, it was found that the majority of the Arab population lived on farms which did not guarantee a subsistence minimum.[65] Central government planning was crucial, particularly in land conservation and reclamation—the latter requiring costly expenditure on irrigation. The government, however, had conceived no comprehensive policies in these areas, and the Jewish Agency, for its part, was "opposed to any large scale measures on the part of the Government to intensify or develop *fellahin* farming unless this involved the transference of some of the land in question to the Jews."[66] Even if the most ambitious proposals for irrigation, put forward by various Zionist writers, had been realized, the additional cultivable land would barely have been sufficient to absorb the increase in the Arab population.[67] Thus the uprising of 1929 (and more especially the rebellion of 1936–39) was related to the overall ineffectiveness of the mandate administration to cope with the fundamental economic grievances of the peasantry. Implicitly, the Jewish national home was called into question, for extensive planning and expenditure on the Arab sector of the economy would seriously retard the rate of the Zionists' progress in their sector.

The peasants' and workers' reaction, however, was not simply due to an oppressive mandate policy; it was also related to the failure of the Arab leadership to obtain meaningful concessions from the British whereby the position of the masses would be adequately safeguarded. Obviously, the existence of shared interests between the lower and upper classes cannot be denied. The Arab Congresses, as we have seen, treated economic questions seriously, and the Supreme Muslim Council established a "national fund" to purchase land which would otherwise be bought by Zionists. The end of the mandate, or more precisely, the termination of the scheme for the Jewish national home was a common national goal.

Nevertheless, the perspectives of the upper class and the peasantry were quite different in another sense. The former sought a resolution to the question of political power, while the latter struggled to alleviate their

65. Great Britain, Colonial Office, Palestine, *Report on Immigration, Land Settlement and Development* (Parliamentary Papers, Cmd. 3686–87; London, 1930) [Hope Simpson Report].

66. Barbour, *Nisi Dominus,* p. 121.

67. Warriner, *Land and Poverty,* pp. 58–60.

economic plight. Representative institutions would secure the interests of
the upper class which would then enjoy the privilege of rule in an independent Palestine; hence the basis of political action of the Arab leadership
was direct negotiation with the British for a democratic constitution. The
basis of political action for the peasantry was through violence so long as
political negotiations and the demands for economic stability proved fruitless. A strong movement among the peasantry was perhaps the more radical
approach, for the transfer of political power from the mandatory to the
upper classes did not necessitate the betterment of the peasants' living
conditions. It might, therefore, be said that—given the conditions under the
mandate—the failure of the nationalist program was largely due to the
inability and unwillingness of the Arab leadership to co-opt the peasants'
full support in bringing about the destruction of the mandate. The upper
classes could not think in terms of *being obligated to* the lower classes in the
context of a total national struggle; they could only feel *some* obligation *for*
the lower classes insofar as this did not conflict with their own vital
interests. In other words, the potential of the Arab peasants and workers
within the total power profile was never exploited by the leadership. In
times of crisis, such as 1929 (and again in 1936–39), the Arab leadership
seemed to shrink in horror at the prospect of violence from below. On the
second day of rioting in August, 1929, a manifesto was issued by the Arab
leaders to their people:

> We call upon you O Arabs in the interest of the country, which you
> place above all other considerations, to strive sincerely to quell the
> riot, avoid bloodshed and save life. We request you all to return to quiet
> and peace, to endeavour to assist in the restoration of order and turn a
> deaf ear to such unfounded reports and rumours. Be confident that we
> are making every possible effort to realize your demands and national
> aspirations by peaceful methods.[68]

In the months which followed, the Arab Executive lost much of its credibility with the Palestinians as efforts to realize national aspirations through
negotiation were again made in vain.

ZIONIST STRATEGY AND BRITISH POLICY

The disturbances of 1929 resulted in a commission of inquiry, a special

---

68. Cited in Mogannam, *The Arab Woman,* pp. 174–75; The manifesto was issued
by Musa Kazem al-Husayni, al-Hajj Amin al-Husayni, Raghib al-Nashashibi,
Mustafa al-Khalidi, and Aref Dajani.

report, and a White Paper. The Shaw Commission recognized that the tension in Palestine had been aggravated by the failure of the British government to meet its commitment to the Arabs and that Arab fears stemmed from the threat of ultimate economic domination by the Jews. The commissioners advised a more stringent control of immigration to prevent the recurrence of the economic disequilibrium of the mid-1920s and predicted the creation of a landless class of Arabs as a consequence of the lack of protection in the law for tenants involved in land sales to the Zionists. Curiously, the commission regarded the issues of immigration and land sales as incidental matters which could be remedied without basically affecting British policy as a whole.[69] The second investigation, conducted alone by Sir John Hope Simpson, also drew attention to the lot of the peasantry. Hope Simpson found fault with the Zionist Organization's methods of land purchase and settlement and with the gradual creation of an extra-territorial Jewish enclave from which all Arabs were excluded.[70]

The British government then issued its statement of policy in the Passfield White Paper of October, 1930. The weight of evidence of the Shaw and Hope Simpson reports determined the line of Colonial Secretary Lord Passfield's new policy. Although he stressed that Arab and Jewish aspirations were "in no sense irreconcilable," Lord Passfield argued that under existing conditions "there remains no margin of land available for agricultural settlement by new immigrants."[71] Accordingly, stricter land-transfer and immigration controls were recommended. The White Paper was greeted, predictably, with joy by the Palestinians and with anger by the Zionists. The Arab delegation which went to London to seek new constitutional arrangements was thwarted by the strong parliamentary opposition and organized Zionist reaction to the White Paper. Finally, in February, 1931, Prime Minister James Ramsey MacDonald virtually repudiated the Passfield White Paper in a letter to Chaim Weizmann in which he stated that "the obligation to facilitate Jewish immigration and to encourage close settlement by Jews on the land remains a positive obligation of the mandate and it can be fulfilled without prejudice to the rights and position of other sections of the population of Palestine."[72] (Later, in 1936, the British government again retreated under similar pressure from a plan

69. Great Britain, Colonial Office, Commission on Palestine Disturbances of August, 1929, *Report of the Commission* (Parliamentary Papers, Cmd. 3530; London, 1930) [Shaw Commission Report].

70. Hope Simpson Report.

71. Great Britain, Colonial Office, Palestine, *Statement of Policy by His Majesty's Government in The United Kingdom* (Parliamentary Papers, Cmd. 3692; London, 1930) [Passfield White Paper].

72. For the text of the MacDonald Letter, see Laqueur, *Israel-Arab Reader,* pp. 50–58.

proposed by High Commissioner Arthur Wauchope for a Legislative Council in which the Arab community would have a favorable—14 out of 28 seats—share of power.) The upshot of MacDonald's letter was a serious political setback for the Arab Executive. As in 1921, the pattern of crisis and setback was repeated, and the unity of the Arab leadership was dissipated.

The moment of this occurrence could not have been worse for the Arab community. The Jewish community was on the threshold of a new stage of rapid development and expansion. The social, economic, and political structure of the Yishuv revealed the solid foundations of a dynamic sub-national government. Morever, in the elections of the Jewish Agency for 1933, the Labour group of the Histadrut led by David Ben-Gurion gained control. This was to mark a shift in Zionist strategy away from the current gradualist approach to Jewish statehood.[73] The Labour Zionist leader, Chaim Arlosoroff, had made a careful assessment of the Zionist position in a letter to Weizmann in June, 1932. He believed that the Arabs were no longer strong enough to destroy the position of the Jewish community or to frustrate the growth of the national home. Zionist strategy at the next stage, therefore, would be to preclude the possibility of the establishment of an Arab state in Palestine by ensuring that the relationship between Jews and Arabs be based upon the balance of real power being in the Jews' favor. Under the present circumstances, he concluded, this could not be realized "without a transition period during which the Jewish minority would exercise organized revolutionary rule."[74] The entire apparatus of the state, including the miltary, would fall into the hands of the Zionist minority. On the military side, a beginning had already been made with the formation in 1929 of an underground force known as the Haganah, which was to be the nucleus of the future Israeli army. Illegal Jewish immigration, which had a political purpose, commenced in the mid-1930s, and by 1937 a Committee of Illegal Immigration was founded by Labour leaders and the Haganah High Command.[75] On the diplomatic front, the new policy culminated in the Biltmore Program of May, 1942, which made public the Zionist demand for a Jewish state. From 1933 onward, events in Europe exercised an indirect but ever-increasing influence upon developments in Palestine. It has been said, with little distortion, that if Herzl was the Marxist theorist of Zionism, then Hitler was the Leninist prime-mover of the Jewish state.

73. Ben Halpern, *The Idea of the Jewish State* (Cambridge, Mass., 1961), p. 44.

74. Cited in Walid Khalidi, "Plan Dalet," *Middle East Forum,* November, 1961.

75. Jon Kimche and David Kimche, *The Secret Roads* (New York, 1955), pp. 23, 27.

Meanwhile, the Palestinian struggle against the mandate was not aided by the appearance of political parties within the Arab community; if anything, the community was more fragmented than ever. Now, instead of the two major factions, the Husaynis and the Nashashibis, there were six separate groups, each identified with a powerful Muslim family. The one party with a definite political ideology was the Istiqlal which formed part of the Arab nationalist movement in Syria, Lebanon, and Iraq. Istiqlal enjoyed the support of many of the younger generation of intellectuals, who were dedicated anti-imperialists. During World War II, when it was the only viable Arab political party (or faction) in Palestine, Istiqlal, suffering the familiar weakness of "regionalism," could not rally country-wide backing to its banner; the party's president, Awni Abdul Hadi, was a prominent member of a large clan whose influence centered about the Jenin-Nablus region.

The plague of interfactional bickering which characterized the years prior to the rebellion in 1936 first broke out over the Islamic Congress held in Jerusalem in December, 1931.[76] The congress was the inspiration of al-Hajj Amin al-Husayni who had observed the importance of making "the Palestine problem" an international issue in much the same way Herzl had attempted to internationalize "the Jewish problem." Invitations were sent to Muslim Associations throughout the Arab world, including the Shi'i Ulema of Syria and Iraq. The congress, therefore, probably better represented Muslim public opinion on the Palestine question than did the Arab governments. Resolutions were duly passed condemning Zionism, the mandates, and colonialism in general. Nevertheless, the congress aroused the hostility of al-Hajj Amin's political rivals, and Raghib al-Nashashibi summoned a counter-conference to express the opposition's lack of confidence in the mufti's leadership. The congress itself may have been gratifying as a gesture of universal Muslim sympathy, but it also revealed a corresponding defect, namely, the tendency of the Palestinian leaders to rationalize the internal weakness of their community by concealing weakness behind a façade of powerful external support.

THE ARAB REBELLION

As the high-water mark of Palestinian resistance to the mandate was reached in 1936–39, the social and economic structure of the Arab com-

76. See H. A. R. Gibb, "The Islamic Congress at Jerusalem, December, 1931," *Survey of International Affairs: 1934* (Oxford, 1935), pp. 99–109.

munity was clearly an added source of weakness to the already disadvantageous position of the community within the power profile. By 1935–36 a situation that was the logical outcome of the events of the preceding years had materialized. Violence was one of its manifestations, for the Palestinians had realized that they must either endure perpetual submission or break the law. Under the terms of the mandate, Britain permitted mass Jewish immigration into Palestine; by the time of the outbreak of rebellion, the Jewish community constituted close to 30 per cent of the total population. The trend of the previous three years (the 1933 total of immigrants was 30,327; 1934, 42,359; and 1935, 61,854) was such that the numerical relations in the country could be transformed within a decade. The threat of that prospect was the immediate cause of the Arab leaders' calling a general strike in April, 1936, to be continued until the mandatory government abolished the Jewish immigration schedule.

The strike was endorsed by all political factions, and a permanent ten-man executive, known as the Arab Higher Committee, was formed to conduct the operation. Other factors contributed to the leaders' decision to adopt this more drastic form of direct action against the government. One was the ill-fated negotiations for a Legislative Council alluded to above. Another was the depressed state of the economy which was attributed to the excessive rate of immigration. Finally, there were the examples of successful nationalist struggles in neighboring countries.

The aim of the strike was to paralyze the country's economy and thereby wring reluctant concessions from the British; it had the paradoxical result of strengthening the economic autonomy of the Yishuv. Jewish commercial enterprises were able to take up the sudden slack in both the private and public sectors of the economy, while Jewish labor worked on various government security projects such as the northern fence designed to keep out infiltrators from Syria. A general strike, therefore, could scarcely have the desired consequence when a highly organized and largely self-contained one-third of the population could act as a buffer in the crisis and even derive benefit from it. That this was possible at all was due to the favored position of the Yishuv within the structure of the mandate.

The strike was a direct challenge to British authority, and created the likelihood of a complete breakdown of public order resulting from the revolt among the rural population in the hills. The bands of guerrillas were poorly equipped and unorganized, their only advantages being an intimate knowledge of the terrain where they operated and the sympathy of the villagers among whom they found ready refuge. The forces available to the government were infinitely superior, and by the end of August, 1936, some 20,000 troops had been seconded to Palestine to join the offensive against the rebels. The high commissioner, Arthur Wauchope, initiated a series of stringent emergency regulations: strike leaders and prominent members of the labor movement were arrested and interned or deported, collective punishments were meted out to entire villages suspected of harboring guerrillas, and house-to-house searches for weapons and ammunition were made with the intent to disarm the Arab population. At the same time the government permitted the Jewish defense establishment to expand, and, later, Haganah recruits were deployed with British troops in northern Palestine.[77] In the gravest crisis, despite the failure to meet its obligations to the Palestinians, the British government chose the dark path of repression rather than concession. To keep the mandate intact, violence was countered with violence. The lesson was not lost upon the Zionists, but where the Palestinians' option of rebellion failed, the Zionists' would later succeed.

The Arab Higher Committee continued to believe that a political solution was possible; the cessation of Jewish immigration, for example, would put an end to the Jewish national-home scheme and an end to the Palestinians' worries. The committee had little influence upon the guerrilla activities in the hills, but it made no concerted effort to coordinate all forms of resistance for the sake of exerting the maximum pressure on the government. After six months, the strike ground to a halt. Not a single concession had been won, only the promise of yet another royal commission. In calling off the strike, the Higher Committee heeded the plea from the rulers of Iraq, Transjordan, and Saudi Arabia to end the disorders and trust in Great Britain's declared intention to do justice. But justice to whom remained to be seen.

The main conclusion of the Peel Commission Report of 1937 was starkly simple: the mandate was unworkable, since Britain's obligations to the Jews could only be fulfilled by a policy of repression against a resentful Arab population. However, the report's main proposal, namely, the partition of Palestine into an Arab state and a Jewish state,[78] was equally unworkable, for from the Palestinian viewpoint, "it conceded the essence of the Jewish claims, although on a smaller scale than they demanded. It involved exactly the same dangers to the Arabs, and not even on a smaller scale, since if the Jews once got a foothold it would be difficult to stop them advancing."[79]

The report, in fact, signaled the renewal of sporadic resistance which continued into the summer and fall of 1938. After the murder of a British

77. Hurewitz, *Struggle for Palestine,* p. 93.
78. Great Britain, Colonial Office, Palestine, *Report of the Palestine Royal Commission* (Parliamentary Papers, Cmd. 5479; London, 1937) [Peel Commission Report].
79. Hourani, "The Decline of the West in the Middle East," p. 45.

district commissioner in September, 1937, the government brought all its resources to bear on the Palestinians in order to crush the rebellion once and for all. The Arab Higher Committee was declared illegal and dissolved. Most of its members were arrested and deported to the Seychelles, but al-Hajj Amin managed to escape to Lebanon. The Supreme Muslim Council was placed under the direct supervision of the mandatory government, and the Arabic press was muzzled. Detention camps were filled with political prisoners, and some were summarily tried and executed. The casualties of the rebellion exceeded 7,000 dead and wounded Palestinians. The Palestinian nationalist movement had collapsed; it was never fully to recover.

During the last decade of the mandate, Palestinians reaped the bitter harvest of their struggle against British policy and Zionism. The community was crippled, its will paralyzed, and with that the means to continue the resistance perished. The Palestinian leaders either had been deported, had taken refuge in neighboring Arab countries, or had remained in Palestine but under close government surveillance, prohibited from any political activity. The mandatory government made no attempt to cultivate the support of prominent Palestinians who would have collaborated with them within the terms of the mandate.

Consequently, the initiative for the Palestine problem passed outside the country and left a widening gap between the people and the center of political authority. This was due, in no small way, to al-Hajj Amin al-Husayni, who turned to Germany for aid in an effort to remove all challenge to his personal direction of Palestine's affairs. In 1944, a Palestinian delegate attended the Alexandria conference of Arab states, out of which emerged the Arab League. Henceforward, the major political decisions concerning tactics against the mandate and the Zionists were taken in Cairo. This development undoubtedly gave the Palestinians an important outlet through which their views reached the international community, but it did nothing concrete by way of strengthening the Arab community or making it more cohesive. When the final show of strength came, as it was bound to do, the Jewish community was far better prepared to seize the option of violence and make it count decisively.

The final decade of the mandate was marked, in fact, by the complete internationalization of the Palestine problem. The Palestinians went to the international community via the Arab League and the Zionists went the same road via the government of the United States.[80] As Britain's will to

80. An excellent study of Zionist diplomatic activities in the United States during the Second World War is to be found in Richard P. Stevens, *American Zionism and U.S. Foreign Policy, 1942–1947*, (New York, 1962).

govern was weakened by her own enfeebled condition following the Second World War and by the determined battle of attrition which Zionists waged against the White Paper of 1939, a new balance of forces gradually emerged. Finally, in the United Nations, a return to the principle of partition was approved, but only after an intensive diplomatic battle in which a Zionist victory was assured by massive reinforcement from Washington. The Palestine war of 1948 confirmed the existence of Israel as an independent state. The mandate had been buried without honor. Three tragic decades of ill-conceived British policy did not resolve the mandate's inherent contradictions and antagonisms, and two decades later, the River Jordan still flows through an unholy land.

8. The Revolt of 1936: A Chronicle of Events

Barbara Kalkas

On the eve of the Arab rebellion the Arabs of Palestine were concerned less about latent cleavages between the two resident populations in their country than they were about the fulfillment of the British promise of independence given, they believed, in the course of the First World War. Despite the progressive alienation of farm land to the various land funds, farmers had not attempted concerted political action to arrest the process. Despite dual pay scales—Jewish and "non-Jewish"—and ethnic quotas for many jobs, Arab workers for the most part avoided political articulation. Despite higher prices and unemployment following three years of record-breaking European immigration into Palestine, Palestinian ladies retained their *chic* Jewish dressmakers and continued to use European imports from the Jewish-owned retail stores which dotted Palestinian cities. Although Arabs recognized the connection between the economic problems facing their country and rampant immigration and land alienation, if they recognized a cleavage, this cleavage was between Palestinians and their colonial rulers—the British—not between Palestinians and the Zionists, who were seen as only secondary parties to the problem.

In the months preceding the 1936 rebellion, Palestinian Arabs were engaged in yet another attempt to attain political independence under provisions of the Palestine "Class-A" mandate. Late in the fall of 1934 another of the Arab delegations had approached the British high commissioner, Lt. Gen. Sir Arthur Wauchope, requesting the formation of a Legislative Council as a first step toward Palestinian self-government envisioned in the mandate. A year later the delegation, called the United Front, again submitted its demands to Wauchope. Designed to alleviate the "landless Arab" problem and to better regulate the flow of immigrants into the country, the so-called "November Demands" requested:

1. The establishment of democratic government in accordance with the Covenant of the League of Nations and Article 2 of the Palestine Mandate.

2. Prohibition of the transfer of Arab lands to Jews and the enactment of a law similar to the Five Faddan Law in Egypt.

3. (a) The immediate cessation of Jewish immigration and the formation of a competent committee to determine the absorptive capacity of the country and lay down principles for immigration.

    (b) Legislation to require all lawful residents to obtain and carry identity cards.

    (c) Immediate and effective investigation into illicit immigration.[1]

It was stressed that the first demand was the most important. Wauchope, who had been cooperating with the United Front, submitted his proposal for a Legislative Council to the Colonial Office in December, 1935.

The Zionist Organization had opposed the self-government scheme as early as November, 1934, insofar as a legislature might put the national home into question. Their suspicions were not entirely groundless, for under the proposed scheme the Legislative Council would ultimately control immigration and land sales, the building-blocks of the national home. Thus the Zionist Organization successfully blocked the measure in the British Parliament. Zionist opposition to the council was matched in part by that of a growing contingent of Arab militants who had become impatient with the failure of Arab diplomacy. Their feelings were not entirely groundless, insofar as the conservative, upper-class leadership had not gained any concession whatever from the British in thirteen years of on-and-off negotiations. The Jewish militants were similarly impatient, and several political assassinations of Zionist leaders, attributed to the Revisionists, created fears in the "orthodox Zionist" community.

In the few months preceding the disturbances, fear and mutual distrust became increasingly apparent between the two communities. On October 16, 1935, an arms shipment destined for a Tel Aviv Jew and concealed in cement barrels was intercepted in the Jaffa port; the shipment was found

---

1. Great Britain, Colonial Office, *Report by His Majesty's Government in the United Kingdom of Great Britain and Northern Ireland to the Council of the League of Nations on the Administration of Palestine and Trans-Jordan for the Year 1935* (Colonial no. 112; London, 1936), p. 15 (series cited hereafter as *Palestine Report*).

to contain 800 rifles and 400,000 cartridges. Many Palestinian Arabs, particularly members of the sizable petit bourgeoisie of Jaffa, staged a strike on October 26. They had called the work stoppage to draw attention specifically to what they believed to be the gradual arming of Jews in Palestine. In fact, Zionists suspected Arabs of the same activity, pointing to the program of the Holy Martyrs, a group of parapolitical religious-national revolutionaries. Accounts of the daring exploits of these rebels had been a regular feature of the Arab press, and the flair of the shaykh who headed the group, Shaykh Izz al-Din al-Qassam, led to his being cast as a romantic survival from the legendary past. In late November, British police had routed the revolutionary group near Jenin, killing the shaykh, and several of his followers. Remnants of the group reformed in the hills as the Holy Martyrs, proclaiming that they would collect money to buy arms to purge Palestine of alien influences (that is, British and Zionist). In mid-April of the following year, one of the isolated operations of these revolutionaries set off a wave of Jewish retaliation; Arab counter-retaliation eventually took the form of a general strike which lasted six months.[2]

THE OUTBREAK OF VIOLENCE

On the night of Wednesday, April 15, 1936, the Martyrs held up a convoy of ten cars traveling the Nablus-Tulkarm road and robbed the passengers. They escorted three of the Jewish passengers to the back of a truck and shot them. One was killed instantly, one later died of his wounds, and the third survived. The following night prowlers broke into the house of two orange-grove workers near Petah Tiqva, a Jewish settlement to the northeast of Tel Aviv. The intruders fatally shot the two Arab occupants of the house at close range in apparent reprisal for the Martyrs' murder of Jews the night before.

At noon the following day, services were held in Tel Aviv for the

2. The account of the disturbances presented in this essay is based upon day-to-day accounts in the *New York Times;* the *Times* (London) (all citations are to the Royal edition); *Manchester Guardian Weekly; Palestine and Transjordan;* and various British government reports. Different accounts of the outbreak of violence are given in Christopher Sykes, *Crossroads to Israel* (Cleveland, 1965), p. 148; and the *Times* (London), April 24, 1936, p. 7. Nevill Barbour, whose own account of the outbreak closely follows that of the official *Palestine Report, 1936,* adds, "attempts made by the Jewish Agency to dispute the accuracy of this account were completely refuted by the Accredited Representative before the Permanent Mandates Commission (*Minutes, 32nd Session,* p. 145)" (Barbour, *Palestine: Star or Crescent?* [New York, 1947], p. 196n).

Martyrs' victim. Although police had prohibited eulogies at the funeral, Tel Aviv municipal officials joined the crowds calling for vengeance: "We don't want this government; we want a Jewish army."[3] This call triggered anti-Arab demonstrations in Tel Aviv which culminated in an attempted march on Jaffa, Tel Aviv's Arab counterpart to the south. Diverted by police and following calls from the crowd, the mob moved to the Tel Aviv City Hall, where more speeches were delivered. The police, having been attacked as they attempted to disperse the demonstrators, fought back and actually fired into the crowd. Four persons were shot and thirty beaten. To prevent further problems, authorities blocked off Allenby Square, and extra police were assigned, although Tel Aviv officials protested the presence of "non-Jewish" (that is, British) police in their city.

Friday and Saturday, Jews in Tel Aviv picketed businesses which hired Arabs, and several Arabs were assaulted. The British government *Palestine Report* recorded some of these assaults, which occurred in Jaffa as well as in Tel Aviv, but added that "during the 17th and 18th of April no case of reprisal on the part of the Arabs was reported to the police."[4] Wisely, the Arabs had been restrained, but they planned a demonstration for Sunday to protest events of the previous several days in the Tel Aviv area.

At nine o'clock Sunday morning (April 19), Arabs gathered in front of the Jaffa municipal offices while their leaders attempted to obtain a parade permit. Denied the permit, the gathering became a mob. Three Jews, one of whom was working in the area, were killed in the scuffle. The crowd moved toward the Tel Aviv road, hurling objects at cars and buses. Disorder continued until nightfall, by which time nine Jews and two Arabs had been killed and forty Jews and ten Arabs injured. Similar, though less bloody, demonstrations occurred simultaneously in Tulkarm and Nablus. During these disturbances the two Semitic populations in Palestine, already ideologically separable, began to separate spatially. The traditional Near Eastern mosaic pattern began to be rearranged, with even the ill-reputed Jaffa lightermen helping the majority of Jaffa's Jewish community to their Tel Aviv refuge. The populations were moving both ways; apparently it was obvious to them that the disturbances of the weekend would not subside immediately.

The high commissioner's reactions were more temperate. In a radio broadcast Sunday evening, Wauchope announced that he had put the 1931 Palestine (Defense) Orders-in-Council into effect. At first he applied these emergency regulations only in Jaffa and Tel Aviv, cordoning off these cities, regulating the sale of contraband, and imposing a curfew. Although

3. *Palestine Report, 1936*, p. 7.
4. *Ibid.*

he did suspend certain civil rights, he did not declare martial law. The district commissioner of Tel Aviv, however, authorized the formation of a Jewish supernumerary force to protect the city, granting it permission to use arms already stored in Tel Aviv.

Incidents in Tel Aviv on Friday and Saturday dramatized to Arabs throughout Palestine the new-found confidence of the Zionists in their internationally protected status as members of the "national home." Palestinians were alarmed at the racial overtones of the recent events. They were being blatantly attacked by foreigners who were not only living in their country but were publicly stating their plans to take it over. Despite the unpopularity of the Legislative Council scheme itself, many Arabs resented its being shelved by Parliament. Now the foreigners were forming an army, sanctioned by the British authorities, who in the meantime were controlling their country. The refusal of authorities to grant a parade permit was the straw that broke the camel's back. Petitions to London had been ineffective, and protest was not allowed; the only course left was civil disobedience.

THE ORGANIZATION OF THE NATIONAL STRIKE

Although the coordination of a single set of Arab demands to the British government and the complementary formation of an organization to articulate these demands had begun by the time of the Jaffa riots, neither organization nor demands were firmed-up until a week later. In fact, the final organization of the Arab strike and its overall process can be understood only in terms of contrapuntal movements among the Zionists, the authorities, and the Palestinian Arabs between mid-April and the beginning of May. Arab leaders knew that the strike and disturbances were highly destructive to the national movement and at times wished that they could be stopped. Instead, actions of the authorities and the Zionists exacerbated Arab grievances at the grass roots. This led to a hardening of the line at the top, while simultaneously fostering dissension at the base of the national movement. The chronology of British, Zionist, and Arab moves during this period explains the closing of each side's ranks and subsequent alteration of each side's position vis-à-vis the others by the end of the strike.

From Sunday to Tuesday, April 19 to April 21, Arabs in almost every city in Palestine set up autonomous "national strike committees" in response to the Tel Aviv violence and official handling of it. Members of these committees were for the most part small businessmen and professionals, inexperienced in politics but shocked into action by the

Tel Aviv riots and assaults. While Arabs perceived this violence to be a result of British administration, their efforts to protest British policy were in no way concerted at this stage. Each committee had its own demands which centered around (but did not necessarily include and were not necessarily confined to) the limitation of immigration, the regulation of land sales, and the establishment of self-government in Palestine. The committees were formally united, and their demands regularized into a single program about a week after the Tel Aviv riots when the Supreme Arab Council (later called the Arab Higher Committee) was formed to coordinate the strike at the national level. The demands and strategy did not reach their final form until mid-May, long after most Arabs had originally assumed the strike would end.

The day after the Jaffa riot, Monday, April 20, community leaders in Jaffa met again with members of the Arab community there to discuss plans for protest of the incidents both in Tel Aviv and their own city. Like the *ad hoc* "national committee" meeting in Jerusalem on the same day, the Jaffa committee borrowed the demands and strategy formulated by the Tulkarm committee the day before. Assuming that the country could prosper only as a result of economic cooperation between the Muslim/Christian and Jewish communities, they decided as Arabs to boycott Jews until the Jewish community assented to the regulation of land sales and immigration in Palestine. All Arab shops would be closed, and no Arab was to perform his customarily low-cost services to Jews until an understanding was reached.

While the Nablus committee was similarly constituted and while it also employed the strike strategy, it adopted the United Front's November Demands to the British as its platform. Members incorporated the demand for a responsible national government in Palestine; they directed their grievances toward the authorities who fostered the national-home policy at the expense of the Arabs rather than toward the Jewish community as such. They protested the continued unregulated land sales and large-scale immigration which endangered Arab civil and national rights. The Nablus strike committee joined with the Palestine Arab Party in appealing to Syrian nationalists for support of their actions.

By Tuesday, April 21, Arabs in Gaza, Jenin, Hebron, and Haifa had set up committees and called strikes. The same day the United Front met in Jerusalem to reaffirm the demands of the Nablus committee. The following day it announced that it too would strike: the delegates postponed their trip to London until the strike was settled. In Jaffa, stores closed as a result of the Sunday riot remained closed, and by Tuesday the entire Arab sector of Palestine (with the possible exception of Haifa) was closed to business.

Peaceful civil disobedience had begun, but isolated violence continued and the government responded. On Monday, April 20, a group of three hundred Hourani migrant workers invaded several Jewish quarters in Jaffa and burned the Yemenite quarter to the ground. Five Jews and two Arabs were killed. Authorities divided the city into police districts, called for reinforcements, and rounded up all known Communists, who were adjudged responsible for the disturbances at this time. Fearing an Arab invasion of Jerusalem, authorities took similar measures there. Zionist officials reported to the district commissioner in Tel Aviv and were cautioned against arousing their followers. Wauchope summoned Arab leaders to his offices in Jerusalem, giving them similar advice. He suggested that if Arabs had complaints, these should be aired in London on the United Front's proposed trip. He added that the authorities could not be held responsible for injuries or deaths of persons involved in riots, and the following day notices to this effect were posted all over Palestine. Apparently the government was prepared to take full advantage of its avowed non-responsibility: as a result of a police charge on a riot in Jerusalem on Wednesday, the twenty-second, eight Arabs were killed and fifty-eight wounded.

While Arabs vainly attempted to amalgamate the scattered local committees on Tuesday the twenty-first, the Tel Aviv Executive Council (which had been meeting since the previous afternoon) issued a set of demands to the government. It wished the government to transfer its offices from Jaffa to Tel Aviv, and it requested that the authorities feed and provide land for the settlement of Jews who had sought safety in Tel Aviv. Some even wanted the declaration of martial law, but Wauchope counseled patience and reason, cautioning both Arab and Zionist leaders not to agitate their followers. On Wednesday, April 22, the high commissioner discussed with Tel Aviv leaders means by which the two hostile populations might be separated and thus restrained from further confrontations. The London *Times* commented, "The question arises whether a permanent no-man's land shall be maintained between the two populations."[5] Wednesday had passed relatively quietly in both Jaffa and Tel Aviv, but the following morning Mr. Thomas, the colonial secretary, echoed Wauchope's plea for a return to reason and order.

At this point Zionists brought the conflict into the international arena. Speaking before the First World Congress of Jewish Physicians meeting in Tel Aviv, Dr. Chaim Weizmann likened the Arab-Zionist hostilities to the struggle between barbarity and civilization. Noting Zionist dedication of purpose, he assured the physicians that civilization would not fall

5. April 29, 1936, p. 13.

to "the forces of destruction, the forces of the desert."[6] David Ben-Gurion, then chairman of the Jewish Agency for Palestine, told leaders of the American Jewish community that the strike necessitated a vigorous campaign for increased immigration to Palestine. Zionist resolution would be made clear to the world, he said, and the Jews would prove that Palestine's economic absorptive capacity far outstripped that which the Arabs claimed. These statements provoked Palestinians to further political organization. The following day Sulayman Tuqan, mayor of Nablus, addressed representatives of about 30 villages in an organizational meeting called to refute Weizmann's and similar charges. Meetings were also held in Jenin and Tulkarm.

The authorities responded on April 24 by cutting telephone and telegraph communications between Palestine and surrounding states, explaining that this would inhibit activists' rumor-spreading; this action created, in effect, a news blackout on the Palestine situation. The government issued another warning to would-be rioters that the crowd-control police would be armed. If crowds attacked police or even refused to disperse on orders, the police were authorized to shoot. The next day police brought machine guns and armored cars into Tulkarm to control a demonstration there. Since the frightened crowd dispersed immediately, they did not use these weapons. Yet sporadic violence continued throughout the week. Arabs and Jews still stoned one another's motor vehicles, vandalism continued, and there were riots in major Arab cities. Support for the strike was growing, uniting disparate segments of the Arab population of Palestine. Several hundred veiled Muslim women staged a protest parade in Gaza on April 25, and on the same day the Haifa boatmen went on strike, despite the difficulties of organizing them previously.

Order emerged on April 25. At this time representatives of the six Arab national political parties in Palestine met in Jerusalem to establish the Supreme Arab Council. The coalition, later called the Arab Higher Committee, included the members of both the United Front and the Istiqlal (Independence) Party, which, up to then, had not been allied with the United Front. In a statement delivered to the high commissioner, the council adopted the November Demands of the United Front in a slightly altered form:

1. Stoppage of Jewish immigration.
2. Prohibition of land sales to Jews.

---

6. Cited in Matiel E. T. Mogannam, *The Arab Woman and the Palestine Problem* (London, 1937), p. 295.

3. Formation of a national government responsible to the representative council.[7]

The third demand, calling for Palestinian independence, subsumed the other two, but the council indicated that they would accept a government statement that immigration would be suspended as a signal to begin negotiations to end the strike. The authorities were due to announce the Jewish labor quota for the next six-month period in several days.

The Supreme Arab Council was a coalition representing every faction of the Palestinian Arab bourgeoisie.[8] Composed of mature men, some of whom had served in the Ottoman Parliament, the committee theoretically was to be the base of the proposed Palestinian Parliament. The committee members were nationalists, and the business of the coalition was to translate and direct Palestinian desperation into constructive political articulation through the language of nationalism. At the local level, most strikers were not politicized—this was the first time most strikers had attempted political action—and therein lay a weakness of the national movement. The committee members were moderates, if not conservatives, but they maintained a popular base by co-opting younger and more militant groups. Thus, as the strike progressed, the Arab demands were amended, and the original coalition was opened to include possible dissenters. In the process the Arab Higher Committee unified interest-based and regionally based national-strike committees into one, albeit loosely woven, organizational fabric. Finally, members of the coalition were experienced in negotiations

7. *Times* (London), April 29, 1936, p. 14.

8. The original officers of the Higher Committee were al-Hajj Amin al-Husayni, who was the grand mufti of Jerusalem and who supported the Palestine Arab Party, president; Awni Abdul Hadi, who was a lawyer and head of the Istiqlal Party, secretary; and Ahmad Hilmi Pasha, who was a manager of the Arab Nation Bank (an institution founded to finance Palestinian smallholders whose land might otherwise be alienated), treasurer. Original members of the committee included Jamal Husayni, a cousin of the mufti and formal head of the Palestine Arab Party; Raghib Nashashibi, a former mayor of Jerusalem and former member of the Ottoman Parliament who was associated with the National Defense Party; Abd al-Latif Salah, a lawyer from Nablus who led the National League; Dr. Husayn Khalidi, a physician who was mayor of Jerusalem at the time of the strike and was a founder and leader of the Islah (Reform) Party; Ya'qub Ghusayn, a landowner and entrepreneur who was on the Board of Directors of the Arab Nation Bank and was associated with both the Young Muslims Association and the Arab Youth Executive Congress; Ya'qub Faraj, a member of the Arab Executive, the deputy mayor of Jerusalem, and an important member of the Arab Orthodox Christian community, who was on the central committee of the National Defense Party; and Alfred Rock, an entrepreneur engaged in orange growing and shipping, who was associated with the Palestine Arab Party and was an active member of the Arab Roman Catholic community.

with the British. Acting as a representative "government," the committee was responsible for negotiations with Great Britain and other governments. As a national government, the Arab Higher Committee succeeded; as the planning arm of a war of liberation it failed, but not by far.

The committee was able to unify disparate groups among Palestinians by acting as an intermediary to aid in the articulation of demands in a manner which the authorities would understand. For example, 25 Bedouin chiefs from Beersheba came to Jerusalem on April 29 to discuss a petition they intended to submit to the high commissioner. The petition had originally called for the cessation of immigration and land sales, but in the course of the discussion the Bedouins amended their statement to include the demand for a responsible government. While the committee coordinated the submission of demands, it imposed neither its form of demands nor its own ultimata on the various petitioners. Thus the committee let stand both the Bedouin demand that the government grant pardons to the imprisoned participants of demonstrations previous to 1936 and their threat to implement their demands themselves by force if the government failed to accede.

Hasan Sudqi Dajani, a Jerusalem municipal councilor, had been excluded from the Arab Higher Committee because of his presumed militance. He had organized the Motor Transport Strike Committee as an adjunct to the Arab Car Owners and Drivers Association, of which he was an officer. The Owners and Drivers were a unionlike organization of small capitalists who drove buses, taxis, and trucks, using chauffeuring fees to make payments on their vehicles. By late April the Motor Transport Strike Committee, headed by Dajani and Salah Abduh, had incorporated the withholding of taxes in their ultimata. On May 1, Dajani issued a manifesto to the Arab people on behalf of his strike committee, calling for Arabs to withhold their taxes until the authorities agreed to limit immigration. By May 5, several national-strike committees had taken up the call. Here cleavages among strikers first appeared; some of the younger and more militant strikers were ready to condemn the Higher Committee for not taking more radical action.

The government ordinarily announced labor quotas around the first of May, but since the announcement had not yet been made on May 5, the Higher Committee issued another mild memorandum to the high commissioner early that day. The members were summoned to Wauchope's office where he stated that he "was confident that none of you gentlemen associate yourselves with this [Dajani's] manifesto or any illegal act."[9] He expressed the authorities' desire that the strike cease since it caused

9. Statement outlined in Mogannam, *Arab Woman*, pp. 297–98.

"needless suffering,"[10] and asked that the committee disband itself. He urged them to present their demands in London as planned. The committee responded that they would not leave Palestine until immigration was suspended; they would not stop protesting until the government gave some indication that it would negotiate the formation of a responsible national government.

The same day Dajani and Abduh were arrested. But at 5:30 that afternoon the Higher Committee issued a second memorandum to the high commissioner, this time incorporating the Motor Transport Strike Committee ultimatum on the withholding of taxes. The committee again stated that it would accept the cessation of immigration as an indication of the authorities' good faith and would stop the strike if immigration were suspended. In its memorandum the Higher Committee noted that the stoppage of immigration was far from unprecedented at times of disorder in Palestine:

> The Arab people had hoped that the British Government would adopt a just policy and assist the Arabs in the realization of their [national] aspirations. But the Government had not even stopped Jewish immigration, as Sir Herbert Samuel and Sir John Chancellor did following the disturbances in 1921 and 1929.[11]

Although the younger militants saw this statement as unduly conservative, the British government regarded it as attempted blackmail. They explained that in addition to the constant reminders from the Jewish Agency, the Permanent Mandates Commission had recently expressed concern over the well-being of Jewish refugees from Germany.

But by May 7 the die had been cast. The Higher Committee called a meeting in Jerusalem of representatives of the various national-strike committees and the militants.[12] The meeting of 150 representatives produced another memorandum for the high commissioner. More succinct than the last, it read:

> The Conference unanimously resolves:
>
> (i)   That the Arab [Palestinian] Nation should continue the strike until

---

10. *New York Times,* May 6, 1936, p. 16.

11. Entire document reprinted in Mogannam, *Arab Woman,* pp. 298–99.

12. They included Dajani (who had recently been released from jail), Ibrahim Shanti, editor of Al-Difa' (an Arab daily) and Akram Zu'aytar, a community leader from Nablus.

the British Government introduces a basic change in its present policy
which will manifest itself in the stoppage of Jewish immigration.

(ii) That the Arab Nation should refuse to pay taxes as from May
15, 1935, should the British Government fail to introduce a fundamental
change in its policy which will manifest itself in the stoppage of Jewish
immigration.[13]

This, the final manifesto of the Arab Higher Committee, put forth conditions for ending the strike. Stoppage of Jewish immigration (not
necessarily the *permanent* stoppage) was not the primary Palestinian
demand but rather a precondition for the strike's end. When the British
government changed its pro-Zionist immigration policy, Arabs would
abandon the strike and begin negotiations with the British on their
previous demands, foremost among which was the establishment of a
responsible national government.

Throughout May, group after group in Palestine voted to support the
strike. Members of the Jerusalem Chamber of Commerce went on strike
May 12. The All-Palestine Conference of Arab Students was organized
in Jaffa on May 13. Their resolution included the three demands of
the Higher Committee and the civil-disobedience ultimatum. Like the
Bedouins in late April, they demanded the release of political prisoners
jailed prior to 1936. They also demanded that the government nullify
land transfers that had occurred in the last five years (since the John
Hope Simpson Report), and that it repeal the collective-punishment
ordinance. They even demanded that the Palestinian Boy Scouts be
allowed to break off from the British association. On May 17 the Arab
National Guard issued a proclamation urging universal support for the
strike. The document called to the attention of conservative villagers that
Great Britain was no longer a friend or protector of Islam, if in fact it
ever had been. Palestinian resistance to British rule must persist, they
said, even to the point of national self-extermination.[14] The authorities
confiscated the document the day it was issued.

Arab government officials increasingly showed support for the strike.
Although they did not strike themselves, Arab police initiated a strike-
relief fund early in June. Arab mayors meeting at Ramallah May 30
voted on whether they should call strikes of their municipal governments.
The mayors of Jaffa, Nablus, Lydda, Ramle, Jenin, Tulkarm, Bethlehem,
and Shefa'amr voted to strike as of June first. Mayors of Jerusalem, Acre,

13. Document reprinted in Mogannam, *Arab Woman*, pp. 300–1.
14. *New York Times*, May 18, 1936, p. 1.

Gaza, Safad, Majdal, Nazareth, Beersheba, Ramallah, Beit Jala, and Khan Younis voted to strike the next week if the government did not accede to the Higher Committee demands. These strikes went off as scheduled.

On June 30, one month after the mayors' meeting, 137 Arab senior officials submitted a memorandum to the government indicating their endorsement of the Palestinian demands and urging the government to follow suit. In July, 1,200 second-division Arab civil servants presented a similar memorandum. From mid-June on, Palestinian Muslims had criticized al-Hajj Amin al-Husayni for not encouraging officials of the Muslim religious courts to strike. Though they did not strike, they presented a memorandum to the government in July, reminding the "British officials of the revenge of God the Almighty."[15]

As Palestinian unity behind the demands developed, so did foreign sympathy for Palestinians. Middle Eastern and American Arabs, Christian missionaries, and public figures far removed from either Palestine or the Arab world, including Pandit Nehru, issued statements sympathetic to the Palestinians. The prime minister of Egypt, Nahhas Pasha, and the rector of al-Azhar led Egyptians in a fund drive which collected more than £E 12,000 to support the strikers. This support was by no means overwhelming, but it represented the first large-scale support ever given to Palestinians in their quest for self-determination.

THE GOVERNMENT RESPONDS: USE OF CIVIL POWERS

Although the authorities were never tolerant of the disorders, their actions to put them down became increasingly drastic as the strike proceeded. This was particularly true following the Arab memorandum concerning the nonpayment of taxes. Reluctant to resort to force of arms in what was essentially a political matter, Wauchope attempted to repress dissent under provisions of Palestinian civil law and the 1931 Palestine (Defense) Orders-in-Council. As disturbances continued, the authorities' powers were extended through successive amendments of these emergency regulations. Mass arrests, collective fines, and demolitions were characteristic of government actions at this time. By midsummer the courts were questioning the legality of these government actions.

15. Senior officials: Great Britain, Foreign Office, Palestine Royal Commission, *Report of the Palestine Royal Commission* (Parliamentary Papers, Cmd. 5479; London, 1937) [Peel Commission Report], pp. 401–3; Religious court officials: *ibid.,* p. 99.

Under Palestinian civil law, the high commissioner had the power to suspend newspapers, arrest agitators, and levy collective fines on villages and quarters of cities in violation of the law. In times of civil disorder the high commissioner could also invoke provisions of the 1931 Palestine (Defense) Orders-in-Council. These laws empowered him to impose censorship and curfews, authorize searches and seizures without a warrant, and regulate the sale of contraband. The night following the Jaffa riots these regulations were put into force. A month later, on May 22, the regulations were amended to authorize the detention of persons suspected of illegal actions. On June 2, the strike was declared illegal. Two days later, the regulations were again amended to authorize forced opening of businesses and detention of strikers in camps.

At the outset of disturbances the authorities had assumed that the Arab masses were still loyal and that Fascist and Communist propagandists were responsible for Arab anti-British sentiment. In view of this, the authorities hoped that arrest and detention of such agitators would curtail the disturbances. In the several days preceding May Day, police arrested all known Communists in Palestine (the group included 15 Arabs and 66 Jews). Despite these preparations, May Day did not go quietly. A Haifa demonstration of 2,000 persons turned into a riot when the crowd attacked the police. The police fired into the crowd, killing 2 Arabs and injuring 15. There were similar demonstrations in other Arab cities. In all these and in the subsequent framing of the Arab demands, youthful Arab nationalists played decisive roles. Thus the attention of the government turned to the "youthful militant."

The government made its first arrests of members of the resistance when, after several local national-strike committees had adopted the nonpayment of taxes provision of the Motor Transport Strike Committee manifesto issued May 1, the authors of the manifesto, Salah Abduh and Hasan Sudqi Dajani, were detained. By May 13, over 600 persons (mostly Arabs) had been arrested as a result of the disturbances. On May 23, following the Higher Committee's rejection of the Royal Commission, Wauchope authorized the arrest of 61 Arab "agitators," among whom were 40 heads of local national-strike committees. The next day Dajani was arrested a second time, along with four Arab journalists whose papers had published the Higher Committee's manifesto. Others, including Fakhri Nashashibi, were required to report to Jerusalem authorities three times daily.

By the beginning of June the authorities had transformed the Royal Air Force billet near Jaffa at Sarafand into a new concentration camp. The other camp at Auja al-Hafir was so full that it could not accommodate any more prisoners. Later it was explained that Sarafand was more accessible than the other camp, which was located in the Sinai. By the beginning of June, 37 more leaders had been sent to Sarafand, including Awni Abdul Hadi of the Higher Committee and Asem Sa'id, Jaffa's 70-year-old mayor. On June 19 Mr. Ormsby-Gore announced that 2,598 persons had been arrested in Palestine as a result of the strike. Of the 1,823 Arabs who had been tried, 1,206 had been convicted; another 281 awaited trial. Of the 418 Jews who had been tried, 328 had been convicted; 76 more awaited trial. By the nineteenth, 81 Arab leaders had been imprisoned at Sarafand. At least 122 other leaders were under suspicion at that time, "most of whom [were] to be deported to Sarafand within the week."[16] By the end of the disturbances these figures must have increased considerably; official figures, however, are not consistent. At one point during the strike more than 400 leaders of strike committees were in prison;[17] yet without these leaders the strike continued.

Failing arrests, the high commissioner still had the power under civil law to impose collective fines on settlements. This power was said to be based on historical Ottoman prerogatives. The authorities' resurrection of these antique laws (dating back to the barter economy) occasioned jokes among the Arabs. Early in May the authorities announced that collective fines would be levied against villages and towns where resistance was encountered. The collection of fines began in mid-May in the northern district with government confiscation of 193 houses as punitive fines. On June 12, public laws concerning the imposition of these fines were augmented by new emergency regulations, and by mid-July fines had been levied on most major Arab settlements. Apparently the collections were made routinely until July 23, when Gaza officials made an appeal to the Palestine Supreme Court to set aside its £P 1,000 fine. The city was being punished for sabotage of railways and telephone lines in the area.

On July 31, Judges McDonnell and Manning ruled that the emergency

16. Great Britain, *Parliamentary Debates*, (Commons), 5th ser., vol. 313, (June 19, 1936), col. 1320, by Ormsby-Gore (cited hereafter as *Debates, Commons*).

17. Mogannam enumerated some of these: "Faiz Bey Haddad, Chairman of the National Committee of Jerusalem; Fakhri Bey Nashashibi, formerly Assistant Mayor of Jerusalem; Izzet Effendi Darwaza, General Director Awkaf; Nebih Bey al Admeh, a leading member of the Istiklal Party; Abdul Hamid Effendi Shuman, General Manager of the Arab Bank; . . . Ajaj Effendi Nuwaihed, Editor of the *Arab Weekly;* Ibrahim Effendi Shanti, Proprietor and Editor of *Ad-Difaa* newspaper; Rasheed Effendi Al Haj Ibrahim, Manager of the Arab Bank, Haifa; Ahmed Effendi Shukairi, Advocate of Acre; Hanna Effendi Asfour, Advocate of Haifa; Dr. Mustapha Busknak, Local Director of Awkaf, Nablus; Subhi Bey Al Khadra, Advocate and Local Director of Awkaf, Acre; . . . and many other Doctors and Advocates" (*Arab Woman*, pp. 305–6n.)

regulations of June 12 were not constitutional insofar as they were not subject to appeal by the victims. Furthermore, the chief justice, Mr. McDonnell, censured procedures by which officials took their actions. An unauthorized person—the assistant district commissioner—had authorized the fine. Regulations did not allow for levying fines in cash; rather they had to be levied in kind. Finally the regulations were not retroactive, and the Gaza fine, levied for sabotage which took place before the regulations were enacted, was set aside. The court urged the authorities to restrain their applications of emergency measures. It was assumed that the judgment would annul similar fines on other cities. On August 1, another collective-fines ordinance was published; this one was retroactive to April 19 and allowed the payment of fines in cash. By September 14, fines equaling $90,000 had been levied in 28 towns—yet rural resistance continued unabated.

It was suggested on May 28 that the rural area surrounding Nablus, a stronghold of resistance to the collection of punitive fines, be evacuated of civilians and bombed. This action was not taken in Nablus, but a similar strategy was suggested for the city of Jaffa. Throughout the strike the old city of Jaffa had been entirely outside government control. The old quarter of Jaffa offered special problems to the authorities. Built on a mountainous promontory overlooking the harbor, the walled quarter was an impenetrable fortress. The strike had begun in Jaffa, and militant youth there were encouraged by the Jaffa boatmen, who lived mainly in the old city. A haven for snipers and manufacturers of homemade bombs, Jaffa could not be patrolled on foot. The narrow streets, so steep that in places they were constructed as stairways, prevented the use by police of armored motor vehicles. In early June police had considered sealing the city with barbed-wire barricades, placing it under seige.

Royal Air Force planes traveling over Jaffa on June 16 dropped leaflets into the old city announcing to residents the government's intention to execute a sweeping "urban-renewal" program there. The work would begin immediately since a corps of Royal Engineers happened to be in Palestine at the time. Most of the old city would be demolished, ridding the place of congested and unsanitary housing, all for the benefit of the inhabitants. Two wide boulevards, flanked with spacious, modern buildings, were to be cut through the old quarter in the direction of the Jaffa port. Residents questioned the government's sudden philanthropy, suggesting that the demolition of their quarter was a military rather than town-planning effort.

Although demolition had been scheduled to begin June 16, the government delayed work two days while it considered the fate of a small mosque in the path of destruction. Meanwhile, residents were forced to evacuate the quarter, most of them to take up housekeeping in orange groves to the east of the city. The government planned to compensate the 6,000 displaced persons at the rate of 20 mils (five English pence) per person per week, and some persons were even given shelter in public buildings. By five o'clock on the morning of June 18 the city had been searched and sealed, and police were stationed at all gates. In the next few days structures were blown up, cluster by cluster, layer by layer. The London *Times* reported that by Sunday, June 21, the demolition deemed necessary by the town-planning effort had been accomplished. The Hourani quarter and much of Jaffa's old city had been eliminated.[18]

On June 26 the government circulated a second batch of notices:

> In accordance with the scheme for opening up the Old City of Jaffa your house may be demolished.
>
> You are therefore required to vacate it before 7 p.m. on Sunday 28th June, 1936.
>
> No claim for compensation in respect of furniture or effects left in your house after that hour will be considered.[19]

On June 27 several homeowners filed motions with the Palestine Supreme Court to protest this measure. On July 1, Mr. Ormsby-Gore announced in Parliament that the demolition was necessary for the defense of Palestine. One case came to court July 3, after the owner's house had been demolished. The chief justice, Mr. McDonnell, and the senior puisne judge, Mr. Manning, ruled first that the government ought to have made clear that the demolition had been necessitated by the military emergency in Palestine, not town-planning as the government had claimed (the English phrase "scheme for opening up" had misleadingly been rendered "town-planning scheme" in Arabic); second, that the legal provision under which such demolition was to take place allowed the authorities to "pull down" structures in accordance with normal wrecking procedures but not to blow them up with dynamite; third, that although only the Jaffa district commissioner had the power to authorize such "pulling down," this official claimed he had not authorized the action (in fact, no leaflets or papers showered on, or served on, Jaffa residents were signed by any government official, nor was it even indicated which office had sent them

18. June 22, 1936, p. 14.

19. The notices are reprinted along with two decisions for the case in *Palestine and Transjordan,* July 11, 1936, supplement. A less detailed but more available account appears in the *Times* (London), July 6, 1936, p. 13.

out); fourth, that the government was bound to make full compensation for damages whether or not effects had been removed by the appointed hour; and finally, that some of the houses demolished, including the house in question, were not even sited on parcels destined for "renewal." Thus, while the court did not overrule the government's action, it did severely censure the means by which it was taken and waived court costs for the petitioner.

Efforts to Mediate: Arab-British Deadlock

Whereas in May the Higher Committee followed the precedent set by the United Front, confining negotiations to Palestine and negotiating functions to Palestinians, in June and the months following the most important negotiations either took place outside Palestine or utilized services of non-Palestinians. From late June through mid-July representatives of the Higher Committee traveled from capital to capital, concentrating their efforts in London. The Higher Committee's May 7 manifesto had set the stoppage of immigration as a signal to end the strike and begin negotiations on the national demands. The authorities, however, called for an end to the strike as a signal for an inquiry into Arab grievances, foremost among which they understood to be the insufficient restriction of immigration. This deadlock continued until late August when mediation efforts of the Iraqi foreign minister showed signs of success.

A few days before the announcement of the labor quota, the high commissioner stated that the government would appoint a royal commission to investigate the merits of the Palestinian case. On May 18 he announced the quota. The 4,500 certificates allotted (4,000 to the Jewish Agency and 500 to the government department of immigration) represented a dramatic increase[20] over the 3,250 certificates issued in the previous six-month period. The official London announcement of the royal commission was made the same day. Two days later, on May 20, the Arab Higher Committee issued a proclamation indicating that it would not accept the appointment of another commission in lieu of government stoppage of immigration. Had the authorities only followed recommendations of the previous commissions, that is, limited immigration, regulated

20. The Zionist *Palestine Economic Review* explained, "the 4,500 quota should result in the immigration of a larger number of individuals, as each certificate allotted to married men covers a whole family unit" (Vol. I, No. 6–7 [June–July, 1936], p. 6).

land sales, and established a responsible national government, Arabs would not have gone on strike in the first place. If the authorities agreed to follow only the recommendation regarding immigration, the Higher Committee would call off the strike and commence negotiations on the national demands. Instead of a British commission, it suggested another *international* inquiry into the mandate. It also recommended that a plebiscite be held to decide whether the mandate should be continued.[21]

Concurrent with their official rejection on May 28 of the proposed royal commission, the Higher Committee cabled the League of Nations Permanent Mandates Commission to ask for an official investigation of the Palestine disturbances. These began immediately. Mr. H. H. Trusted appeared as the British delegate during the first ten days of June. He said little, explained nothing, and the League did nothing. During the inquiry it became clear that he was not entirely familiar with events in Palestine. Anyone having acquaintance with the subject was in Palestine or London attempting to deal with it. The official explanation of British intransigence ran that the chairman of the commission was Italian and was thus considered a belligerent in the Palestine disturbances (the current British explanation of the strike was that it had been brought on by Italian propaganda).

Meanwhile the Zionist Federation of Great Britain and Ireland filed a statement with the League commission, holding that an inquiry was unnecessary and that the "Arab attitude" during the strike demonstrated their unreadiness for self-government. They demanded not only a larger

---

21. But as early as 1919, delegates representing Muslim, Christian, and Jewish communities in the Ottoman province of Syria (Lebanon, Syria, and Palestine) resolved to "reject the claims of the Zionists for the establishment of a Jewish commonwealth in that part of southern Syria which is known as Palestine, and we are opposed to Jewish immigration into any part of the country. We do not acknowledge that they have a title, and we regard their claims as a grave menace to our national, political, and economic life. Our Jewish fellow-citizens shall continue to enjoy the rights and to bear the responsibilities which are ours in common" ("Resolutions of the General Syrian Congress, Damascus, July 2, 1919"; reprinted in appendix G of George Antonius, *The Arab Awakening: The Story of the Arab National Movement* [1938; New York, 1965], pp. 440–42, quote from p. 441. These resolutions along with 1,800 others were presented to the American section of the Inter-Allied Commission (King-Crane Commission), which commented in its report, "with a deep sense of sympathy for the Jewish cause, the Commissioners feel bound to recommend that only a greatly reduced Zionist programme be attempted by the Peace Conference, and even that, only very gradually initiated. This would have to mean *that Jewish immigration should be definitely limited,* and that the project for making Palestine distinctly a Jewish commonwealth should be given up" ("Recommendations of the King-Crane Commission with regard to Syria-Palestine and Iraq"; reprinted in appendix H of Antonius, *The Arab Awakening,* pp. 443–58, quote from p. 450; italics added).

volume of immigration into Palestine but also an extension of the national home into Transjordan. The Permanent Mandates Commission inquiry was resumed in late August, with the British still refusing to make an official statement until the Peel Commission made its inquiry. The League could not act on petitions it received until Britain made an official statement. It did not discuss the 1936 disturbances until its 32nd session in the summer of 1937.

At the end of May and beginning of June the Higher Committee engaged in intensive talks with the high commissioner. On June 3, the high commissioner flew to Amman to discuss the situation with Amir Abdullah of Transjordan. The *New York Times* speculated that Abdullah, as the most vulnerable Arab statesman, might make an easy ally in negotiations. As the principal exponent of a "Greater Syria," a united Arab state, Abdullah and his vision might be made to work for Britain. Speculation ran high that the disorders would soon spread from Palestine into Transjordan, and the amir was already having trouble with his Bedouins. But he replied that he would be unable to act as an intermediary unless empowered to make certain concessions to the Higher Committee. Wauchope flew back to Jerusalem June 6.

On June 7, al-Hajj Amin al-Husayni, Mayor Khalidi, Awni Abdul Hadi, and two others flew to Amman to confer with Abdullah. On their return the same day, Awni Abdul Hadi was arrested. Baiting the high commissioner, the mufti, al-Hajj Amin, reportedly

> informed Sir Arthur that the only solution that the Arabs would accept would be that the Jews in Palestine who entered the country since the World War should be sent out. Arabs would then buy land with funds from "Palestine Tickets."[22]

The joke ran that if Zionists could colonize Palestine, displacing Arabs, why couldn't Arabs launch a bond drive for the recolonization of their country? If Arab civil rights were unimportant to the authorities, the rights of the Zionists ought not to be important either. Several Arab newspapers had in the meantime printed rumors that the government was ready to concede on immigration. On June 9, Wauchope suspended these newspapers, denying that the authorities would concede anything. The Higher Committee's statement issued the same day declared that negotiations were impossible at the time, as the government's actions precluded them.

In a statement before the Supply Committee on June 19, the colonial secretary, Mr. Ormsby-Gore, reaffirmed the British position on continued

22. *New York Times,* June 8, 1936, p. 10.

immigration and British commitment to the national-home policy. On
June 29, the Higher Committee answered the colonial secretary. They
particularly stressed that a national government responsible to all segments
of the Palestine population must be established. They further suggested
that Zionist plans endangered the Muslim Holy Places in Jerusalem,
particularly the Haram al-Sharif. Finally they protested the "use of
armed forces against an unarmed people."[23] The Arabs and British were
talking past each other.

On July 13, Wauchope again went to Amman to confer with Abdullah.
In view of the deadlock, the Associated Press asked Abdullah whether
he would mediate to end the strike even if the authorities refused to
concede on immigration. He answered:

> No, we cannot interfere. . . . But a man does not hate himself. And all
> Arabs will hold on with their teeth until the British Government realizes
> the justice of Arabian claims for independence, economic security,
> freedom from the rising tide of Jews who have smothered the Palestinian
> Arab by absorbing his land. If there had been no Balfour Declaration,
> Jews would have come under an Arabian Government in Palestine.
> They would have been welcome.

The interview also contained the first public statement on what concession
on immigration would be considered an acceptable invitation to negotiations on the national demands.

> Now to find any solution, Jewish immigration must be limited to 30%
> of the present Jewish population if any room is to be left at all for
> the Arabs.[24]

Meanwhile, early in June several representatives of the Higher Com-
mittee had departed from Palestine to make the circuit of foreign capitals.
On July 2, the delegation presented the Palestinian case in full to about
one hundred members of Parliament. Several days later they set up an
Arab information office in London. On July 14 the delegation met with
Mr. Ormsby-Gore to present their interpretation of the events in Palestine.
On July 20, Ormsby-Gore announced the membership of the royal commission of inquiry, but did not release the terms of inquiry until several
days later. Since the members of the commission were experienced in

23. *Times* (London), June 29, 1936, p. 14; see below, "The Mobilization of the
Military," for a discussion of the use of military forces.
24. *New York Times,* July 14, 1936, p. 9.

colonial affairs, the Arabs were encouraged that the terms of inquiry would be favorable. By July 25, the deadlock in negotiations was obvious, and the Higher Committee met in Jerusalem to discuss strategy. The members decided that they would cooperate with the commission if its terms of inquiry allowed negotiations on their national demands. Awni Abdul Hadi, imprisoned at Sarafand, had a letter smuggled to al-Hajj Amin al-Husayni suggesting that Arabs boycott the commission if its terms kept negotiations within the framework of the mandate and precluded negotiations on their national demands.

On July 27, the one hundredth day of the strike, the Higher Committee issued a congratulatory statement to strikers and appealed for support from non-Palestinians. The day was proclaimed a national day of prayer. It was rumored that London was prepared to enter negotiations. But on July 29 Mr. Ormsby-Gore announced that the commission's inquiry would be bound by the terms of the mandate; the *New York Times* recorded that while Arabs were disappointed, "Jews were not displeased."[25] On August 1, there was a meeting in Jerusalem of unidentified members of the Arab elite. As usual it was reported that enthusiasm for the strike had waned, and the leaders wanted out.

On July 23, however, Abdullah had extended another invitation to the Higher Committee to come to Amman, and the committee had accepted. It was assumed that Abdullah would convince the British to make concessions on the terms of inquiry and that the Palestinians would accept the new terms and call off the strike. The question remained whether the militants would accept the plan. On August 4 a party of 26 Palestinians, including the Higher Committee and interested mayors, met with Abdullah in Amman to discuss the acceptance of the royal commission. By August 7 it was known that Abdullah had stressed that the British would ultimately stop the strike with brute force regardless of the justice of the Palestinian demands. He suggested that the committee call off the strike unilaterally. In return, the committee could count on his efforts to achieve concessions.

On August 8 it was rumored that Abdullah's mediation attempt had not worked. By August 11 the Higher Committee issued another proclamation condemning the terms of inquiry and stressing that Palestinian independence was long overdue. Although the Higher Committee also called a congress of representatives of local national-strike committees to meet in Jerusalem August 20 to discuss Abdullah's offer, by August 15 newspapers printing explanations of Abdullah's proposal were publicly burned. On August 17 two Jewish nurses were murdered in Jaffa, and, as a result, the authorities extended the Jaffa curfew to 21 hours and prohibited the scheduled Jerusalem congress.

25. July 30, 1936, p. 4.

On August 18 Nuri al-Sa'id (the foreign minister of Iraq) met with King Ghazi, Yasin Hashimi (the Iraqi prime minister) and Sir Archibald Kerr Clark (the British ambassador to Baghdad) to discuss Nuri's possible role as a mediator in the strike. On August 20, Nuri stopped off in Jerusalem "on his way to Europe." In Palestine he interviewed members of the Higher Committee for four days, including (with government permission) those interned at Sarafand. His plan for settlement was to stop the violence and wait for a suspension of immigration, then—and only then—to negotiate with the commission. What differentiated Nuri's scheme from Abdullah's was that Palestinians would still hold the trump card: the strike.

On August 23 the first apparent breakthrough in the strike occurred. The *New York Times* reported:

> — Jerusalem, Aug. 22 (wireless) This correspondent learned tonight on the most reliable authority that it now has been definitely decided to order a stoppage of immigration from the time of the arrival of the British Royal Commission coming to investigate the Palestine disorders until after all the work in connection with the investigations and recommendations has been completed.[26]

The same day 25 prisoners were released from the Sarafand concentration camp.

Nuri then consulted with leaders in Amman and Cairo on August 25 and 26. The Higher Committee was to discuss the scheme privately on the twenty-fifth. On August 24, Awni Abdul Hadi had developed problems with his teeth. At Nuri's request he was permitted to see a dentist in Jerusalem and was then allowed to stay on to participate in the talks. On August 26, the Higher Committee communicated with Nuri, then in Alexandria, their desire to meet with him again. But *Falastin,* an Arab daily in Palestine, reported that the militants would accept no scheme which would not eventuate in full independence for Palestine. On August 29 leaders of national-strike committees announced to the Higher Committee that they would accept the commission on Nuri's terms. The *New York Times* reported that Nuri said he had "reasons to believe that Government would order the stoppage of Jewish immigration as soon as acts of violence cease."[27] On August 30 the Higher Committee published a proclamation indicating that it had accepted Nuri's offer of mediation.

Negotiations have taken place between the Arab Higher Committee and

26. August 23, 1936, p. 10.
27. August 28, 1936, p. 3 (dated Jerusalem, August 27).

Nuri Pasha Es-Said, the Foreign Minister of Iraq, for several days, during which all points relating to the Palestine Arab Case were discussed in an atmosphere of confidence and frankness, as a result of which a complete understanding has been reached and the unanimous approval for the intervention of the Iraqi Government and the Arab Sovereign Princes has been given with complete confidence and satisfaction. The said minister will therefore conduct the necessary official correspondence in this matter, while at the same time the Arab Higher Committee will submit this proposal to the public at a congress of the National Committees for confirmation.

Meanwhile the general strike will continue with the same steadfast conviction hitherto shown until these negotiations are placed on a firm basis, which will secure to this nation its existence, and will fulfil its rights and hopes if God so wills it.[28]

Ibrahim Pasha, the Transjordanian premier, had been in Palestine since mid-August, and Fuad Hamzah, the Saudi Arabian undersecretary for foreign affairs, was rumored to be on his way.

COMPLETING THE TRIANGLE:
ENTER THE ZIONISTS

Unlike the Arab nationalists, at the outset of the strike Jewish nationalists were blessed with an ongoing organization. This organization went to work immediately following the Jaffa demonstrations on April 19, and, like the Higher Committee, formulated demands and participated in diplomacy both inside and out of Palestine. While at first Zionist demands centered on the speedy cessation of the strike (preferably through the use of martial law) and small concessions to bolster the status of the national home under attack, later these demands quieted. They gave way to efforts of the diplomatic wing to disseminate a Zionist interpretation of the Palestine events. This interpretation obscured the primary Arab demand for independence, substituting for it an anti-Semitic desire on the part of the Arabs to stop Jewish immigration to Palestine and, with the help of the strike, to strangle the yet embryonic national home there. Efforts to mediate and negotiations for a settlement of the strike were in actuality not bilateral, but trilateral: the Zionists completed the triangle.
Following the Jaffa riots on April 19, the authorities had sanctioned

28. *Palestine and Transjordan*, September 12, 1936, p. 4.

the formation of a Jewish supernumerary force to protect Tel Aviv, permitting it to use weapons already stored there. Two days later the Tel Aviv Executive Council issued a set of formal demands to the authorities. The authorities had dismissed these, counseling patience. On May 7, the day the Arabs voted civil disobedience, the Executive Council repeated its demands that the government move the courts and government offices from Jaffa to Tel Aviv, that it give special considerations to strike victims, and that it offer greater protection to the city. On the following day, May 8, the government offices were moved.

Throughout May, Zionist officials grew increasingly impatient with the authorities' reluctance to intern or exterminate all rebels and repeatedly argued for the imposition of martial law. On May 14 the demands of the Executive Council were again submitted to the high commissioner by a deputation led by Tel Aviv's Mayor Dizengoff. The deputation

strongly criticized the Palestine government for not taking strict measures in the country's present condition. Mayor Dizengoff said he was speaking on behalf of 150,000 Jews in Tel Aviv who wanted to know whether or not they have a high commissioner.

The deputation further demanded a Jewish army which could function in the event the government found itself "too weak" to do so. In response the high commissioner praised the delegation's

exemplary behavior and self-control, . . . [and] requested Jews to fortify themselves with more patience.[29]

Although the authorities displayed the forces under their command by holding a military parade in Jerusalem on May 17, Zionists repeated their criticisms of Wauchope's policies. But the *Palestine Post* noted philosophically that even the extermination of the entire Jewish population of Palestine would not change history since Europe stood behind the national home.[30]

The Tel Aviv Executive Council had repeatedly complained that the Jaffa boatmen's strike had severed Tel Aviv's link with the outside world — a link without which the city could not survive. They demanded permission to build a jetty at the mouth of the Yarkon River to eliminate

29. *New York Times,* May 15, 1936, p. 16.
30. *New York Times,* May 18, 1936, p. 11.

Jewish dependence upon the "Arab" port at Jaffa. Dampened festivities
at the Levant Trade Fair in Tel Aviv had dramatized the importance of
a port to the city. Although the fair had opened as scheduled on May 1,
the opening of the pavilions had been delayed a week. Much of the
merchandise to be displayed was either inaccessible in the Jaffa port area
or had been rerouted through the Haifa port, where Jews as well as Arabs
unloaded ships. Because of the disturbances, attendance at the fair was
little more than half that of the previous trade fair (320,000 as opposed
to 600,000 in 1934).

Thus the authorities approved the building of a port at Tel Aviv, in
spite of the high surf there, which engineers said would hamper loading
and unloading operations. On May 19 the government allowed the first
ship to be unloaded at Tel Aviv. Between May 26 and June 2 municipal
officials made £P 76,000 in subscriptions available to the public to finance
the port. On June 4 the government officially approved plans to build the
jetty and dredge the river mouth. With this, and the announcement on
May 28 that the government would furnish a Jewish youth force with
weapons, Zionist opposition to official policies in Palestine appeared
to subside.

In fact, this opposition took on a new character. Having purged itself
of negative demands, the policy became "constructive." Zionists now
appealed for increased Jewish immigration and settlement in Palestine
and for the reaffirmation of the Jewish rights guaranteed under the
mandate. Thus on May 28 the Jewish Agency petitioned for official
British encouragement of settlement in Palestine. The Pro-Palestine
Federation (of America) reminded the British authorities of the plight of
German Jewry, urging support for the Palestinian haven for victims of
European anti-Semitism. The Zionist Federation of Great Britain expressed fears for the safety of Palestinian Jewry, urging the arming of
Jews there. On June 21 the Jewish Agency Executive called for a world-
wide mobilization of "their forces for a well-balanced political effort and
strengthened constructive endeavor to protect the Jewish population in
Palestine."[31] The next day the United Palestine Appeal announced its
intention to raise $3.5 million to aid in the endeavor.

By mid-August, and with the increasing success of Arab attempts to
begin negotiations for a settlement of the strike, Zionists made several
decisive political moves aimed at obscuring the primary Arab demand for
independence. Participants in the First World Jewish Congress, meeting
the second week of August in Geneva, called attention to the right guaranteed under the mandate for Jews to immigrate to Palestine and resolved

31. *New York Times*, June 22, 1936, p. 1.

to urge the League of Nations and the British government not to alter the status of the Balfour Declaration in the mandate. On August 17 the Zionist National Council, meeting under the leadership of Mr. Isaac Ben Zvi, resolved to "mobilize world Jewish opinion against even a temporary suspension of the immigration which is so essential to its conception of Zionism."[32]

On August 21 Mayor Dizengoff castigated the government for not taking more strict measures against the Arabs and accused authorities of "blocking the national home." On August 24, a Zionist delegation again urged the high commissioner to impose martial law. Referring to the *New York Times* report that the authorities would shortly suspend immigration to facilitate Nuri al-Sa'id's mediation, Dr. Chaim Weizmann called for Jews to "exercise all moral pressure, which is the only weapon at their disposal against such an astonishing action."[33] And so the litany continued.

MOBILIZATION OF THE MILITARY

Caught between two irreconcilable sets of demands, Wauchope had no choice but to take the middle road. While wielding the civil powers at his command in no uncertain terms, he also made restrained use of his military authority. By midsummer, however, the authorities were straddling the fine line between civil repression and outright martial law. Wauchope's initial restraint had proved reassuring to neither the Arabs nor the Zionists, and from May through September, unit after unit of the British army entered Palestine. In the early part of the strike this military force did not sufficiently intimidate the rebels; by June the scene of conflict had shifted to the countryside, where orthodox military methods were ineffective in the control of guerrilla warfare. By September, after a series of high-level political maneuvers, the decision was made in London over Wauchope's head to issue a proclamation which would facilitate the imposition of martial law. With the presence of over 20,000 troops in Palestine, civil disobedience had no chance of success.

In the early part of the strike military techniques and personnel were used sparingly. Cities where disturbances occurred were cordoned off and patrolled by "occupation" police. After April 25 the police were armed and empowered to use their guns in crowd control. By June 2 military reinforcements were empowered to work as police in crowd control and

32. *Times* (London), August 18, 1936, p. 10; compare *New York Times,* August 14, 1936, p. 2.
33. *Times* (London), August 27, 1936, p. 12.

preventive patrols. But as the disturbances proceeded unabated, the authorities called in increasing numbers of police and military. As of December 31, 1935, the Palestine police force had consisted of 2,576 men, of whom 1,465 were Arabs, 746 were British, and 365 were Jewish. By the end of 1936 the forces had been increased by almost 1,000 men to include 1,902 Arabs, 930 British, and 484 Jews. In addition, 3,000 Jewish supernumerary police were authorized in 1936, more than 2,000 of whom were in action by June 24.

The Palestine Defense Force (British regulars) normally consisted of 1,970 men, most of whom were in the two infantry divisions stationed in Palestine. By May 10 the first reinforcements of 300 infantrymen arrived in Palestine. On May 21 a battalion of Seaforth Highlanders left Egypt for Palestine. By the beginning of June, the Royal Scots Fusilers, the Loyal Regiment, and the Cameron Highlanders were all in Palestine. On June 2, the Second Battalion of the Bedfordshire and Hertfordshire Regiment arrived; on June 7 the First Battalion of the York and Lancaster Regiment arrived from Alexandria; on June 9 the Second Battalion of the Cheshire Regiment arrived from Egypt; on June 28 the Eighth Hussars (mechanized cavalry) arrived in Palestine. This made a total of nine battalions over and above regular troop strength in Palestine. Almost two brigades of regular British troops were operating in the country by the end of June.

At the end of August, the First Battalion of the King's Own Scottish Borders sailed from Malta. Royal Navy personnel even participated in land operations, aiding in the Jaffa demolitions and policing Haifa and Nablus. When Arab railroad operators went on strike, naval personnel operated the trains. These personnel were further aided by 700 members of the Royal Air Force. Meanwhile, troops from other parts of the Mediterranean were being redeployed to Egypt to beef-up depleted forces there. Troops came with full battle equipment, including tanks, armored cars, and machine guns. In a Questions Session in Commons, Mr. Gallacher asked Mr. Duff Cooper, secretary of state for war, the number of casualties in the entire British Imperial Army so far in the year. As of July 14 there had been 33, all of which had occurred in Palestine.

At the inception of the disorders, these troops were used primarily as police reinforcements in the cities to handle unruly crowds. By mid-June, however, the scene of disorders had spread to the countryside, and sabotage in the rural areas became increasingly well-organized and aggressive as the strike progressed. Peasants had joined other rebels who occupied themselves by sniping at Jewish colonies, police patrols, and police billets. Many of these rebels intimidated rich farmers, extorting contributions to the strike fund and forcibly dissuading conservatives from open opposition to the strike. Rebels bombed railways and held up convoys of vehicles traveling the roads. Little boys were encouraged to keep roads well-strewn with nails, large pieces of scrap metal, and stones.

But just as urban violence occurred when troops or police used force to break up protest demonstrations, most rural violence occurred when troops attempted to collect fines, conduct searches and seizures, or demolish houses. Here the military encountered grave difficulties in the control of the resistance movement, which fought not so much to express national convictions as to defend its own property. Particularly after the May 7 declaration of the Higher Committee, conflict centered in Arab or predominantly Arab areas and—as in the cities—most rural violence appeared between the Arabs and police. Participation of Jews in open conflict, either as victims or as perpetrators of terrorism, was relatively small.

On July 6 the military announced a "comb out" in progress in the rural area bounded by Jerusalem, Nablus, Tulkarm, and Lydda. Up to this time strategists had assumed that resistance to British authority was reducible to intimidation of the peasantry by "marauding bands." Four thousand troops participated in the "comb out," utilizing machine guns and tanks. While this formidable army passed through the area searching homes for contraband and arresting members of the populace, RAF planes dropped leaflets reminding the "natives" that Britain would protect them against intimidation if they stopped the strike. By the end of the operations the following day, officials announced that troops had encountered only small pockets of resistance but that the area was under control. In an engagement July 8 in the area declared "combed out," six Arabs were killed and one wounded. The London *Times* correspondent again identified the problem:

> The lesson to be gained from the operations seems to be that although the troops, thanks to their superior number and efficient organization, are able to deal promptly with marauders when they try to attack, they are faced with an extremely difficult task when they try to seek them out.[34]

Encounters and operations of this sort continued in Palestine until 1939. As the 1936 disorders progressed, the authorities used more force. By August troops were using the RAF as cover rather than for leafletting. By September the resistance had shot down at least one of the planes. The authorities found these miltary difficulties embarrassing—doubly so thanks to continual reminders of the threatened status of the British-guaranteed national home. Rumors surrounding Nuri's mediation attempts brought these reminders to a crescendo. Matters came to a head on August

34. July 8, 1936, p. 14.

31 with the *Palestine Post's* publication of an inflammatory article on Nuri's mediations. According to the London *Times,* the article said in part that

> all the proceedings of the last few days' hiatus have shifted the centre of gravity in the administration of the country, in the public mind at all events, from Government House to the Headquarters of the Moslem Supreme Council.[35]

In London, on September 1, Chaim Weizmann wrote a letter to Mr. Ormsby-Gore, imploring him not to allow a suspension of immigration into Palestine and enclosed a copy of the *Palestine Post* article.

On September 2 the British Cabinet met in special session to discuss recent European events and a dispatch from Sir Arthur Wauchope, the high commissioner in Palestine. Only 14 of the 21 Cabinet members were present. Some, including the prime minister, were on holiday; one had the chicken pox. The meeting lasted four hours. After the meeting Mr. Ormsby-Gore answered Weizmann's letter, disavowing any statement that the authorities intended to suspend immigration.

> No such terms have been agreed to either by the High Commissioner or by His Majesty's Government. Moreover there is no foundation for the suggestion which is referred to in the letter addressed August 31 by the Jewish Agency to the High Commissioner that the High Commissioner has authorized Nuri Pasha to give assurances regarding measures including the suspension of immigration to be taken after the cessation of the disturbances. Not only has Nuri Pasha not been authorized to give any assurances, but, Sir Arthur Wauchope states, he has not asked for any such authority.[36]

The same day, war games at Sussex were abruptly canceled. The First Division (15,000 strong) was given orders to proceed directly to Palestine. This division consisted of twelve infantry battalions, including artillery. Friday night, September 4, the government called out reserves to augment the English forces. Commenting on these moves, the London *Times* reported "Arab despair" and "Jewish satisfaction."[37] The high commissioner, however, continued to oppose the imposition of martial law in Palestine. The next day he met with British military authorities and conferred with Abdullah in Amman. He pleaded with the amir to use his

35. September 1, 1936, p. 12.
36. *Times* (London), September 4, 1936, p. 12.
37. September 5, 1936, p. 10.

offices to call off the strike before the declaration of martial law. Abdullah regretted that he could do nothing until the government agreed to negotiate with the Higher Committee. On September 5 and 6 the Higher Committee met in Jerusalem. They counseled Arabs to remain calm.

On September 7 the government issued a policy statement giving its official interpretation of the events of the strike and disorders. The proclamation implied that Nuri's mediation efforts had failed because the Higher Committee refused to call off the strike. It declared that agreement with the Arab demands would constitute an abrogation of the mandate. Therefore it officially announced the calling-in of troop reinforcements and the appointment of Gen. J. G. Dill as commander of these forces.[38]

Astonished, the Higher Committee met on the seventh and eighth to discuss strategy. They announced that they had empowered Nuri to negotiate in their stead with the authorities and had been waiting for the authorities to contact Nuri. With the Higher Committee still meeting on the ninth, al-Hajj Amin al-Husayni, Raghib Nashashibi, and Moshe Sharett (from the Jewish Agency) went to Wauchope's office to dispute the accuracy of certain details in the government's policy statement. Apparently Wauchope was interested in the Palestinians' charges. He held intensive meetings with the Higher Committee throughout the following three days.

The Higher Committee issued another proclamation on the thirteenth, making the following statements: (1) The rioting began in Tel Aviv and was not started by Arabs. (2) The strike was called to dramatize the Palestinian demand for independence. (3) Many illegal acts committed by Arabs were committed in response to repressive acts on the part of troops. (4) By Mr. Ormsby-Gore's own admission, intimidation played a very small role in the Arab resistance to colonial authority. (5) The government's promise of a royal commission was not sufficient to end the strike because the government regularly failed to follow the recommendations of its commissions. (6) The intervention of the Arab monarchs and Nuri's mediation have not failed, since their offers still stand. Nuri was then engaged in talks with other governments on the Palestine situation. The proclamation continued with the statement that

the Committee asked the continuance of the strike only until the other parties had accepted the principle of intervention, which principle had been accepted by the Committee.[39]

38. September 7 declaration reprinted in the *Times* (London), September 8, p. 12. Dill had been the director of military operations and intelligence in the War Office.

39. *Palestine and Transjordan,* September 19, 1936, pp. 5, 8.

The same day General Dill, commander of emergency forces in Palestine, arrived. It was announced that Lt. Col. F. H. Kisch had been appointed the Jewish liaison to the British military in Palestine.

On the eighteenth of September, eight British Cabinet members and several military advisers met to consider a proclamation enabling the high commissioner in Palestine to declare martial law. A dispatch from Wauchope indicated that negotiations were again in sight. Thus, action on the proclamation was delayed. Meanwhile the Higher Committee engaged in negotiations with the kings of Iraq, Saudi Arabia and Trans-jordan. But since no concrete program had been submitted to the British authorities within a week, London approved the Palestine Martial Law (Defense) Order-in-Council on September 26. The declaration, published September 29,[40] empowered the high commissioner to execute actions, such as the declaration of martial law, which were not subject to appeal. Although Wauchope was thus empowered to declare martial law, he never exercised his power.

PROPOSALS FOR A SETTLEMENT AND ARAB INTERVENTION

The Higher Committee was in a most difficult position. Palestinians had been on strike for more than five months in order to achieve a position from which they could negotiate changes in British policy. The strike had indeed mobilized Palestinians, but the colonial authorities refused to make a move toward negotiations. Instead they would soon declare martial law and forcibly put down resistance. It was questionable whether continuance of the strike would enhance the Palestinian position before the royal commission, although it had altered British opinion of the mandate. The Zionists, on the other hand, had profited by the strike; as the underdogs they had gained both world sympathy and significant concessions affecting their status in Palestine. In September their international diplomatic efforts took on an even more constructive appearance as they put forth proposals for a settlement of the Palestine conflict.

The events following Nuri's attempts at mediation were a replay of events of the previous month. In issuing the August 30 proclamation, the Higher Committee had again called for a congress of representatives of local national-strike committees. This was to be held in Jerusalem on September 17. On the fourteenth the committee deliberated on the termination of the strike. By this time the government had announced

40. Text of declaration in the *Times* (London) September 30, 1936, p. 11.

that it would compensate homeowners and renters of demolished Jaffa property, and this was a concession of sorts. But on September 7 Wauchope had ordered that the planned congress not be held, presumably because of possible rioting in Jerusalem. Tension in Palestine, which had diminished following the August 30 proclamation of the Higher Committee, increased sharply after the government's September 7 order.

On the sixteenth the Higher Committee again discussed strategy and announced that instead of proceeding to Jerusalem for the congress, delegates of the local national-strike committees should assemble at the offices of their respective district commissioners. At the meetings on the seventeenth the district commissioners reread a statement that the high commissioner had delivered to the Higher Committee on the twelfth. This statement reminded strikers of impending martial law in Palestine and concomitant penalties for disobeying the law. Like the Higher Committee the week before, strike leaders repeated that they could not assure the government that the strike would cease unless they knew of the government's intention to enter into negotiations at the strike's end. Arab leaders meeting with the Jerusalem district commissioner informed him that even if they were to terminate the strike, their constituents would not follow the order. Strikers in the cities and rebels in the hills awaited the concession on immigration. On the seventeenth, Wauchope and General Dill conferred with members of the military and flew to Amman for a conference with Abdullah.

But the strike leaders knew that to continue the strike past this point might well work against the national interests of the Palestinians as it had already worked against the economic interests of the strikers. The Spanish Civil War had eliminated competition from Spain in the citrus market, and citrus prices had increased 60 per cent. Zionists were ready to corner the market. Arab jobs, including picking, packing, loading, and transporting, would revert to nonstrikers, and missing one season would mean that most Arab growers would fail to make payments on their farms. Their land then would be alienated, as Zionists were ready buyers. Toward the end of September more troops would arrive in Palestine, with money to spend. This would be added to Zionist coffers if the Arabs did not end the strike. Finally, funds provided for the resistance were running out. With the government holding firm, the only hope for negotiations lay with the royal commission. With the Palestinian people holding firm, the only hope for ending the strike lay with intervention by the heads of the semi-independent Arab states. Thus, since June the Higher Committee had hung its hopes on the intervention of other Arab states, but there was always the possibility that their efforts, like Nuri's, would be discredited.

Thus the Higher Committee drafted the appeal which heads of independent Arab states would make to Palestinians to end the strike. The committee was in contact with the Saudi Arabian and Iraqi consulates in Cairo and Haifa respectively and apparently with representatives in Jerusalem of King Abdullah and Amir Yahya of the Yemen. On September 24 the committee agreed on the wording of the appeal and sent the draft to the various Arab capitals. On September 28 it was known that the four governments had agreed in principle to the draft, although some wanted alterations in its exact wording. Shaykh Qassab of Saudi Arabia arrived in Palestine from Cairo bearing a letter from King Ibn Saud explaining his alterations to the appeal. Other changes in wording were to be made by the monarchs concerned and agreed to by the committee.

Meanwhile the Zionists had also been formulating plans for a settlement. At a conference of Anglo-Jewry in London, Jewish Agency representatives stated that the government ought to put down disturbances forcibly rather than to allow Palestinians to state their case before another royal commission. On September 11 Mr. Bevin suggested in a letter to the editor of the London *Times* that Palestinians repeat in Iraq, an *Arab* country, the process by which Zionists had "improved" Palestine. Reconstructing irrigation works in Iraq destroyed by a series of barbaric invasions from the East, Palestinians too could "make the desert bloom," in the process restoring Iraq's former grandeur.[41]

The Round Table Plan, generally associated with Chaim Weizmann, had evolved in late August and early September in the letters to the editor section of the London *Times*. In a letter published August 28, Mr. Israel M. Sieff proposed a round table conference between Arabs and Jews in Palestine. Three days later Lord Winterton concurred, as did Lord Lugard on September 2. On September 4, Chaim Weizmann accepted the proposal.[42] The *Palestine Post* of September 6 and October 5 sketched out the plan. It was based on the assumption that Palestinians and Zionists were the true protagonists in Palestine and the mandatory authorities were simply overseers. Petty squabbles occur in the best of families and the two Semitic cousins ought to reason out their differences in a civilized manner, face to face over the peace table. For the September 17 (Jewish New Year) edition of the *Palestine Post,* Weizmann wrote a piece entitled "Palestine To-Day, the Common Fatherland for Arab and Jew." Whereas the plan was intuitively appealing, it substituted racism and the "clash

41. September 7, 1936, p. 7 (Inskip); September 11, p. 10 (Bevin).

42. The *Times* (London), August 28, p. 8 (Sieff); August 31, p. 13 (Lord Winterton); September 2, p. 11 (Lord Lugard); September 4, p. 13 (Weizmann).

of nationalisms" for the Palestinians' will not to be colonized. It thus obscured what had been a primary Palestinian goal from 1916 on: self-determination. The Palestinians felt that since the British had promised Arab independence but in the same breath brought Zionism to Palestine, the only lasting settlement would be one reached through negotiations between Palestinians and the British, not between Palestinians and the Zionists.

In the first week of October the Higher Committee continued its deliberation sessions. Awni Abdul Hadi returned to Jerusalem from a two-day trip to Amman where he had seen Abdullah and conferred by telephone with the Iraqi prime minister. On October 3 it was announced that the kings would appeal for cessation of the strike only if the government granted an amnesty to persons arrested for noncapital offenses during the disturbances. On October 8 the Higher Committee received the following appeal from Abdullah, Ghazi, and Ibn Saud:

> To our Sons the Arabs of Palestine (through the Arab Higher Committee) — We have been greatly pained by the prevailing situation in Palestine. We, together with our brethren the Kings and the Emir, call upon you to resort to quietness in order to prevent bloodshed, confident in the good intentions of our ally, the British Government, which has declared its desire to administer justice. Rest assured that we shall continue our efforts for the purpose of assisting you.[43]

For the third time the Higher Committee called a congress of delegates of national-strike committees, this time with success. On October 9 and 10 the Higher Committee read and discussed the appeals with delegates, along with constraints on them to end the strike. The congress voted to accept the appeal and to publish it on Sunday, October 11, along with their acceptance of it. Monday, October 12, was the anniversary of Muhammad's journey to Jerusalem, a holy day. Though the holiday was a Muslim affair, many Christian Arab churches also held thanksgiving services.

Order but not amity was restored. Many shops had opened the week before. By the end of the week business was back to normal: locks on shutters had been unstuck, keys lost since April remade, and wares dusted off. In the holiday atmosphere proprietors enthusiastically bargained with patrons and watched out for affluent British troops in the

---

43. *Palestine and Transjordan,* October 17, 1936, p. 5. This is the wording of King Ghazi's appeal. British sources normally reprint either Saud's or Abdullah's wording, in which "our friend" is substituted for Ghazi's "our ally."

market for souvenirs. There was speculation over the troop withdrawal, but by the end of the year withdrawal was complete.

The strike and disturbances had exacted a terrible price. Officially, there were 314 dead and 1,337 wounded. The civilian dead included 187 Arab Muslims, 10 Arab Christians, and 80 Jews; police fatalities included 7 British, 8 Muslim Arabs, and 1 Jew; and military fatalities included 21 British. Among the wounded civilians were 768 Muslim Arabs, 55 Christian Arabs, and 308 Jews; police personnel wounded included 40 British, 41 Muslim Arabs, 13 Christian Arabs, and 8 Jews. Military personnel wounded included 104 British. In these figures Arab casualties are significantly undercounted.[44]

The popular Arab reaction to the strike's end was that it had actually failed. There was little confidence that the government would address itself to even the minimum Palestinian demand. As early as October 11 it was proposed that Palestinians redouble their efforts to regulate land transfers. A buy-Arab, sell-Arab campaign to eliminate Jewish middlemen was suggested to bring home to the British colonial authorities—and to the Zionists—the dual obligation of the mandate. But the guerrillas in the hills dispersed, some say to participate in the orange season. On October 26 Fawzi al-Din al-Qawiqji and his forces were surrounded by British troops but were allowed to escape to Syria. Many Arabs took this, as well as the granting of suspended sentences to rioters, as government acts of faith. Zionists also had mixed feelings about the strike's end. Many would rather it had been put down by force, and most disliked the idea of the Arab monarchs' intervention. The intervention established a "dangerous precedent" insofar as Palestine might identify with, or be identified with, independent Arab states.[45]

The Peel Commission arrived in Palestine on November 5, 1936. On the same day the secretary of state announced a new labor schedule. The 1,800 quota was considerably below the previous one; the government justified the drop by citing Palestine's lowered economic absorptive capacity and made an abusive allusion to the Arab demand for cessation of Jewish immigration. In fact the strike and volume of immigration previous to it *had* greatly reduced the absorptive capacity roughly to the level suggested by the quota size; the reduction of the quota was, therefore, not a concession. Arabs boycotted the Peel Commission, in effect allowing Zionists to use it as a forum to present their demands. Again the Arab monarchs intervened, urging Palestinians to present their case before it was too late. This they finally did in January, 1937, in the last ten days of the hearings.

44. *Debates, Commons,* vol. 316, (October 29, 1936), 5th ser., col. 13, by Ormsby-Gore; see also *Palestine Report, 1936,* pp. 19–20.

45. *Times* (London), October 13, 1936, p. 10.

Although the Peel Commission reaffirmed the national home as an obligation of the mandate, its recommendations went beyond recommendations of other commissions of inquiry. It concluded that the mandate did include contrary obligations, and that efforts to implement recommendations of other commissions within the framework of the mandate had failed utterly. Political as well as economic absorptive capacity ought to be considered in the granting of immigration quotas, and these ought to be limited. Land sales in certain areas ought to be regulated. The commission did not endorse Palestinians' demand for self-government. Its conclusions, like its (*de jure*) limitations in the terms of inquiry, were couched entirely within the framework of the mandate. Thus the Peel Commission did not fully investigate the substance of Palestinians' claims to Palestine. Moreover, it observed that schemes for self-government in 1922 and 1935 had ended in discord. Abandoning hopes for an eventual Arab-Zionist entente in Palestine, it suggested partition.[46]

Until the end of July, 1937, Palestinians and non-Palestinian Arabs condemned the plan. Raghib Nashashibi, who had since broken off from the Higher Committee, condemned it on July 11, and on the twenty-third the Higher Committee followed, restating the Arab demands. Initially Zionists soundly rejected the partition plan, Weizmann holding that it would "crystallize" the national home within but a fraction of its true boundaries. Others went further, making specific territorial counter-demands. Although the Zionists eventually accepted a partition plan, the Arabs never did.

By late September guerrilla warfare had again erupted in Palestine. Empowered by another (Defense) Order-in-Council, the high commissioner outlawed the Higher Committee and the local national-strike committees. Authorities swore out warrants for the arrest of the leaders. Al-Hajj Amin and Jamal Husayni fled to Lebanon and Egypt respectively, but Mayor Khalidi, Ya'qub Ghusayn, Ahmad Hilmi Pasha, and Fuad Saba (editor of *Palestine and Transjordan*), and others were exiled to the Seychelles. By mid-October, 100 Arabs had been arrested. These actions ushered in yet another period of rebellion, which lasted until 1939.

The general strike of 1936 was more than simply a continuation of Palestinians' protest against the British sanction of Zionist colonization of their country and hence the dispossession of the Palestinians from their land. Several new features entered the Palestine conflict at this time. The intervention of the semi-independent Arab states marked a step toward

---

46. See Peel Commission Report. A partial transcript of the proceedings of the commission may be found in Great Britain, Colonial Office, Palestine Royal Commission, *Minutes of Evidence Heard at Public Sessions* (Colonial no. 134; London, 1937).

Arab unity and as such constituted a diplomatic victory. In late December
of 1936 Arab heads of state considered the formation of an Arab federation.[47] This unity was an attempt to counterbalance international Zionist
pressures on the mandatory power. The strike marked the first appearance
of Third World support for the Palestinian case. But it also marked the
first appearance of a Jewish Army in Palestine and, toward summer's end,
organized Jewish terrorism. It signaled further geographical as well as
ideological separation of Arabs and Zionists in Palestine, to be "crystallized" in later partition suggestions. It marked the first appearance of
the Round Table idea of direct negotiations. These developments led to
new Zionist strategies for the attainment of Palestine.

47. *Times* (London), December 29, 1936, p. 11.

9. Arab "Disturbances" and the Commissions of Inquiry

Richard N. Verdery

While the general history of the British mandate for Palestine has been expertly recounted by several writers—perhaps most judiciously by John Marlowe and Christopher Sykes—an examination of the several official investigatory commissions, their reports, and the fate of their recommendations throws the complicated political history of the mandate into what may be an interesting perspective. Investigatory commissions were employed by the British government in connection with the four occasions before the outbreak of the Second World War when the level of violence in Palestine became too high to be handled by ordinary administrative means: in 1920, 1921, 1929, and 1936. This essay will not deal with the Anglo-American Committee of Inquiry of 1945–46, for by the close of World War II, if not before, the Palestine problem had ceased to be one which Great Britain could handle alone and had become inextricably entwined with American and global politics.

The pattern appears similar in all four outbreaks of violence for which commissions were convened: Arab discontent with the imposed British regime, and more particularly with the threat which Zionist immigration carries, leads to an outbreak of violence by unorganized Arab peasants or urban poor in which Jews are killed or injured. The well-armed British are not attacked until 1933 and after. The subsequent investigation quickly discovers that the real cause of the outbreak is intensely political and that the Balfour Declaration and the mandate based thereon are completely unacceptable to the Arabs. The commission, in the best tradition of British fair play, makes recommendations which it is hoped will allay local Palestinian fears, but still retains the terms and spirit of the hated Balfour Declaration. Then follows an intense period of lobbying in London, with pro-Zionist letters to the *Times,* a few pro-Arab

275

rejoinders, a spirited debate in Parliament, and then a White Paper announcing what the policy in Palestine is to be. The Arabs of Palestine usually reject the new variant upon the old policy; early in the British regime they adopted a passive-resistant attitude which was to serve them very ill indeed. The Zionist reaction is usually more flexible, thanks largely to the supple diplomatic mind of Dr. Chaim Weizmann, who managed to keep extremists in the background during the years up to World War II. Thus, after each crisis, we see the British government either issuing palliatives to the Palestinian Arabs or rejecting (in the cases of the Shaw and Peel Commissions and Sir John Hope Simpson's mission) the recommendations of their commissioners, due to the impossiblity of putting these into effect while still holding to the spirit of the Balfour Declaration.

DISORDERS IN JERUSALEM: 1920

The first sign of Arab discontent with the new order imposed by Great Britain in Palestine after the defeat of the Ottoman Empire in October, 1918, occurred in April, 1920. On the occasion of the local festival of the Prophet Moses, revered by Muslims as well as by Jews, which entailed a procession from outside the walls of Jerusalem in through the Jaffa Gate, a minor incident led to a fatal stabbing and then to general assaults by Arabs upon Jews in the streets. Nine persons were killed and over 200 seriously wounded; order was restored by the military, who were present in sufficient force to prevent the spread of violence beyond the city of Jerusalem itself. Since the military occupation which had taken over from the departing Turks was still in force, a military court was convened, consisting of Major General Palin, Brigadier Wildblood, and Lieutenant Colonel Vaughan-Edwards. Legal counsel was a Mr. McBarnet, seconded from the Egyptian Service. Their terms of reference were

> To record evidence as to the circumstances which gave rise to the disturbance which took place at and near Jerusalem on the occasion of the Nebi Musa Pilgrimage on the 4th April and following days and as to the extent and causes of racial feelings that at present exist in Palestine.

The report of the Palin Commission was never published and was regarded as a confidential document. It was consulted, however, by subsequent commissions, and the above information upon it is derived from the report of the 1929 Shaw Commission.[1] One can only guess at the reasons for suppressing the Palin Report: the natural tendency of the military official to avoid damaging publicity or the desire not to rock a boat whose voyage was to be over in a few months.[2] It seems most probable that the imminence of the San Remo Conference, which took place April 19–26, 1920, may have had much to do with the confidentiality of the Palin Report. San Remo was the occasion for finally awarding the postwar mandates to the victorious powers, and the publicizing of intercommunal violence in Palestine, in the presence of a substantial army of occupation which had been there for two and a half years, would certainly have been unwelcome to the British government as it was about to "accept" the League of Nations' mandate for the Holy Land.[3]

MAY DAY RIOTS: 1921

The riots of 1921 were the first to disturb the surface of the new civil government in Palestine sufficiently to require a commission of inquiry. The mandate for Palestine had been assigned to Great Britain in April, 1920, by the Conference of San Remo, which was to lead to the Treaty of Sèvres. Turkish military resistance to the Greek occupation of western Anatolia and the growing rift between the nationalist government in Ankara and the sultan's government in occupied Constantinople, forced a postponement of a formal conclusion of World War I with Turkey. The Treaty of Sèvres was never ratified, formal peace with the Allies being embodied in the 1923 Treaty of Lausanne (in which the mandates are not mentioned); the arrangements made at San Remo in 1920 for the Arab provinces of the Ottoman Empire were what Britain and France put into effect.

For two and a half years, from December, 1917, to June, 1920, Palestine had been governed by the British Army and its Occupied Enemy Territories Administration (OETA) South. This military government had developed a reputation in Zionist circles for uncooperativeness with the Zionist Commission and for willful opposition to the principle of the

---

1. Great Britain, Commission on the Palestine Disturbances of 1929, *Report of the Commission* (Parliamentary Papers, Cmd. 3530; London, 1930) [Shaw Commission Report], p. 12. See also Ronald Storrs, *The Memoirs of Sir Ronald Storrs* (New York, 1943), pp. 346–49; Storrs was military governor of Jerusalem at the time of the 1920 outbreak.

2. Civilian rule for post–World War I Palestine began July 1, 1920.

3. The mandate for Palestine was officially awarded by the League to Great Britain on July 24, 1922.

national home embodied in the British government's official policy, the Balfour Declaration. Sir Herbert Samuel had accordingly been selected as the first civilian governor (in deference to the new system of mandates, his official title was to be high commissioner) and took office from OETA's General Louis Bols on July 1, 1920. At the time of the 1921 May Day riots, then, a civil administration had been in office ten months.

Despite the lack of legal clarity in the position of Palestine in 1921, His Majesty's government was set upon the Balfour Declaration as a policy, and had been since November 2, 1917. At first, for obvious reasons of the military morale of the Arab rebels under Faysal (before the surrender of the Ottoman Empire), and later because of General Allenby's political prudence and his desire to adhere to the Hague Convention about military occupation governments, the Balfour Declaration was not officially published in Palestine. In fact, it was not officially acknowledged there until the extinction of OETA and the proclamation of civilian rule under Samuel.[4] This naturally did not prevent knowledge of the Balfour Declaration from circulating unofficially in Palestine; it simply added to the uneasiness of the Palestinian Arabs who heard about it in roundabout fashion and consequently feared the worst.

The political climate in Palestine and the Arab East in general was also perceptibly heated by the rapid expulsion of King Faysal from his throne in Damascus in July, 1920, after the final decision made at San Remo the previous April to award the mandate for Syria to France. A serious revolt had broken out in Iraq at almost the same time against the India Office style of direct British rule there. Simultaneously, Egyptian relations with Great Britain were under considerable strain, although the outright disorders that had flared up in 1919 had been quickly suppressed by British military authorities, martial law having been in effect since 1914. The French had installed themselves in Syria and Lebanon and enjoyed an accord with the Maronites; the other major communities— Muslims, Orthodox Christians, and Druse—felt varying degrees of hostility and resentment to the French occupation, and in Syria a serious general rebellion against the French regime was to break out in 1925.

In order to clarify the affairs of the new mandates, His Majesty's government sent the new colonial secretary, Winston Churchill, to Cairo in March, 1921. Here a two-week long conference was held in which it was decided to offer the throne of Iraq to Faysal, and to confirm his brother 'Abd Allah as Amir in Transjordan, which was at the same time

4. John Marlowe, *The Seat of Pilate: An Account of the Palestine Mandate* (London, 1959), p. 27; J. M. N. Jeffries, *Palestine: The Reality* (London, 1939), p. 218.

removed from the sphere of operations of the prospective national home for the Jews in Palestine. "Thus were British obligations to the House of Husain belatedly honoured, without prejudice to France, without much immediate prejudice to the Zionists, and without any apparent prejudice to British imperial interests."[5]

The above political background was the setting for the intercommunal riots which started on May Day, 1921, in Jaffa, and which later spread to various parts of the Palestinian countryside. The affair began as a clash between an authorized Zionist May Day parade and an unauthorized group of marchers from a Communist splinter highly unpopular with the bulk of the Zionists at the time. The Communist group and other marchers were shunted out of the main line of march by police action onto a strip of beach between Tel Aviv (then a Jewish suburb of Jaffa) and the northern outskirts of Arab Jaffa. Arab onlookers began to stone the demonstrators and then to fire on them from houses; the fire was returned by householders in Tel Aviv, and what had started as a political disturbance between Jewish factions took on the character of a race riot between Arabs and Jews. Before order could be restored, an Arab mob in the center of Jaffa had killed thirteen, and wounded several other, newly landed Jewish immigrants in the immigration hostel. A few days later, while order was still being restored in Jaffa, there were attacks or attempted attacks by excited Arab peasants upon the Jewish settlements of Hadera and Petah Tiqva. These seem to have been acts of almost pure hysteria, sparked by rumors to the effect that Jews were killing Arabs in Jaffa and even more baseless rumors that the Jews of Hadera were holding their Arab agricultural laborers prisoner. No Jews were killed in the attempt on Hadera (on the coast between Haifa and Jaffa). The Arab attackers were repulsed by an RAF airplane; three were killed and three wounded.

Haycraft Commission

The commission of inquiry later known as the Haycraft Commission after its chairman, Sir Thomas Haycraft, chief justice of Palestine, was appointed by the high commissioner a week after the outbreak. Its terms of reference were simply to "inquire into the recent disturbances in the town and neighbourhood of Jaffa and to report on them."[6] This

5. Marlowe, *Seat of Pilate,* p. 61.
6. Great Britain, Foreign Office, Palestine Commission on the Jaffa Riots, 1921, *Palestine Disturbances in May 1921: Reports of the Commissioners of Inquiry with Correspondence Relating Thereto* (Parliamentary Papers, Cmd. 1540; London, 1921) [Haycraft Commission Report] p. 2.

was a commission internal to the Palestine government: the other members were Harry Luke, deputy governor of Jerusalem, and J. N. Stubbs, a member of the Legal Department. Their report, published as a command paper, is a document which, in its careful preparation, its tendency to range beyond the narrow terms of reference originally given to its authors, and in the remarkably slight effect which it had upon the subsequent conduct of policy, resembles its successors.

The commission concluded that the Arab-Jewish character of the riots was completely unpremeditated and was unforeseen by the government authorities. A certain amount of friction had been expected, but only between the two Jewish groups of May Day marchers, and reasonable precautions for such a minor fracas had been taken. When the intercommunal violence flared up, however, the police rapidly revealed themselves to be inadequately trained for serious riot duty, insufficient in numbers in the country as a whole, and not to be counted upon to do their duty against members of the community—Jewish or Arab—from which they were recruited. The evidence taken was quite clear in showing that the Arabs had fired the first shots, and had—so far as the actual riots and violence were concerned—been the aggressors in almost every instance. The performances of individual officers, British, Jewish, and Arab, were briefly examined in the report, and blame or praise assigned.

Faced with an unpremeditated and unanticipated communal riot to explain, Chief Justice Haycraft and his colleagues interviewed scores of witnesses during the weeks that the commission sat and came to a number of interesting conclusions. First of all, the commission judged that there was no question of there being any sort of plan to the riots; this was shown by the rapid spread of violence from Jaffa to the neighborhoods of Petah Tiqva, Hadera, Tulkarm, and Qalqilya, all (except the first) relatively remote from Jaffa in that period before there were good roads in the country and methods of rapid communication. A further conclusion stemming from this phenomenon was that anti-Jewish feeling was widespread in all sections of the Arab population.[7] If this were the case, how was the rise of such a violent sentiment, compounded of resentment and fear (as in the case of the peasants who marched on Hadera to liberate the Arab field hands rumored to be held there by the Jews) to be accounted for, given the almost complete absence of Arab-Jewish violence in the years from 1880 to 1920?[8] Zionist spokesmen were at pains in their

---

7. *Ibid.,* p. 45.

8. The chief form of violence endured before World War I by Jews living in Palestine seems to have been plundering raids by Bedouins upon outlying agricultural settlements. This was a dangerous nuisance, but one to which Arab peasants were equally subjected, and it had almost no political overtones.

testimony before the commission to deny any connection between Zionist activity and the riots, and thus to create the impression that the Palestinian Arabs had no legitimate grievance against the Zionists and were simply, ingrainedly, anti-Semitic.[9] The commission of inquiry, however, rejected this line firmly and attributed Arab discontent with, and hostility toward, the Jews to political and economic causes, especially the issue of Jewish immigration into Palestine, and also to the Arabs' "conception of Zionist policy *as derived from Jewish exponents.*"[10] As in the first riot the previous year, animosity on the part of the Palestinian Arabs had been directed against Jews, not against the British government: "we consider that any anti-British feeling on the part of the Arabs that may have arisen in the country originates in their association of the government with the furtherance of the policy of Zionism."[11]

The commission summarized the various grievances ventilated before them by Arab witnesses: Great Britain was partial to Zionists in taking over the administration of Palestine after the rout of the Turks; the government "has, as its official advisory body, a Zionist Commission"; there were an undue number of Jews in government service in Palestine; part of the Zionist program was to flood Palestine with people abler than the Arabs, who would gain the upper hand; Jewish immigrants were an economic danger, and more competitive; Jewish immigrants were arrogant and contemptuous toward the Arabs; and the laxness of government supervision of immigration had permitted the entry into the country of "Bolshevik" Jews.[12] The investigators felt that the Zionist Commission had created "profound distrust" among the Arabs. The obvious apprehension of the Arabs with regard to Jewish immigration is significant, especially when one considers the relatively small number of Jews who had immigrated since the close of hostilities with the Turks.[13] This suggests that the Arabs of Palestine were, even in 1921, very largely alive to the ultimate goal of the Zionists—a Jewish state in Palestine, to be achieved after immigration under British aegis had swelled the ranks of the Palestinian Jews into a much larger proportion of the population than they represented at the time of the Haycraft Commission.

The commissioners also took testimony from Dr. David Eder, acting chairman of the Zionist Commission, which had come to Palestine in

9. Haycraft Commission Report, p. 44.

10. *Ibid.,* p. 59 (italics added).

11. *Ibid.,* p. 44.

12. *Ibid.,* p. 51.

13. The Peel Commission Report shows a total of 14,663 legal Jewish immigrants from September, 1920, through December, 1921 (Great Britain, Foreign Office, Palestine Royal Commission, *Report of the Palestine Royal Commission* [Parliamentary Papers, Cmd. 5479; London 1937], p. 279).

the spring of 1918 before General Allenby's decisive defeat of the Turks. They reported that

> [in Dr. Eder's] opinion there can only be one National Home in Palestine, and that a Jewish one, and no equality in the partnership between Jews and Arabs, but a Jewish predominance as soon as the numbers of that race are sufficiently increased. . . . We do not comment upon [Eder's] opinions because the discussion of the questions raised is not our concern, but it is relevant to our report to show that the acting Chairman of the Zionist Commission asserts on behalf of the Jews those claims which are at the root of the present unrest, and differ materially from the declared policy of the Secretary of State [for the Colonies] and the High Commissioner for Palestine. It is perhaps worth noting as an instance of the diversity of manner in which Jews and Arabs look upon the same questions, that, whereas Arab witnesses denounce the Government of Palestine as a Zionist Government, Dr. Eder stigmatises it as an Arab administration.[14]

An immediate result of the 1921 riots was the suspension of Jewish immigration by the high commissioner.[15] This was a prudent and natural step for the head of the Palestine government to take, given the reports from officers at the scene of the disturbances. For example, on May 4, three days after the initial riots, Colonel Byron, commanding troops in the Lydda area, reported that

> as far as the Moslem population were concerned, they were very anxious to receive some declaration on the question of immigration. I gathered such information from both parties, i.e., the notables here [Jaffa], and Mr. Dizengoff, the Mayor of Tel Aviv.[16]

Colonel Byron ordered on the spot that no Jewish immigrants were to land at Jaffa until further notice, and a cable dated May 14 from Samuel, the high commissioner, backed him up.[17]

Samuel was a first-rate administrator and an impeccable British civil servant. But although suspension of immigration seemed the fairest and

---

14. Haycraft Commission Report, p. 57.

15. Great Britain, Colonial Office, *An Interim Report on the Civil Administration in Palestine during the Period 1st July 1920–30th June, 1921* (Parliamentary Papers, Cmd. 1499; London, 1921), p. 8.

16. Haycraft Commission Report, p. 35.

17. *Ibid.*

the most sensible thing for such an official to do at the time and although most other British officials might have done the same, Sir Herbert earned more than his share of Zionist reproach because he was a Jew and a Zionist, and the Zionists expected him to act always and only in their interests. They were not interested in British fairness, and to detect it in one of their own, and in a matter so closely touching Zionist doctrine, seemed unforgivable.

The order suspending Jewish immigration into Palestine was revoked after two months, but from this point until 1936 immigration was to be regulated by a new principle, that of the economic absorptive capacity of Palestine.

Churchill White Paper

It has been recognized by scholars in the field, as it was earlier recognized by the administrators called upon to try to apply it, that the Balfour Declaration was far from clear and self-explanatory. In a largely successful effort to make its interpretation of the declaration prevail, the Zionist Organization, with a permanent staff in London, had been continuously in contact with the Colonial Office and with other key people and offices. The guiding light of the organization, and its most brilliant, persistent, and effective propagandist, was Dr. Chaim Weizmann, at that time president of the Zionist Commission in Palestine. Competing with the Zionists for official London's attention from August, 1921, to June, 1922, was a delegation of Palestinian Arabs, who attempted, for the first time in the years of Britain's stewardship over their country, to influence British policy at its source, rather than in Palestine. The delegation consisted of six members, and officially represented the Moslem-Christian Association, though claiming with some justification that it spoke for the bulk of the Arab people of Palestine. Through persistent lobbying, both in Westminster and briefly at the League of Nations in Geneva, the delegation succeeded in getting the colonial secretary, Winston Churchill, to attempt a clarification of the Balfour Declaration policy.

This document, often referred to as the Churchill White Paper of 1922, summarized British policy clearly on some points: the Balfour Declaration was reaffirmed as not subject to change, and the vital topic of immigration of Jews was qualified to the extent that it "will not exceed the economic capacity at the time to absorb new arrivals."[18] In less precise but more

18. Great Britain, Colonial Office, Palestine, *Correspondence with the Palestine Arab Delegation and the Zionist Organisation* (Parliamentary Papers, Cmd. 1700; London, 1922) [Churchill White Paper], p. 19.

emotive passages, the White Paper made the ringing declaration that the Jewish people "should know that it is in Palestine as of right and not on sufferance," while at the same time disclaiming any intention of making Palestine "as Jewish as England is English."[19] All citizens of Palestine were to regard themselves as Palestinians; the government did not contemplate the disappearance or subordination of the Arab population, language, or culture; self-government was to be fostered, with a Legislative Council to be set up immediately with a majority of elected members, from which an advisory Immigration Board would be chosen (this last stipulation was never put into effect, however, as elections were boycotted).

SUSPENSION OF VIOLENCE: 1921–1929

There were no serious nationalist outbreaks in Palestine on the part of the Arabs from 1921 to 1929. The reasons for this lull in overt hostility to Zionism must be, in part at least, a conjectural matter. In the early stages of the mandate, the idea of an investigative commission did not yet provoke cynicism or bitterness among the population. The Haycraft Commission took testimony over a period of several months, and its report was made public in October, 1921. At that time the representatives of the Palestinian Moslem-Christian Association were in London and Geneva, lobbying against a Zionist interpretation of the mandate for Palestine, a document which was finally issued in July, 1922, not long after the appearance of the Churchill White Paper in June. Arab public opinion in Palestine, without any firm leadership at this time, appears to have settled down after the 1921 riots, at least until a reaction could be forthcoming from the Haycraft Commission and the Arab delegation of lobbyists could return to the country.

Arab reaction to the Churchill White Paper was not violence, but a refusal to participate in elections to the Legislative Council announced in that document. Pressure was also exerted upon eight Muslim and two Christian Arabs, men of some prominence in the community, who had been invited, after the failure of elections, to take part in a nominated Advisory Council; under this pressure from their compatriots, the Arab notables withdrew. Thereafter, Palestine was governed by the high commissioner, assisted by an Advisory Council composed solely of British

19. *Ibid.,* p. 18.

officials.[20] These British officials at times included British Jews sympathetic to Zionism; at no time were Arabs included.[21]

By thus boycotting the British offer of at least a semblance of self-government, the Arabs of Palestine closed off a vital channel of communication with the Colonial Office. This was a tactical error which was to be repeated: boycott became a consistent Palestinian Arab response to investigatory commissions and later offers of self-government. Characteristically, the Zionists, perhaps more sophisticated in the give-and-take of European politics, saw the value of even partial victory and accepted the Churchill document,[22] although there were grumblings from those less farsighted than Weizmann.[23]

The outbreak of 1921 pointed clearly to one thing upon which Arab grievances focused: the fact that Jewish immigration was in no way under the control of the majority of the local population. Even though only about 10,000 authorized Jewish immigrants had landed in Palestine from September, 1920, to April, 1921,[24] the Arabs correctly took this to be a harbinger of many more thousands to come. Small quotas also predominated in 1922 and 1923, but the following year saw another large increase to 12,856 recorded immigrant Jews, and 33,801 Jews immigrated in 1925, the largest number to do so legally until 1933.[25]

20. Fannie Fern Andrews, *The Holy Land Under Mandate,* 2 vols. (Boston, 1931), II, 105–11.

21. Sir Herbert Samuel, high commissioner from 1920 to 1925, was known to have Zionist sympathies although, in the tradition of the British civil service, he tried to govern impartially. Although personnel changed from time to time, it is instructive to note the composition of the first Advisory Council. It included the high commissioner's three-man Executive Council—Chief Secretary Brigadier Wyndham Deedes, Attorney General Norman Bentwich, and Financial Secretary H. Smallwood. Bentwich was a "birthright" Zionist, his father having been one of the original members of the Lovers of Zion group in the nineteenth century (Storrs, *Memoirs,* p. 390). Wyndham Deedes was not Jewish but was sympathetic to Zionism (see Norman Bentwich and Helen Bentwich, *Mandate Memories, 1918–1948* [New York, 1965], p. 32). Smallwood was a colonial official from the Malay States with no knowledge of the Middle East. In addition to the Executive Council members, the Advisory Council also included the five departmental chiefs, two of whom were British Jews; the deputy director of the Immigration Department was also a British Jew (Bentwich and Bentwich, *Mandate Memories,* p. 59).

22. See Chaim Weizmann, *Trial and Error* (Philadelphia, 1949), p. 290.

23. Enzo Sereni and R. E. Ashery, eds., *Jews and Arabs in Palestine: Studies in a National and Colonial Problem* (New York, 1936), p. 61a.

24. *Interim Report on the Civil Administration,* p. 18; this was Sir Herbert Samuel's first report.

25. For statistics showing authorized immigration form September, 1920, to the end of 1936 see Peel Commission Report, p. 279.

Curiously, the unprecedentedly large immigration of 1925 brought no violent reaction from the Palestinian Arabs, despite the fact that 1925 saw the orderly retirement from office of Sir Herbert Samuel and the accession of a figure new and unknown to Palestine, Field Marshal Lord Plumer; there was an interregnum of several weeks between Samuel's departure and Lord Plumer's arrival, and during this time Palestine was politically quiet. One possible explanation is that the Arabs were without adequate leadership in the sense of persons able to organize violence or direct a campaign of demonstrations or even petitions against the British. Then, too, the British administration did not appear easy to dislodge. The British Empire may not have been as strong in 1925 as it was before World War I, but this was not obvious to unsophisticated subjects in outlying parts of that Empire. Also there was an element of continuity in the presence of Ronald Storrs, governor of Jerusalem, who was deputized high commissioner during the interregnum. A firm believer in the equality of British obligation to the two communities of Palestine, Storrs's intentions were suspected by both sides. He was deeply distrusted by the Zionists because of his background as oriental secretary to the British Residency in Cairo when that office had been held by Lord Kitchener and because of his connections with the Arab revolt of the war years. Although Storrs left Palestine in 1926, early enough to retain an optimism about the eventual possibility of a binational state and unshaken in his faith in the efficacy of British fairness, he was subjected to attacks by Zionist leaders to such a degree that many Arabs may have believed that he was really on their side.[26] In any case, his presence during the interregnum may have helped avert a third outbreak of communal violence at that time.

When Lord Plumer himself assumed office, he proved to be a person of such formidable character that order was maintained almost by force of his personality. Civil peace continued throughout Lord Plumer's term of office. Due to the desire on the part of the Palestine administration to economize and the mistaken judgment that the last had been seen of violent resistance to the establishment of the national home for the Jews in Palestine, security forces were reduced to what was to prove to be a dangerously low level.

It ought to be borne in mind that the years 1926 to 1930 were difficult for the Palestinian economy; this is reflected in the sharp drop in recorded immigration from 13,081 in 1926 to 2,713 the following year. The peaks of 1924–26 had been caused by political and economic pres-

---

26. Storrs's general attitude toward the problems of Palestine may be gleaned in his *Memoirs*. An illuminating assessment of him is made by Christopher Sykes in *Cross Roads to Israel* (London, 1965), pp. 39–40.

sures upon the Jews of Poland, but the large numbers of Jews who immigrated in those years put a strain upon the absorptive capacity of Palestine, and a few thousand Jews even began to emigrate elsewhere under the pressure of hard times. This phenomenon in turn may have influenced the Palestinian Arabs to feel that the Zionist experiment was collapsing of its own weight, and that—sooner rather than later—the Jews would leave.

THE WAILING WALL CRISIS AND ITS AFTERMATH: 1929–1932

The crisis, when it came, was bloodier and more widespread than the outbreaks of 1920 and 1921. Tensions were building in both Palestinian communities in 1928, attentions being fixed upon the Wailing Wall where Jews were attempting to enlarge their long-admitted right to pray at the Wall and where Muslim Arabs were conducting building operations which might disturb worshippers or otherwise alter the *status quo*. There were demonstrations and counterdemonstrations at the Wall in August, 1929, and on August 17 blood began to flow.

A Jewish youth was stabbed to death in an affair of the most minor property trespass—a football had been kicked by accident into an Arab's garden. The boy's funeral became the occasion for a large Zionist demonstration. On succeeding days Arab peasants began to arrive in Jerusalem, as was usual on Thursdays and Fridays, but many of them were noticed by the police to be carrying heavy staves. The police chief ordered the disarming of people entering the city but countermanded the order later after deciding that such a course of action would be difficult to enforce—doubtless because British security forces were insufficient for the task (as had been the case in 1921, Arab and Jewish policemen were to prove unreliable in dealing with rioters of their own groups). Immediately after countermanding the disarmament order, the acting commandant of police called on the mufti of Jerusalem, al-Hajj Amin al-Husayni, and asked him to explain why so many villagers were entering the city so armed. Al-Hajj Amin replied that it was for self-protection in the event of Arab-Jewish disturbances, a reasonable explanation given the extreme tension and the sporadic fighting which had occurred the previous week between Arabs and Jews. The commandant was satisfied as to the good faith of the reply, and Friday prayers in the Haram area took place as usual on August 23. Notes were taken of the sermons preached, which were "of a pacifying character," but some of the congregation shouted the official speakers down. After noon prayers, the Muslim congregation dispersed through the old city, armed with their staves, and began attacking any Jews they found. The police restored order with difficulty and had to open fire. Calm was imposed after several Arabs were killed and others wounded, but the disturbances spread to outlying parts of Palestine as soon as rumors got abroad of the events in Jerusalem.

A brutal massacre of Jews in Hebron took place the next day, accompanied by desecration of synagogues and an attack on a Jewish hospital which had provided treatment for Arabs. The Jewish town of Safad was attacked late in the following week, despite the alertness of a British police officer and the presence of British-officered troops from the Transjordan Frontier Force. (The British high commissioner was away on leave when the outbreaks started. His deputy immediately cabled for reinforcements from Transjordan, Egypt, and Malta.) Many Jewish kibbutzim were attacked, and six were totally destroyed. The toll was officially recorded as 133 Jews killed and 339 wounded, while 116 Arabs were killed or died of wounds and 232 were hospitalized. In this outbreak some Jews, sorely provoked, did retaliate; two mosques were desecrated, and the imam of one of them and six other people were murdered. Many of the Arab casualties were the result of police or army action; some of the Jewish casualties may have been also.[27] Twenty-seven death sentences were meted out, one of them to a Jew; three Arabs were hanged, and the other sentences were commuted.[28]

Shaw Commission

After peace was restored, the causes of the outbreak had to be investigated. This time, in keeping with the seriousness of the events, the secretary of state for the colonies appointed a commission headed by a distinguished colonial civil servant with no previous connection with Palestine and composed of parliamentary representatives of the Conservative, Liberal, and Labour parties. A word is in order here about Lord Passfield, the colonial secretary at the time: he had been, before being made Lord Passfield, Sydney Webb, the famous Fabian socialist thinker and writer. It is clear that he was anti-Zionist, perhaps the only colonial secretary to be obviously so during the mandate period. Christopher Sykes believes he was anti-Semitic also and explains the anomaly in terms of

27. The official description of the 1929 riots is found in the Shaw Commission Report, pp. 55–56.
28. Peel Commission Report, p. 68.

the Webbs' contacts with continental socialism where *Jew* tended to be equated with *capitalist,* at least in some circles.[29]

The Shaw Commission, named after its chairman, Sir Walter Shaw, a retired chief justice of the Straits Settlements, concluded after two months of hearings in Palestine and in London that the disturbances of 1929 were unpremeditated, were precipitated by wanton attacks of Arab peasants upon Jews perpetrated in the heat of political and religious tension, and did not have the character of a revolt against British authority. During the hearings, the scope of the inquiry seems to have broadened beyond Lord Passfield's terms of reference, which were "to inquire into the immediate causes which led to the recent outbreak in Palestine and to make recommendations as to the steps necessary to avoid a recurrence."[30]

Paul Hanna notes that "the ground of the investigation was shifted until it became to a considerable extent an examination of the validity of the national home policy."[31]

The commission called for a clearer definition of British policy and unambiguous affirmation that the government would stand by that policy. Specifically, the government was asked to define clearly the passages in the mandate (reflecting the Balfour Declaration) having to do with safeguarding the rights of the non-Jewish communities, that is, the Arabs, and to give firmer guidance on the policy to be followed in land and immigration.

In the immigration field, the large immigrations of the years 1925 and 1926 were viewed as excessive, and it was advised that immigration on this scale be prevented in the future. The mandatory government, rather than the Jewish Agency for Palestine, should regulate the award of individual immigration certificates. (The certificates for laborers or immigrants without a certain amount of capital had been turned over to the Jewish Agency by the Government Immigration Department, and the agency in turn passed these permits to immigrate to Palestine on to Histadrut, which allegedly saw to it that the eventual recipients were all good Zionists of the correct political complexion.)[32] The feeling of Arab apprehension over Jewish immigration was also cited as a contributing factor in the outbreak.

With regard to the problem of land, the report called attention to the unsuccessful attempts in 1920 and 1921 to protect Arab peasant cultivators from being driven off the land by indiscriminate sales to Jews or

---

29. Sykes, *Cross Roads,* pp. 139–40.
30. Shaw Commission Report, p. 3.
31. *British Policy in Palestine* (Washington, D.C., 1942), p. 99.
32. Shaw Commission Report, pp. 102–5.

Jewish groups. The land-tenure system in Ottoman Palestine had been chaotic; much of the land was tilled by tenants or day laborers, and it was a simple matter for a prospective purchaser to buy up large tracts from absentee landlords, specifying that the land was to be delivered clear of squatters or tenants. The Arab landlords, more interested in their investments than in resisting Jewish colonization in Palestine, could and did turn the peasants off the land; in that way the peasants were not being evicted by foreigners but by their own countrymen. The report of the Shaw Commission states flatly that "there is no alternative land to which persons evicted can remove. In consequence a landless and discontented class is being created. . . . Palestine cannot support a larger agricultural population than it at present carries unless methods of farming undergo a radical change."[33]

Notice was taken of Arab resentment at a lack of participation in the governmental process by this commission, and the Arab rejection of the 1922 Legislative Council offer was regretted. Arab demands for participation were recognized as strong.[34] The Shaw Report, however, made no concrete constitutional proposal.

The report of the Shaw Commission was published in March, 1930, signed by all members, but with a variant opinion by Mr. H. Snell, a Labour member of Parliament, who took a pro-Zionist tack and charged the mufti with more responsibility for the bloodshed than did the rest of the commission. His recommendations, however, seem in retrospect unrealistic:

> What is required in Palestine is, I believe, less a change of policy in these matters than a change of mind on the part of the Arab population, who have been encouraged to believe that they have suffered a great wrong and that the immigrant Jew constitutes a permanent menace to their livelihood and future. I am convinced that these fears are exaggerated and that on any long view of the situation the Arab people stand to gain rather than to lose from Jewish enterprise.[35]

Hope Simpson Report

Something of Lord Passfield's views were known in official circles, and a joint letter cautioning the government against a change of policy appeared

---

33. *Ibid.*, p. 162.

34. They were also legitimate by any sort of democratic standard. The 1931 census showed that "non-Jewish communities" constituted almost 79 per cent of the population of Palestine, despite twelve years of Jewish immigration. (Peel Commission Report, p. 404).

35. Shaw Commission Report, p. 174.

in the London *Times* months before the Shaw Report was published. It was signed by Lord Balfour, Lloyd George, and General Smuts.[36] When the report appeared, its pro-Arab tone and recommendations gave the Zionists and their supporters pause—and time for study, as government policy was not announced at the same time. In order to back up the Shaw Report's statement that no spare land existed in Palestine for immigrant settlers, the Colonial Office dispatched in May, 1930, a land and resettlement expert, Sir John Hope Simpson, who had been working with the League of Nations on the difficult "transfer of populations" between Greece and Turkey. Basing his figures on a rather superficial aerial survey, Hope Simpson revised sharply downward the estimated amount of cultivable land available for Jewish settlement without prejudice to Palestinian Arab interests: from 10,592,000 *dunums* to 6,544,000.[37] In the field of possible industrial development, Hope Simpson was very cautious; it must be recalled here that British colonies (and Palestine had many of the earmarks of a colony even though it was formally a mandated territory) were supposed to pay their own way. Given the several bad years prior to the 1929 investigation, it was natural for Hope Simpson to take a guarded, circumscribed view that major industries would not be attracted to Palestine and that such development as could take place must concentrate upon small enterprises geared to the local market.[38]

Passfield White Paper

A policy document was issued at the same time as Sir John Hope Simpson's report, known informally as the Passfield White Paper. As regards the all-important question of the availability of land for "close settlement," that is, agricultural colonization, the White Paper echoed Hope Simpson's judgment that "there is at the present time and with the present methods of Arab cultivation no margin of land available for

36. *Times* (London), December 20, 1929, cited in Sykes, *Cross Roads,* p. 141.
37. One metric *dunum,* introduced in mandate times, is one-quarter acre or 1,000 square meters; 1,000 dunums is equal to one square kilometer. The figure of 10.5 million dunums was the estimate of the cultivable areas in the inhabited hills and the so-called Five Plains of Palestine. A cadastral survey in progress while Hope Simpson was in Palestine put the cultivable areas of the same regions at the 6.5 million figure. Both estimates omitted potentially cultivable lands in the then waterless Negev. Various Zionist estimates of the cultivable area of Palestine ran from 12 to 17 million dunums. (See Great Britain, Colonial Office, Palestine, *Report on Immigration, Land Settlement and Development* [Parliamentary Papers, Cmd. 3686–3687; London, 1930] [Hope Simpson Report], pp. 22–23; and Peel Commission Report, p. 71).
38. Hope Simpson Report, pp. 106–18.

agricultural settlement by new immigrants, with the exception of such undeveloped land as the various Jewish Agencies hold in reserve."[39] The remedy, in the eyes of the Colonial Office, was to improve Arab methods of farming on land already held by Arabs and to let the Zionists fill up the reserves of land already purchased but not yet settled by Jewish pioneers. While this was going on, Jewish immigration could be held down to a more controllable scale, and control was to be more firmly exercised, not by Histadrut but by the Palestine administration.[40]

Criticism was directed by the White Paper at the Palestine Foundation Fund (Keren Hayesod), whose policy was to declare that any labor hired by Jewish agricultural colonies indebted to the fund must be Jewish labor. A similar clause in the constitution of the enlarged Jewish Agency for Palestine stated that all lands acquired should be the inalienable property of the Jewish people and could not be reacquired by non-Jews. This exclusive attitude was contrasted in the White Paper with the expression of the Zionist Congress of 1921 of a desire "to live with the Arab people in relations of friendship and mutual respect, . . . and to develop the homeland common to both into a prosperous community which would ensure the growth of the people."[41] The White Paper also renewed the offer rejected by the Arabs in 1922 of a Legislative Council.

The Passfield White Paper was noteworthy for the expression of pique on the part of the government that neither side in Palestine was sympathetic to the heavy burden being borne by the mandatory power, a burden which the government was trying to carry as evenhandedly as possible.[42] (The fact that the burden of the mandate for Palestine was self-imposed was deliberately hidden; the appeal for sympathy might have made the two opposed sides smile ironically had they both not been so deadly serious.)

The White Paper of 1930 was greeted by a vigorous and well-coordinated campaign of protest in the British press and in the houses of Parliament. The most severe pressure was put upon the government by the parliamentary opposition, headed by surviving members of the wartime coalition government of Lloyd George which had been party to the issuance of the Balfour Declaration. The Labour government of Ramsay MacDonald which was in power had been elected in 1929 with only a thin margin of seats over the Conservatives. The Zionist attack upon the

39. *Ibid.,* p. 141.
40. Great Britain, Colonial Office, Palestine, *Statement of Poicy by His Majesty's Government in the United Kingdom* (Parliamentary Papers, Cmd. 3692; London, 1930) [Passfield White Paper], pp. 18–22.
41. Cited in *ibid.,* pp. 17–18.
42. *Ibid.,* pp. 4–5.

Passfield White Paper was skillfully couched in terms of it being a repudiation of wartime commitments issued by a national coalition government; this attack, led by former members of that coalition, made the uncertain Labour government far more uncomfortable than would threatened resignations of top Zionists like Chaim Weizmann and Lord Melchett from their posts.

MacDonald "Black Letter"

Faced with a barrage of criticism of the new policy statement, the government first quietly withdrew its support from the recommendations of the Shaw Commission and of Sir John Hope Simpson and later practically reversed the policy changes enunciated in the Passfield White Paper. It did this, however, in a manner intended to disguise the completeness of the retreat: the prime minister wrote a letter to Weizmann "clarifying" the White Paper for him but in reality capitulating to the pressures which the Jewish Zionists and their more politically powerful Gentile supporters in the British Parliament had brought to bear. MacDonald's letter was read into Hansard, and thus became public property and — firmly but unofficially — British government policy in Palestine. The difference in tone between the White Paper of 1930 and the "Black Letter" of 1931, as the Palestinian Arabs termed it, is perhaps the most important contrast between the two documents. Whereas the Passfield White Paper and the commission reports that preceded it had conceived matters in terms of inhabitants of Palestine both Arab and Jewish, the MacDonald letter reaffirmed that the mandate for Palestine reflected an obligation to the Jews of the world as a whole, not merely to those resident in, or currently eager to immigrate to, Palestine. The letter further eased government strictures upon Zionist-demanded Jewish labor for Jewish enterprises and permitted the further acquisition of land in Palestine by Jews or Jewish agencies:

> The Labor government, like its predecessors, adhered to the unsuccessful policy of attempted compromise between the aims of Arab nationalism and Zionism. Such a program, based upon recognition of equal obligations to Arabs and Jews, could have a satisfactory outcome only in the creation of a unitary, binational state, and that goal was entirely foreign to the desires of either community in Palestine. . . . The Passfield Paper and the MacDonald letter were particularly unfortunate applications of the general British policy, for they convinced first the Arabs and then the Jews that sufficient agitation and pressure could alter the intentions of the mandatory. The whole philosophy of compromise was at fault.

The effort of the London government to be both pro-Arab and pro-Zionist within the limited confines of the Holy Land was fraught with danger alike to the Arabs, the Jews and the British.[43]

If the wording of the Shaw Commission Report, the findings of Sir John Hope Simpson, and the Passfield White Paper's indications of a new turn in British policy gave the Arabs momentary hope, such hope as they may have felt was to be violently dashed by Ramsay MacDonald's letter of clarification to Weizmann. While criticized by more extreme Zionists for being satisfied with a mere letter, Weizmann wrote,

> I considered that the letter rectified the situation . . . and I so indicated to the Prime Minister. . . . Whether I was right or not in my acceptance may be judged by a simple fact: it was under MacDonald's letter to me that the change came about in the Government's attitude, and in the attitude of the Palestine administration, which enabled us to make the magnificent gains of the ensuing years. It was under MacDonald's letter that Jewish immigration into Palestine was permitted to reach figures like forty thousand for 1934 and sixty-two thousand for 1935, figures undreamed of in 1930. Jabotinsky, the extremist, testifying before the Shaw Commission, had set thirty thousand a year as a satisfactory figure.[44]

The Period of the Arab Revolt: 1933–1939

One of the decisive events in the history of the Palestine mandate was the accession to power in Germany of Hitler. Almost overnight the atmosphere of liberalism and assimilationism which the Jews of Europe had breathed in varying amounts changed to an air charged with fear, uncertainty, and disbelief — at first — that Hitler meant what he said. The pressures placed upon German Jews, and by repercussion upon the Jews of Eastern Europe, were felt almost simultaneously in Palestine, and the jump in immigration was dramatic. The Arabs, naturally, viewed these developments with alarm, and whatever faith they may have had in the impartiality or pro-Arab stance of the British government evaporated after MacDonald's letter to Weizmann.

The tenor of Palestinian political life continued upon a gradual downward slope in the direction of further communal strife. The Jewish

43. Hanna, *British Policy,* p. 108.
44. *Trial and Error,* p. 335.

community grew in numbers and in economic strength. At least at the beginning of the Hitler period, some German Jews were able to bring modest amounts of money as well as valuable entrepreneurial skills. The world at this time was in the depths of the great depression, and chances for safe investment were rare. However, the Palestinian economy boomed while other economies foundered as Jewish capital coming into Palestine created a rise in investments. But the flow of funds into Palestine was selective in bestowing its benefits. The most attractive sectors of the economy were citrus groves along the Mediterranean coast and urban real estate in Tel Aviv, Haifa, and Jerusalem. General agriculture, especially the less-efficient peasant agriculture of the Arab villages, was a distressed sector while citriculture and the building trades were booming.[45]

All these factors — the accelerating step-up in Jewish immigration, growing economic disparities between the Jewish centers and the Arab villages and quarters, and the widespread and growing distrust of the British administration — led to still another outbreak of bloodshed and violence in the fall of 1933. The various Arab groups and committees had coalesced by this time into an Arab Executive Committee inspired, though not yet headed, by al-Hajj Amin, the mufti of Jerusalem since 1921. This committee issued a manifesto to the Arabs of Palestine in March, 1933, denouncing the British as the cats-paws of the Zionists and calling for Arab noncooperation with the mandatory government and a boycott of British and Jewish goods and institutions. The Arab press took a more militant tone about this time: press attacks upon the administration grew in virulence, and even the Arab Executive Committee itself was not spared. A demonstration called in October, 1933, in Jerusalem was prohibited by the authorities, but was held in spite of the ban. Heads were bloodied, but no one was killed. A more serious antigovernment riot in Jaffa two weeks later resulted in the death of 27 Arabs and over 200 lesser casualties; among the wounded was Musa Kazim al-Husayni, the octogenarian head of the Arab Executive Committee, who died a few months later. No full-dress commission was ordered out to Palestine to

45. "The amount of Jewish capital invested in land-purchase, in the development of citriculture, and in industry and transport was £2,833,000 in 1932 and £5,360,000 in 1933. The imports of capital goods for the equipment of agriculture, industry and transport . . . was £2,422,000 in 1932 and £4,060,000 in 1933. The financial element which the National Home had always needed for its success—the investment of money in it not as a missionary enterprise but as a 'going concern'— had already begun to materialize before 1933; but now its continuance and expansion seemed assured" (Peel Commission Report, p. 82). The figures were supplied to the Peel Commission by the Jewish Agency for Palestine; see also A. M. Hyamson, *Palestine under the Mandate, 1920–1948* [London, 1950] p. 130).

investigate this outbreak. All accounts are united on the fact that the disorders of 1933 were clearly fomented by the Arab Executive Committee and were directed solely against the British; there were no Jews slain, although some Jewish property was destroyed.[46]

The high commissioner who succeeded the civilian Sir John Chancellor in 1931 was, like Lord Plumer, a professional soldier of high rank and distinction. Although this appointment perhaps reflected the home government's wish for a period of tranquillity as in the years of Lord Plumer, Major General Sir Arthur Wauchope was fated to be in charge of the government of Palestine during the most severe outbreak of all, a period correctly known as the Arab rebellion. Wauchope as high commissioner appears to have been eager to please everyone, an impossible undertaking at that late stage of the mandate.[47] He tried with great persistence to move away from the authoritarian government by fiat which mandatory Palestine had become after the Arab rejection of an elected Executive Committee in 1922, and he kept pressing for a Legislative Council, both in reports and correspondence to the Colonial Office and before the League of Nations in Geneva. This time, aware of the opportunities which they had lost since 1922, the Arabs of Palestine were cautiously receptive, while the Zionists, under great and mounting pressure from the events in Europe, no longer felt they could take the risks of accepting a British offer of representative government while they were yet in the minority.[48] Wauchope kept trying, the Arabs kept agonizing: if they accepted, then they gave up their attitude, fondly cherished since the Turkish defeat, of nonrecognition of the British mandate; if they refused, they stood to continue to lose ground to Zionist immigration, hard work, abundant capital, and sense of mission.

Again, as in 1930–31, the pattern was one of cautious recognition on the part of the British (this time by the high commissioner) of a certain amount of justice on the side of the Arabs, followed by parliamentary maneuvers in which partisan British political issues were manipulated adroitly by the Zionists, both Jews and Gentiles, and the Arab case in question was defeated. So it appeared to the Arabs of Palestine, at least, when Wauchope's scheme for a Legislative Council was aired in Parliament and defeated in the spring of 1936.[49]

46. Sykes, *Cross Roads,* pp. 175–76; Peel Commission Report pp. 83–85; Hyamson, *Palestine under the Mandate,* pp. 131–32. The 1933 outbreaks are described in detail in the *Palestine Gazette,* Extraordinary, no. 420 (February 7, 1934), pp. 89–105.

47. Hyamson, *Palestine under the Mandate,* p. 143; Sykes, *Cross Roads,* pp. 174–84.

48. See Sykes, *Cross Roads,* p. 177, for a thoughtful and lucid discussion of Zionist attitudes toward representative government in the mandate period.

49. Peel Commission Report, pp. 89–92.

This rejection by the British Parliament of representative government for Palestine was one of the major contributive causes of the Arab rebellion of 1936, although the members of the royal commission who came to investigate the "disturbances" were careful to point out that the action of Parliament merely aggravated the cause. Also seen as significant by the commissioners was the attainment of nominal sovereignty by Palestine's neighbors — Syria, Lebanon, and Egypt — all in 1936. (Iraq had achieved sovereignty in 1930.)

The occasion for the outbreak of rebellion in April, 1936, was a handful of sporadic attacks by individual Arabs upon Jews, retaliatory attacks by Jews on Arabs, and the swift spread of rumors that Arabs had been killed. This led to actual murders of Jews and a general heightening of tension; curfews were proclaimed in Jaffa and Tel Aviv, and emergency regulations were put into effect by the administration.

Within a week, all the Arab political parties, usually at bitter variance one with another, had formed a united front which became known as the Arab Higher Committee, presided over by al-Hajj Amin al-Husayni. The Arab Higher Committee called for, and got, a general strike of Arabs, in business, government offices, transport, and other services. The strike was to continue until the British administration acceded to Arab demands that Jewish immigration be prohibited, that transfer of Arab land to Jews be forbidden, and that a national government be established responsible to a representative council. After a month of quite effective strike, the government in London announced a royal commission "which, without bringing into question the terms of the Mandate, will investigate causes of unrest and alleged grievances either of Arabs or Jews."[50] In the meantime, public order had deteriorated even further, and incidents of sniping at police, soldiers, Jews, and Arabs not participating in the strike grew in number. Troops were sent from Egypt and Malta, but no very aggressive effort was mounted to get at the armed bands in the countryside; the added troops were used to guard communication lines and public buildings. An unprecedented situation arose with the petitioning of the high commissioner by almost all the senior Arab government officials, and later by some 1,200 junior Arab members of the administration, a petition which put the cause of the disturbance as a "loss of faith in the value of official pledges and assurances for the future" and recommended the stoppage of Jewish immigration.[51]

Despite the build-up to some 20,000 troops in Palestine by September, 1936, the high commissioner still appeared reluctant to press the rebels

50. *Ibid.,* p. 98.
51. *Ibid.,* p. 99.

too harshly. The strike was finally ended by diplomatic means. British pressure was put upon the governments of the surrounding Arab states— a fateful but perhaps inevitable drawing of these governments into the Palestine problem—to urge their fellow Arabs in Palestine to end the strike and cease firing and to permit the royal commission to make its investigation and recommendations. In conjunction with economic difficulties, this pressure from abroad was ultimately successful, the Palestine Arab Higher Committee called off the strike, and the commission conducted its researches in Palestine from November to the following January. Throughout most of this period, however, the Arabs of Palestine boycotted the proceedings of the royal commission, and only gave up this, by then familiar, tactic under further pressure from Arab neighbors.

The Peel Commission

The Peel Commission, named for William Robert Wellesley, Earl Peel, was the ablest and most illustrious of the bodies which were appointed during the mandate over Palestine to investigate the recurring evidences of bitter unrest and to make recommendations on how such unhappy symptoms might be avoided.

The report of the commission stated matters quite plainly, in the lucid prose of Professor Reginald Coupland, who was largely responsible for the writing of the report:

> After examining this and other evidence and studying the course of events in Palestine since the War, we have no doubt as to what were "the underlying causes of the disturbances" of last year. They were:
>
> (i) The desire of the Arabs for national independence.
>
> (ii) Their hatred and fear of the establishment of the Jewish National Home.
>
> We make the following comments on these two causes:
>
> (i) They were the same underlying causes as those which brought about the "disturbances" of 1920, 1921, 1929 and 1933.
>
> (ii) They were, and always have been, inextricably linked together. The Balfour Declaration and the Mandate under which it was to be implemented involved the denial of national independence at the outset. The subsequent growth of the National Home created a practical obstacle, and the only serious one, to the concession later of national independence. It was believed that its further growth might mean the political as well as economic subjection of the Arabs to the Jews, so that, if ultimately

the Mandate should terminate and Palestine become independent, it would not be national independence in the Arab sense but self-government by a Jewish majority.

(iii) They were the only "underlying" causes. All the other factors were complementary or subsidiary, aggravating the two causes or helping to determine the time at which the disturbances broke out.[52]

After a detailed and masterly dissection of the operation of the Palestine mandate from its inception to 1936, the Peel Commission made its recommendation: the mandate should be abolished and replaced with a treaty relationship, such as had just been accomplished in Syria and, earlier, in Iraq, and the territory of Palestine should be partitioned into a Jewish state and an Arab state. The Holy Places in and around Jerusalem should form a mandatory enclave administered by the British government.

The proposed Jewish state would include the northern part of Palestine, that is Galilee, and the coastal plain from Tel Aviv north to the Lebanese border, with a small area to the south of Tel Aviv, cut off from the main part of the Jewish state by Arab Jaffa and a corridor thereto from Jerusalem. The Arab state was to consist of the rest of Palestine. It was expected that both states would be granted almost immediate independence. The Arab state, which would be poorer than the Jewish state in land and in almost every other way, would receive a subvention from the British treasury and from that of the Jewish state. A far from satisfactory feature of the Peel plan for the Zionists was the inclusion at the initial stages of the partition of some 225,000 Arabs then resident in Galilee; this implied a transfer of populations akin to the unhappy Greco-Turkish settlement.

The partition scheme proposed by Peel and his committee was rejected by the annual Zionist Congress, which met in Zurich a month after the report's publication and discussion in Parliament, where it had been given moderate government backing. The Zionists accepted the principle of partition, but objected mainly to the narrow confines of the proposed Jewish state. The Arab Higher Committee rejected partition out of hand, and the rebellion was resumed almost at once. John Marlowe believes that the British government would not have come out for partition if it had not thought that the surrounding Arab states would approve; he assumes diplomatic soundings had been taken and a climate favorable to partition of Palestine had been ascertained to exist.[53] The Arab Higher

52. *Ibid.,* p. 110–11.
53. Marlowe, *Seat of Pilate,* p. 147.

Committee's intransigent rejection, however, gave the other Arab rulers pause, and they subsequently rejected it also.

It may be remarked in passing, also, that one of the obvious reasons for parliamentary opposition to the Peel Report was the fact that the report was issued at the same time as a government White Paper on policy recommending the partition scheme in principle,[54] and a letter to the League of Nations requesting the Permanent Mandates Commission of that body to study the Peel Report—all this before any debate had taken place in Parliament on the report. Parliament eventually compromised on a proposal made by Winston Churchill that the subject of partition be studied by the League of Nations and the League's recommendation taken into consideration by Parliament.

The Arabs of Palestine, however, remained resolutely opposed to the decision to partition their country, and one of the most active and vocal denouncers of the new policy was al-Hajj Amin. Here again, as in the days of the OETA, a significant Arab miscalculation of British intentions occurred. Since, in the view of the Arabs, it was so patently not in the Arab interest for the British to partition their country, they could not believe that the latest White Paper was to be taken literally. To clinch this Arab belief that the British did not really intend partition, they saw al-Hajj Amin retained in his post as head of the Supreme Muslim Council and the General Waqf Committee, although he could have been removed from both positions at the instance of the high commissioner.[55] There was therefore no reason for the Palestinian Arabs to accept the British policy; this attitude was strengthened by representations of solidarity from neighboring states. The guerrilla warfare in the hills continued and was only brought under control after the Munich Pact of September, 1938, when British troops could be released for duty in Palestine.

Woodhead Commission

The storm of criticism of the Peel scheme for partition from Zionists and from Palestinian and other Arabs must have primed the Woodhead Commission, which, after a long postponement due to the revival of the

---

54. Great Britain, Colonial Office, *Statement of Policy* (Parliamentary Papers, Cmd. 5513; London, 1937).

55. Al-Hajj Amin was removed from these posts September 30, 1937, and soon fled to Lebanon, after the assassination of a British district commissioner. This particular act of terrorism, to which the mufti was not directly linked, was used as the occasion to call upon new emergency powers by the high commissioner. Six other Arab leaders were arrested and deported at this time.

Arab rebellion, finally held its inquiries in Palestine from April to August, 1938. The Woodhead Commission was a technical group sent out to propose concrete steps for the actual partition. It produced three alternative plans with respect to boundaries, but was unable to agree upon boundaries that would afford a reasonable prospect of the eventual establishment of self-supporting Arab and Jewish states.[56] The Woodhead Commission Report of 1938 signaled the abandonment of the Peel proposal to partition Palestine.

At this juncture, with 20,000 British troops in Palestine suppressing with difficulty a popular uprising of Arab peasants, and with the outbreak of a general European war obviously imminent, the British government appears to have decided to impose a policy on Palestine which would be sufficiently palatable to the Arabs of the Middle East to keep them quiet. It did go through the motions of calling a Round Table Conference in early 1939, inviting to London not only Palestinian Arabs but also representatives of the neighboring Arab countries and representatives of the Jewish Agency for Palestine. Given the high political temperature in Palestine at the time, failure to come to an agreed-upon formula acceptable to both Zionists and Arab nationalists was almost a foregone conclusion; the delegates refused to sit together, and British officials were forced to carry messages from room to room. When the conference failed, in April, 1939, the government issued a statement of policy which was to hold throughout the Second World War, a document known as the MacDonald White Paper, or, to the Zionists, the "Black Paper."[57]

MacDonald White Paper

In the MacDonald White Paper, the government declared that it was not part of their policy to create a Jewish state in Palestine. Rather, they envisioned a binational state which would be granted independence and a treaty with Great Britain after the establishment of "such relations between the Arabs and the Jews as would make good government possible."[58] Such an independent Palestine could become possible ten years from the time of the issuance of the White Paper, with a Palestinian (including

56. Great Britain, Colonial Office, Palestine Partition Commission, *Report of the Palestine Partition Commission* (Parliamentary Papers, Cmd. 5854; London, 1938) [Woodhead Commission Report].

57. Great Britain, Colonial Office, Palestine, *Statement of Policy* (Parliamentary Papers, Cmd. 6019; London, 1939) [MacDonald White Paper], p. 4.

58. *Ibid.,* p. 6.

Arabs and Jews) and British joint commission to review matters within five years and suggest a constitution. The hoped-for constitution was to contain provisions that would safeguard access to the Holy Places and protect religious interests all around; would see to "the protection of the different communities in Palestine in accordance with the obligations . . . to both Arabs and Jews and for the special position in Palestine of the Jewish National Home"; and would safeguard British security requirements.[59]

Turning to immigration, the government finally abandoned the pre-occupation—operative since 1922—with the economic absorptive capacity of Palestine and admitted that it would take into consideration political matters as well. While not agreeing to the stoppage of Jewish immigration entirely, it set a maximum of 75,000 immigrants over the next five years (10,000 per year as regular settlers and 25,000 as refugees), assuming the economy could absorb them. After 1944, no further Jewish immigration would be permitted unless the Arab community agreed. With regard to land transfers, the high commissioner was given wide powers to prohibit and supervise the sale of lands; what was intended here was to insure internal tranquillity in Palestine by avoiding the creation of a large body of landless ex-peasants. The whole question of the sale of land to the Jews was one of the sorest points of friction throughout the mandate period, made sorer by the fact that patriotism so often lost out to private cupidity when an Arab landlord was offered a high price for his land. The acquisition of land by the Zionists continued through the Second World War, despite the policy set forth in the White Paper of 1939.[60]

The MacDonald White Paper, which was to be British policy in Palestine for the duration of the war which everyone knew was imminent, was an attempt to keep nascent Arab national feeling temporarily placated, if not actually satisfied. The Zionists were embittered at its terms, but accepted the fact—obviously known to the British government as well—that the Jews of Palestine would have no choice in the coming struggle with Hitler but to support the British side loyally, if the Jewish national home were, with the termination of the war, to retain the direction of its growth into a Jewish state.

With the issuance of the 1939 MacDonald White Paper, the history of interwar Palestine comes to an end. The British administration and the

59. *Ibid.,* p. 7.

60. Marlowe says that the Jewish National Fund bought, in the period 1940–46, 50,000 dunums of land in parts of Palestine open to Jewish land purchase under the 1939 White Paper policy and 275,000 dunums in areas where Jewish purchase was restricted or prohibited (*Seat of Pilate,* p. 169). This largely illegal growth doubled Keren Kayemeth's holdings during World War II.

government in London prepared for the war and were too preoccupied to send investigatory commissions. The Palestinian Jews and the larger Zionist community bowed to the inevitable restriction on immigration for the duration of the war, although many clandestine immigrants—the fortunate ones—made the journey from Europe. The Palestinian Arabs, their peasants' revolt spent, and their titular leader a fugitive, relapsed into political quiescence. The struggle between two communities on Palestinian soil subsided beneath the surface, to boil up again after the war, when investigations of the problem would be renewed on an international scale.

PART IV

Sovereign Conflicts

The collapse and ultimate failure of the Palestinian resistance, though evident in 1936–37, was consummated with the triumph of the Zionists politically and militarily in 1947–48. The unwillingness or incapacity of the British colonial administration of Palestine to employ the same repressive measures to thwart the Zionist drive which they employed to thwart the Palestinian drive for an independent Palestine, combined with the enormous pressures of the United States and other Western publics, led Britain to relinquish the mandate regime over Palestine. Having denied the Palestinians the right of self-determination—now denying to both Arab and European in Palestine the same right—Britain transferred the question of the disposition of Palestine to the United Nations. The latter dispatched yet another committee of inquiry which in due course submitted two reports, one favoring partition, a scheme proposed earlier by the British Peel Commission, and the other favoring independent status. The General Assembly of the United Nations on November 29, 1947, recommended partition. The following day the final confrontation between the two communities of Palestine—the European and the Arab—took the shape that culminated on the fifteenth of May, 1948, in the proclamation of the state of Israel. The Arab states then in independent status tried unsuccessfully to come to the assistance of the Arab people of Palestine. The brief and inconclusive hostilities between Israel and the adjacent Arab states were terminated by the conclusion of the armistice system with separate agreements between Israel, on the one hand, and Jordan, Syria, Egypt, and Lebanon, on the other.

While the old issues that pitted the two communities in Palestine against one another remained to plague the world, newer issues arose between sovereign states whose relationships are governed, unlike the previous

305

issues, by international law and norms. The Arab states adopted policies toward Israel which could have stemmed from their appreciation of the forces at work in the Arab world, or from the general international inter-action, or from the specific background of the conflict over Palestine. Bound as they were by bonds of kinship, loyalty, and national aspirations to the Arab people of Palestine, they had to take these factors into account in determining their policy or policies toward Israel. Michael C. Hudson, Associate Professor of Political Science and Director of the Middle East Center at Johns Hopkins School of International Studies, is intimately familiar with Arab political processes and has contributed several essays on the Palestinian movement in addition to his major study, The Precarious Republic: Political Modernization in Lebanon. *In his essay he analyzes the conditions under which the policies of the adjacent states have been formulated and reformulated and discusses the factors that hinder the consistent implementation of an Arab policy toward Israel.*

While the Arab states may have adopted policies in response to specific issues of contention, it is quite clear that inner forces propelled these same states to the adoption or lack of adoption of certain policies. The same can be said with regard to Israel's Arab policy. Miss Janice Terry is an Assistant Professor of History at Eastern Michigan University. Her analysis of Israel's policy toward the Arab states reveals that it too was based on several assumptions, drives, and aspirations. These combined to pro-duce a specific policy with specific characteristics that may or may not have hindered the process of settlement between the contending states.

The absence of a settlement between the Arab states and Israel, ir-respective of the factors that have combined to preclude such a settle-ment, is noted by all concerned. The contrary is obvious. The relationship between Israel and the Palestinians and between Israel and the Arab states has fluctuated from watchful tension to eruption of armed con-flict. Twice since 1949 the area witnessed the outbreak of war, and each time the conflict engulfed more humanity and precipitated energetic external intervention. The June war of 1967, however, produced altera-tions that may turn out to be quite fundamental in thwarting the chances for peaceful settlement. The military occupation of eastern Palestine (the West Bank) and southeastern Palestine (the Gaza Strip) completes the Israeli occupation of Palestine proper. The additional occupation of the Golan Heights and Sinai produce territorial dilemmas and questions between Israel and Syria and the United Arab Republic that transcend the original issues involved in the Palestine conflict. The fate of these territories is as yet unknown; although the weight of the international community is squarely placed against any alteration of the status of these territories as a result of their military occupation, one part of eastern

Palestine, namely Jerusalem, was in fact and in law annexed by Israel despite the counter-resolutions of the United Nations. This volume has dealt with events pertaining to Palestine. Therefore the Israeli annexation of Jerusalem deserves our attention if for no other reason save the fact that such a transformation has made a difficult conflict more intractable. Malcolm Kerr, Professor of Political Science at the University of California at Los Angeles, has written extensively on political and cultural questions pertaining to the Arab world. His previous contributions include Islamic Reform *and* The Arab Cold War, *as well as many writings on the Arab-Israeli conflict. His essay on the changing political status of Jerusalem confines itself to Jerusalem's political transformation against the background of the United Nations recommendations and the city's political history since 1948.*

10. The Arab States' Policies toward Israel

Michael C. Hudson

Arab government policies and behavior on the Palestine-Israel question in the period 1949–1967 do not win high marks by the criteria of foreign-policy evaluation. If the Arab states' objective was the destruction of Israel, they failed; if it was economic strangulation, they failed; if it was accommodation through assimilation of displaced Palestinians, they failed; and if it was containment, they failed. These failures were due more to political than military weakness. The Arab policy-making elites were unable to arrive at a coherent set of policy objectives for any significant period of time, nor were they able to achieve more than limited success in implementing the plans that were formulated.

The purpose of this essay is to inquire into these political infirmities. I shall begin by sketching the main aspects of Arab policy and behavior toward Israel and the Palestinians from 1949 to 1967. I shall then try to explain this behavior in the context of events by analyzing Israeli policies, the growth of populism and instability in Arab domestic politics, and the dynamics of Arab interstate relations.

PRINCIPAL FEATURES OF ARAB POLICY

The main dynamic elements in the Palestine struggle, both before and after 1949, were intrusive Jewish nationalism with its support bases in Europe and the United States and reactive defense by the Palestinian Arab community and its allies in the other Arab states. With the collapse of effective indigenous Palestinian opposition during the winter of 1947–48, the neighboring Arab governments came to play the principal role in the defense of Palestine. Their belated entry into Palestine after the

termination of the British mandate on May 15, 1948, undoubtedly helped
deny to the Jews some of the territory promised to the Palestinians
under the United Nations partition resolution of November 29, 1947,
but the effort was not sufficient to the need. After the war a new situation
existed in which the 1949 armistice agreements largely superseded the
partition plan as the basis for Arab-Israeli relations. Having taken on
the defense of Arab Palestine, the governments of Egypt, Transjordan,
Syria, and Lebanon assumed partly by default and partly through calcula-
tion the responsibility for the remaining territory. A communal or civil
struggle for mandate Palestine had been transformed into an interstate
problem. To be sure, the Arab governments wished to preserve as much
of Palestine as possible for its Arab inhabitants; but the two succeeding
decades were to make it painfully clear, particularly to the Palestinian
Arabs, that these governments did not place the recovery of Palestine
above all other interests and commitments.

The Arab governments, as new custodians of the Palestinian patrimony
and as the weaker parties in the conflict, relied more heavily upon various
U.N. resolutions than did Israel. Israelis were to emphasize heavily the
international legal legitimacy bestowed upon the new Jewish state by the
U.N., but they consistently ignored or thwarted U.N. directives on resettlement, truce supervision, and refugee matters. The Arab governments,
however, grasped at whatever favorable straws the international community would extend. One of these, ironically, was the partition plan so
firmly rejected by the Arab states in 1947.[1] Of course, there was not the
slightest incentive for Israel to consider reverting to partition, so long
as it was prosperous and secure within the 1949 armistice lines. As long
as the Arab governments were weak and passive, they had nothing significant to offer Israel and her Western backers in return for the limited
rollback of Israel's frontiers.

More important U.N. documents were the series of armistice agreements concluded on Rhodes between February and July, 1949, under the
auspices of the mediator Ralph Bunche.[2] Article II, section 2 of these
documents summed up the operative Arab government position:

No provision of this Agreement shall in any way prejudice the rights,

---

1. United Nations, General Assembly, Resolution no. 181, Session II, November
29, 1947.

2. United Nations, Security Council (S/1264/Rev. 1) [Israel-Egypt], February 24,
1949; (S/1296/Rev. 1) [Israel-Lebanon], March 23, 1949; (S/1302/Rev. 1)
[Israel-Jordan], April 3, 1949; and (S/1353/Rev. 1) [Israel-Syria], July 20, 1949.
Iraq, having withdrawn its troops from Palestine, did not conclude an armistice
agreement.

claims and positions of either Party hereto in the ultimate peaceful settlement of the Palestine question, the provisions of this Agreement being dictated exclusively by military considerations.

In the Arab view, Israel had won a military victory by force of arms, and the Arab governments took care to leave the way open for future redressment of the military settlement without compromising what they regarded as their just claims. The Arab governments were influenced in this stand by the indignation of Arab public opinion. The Israelis, who felt that their foothold was precarious and the new frontiers still awkward, were doubtless equally unwilling to commit themselves to a permanent settlement.

Implicit in the armistice agreements was the Arab decision not to recognize Israel, even in a *de facto* sense. Israel was "occupied Palestine." Frontiers were to remain closed. Commercial relations were prohibited. Postal and telephone communications with Israel were severed. Direct diplomatic or political contact was virtually nonexistent. Israel was isolated from its immediate environment in a manner unprecedented among nations in the modern world. This isolation of Israel was effective for a time; Israel was almost completely thwarted in integrating itself commercially, socially, or politically into the region. For Israel the price was heavy in some ways. Arab isolation policies made Israel a ghetto in the Middle East. The hostility created a certain psychological strain. Economic isolation led to a restructuring of trade patterns, with a continued and heavy dependence on the West for markets and financial assistance. Israelis who desired to see the new state take root in the region were disappointed. But not all Israelis were disappointed with the "success" of Arab isolation policy, for the Arab policy contributed to national solidarity: it diminished the likelihood of the widely feared "Levantinization" of Israel; it solidified linkages with Western governments and world Jewry; it engendered a spirit of discipline, sacrifice, and preparedness that was useful in counteracting factionalism within the Israeli body politic. Thus, both sides derived benefits from deferring a permanent solution to the Palestine conflict.

Another U.N. resolution upon which the Arab governments placed importance was that which in December, 1948, established a Conciliation Commission to work toward "a peaceful adjustment of the future situation in Palestine." But the most important section resolved that

the refugees wishing to return to their homes and live at peace with their neighbors should be permitted to do so at the earliest practicable date, and that compensation should be paid for the property of those choosing not to return.[3]

It was this expression by the international community of the refugees' rights that underlay the Arab policy of resisting their formal political assimilation in the countries to which they had fled. The degree of assimilation varied from one state to another. Jordan was exceptional in granting them citizenship; but in general the Arab governments resisted pressures by Israel, the Western powers, and indeed some Palestinians themselves, for liquidation of the Palestinian political identity. The Arab states accepted and generally cooperated with the United Nations Relief and Works Agency (UNRWA) as a means of providing the barest human necessities for the refugees without compromising their right to return. We cannot evaluate the proportions of altruism, cynicism, and skepticism among the makers of this policy, except to note the interests and values involved. The policy conformed to the widespread sentiment, among both Palestinians and other Arabs, that the struggle must go on; thus it reflected an important domestic pressure. For different reasons, Israel made no particular effort to mitigate the grievance by accepting more than token numbers of refugees in its own territory, and it found an effective weapon for discrediting Arab governments abroad with the dubious claim that they were using the refugees as a political pawn.

The Arab states' position, framed as it was by volatile public opinion and by U.N. declarations made under varying political-military conditions in Palestine, was thus not a model of consistency or clarity. At this point the Arabs probably would have accepted a settlement along the lines of the previously rejected partition resolution. Even though the armistice agreements terminated the fighting, they did not end the state of belligerency between Israel and the Arab states. The Arab states were too weak militarily to make war and too weak politically to make peace. The U.N. Truce Supervision Organization (UNTSO) was able to observe and terminate border incidents as they occurred, but these incidents were chronic and could not be prevented by UNTSO. At the same time, the Arab states supported U.N. resolutions on the refugees, resolutions that were meaningful only in the context of a more general settlement that neither side felt was possible. Finally, there remained the anguish suffered by the Arabs as a result of the implantation of Israel; their primordial anger, although inchoate and unorganized, held explosive potential in

3. United Nations, General Assembly, Resolution no. 194, Sec. 11, Session III, December 11, 1948.

Arab politics. This feeling could not be assuaged by armistice, resettlement, compensation, or even the 1947 partition. It could only be suppressed, and the Arab governments—however much they may have desired a settlement—lacked the strength and the skill to suppress it completely. Illogical as the overall Arab stance may have been, it did allow them to use the meager weapons of the weak: the withholding of recognition, acceptance, and normalization of relations. These were benefits the Israelis would have to bargain for; they could not be granted as preconditions for negotiations, for the Arabs had nothing else to offer.

Instruments of Inter-Arab Policy

In an effort to improve the coordination of their efforts over Palestine, the Arab states strengthened several instruments of common action and created others. On the regional level the Arab League and its specialized structures, such as the Boycott Office, were of primary importance. On the international scene, the Arab states achieved a substantial measure of unity in U.N. voting on matters related to Palestine, but their diplomatic efforts to influence governments and world public opinion were inadequate.

The League of Arab States was founded in 1945 to strengthen relations among the sovereign signatories and to coordinate their policies, particularly in nonpolitical activities.[4] Its efforts to organize the defense of Palestine in 1948 had been strenuous but unsuccessful, and its later work toward Arab coordination against Israel fell far short of its goals. Nevertheless, the League provided some institutional machinery for implementing the policy of isolating Israel.

The most effective League operation was the economic boycott of Israel. The boycott began in December, 1945, to prevent Jewish smuggling into mandate Palestine, and after the establishment of Israel it was elaborated into a full-time office with headquarters in Damascus. The function of the boycott was to discourage foreign companies from doing business with Israel by denying them access to Arab markets. By 1962 there were some 80 companies on the blacklist. The boycott may have caused some economic distress in Israel, but this was probably minor. It did not prevent Israel from achieving one of the highest growth rates in the world. Nor did it inhibit close trade relationships with the West; in fact, by closing off Arab markets it probably encouraged such trade. And if the boycott

4. Robert W. Macdonald, *The League of Arab States: A Study in the Dynamics of Regional Organization* (Princeton, 1965), pp. 42–43.

intended to mobilize American business interests to pressure the U.S. government to soften its pro-Israel position, again it failed. The Arab states themselves may have suffered some economic damage, but this was minimized by the pragmatic considerations that frequently underlay blacklist decisions. Arab states did not deny themselves, for example, the benefits of banks and airlines that did business with Israel. Companies that went beyond "routine" business relationships, however, were penalized, as in the cases of the Ford Motor Company and Coca Cola, both of which decided to build plants in Israel. Nevertheless, the boycott symbolized an Arab position that did foreclose important development opportunities for Israel and contributed to its chronic balance-of-trade deficit. The main area of boycott effectiveness, suggests Robert Macdonald, was in keeping the Palestine issue alive before the Arab public: it was a hindrance to those forces working for the gradual acceptance of Israel.[5] Significantly, it was one of the few activities that survived, almost unscathed, the factionalism that weakened much of the League's work.

The League sought to hinder Israel's development in other small ways. Israelis were denied entry to Arab countries, and in several states the prohibition was extended to Jews, whatever their nationality. Outside the Arab world itself, Arab missions sought to counteract Israeli influence. Two important battlegrounds in this struggle were the Afro-Asian countries and the United States. Thwarted in its effort to gain access to the Arab world, Israel undertook a systematic development of commercial and technical aid and military assistance programs in certain African countries such as Kenya and Ethiopia. The Arab states, especially Egypt, tried to compete in these fields, and Egypt's powerful radio, directed especially toward Africa's Muslims, broadcast pro-Arab propaganda to a large audience. Egypt's blockade of the Suez Canal to Israeli goods and shipping, on grounds of the state of belligerency, retarded Israel's commercial links with Asia. Even after Israel succeeded in securing access to the Gulf of Aqaba in the Sinai-Suez war of 1956–57, the port of Elath received only a small percentage of Israeli imports. In the diplomatic sphere, the Arabs were successful in excluding Israel from membership in the nonaligned bloc of Third World nations, an effort that had begun with President Nasser's appearance at the Bandung Conference in April, 1955.

The Arabs also tried to carry on the struggle with Israel through propaganda in the West. In addition to embassies and consulates, Arab Information Offices were established. In the United States, for example, such offices in New York, Washington, and several other cities distributed

5. *Ibid.,* pp. 119–20.

a monthly magazine, the *Arab World,* and various bulletins and pamphlets. Compared to the Israeli operation, which was closely coordinated with the American Jewish organizations, these efforts were of little value. To most Americans, Palestine was an issue settled and forgotten, and their image of the Arab was hardly favorable. Arab spokesmen complained about unfair treatment in the U.S. mass media but were not very skillful in their efforts to change it.[6] Even though the Arabs had potential influence through U.S. businesses with interests in the Arab world, they were ineffective in developing it. Indeed, American oil companies, fearing attacks by Jewish groups, were nervous about becoming identified with the Arab side in debates on the Middle East question. If the Arab League made any effort to mobilize the American Arab community to exert political pressure, it was not effective.

The Arab states did show a high degree of unity in their voting patterns in the United Nations, particularly on Palestine-related questions but also on a range of other issues. One study, for example, reported that, along with the Soviet and Western voting blocs, "the Arabs are almost always among the most cohesive. Their unity has disintegrated somewhat since 1947 (when Palestine was so important), but it partly returned in 1961."[7] During the first twelve sessions of the General Assembly, Arab League members had an internal-cohesion voting score of 90.2 per cent.[8] And even with inter-Arab splits, such as that over the Baghdad Pact from 1955 on, the Arab League Council exercised a high degree of coordination over Arab-state voting. Arab delegations occasionally diverged, but never on Palestine questions. Even dissidents on inter-Arab affairs such as President Bourguiba of Tunisia did not deviate on matters of principle involving Palestine. Arab delegations were also active, though not decisive, in bringing about several condemnations of Israel by the Security Council for truce violations. However impressive this solidarity and such efforts may seem, their practical effects were very limited. And diplomatic initiatives by the Arab states, such as their efforts in 1961 to obtain a resolution supporting Arab property rights in Israel, were

---

6. See, for example, the following studies by Michael W. Suleiman: "The Arabs and the West: Communication Gap," *Il Politico,* XXXII (1967), 511–28; "An Evaluation of Middle East News Coverage in Seven American Newsmagazines, July–December, 1956," *Middle East Forum,* XLI (1965), 9–30; and "American Mass Media and the June Conflict," in *The Arab-Israeli Confrontation of June 1967,* ed. Ibrahim Abu-Lughod (Evanston, Ill.: Northwestern University Press, 1970) pp. 138–54.

7. Hayward R. Alker, Jr., and Bruce M. Russett, *World Politics in the General Assembly* (New Haven, 1965), p. 256.

8. Macdonald, *League of Arab States,* pp. 252–53, citing Thomas Hovet, *Bloc Politics in the United Nations* (Cambridge, Mass., 1960), p. 62.

unsuccessful. Israel was repeatedly condemned, UNRWA appropriations were repeatedly approved, but Arab diplomacy was unable to alter the *status quo* in Palestine in its favor. Even growing support from the Soviet Union failed to improve the Arab situation.

Outside efforts to reach a solution were received with suspicion by both the Arab governments and Israel.[9] The Arab governments convened in Beirut in the spring of 1949 in hopes of working out a refugee plan under the auspices of the U.N. Conciliation Commission for Palestine (CCP), but they would not accept substantial resettlement, while Israel remained opposed to repatriation. In the same year, the CCP created the Economic Survey Mission for the Middle East, headed by Dr. Gordon Clapp, to begin drawing up plans for water and land development on a cooperative basis. But neither these initiatives nor the plan promoted by President Dwight Eisenhower's representative, Eric Johnston, during 1953–55, came to fruition. A technical committee of the Arab League did in fact approve a modified version of the so-called Johnston Plan, modeled on the U.S. Tennessee Valley Authority, but border conditions on the Israel-Jordan and Israel-Syria armistice lines at the time were so volatile that the plan failed: Israel first rejected it because of proposed U.N. participation, while the Arab governments would not accept it otherwise.[10] In 1961 another major U.N.–sponsored effort, the mission of Dr. Joseph E. Johnson, president of Carnegie Endowment for International Peace, met a similar fate. Johnson, who had the informal backing of President John F. Kennedy, proposed a gradual settlement under which individual refugees, free of any pressure, would express their wishes on repatriation or resettlement. Israel rejected the notion of anything but token repatriation, and the Arab states, even the "moderate" ones, closed ranks against it for the opposite reason.[11]

In the military domain, formal collective-security action by the Arab states proved to be not only inadequate but highly dangerous. Arab defense coordination, discussed below, was more a product of inter-Arab political quarrels than of rational analysis of the Israeli threat. Beyond the Arab League machinery itself, the first major effort to establish a joint military command occurred only two days before Israel's invasion of Sinai in October, 1956, when Jordan belatedly joined the Syrian-Egyptian defense pact of October, 1955, itself a response to the British-inspired Baghdad Pact. It was not enough time to organize an effective

---

9. Don Peretz, *Israel and the Palestine Arabs* (Washington, D.C., 1958), chap. 2.

10. Fred J. Khouri, *The Arab-Israeli Dilemma* (Syracuse, 1968), pp. 142–43.

11. See Joseph E. Johnson, "Arab vs. Israeli: A Persistent Challenge to Americans" (Address to the 24th American Assembly, New York, October 24, 1963).

joint-military effort against Israel, as Israel's swift military success clearly
showed. This dismal history repeated itself exactly a decade later: Egypt
and Syria signed a defense agreement on November 4, 1966, to strengthen
a joint military command envisaged by the first Arab summit conference
of January, 1964. Once again, as violence escalated, the reluctant Jordanians belatedly signed on—this time less than a week before Israel's pre-
emptive strike of June 5, 1967. The same domestic forces that stimulated
sporadic pact-building also frustrated the institutionalization of alliances.

Policy toward the Displaced Palestinians

Over 700,000 Arabs fled their homes during the turmoil and warfare
surrounding the establishment of Israel in May, 1948, and took up residence in the West Bank (formally annexed by Jordan in 1950), Transjordan, Gaza (administered by Egypt), Syria, and Lebanon. Relations
with Israel constituted the most obvious aspect of the Arabs' Palestine
policy, but relations with the displaced Palestinians were also significant
in the long run. Deliberately or accidentally, the Arab governments came
to accept the designation of the Palestinians as *refugees* whose claims were
essentially *private* (rooted in the involuntary deprivation of property
and livelihood) rather than *public* (consisting in the right of national
political self-determination in Palestine). Past miscalculation and military
defeat, as we have seen, placed the Arab states in an awkward position
on the matter of political self-determination for the Palestinians; ambiguity existed as to whether all of Palestine, partition Palestine, or
armistice Palestine was the Palestine in which self-determination obtained.
Given the reality of a powerful and intransigent Israel that enjoyed substantial international support, it is understandable that the Arab governments should have found the General Assembly's 1948 formula about
refugees (embodied in resolution 194) the most realistic framework in
which to operate. The fact that the issue of an independent Arab Palestine
state was also enmeshed in the rivalry between Egypt and the Hashemite
Kingdom in Jordan further complicated the Palestinian political cause.

If the Arab governments found it expedient to underplay long-standing
Palestinian political claims, they did not go to the extreme of eliminating
the Palestinian communal identity by forcing, or permitting, assimilation.
There is little doubt that important elements among Arab elites would
like to have seen assimilation, both on humanitarian and pragmatic
political grounds; nor is there doubt that substantial American economic
aid would have been made available for such purposes. But to most Arab
leaders resettlement without the choice of repatriation was morally un-

acceptable. An equal deterrent was the high political risk of accepting such a policy. According to one student of the problem, "No Arab government dared to initiate a resettlement project. The very word was associated by nationalists with defeat by Israel and with 'Western imperialism.' "[12] Unable to surmount either horn of the dilemma, the Arab governments and the international community left the Palestinians in the limbo of refugee status, providing only the minimum resources for relief and rehabilitation.

The General Assembly created the United Nations Relief and Works Agency for Palestine Refugees (UNRWA) in December, 1949. Its mission was twofold: (1) to carry out relief and works programs in collaboration with local governments and (2) "to consult with the interested Near Eastern Governments concerning measures to be taken by them preparatory to the time when international assistance for relief and works projects is no longer available."[13] The second objective made clear that the establishment of UNRWA not be taken as a substitute for a settlement. While there were consultations between UNRWA and the Arab governments about the ultimate transfer of responsibility for the refugees to the host governments, these came to nothing.

The Arab governments did cooperate with UNRWA in the spirit and letter of the second objective. UNRWA maintained good relations with the host countries despite the inevitable administrative problems, notably those with respect to verifying registration lists and those resulting from the tensions of domestic and inter-Arab politics.[14] This difficult job was accomplished with a high degree of efficiency up to and through the June, 1967, war. Structurally, UNRWA was a national government with a personnel of over 11,500, of whom less than 150 were non-Arab; of the Arab employees "virtually all are refugees."[15] Although manned largely by Palestinians, except in the top positions, financially UNRWA was only marginally supported by the Arab states: total Arab-state contributions to the UNRWA budget over the 1950–67 period amounted to about 2 per cent of the total, and for the fiscal year 1966–67 the figure was around 4 per cent.[16] The Arab governments argued that they bore no

12. Peretz, *Israel and the Palestine Arabs*, p. 21.

13. United Nations, General Assembly, Resolution no. 302, Session IV, December 8, 1949.

14. See, for example, the commissioner-general's comments on these matters in United Nations, General Assembly, *Report of the Commissioner-General of the United Nations Relief and Works Agency for Palestine Refugees in the Near East*, Suppl. 13, June 30, 1967, Session XXII, pp. 6–8.

15. *Ibid.*, p. 90.

16. Calculations from *ibid.*, Annex I, Table 20, pp. 77–82.

responsibility for the plight of the Palestinians and that such contributions as were made to UNRWA were beyond the call of duty. That argument, while debatable, was more plausible than Israel's similar disclaimer of responsibility; but the Israelis contributed far less to UNRWA than did the Arabs. Total Israeli contributions to UNRWA, 1950–67, were $406,-547 (the total Arab contribution was $16,863,082) which may be compared to the contributions of the Arab host countries: Jordan, $1,891,833; Gaza Authorities (Egypt), $1,999,919; Syria, $1,529,443; and Lebanon, $728,967. The major contributors, of course, were the Western nations, notably the United States which contributed over $411 million, or nearly 70 per cent of the agency's revenue from 1950 through 1967.[17]

Contributions to UNRWA do not tell the whole story of Arab government aid to the displaced Palestinians, because these governments made annual contributions that were substantially higher than their contributions to UNRWA directly to refugees for education, social welfare, housing, security, and other services. In 1966–67, for example, the relative contributions were as depicted in the table below.

Arab Government Contributions to UNRWA and Directly to Refugees
1966–67 (in dollars)

Contributions	Lebanon	Syria	Gaza Authorities (Egypt)	Jordan
To UNRWA	$ 45,531	$ 93,742	$ 273,494	$ 170,822
To Refugees Directly	841,233	2,649,851	2,514,000*	3,128,284
Total Contributions	886,764	2,743,593	2,787,494	3,229,106
Number of Refugees**	160,723	144,390	316,776	722,687
Total aid per Refugee	$5.52	$19.00	$8.79	$4.56

SOURCE: *Report of the Commissioner-General, UNRWA,* 1966–67, Tables 20 and 22.

*1965–66 data.

**Grand total of those registered; includes refugees not receiving rations or living in UNRWA camps.

17. Over a similar time period (1946–64) the U.S. government also provided Israel with over $363 million in economic grants, which when combined with economic loans amounted to nearly $997 million in aid (U.S. Agency for International Development, "U.S. Overseas Loans and Grants," special report prepared for the House Foreign Affairs Committee, March 3, 1965).

When the Arab governments' aid to refugees is divided by the number of refugees in each host country, it is possible to ascertain roughly how much each government was spending per refugee. The Syrian government provided the most aid per capita, around $19.00, followed at some distance by the Egyptian authorities in Gaza ($8.79), Lebanon ($5.52), and Jordan ($4.56). When deductions are made for Arab government contributions to the UNRWA budget of 1966–67, we find that the non-Arab states were providing about $24.30 per refugee as compared to the individual Arab-state contributions, made through UNRWA and directly, presented in the Table above. The Syrians were thus in effect, making a matching grant of over two-thirds the non-Arab, world contribution; the Egyptians one-third; the Lebanese over one-fifth; and the Jordanians over one-sixth. By comparison, Israel, assuming it had a certain responsibility for *all* the refugees it created, contributed through UNRWA a little over 11 cents per refugee.

I have attempted to show that the Arab governments' contribution to the destitute Palestinians was by no means negligible, particularly in light of the limitations of resources and political constraints. Nevertheless, the Palestinians had many good reasons to feel they were strangers, and they suffered many hardships in the host countries. Some were social: one young Palestinian recalls, for example, that his Lebanese schoolmates taunted him about his Palestinian accent so much that he felt compelled to speak Lebanese Arabic. Some were economic: displaced Palestinian peasants were unable to find farm work. Many found menial work outside the camps on the fringes of the cities, but often there were legal barriers and job discrimination. Some were political: the local authorities in every host country tried to curtail organized political activity because they feared Palestinian interference in domestic affairs and, perhaps even more, Palestinian provocations of Israel. Refugee status deprived or impaired Palestinians' conventional political rights to organize parties, vote, and travel outside the country. The most debilitating aspect of the Arab states' treatment of the Palestinians, however, was probably psychological. For the many middle- and upper-class Palestinians not confined to camps, hopelessness was not a crushing problem, and many thousands—virtually the entire urbanized sector—did outstandingly well in commerce and the professions in the host countries. But for those in the camps the hopelessness of life, more than the squalidness, was immense. It is interesting that only the educated Palestinians placed major blame on the Arab governments for their plight.[18] Ironically, UNRWA's extensive educational

18. Fred C. Bruhns, "A Study of Arab Refugee Attitudes," *Middle East Journal,* IX (1955), 130–38.

program was as powerful an incentive as the inconclusive and temporizing policies of the Arab states in stimulating the Palestinians to reorganize and begin once again to assert themselves politically.

THE DYNAMICS OF ARAB BEHAVIOR

While it is important to try to identify the main issues and the positions taken by the Arab governments, it is equally necessary to observe Arab actions in the context of the developing situation. The conflict arena was not static between 1949 and 1967, and Arab behavior was *ad hoc* rather than coherent, particularly because the Arabs were weak and disorganized. The conflict twice escalated drastically during Israel's first 20 years of sovereignty: The first "active" phase was from around February, 1955, through March, 1957, and was marked by the Sinai-Suez war, while the second began in 1966, extended through the 1967 June war, and by the end of 1970 had not ended. Three developments help explain the escalation: (1) the Israeli policy of massive retaliation and violent provocation; (2) internal political ferment that led to the weakening of "moderate" elements; and (3) inter-Arab rivalries, partially the result of great power maneuvering, that triggered governmental activism.

The first active phase was preceded and initiated by severe Israeli provocations against Egypt, the Gaza raid of February, 1955, being particularly crucial. It followed upon a political convulsion, traceable to the 1948 Palestine war, which saw the overthrow of some pro-Western factions and the emergence in one country, Egypt, of a revolutionary government. It came as Egypt and Iraq, with their respective allies, struggled for hegemony in the Arab East. It was linked to Britain's collapse as the main colonial power in the area and the intrusion of the Soviet Union. The second active phase was initiated by Israel's unilateral diversion of Jordan River waters in 1963–64 and by new punitive actions against Jordan and Syria. By early 1966 there were two additional revolutionary governments, Syria and Iraq, arrayed against Israel—the former being especially provocative—and the non-revolutionary states of Jordan and Lebanon were under strong pressure to become militant. Palestinian guerrilla activities were beginning to add to this pressure. This phase was preceded by a period of greater than usual confusion in Arab-state relationships, marked especially by rivalry among Egypt, Syria, and Iraq; the Egyptian-Saudi struggle in Yemen; and the continuing friction between Jordan and Egypt. The American decision to stop courting Nasser and to help strengthen the influence of King Faysal of Saudi Arabia propelled

Egypt toward the Soviet Union and a more adventuresome position on Palestine, while the U.S. became increasingly identified with Israel.

Israeli Massive Retaliation and Provocation

The Arab governments and Israel have been so strident in blaming each other for the Palestine problem that world opinion has come to treat such arguments as sterile and tiresome. Nevertheless, there is a great deal of truth to them: the contenders have found themselves locked in a cycle of response and counter-response. It is useful to examine this interrelationship over time.

On the basic issues, as we have seen, there was very little movement from 1949 to 1967. There was only one period in which either party showed any signs of flexibility. This period began with the officers' coup in Egypt in July, 1952, and ended wth David Ben-Gurion's return to the Israel Cabinet in February, 1955. We are told by a former U.S. intelligence agent that General Muhammad Nagib, figurehead leader of the Free Officers, informed the United States within hours of the July, 1952, coup that he "wasn't interested in Palesine."[19] Nasser, the real power in Egypt, also expressed interest in a settlement, and the American government for a time had hopes that he would keep the Arabs under control.[20] Nasser was also reported to be interested in encouraging indirect contacts with Moshe Sharett, who succeeded Ben-Gurion as prime minister in December, 1953.[21] Fred J. Khouri cites Israeli press reports issued in 1961 of clandestine meetings which occurred in Paris between Egyptian and Israeli representatives during 1954; the representatives sought to arrange an informal normalization of border relations and open the way to later negotiations on other outstanding issues.[22] No significant results came of these contacts, and the climate for accommodation worsened rapidly with the return of Ben-Gurion and the escalation of border conflicts between Egypt and Israel.

At the tactical level, however, there was a great deal of movement: the vicious cycle of provocation and reprisal kept the situation inflamed even during the relatively passive phases of the conflict. The pattern of

19. Cited in Miles Copeland, *The Game of Nations* (London, 1969), p. 62.

20. *Ibid.,* pp. 56–57, 129–30.

21. Jean Lacouture and Simonne Lacouture, *Egypt in Transition* (London, 1958), p. 233.

22. *Arab-Israeli Dilemma,* pp. 300–1.

incidents culminating in the Israeli invasion of Sinai in 1956 usually involved individual Palestinians or small groups crossing the armistice line to recover property or commit acts of revenge; these actions periodically led to bloody reprisals by the Israel Defense Force, in which whole villages were punished for the individual provocations. Such incidents occurred principally along the Jordan border, where refugees or villagers were often situated adjacent to their own farms and houses, which had been appropriated by Israeli settlers. However understandable the Arab incursions may have been, they were intolerable to the Israelis, who chose to regard them as planned guerrilla activities. In January, 1955, Maj. Gen. Moshe Dayan wrote that

> Thefts, robbery, hold-ups and eventually murder and sabotage became of frequent occurrence. . . . There can be little doubt that much of this guerrilla war is of a military character. . . . From 1949 to the middle of 1954 there have been an average of 1,000 cases of infiltration per month along the several frontiers.[23]

The accounts by U.N. truce-supervision officers, however, suggest that most of the incidents were not organized by Arab governments and that these governments in fact sought to curb them and to cooperate in bringing infiltrators to justice.[24] The Israeli response was often devastating, and it was not softened by the frequent condemnations by the U.N. Security Council. Israel's reprisal raids—such as those on the Jordanian villages of Qibya in October, 1953 (75 villagers killed); Nahhalin in March, 1954 (14 killed); and Qalqilya in October, 1956 (48 killed)—deepened the bitterness of the Palestinians. They confirmed the image the Israelis had created for themselves during the 1948 fighting when, on April 9, 1948, they had massacred between 250 and 350 civilian residents of the village of Deir Yassin. At the cost of exacerbating hatred at the popular level, the Israelis probably succeeded in "teaching a lesson" at the governmental level, for Jordan did what it could to discourage incidents.

Israel's problem with Egypt, however, was more complicated. Here too there were the usual incidents during the immediate postwar years, although fewer than on the Jordan border. In military terms, Egypt alone had the potential to threaten Israel's territorial integrity. In political terms,

23. "Israel's Border and Security Problems," *Foreign Affairs,* XXXIII (January, 1955), 260–61.
24. See, for example, E. L. M. Burns, *Between Arab and Israeli* (New York, 1963), pp. 33–68; Kennett Love, *Suez: The Twice-Fought War* (New York, 1969), pp. 86–87.

the threat was even more ominous, at least to the dominant hard-line school of thought represented by Ben-Gurion. Ben-Gurion's comment after the Sinai campaign is revealing:

> I always feared that a personality might rise such as arose among the Arab rulers in the seventh century or like [Kemal Atatürk] who arose in Turkey after its defeat in the first World War. He raised their spirits, changed their character, and turned them into a fighting nation. There was and still is a danger that Nasser is this man.[25]

Furthermore, Israel still had two important grievances against Egypt. Since the 1948 war Egypt had blockaded the Suez Canal to Israeli shipping and contraband, and since 1950 it had applied, more in theory than in practice, the same prohibitions at the Straits of Tiran, entrance to the Gulf of Aqaba. The possibility of good Egyptian-American relations may also have been thought by the hard-liners to represent a threat to Israel's long-term security. Such calculations may explain the series of unusual Israeli provocations against Egypt that culminated in the Sinai-Suez war. In July, 1954, during the Sharett ministry, but unbeknown to Sharett or Defense Minister Pinhas Lavon, Israeli agents carried out sabotage against U.S. government installations in Egypt, presumably to alienate the United States from Egypt. The plot backfired and set off the famous "Lavon affair" in Israel. It also helped abort Sharett's initiative of sending an Israeli freighter, the *Bat Galim,* to test the Egyptian blockade in September, 1954.[26] In July, 1954, the Israeli army chiefs, Dayan and Shimon Peres, persuaded France to begin supplying arms secretly. On February 21, 1955, Ben-Gurion returned to the Cabinet as defense minister, and on February 28 Israel carried out a major raid on Gaza that Nasser called "the turning point" in Egyptian-Israeli relations.[27]

The "lesson" of the Gaza raid was not simply that the Arabs must prevent marauders from entering Israel, as was the case on the Jordan border and in the Syria-Israel demilitarized zones. The Egyptian-Israeli frontier had been relatively free of such incidents. The Gaza raid signaled to the Egyptians that Israeli intentions extended beyond the maintenance of the *status quo* and involved attaining freedom of navigation, acquisition of further territory, and the stifling of any pan-Arab, anti-Israel movement that might accompany Cairo's growing influence in the area. It also revealed that the Egyptian armed forces were dangerously inadequate.

25. Cited in Love, *Suez,* p. 676.
26. *Ibid.,* pp. 74–75.
27. *Ibid.,* p. 83; Burns, *Between Arab and Israeli,* p. 18.

During the remainder of 1955, Egypt, on the one hand, maintained a posture of diplomatic flexibility and accommodation toward Israel and gave sympathetic attention to the proposals advanced by John Foster Dulles in August and Anthony Eden in November. On the other hand, it also began to stiffen its military posture. As humiliating incidents continued, Nasser in August authorized the use of Palestinian guerrillas (fedayeen) in officially instigated reprisal raids.[28] The fedayeen operations represented a major shift in Egyptian policy: for the first time Israeli violence was countered with Arab governmental force. The Egyptians also began an earnest search for weapons. After an unsuccessful effort to get them from the United States, they obtained them through the Soviet Union, in the famous Czech arms deal of September 27, 1955.

Simultaneously, Nasser's relations with Britain and France were in decline as a result of British initiatives to build an anti-Nasser bloc through the Baghdad Pact and French hostility at Egypt's support for the Algerian rebellion. America's and Britain's cancellation of their promised financing of the Aswan Dam led to another bold move by Nasser, the nationalization of the Suez Canal Company on July 26, 1956. The story of Israeli, French, and British collusion to chase Nasser out of office through a joint invasion of Egypt has been told elsewhere in fascinating detail.[29] Here it need be observed only that Egyptian policy was reactive rather than provocative and that it sought to build both diplomatic and military defenses against what it rightly interpreted as a systematic effort by the Israeli "hawks" to improve the status quo of the 1949 accords. Nasser kept the Israelis from using the Suez Canal but lost control of the Straits of Tiran. In the military sphere Egypt's efforts proved completely inadequate, but in the political sphere its bold—if risky—stands against Israel and Western imperialism defeated the efforts to eliminate him. Indeed, Nasser emerged as a stronger political figure in the Arab world than he had been before the crisis.

The Sinai-Suez war brought several years of relative calm to Israel's border with Egypt, through the imposition of the United Nations Emergency Force on the Egyptian side of the line. The Jordanian front too remained relatively quiet, and the Lebanese continued their policy of noninvolvement. But the war had not alleviated the main causes of the Arab-Israeli conflict. Israel showed no change in its unyielding position with regard to Arab claims and U.N. resolutions, and the Arabs, for their part, rigidly maintained their refusal to accept the legitimacy of Israel. The

28. Love, Suez, pp. 84–86.
29. See, for example, ibid.; Anthony Nutting, No End to a Lesson (London, 1967); and Hugh Thomas, Suez (New York, 1967).

Arab states continued to press the boycott, uphold the claims of the refugees, and maintain a constant flow of vituperative propaganda.

The scene of conflict shifted to northern Palestine, and it was Syria's border with Israel that became the origin of the second active phase of the Arab-Israeli dispute. Two disputes crystallized during the period from late 1957 through 1964, both involving new Israeli challenges to the 1949 *status quo*. The minor dispute was over control of the demilitarized zones and Lake Tiberias. Israeli efforts to cultivate in the DMZs were considered by Syria as violations of article 5 of the Syrian-Israeli armistice agreement, which stated that the purpose of the DMZ arrangement was to minimize friction and provide for "the gradual restoration of normal civilian life in the area of the Demilitarized Zone, without prejudice to the ultimate settlement." On a number of occasions Syrian artillery on the Golan Heights shelled Israeli settlements beyond the immediate area of an incident, and the Israelis mounted heavy counter-reprisals.[30] The major dispute developed during 1963 when Israel began its project to divert Jordan River waters for irrigation in the Negev. A decade earlier Israel had been dissuaded by the United States from a similar unilateral undertaking. Syrian and joint Arab efforts to counter this project were unsuccessful, for reasons discussed below. Once again the Arab governments — the weaker party—were pushed by Israeli initiatives into *ad hoc* and ineffectual responses.

Israel's northern initiatives in the early 1960s led to results similar to those of 1956. Once again there were raids by Palestinian *fedayeen,* sanctioned and encouraged by an Arab government, Syria. Once again there was an acceleration of the arms buildup, in Syria and Egypt. Once again Israel mounted massive reprisal raids. The sequence of events leading up to the June war has been adequately described elsewhere.[31] It is sufficient here to note that Israel's raid on the Jordanian village of Sammu' on November 13, 1966 (18 dead, 134 wounded); its air raid against Syria on April 7, 1967; and its reported intention to invade Syria were successful in provoking the U.A.R. to build up its forces in the Sinai, announce reimposition of its closure of the Straits of Tiran, and demand withdrawal of the United Nations Emergency Force. All this was sufficient pretext for Israel to launch its strike on June 5.

30. Khouri, *Arab-Israeli Dilemma,* pp. 222–25; see also Carl von Horn, *Soldiering for Peace* (New York, 1966), chap. 10.

31. Charles W. Yost, "The Arab-Israeli War: How it Began," *Foreign Affairs,* XLVI (January, 1968), 304–20.

Internal Political Ferment

The most significant political event of the century in the Arab East, as elsewhere in the Third World, has been the politicization of the masses. This process and the concomitant struggle for independence from British and French colonialism began in World War I, gathered momentum after World War II, and has not yet ended. Because development occurred unevenly and caused severe social, economic, and psychological disruptions, it did not bring about stability and liberal democracy, as many Arabs and Western observers expected. Instead it led to tension, ferment, and violence. According to one systematic tabulation of domestic instability and events of violence over the 1948–67 period, Syria experienced 20 successful or unsuccessful coups; Iraq, 16; the U.A.R., 8; Jordan, 3; and Lebanon, 2. The numbers of deaths from political violence recorded by the press during this period were as follows: Iraq, 6,300; Syria, 1,800; the U.A.R., 478; Lebanon, 375; and Jordan, 74.[32] Rule passed uneasily from traditional to liberal-bourgeois to military-reformist elites in several Arab states, yet genuine social revolution remained elusive.[33]

While social mobilization was enlarging the political arena, traditional-elite rivalries were intensified. Issues such as imperialism and corruption fueled the conflict, but none was more important than Palestine. Palestine became the running sore of Arab politics, the refugees a symbol of weakness, stupidity, humiliation, and guilt. The loss of Palestine was a touchstone for opposition politicians from the conservative right, represented by the Muslim Brotherhood, to the radical left, represented by the Ba'ath socialists. The Palestine issue contributed to violent upheavals in every country bordering on Israel. Egypt, already racked by anti-British and antiregime turmoil, had suffered the most humiliating defeat in the Palestine war. On December 4, 1948, Nukrashi Pasha, the prime minister, was assassinated by a Muslim Brother. From 1949 through the officers' coup in 1952, Egyptian politics seethed with assassination and turmoil; much of it originated with the Muslim Brotherhood whose dedication to the Palestine cause had been shown by their militant guerrilla fighting during the war.[34] The government, which feared subversion not only by

---

32. From data compiled under the direction of Charles L. Taylor and Michael C. Hudson for the revised *World Handbook of Political and Social Indicators,* forthcoming, under the auspices of the Yale World Data Analysis Program.

33. See Manfred Halpern, *The Politics of Social Change in the Middle East and North Africa* (Princeton, 1963).

34. Richard P. Mitchell, *The Society of the Muslim Brothers* (London, 1969), pp. 55–58, 70.

extremist sections of the brotherhood, but also by a broad, if amorphous, nationalist movement, had been seriously compromised by the scandal over defective ammunition supplied to Egyptian forces in the Palestine war. Syria, similarly embarrassed by scandals over conduct of the war, experienced three *coups d'état* in 1949 alone, and many more were to follow.[35] And, in the clearest expression of Arab mass discontent, King Abdullah of Jordan was assassinated on July 20, 1951, in Jerusalem by a Palestinian student.

The tragedy of the Palestine war spawned, or gave fresh impetus to, a number of revolutionary parties and secret societies. Displaced Palestinians were often active in the leadership of groups such as the Arab Nationalist Movement, the Ba'ath Party, and the Syrian National Social Party. Despite constant and vigorous efforts by the Jordanian regime to curb activity, pan-Arab cells and cliques with a militant Palestinian position continued to develop in Jordan, and they found support from regimes hostile to the Hashemite government, especially from Egypt.

The Palestine defeat had also given impetus to active intervention by the military. President Nasser's combat in Palestine may not have made him a partisan of the Palestine cause per se, yet it seems to have been important in galvanizing him to reform the corruption so manifest in Egypt.[36] The officers' coup in Egypt was not the first of such interventions. In addition to the 1949 coups in Syria, reform-minded officers seized power in Iraq in 1958, 1963, and 1968, and again in Syria in 1963 and 1966. Each takeover displayed a more radical expression of the basic ideological tenets of Arab unity, socialism, and Palestinian militancy: the Ba'ath was more radical than Nasser or Qasim on these matters and the neo-Ba'ath more radical than the Ba'ath. The trend was to an increasing populist influence on national leadership. The militants on Palestine probably benefited from this trend more than Arab nationalists or socialists.

Radical populism had "spillover" effects in states such as Jordan and Lebanon, not yet officially "progressive." Both King Husayn and the Lebanese authorities had to show popular support for Palestinian militancy, even while their security services strove to curb border raids and subversive activities. But the relationship between popular militancy on Palestine and governmental behavior was indirect, delayed, and complex. Even the "revolutionary" governments sought to temper and control it, for their leaders had a variety of internal goals to serve as well. Usually

35. Patrick Seale provides details (*The Struggle for Syria* [London, 1965], pp. 33, 41–44).

36. Copeland, *Game of Nations,* p. 56; Gamal Abdel Nasser, *The Philosophy of the Revolution* (Buffalo, 1959), pp. 28–29.

these governments gave little more than lip service to the demands for liberation. It was not until 1961 that an Arab government—Iraq under General Qasim—made any more-than-routine proposals for resumption of military preparations. Qasim's offer to train a Palestine army was interpreted by some observers, however, as a maneuver to counter his Arab nationalist critics at home and to challenge Egypt and Jordan for the prestige of representing Palestinian interests.[37]

With the ascendency of Ba'athist and pan-Arab nationalism in Iraq and Syria in 1963, Egypt, whose own revolutionary pan-Arab influence was on the wane following the Syrian succession of 1961, felt the sting of radical rivalry. Palestine was of course one of the major inflammatory issues. President Nasser is said to have fully realized the perils of escalating radical rhetoric under these conditions, and his management of the summit conference of January, 1964, was an effort to avoid being either outflanked in militancy or sucked into another losing war. But the rhetoric of liberation warfare was beginning to generate unintended consequences. Establishment of a Joint Command and a Palestine Liberation Organization (PLO), while intended simultaneously to exploit and contain militancy, proved a dangerous step for governments whose structures were inadequate for controlling an issue of such high salience to the Arab public.[38]

Not only had the number of "progressive" Arab regimes increased between the first and the second active phases of the Palestinian conflict but a new militancy was also taking root within the Palestinian Arabs themselves. Long before the establishment of the Palestinian Liberation Organization, groups of Palestinians had begun to plan and organize a resistance movement that would attempt to restore Palestine to the Palestinians and build there a secular state for Muslims, Christians and Jews. The men who established Fatah, the Palestine Liberation Movement, in 1956 doubtless were in full agreement with Musa al-Alami, a leading Palestinian liberal, who in 1949 had condemned the Arab governments for their handling of the Palestinian case.[39] But they rejected Alami's call for

---

37. Majid Khadduri, *Republican 'Iraq* (London, 1969), p. 187.

38. Maxime Rodinson, *Israel and the Arabs,* trans. Michael Perl (London, 1968), pp. 163–71.

39. "In the face of the enemy the Arabs were not a state, but petty states; groups, not a nation; each fearing and anxiously watching the other and intriguing against it. . . . The structure of the Arab governments was old-fashioned and sterile. The regimes did not even understand the situation, or the importance and danger of the hour, or the course of events. They did nothing positive in accordance with the exigencies of the situation" (Musa al-Alami, "The Lesson of Palestine," *Middle East Journal,* III [1949], 373–405).

Arab unity as a means of liberating Palestine because they felt that Arab unity could only come after the intruded Zionist enclave had been eradicated. The collapse of the Egyptian-Syrian union in September, 1961, confirmed this position and gave impetus to Fatah and the other Palestinian organizations that were forming all across the Arab world. Fatah launched its first armed attack into Israel on January 1, 1965. Thereafter it enjoyed the sponsorship of the Ba'athist government of Syria, from whose territory it launched most of its border raids. While the Palestinian resistance movement exerted no significant populist pressure in the Arab world until after the 1967 war, it was crucial in exacerbating the border tensions and intensifying the anti-Israel opinion that eventually pulled three Arab governments into direct conflict with Israel.

On the eve of the June, 1967, war, the pressure of Arab populism, fanned both by radical Syria and conservative Jordan (for conservative, pro-Western governments also exploited the Palestine issue), helped induce Nasser to make his threatening gestures toward Israel.[40] History, intelligence, instincts may all have counseled caution, but the power of popular sentiment was such that even Gamal Abdel Nasser, the strongest Arab leader, appears to have calculated that a military defeat would be easier to withstand than the consequences of being soft on the Palestine issue.[41]

Inter-Arab Rivalries

Aside from its domestic ramifications, Palestine had also become a bone of contention in inter-Arab politics. Egypt's natural hegemony, particularly after the rise of Nasser, gave it a special interest in Palestine, but Egypt was challenged by the Hashemite regime in Jordan and by the revolutionary regimes that arose in Iraq and Syria. The conduct of the 1948 war had been seriously impaired by Egyptian-Jordanian rivalries. Glubb Pasha, commander of the Transjordan Arab Legion, notes repeatedly the lack of Egyptian cooperation (such as the Egyptian seizure of an ammunition ship destined for Transjordan) which he ascribes in part to inefficiency and in part to politics.[42] Glubb's summary of Jordanian-Egyptian friction is worth quoting:

40. Malcolm Kerr, *The Arab Cold War 1958–1967: A Study of Ideology in Politics* (2d ed., New York, 1967), p. 169.

41. Copeland, *Game of Nations,* pp. 236–39.

42. See Sir John Bagot Glubb, *A Soldier with the Arabs* (New York, 1957), pp. 91–92, 133, and chaps. 6–12.

The real fact was that the Egyptian government had led the Arab League to war in May 1948 against the advice of Jordan. Egyptian leadership had ended in a fiasco, whereas the Arab Legion had gained in prestige and had actually saved a considerable part of Palestine. It was necessary for Egypt to find an excuse for her failure. She was also intensely jealous of Arab Legion successes, contrasted with her defeats. These two factors were further accentuated by King Farouq's jealousy of King Abdulla, and by the general anti-British trend of Egyptian policy. For the army which had outshone that of Egypt was the army of King Abdulla, and it had been trained and led by British officers.[43]

For their part, the Egyptians suspected that Transjordan was the tool of British policy and that its counsels of "moderation" and "realism" constituted a sellout of the Palestine cause. Furthermore, there was resentment among Egyptian officers that the Arab Legion had not deployed its forces as aggressively as might have been possible, for example in the fighting for Jerusalem, Lydda, and Ramle. Nasser himself was suspicious of the Jordanians and is quoted as remarking:

> Before leaving Gaza we received some strange instructions: we were told to march to the relief of the Jordan army which was in trouble near Bab el Wad. . . . We thought it was strange to be shorn of a quarter of our fighting troops by throwing them into the hornets'-nest at Bab el Wad.[44]

The Egyptians were not alone among Arabs in condemning King Abdullah's ambitions to establish himself as the ruler of a Fertile Crescent state in Syria, including Arab Palestine. Abdullah was also accused, with reason, of readiness to conclude a permanent settlement with Israel, conceding more to the Jews than the other Arabs cared to. In fact the king had held talks with Israeli officials both before the war and after it, in the latter case ceding to the Israelis a strip of border territory. And in December, 1948, when Palestinian notables met in Jericho to call for unification with Transjordan (to which the Transjordan Parliament readily assented), the "treachery" of King Abdullah was confirmed in Egyptian eyes because the annexation subverted the All-Palestine Government, established in September, 1948, led by the mufti of Jerusalem, and sponsored by the Egyptian-dominated Arab League. The Syrian

43. *Ibid.,* p. 243.
44. Cited in Lacouture and Lacouture, *Egypt in Transition,* p. 139.

government was equally hostile, because King Abdullah's ambition to establish himself at the head of a Fertile Crescent state was anathema in Damascus. Saudi Arabia, whose ruling family had evicted the Hashemites from Mecca and Medina in 1924, had no reason to be pleased with this outcome either. The Palestine issue continued to divide Jordan and Egypt long after the main actors in the 1948 debacle had been swept away by assassination or revolution, and Israel's military victories in 1956 and 1967 were again facilitated by the failure of these key Arab states to cooperate with each other.

Virulent as it was, the Egyptian-Jordanian rivalry was a minor theme in the growing inter-Arab quarrels that foreshadowed the 1955–57 "active phase" in the Palestine conflict. The friction between Egypt and Iraq was more important. Cairo and Baghdad represented two contradictory trends in the rapidly changing Arab world. Domestically, Egypt had become a modernizing military oligarchy; younger officers and civilian professionals were the new political elite; their ideology was technocracy and reform. Iraq, however, remained a traditional oligarchy under the control of the wealthy landowners, tribal chiefs, and businessmen associated with Nuri al-Said and the Hashemite monarchy. The ideology was "liberal," but popular participation was, in fact, very limited. Externally the two capitals differed even more profoundly. The new Egypt was vigorously anti-imperialist. With the Suez Canal Zone evacuation agreement of 1954, the officers' regime reaped the fruits of a half-century of struggle against the British presence. The new regime was also in the process of staking out for itself a leading role in the world of the newly independent Afro-Asian states which were just beginning to develop a sense of separate destiny in a world dominated by the Cold War. Nasserist ideology viewed Israel as a manifestation of Western imperialism.[45] Nasser's doctrine of "positive neutralism" called for building a bloc of nonaligned Arab states, the first step in a mission that might eventually embrace Africa and the Muslim world.[46] Toward that end, the regime utilized not just traditional diplomacy but also the techniques of modern propaganda, economic and cultural representation, and clandestine activities throughout the Arab states.[47]

Iraq's external posture was quite another matter. Nuri al-Said, its strongman, and the royal family maintained close and friendly ties with Great Britain; British imperialism was no longer an issue to them. Rather

45. Nasser, *Philosophy of the Revolution*, pp. 64–70.

46. *Ibid.*, pp. 59–62.

47. Charles D. Cremeans, *The Arabs and the World: Nasser's Arab Nationalist Policy* (New York, 1963), pp. 32–46.

than shunning political relations, Nuri al-Said accepted British overtures to establish the Baghdad Pact, which eventually linked Pakistan, Iran, Iraq, and Turkey in a defense alliance with Britain. Iraq also had an interest in dominating at least the Fertile Crescent area of the Arab world, an interest that was sharpened by the rise of the revolutionary regime in Egypt. Locked in a struggle for influence of Arab public opinion, Iraq and Egypt were equally vehement in their rhetoric about upholding Arab rights in Palestine. Neither regime wished to suffer politically by making any conciliatory initiatives in the matter, even though both may have been ready to normalize relationships with Israel, and neither was capable of retrieving those rights through force. Thus, inter-Arab rivalry helped create a situation in which neither regime could afford to make gestures of peace, nor could they possibly cooperate to make war against Israel. When Israel, Britain, and France launched their attack on Egypt in October, 1956, the assistance Egypt received from Iraq and Jordan, and even from its allies, Syria and Saudi Arabia, was nominal and insignificant.

Inter-Arab rivalries reached another peak of disunity just prior to the second escalation of the Palestine conflict. Compared to the 1955–57 period, this pattern of disunity was more complex, since it involved both rivalries between progressive and conservative forces and rivalries among progressive forces themselves.[48] But the results were the same: competition in rhetoric, a tendency toward dangerous gambles, and a diminution of cooperative behavior in the face of Israeli initiatives. President Nasser's bid for ascendency in the Eastern Arab world received a sharp setback on September 28, 1961, when Syria seceded from its union with Egypt in the United Arab Republic. Egypt blamed both reactionary forces and its erstwhile colleagues in union, the Ba'athists, for the breakup. Egypt's embroilment in the 1962 republican revolution in Yemen also tended to weaken Nasser's reputation and influence. Meanwhile, the days were numbered for the governments of Iraq and Syria, which opposed Arab unity and socialism; in February and March, 1963, Arab unionists and socialists of the Ba'athist persuasion seized power in both countries. Ideologically, it seemed that a new era of cooperation, even unity, was in the offing, but factional competition negated such a possibility.

For Egyptian strategists the rise of the Ba'ath Party was a mixed blessing indeed, for it was a competing movement, more revolutionary than Nasser and possessing more mass appeal than the fallen bourgeois oligarchs of Iraq and Syria. In Iraq, pro-Nasser factions took control

---

48. See Kerr, *Arab Cold War,* for the best account of these rivalries.

but were prevented by the precariousness of their position from achieving the degree of coordination with Egypt that they desired. Indeed, their concern with maintaining a balance among radicals and traditionalists and among Nasserists and Ba'athists, while trying to resolve the Kurdish question and oil disputes, left the leadership unprepared to render effective assistance in the 1967 June war.[49] In Syria, the Ba'athist government sought to suppress pro-Nasser factions bidding for power while at the same time seeking to share Nasser's influence on the pan-Arab ideological level. Nasser's own caustically stated reservations about links with the Ba'ath are revealed in the transcript of the unity talks of spring, 1963.[50] Relations between Cairo and Damascus were cool, to say the least, up until the eve of the June war. When pro-Nasser officers in Iraq wrested power from the Ba'athist officers, relations between Iraq and Ba'athist Syria became openly hostile. When Iraq joined Egypt and Syria in the ranks of the "progressive" states, Jordan, maintaining the longest border with Israel, was more isolated than ever in the Arab world; at this point it could seek support only from its hereditary rival, the Saudi Arabian monarchy.

The time was opportune for Israel to begin to divert waters of the Jordan River. That provocation, as we have seen, brought all the Arab states together in January, 1964, in the first of a series of summit conferences. The unity displayed at this meeting was in fact illusory. Objectively, the situation required cooperation, and the summit meeting temporarily achieved this on a symbolic level. Each government individually, however, perceived—correctly—that a confrontation between any of them and Israel would be disastrous and that a joint confrontation, with only a marginal chance of success, could hardly be depended upon, given the rivalries between them. Each Arab leader knew very well that every other leader shared the common suspicion. The rational course, therefore, was to do as little as possible consistent with the demands of internal populism and inter-Arab ideological competition. It was not surprising, therefore, that nothing came of the Arab scheme to undertake a counterdiversion of the Jordan River headwaters.

As inter-Arab antipathies continued to ripen, however, this inertia gave way to an adventurous and unstable posture. The Yemen involvement exacerbated Saudi-Egyptian relationships, as did Saudi interest in an association of Islamic states, a successor to the Baghdad Pact. Egyptian

49. Khadduri, *Republican 'Iraq,* p. 290.
50. See Walid Khalid and Yusuf Ibish, eds., *Arab Political Documents, 1963* (Beirut: American University Beirut, Department of Political Studies and Public Administration, 1963), pp. 75–217.

backing of the PLO, which was proving more successful than expected in inflaming Palestinian-Hashemite grievances, further strained King Husayn's relations with Cairo. Husayn was to retaliate by accusing Nasser of hiding behind UNEF. And the displacement of the Ba'athist regime of General Amin al-Hafiz in Syria by a militant, younger neo-Ba'ath faction, opposed to cooperation with Nasser, breached the system of tacit coordination by which the Arab states had maintained a passive stance on Palestine. The new Syrian regime, influenced by the Algerian war and other "liberation struggles" was the first Arab regime to take the initiative of risking vital state interests for the cause. President Nasser, seeing the danger ahead, rushed to conclude a defense alliance with the neo-Ba'athists in June, 1966, presumably on the assumption that he would thus gain some control over Damascus. The outcome, however, was different: Syria fomented attacks against Israel, and Nasser, to defend Damascus, was precipitated into the June war. An observation by Malcolm Kerr aptly summarizes the situation:

> A longstanding Western myth holds that the Palestine cause unites the Arab states when they are divided on all else. It would be more accurate to say that when the Arabs are in a mood to co-operate, this tends to find expression in an agreement to avoid action on Palestine, but that when they choose to quarrel, Palestine policy readily becomes a subject of dispute.[51]

One might add that in a situation of political turmoil dispute leads to escalation.

THE ARAB STATES IN 1967

Israel's provocations against Egypt in 1955 and 1956 opened up the Straits of Tiran, but stimulated a spate of *fedayeen* raids and an Egyptian military buildup, neither of which was very costly to Israel. Israel's initiatives of the 1960s, however, led both to benefits and costs of a different order. Israel occupied all of Jerusalem and all of Palestine; it gained direct control of the Straits of Tiran, closed the Suez Canal, acquired a vast security zone in the Sinai, and dealt a far more serious blow to President Nasser and his pan-Arab influence than it had in 1956; it acquired more defensible frontiers with Jordan and Syria; and it im-

---

51. *Arab Cold War*, pp. 151–52.

proved its value as a strategic asset of the United States. The only significant cost, aside from the manageable problems of ruling a large Arab population, was the impetus Israel's victory gave to the development of the Palestinian resistance movement.

Palestinian resistance activity differed from the Arab governments' behavior on Palestine in two important ways. First, Palestinian guerrilla action was not constrained by the limitations of state interest and domestic politics that made Arab governmental policy on Palestine either passive or *ad hoc*. Second, it was based on a simple and coherent program—the elimination of the Israeli state by force and the establishment of a secular, democratic state of Palestine—and thus differed from the ambiguous, multiple, and contradictory goals of the various Arab regimes.

The Arab governments were the main losers in 1967, and for the first time in the three Palestine wars their losses were significant. This essay has tried to discover why they failed and why they seemingly repeated past mistakes. Apart from their relative military weakness, the main factors were political. The immediate cause was ambiguity of goals and conflict of interest in the face of Israel's forcible initiatives at improving the 1949 *status quo*. The underlying causes were the weakness of national governmental structures in the face of a growing populism that inflamed the Palestinian issue among the Arab public and the centrifugal tendencies inherent in the inter-Arab state-system. Containment, as Cecil Hourani has suggested, may have been the soundest policy for the Arab coalition, faced as it was by Israel's constant challenge,[52] but these divisive factors made the consistent pursuit of such a policy difficult indeed.

52. "The Moment of Truth: Toward a Middle East Dialogue," *Encounter*, XXIX (1967), 3–14.

11. Israel's Policy toward the Arab States

Janice Terry

━━━━━━━ Zionist and Israeli relations with the Palestinians and the Arab states divide into five major periods. The first dates from the Zionist Congress held in Basle, Switzerland, in 1897 through the period of the British mandate of Palestine from 1922 to 1948. The second begins with the creation of Israel in 1948 and ends in 1954 with the emergence of Nasser as a dominant Arab leader. The third period, 1954 to 1956, was culminated by the Suez crisis. The fourth period lasted from 1957 until the escalation of hostilities in the spring of 1967. The fifth period is the current one, beginning with the June, 1967, war. Throughout these five periods the policy of Zionist and Israeli leaders toward the Palestinians and the Arab states has been ideologically consistent but flexible in terms of political exigencies. The Zionists and Israelis, unlike the Arabs, have, at several junctures accepted limited objectives and have developed practical short-range policies, which over the course of the twentieth century have served the long-range aspiration of the Zionist movement— namely, to establish and secure an exclusivist Jewish state in the area known as Palestine.

EARLY ZIONISM AND
THE MANDATE: 1897–1948

Early Zionist attitudes toward the Arabs established the ideological pattern for Israeli policy. The first Zionist leaders promoted the view that Palestine and the Middle East was a culturally underdeveloped area with few well-defined and formalized social institutions. The area was perceived as a "backwater" of the Ottoman Empire, itself viewed as weak and

337

dying. Zionist leaders asserted that the establishment of a Jewish state in Palestine, led and built by European Jewry, would not only alleviate the centuries-old problem of anti-Semitism in Europe but would also infuse a new life into the Middle East. The proposed Jewish state was to be the carrier of Western culture and technology into the area.

Herzl, in his novel *Altneuland* [Old newland], voiced his belief that the Arabs would come to accept the Jewish settlers as benefactors. Initially, Weizmann too seems to have thought that those Arabs with whom the Jews would have primary contacts could easily be persuaded of the benefits European Jewry would provide for Arab and Jew alike.[1] He seemed to regard the area as a cultural monolith and evidenced little awareness of the complexity of Middle Eastern social institutions or the differences among nomadic, village, or urban life styles. Weizmann's first visit to the Middle East in 1907 reinforced his European stereotype: at the time of this visit, he remarked that he hoped Zionism could "bring civilization back" to the area.[2]

Zionist territorial objectives were made explicit at an early date, and consistent with the Zionist vision, the boundaries of the state of Israel have been systematically enlarged to encompass most of the area originally sought, as well as additional territory in the Sinai which was deemed necessary to the maintenance of defensible frontiers. The Zionist plan of 1919 had included territory from the eastern portion of the Sinai to Sidon in southern Lebanon and the southern section of Syria, and from the Mediterranean to a point just west of Amman. Israeli leaders are firmly committed to the policy of the ingathering of the Diaspora, or all of the Jews living outside Israel, and have urged the immigration of those communities. Thus, in addition to defense considerations, questions of the ultimate size of the population and the boundaries of the state indicate that Israeli leaders have historically foreseen progressive frontier adjustments.

Few of the early Zionists believed that the proposed state or its Jewish inhabitants would become an integral part of the area. Weizmann stressed that "the Jews who went to Palestine would go to constitute a Jewish nation, not to become Arabs or Druses or Englishmen."[3] He even categorized those Jews living in Palestine since Roman times as "useless."[4]

---

1. Chaim Weizmann, *Trial and Error: The Autobiography of Chaim Weizmann* (Philadelphia, 1949). The Lloyd George Papers in the Beaverbrook Library, London, and the Reginald Wingate Papers in the Sudan Archive, Durham, contain numerous letters from Weizmann concerning Zionist attitudes toward the Middle East.

2. Weizmann, *Trial and Error*, p. 149.

3. *Ibid.*, p. 189.

4. *Ibid.*, p. 125.

This was to be echoed by David Ben-Gurion when he stated that the Oriental Jew had to be made "to acquire the superior moral and intellectual characteristics of those who created the State."[5]

Two principal objectives of the Zionist movement during this period were to engage and mobilize support for the national-home scheme—that is, to lay the foundations for the establishment of a Jewish state in Palestine—and to displace indigenous Palestinians from areas that were essential to the growth and development of the Jewish state.

In their attempts to gain British support for the proposed Jewish state, Zionist leaders emphasized the close relationship between Zionist aims and the imperial interests of Great Britain and expressed a desire to support British administration of the area. Zionist leaders suggested that the so-called "Arab problem" would be easily solved. Weizmann appears to have concluded that those people who were in the area would be likely to move into other Arab states as the Jewish population in Palestine increased. Concerning the Palestinians he observed, "those who wish to remain here can of course do so. . . . but for those who do not so wish, there is Egypt, there is Syria, and there is the great desert from whence they originally came."[6]

The diplomatic efforts of Weizmann and other Zionist leaders in London before and during the First World War culminated in the issuance of the Balfour Declaration which announced British support of the "establishment in Palestine of a national home for the Jewish people." This statement did not meet Weizmann's expectations, but he continued his strategy of elaborating the confluence of Zionist and British interests in Palestine. Even before the mandate for Palestine had been awarded to Great Britain, the Zionist Organization sent a commission—headed by Weizmann and including Major Ormsby-Gore and Major de Rothschild — to Palestine with the intention of establishing administrative links between the military government under General Allenby and the various Zionist and Jewish organizations and institutions in the area.

The Zionist leaders, for obvious reasons, concentrated their diplomatic efforts in London. Weizmann, however, did meet in Paris with Prince Faysal of Syria during the peace negotiations. Weizmann was hopeful at this time that some sort of agreement might be obtained with Faysal, but

---

5. *Divrei Haknesset* [Knesset stenographic record], October 24, 1960; cited in Michael Selzer, *The Aryanization of the Jewish State* (New York, 1967), p. 65.

6. Cited in Humphrey Bowman, *Middle East Window* (London, 1942), p. 284. For more complete details on the early history of Zionism in Palestine and on the British mandate see Christopher Sykes, *Cross Roads to Israel* (London, 1965).

when territorial and political demands were rejected and Faysal lost
Syria to the French, these hopes disappeared.[7]

The years of the mandate were characterized by an unwavering pursuit
on the part of the Zionist Organization of the Jewish national home and
an equally consistent unwillingness on the part of the Palestinian people
to acquiesce to the fate envisioned for them by the Zionist movement.
Once it became clear to the Zionists that their earlier plans for the existing
Palestinian population were not be realized, the policy became one of
attempting to achieve dominance over the opposition and a firm hold on
the land itself. In general this was effectuated in cooperation with the
British. British policy in the area, however, was influenced by the need
to maintain stability in the face of a rising and increasingly articulate
Arab nationalist movement. Although the British government failed to
act on the recommendations of the several commissions of inquiry which
were sent to Palestine during the mandate period, immigration quotas were
periodically modified in response to Arab unrest. The divergence of British
and Zionist interests was particularly apparent after the issuance of the
McDonald White Paper of 1939.

The vitality of Arab nationalism in this period, with its demands for
an independent Palestinian state, was underestimated both by the British
and the Zionists. Many Zionists, in fact, saw the British presence as the
principal stimulus to Arab nationalism. The independent states which
eventually emerged from the mandates over the Arab Middle East were
viewed by many Zionists largely as the creations of the Western powers,
particularly France and Great Britain.[8] Arab demands in this period
support the interpretation that Arab nationalism was primarily an anti-
imperialist movement and only secondarily anti-Zionist, or anticolonialist.

World War II brought the Zionists and the British again into closer
alliance, but the Zionist Organization recognized that British influence
in the Middle East was waning. Given these circumstances, Zionists began
to concentrate their efforts for support in the United States. The Zionists
adopted this policy assuming that as British influence in the Middle East
declined, American influence would increase. Thus it was the United
States which could best aid Zionist aspirations for an independent state
and which could, if possible, gain Arab acceptance of such a state.

---

7. Weizmann, *Trial and Error*, p. 235.

8. Abba Eban spoke of Arab independence occurring "less as a result of their
own sacrifice and effort than as a consequence of international influence in two
world wars" (speaking to the Jewish Theological Seminary, New York, February
29, 1952, in *Voice of Israel* [New York, 1957], p. 70); see also, Weizmann, *Trial and
Error*, p. 235.

At this juncture, the opposition of Arab governments to the proposed Zionist state was well known. This opposition did not commonly deter Zionist aspirations since Great Britain remained the dominant force in the area and could check those movements on the part of Arab governments or leaders which appeared to threaten its interests. Once the checks of the Western powers on Arab opposition appeared to be diminishing, the Arab states were informed by the Zionists that any attempt to thwart their goals would be dealt with in a severe manner.

The Creation of Israel to the Emergence of Nasser: 1948–1954

With the 1947 British announcement of the intention to terminate their mandate in Palestine, the Zionists took immediate steps to bring to fruition their long-held aspirations for an independent Jewish state. Opposition to the proposed state of Israel by the Arab governments was much publicized. Many Zionists, affected not only by their Western images of the backward and violent Arab but by their experiences or knowledge of the horrors perpetrated upon the Jewish communities in Nazi-dominated Europe, believed that the Arab armies planned to overrun Palestine and slaughter the Jews. They were determined that such an event would not occur and were, to an extent, exhilarated by the knowledge that they were in control of their own futures.[9]

The establishment of an independent Israel and its recognition by numerous states, including virtually all of the West, was a victory for the Zionists. However, a resolution of the conflict was not achieved even after the Israeli military victory over the opposing Arab armies. The Palestinians and the Arab governments refused to acknowledge their final defeat or Israel's military success as signifying the end of the conflict. Israel's policy toward the Arab states in this period was to a large extent determined by two factors: (1) the territorial aims of the Zionist movement had not yet been achieved, and (2) the Palestinian population, again, did not acquiesce to its displacement from its homeland. The observation has been made that Israel's Arab policy, thus, had three objectives:

> first, to break the back of what remained of Palestinian resistance; second, to serve notice to the adjacent states that, should they harbor Palestinian resistance movements in territories under their jurisdiction,

9. David Ben-Gurion and Moshe Pearlman, *Ben-Gurion Looks Back: In Talks with Moshe Pearlman* (New York, 1965), pp. 9, 28.

they would automatically invite intervention by Israeli armed forces in
in their domestic affairs; and third, to maintain a high but tolerable
level of tension on Israel's frontiers in order to serve the internal political
purposes of the new state—namely, strengthening the bond of its citizens
and consolidating its hold over external supporters.[10]

Acting upon these premises, Israeli leadership concluded that only
military prowess would make the Arab states accept Israel as constituted
after 1948. Israelis viewed Arab opposition as largely unrealistic and
irrational. However, Israel was content to forego a large-scale military
confrontation with opposing Arab states as long as those states were
predominately engaged with internal problems and inter-Arab conflicts.
These divisions created a situation in which a precarious balance of power
existed between Israel and the Arab states, but which enabled Israel to
concentrate on its own internal development.

The period from 1948 to 1954 is marked by the development of Israeli
institutions and the building up of a military capable of defeating potential
Arab attacks. The army was frequently depicted as being an excellent
socializing force for the Jewish immigrants from diverse backgrounds.
Ben-Gurion remarked that "the persistent antagonism of the Arabs before
the establishment of the State led to a more cohesive Jewish community
in the country. . . . Since then, continued Arab enmity has been a stimulant
to the development of Israel."[11] The Arab boycott, which was a relatively
minor deterrent to Israeli economic growth, produced similar results in
fostering autonomous development.[12]

The Israeli leadership maintained that the Arabs desired not only the
eradication of the state of Israel but also of its people. Although Israeli
policy statements directed to the West emphasized the willingness of
Israel to live at peace with its Arab neighbors, the Israeli people continued to evidence extreme suspicion toward the Arab governments. Arab
leaders were viewed as being corrupt and undemocratic. In general,
Israeli leaders held that it would be either futile or impossible to enter
into negotiations with the Arabs. King Abdullah of Jordan was considered
the one exception. For a short period of time, Israeli leaders hoped to
negotiate a separate peace with Abdullah. From this hope grew the secret
negotiations between Israeli leaders and Abdullah, but Abdullah's assassination in 1951 halted all such negotiations.[13]

10. Ibrahim Abu-Lughod, "Israel's Arab Policy," in *The Arab-Israeli Confrontation
of June 1967: An Arab Perspective,* ed. Ibrahim Abu-Lughod (Evanston, Ill., 1970),
p. 71.

11. Ben-Gurion and Pearlman, *Ben-Gurion Looks Back,* p. 152.

12. *Ibid.,* p. 154.

13. *Ibid.,* p. 157.

In Israeli eyes the unreasonableness of Arab leaders was demonstrated by the unwillingness of that leadership to take firm steps to resettle the Palestinian refugees. The Israelis contended that they had little responsibility for the refugees and that the refugees could be assimilated without difficulty into the neighboring Arab states if the will to do so was evidenced by Arab leaders. Israeli assimilation of thousands of Jews from diverse backgrounds was used as an example of what could be done.[14] The continuation of refugee camps, with their high rate of population growth, was interpreted by the Israelis as a concerted attempt by the Arab leaders to foster opposition to Israel and to create a situation in which the acceptance of Israel would be highly unlikely. Israelis generally did not consider the refugees to be their problem. The failure to settle them in Arab states was seen to be a failure of the Arab states and the United Nations.[15] (No differentiation was made between Jewish immigrants who came willingly to settle and create a new life in Israel and refugees who, for whatever reason, had left their homes in Palestine and wished to return to them.)

Consistent with its belief that only the threat of force would persuade the Arab states to sue for peace and restrain Palestinian political and guerrilla activities emanating from within their borders, Israel in the period 1948 to 1954 applied a policy of systematic attack and reprisal along the Jordanian, Syrian, and Egyptian armistice lines. Similarly, Palestinians living in Jordan and in the Gaza strip engaged in periodic, unofficial raids on the Israeli border. The failure of this Israeli policy was apparent by 1953 when, "instead of suing for peace [the Jordanian government] began to take more seriously the task of arming the Jordanian population, particularly in those areas adjacent to Israel."[16]

NASSER AND THE SUEZ
CRISIS: 1954–1956

With the appearance of Nasser as a possible agent of Arab union, the focus of Israel's Arab policies shifted from Jordan to Egypt, which was seen as the primary threat to Israel's boundaries and continued existence.

14. Golda Meir, address to Socialist International, Vienna, July 3, 1957, in *This Is Our Strength* (New York, 1962), p. 96; see also Levi Eshkol's statement in the Knesset concerning the social situation in Israel, December 8, 1964, in *The State Papers of Levi Eshkol* (New York, 1969). pp. 21–22.

15. Eban, to the General Assembly of the United Nations, December 1, 1952, in *Voice of Israel,* pp. 108–10. For a more detailed discussion of the proposed solutions for the resettlement of refugees see Fred Khouri, *The Arab-Israeli Dilemma* (Syracuse, 1968).

16. Abu-Lughod, "Israel's Arab Policy," p. 73.

Border incidents and actual military confrontations increased after 1954.

The famed Lavon Affair which in 1954 sought to "indicate Egyptian internal instability,"[17] and which might have led "the United States and Great Britain to suspect a growing Egyptian terrorism directed against them and their nations," was instigated by Israeli intelligence, apparently without the knowledge of Pinhas Lavon, the defense minister. The scheme to explode bombs at United States offices in Cairo to demonstrate anti-Western feelings within Egypt has been described as a "classic example of agent provocateur techniques."[18] The prompt Egyptian discovery of the plot, which was eventually publicized by the Israelis in 1960, caused an upheaval in the Israeli government and ruling circles that lasted for years. However, the discovery of the plan, while indicating the difficulty of direct intervention in Arab politics, did not deter the desire of portions of Israeli leadership to effect a change in the government of Egypt and/or in Egypt's relationship to the West.

At this time there was a division among Israeli leaders themselves. Moshe Sharett, who was prime minister from 1953 to 1955, advocated moderation and established a dialogue with certain Egyptians. Sharett anticipated that these talks would result in the acceptance of the *status quo* and *de facto* recognition of Israel by the Arab states, with Egypt under Nasser taking the lead. However, a section of Israeli leaders, dominated by Ben-Gurion, viewed these developments with alarm. Lavon resigned in the aftermath of the failure of the intelligence plot, and Ben-Gurion became defense minister. He maintained that security was to be the mainstay of Israeli policy.[19] Largely on Ben-Gurion's insistence, Israel launched a large-scale attack on Gaza in February, 1955; the attack was intended not only to stop *fedayeen* activities based in Gaza but to demonstrate Egyptian vulnerability.[20] After the July elections, Ben-Gurion again became prime minister. Sharett remained as foreign minister until 1956 when he was succeeded by Golda Meir, who had a reputation for being a close adherent of Ben-Gurion's policies to force a solution to the conflict through a military victory.

The Egyptian arms agreement with Czechoslovakia in September, 1955, intensified alarm in Israel, although the arms deal was a direct response by the Egyptians to the Israeli attack on Gaza in 1955. Israeli leaders foresaw increased Soviet activity and support for the Arab states, par-

---

17. Terence Prittie, *Eshkol: The Man and the Nation* (New York, 1961), p. 195; see also Ben-Gurion and Pearlman, *Ben-Gurion Looks Back*, pp. 206–15.

18. Terence Prittie, *Eshkol: The Man and the Nation* (New York, 1969), p. 195.

19. David Ben-Gurion, *Israel: Years of Challenge* (New York, 1963), pp. 68–69.

20. *New York Times,* October 24, 26, 1960; excerpts from the Diary of Moshe Sharett, *Jerusalem Post,* October 31, 1965.

ticularly for Nasser's government. The influx of Soviet arms and advisers into the Middle East was thought to have caused a change in the balance of power in the area. Israeli leadership recognized that action against the borders of the Arab states would not be adequate to execute a change in the balance that a Soviet-Arab *détente* seemed to indicate.

The economic difficulties of the state and of shipping in the area also became clear at this time. The Israelis sought to increase their foreign trade and were beginning to feel Arab deterrents to that goal. As early as October, 1955, plans were being formulated in Israel to capture the Straits of Tiran in order to ensure safe Israeli shipping to the port of Elath.[21] The opportunity to ensure that shipping, and perhaps to change the government in Egypt presented itself after Nasser nationalized the Suez Canal. The British and the French were determined to regain control of the canal, while simultaneously removing Nasser whom they, too, had come to view as a threat to Western hegemony in the Middle East. Here the Israelis, as in the past, saw a confluence of interest. The Israelis were willing allies to the British and the French in this venture. The tripartite invasion of Egypt in 1956 was the result of that alliance. Out of the military victory over Egypt, Israel expected to gain freedom for Israeli navigation in the Suez Canal and the Gulf of Aqaba, and a cessation of resistance activities along the Gaza Strip. It also anticipated the speedy downfall of Nasser with a concomitant increase of prestige for Israel.[22]

With the 1956 victory, Israel gained the use of the Gulf of Aqaba, which had been denied Israel under the terms of the Egyptian-Israeli armistice agreement of 1949. Some measure of peace was achieved along the Gaza border, largely as a result of the stationing of the UNEF on the Egyptian border. But Israel failed to attain either the passage of Israeli shipping through the Suez Canal or the removal of Nasser. In fact, Nasser's influence in the Middle East was considerably heightened after the tripartite aggression. Thus, he proved to be a greater threat than before.

Israelis depicted Nasser as a power-thirsty tyrant who constituted the greatest threat to Israel.[23] Behind much of the Israeli rhetoric concerning Nasser lay the possibly correct supposition that Nasser's charismatic leadership had the potential to sway and control other Arab governments

21. Moshe Dayan, *Diary of the Sinai Campaign* (New York, 1967), p. 12.

22. *Ibid.*, pp. 203, 206; see also Kenneth Love, *Suez: The Twice-Fought War* (New York, 1969); Terence Robertson, *Crisis: The Inside Story of the Suez Conspiracy* (New York, 1965).

23. Eban, to the General Assembly of the United Nations, November 1, 1956, in *Voice of Israel*, pp. 276–92. Golda Meir, address to the National Press Club, Washington, D. C., December 11, 1956, in *This Is Our Strength*, p. 79; David Ben-Gurion, *Israel: Years of Challenge*, p. 150.

and their policies vis-à-vis Israel. Furthermore, it was possible that Nasser might institute an Arab union with the potential to destroy the state of Israel or that he might secure implementation of the U.N. resolution 194 calling for the choice by Palestinians of either repatriation or compensation.

CONSOLIDATION AND
DEVELOPMENT: 1957–1967

Although the tensions persisted during the period from 1957 to the winter of 1967, armed conflict between the Arabs and the Israelis was relatively minimal. This tranquillity was largely the result of a purposeful avoidance of direct confrontation. Both protagonists turned to a renewed concentration on internal development. The basic attitudes toward the opposition, however, did not change but in fact ossified. In Israel this hardening of attitudes was demonstrated by a *Maariv* Round Table held in 1963. Noted Israelis at this time remarked that a conclusion of the conflict would be an extremely difficult task. Not the least of the difficulties was seen to be the division of the Israelis themselves over the territorial issue. The discussion revealed that there was a portion of the Israeli population which was determined to gain the historic boundaries of *Eretz Israel*.[24] Others forecast an alteration of Israel's 1948 boundaries to include more territory and to provide more adequate lines of defense.

During this period attempts to temper the Arab-Israeli conflict originated primarily from outside the area. These included plans to finance the resettlement outside Israel of the refugees and schemes such as the Johnston Plan for the increased use of available water from the Jordan River for irrigation. Such plans aimed to increase the agricultural productivity both of Israel and the neighboring Arab states; it was thought, particularly in the West, that if the economic difficulties of both sides were lessened, political tensions would be reduced. However, in general, these plans resulted instead in a heightening of the riparian dispute and increased armed conflict, particularly between Israel and Jordan.[25] No compromise acceptable to all parties involved concerning the division of water resources

24. "How to Speak to the Arabs, a *Maariv* Round Table," August, 1963, in *Middle East Journal*, XVIII (Spring, 1964), 143–62. The most militant viewpoint was taken by the poet Yetzhak Shalev who remarked regarding the Arab states, "The people of Israel are not obliged to respect these 'nations' and these 'kingdoms' which blossomed from the . . . mouth of Lawrence and his friends. . . . The Arab nations' ownership to their land was invented and signed in the Foreign Offices . . . of Britain and France" (p. 162).

25. Basheer K. Nijim, "The Jordan Basin and International Riparian Disputes: A Search for Patterns" (Paper delivered at the Middle East Studies Association conference, Columbus, November, 1970); Khouri, *Arab-Israeli Dilemma*.

could be reached. When no decision could be taken jointly, Israel went ahead in 1963 with a unilateral plan to divert the Jordan waters for its own use. Israeli leaders were able to plan and carry out this diversion largely because of Israel's superior military might and the ineffectualness of the surrounding Arab governments in countering Israeli activity. Then, too, no outside forces, either from within the United Nations or from the superpowers, put pressure on Israel to halt this activity.

The main focus of military confrontation during this period, however, was between Israel and Syria. The source of this renewed hostility was Israeli attempts to cultivate the demilitarized zones. When Israel attempted to cultivate these areas through the Nahal kibbutzim, paramilitary agricultural settlements, Syria responded by shelling the area. This created a situation in which Israel felt justified in retaliation, resulting in a steady escalation of border incidents. Once again the Israeli decision to test the 1948 demilitarized zones and Arab maintenance of the armistice agreements was largely based on Israeli military power and the confluence of United States tacit support, or at least inaction, together with the weakness of the Arab governments.

As the irrigation schemes and plans for refugee resettlement originated largely outside the area itself, they had little support from within the Arab states or Israel, and none at all among the Palestinians. In particular, Israeli leaders were anxious to safeguard Israel's interests against possible diminishment by the superpowers or other international bodies. They were wary of outside nations or organizations attempting to force a solution to the conflict based on their own precepts. Israeli leaders believed that a solution had to emanate from within the area and had to be negotiated by those they considered to be the protagonists to that conflict, namely the Israeli government and the Arab governments.

Israeli leaders, therefore, evidenced a high degree of suspicion toward the United Nations, particularly after the inclusion of the newly independent Asian and African nations, many of which regarded the Arab states as Third World allies. While summarizing Arab strategy against Israel in 1965, Eshkol publicly recognized Arab attempts to gain African and Asian support:

> The Arab countries are conducting the struggle against us in three spheres; the building of a military force, an international campaign to damage our prestige and standing, and a plan to sabotage Israel's development. . . .
>
> In addition, we must pay heed to ideological developments in the Arab camp such as the identification of Israel with colonialism.[26]

26. Eshkol, address at the tenth convention of Mapai, February 16, 1965, in *State Papers,* p. 36.

To counter Arab influence in Africa and Asia, Israel began an extensive aid and informational program.[27]

By 1965, Israeli economic problems were becoming more acute, since German reparations and aid, which had provided a tremendous source of capital for investment and development, had ceased. Unemployment rose, the balance of payments, always a problem for Israel, worsened, and domestic discontent increased, particularly among labor.

The years 1965 and 1967 were spent in a reevaluation by Israel of its international position and in attempts to strengthen its relations with the United States.[28] There was a split among Israeli leaders over what stance Israel should adopt with regard to the Arab states and Israel's Western allies. Moshe Dayan and others argued that military victory would be the only method by which the Arabs would ultimately accept Israel. This was based upon the premise that the only thing the Arabs really respected was force and that no amount of outside pressure or realignment could change that. It also assumed that the Arabs were nationalists and would not easily give up their claims to Palestine which they perceived to have been an integral part of their territory.[29]

Abba Eban, on the other hand, proposed that Israel adopt the more difficult and longer range project of attempting to fragment further the Arab states and their loose alliances and thereby gain by degrees the tacit acceptance of the individual states.[30] This policy, of course, would involve increased Western aid; it was hoped that the West would furnish military hardware to ensure Israel's military superiority as well as economic aid. It was also hoped that the West could pressure the Arab governments to react favorably to Israel's demands. After some debate Eban's plan to gain additional Western aid and to utilize and exacerbate inter-Arab rivalries was acted upon. The Israeli policy was to be four-pronged: (1) to gain more commitments from the West, particularly the United States; (2) to continue development projects regardless of opposition; (3) to use the existing Arab conflicts to the best possible advantage;

---

27. Mordechai Kreinin, *Israel and Africa: A Study in Technical Cooperation* (New York, 1964); Sanford Robert Silverburg, "Israeli Military and Paramilitary Assistance to Sub-Saharan Africa: A Harbinger for the Role of the Military in Developing States" (M.A. Thesis, American University, 1969).

28. An account of this activity, particularly with regard to the United States, is found in Abu-Lughod, "Israel's Arab Policy."

29. Maxime Rodinson, *Israel and the Arabs,* trans. Michael Perl (London, 1968), p. 65.

30. Abba Eban, "Reality and Vision in the Middle East," *Foreign Affairs,* XLIII (July, 1965), 626–38.

and (4) to maintain a clear-cut military superiority.[31] In 1966, Israeli leaders toured the West in order to gather support; simultaneously incidents along all the borders increased. With this situation, the Israeli leaders asked for, and generally received, armaments to maintain military dominance and continue to mount massive retaliation raids in order to demonstrate that superiority.

During 1967 the attacks and retaliations along the borders steadily escalated. Many of the attacks which emanated from Arab states were mounted by irregulars or *fedayeen* and had no official support from Arab governments. Arab governments in general attempted, when possible, to limit or suppress these attacks. However, Israeli leaders, as in the past, maintained that the Arab governments were responsible for the *fedayeen* raids and that as long as they continued Israel would retaliate at the places of its choosing, at the time of its choosing, and in much larger force than the original attacks.[32] Thus, the largest battle since 1956 occurred between Israel and Syria on April 3, 1967; this precipitated the further escalation of attack and response which led to the June war.

THE 1967 JUNE WAR
AND ITS AFTERMATH

The increased armed conflict along the Arab-Israeli frontiers tended to strengthen the importance of Arab efforts at collaboration. Faced with a powerful opponent, the governments of the bordering Arab states felt threatened and recognized that separately they would be unable to stem the effectiveness of Israeli raids and penetrations. Their efforts in the past to concert their response to increasing Israeli pressure were on the whole unsuccessful; with the heightened tensions of April and May and the hardening of Israeli positions, the three Arab states bordering upon Israel managed to reach some accords on unified action in case of military encounters with Israel. The seeming agreement played into the hands of Israeli hard-liners who had been pressing for a more systematic and vigorous military intervention than Prime Minister Eshkol seemed to have been willing to undertake. With the Egyptian request

31. For a summary of these aims, see Eshkol, broadcast to the citizens of Israel at the approach of the Jewish New Year, September 11, 1966, in *State Papers*, pp. 57–66.

32. Eshkol, broadcast on Remembrance Day for those who fell in defense of Israel, May 13, 1967, in *State Papers;* Eshkol said, "we were able to respond at a place, time and by a method of our own choosing" (p. 71).

for the withdrawal of United Nations forces, the subsequent declaration reinstituting the blockade to Israeli shipping through the Straits of Tiran was construed by Israel to be a serious violation of previous accords and was viewed as an indication of aggressive intent on the part of the United Arab Republic.[33] Prime Minister Eshkol had stated that "any interference with freedom of passage in the Gulf and the Strait constitutes a gross violation of international law, a blow at the sovereign rights of other nations and an act of aggression against Israel."[34]

The internal political moves in Israel, the heightened tension within the Arab states, and the feverish activities on the part of most interested parties led in the end to the escalation of events to the point when war became inevitable.[35] The replacement of Eshkol by Moshe Dayan as minister of defense was a signal that Israel had resolved to go to war.

The June war which followed has been discussed in numerous studies. What is important here is not the chronicle of the wartime events but the Israeli policy after that victory. It was widely believed among Israelis, once Israeli military superiority had been clearly demonstrated, the Arabs would recognize the futility of further opposition to Israel, direct negotiations would take place, and after a few boundary alterations had been made there would be a permanent peace treaty adhered to by all involved parties. Notably, the necessary boundary alterations were not initially spelled out but were left open for negotiations between Israeli and Arab officials.[36]

In the halcyon days following the initial military victories, Israeli leaders and citizens called for direct negotiations with the Arab states, without first delineating what their optimum demands were in terms either of possession of territory or political concessions.

> If the Arabs are ready for peace, there is no reason why they should not agree to talk with us about it. If they don't want peace, third-party

33. Eshkol, *Weekly News Bulletin,* May 9–15, May 22, 1967; Rodinson, *Israel and the Arabs,* p. 195.

34. Statement in the Knesset, May 23, 1967, in *State Papers,* p. 93.

35. Eban, to the Security Council of the United Nations, June 6, 1967, in *Voice of Israel,* p. 300.

36. Eban, to the Security Council of the United Nations, June 6, 1967 in *ibid.,* pp. 310–11; to the General Assembly of the United Nations, June 19, 1967, in *ibid.,* 335–36; Eshkol, statement in the Knesset, June 12, 1967, in *State Papers,* pp. 122, 134. For a description of the events leading up to the 1967 war and of the war itself, see the chronology in the *Middle East Journal,* XXI (Summer and Autumn, 1967); Charles Yost, "The Arab-Israeli War: How it Began," *Foreign Affairs,* XLVI (January, 1968), 304–20; Nadev Safran, *From War to War: The Arab-Israeli Confrontation, 1948–1967* (New York, 1969); Theodore Draper, *Israel and World Politics: Roots of the Third Arab-Israeli War* (New York, 1968).

mediation would only serve as a screen behind which the Arab states could pursue their policy of non-recognition of Israel and belligerency toward it. . . .

There are today indications that at least part of the Arab leadership is aware of the futility of attempting to return to the untenable conditions that prevailed in this region for so many years. They—like we—would probably prefer to see a "new deal" for the peoples of the Middle East.[37]

It did not appear necessary to delineate these demands when the deficiencies of both the Arab military and governments had been amply demonstrated. Most Israelis apparently believed that the Arabs, acting rationally in the face of force, would be convinced that at long last there was no other alternative but to sit down in face-to-face negotiations and enter into a peace treaty which would recognize the sovereignty of Israel.

It was felt that King Husayn of Jordan, of all the Arab leaders, would be accessible. With the decline of Nasser's prestige owing to the loss of the war, it would be considerably easier for Husayn to negotiate directly, even if Nasser refused to do so. Many also felt that Nasser's final downfall was imminent. After Nasser's initial resignation, Israelis demonstrated joyously in the streets of Tel Aviv while Egyptians cried for his return in the streets of Cairo. Indeed, it appears that the Israelis miscalculated the impact that their military victory would have. They anticipated an Arab acceptance of Israeli superiority while, in point of fact, the Israeli victory by exposing the weakness of the Arab governments served to encourage further the already vigorous Palestinian resistance movement.

By the autumn of 1967 it was readily becoming apparent that Israel was no more near the "peace" it sought than before the war. While some portion of Arab leadership was willing to negotiate, it was difficult for them to do so because of fierce popular opposition to acceptance of a militarily superior and expansionist Israel. Nor were the Israelis able to agree among themselves over which occupied territories were negotiable and which were not.

Though Israelis were either unable or unwilling to delineate the desired territorial map, there was some agreement about a portion of that map. The annexation of Jerusalem commanded total Israeli support. The eventual annexation of the Golan Heights and the Gaza Strip seem to command support across the wide spectrum of Israeli political life. If population settlements signify real intentions, then Israeli settlements along the West Bank and in Sinai—so far about 20—suggest clearly that a dominant wing of Israeli society wants to create "new facts" that have to be taken into account should a "peace" treaty be negotiated and contracted.

37. Eshkol, public statement, June 27, 1967, in *State Papers,* pp. 138, 140.

The territorial question in its full dimension remains unclear; two possible approaches have generally and simultaneously been followed. One, the Allon Plan, envisages certain annexations—such as Jerusalem—in addition to areas which while juridically part of a neighboring sovereign state should remain free of Arab military forces; Israel would "protect" the area by ringing it with strategically placed military-agricultural settlements. The alternative approach associated with Dayan relies essentially on the creation of "new facts." Each new fact becomes in time non-negotiable and the protraction of "peace" discussions simply becomes a convenient means of establishing the new realities.

Both approaches, in addition to prolonging the Arab-Israeli impasse, have reinforced Israel in its resolve not to publicize its territorial aspirations. As the period between the military victory and direct negotiations with the Arabs extended, the Israeli demands hardened. More and more territory was announced to be non-negotiable by at least some portions of the government.[38] The hopes for the separately negotiated peace with King Husayn proved abortive. The rapid and extensive growth of the armed Palestinian resistance based in Jordan prevented Husayn from negotiating with the Israelis and maintaining his throne at the same time.

The battle at Karameh in March, 1968, demonstrated not only that the Palestinian resistance could capture the imagination and support of the Arab masses but that it had the ability to exert pressure against capitulation by the Arab regimes. And the further growth of the Palestinian resistance served the additional purpose of projecting the Palestinians once more as a primary party to the Arab-Israeli conflict. Israel therefore had to evolve a new policy.

The Israeli government is still formally committed to the doctrine that the conflict is between sovereign states; lacking political sovereignty, the Palestinians are not a party to any negotiations it wishes to conduct. Certain sections of Israeli society, however, began to question the wisdom of this rigid position and publicly demanded its modification. As Arie Eliav, secretary-general of the Labor Party, expressed the problem:

> The first thing we have to do is to recognize that the Palestinian Arabs exist as an infant nation. It is there. We have to recognize them. The sooner we do it, the better it will be for us, for them, for eventual peace.[39]

Certain socialist groups such as Matzpan have also advocated dealing directly with the Palestinians, but such statements and groups do not, as

38. Moshe Dayan, in *Jerusalem Post,* January 17, 1969.
39. Interview on January 28, 1970, *Time,* January 28, 1970.

yet, represent more than a small minority within Israeli political thought. The governing circles have been practically unanimous in their attempts to ignore the Palestinians or to deny their existence. The government has maintained the policy that the Palestinian resistance can, and should, be controlled by the Arab governments. It is with those governments that Israel hopes to engage in direct negotiations. If the Arab governments do not control the Palestinian armed resistance, the Israelis will continue to hold those governments responsible for all damages done and will retaliate against the Arab states.[40]

Other attempts have been made to foster peace by gaining outside support and by placing outside pressure upon the Arab states for direct negotiations. Israeli peace groups emerged after the 1967 war. One of them, the Association for Peace, issued a series of pamphlets on peace proposals and alternatives for the Middle East. These proposals and others are based on the assumption of the continued existence of an exclusivist Zionist state and the dominance of Israel as an economic, social, and technical leader in the Middle East.[41]

Israeli government policy toward the Arab states since the autumn of 1967 has been unyielding. Israelis have shown an increased determination to maintain the occupied territories which are considered more defensible boundaries. Military preparedness and the stockpiling of armaments have steadily risen. After 1968, Egypt was once again viewed as the primary threat to Israeli military dominance and as the key to the future acceptance of Israel by the Arabs. For this reason, the hostilities along the Suez Canal increased, as did Israeli military incursions deep within Egyptian territory. The underlying motivation behind these advances was to again demonstrate Israel's ability to conquer Egypt and to force Egypt into direct negotiations. Egypt responded by obtaining added Soviet aid and armaments. When Soviet support seemed limited, Nasser appeared to become more open to a settlement with Israel. In reaction to Soviet aid to Egypt, Israel asked for, and received, increased United States military aid to counter the Soviet presence in the Middle East.[42] The escalation mounted steadily until there was a state of undeclared war along the entire length of the Suez Canal.

When this reached what the United States considered to be an untenable proportion, peace initiatives from within the United States government

40. For statements on this stance, see *Jerusalem Post*, October 15, 1967; Golda Meir, interviewed by Frank Giles in the *Sunday Times* (London), June 15, 1969.
41. Association for Peace, *The Middle East in the Year 2000*.
42. Embassy of Israel, Washington, D. C., statements of March 26, 1970; July 7, 1970; August 13, 1970; Moshe Dayan, in *Christian Science Monitor*, December 2, 1970.

were launched in December, 1969, and July, 1970. Once more, the superpowers evidenced a willingness to attempt to pressure a solution upon a conflict which they believed was uncontrollable and which threatened to expand to international proportions. Neither the Arabs nor the Israelis were eager to accept these plans, which were associated with Secretary of State William Rogers. The Palestinians for their part refused to have anything to do with the peace initiative, nor were they included as primary participants in the proposals.

Eventually, the Arab states, recognizing their military inadequacy, accepted the Rogers' plan. Israel was reluctant to place its future in the hands of alien governments. However, faced with pressure and assurances by the United States, its foremost supporter and main supplier of arms, the Israeli leadership acceded to the Rogers' plan. This acceptance was achieved only at a substantial political cost within Israel. It precipitated a split in the Cabinet along with several resignations. The cease fire and alleged contraventions of the cease fire halted the possibility of negotiations. Nasser's death further delayed negotiations and, ironically, removed what Israeli leaders had previously regarded as their greatest enemy at the very time it appeared that he was willing to effectuate a compromise. Thus the current situation finds the Israeli leadership determined to maintain its present territorial positions while seeking additional United States and Western help. That assistance is essential in order to defray the increased military and economic expenditures necessitated by holding the occupied territories and the continuation of the strongly fortified and guarded boundaries.

12. The Changing Political Status of Jerusalem

Malcolm H. Kerr

By the close of the British mandate in Palestine, the city of Jerusalem had grown far beyond its traditional dimensions as an old walled town of narrow lanes, crowded houses and shops, and the ancient shrines of three religions. Almost 100,000 Jews had settled in the modern sector expanding to the west of the walled city; approximately 40,000 Christian and Muslim Arabs also lived outside the walls, plus another 20,000 within them.[1]

Not only Jerusalem's mixed population but more particularly the abundance of Jewish, Muslim, and Christian religious sites and the worldwide interest in them, encouraged the idea of an international status for the city well before the Palestine war of 1948. Thus the principle of internationalization was recommended by the Peel Commission as part of the plan for partitioning Palestine that it submitted to the British government in 1937. It was also recommended by an Anglo-American Commission of Inquiry in 1946. Internationalization was again endorsed by both the majority and minority reports of the United Nations Special Committee on Palestine which were transmitted to the General Assembly in September, 1947.

---

1. Although in medieval times Jews had formed only a miniscule portion of Jerusalem's population, their number had gradually increased to the point where it reached about half the total population in the middle of the nineteenth century. Zionist immigration from Eastern Europe had produced a Jewish majority in Jerusalem well before 1900. The establishment of Israel in 1948 and the subsequent location of its capital in Jerusalem caused the Jewish population to rise rapidly, reaching 200,000 by 1967, while the Arab population on the Jordanian side remained almost constant, rising by 1967 to only 67,000; about 6,000 of these Arabs left Jerusalem during and after the June war.

THE FAILURE OF
INTERNATIONALIZATION: 1947–1967

The General Assembly's resolution of November 29, 1947, recommending the partition of Palestine into an Arab state and a Jewish state,
provided that the city of Jerusalem and the area surrounding it (including
Bethlehem) be set aside as a separate international enclave administered
under United Nations authority. The resolution instructed the Trusteeship
Council to prepare a statute.

The Jewish Agency for Palestine, representing the Palestinian Jewish
community and allied international Zionist organizations, reluctantly
accepted the principle of internationalization as a necessary price for
obtaining support in the assembly for the partition plan as a whole; the
Arab states opposed the overall plan and with it the internationalization
of Jerusalem, demanding the recognition of Palestine as an integral,
independent state with an Arab majority. By the time the Trusteeship
Council had proceeded to draft its statute, however, the whole notion of
an orderly implementation of the partition resolution had practically
dissolved. The British mandatory authority was in the process of dismantling itself, and in the absence of any other outside force, Arabs and Jews
in Jerusalem and the rest of Palestine were engaged in securing what
positions they could by military means.

As the United Nations turned its attention, amidst much confusion,
in the spring of 1948 to consideration of the emergency and of possible
alternatives to the partition plan, the drafting of the Trusteeship Council's
statute remained incomplete. An "advance group" of the Palestine Commission established by the General Assembly arrived in Jerusalem in
February but found itself obstructed by the British authorities and largely
ignored by the combatants. On May 6 the assembly requested the British
mandatory government—then on the verge of expiration—to appoint a
municipal commissioner of Jerusalem. Harold Evans, a Quaker from
Philadelphia, was appointed; he eventually made his way to Cairo, where
he remained, declaring that his pacifist convictions deterred him from
assuming his functions in Jerusalem as long as hostilities raged there,
since he could not accept the protection of a military escort.[2]

The Spanish diplomat Pablo de Azcarate, head of the "advance group,"
was appointed temporarily in Evans' place and spent the next weeks
rather irrelevantly scurrying between the Arab- and Jewish-controlled

2. Pablo de Azcárate, *Mission in Palestine, 1948–1952* (Washington, D. C., 1966),
p. 50.

parts of the city observing the events that determined its fate for the next 19 years but which were altogether beyond his influence.

With the end of the Palestine war, other resolutions at the United Nations were to follow. The General Assembly reiterated its support for internationalization of Jerusalem in December, 1948, and again more particularly on December 9, 1949, when it once more requested the Trusteeship Council to draw up a statute. On April 4, 1950, the council accordingly adopted a plan under which Jerusalem would be ruled by a regime consisting of a governor and supreme court appointed by the council, and a legislative council of both appointed and elected members. The Trusteeship Council proposed to put the plan into operation at an opportune time to be determined by itself. In view of opposition from both Israel and Jordan, however, that time never arrived; the plan was referred back to the General Assembly, where it failed to receive further endorsement.

The fate of Jerusalem was determined not at the United Nations but by the protagonists on the spot. Well before the departure of the British high commissioner on May 15, 1948, the bulk of the modern part of the city to the west of the walls was in the hands of the Jewish Haganah and was being administered by local Jewish civil agencies, while most of the walled city and its northern and eastern environs were governed and defended by Arab irregular forces. The prosperous Arab minority living in the western part of Jerusalem had already fled; within the old city, the 2,500 members of the traditional Jewish quarter held out, defended by troops of the Haganah, until after the termination of the mandate when the Transjordanian Arab Legion arrived and obliged them to surrender.[3] Apart from this exchange of refugees—a relatively minor tragedy in comparison to the hundreds of thousands uprooted elsewhere in Palestine—the city was thus partitioned by the fortunes of war along lines corresponding substantially to the distribution of its Jewish and Arab population.

This division was confirmed on a *de facto* basis by the Israeli-Transjordanian armistice agreement of April, 1949, an agreement which regulated relations between the two states for the next 18 years. As each of the two moved to incorporate the portion of the city that it controlled as an integral part of its own national territory and to seal it off from the

3. Men of military age were made prisoners of war and were released to Israel under an exchange agreement in 1949. All the others were escorted out of the old city into Israeli-held territory. According to de Azcarate, the U.N. representative who observed the proceedings, the surrender operation was carried out with remarkable decorum (*Mission in Palestine*, pp. 64–79).

other side, the world became accustomed to the notion of two Jerusalems, physically separated only by walls and barbed wire but politically, economically, socially, and psychologically as far removed as New York and Peking.

Neither Israel nor Transjordan was interested in internationalization. In April, 1949, with its application for U.N. membership still pending, Israel's representative at the U.N. gave formal assurance that Israel would pursue "no policies on any question which were inconsistent with . . . the resolutions of the Assembly and the Security Council." In a written statement solicited by the Colombian delegation, he became more specific and declared that Israel would not oppose the internationalization of Jerusalem, a proposal which had been an integral part of the 1947 partition resolution and which had been reiterated in principle in the General Assembly's resolution of December 11, 1948. The assembly's resolution admitting Israel to U.N. membership on May 11, 1949, specifically recalled these two resolutions and noted the Israeli representative's assurance regarding them.[4] Once having gained U.N. membership, however, Israel made clear its unwillingness to consider internationalization. Israel voted against the assembly's resolution of December 9, 1949, which directed the Trusteeship Council to proceed with the drafting and implementation of a statute and meanwhile moved its major governmental offices from Tel Aviv to Jerusalem. The Knesset began meeting in Jerusalem before the end of the year and in January, 1950, proclaimed Jerusalem to have been Israel's capital since the first day of independence.

Meanwhile Transjordan took parallel steps to incorporate into its sovereignty the Palestinian territory it controlled, including the Arab sector of Jerusalem. In 1949, Transjordan changed its name to Jordan, and in April, 1950, its Parliament formally ratified the annexation of Palestinian territory. This action was denounced by Jordan's fellow members of the Arab League, and at one point Jordan even came close to being expelled from that body. (Jordan did not become a member of the U.N. until many years later.) Since the 1948 war the other Arab states had not only become firm advocates of the internationalization of Jerusalem as provided for in the partition plan but had also opposed the ambitions of King Abdullah to turn the Arab defeat to his own advantage. His assassination in 1951 and the early failure of rival Arab plans to organize a viable Palestinian regime centered in Gaza abated this issue, and for the most part thereafter the Arab states ceased to

4. Cited from the official records of the General Assembly and the Ad Hoc Political Committee, in Fred J. Khouri, *The Arab-Israeli Dilemma* (Syracuse, 1968), p. 105.

challenge Jordanian sovereignty on the West Bank and in Jerusalem, save for those occasions when Egypt and Syria sought to capitalize on the discontent of Palestinians with Jordanian policy.

Most U.N. members, including the great powers, continued to disapprove both Israel's and Jordan's unilateral actions. The majority of states establishing diplomatic relations with Israel have refused to move their embassies from Tel Aviv to Jerusalem up to the present day, and throughout the 1948–67 period maintained single consulates in Jerusalem accredited to both halves of the city as if it were a unit. But from 1950 onward, until the Israeli move to annex the Arab sector in June, 1967, the issue of Jerusalem's legal status was left dormant by the international community, on the elementary ground that nothing could be done about it.

The maintenance of the *status quo* along the armistice demarcation line was entrusted to a Jordanian-Israeli Mixed Armistice Commission and to the United Nations Truce Supervision Organization consisting of an international corps of military officers, one of whom was assigned to preside over the commission. It was the MAC's function to investigate alleged violations of the armistice and report its findings; but given its composition, in time the natural tendency was for the Israeli and Jordanian members to conduct themselves as national advocates, and for the UNTSO chairman to cast a deciding vote, based as much on what information the team of UNTSO observers could independently provide as on the claims advanced by his Israeli and Jordanian colleagues.

In Jerusalem itself, the situation lent itself to better control than in many other places along the armistice line. The huge wall of the old city, constructed by Sultan Suleiman the Magnificent in the sixteenth century, formed a major part of the dividing line; strips of no-man's land marked by barbed wire, empty buildings, and other obstacles formed the rest. UNTSO headquarters were located in the former British high commissioner's residence, called Government House, in a large hilltop area of no-man's land outside the city to the southeast, well separated from both sides but independently accessible to each of them. The only point of direct access between Israeli and Jordanian Jerusalem—indeed, the only overland transit route available for foreign travelers anywhere along Israel's frontiers—was a place north of the old city called the Màndelbaum Gate, which was not really a gate at all but a few dozen yards of roadway, walled along each side, with a Jordanian military checkpoint at one end and an Israeli one at the other. Through it shuttled U.N. and consular personnel, an occasional foreign dignitary on a specially arranged trip, and (into Israel but seldom out) foreign tourists. Twice a year, at Christmas and Easter, a flock of Israeli Christian Arab citizens holding special passes were allowed through the gate to visit their relatives in Jordan.

With these physical features, the armistice line in Jerusalem did not lend itself to accidental straying or clandestine infiltration, and it could be quite easily inspected by the members of the UNTSO. There were, however, occasional incidents of small-arms barrages along the walls. (The armistice barred the two sides from stationing tanks and artillery in the area.) Elaborate means were devised to deal with the problem posed by Mount Scopus. This hilltop enclave of several hundred acres, including the grounds and buildings of the Hadassah Hospital and the old Hebrew University but lying a mile inside Jordanian territory, was designated by a truce agreement in 1948 as a demilitarized area under Israeli maintenance in which Israel was entitled to station 120 lightly armed policemen. These were supplied with provisions and replacement personnel once every two weeks by a convoy of Israeli armored trucks inspected and escorted by UNTSO officers in jeeps. The Jordanian military police were naturally suspicious of the possibility of the Israelis smuggling unauthorized weapons or excess personnel into Mount Scopus,[5] but the Israelis were unwilling to be inspected by anyone other than the U.N., and on occasion this led to serious tension. Furthermore, Israel and Jordan each recognized a different map demarcating the boundaries of the enclave itself. However, apart from occasional difficulties, the arrangements continued to function until the June war and became smooth enough that in the week before the war the Israelis amicably agreed to a Jordanian request to postpone their scheduled convoy on grounds that the tensions of the international crisis then raging might jeopardize the convoy's security as it passed through the Arab-inhabited area en route to its destination.[6]

ISRAELI POLICY: JUNE, 1967, AND AFTER

Israel's conquest of the Arab sector of Jerusalem and the rest of the West Bank in June, 1967, might never have been undertaken in the absence of the pretext supplied by Jordanian artillery on the morning of June 5. On the other hand, once the Jordanian shelling gave them the opportunity, it seems clear that the Israeli government and army were only too eager to make the most of it.

Immediately following the first Israeli air attacks on Egypt early on the morning of June 5, Prime Minister Eshkol communicated with King

---

5. The vigor with which the Israeli garrison on the hilltop returned Jordanian fire in June, 1967, suggested to some that such smuggling had indeed occurred (see Randolph S. Churchill and Winston S. Churchill, *The Six Day War* [Boston, 1967], p. 124).

6. *Ibid.*, p. 124.

Husayn through the UNTSO, promising not to be the first to open hostilities; but by the time Husayn received the message, small-arms fire had already broken out, and soon afterward Jordanian artillery opened up both on Israeli Jerusalem and on the Tel Aviv area, as if to indicate Husayn's reply. The commitment of Israel's main forces to the Egyptian front and the uncertainty of what would happen there was initially bound to make the Israeli military command cautious about becoming involved with Jordan. Eshkol's statement on June 5 that Israel had no territorial ambitions—a statement he must have regretted the moment Jerusalem had been captured—seems to strengthen the impression that Israel's overwhelming concern at the time was to crush the Egyptian forces, with all other objectives only hypothetical. According to journalists' reports, notably the Churchills' quotation of General Uzzi Narkiss'. diary,[7] the Israeli General Staff allotted very limited forces to Narkiss' command and made a point of refusing authorization for him to cross the armistice lines until the afternoon of the fifth, several hours after the Jordanian bombardment had begun and after confirmation of the success of the air attack on Egypt. One of the two paratroop battalions that invaded the old city on the seventh had originally been destined for an air drop in the Sinai.

But if the Israelis did not initially expect to fight in Jerusalem, they certainly did not lack enthusiasm for the operation as such. The first Jordanian shells had scarcely fallen shortly after 9:00 A.M. when General Narkiss reportedly exclaimed to Mayor Teddy Kollek: "You may well be mayor of a united Jerusalem."[8] And when General Haim Bar-Lev, the deputy chief of staff, finally authorized General Gur to attack the old city on June 7, he said, "We are already being pressed for a cease-fire. We are at the Canal. The Egyptians have been carved up—don't let the Old City remain an enclave."[9]

Authoritative U.S. government sources have stated orally that at 2:00 A.M., June 6 (when the main Israeli thrust into Jordanian territory was just beginning), King Husayn asked the United States to try to obtain a cease fire from Israel—a belated acquiescence in Eshkol's appeal of the day before. This time Eshkol refused, remarking that Israel had no interest in the survival of Husayn's throne.

Thus, from the moment when it became militarily safe and politically plausible, the Israelis proceeded without further inhibition to occupy what Jordanian territory they could—most notably, Arab Jerusalem. With Israel's lightning success in Egypt, the Jordanians no longer posed

7. *Ibid.,* p. 128.
8. *Ibid.*
9. *Ibid.,* p. 139.

a strategic threat; and with Husayn's appeal for a cease fire, they no longer even posed the threat of a security nuisance. But other considerations had come into play, reflected in the declaration made to Narkiss at midnight June 5–6 by the chief rabbi of the Israeli Army, General Goren: "Your men are making history—what is going on in Sinai is nothing compared to this." Narkiss got the point: he advised Goren to have his *shofar* (ram's horn) ready.[10] Soon after Israeli forces reached the Wailing Wall on the morning of the seventh, a collection of Israeli leaders assembled there, and Rabbi Goren led prayers.

The whole Israeli population, and countless Jews abroad, were deeply stirred by their sudden and seemingly miraculous access to the old city. Israel had gone to war, in Egypt, on grounds of all-important security considerations, but once Israel had emerged victorious on all fronts, the most significant result in the minds and emotions of Israelis and other Jews seemed to lie not in Sinai but in Jerusalem.[11]

Since June, 1967, the main concern of the Israeli government has been to assert its claim to permanent control of Arab Jerusalem as fully as possible. While the aim has been unequivocal, the tactical requirements of achieving it have been varied.

The legal and administrative framework for Israeli policy was established on June 27 and 28, 1967, barely three weeks after Israeli forces first crossed the armistice demarcation lines into Jordanian Jerusalem. A law enacted by the Knesset on June 27 authorized the minister of the interior to proclaim the enlargement of municipal boundaries and to apply, in designated parts of occupied territory, the same legal jurisdiction and administration in force in Israel itself. The next day the minister took this step with regard to Arab Jerusalem and surrounding areas, incorporating it under the administration of Mayor Teddy Kollek of the Jewish city.

The Jordanian government, of course, protested bitterly at this unilateral transformation of the status of occupied territory and noted that under the international laws of war expressed in the Hague Convention of 1907 the occupier is obliged to maintain the existing legal and administrative structure of the occupied territory. (Israel did so elsewhere on the West Bank.) The United Nations General Assembly supported the Jordanian claim in two resolutions passed without dissent on July 4 and July 14 denying Israel's right to alter unilaterally the legal status of the city.

10. *Ibid.*, p. 133.

11. Note, for example, the title of Walter Laqueur's book *The Road to Jerusalem* (New York, 1968), the contents of which focus almost entirely on the buildup of the May crisis between Israel and Egypt; what led Israel into East Jerusalem is not discussed at all.

The Israelis took pains to formulate their action in technical terms other than those of a simple annexation, although the practical effect was virtually the same. Words such as annexation, territorial extension, and sovereignty were avoided; instead, they spoke of "reunification of the city" and of the extension of the administrative jurisdiction of the Israeli municipality. East Jerusalem (as it is now called) is an integral part of a united Israeli city, but whether it is officially regarded as an integral part of Israel itself has not been altogether clear. Are Arab inhabitants of East Jerusalem Israeli citizens? Must they renounce Jordanian citizenship? Can they vote in Israeli national elections? Can they apply for foreign travel on Israeli passports? Can they reclaim properties in Israel that they lost in 1948 on the ground that they are no longer "absentees"? So far, the answers to all these questions appear to be in the negative, although not explicitly or definitively so.

The reasons for this technical ambiguity are obvious. On the one hand, the Israeli government wished to lose no time in establishing the incorporation of Arab Jerusalem as a *fait accompli* and thus to put it beyond international discussion before diplomatic pressures might build up against it. On the other hand, Israel wished to avoid being in obvious and direct violation of international law, and did not wish to undercut the credibility of her professed interest in a negotiated peace with Jordan by slamming the door before the eyes of the world on any discussion of Jordanian interests in the old city. While Israel's control of East Jerusalem is declared to be non-negotiable, the precise legal framework of that control remains at least theoretically subject to some face-saving adjustment on behalf of the Jordanians, if and when they agree to full peace negotiations. Thus, Israel can continue to proclaim, and some may continue to believe, that "all Israel wants is peace."

Meanwhile, on the level of practical action in Jerusalem itself, Israeli policy has shown the same mixture of implementation of the *fait accompli* on the one hand and occasional moderating gestures designed to avoid jeopardizing that *fait accompli* on the other.

The first step taken, even before the dust of the fighting had settled and several weeks before the legal incorporation of the Arab city into the Jewish one, was to introduce unalterable physical changes. Walls, houses, and other barriers along the old armistice line were quickly torn down; streets leading across the line were widened and repaved; 135 houses of the Magharibah quarter opposite the Wailing (Western) Wall within the old city were demolished, and their 600 residents evacuated in order to clear a wide area for worshipers to stand in. A plastics factory was also demolished to facilitate access to the Wailing Wall area from the Jewish side of the city. Israelis poured into the old city by the thousands to shop, sightsee, visit the wall and the remains of the old Jewish quarter, and to make contact with the enemy population; the Israeli city was meanwhile opened to Arabs. Much publicity was given to the notion of "reunification" and friendly contact between Arabs and Jews, in the manner of long-lost cousins.

With the formality of municipal unification, other steps followed. The administrative personnel of the Jordanian city, below the highest ranks, were amalgamated into the Israeli city bureaucracy; the Israeli social services, water supply, telephone system, electric grid, etc., were extended to the Arab sector; the Jordanian municipal council was dissolved and its members invited to take seats within the much larger Israeli council. (They of course declined.) Arab schools were placed in the same status as those in Israel, and subjected to the curricular and other regulations of the Israeli Ministry of Education.

The economy of East Jerusalem was separated from that of the occupied West Bank and joined to that of Israel. Jerusalem Arabs were subjected to Israeli taxes and commercial regulations; Israeli currency replaced that of Jordan; Jordanian banks were closed and branches of Israeli ones opened; trade with the West Bank was restricted and was subject to import controls, while trade with the Israeli hinterland was opened up. Members of the professions were obliged to qualify for Israeli licenses and conform to Israeli regulations—in the case of lawyers, this meant acquiring a proficiency in Hebrew. Homes and properties of some of the Arabs who fled or were absent during the fighting were placed under the control of the Israeli Custodian of Absentee Property for assignment for use by Israelis.

Other changes followed. A Muslim girls' school in the old city became the seat of the High Rabbinical Court; a hospital became an Israeli police station. In January, 1968, the Israelis expropriated 838 acres of former Jordanian territory and shortly afterward published plans for its redevelopment—including the settlement of substantial numbers of Jewish residents. Part of the area consisted of the pre-1948 Jewish quarter within the old city; a larger part consisted of land further north, between the Jewish new city and Mount Scopus. The distribution of title to the land became the subject of an argument at the United Nations between Jordanian and Israeli spokesmen,[12] but it seemed clear in any case that the effect of the

12. The Jordanians claimed that of the total, 91 per cent was the property of private Arab individuals and firms, 8 per cent was public domain, and only 1 per cent was Jewish-owned (even the land in the former Jewish quarter, they insisted, had always been substantially owned by Arabs). The Israelis asserted that one-third of the total area was Arab-owned, one-third state-owned, and one-third Jewish-owned (Security Council meeting of May 3, 1968, in *U.N. Monthly Chronicle*, V [June, 1968], 8–12).

plan would be to introduce a substantial and continuous Israeli human presence in East Jerusalem in locations partially surrounding the Arab population and thereby to diminish the contiguity of the latter with other Arab communities nearby on the West Bank.

These measures may all seem unambiguous in their design and effect—namely, to solidify and regularize an Israeli presence in East Jerusalem that might otherwise rest on no more than a military occupation and a dubious diplomatic claim. But in advancing these steps, the Israeli administration of Mayor Kollek has taken evident pains to minimize the harshness of their impact on the Arab residents, the better to reconcile Arab opinion to the new arrangements and avoid explosive reactions. Thus, for example, while Israeli taxation rates decreed after the annexation would have been extremely onerous if applied strictly, in practice they were only partially enforced. Likewise, the compulsive penchant of the Israeli Army for summarily blowing up the houses of persons suspected of complicity with *fedayeen* activities, practiced so freely in the occupied territories, was brought under considerably greater restraint in Jerusalem at the insistence of the mayor. And again, after the initial stimulation of Muslim fears for the sanctity of their shrines and mosques by the callous behavior of some Israelis shortly after the war,[13] an effort was made to alleviate anxieties.

Despite these and some other indications of the mayor's desire to earn the confidence of the Arab inhabitants, that desire was bound to operate within certain limits imposed by both the practical effects of the annexation and some overriding considerations of policy. Some economic hardships were inevitable: the loss of business and employment in the hotel, transportation, and other tourist industries; the closing of banks and cutting off of transactions with the Jordanian East Bank and other Arab states; the higher prices prevalent in Israel and higher taxes even if not fully collected; the loss of employment opportunities by members of the professions. To what extent Israeli policy was really designed to exacerbate or to minimize some of these problems was a matter of opinion; there were many instances alleged, however, of Arab businesses suffering a confiscatory level of inventory tax, of Arab tourist agencies being driven out of business by concerted Israeli competition, and so forth. Arab

---

13. General Goren, the chief rabbi of the Israeli Army, gave offense by conducting prayers in the enclave of al-Haram al-Sharif, adjacent to the Dome of the Rock, and by speaking of building a temple there. Muslim leaders protested the free and casual entry of the Israeli public into mosques during times of worship. Islamic institutions were initially placed under the authority of the Israeli Ministry of Religious Affairs, headed by the National Religious Party member, Zerah Wahrhaftig; subsequently, they were transferred to the more pragmatic authority of the Ministry of the Interior.

members of the professions, and of well-educated and upper-income status generally, professed to see an Israeli policy of squeezing them out and encouraging them to leave Jerusalem, in order to deprive the Arab population of commercial and social as well as political leadership. It was noted that among the 14,000 or so Arab refugees of 1967 admitted back later in the summer to the West Bank, scarcely any were Jerusalem residents, thus maintaining the exclusion of the 8 or 10 per cent of Jerusalem's Arab population which had left or been away during the fighting; it was natural for Arabs to suspect, and probably correctly, that the Israelis would be glad to see this exodus continue.

One thing the Israelis could not tolerate under the format of their unification of the city was an autonomously organized Arab political leadership. The dissolution of the Jordanian municipal council, the dismissal of the mayor, and the refusal of the members of the council to take the seats offered them by the Israelis in the unified council, left the Arab community without any recognized political structure. A few weeks after the annexation a group of notables, including the ex-mayor Rouhi al-Khatib and the president of the Islamic Court of Appeals, Abdel Hamid al-Sayeh, constituted themselves as a body claiming to speak for the Arab community, protested vigorously against the Israeli measures of annexation, and organized a one-day strike. Khatib, Sayeh, and two others were deported, and some other strikers were dealt with vigorously by the Israelis. In the two years that followed there were occasional protest marches and strikes as well as one or two brief clashes between Arab and Israeli citizens in the wake of terrorist incidents. None of these led to sustained disruptions of the peace of the city, nor did any overt Arab political leadership or organization emerge from them. The Israelis, who normally restricted their security measures in the Arab sector to a few lightly armed military patrols, made it clear that as long as quiet continued they would lean over backward to leave the Arab community to its accustomed ways of life, but that they drew the line at any challenge to their complete authority over all parts of the city.[14]

Not only were the Israelis concerned to make clear the fullness of their authority over the Arab community of Jerusalem, but for different reasons they took pains to exclude any role claimed by the United Nations and its Truce Supervision Organization. With the events of June, 1967, the Jordanian military presence of course disappeared, and the complicated arrangements regarding demilitarized zones, force levels, passage through

14. For an excellent review of attitudes and conditions among the Jerusalem Arabs a year after the war, see Michael C. Hudson, "A City Still Divided," *Mid-East,* VIII (September, 1968), 20–25.

the Mandelbaum Gate, and the Israeli convoys to Mount Scopus lost all practical significance. But the U.N. Secretariat in New York and UNTSO headquarters in Jerusalem did not accept the Israeli contention that the Jordanian-Israeli armistice of 1949 was legally defunct and their own mission terminated. (Indeed, the Security Council's resolution of April 27, 1968, which vainly called upon Israel to desist from holding its military parade in Jerusalem on May 2, purported to be based in part upon the judgment that the parade violated provisions under the armistice.)

This anomalous situation, on top of the long-accumulated Israeli attitude of resentment and distrust of the United Nations, accounts in large measure for the events at the UNTSO headquarters during and after the June war. Jordanian forces on June 5 briefly occupied the grounds sur- rounding Government House, in violation of its demilitarized status, until they were driven off by Israeli troops. The latter forcibly entered the building, detained UNTSO Commander Odd Bull and his staff, and later escorted them to Israeli territory where they were allowed to set up temporary quarters. General Bull and Secretary-General U Thant spent the next two months attempting to negotiate with the Israeli Government for return of the property to U.N. hands and succeeded at length, in August, in acquiring the buildings and a fraction of the surrounding land. The intervening time provided ample opportunity for the Israeli authorities to ransack and photograph the confidential files within the headquarters (presumably containing, for example, minutes of secret discussions between U Thant and Nasser).

Israeli Claims to Jerusalem

The legal status of the city of Jerusalem has been a tangled one ever since the termination of the British mandate in 1948. The creation of an international regime never having taken place and Israeli and Jordanian control having been firmly established over the two halves of the city in the process of hostilities in the spring of 1948, the unilateral claims of these two powers to sovereignty in their respective zones have nonetheless gone unrecognized until the present day by the United Nations and most of its members.

Technically speaking, the legal status of the city has been subject to the same indeterminateness as all other portions of former Palestine outside the area alloted to Israel under the partition plan. Israeli claims to Acre and Beersheba and Jordanian claims to Nablus and Hebron, are all founded tenuously on the failure of the Palestinian Arabs in 1948 to create the regime envisaged by the partition scheme and on the fortunes of war reflected in the 1949 armistice. The armistice lines were drawn explicitly as military rather than political frontiers and without prejudice to the disposition of territory under a peace treaty. They were solidified, however, by 19 years of the normal exercise of sovereignty by Israel and Jordan and by the exercise of citizenship by the inhabitants and thus acquired a measure of legitimacy on the principle of prescription. All this could also be said of western and eastern Jerusalem, with the major difference, of course, that here it was the United Nations itself rather than the non-existent Palestinian Arab state that had an internationally recognized claim to them.

An argument commonly advanced in Israel's favor since the June war has been that Jordan's presence in eastern Jerusalem after 1948 had stemmed only from military occupation, and that since the state of war in 1948 was never officially terminated, and was in fact reactivated by Jordanian artillery fire on June 5, the judgment of war in 1967 should be considered as authoritative as that in 1948. This argument assumes, of course, that the Israeli-Jordanian armistice of 1949 died with the 1967 hostilities and was replaced by the cease-fire agreement which left the entire city in Israeli hands — a point that may carry some logical and practical weight but little legal persuasiveness since it is unilaterally maintained, neither Jordan nor the United Nations having recognized the termination of the armistice provisions. More significantly, however, such an Israeli claim amounts to an attempt to have the best of both sides of a contradiction. If Israel after 1949 claimed sovereignty over West Jerusalem and not only a temporary right of occupation, how could Israel deny equal sovereignty to Jordan over East Jerusalem?

Furthermore, the above argument advanced over Jerusalem should logically apply with no greater or lesser force to the rest of the West Bank. Indeed, if the Israeli government should ever unilaterally declare the annexation of further West Bank territory, it will presumably attempt to make a similar case, declaring the 1967 war to have been merely a belated continuation of the 1948 one and thus entitling it to exercise the same sovereignty in, say, Latrun or Qalqilya as it does in Acre and Beersheba. Since 1967, it has not done so. It has maintained a military occupation, accepting the international laws of war regarding the administration of occupied enemy territory by leaving intact the existing administrative and legal institutions of the Hashemite Kingdom of Jordan.

Even assuming the absence of a fully valid Jordanian claim to either East Jerusalem or the West Bank, this would not mean a vacuum of legitimate interests for Israel to move into. If Jordan's claim is suspect, there remain the unfulfilled claims (established in the 1947 partition plan) of the Palestinian Arab population and the international community, respectively. The declared interest of the international community applies equally to East and West Jerusalem; and while Israel may well claim a residual right as the custodian of self-determination in the western sector with its Jewish population, it can hardly claim it in the Arab-inhabited eastern part. The principle of self-determination is admittedly something of an abstraction in many parts of the world where populations are geographically mixed and national units difficult to define objectively. It is, however, a principle enjoying the legal recognition of the United Nations Charter and is not irrelevant to the argument in those cases in which a reasonable identification of geographic and ethnic distinctions can be made. Thus, while there is no conclusive way of deciding to what extent Arab inhabitants were really practicing self-determination as citizens of Jordan, it requires no great genius to perceive that in becoming subjects of Israel they enjoyed no self-determination at all. East Jerusalem is not, as some seem to imagine, simply a large empty space around the Wailing Wall.

Whatever the legal basis of Jordanian rule in East Jerusalem before the war may have been, there was no doubt among the overwhelming majority of members of the United Nations that Israel's authority there after the war was limited to that of military occupation as defined in the international laws of war. The steps taken by the Israeli government on June 27 and 28, 1967, were flatly disapproved in the resolution of the U.N. General Assembly on July 4, which declared invalid "measures taken by Israel to change the status of the city" and called upon Israel to rescind them. The resolution passed by a vote of 99 to 0 with 20 abstentions. Israel's rejection of the resolution led to its reaffirmation by the General Assembly in a further resolution on July 14.

On May 21, 1968, the Security Council adopted a similar position, in a resolution partly prompted by Israel's expropriation of land inside East Jerusalem. The resolution deplored Israel's failure to comply with the General Assembly's two resolutions, reiterated the inadmissibility of the acquisition of territory by military conquest, and declared invalid "all legislative and administrative measures and actions taken by Israel, including expropriation of land and properties thereon, which tend to change the legal status of Jerusalem." The council urgently called upon Israel to rescind and desist. The Israeli delegate at the council declared that the resolution was neither practical nor reasonable, that it disregarded Israel's basic rights (but he did not specify these), and that it sought to violate the natural unity of Jerusalem against the wishes of its citizens (surely an odd reference to the Arab population, whom the Israelis had carefully avoided consulting about the future of the city). With this rejection, the matter rested.

The United States abstained on both General Assembly resolutions and on that of the Security Council. It did not, however, accept the validity of Israel's actions. On June 28, 1967, immediately following the annexation measures, the State Department referred to Israel's "hasty administrative action" and declared: "The United States has never recognized such unilateral actions by any of the states in the area as governing the international status of Jerusalem."[15] Ambassador Goldberg stated in the General Assembly on July 14: "We insist that the measures taken cannot be considered as other than interim and provisional, and not as prejudging the final and permanent status of Jerusalem." Nonetheless, in explaining his delegation's abstention, Goldberg went on to imply that Israel's actions might indeed be accepted as only provisional, and not as outright annexation.[16] In the Security Council debate on May 9, 1968, leading to passage of the May 21 resolution, Goldberg expressed similar views. The U.S. did not accept or recognize unilateral actions, including expropriation of land and other Israeli measures, other than on a provisional basis; such actions could not alter Jerusalem's present legal status nor prejudge its permanent one.[17] Again, however, by purporting to accept these measures as provisional, the U.S. saw fit to abstain on the resolution.

Alongside the legal controversies over Israel's policy in Jerusalem, there are moral ones. The chief objects of discussion on this level have been the questions of whether it is not a blessing for cities to be united rather than divided, whether Israel or Jordan is a more responsible custodian of alien religious interests, and whether Jews or Muslims care more deeply about their Holy Places.

On general social and political grounds, the argument on behalf of a united city is a highly specious one. The euphoria about "reunification" as an inherent virtue, with its conjuring up of images of Arabs and Jews falling into one another's arms, amounts to no more than silly mysticism, unless it be a calculated manipulation of ignorance; it overlooks the elementary cleavages of identity and allegiance between the two populations that the armistice line had divided, one of which had now suddenly seized the opportunity to subjugate the other. Would a Jordanian conquest of Jewish Jerusalem have been equally celebrated as an act of "reunification"? The previous division of the city has been compared, in its supposed tragedy, to the division of Berlin. A more suitable comparison might be made to El Paso, Texas, and Juarez, Mexico, happily separated by the Rio Grande and an international frontier. Like them, West and

15. *Department of State Bulletin*, LVII (1967), 60.
16. United Nations, General Assembly (A/PV 1554), July 14, 1967.
17. *United Nations Monthly Chronicle*, V (June, 1968), 21.

East Jerusalem are populated by different nationalities, each with its own ethnically homogeneous hinterland to which it is most naturally joined. From the point of view of minimizing communal violence and enhancing the opportunity of Arabs and Jews to tend constructively to their own affairs, it was surely a blessing that in 1948 the two parts of the city's population happened to be as substantially segregated from one another as they were, with only a few thousand Jews and Arabs being uprooted from the eastern and western sections of the city respectively and with the walls of the old city providing a natural barrier along a good part of the armistice line. At least that meant that Arabs and Jews were unable to throw stones at one another or beat one another up, as happened on occasion both before and after the 19-year period of division.

What complicates this tidy argument is the problem of the religious shrines, distributed as they are without conformity to the location of populations. Neither side treated with perfect virtue the shrines of its adversary: thus, for example, it is reported that a Jewish cemetery on the Mount of Olives became the site of a Jordanian military installation, while the Muslim cemetery in Ain Karim was used by some Israelis as a latrine.[18] Such cases, however, are of very minor importance compared to the problem posed by the Wailing Wall and, to some extent, memories of the traditional pre-1948 Jewish quarter within the old city. For the strength of Jewish attachment to these places, so dramatically evident in the days following the 1967 war, now stands as an enormous barrier to any willingness by Israel to relinquish the control it has gained over the old city. On the other hand, the presence adjacent to the Wailing Wall of the Muslim sanctuary called al-Haram al-Sharif, containing the Aqsa Mosque and the Dome of the Rock and constituting the third holiest shrine in Islam after Mecca and Medina, also provides a barrier to Muslim acquiescence in Israel's control. It is easy for both Jews and Muslims to belittle one another's attachments by characterizing them as politically inflated. Certainly these attachments are exploited politically, but to belittle their emotional force is a serious mistake.

The historical circumstances of these shrines and of the events just after the June war illustrate the clash of emotions involved. The Haram al-Sharif stands on what is traditionally considered the site of Solomon's Temple, of which the Wailing Wall (in Jewish parlance, the Western Wall) is believed to be the remnant. Since the seventh century the whole area has been under Islamic jurisdiction; and while the wall itself is not

18. The latter and other cases are cited by Evan M. Wilson, former United States consul-general in Jerusalem, in "The Internationalization of Jerusalem," *Middle East Journal*, XXIII (Winter, 1969), 3–4.

revered by Muslims, it falls within a revered site and for many centuries has formed part of a legally inalienable charitable Islamic endowment *(waqf)* that included the closely surrounding houses of the Magharibah quarter, whose inhabitants were the beneficiaries of the endowment. Thus the wall was the property of an Islamic institution, whose authorities traditionally allowed individual Jews to come to pray but jealously resisted efforts of the rapidly growing Jewish population in modern times to establish the right of organized communal worship at the wall, let alone proprietary title to it. In part, their resistance stemmed from the proximity of the Haram, whose sanctity and decorum might be jeopardized by the development of a competing non-Muslim place of public worship in its midst; in part, from the traditional subordination of Jewish and Christian religious sites in Palestine to the benevolent custodianship of local Muslim authorities (the keys to the Church of the Holy Sepulcher and several other Christian shrines, for example, have customarily been in Muslim hands); and, in part, from an unwillingness to tolerate the erosion of the proprietary rights of the *waqf* for which they were responsible. The people of the district, and the Muslim religious authorities themselves, were long accustomed to the presence of a small number of Jewish worshipers in their midst and at their sufferance but not to the notion that the wall or the neighborhood was subject to any competing claims of jurisdiction. Thus, throughout the years of the Ottoman Empire and the British mandate, Jews at the wall were not entitled to bring chairs to sit on or to sound the *shofar*. From 1948 to 1967, Jews were unable to visit the wall at all; the inhabitants of the Jewish quarter in the old city had been deported across the line into Israel, and although an armistice provision called for the right of visitation from the Israeli side, the Jordanians failed to honor it.

Thus, by 1967, it might be said that for Israelis the wall was a symbol of aspirations denied. Most Israelis had never seen the wall or the old city; many were nonreligious, yet nonetheless mindful of such biblical phrases as "If I forget thee, O Jerusalem, let my right hand forget its cunning," which had long since taken on an equally potent character of secular political symbolism. Those with memories of the mandate period and before could well recall that the wall, like the land of Palestine itself, was a place to which Jews were expected to go only on the sufferance of alien authority, to stand meekly and unobtrusively in the midst of an unfriendly majority. It was a remaining symbol of the insecurity of the Diaspora, though situated at the very heart of *Eretz Israel* itself.

What made this symbolism meaningful in June, 1967, was the psychological aspect of the crisis that the Israelis had just undergone: deep apprehension as the surrounding Arab armies mobilized, a sense of vulnerability strengthened by memories of the tragedies of modern Jewish history, a feeling of helpless isolation in confronting Israel's more numerous enemies—and then, a lightning bolt of deliverance on the week of June 5 and the exhilaration of collapsing anxiety.

The wall offered the ideal object for the expression of this exhilaration. What had been Muslim became Jewish; where a few Jews had stood with crowds of Arab children looking on, and where they had subsequently been excluded altogether, thousands could now gather, post a sign saying *Bet Knesset* (A Temple) on the wall, and—for the first time in almost two millenniums—hear the sound of the *shofar*. The patronizing authority of the Muslim *waqf* authority, and the stares of Arab children, had vanished in the cloud of dust arising from the demolition of the surrounding hovels of the Magharibah quarter. Arabs praying in the two mosques of the Haram above the wall, within the Temple Mount, would henceforth do so at the sufferance of Jewish authority, and under the eyes of Jewish bystanders.

The ceremonies of celebration at the Wailing Wall, the summary disposal of the Magharibah quarter, and the annexation of Arab Jerusalem thus seem to have represented in Israeli (and other Jewish) minds not simply the expression of a religious sentiment but a second political and emotional declaration of independence, comparable to the declaration of May, 1948, proclaiming Israeli statehood. Regardless of the distribution of population in Jerusalem, requirements of international law, or the added difficulties in persuading the Arabs to make peace, Israeli opinion almost universally threw reason to the winds and regarded the annexation as a non-negotiable, irreversible act. In this, their own government took the lead.

Thus, the Israeli justification comes down to a simple claim of emotional commitment—that Israelis care more deeply about the old city than Arabs do, or at least so deeply that Arab sentiment must perforce be sacrificed. In the arena of political argument this is perhaps the strongest kind of claim because it is so insistent; it is the most unanswerable, because it is so unreasoning. In the arena of political struggle, as distinguished from mere argument, there seems little to pit against it save either the threat of overwhelming military force or a decision to concede the issue. Unhappily for the Arabs, in recent times they have possessed scant ability either to wield force or to abandon their own claims.

PROPOSALS AND PROSPECTS
FOR THE FUTURE

It is clear that no scheme for agreement on the future of Jerusalem can make any sense apart from the context of the solution of the issues regarding the rest of the West Bank—that is, apart from either a general agreement between Israel and Jordan or a settlement directly between Israel and the Palestinian Arabs independently of Jordan. Whether Arab claims are represented by Jordan or by leaders of the Palestinians themselves is another question, although it might have some relative effect on the nature of any agreement about Jerusalem.

It is also obvious that schemes calling for the unilateral control of one party over the interests of others are not going to win acceptance. Peace on the basis of today's *status quo,* that is, on the basis of full Israeli control of the united city, is an illusion; so is peace on the basis of a simple return of the old city to Jordan. Here we are faced, realistically speaking, with some imbalances. The city as a whole has a 75 per cent Jewish majority; most of it has functioned since 1949 as Israel's capital; and since 1967 it has been under complete Israeli military and administrative control. The eastern sector of it, including the old city and other areas outside the walls, is homogeneously Arab in its population and has been the natural economic center of the West Bank and for these reasons would most logically belong under Jordanian or Palestinian sovereignty; but the presence of Judaism's most important shrine in the heart of the old city renders Arab sovereignty out of the question so far as Israel is concerned.

Speaking for myself, I have no hesitation in saying that I consider the Jordanian demand for a return to the pre-1967 boundaries in Jerusalem to be fully justified and that the pre-1967 arrangements made much better sense, in terms of the elementary welfare and political entitlement of all concerned, than what Israel has imposed since then. The partition of the city, even with walls and barbed wire to divide it, does not offend me morally or aesthetically; it is not properly analogous to Solomon's proposal to cut the baby in two but to putting different categories of creatures in their own unique habitats. While some problems of the pre-1967 division no doubt invited correction, such as the inaccessibility of the Wailing Wall to Jews and the Israeli Army's desecration of the Armenian Church of St. Savior on Mount Zion and of the Dormition Abbey, these problems could scarcely be isolated from the general conflict between Israel and the Arabs. Conversely, were the general conflict settled to any significant degree, these problems could presumably be settled as well.

Neither these personal judgments nor the clear conscience of Arabs who demand that Israel return the old city to their control, however, can make much difference so long as Israel remains militarily and diplomatically strong enough to enforce its own preferences. Nor, unfortunately, can the simple reinvocation of the commitment of the General Assembly and the Trusteeship Council to internationalization of the whole Jerusalem area make much difference, despite the fact that this commitment has been a matter of continuous formal record since 1947. Given Israel's adamant and successful obstruction of the U.N. position from the beginning of its existence as a state, even when its own stake in the city was much less and its international position much weaker than today, it is hard to see that a fresh exercise in beating Israel with the same little stick can advance the cause of either peace or justice. For peace, we need agreement; for justice, we need not merely words but the actual restitution of rights to those who have been deprived of them.

A plan that will have any chance of success must be one that responds significantly to the most essential interests of both Israel and Jordan (or whatever other party may come to represent the Palestinians) as these parties themselves conceive these interests and one that can seem preferable in the eyes of both to the *status quo*. In addition to their interests, however, an international interest ought also to be represented, not only because Christian denominations have not always felt secure in the manner in which either Israel or Jordan has dealt with their shrines and institutions but also because an international presence is a useful cushion to ease the mistrustful relationship between Arabs and Israelis. The U.N.'s presence in the form of the UNTSO before 1967, however modest, was certainly an asset; it would be only sensible to expand and build on it.

Among the various proposals for the solution of the Jerusalem problem since the June war, only one makes much sense to me. This is the scheme for creation of a limited international enclave proposed by Evan M. Wilson, former United States consul-general in Jerusalem.[19] In some respects Wilson's proposal recalls a plan submitted to the General Assembly by the Palestine Conciliation Commission in 1949, which the assembly at the time shelved without a vote but which might well be reconsidered. The PCC had recommended that Jerusalem continue to be divided between Israeli and Jordanian jurisdiction but that a United Nations commissioner, assisted by a consultative council equally composed of Arabs and Jews, supervise the demilitarization of the city and assure the protection and accessibility of religious shrines of all faiths. In other respects Wilson's plan is more similar to the general internationalization of Jerusalem envisaged in the Palestine partition plan of 1947.

Wilson would limit the internationally administered area to a zone comprising the old city and southward to Mount Zion and eastward to the Mount of Olives plus a separate enclave containing Government House. Sovereignty over this area would be retained by the United Nations, which would appoint its own special representative to serve as chief

19. *Ibid.*, pp. 1–13. See also Evan M. Wilson, *Jerusalem: Key to Peace* (Washington, D.C., 1970).

executive officer; municipal administration would be entrusted to a locally elected city council. The U.N. special representative would guarantee access to and maintenance of the Holy Places with the assistance of a police force under his authority. Freedom of movement between the international zone and Israeli and Jordanian territory, respectively, would be encouraged by the United Nations but would be subject to the control of each government.

As Wilson points out, this plan would have some plausible appeal to both Israel and Jordan, while still being modest enough in scope to be capable of practical administration. Israel's presence in the new city would be legitimized, and foreign powers would no longer hesitate to move their embassies to Jerusalem. Jordan's consent to the arrangement, without the return of Jordanian authority to the old city itself, would be an important attraction for Israel, for it would both facilitate a general peace agreement with Jordan and assure the continued access of Israelis to the old city and the Wailing Wall under secure arrangements. For Jordan, it would mean less than what it had before 1967 but considerably more than it has any hope of attaining by its own devices, and probably as much as it can realistically expect ever to obtain with the diplomatic assistance of the international community. For Arab Muslims and Christians, as for Israeli Jews, it would mean security of access to their Holy Places in the old city without dependence on the benevolence of erstwhile enemies.

I have referred just above to the diplomatic assistance of the international community. Whether this can be mustered in sufficient support of this or any comparable plan is an open question and probably depends above all on the weight the United States government is willing to throw into the balance. American diplomatic officials have regarded the Jerusalem question as the most difficult single issue involved in their effort to promote compromise peace terms between Israel and Jordan; the great stumbling block clearly is the reluctance of the Israelis to think in terms of any civil authority in the old city other than their own. (Conversely, while the Jordanian government has avoided indicating in public any reduction of its claim to restoration of its prewar position in the city, it is widely believed to be interested in private in anything that might get the Israelis out.) Persuading Israel to accept a scheme such as Wilson's need not be impossible—although the odds in its favor do not seem very great—but it would require some unmistakably forceful American advice of the "Dutch uncle" variety, that is, of the kind that President Eisenhower used with Prime Minister Ben-Gurion in the days after Suez.

So far there has been no indication of such intentions in Washington. The practice of the Johnson administration in not even voting on U.N.

resolutions that criticized Israel's actions in Jerusalem may not have reflected approval of Israeli policy, but it did reflect an unwillingness to subject Israel to any meaningful pressure or to inhibit Israel from exploiting its military victory for whatever bargaining purposes it chose. At this writing the Nixon administration has become actively engaged in the search for a peace formula. In Jerusalem as elsewhere, if the U.S. government believes that compromise terms are essential, sooner or later it must attempt to promote a balance of bargaining power that will make compromise possible.

PART V

International Perspectives

No other country's destiny was so determined by international pressure as was that of Palestine, and perhaps no other conflict has been so dramatically affected by competitive international intervention as has the Arab-Israeli conflict. The particular setting of the struggle over Palestine in an area that has been significant historically, politically, economically, and strategically has contributed considerably to the international attention which it has received. A discussion, therefore, of the perspectives which governed various powers' policies and conduct toward either conflict becomes imperative for an understanding of the evolution of the confrontation and perhaps of its implications for the world.

Subsequent to the passage of a resolution in November, 1970, favoring the resumption of discussions between Israel and the Arab states under the auspices of Ambassador Gunnar Jarring, Abba Eban, Israel's foreign minister, is reported to have said that if the Arab states propose a resolution stating that the earth is not round, undoubtedly they would get enough support to have it approved by the United Nations. He suggested quite strongly that the presence of so many African and Asian states in the world organization has worked to the advantage of the Arabs and thereby implied that the continuing support of the world organization for the Palestinians and Arab states is in part related to the political influence of the representatives of the Third World in that body.

Regardless of the degree of accuracy of that statement and its implication, there is no doubt but that over the years the Palestinians and the Arab states acquired greater support and understanding for their position throughout the world, especially in Africa and Asia. When the United Nations deliberated the Palestine question, the Afro-Asian members of that body hardly exceeded a dozen states. It was evident in 1947 when voting on the partition scheme was underway that the few Afro-Asian member states were quite hostile to the proposal; eventually only the Philippines and Liberia voted in favor of the scheme, and then only under pressure, primarily from the United States. The resultant favorable vote for the partition scheme reflected the primacy and predominance of the European-American membership of the United Nations. The gradual emergence of independent states in the Afro-Asian world eventually was reflected in the altered weight and patterns of voting in the United Nations; it is almost certain that were the partition scheme presented now to the United Nations it would be defeated by a coalition of Afro-Asian and nonaligned states.

The differential behavior, attitudes, and policies of both major concentrations—the European-American and the Afro-Asian—are based on fundamental assumptions of right, justice, and Realpolitik. European-American support for Zionism and subsequently for Israel has been attributed variously to Christian guilt over the persecution of the Jew in Europe, to European colonial schemes which were well served by the Zionist settlement, to the unusual influence and pressures which Zionists have been able to exert, and to the seeming coalescence of the national interests of one or another of the decisive European-American powers with those of Zionism or of Israel. On the other hand, Afro-Asian support for the Palestinians and the Arab states has been attributed primarily to the hostility of the Afro-Asian states to European colonialism, which was perceived to have been chiefly responsible for the transplantation of a European community into the Arab world. Another reason, one which is becoming increasingly more clear, is that of color; European-American support to European Jews in establishing a state in Palestine was viewed by many Afro-Asian spokesmen as stemming essentially from the color prejudice of those states, a prejudice that works to subordinate the interests of non-whites. Whatever degree of validity these and other reasons may possess, they have played some role in shaping the foreign policy and behavior of the major world powers.

The four essays in this part are intended to highlight the roles which the great powers have played in the Palestine conflict and in the Arab-Israel conflict and to indicate the attitudes and perspectives which underlie the behavior of some Asian and African states. Great Britain's tremendous role in the disposition of Palestine is both implicit and explicit throughout the narration in this volume. But that role was played within a specific historical context; with the waning of the mandate over Palestine and the obvious decline of Britain subsequent to the Second World War, Britain was eased out and then ultimately replaced by the United States as the decisive power in shaping the destiny of Palestine.

Prior to 1939, the United States had had some interest in the Middle East, in Palestine, and in Zionism; but that interest was neither consuming nor decisive in shaping American policy. The emergence of the United States as the major power subsequent to the war made it possible for America to play the critical role in the Palestine and the Arab-Israeli conflicts. The Zionist adoption of the Biltmore Program in 1942 signified, among other things, that power within international Zionism had shifted from Europe to the U.S. From 1945 onward, the initiatives of both American Zionists and the American government became critical for any kind of settlement in Palestine and, subsequently, between Israel and the Arab states.

The concern in the United States for the fate of European Jewry may have been an important factor in determining American support for increased immigration into Palestine; Zionist financial and political power as well as their influence on the media may also have assisted in inducing greater measures of support on the part of the U.S. for the eventual establishment of an Israeli state. Surely, the political weight of Jews in urban areas is important in determining the outcome of closely contested presidential elections. But the consistent support which various administrations have rendered to Israel cannot be explained by these reasons alone. The postwar policy of the U.S. in the Middle East was in part related to its global "containment" policy. In the Middle East that policy was expressed as an effort to suppress revolutionary and semi-revolutionary movements that had the potential of disrupting economic and political systems held to be favorable to the maintenance of American economic interests there. It is important in understanding the dynamics of American policy in the region to view it against its proper global and regional framework. Richard Cottam, Professor of Political Science at the University of Pittsburgh, has long concerned himself with the Middle East and the course of American policy and is the author of Nationalism in Iran and Competitive Interference and Twentieth Century Diplomacy. While the intention of the analysis in his essay is to clarify what was the policy of the U.S. concerning Palestine proper, quite appropriately Cottam discusses the evolution of that policy, especially in relation to the cold war "containment" policy, and demonstrates the extent to which U.S. policy in the Middle East has been responsive to a multitude of pressures.

Considerable material has been written on the Soviet Union's policy toward the Arab states and toward the Arab-Israeli conflict. Little has been written on its policy toward the Palestine conflict itself, and that which has been written is not of much significance. In part, the relative recency of the active participation of the Soviet Union in the affairs of the Middle East, may account for the paucity of serious and impartial *discussions of the now critical role of the Soviet Union in that area. It has always been recognized that the Soviet Union had a long-standing interest in the Middle East, although its interest in its hinterland, the Arab world, was not as great as it was with its Turkish-Iranian portion.*

Unsusceptible to the kind of domestic pressure-group politics so characteristic of the United States, the Soviet Union has been able to pursue a foreign policy primarily determined by its consideration of Soviet state and/or ideological interests. The long course of Soviet policy toward the Arab world, toward Palestine, and toward the Palestine conflict itself clearly evidences the primacy of its ideological postulates almost up to 1955 when it responded to Egypt's major initiative for effective interaction. The thrust of Soviet policy in the post-revolutionary decades had anti-imperialist objectives. Most major problems of the Arab world were attributed to its colonial status; the significance of the Arab world from the standpoint of the Soviet Union stemmed from the support it provided, in its colonial form, to the strength of world imperialism. Hence the major objective of Soviet policy was to assist the revolutionary forces in their drive against imperialism. Yet the anti-imperialist forces in the region were led essentially by bourgeois nationalist elements which, more frequently than not, wished some kind of accommodation with the colonial powers. This perception led the Soviet Union to view the nationalist forces with a degree of suspicion and hostility that was not modified significantly until the 1950s.

It was within that framework that Soviet policy toward Palestine and the Palestine conflict was fashioned. Accordingly, Soviet policy showed special hostility first, and most consistently, toward Zionism, but it was frequently hostile to the Palestine nationalist leadership as well. The Soviet Union insisted throughout the mandate that the conflict in Palestine was a result of its control by the British and that therefore the essential task of the revolutionary forces of Jews and Arabs in Palestine was to harness their energy to oust British imperialism and attain independence for the country as a whole. In terms of the objective itself, Soviet policy was in accord with the vision for Palestine projected by the Palestinian Arabs. Yet the Soviet Union's activities in Palestine were quite confined. Its objective of assisting in the growth of a vigorous Communist Party eluded realization, and its pressures for a Jewish-Arab collaboration under the aegis of a unified Communist movement came to nought.

By the time the conflict reached the United Nations, the Soviet Union made a final appeal to both Arabs and Jews in Palestine to set aside their superficial and externally manipulated conflict, to collaborate to oust British imperialism, and to assist in overthrowing the bourgeois nationalist leadership of Zionists and Arabs alike. Neither party heeded the appeal, and the Soviet Union then opted for another alternative. It assisted the Zionists, indirectly through Czechoslovakia, by selling them desperately needed arms in 1948. It voted in favor of the Palestine partition scheme and denounced the potential intervention of the Arab states as serving primarily the interests of British imperialism which was endeavoring to perpetuate itself in Palestine. The objective of Soviet policy was quite clear—the end of British presence in Palestine and the dismantling of British bases, irrespective of the shape of the political map to emerge afterwards.

Whether the Soviet Union anticipated the degree of tension in Arab-Western relations that would result from the Arab failure to resolve the Palestine conflict to the Arab advantage is a moot question. Subsequent events accelerated the anti-imperialist drive of the Arab people and the pace of revolutionary development and eventually produced the turmoil which has been so characteristic of Arab-Western interaction since 1948. It was in that climate of hostility that the Arabs began to reorient their thinking as well as their policies; and as they were reorienting their policies, so was the Soviet Union. A certain degree of mutuality of interests ultimately led the more important Arab states to strengthen the interaction between them and the Soviet Union. Ivar Spector, Professor of Russian Civilization at the University of Washington, is the author of The Soviet Union and the Muslim World. *As a resident of mandated Palestine after his emigration from the Soviet Union, he observed closely the operations of the Palestinian Communist movement—both Arab and Jewish. His critical analysis of Soviet policy in this volume encompasses not only the Palestine conflict but also the complex network of Arab-Soviet relations through the June war of 1967.*

Preoccupied with their own struggle for independence from colonialism, Asian nationalist movements were unable to extend much support to the Palestinians in their struggle against British imperialism and Zionism. Arab missions to India and Indonesia in the 1930s, however, were able to obtain much sympathy and some financial support for their nationalist struggle. There was a consistency in the attitude of leading Asian nationalists toward the Palestine conflict; while many sympathized with the plight of the European Jews, they were not persuaded by the solution propounded by Zionists for dealing with that problem. The plight of the Palestinian, on the other hand, was understood in the context of European colonialism and expansionism. The Palestine conflict that was viewed with such complexity in Europe, was perceived much more simply in Asia. To a large extent, the view of the question as one typical of the relations of technologically backward Asian societies struggling against the technologically superior European colonial system determined the attitude of Asian states toward the conflict in Palestine as well as toward Arab relations with the West. It was therefore not accidental that the more critical Asian states consistently supported the Arab position in international councils.

Though Israel has managed to make some gains in terms of support in certain parts of Asia, it continues to be viewed primarily as a regime dependent on the West and one which more frequently than not acts to advance the interests of the West in the Middle East. The tremendous cooperation between Egypt, India, Indonesia, and to some extent China, in launching the doctrine of nonalignment and the deliberate exclusion of Israel from most Asian gatherings served to reaffirm the perspective that Israel continues to survive largely at the expense of Asian Palestinians and with the support of Western colonialism. The difficulties which Israel encountered in effecting positive relations with Asian states have been discussed repeatedly, particularly by responsible Israeli spokesmen such as Walter Eytan, Israel's former ambassador to London. M. S. Agwani is Professor and Head of the Department of West Asian Studies at the School of International Studies of Jawaharlal Nehru University, New Delhi and author of Communism in the Arab East. *In his essay in this volume he analyzes the Asian perspective which determined the policies of the Asian states, particularly that of India, toward Zionists and Arabs in Palestine and toward Arab-Israeli relations.*

With the exception of South Africa, three African states were sovereign when Israel declared its statehood—Egypt, Ethiopia, and Liberia. Eventually the countries constituting the major portion of the African continent attained sovereign statehood and began to play an effective role in international politics. Both Israel and the Arab states early recognized that that continent represented the last of the uncommitted on the Palestine conflict, and both exerted considerable efforts to obtain necessary support for their respective positions or to get the African states to withhold assistance from the other. Yet the increasing drive of militancy and radicalism in the Arab world has its counterpart in portions of Africa, and increasingly the more radical of the African states were drawn to the Arab position. Thus it was not accidental that the major support for the Arabs came from Nkrumah, Nyerere, Sékou Touré, and like-minded leaders of Africa. North Africa naturally played a critical role in cementing African support for the Arab position, and the increasingly African orientation of the North African states, particularly Egypt, was instrumental in securing political commitments of many African states to the Arab states and to the Palestinians. It is fairly obvious that several factors underlie African support of the Arabs. Like the Asians, many Africans tend to view Israel as a settler regime and to parallel the Israeli experience to European settlements in Africa; the European origin of Zionism and its links with European colonialism have played an important role as well; and the link along radical political lines between several of the Arab states and several of the African states clarified issues of contention in the worldwide struggle for supremacy and control; a struggle in which the primarily Afro-Asian forces were pitted against European-American systems. Within that context, Israel was placed more frequently than not in the camp of the European-American system. More recently, the issues separating the Arabs and Israelis acquired still larger dimensions by crystallizing them along color lines as can be seen in the considerable black support in the United States for the Arabs. Ali A. Mazrui, Professor and Head of the Department of Political Science at Makerere University College of East Africa, is perhaps Africa's leading political theorist and is the author of Towards A Pax Africana. *In his essay Professor Mazrui treats Arab and Israeli policies not in the ordinary sequential fashion but more significantly in terms of the historic attitudes and perspectives governing black-Jewish relations.*

13. The United States and Palestine

Richard Cottam

There is in American policy toward the Palestine question an enduring quality of innocence. A few Americans were intimately acquainted with the Middle East and Palestine before World War I, and Captain Mahan had already argued the case for the strategic importance of the area. But for the vast majority, interest in the Middle East dates back only to World War II when a recognition that the area was important for American security finally developed. In a very real sense, the Middle East was perceived to be without a history. There was, of course, a vague awareness of the ancient history of the area, in particular biblical history and the Crusades. But virtually nothing was known of the living memories of the inhabitants of the area—European rivalries, the decline and dismemberment of the Ottoman Empire, early Zionism and its clash with the first stirrings of Arab nationalism. As awareness of Palestine and the Middle East developed, the surface picture was accepted as reality. In this reality there already existed a substantial Jewish population determined to establish a Jewish state. British refusal to permit the Jewish refugees from Hitler's nightmare to go to Palestine was seen as a perverse manifestation of *Realpolitik*. Although there was some feeling that Arabs too deserved independence, little sympathy was extended to them, especially since their best-known leader, the grand mufti of Jerusalem, was in Nazi Germany advocating a policy that appeared indistinguishable from that of his hosts. Christian anti-Semitism had long been one of the ugliest aspects of European and American life. But its emergence in an unspeakably grotesque form in Nazism produced in all but the hopelessly insensitive feelings of deep remorse, horror, and not a little shame. Vigorous advocacy of a safe haven for Jews in their ancient homeland helped reduce guilt. Thus America prepared to play an important role in the Middle

387

East and Palestine at a time when the American people and public officials were for the most part without a comprehension of lingering European rivalries and colonialism; of the Arab sense of loss, offended dignity, and bitter hostility to Zionism; and hence of the heavy price necessary to establish and make secure a Jewish state. As American policy unfolded it became apparent that there is little charm in innocence in world diplomacy.

There was, of course, American policy toward the Palestine question before World War II. But the most important observation to be made of American policy in Palestine between the wars is the low level of interest. This was not an area of primary concern. For a brief period immediately following the Armistice there was a sense that Palestine and the Middle East were of relevance for national security. A prevailing view at that time was that the right of national self-determination must be recognized as the core of a postwar settlement if the bases for war were to be eliminated. This was the essence of Wilson's Fourteen Points. The question of Palestine was at heart one of national self-determination, and Wilson did show some personal sensitivity to that fact.

THE ROLE OF INTEREST GROUPS
IN POLICY DETERMINATION

Given a lack of compelling national interest, whether defensive or imperialistic, the role of particular interest groups will be an important determinant of the direction of American policy in an area. The vigor with which an interest-group determined policy is pressed and the direction of that policy will therefore furnish a mirror image of interest-group strength and interest-group interaction. From 1920 until the months just preceding World War II, this was true of American policy toward Palestine. Before 1920, and with the onset of World War II, national-security interests interpose and make far more difficult an accurate appraisal of interest-group influence.

Frank Manuel summed up the interest group—security interaction as of 1948 in *The Realities of American-Palestine Relations* as follows: "In this case the common sympathies of the simple American in the White House, Truman, and the hard bargaining of American Zionists won out over the alarmism of State Department officials, war strategists, oil men, Anglophiles, anti-Semites of several varieties, a small though intense group of Protestant missionaries and a few romantic pro-Arabists."[1] The

1. (Washington, D. C., 1949), pp. 358–59.

list of interest groups and their alliances within the decision-making structure is a fairly accurate one and is as interesting for those excluded as for those included. Of economic interest groups, oil was clearly most important. That oil interests needed the assistance of American officials in gaining and protecting concessions in the Middle East, in building pipelines, and in the transport of oil is easily documented.[2] That American officials regarded the maintenance of Middle Eastern oil in friendly hands as a primary defense interest from World War II on is also easily documented; but the extent to which oil interests influenced American policy with respect to the Palestine question is not. While those writing on that policy tend to deduce the role of the oil interests, their picture depends heavily on a prior assumption of the role of economic interests in American foreign-policy decision-making generally. Certainly oil officials discovered quickly enough the deep resentment of Arab leaders toward what they perceived to be pro-Zionist policies of the American government. But in the interwar period instances of sustained pressure applied overtly by American oil interests seeking to alter American policy are rare indeed. Since visibility generally characterizes the behavior of economic interest groups when specific issues are at stake,[3] there are grounds to suspect that the direct role of American economic interests in an American policy toward the Palestine question have been seriously exaggerated. Manuel, for example, finds no difficulty documenting the specific activity of the other interest groups he mentions, but his description of oil influence is only asserted.

Obviously of great importance is the category of ethnic interest groups. But here there is a striking omission from Manuel's list—the Arab-American. Admittedly, there are far fewer Arab-Americans than Jewish Americans, possibly only one-twentieth the number.[4] Although in some congressional districts Arab-American voters outnumber Jewish voters, throughout the interwar period, and indeed up through 1948, so little was heard from this group that Manuel is in fact justified in ignoring them.

2. See for example the following: Charles W. Hamilton, *Americans and Oil in the Middle East* (Houston, 1962); George Lenczowski, *Oil and State in the Middle East* (Ithaca, N. Y., 1960); Olaf Caroe, *Wells of Power* (London, 1951); and Benjamin Shwadran, *The Middle East, Oil and the Great Powers* (New York, 1955).

3. See on this subject Bernard Cohen, *The Political Process and Foreign Policy: The Making of the Japanese Peace Settlement* (Princeton, 1957).

4. According to U.S. Government census figures for 1960, the number of Americans whose mother tongue was Arabic is around 50,000 whereas the number whose mother tongue was Yiddish is over one million. Assuming similar immigration patterns, this may approximate the overall proportion of Arab-Americans to Jewish Americans.

Explanations of this phenomenon are not difficult to come by. Almost all of this group are Christian. Emigration occurred before Arab nationalism had begun in any way to dull the lines between and within the Christian and Muslim communities and to shift a focus from regional parochialism to greater Syria or the Arab nation. Thus the intensity of Arab indentification was low and sometimes, especially for Maronites, nonexistent. This low intensity of identification in turn made assimiliation into the American society fairly easy.

Manuel is doubtless correct also in his assertions that men he described as "Arabophiles" and "Anglophiles" were important opponents of a pro-Zionist American policy. But of the varieties of men qualifying for this category, only one can be characterized as an interest group—the Christian missionaries who served in the Ottoman empire. The *modus operandi* of this group was well-documented in Harry Howard's *The King-Crane Commission.*[5] There was no paid lobbyist or massive public-relations campaign. Rather the interest group simply served to give its spokesmen access to President Wilson and other men important in the decisional area. An example of a man of major personal influence was Dr. Howard Bliss, president of what is now called the American University of Beirut.

Most of the men Manuel classified as "Arabophiles" or "Anglophiles" were of a different stripe. They were Americans whose official position had placed them in the Arab world and who had empathized with articulate Arabs and/or the British officials who dealt with them. They comprehended the Arab sense of outrage at what they perceived Zionism to be: an imperialist-backed colonialism determined to wrench away an integral part of the Arab world. Such men constituted one of the most important obstacles to the achievement of Zionist aspirations. That Zionists would conclude that Arab anger had been internalized in these men and, indeed, that Manuel would see anti-Semitism in their behavior is only natural. That these same officials would see themselves as simply serving American interests by maintaining the basis of a harmonious relationship with the Arab people is also only natural. But ill-feeling and bitterness were the unhappy consequence.

Most visible of all was the Zionist interest group.[6] Here the *modus operandi* included both personal interventions by prominent American Jews with top decision-makers and direct political pressure on members

5. (Beirut, 1963).

6. Fairly detailed accounts of Zionist activities are available in the following: Manuel, *American-Palestine Relations;* Joseph P. Schechtman, *The United States and the Jewish State Movement* (New York, 1966); Christopher Sykes, *Cross Roads to Israel* (London, 1965); and Ben Halpern, *The Idea of the Jewish State* (Cambridge, Mass., 1961).

of Congress and the president. The interventions of Louis Brandeis with Wilson and of Felix Frankfurter with Wilson and Franklin Roosevelt were particularly effective. Wilson in particular was persuaded on several occasions to make statements affirming his desire for a Jewish homeland. An example of broader pressures was the congressional resolution of 1922 in which a majority of senators and representatives endorsed the concept of a Jewish homeland. The results from Wilson and Roosevelt were far from optimal, however. Despite what appeared on the surface to be clear predominance of the Zionists over all other interest groups, American policy was far from being an energetic advocacy of a Jewish state. In all probability this modest success was due more to public disinterest than to any quiet but powerful countervailing interest.

Striking by their absence were ideological interest groups concerned with Palestine. The area was a natural focus of interest for those taking seriously the liberal slogans of "national self-determination" and "open covenants openly arrived at." A web of secret agreements and understandings had been constructed around the Palestine question, many of them contradictory and most little concerned with granting the national aspirations of the inhabitants of the area. But liberal focus was primarily on Europe where putting into effect the principle of national self-determination was proving to be impossibly difficult. There is little evidence prior to World War II of a concern with Palestine or any part of the Middle East by any substantial number of people other than the Zionists and the area old-hands.

WILSON AND THE KING-CRANE COMMISSION

The period of greatest American concern with the Palestine question was the months between the Armistice and Wilson's illness. These were the days in which the British sought to reconcile their conflicting agreements with the French, the Arabs, and the Zionists concerning the disposition of the Mediterranean provinces of the Ottoman Empire. Even in this period, however, American involvement was more formal than inspired. Wilson's repeated statements endorsing Zionist aspirations were made in response to requests of Zionist leaders, and they did not project a spirit of personal commitment. The president showed little interest in seeing Amir Faysal represent the Arabs in the peace negotiations. For Wilson, plagued with opposition at home, Palestine was simply one peripheral issue among many of the utmost complexity. Armenia, Kurdistan, the Straits, and Anatolia vied for attention in the same area. Confronted with serious Franco-British quarreling over the proper execution of the secret agreements concerning the disposition of the Arab provinces, Wilson announced he did not recognize any of those agreements. He called instead for a fact-finding commission to look into the wishes of the inhabitants of the area.[7] On the face of it, this was the most reasonable of suggestions, and Wilson proceeded to ask Dr. Henry C. King, president of Oberlin College, and Mr. Charles R. Crane, wealthy industrialist and philanthropist, to head the American section of the commission. King and Crane knew little of the issue, but for Wilson this was desirable. He wanted men of stature and competence who were personally disinterested. King and Crane met these criteria. In addition they were fair and open-minded men, and both were fully committed to the concept of national self-determination. But the facts were not at issue. Articulate Arab opinion, restricted at this stage of development to a small minority of the Arab population, was bitterly opposed to Zionist aspirations. Most Arabs wished for independence but should they be compelled to accept a mandate status, the majority would have liked to see the greater Syrian area remain a unit under American or, as the second choice, British rule. Only in the Maronite community was there general preference for the French and for more restricted political units.

Since this situation was well known to the parties primarily concerned, opponents and supporters of the commission were easily predictable. Dr. Bliss was a warm supporter, as was the British senior military commander of the area, General Allenby. Zionist leaders were appalled and acted energetically to head off the investigation. But, typically, Clemenceau handled the situation with aplomb. Recognizing the surface appeal to those Europeans and Americans who looked to the national self-determination formula, Clemenceau delayed naming the French commission while quietly preventing the British from formally appointing theirs.[8] More than once King and Crane assumed the investigation would not take place. But Wilson became convinced that the investigation should take place, and the American delegation proceeded to Istanbul, Palestine, and the greater Syrian area. Their findings were just what could have been expected. Upon completing their investigation, King and Crane cabled Wilson as follows:

> We are recommending for Syria first that whatever administration go in be a true mandatory under the League of Nations; second that Syria, including Palestine and Lebanon be kept a unity according to the desires of a great majority; third that Syria be under a single mandate; fourth

7. Manuel, *American-Palestine Relations*, p. 236.
8. Howard, *King-Crane Commission*, pp. 31–33.

that Emir Feisal be king of the new Syrian state; fifth that extreme Zionist program be seriously modified; sixth that America be asked to take the single mandate for Syria; seventh that if for any reason America does not take the mandate then it be given Great Britain.[9]

There was a nonformal minority, however, consisting of two members of the commission, William Yale and George R. Montgomery. Of the two, William Yale, a highly intelligent observer of the Middle East, moved from an earlier position of opposition to Zionism to one of tepid support. Although recognizing that the creation of a national home for Jews "was entirely contrary to the wishes of the people of Palestine and those of most of the inhabitants of Syria," he argued that the Jews did have "a national history, national traditions and a strong national feeling," and Syrians did not. Therefore although an injustice was being done "to the individuals who inhabit Palestine," no injustice was being done to the Arab nation, in that an Arab nation did not, in fact, exist.[10] His statement reflects the clearly perceived need of somehow reconciling—in the name of national self-determination—Zionist aspirations to the fact that 90 per cent of the Palestine population was non-Jewish.

Mr. Montgomery was not burdened by sympathy for the Arabs. Howard described his report as follows:

He asserted that Moslem empires "grew and prospered only as long as there was loot to be looted and divided." Islam to him contained "no nucleus of unselfishness" which held any hope of a Moslem reformation, since it was vigorous only as it conquered, not as it served, and would not meet "the needs of modern society. . . ."

The dominant issue in Palestine clearly was Zionism, which must be considered not from the point of view of Palestine alone, but from "the standpoint of history, of racial achievements, of Jewish persecution and of anti-semitism." There should be no narrow interpretation of the idea of rights, but "the greatest benefit to the greatest number must be considered." Among Arabs were naturally the elements of jealousy and rivalry and the apprehensions of the private land holders.[11]

According to Howard, the King-Crane Report was very well received by the American delegation in Paris. But Wilson was by then largely incapacitated, and the report was never acted upon. The episode is instructive for a number of reasons however. First, it illustrates the disinclination

9. *Ibid.*, p. 218.
10. *Ibid.*, p. 205.
11. *Ibid.*, p. 196.

of the American people to see in the Palestine case any serious security implications for the United States. The notion that the national self-determination doctrine would bring lasting peace and security did not capture the popular imagination to the point that any substantial pressure was applied in this area. Second, it illustrates the receptivity of liberal Christians to the Arab case when confronted with it. Third, it forecasts the response of American officials concerned with the area to the implications of Zionist objectives. Fourth, it suggests the limits of the strength of the Zionist interest group in the formulation of American policy in the period. Though by all surface indications the Zionists were the strongest of the interest groups, they could not deflect Wilson from initiating an inquiry which had the potential to reduce seriously Zionist attainments.

After the King-Crane episode, official American concern with the Palestine question was negligible. The Zionists demonstrated in 1922 their ability to produce a favorable congressional resolution, but concerned officials apparently were unimpressed. This was a period in which the rhythm of British policy revealed a thematic content. Moved by pressures from Zionist interests, and often by their own conviction that justice to the Jewish people demanded their being allowed to create a Jewish state, leading British statesmen supported the Zionist objective. But British officials in the area were made acutely aware of the costs—both moral and material—of such a policy. Arab people felt a sense of outrage at having a Jewish homeland imposed in the heart of the Arab world, and increasing numbers became determined to resist. This response made for great difficulty in governing the area, and many British officials would have liked to have seen serious modifications made in the policy of support for Zionist objectives. Thus British statesmen felt pressure from both sides of the question. The rhythm of vacillation in British policy reflected an attrition of the original pro-Zionist position resulting from bureaucratic dissuasion followed by a mighty wrench back to a pro-Zionist course as a result of mobilization of strong Zionist pressure on the home front. American Zionists counted among those placing the pressure, but they were largely unsuccessful in their efforts to gain official American support in their campaign.[12]

WORLD WAR II AND
THE PARTITION PLAN

Franklin Roosevelt in 1938, confronted with the fact of Hitler's persecution of the Jews, called for a conference at Evian which "would mani-

12. Manuel, *American-Palestine Relations*, pp. 300–8.

fest before the non-European world the urgency of emigration, chiefly to Palestine."[13] In doing so, Roosevelt demonstrated his lack of understanding of the Palestine question and of the altered situation resulting from Hitler's persecution of the Jews. The rhythm of British policy in Palestine had been totally disrupted by the persecution of the Jews and the increasingly serious perception of threat in Britain from Germany. Ironically, Hitler's persecution of the Jews destroyed the Zionist's leverage. British security called for stability in the Arab world, and Zionism was a primary cause of instability in that area. Consequently, pleasing the Arabs came to be seen as vital to British national security. That Roosevelt, who was otherwise astute, was not aware of this situation is an indication of the American government's basic disinterest in Palestine. Moreover, the meager results of the Evian Conference indicate the weakness of Jewish pressures, the lack of comprehension even among Jews of the desperate nature of Hitler's threat to the Jews, and the Zionist preoccupation with Palestine as the logical emigration point for Jewish refugees. The U.S. government did announce its intention to turn over the German quota of 30,000 to Jewish refugees. But had there been greater pressure and greater awareness of the situation, an amendment of American immigration laws might well have been effected.

With American involvement in World War II came the beginning of the end of American disinterest in the Palestine question. As late as January, 1944, Cordell Hull affirmed the official position that Palestine was a British responsibility.[14] That same year the War Department withdrew earlier objections to a congressional resolution censuring the British White Paper of 1939 which had permitted limited immigration into Palestine for five years after which time the door was to be shut completely; but the State Department asked that Congress not act on the resolution. These contradictory actions symbolized the advent of a new era in American policy. Franklin Roosevelt was determined that the United States should not this time refrain from playing a major role in world affairs. His conversations with Ibn Saud of Saudi Arabia suggested that his areas of concern would include the Middle East. Furthermore he made clear to Ibn Saud that Arab interests would not be ignored in the Palestine question. Four months earlier he had told a convention of American Zionists, "I know how long and ardently the Jewish people have worked and prayed for the establishment of Palestine as a free and democratic commonwealth. . . . If re-elected I will help bring about its realization."[15] American

13. Sykes, *Cross Roads,* p. 223.
14. Manuel, *American-Palestine Relations,* p. 310.
15. As quoted in Sykes, *Cross Roads,* p. 326.

policy quickly reflected the same conflicting pressures that had produced vacillation in British policy.

The changed milieu of American policy was on two dimensions: interest-group activity and questions of national security. As an interest group, Zionists were much stronger. By 1945 the unbearable details of Hitler's genocide policy were known, and Jewish determination that a safe haven be provided in Palestine for the pathetic remnant of a once vital European Jewry was intense. Arab-Americans remained quiet, and little opposition was heard from the Christian missionary element which had been so vocal after World War I. American oil interests in the area, especially in Saudi Arabia, had increased and presumably reflected in their contacts with American officials Ibn Saud's hostility to Zionism.

The major change—one which was damaging to the Zionists—is to be found in the altered perception of American officials of the implications of Zionist policy for American security. Roosevelt's sympathetic remarks to Ibn Saud reflected a realization that an expanded American role in the area must include friendly ties with the Arab states. Sensitivity to this need became far greater among concerned American officials as the prospect of Soviet-American worldwide rivalry became ever more likely.

A beginning of an awareness of the basic dilemma posed by Zionist aspirations penetrated American officialdom. Zionism reflected an urgently felt need of Jews everywhere for their own state and a refuge against the curse of anti-Semitism. But a Jewish homeland in the form of a Jewish state would have to be imposed on an awakening Arab population. Every indication pointed to prolonged conflict and hence instability in the area, unless the sponsors of a Jewish state were to protect the emerging state with sufficient force to compel the Arabs to accept for all time the fact of that Jewish state. Neither the British government nor the American government was willing to pay the price of that kind of guarantee. The alternatives were to disappoint the Zionists or to acquiesce in long-term instability, even though it was understood that the Soviet Union could exploit that instability to its own advantage.

That the rhythm of American policy should now parallel that of British Mandate policy was not surprising. Harry Truman was in many respects typical of the liberal American of that day in his attitudes concerning the Palestine question. As a decent human being appalled by Hitler's barbarity and as a man with an understanding of Jewish fears and aspirations gleaned from close friendships with Jews, Truman was deeply sympathetic to the goal of the Jewish state. As a politician whose election in 1948 was at best problematical, Truman was very much aware of his need for Jewish political support. His receptivity therefore to appeals from American Zionists was great.

Congress was even more responsive. In 1941 sixty-eight senators and two hundred representatives had joined the American Palestine Committee.[16] On December 19, 1945, Congress adopted a resolution calling for the free entry of Jews into Palestine, which was to become the Jewish national home. Throughout the war years, Congress had been a primary target interest of the Zionists. The fact that a majority of Congress was openly supporting their objectives could serve to remind the executive that there were boundaries which could not be crossed.

But American officials concerned with American security interests in the area were far less responsive. As the *Forrestal Diaries* make clear, James Forrestal, James Byrnes, and Robert Lovett in particular were deeply concerned about the dangers to American security in a too-close association with the objectives of Zionism. Truman was not immune to the expressions of caution from his primary foreign-policy and security-policy advisers, and despite his clear sympathy for Zionist objectives his policy could not be one of total support.

Soon after assuming the presidency, Truman announced that he favored the immediate acceptance of 100,000 Jews into Palestine, as proposed by the Jewish Agency, and that he was "communicating directly with the British government in an effort to open the doors of Palestine to those displaced persons who wish to go there."[17] The British countered with a proposal that an Anglo-American Commission be appointed to look into conditions in Palestine and among Jewish refugees. There was little innocence in this proposal. There is not much question that the British assumed that this commission, like the King-Crane Commission, would see the complexities and take a skeptical position regarding Zionist goals. They were half right in their expectations. The commission did see the great cost of an imposed settlement and called for a trusteeship to last as long as deep enmity between Arab and Jew persisted. But the report also called for the admission of 100,000 Jews into Palestine. President Truman embraced only the immigration recommendation, and the British rejected the entire report. The British foreign minister, Ernest Bevin, had become annoyed by American pressure regarding immigration, and fences had to be mended. Truman, therefore, sent a mission under Henry Grady to London to explore the possibility of an Anglo-American settlement plan. The result was a provincial partition plan which was acceptable to the British but absolutely unacceptable to the Zionists. Truman had moved too far to the other side and had to retreat before Zionist pressure.[18]

16. Manuel, *American-Palestine Relations*, p. 309.
17. *Ibid.,* p. 320.
18. Sykes, *Cross Roads*, p. 360.

By April, 1947, the United States was promoting a United Nations commission to investigate the conflict and to propose courses of action. When the majority of that commission recommended a partition plan which the Zionists could live with but which was anathema to the Arabs, the United States became the plan's most avid supporter. The plan was adopted in November, 1947, and the United States pledged support for the solution of internal problems in the successor states. If the Morrison-Grady Plan marked a low point in the Truman administration's support of Zionist objectives, this was the high point.

But the rhythm was to proceed according to the familiar theme. Within the concerned bureaucracy a strong case was made that the decision to partition Palestine was inherently irresponsible. The intensity of Arab hostility was finally comprehended and with it the certainty of open conflict. Robert Lovett expressed the opinion that Jewish preparations were superior and that they would win the first round. But he predicted, prophetically, that the Arabs would turn to guerrilla warfare and the area would see protracted conflict.[19] In the view of State Department officials, military strategists, and oil men, United States interests and security would be adversely affected. Dean Rusk anticipated a conflict in which the Soviet Union would be able to capitalize most profitably.[20] Oil pipeline construction plans were interrupted and fears expressed that the oil, so vital for European recovery, would be cut off.[21] The statement of Herschel Johnson in the General Assembly at the time of the partition decision sounded in retrospect very hollow. He had said, "We do not refer to the possibility of violation by any member of its obligation to refrain in its international relations from the threat or use of force. We assume that there will be Charter observance."[22] Now it was clear that there would be a resort to force.

The decision to partition Palestine was perceived to be an irresponsible one simply because it imposed a settlement on the Arabs against their bitter opposition and yet made no serious provision for the protection of the new Jewish state. Opinions varied as to the ability of that state to survive, but regardless of individual expectations, men of responsibility could not take lightly their role in creating a Jewish state which was then placed on its own with the probability of protracted conflict, if it survived initially. The Joint Chiefs estimated that even were a trusteeship established

19. James Forrestal, *The Forrestal Diaries,* ed. Walter Millis (New York, 1951), pp. 303–4.

20. *Ibid.,* p. 410.

21. *Ibid.,* pp. 356–57.

22. Cited in Manuel, *American-Palestine Relations,* p. 353.

and a Jewish-Arab truce declared, 104,000 troops would be required to provide security.[23]

Expressions of concern for the survival of the Jewish state were coupled with expressions of concern for American security. Zionists, having finally achieved an official promise of statehood to be granted within months, were horrified by the growing concern with the wisdom of that decision inside the government. With minimal support from outside sources and often against active opposition, the Jewish community of Palestine had trained and armed their people and were grimly confident of their ability to defend themselves against the Arabs. Consequently their picture of the forces seeking to reverse the partition agreement was anything but benign. Manuel was probably reflecting this response accurately when he wrote,

> The diplomats, the strategists, the oil men, the Anglophiles and the missionaries thus marched as a solid phalanx against the Jewish aspirations in Palestine. They said or implied that they were the true spokesmen for American interests, and that they alone took the broad view which encompassed American security and the American way of life, and that those Americans who espoused Zionism were placing their own narrow aims above the totality of the national welfare or were the dupes of those who did.[24]

He argued further, and more ominously, that

> Many of them indulged in ancient sentiment with a worn phraseology, anti-Semitism. The Zionist delegations who beleaguered the Departments at moments of crisis were importunate, emotional and "unreasonable." Officials had to brace themselves for those interviews in order to maintain their diplomatic calm during the torrent of strong words. The techniques of pressure politics which the American Zionists used with striking success were resented as an invasion of the inner sanctum where the policy-makers were supposed to chart our course immune from such vulgar influences.[25]

Despite this sense of outrage within the American Zionist community, the nadir of Zionist influence was reached in March, 1948, just weeks before Israel was born, when the American government announced a

23. Forrestal, *Forrestal Diaries,* p. 411.
24. *American-Palestine Relations,* p. 340.
25. *Ibid.,* pp. 337–38.

reversal of its position on the partition plan and suggested an international trusteeship in its place. But the proposal was too late. The momentum of the impending conflict was too great to reverse. When Israeli spokesmen announced the existence of Israel, the United States was the first government to grant the new state recognition.

Zionist and Arab anger at official American vacillation was understandable. But there was an ineluctable quality to the rhythm of that vacillation, exactly parallel to that of the British a generation earlier. It reflected the ability of Zionist pressures to set in motion, or to reverse, a policy. But it spelled out the clear limitations of that influence in the execution of policy. Zionist pressures had to be applied at the points of greatest vulnerability in the decisional process, Congress and the White House. Decisions, however, had to be implemented by the bureaucracy concerned and the flow of events indicates that the thrust of bureaucratic pressures served to alter and even reverse the general decisions. Evidence of oil pressure in this period is elusive, but possibly this is in part the result of a coincidence of views of the bureaucracy and the oil companies. Both saw the Zionist program as fundamentally disruptive of their interests.

The end result was a series of decisions which led to the creation of a Jewish state against the violent opposition of the Arab inhabitants of Palestine and the at least rhetorically violent opposition of Arabs elsewhere. But very little was done to give security to the new Jewish state or to offer some remedy to the Arab material losses and profoundly injured sense of national dignity.

THE OBJECTIVES OF
UNITED STATES POLICY

The birth of Israel coincided with the Berlin Crisis and the crystallization of Cold War attitudes and behavior. American policy in this period was described as one of "containment," and indeed that term is descriptive if viewed as an umbrella under which are clustered a number of discrete policies which together have the thrust of containing the perceived threat from international Communism. The primary import to the Middle East and the Palestine question was that this would be an era of intense American involvement in the area.

Overall American policy in the Middle East can be viewed under three general headings. Of primary importance was the containment of anticipated Soviet aggression. The dangers of overt aggression in the Middle East appeared very real at the end of World War II. In Azerbiajan in Iran, a puppet Communist regime was established and protected by Soviet occupation troops. A strong Soviet propaganda offensive was mounted against Turkey, and Greece was in the throes of civil war with a menacing Communist guerrilla movement. But by 1948 this phase had passed its climax, and the most probable form of Soviet aggression was now perceived to be subversion. To contain this aggressive thrust would be difficult at best in an area such as the Middle East in which profound change was certain to occur. The general policy line that developed was to aid in the creation and maintenance of non-Communist stability in the area. This objective was particularly relevant in the strategically vital Arab world.

The central aspect of containment policy generally, however, was in military deterrence. Nuclear weapons were utilized initially to prevent the Soviet Union from taking advantage of her superiority in conventional forces. With the Soviet development of a nuclear capability there soon appeared what has been aptly called a "balance of terror." A nightmarish aspect of this situation was the danger that through accident the nuclear powers might be involved in nuclear conflict which neither wanted. Technical accident would be easier to deal with and remedy than accidental conflict resulting from an uncontrolled dispute which was peripheral to the main conflict. Accidental war areas of primary danger were of two varieties: the divided nations—Germany, Vietnam, Korea, and China—where a nationalistic urge for unity could easily precipitate localized warfare which could escalate, and disputes which stood independently of the Cold War but which again could easily escalate. Of the latter variety the two most important were the Indo-Pakistan dispute over Kashmir and the Arab-Israeli conflict. Thus a second major objective of American policy was to prevent an Arab-Israeli conflagration which could upset the balance of terror.

The third major aspect of American policy regarding the Palestine question involved satisfying persisting domestic interest-group demands. American Zionists and the oil industry both intensified their concern after 1948. The oil investment in the area had expanded significantly, and the industry was naturally deeply concerned with the protection of its investments. Its objective was to insure in the Arab regimes a sympathetic setting for the maintenance and development of the industry. Anti-American attitudes which resulted from an American policy perceived to be pro-Israeli were thus a major threat.

There were periods after 1948 and after the Suez Crisis of 1956 when the future of Israel appeared to be secure. But Arab border crossings testified to the continuing, even intensifying, Arab refusal to accommodate to the fact of Israel, and whenever Israel's security appeared threatened, the activities of American Zionists in support of Israel would be stepped up. Their *modus operandi* remained the same: Congress and the White House were the natural targets of a group which could persuasively argue that the votes of several million Americans could be determined by this issue. Their problem remained the same: how to reach a bureaucracy which appeared to view American support of Israel as being damaging to American security interests.

There were other economic interests concerned. The Arab boycott of American companies doing business with Israel was designed to put pressure on leading American industrialists to be sensitive to American policy in the area. Evidence of success here does not appear on the surface.

Arab-Americans remained largely quiescent until the June war of 1967. American news-media treatment of that conflict and the overt partisanship of American political leaders were perceived by Arab-Americans as outrageously unfair. Since that time several pro-Arab organizations have been formed, and political activities in both the Maronite and the various Orthodox communities have sporadically appeared. But, even given the very substantial numbers of Arab-Americans, the influence exerted has been minor.

A potentially far more important development in ethnic-group activity has been the increasingly widespread perception by militant leaders of the American black community of an identity of interest between themselves and Arabs. A world view is appearing in the black community in which Zionism is perceived much as it is by Arabs—as an integral part of Western white imperialism. By this view, blacks and Arabs are alike its victims. Zionist perception of this threat is acute, and charges were being made by the spring of 1969 of Arab-black collusion.[26] But there were few signs indicating that the developing interest was sufficiently intense to affect policy.

Ideological interest-group activity was minimal. The liberal, anti-Communist Americans for Democratic Action consistently passed resolutions which were virtually indistinguishable from those passed by liberal Jewish organizations. But there was little or no follow-up pressure. American liberals were remarkably unconcerned with, even unaware of, the fortunes of liberal Arab political leaders. Protests of American policies which were perceived to undermine liberal leaders in other developing areas had no echo in the Middle East. Indeed, when the relatively liberal regime of Nabulsi was toppled in Jordan the *New York Times* editorially rejoiced.[27] American liberal blindness here is easily explained, but not

26. For a series of articles on this subject see the periodic publications *Facts* and *Fact Finding Report,* published by the B'nai B'rith.
27. *New York Times,* April 12, 1957, and again on April 16, 1957.

simply by the fact that many leaders of the liberal intellectual community are Zionists. American liberals were profoundly affected by Hitler's genocide and overwhelmingly sympathetic to the need for a national home for the Jewish people where they could be safe from the anti-Semitism of a Christian majority; given the depths of this conviction, an inability to perceive facts which would create moral ambiguity is only expected perceptual behavior. On the New Left a view of Zionism that paralleled closely that of the militant black leaders began to appear, but here too an intensity of concern seemed lacking.

For American decision-makers there could be no easy compartmenting of the three aspects of American policy. Instead, the decision-making process incorporated the demands flowing from each of the objective areas and attempted to produce an integrated whole. What was needed was a policy that would result in Arab regimes which would be stable, non-Communist, sympathetic to American oil interests, and ready to acquiesce in the existence of Israel. But it would be a serious misinterpretation of the process to suggest that such an integrated objective was articulated or even implicitly sought. On the contrary, the decisional process was consistently *ad hoc,* focusing on serious, discrete problem-areas as they presented themselves. There was to some degree a doctrinal division developing within the concerned bureaucracy; although the goal of non-Communist stability was generally accepted, strategies for achieving the goal varied. How should the revolutionary forces in the Arab world be dealt with? These forces called for a rapid transformation of elite control; a greatly expanded state involvement in planning and development; rapid progress toward Arab unity; a defeat of Western imperialism of which Zionism was seen to be an integral part; and a neutral Cold War stance. Since trends indicated a rapid growth in revolutionary appeal, the central problem for American decision-makers was clear. Real stability was unlikely if revolutionary forces were not accommodated. But if these forces were accommodated, the threat to Israel and to American oil interests would be severe.

POLICY DEVELOPMENT: 1948–1956

Actual policy can conveniently be viewed in four periods. In the first, dating from the end of the 1948 war to the Suez war in 1956, American decision-makers seemed to find a path to stability involving supporting either a traditional elite or a popular revolutionary elite equally acceptable. The Nuri al-Said regime of Iraq, which, despite a large oil income, was most hesitant to encourage change except on the infrastructure level, appeared to satisfy admirably all the demands placed on American policy. It was stable, non-Communist, anxious to ally with the West, protective of foreign oil interests, and only rhetorically opposed to Israel and in favor of Arab unity. The military regime of Egypt was less satisfactory in one regard; it was nonaligned. But compared with its predecessor it was stable, and it dealt severely with its domestic Communists. Egyptians were less intransigent in their opposition to Israel than Eastern Arabs, and there was good reason to believe that this opposition too was in essence rhetorical. Egypt was not then of major concern to the oil interests.

Gamal Abdel Nasser, the emerging leader of the military junta in Egypt, was gaining acceptance as the symbolic leader of Arab nationalism and revolutionary change in the Arab world. This role was obviously highly attractive to Nasser, but in accepting it he accepted important constraints. He would have to satisfy the yearning of the revolutionary Arabs of the East both for Arab unity and the defeat of Israel. When the Ben-Gurion policy of massive retaliation against increasingly numerous Arab border crossings was adopted, Nasser had no choice but to respond—especially after the humiliating raid on Gaza in February, 1955. His initial response, a request to buy arms from the United States, revealed the American dilemma. If the U.S. failed to respond favorably, Nasser, and with him Arab nationalism, would likely look to the Soviet Union. This would affect adversely the goals of creating stability and a favorable climate for the oil industry and, more ominous, would threaten the basically pro-Western stance of Arab nationalism. A favorable response from the U.S. would increase the potential for an Arab-Israeli conflict which would then involve the great powers and would infuriate an important section of the American voting public.

That the policy adopted should seek to avoid a choice was entirely predictable. When Nasser turned to the Soviet Union and Czechoslovakia for arms, the American vacillation that followed again accurately reflected severe goal conflict. But the abrupt cancellation of the exploratory offer to assist in financing the construction of the Aswan Dam was an idiosyncratic manifestation of the John Foster Dulles style. Though Dulles vigorously denied the charge, there is little doubt but that he did precipitate Nasser's decision to nationalize the Suez Canal Company and, thus, the Suez conflict.[28]

Confronted with the Franco-British armed response to Nasser's act, Dulles attempted in vain to avoid the decision to intervene, with or without Israeli collaboration. He succeeded only in effecting a break in com-

28. For a detailed, though bitterly biased, study of the Dulles role, see Herman Finer, *Dulles Over Suez* (Chicago, 1964).

munications with his European allies. That Dulles was acutely aware of the difficulty intervention would pose for American relations with Nasser and Arab nationalism is indicated by his remark to the effect that America could hardly afford to appear in the Middle East walking arm-in-arm with British or French armies.[29] The Franco-British support of the Israeli invasion infuriated Dulles and Eisenhower, and it is possible that the implicit Soviet-American cooperation to force the British and French out was due more to anger than to the compulsion to avoid a Soviet-Arab nationalist marriage. The severe pressure placed on Israel to withdraw to its previous boundaries in exchange for a United Nations force in the Sinai and Gaza and a verbal pledge that the Gulf of Aqaba would be open to Israeli shipping was an obvious effort to capitalize on a generally favorable response of the revolutionary Arabs to American policy.

But what had been momentarily forgotten in 1956 was that the Middle East was in counterpoint to the Cold War theme. The U.S. split with its major allies had to be healed if the containment policy in Europe were to be maintained. A meeting was held at Bermuda in late 1956, and disagreements were put aside. Some effort to bring U.S. Middle East policy into harmony with the policies of America's allies could be expected.

Possibly more significant was the policy suggested by the beginnings of a break in the Egyptian–Saudi Arabian alliance. This unnatural alliance was based on mutual antipathy to the House of Hashem, then dominating Jordan and Iraq. The Saudi hostility, however, was based on dynastic rivalry, whereas the Egyptian enmity was that of the revolutionary for the proponents of the *status quo*. With good reason, the Saudi Arabian government began to perceive a greater threat from the revolutionaries than from the Hashemites. With this came the opportunity to isolate and contain the revolutionary Arab movement—the first stirrings of a doctrine.

POLICY DEVELOPMENT: 1957–1958

A "doctrine" had not really crystallized when the term was incorporated in 1957 into what was called the Eisenhower Doctrine. The actual terms of the Eisenhower Doctrine were somewhat mystifying to the uninitiated. At a time of internal conflict between poles of *status quo* and revolution, and at a time of continuing Arab irreconcilability to the presence of a Jewish state, this doctrine promised economic aid and armed support

---

29. Although Dulles refused to exclude the possibility of the use of force, he tried desperately, as Finer illustrates, to avoid a situation in which U.S. forces would be cooperating with old imperial powers.

to any Middle Eastern state desiring protection against "overt armed aggression from any nation controlled by international Communism." Although the Eisenhower Doctrine was not formally invoked during any of the American interventions in the next year and a half, it was referred to in each.[30] What is fairly clear in these references was the assumption that the Egyptian, Syrian, and, in part, even the Jordanian regimes were under sufficient Communist influence to qualify as "Communist controlled." On the surface the Eisenhower Doctrine seemed strangely irrelevant. There were no Communist-dominated states in the Middle East, and a direct Soviet attack was most unlikely. There were very serious problems in the area, but the doctrine seemed unconcerned with these.

In fact, however, given the broad interpretation of "Communist controlled," the doctrine was very much relevant to the demands placed on the American policy-makers. The oil industry wanted cooperative regimes. Were it not for the revolutionary Arab challenge, these companies could feel fairly secure. Isolating and weakening the revolutionaries thus would be most satisfying to the oil industry. The Zionists feared most of all Nasser and the Arab revolutionaries. They too would be pleased with a policy which replaced or at least isolated such regimes. The probability of renewed warfare and hence of escalation to nuclear conflict would be reduced since there was little likelihood of nonacquiescence to Israel's existence by the more traditional Arab states. Furthermore, the favored regimes were far more explicitly anti-Communist, thus satisfying another general requirement.

There remained, thus, only one serious aspect of desired policy unimproved: the need for internal stability if subversive opportunities were to be reduced in number and appeal. Here the argument could be made that the Eisenhower Doctrine was counter-productive. Arab nationalism was a very strong force, and a basic assumption behind the American role in the Suez crisis appeared to have been that the United States must not abdicate its influence with Arab nationalists. Wouldn't turning to a policy of hostility toward the regime that symbolized Arab nationalism be to risk whatever gains had been made during the painful and costly split with America's allies? The men making American policy did not see the situation that way. For them, Nasser did not necessarily symbolize Arab nationalism. Certainly his regime was no more stable than that of Nuri al-Said, and the Iraqi regime was more than willing to cooperate in an

---

30. For a careful study of the extent to which the Eisenhower Doctrine was officially invoked, see Sarah L. Botsai, "The Eisenhower Doctrine" (M.S. thesis, University of Pittsburgh, 1959).

endeavor to isolate Nasser and to overturn the Syrian regime.[31] Furthermore, by 1957, political engineering was an integral part of America's
modus operandi. Mosaddeq, seemingly the symbol of Iranian nationalism,
had been replaced with American help in 1953, and the successor regimes
were far more stable. Thus an Arab world led by men whose prototype
was Nuri al-Said seemed to the policy-makers to be the answer.

In the spring of 1957 the first of the target leaders, Suleiman Nabulsi
of Jordan, was toppled and a royal dictatorship substituted. Direct evidence
of American involvement in the royal coup is not available. But the widespread belief that American involvement was the critical factor in its
success was determinative of Arab response. Certainly American aid after
the coup was most generous, and the stability of the regime was heavily
dependent on that support.

This, then, was the point at which American policy in fact crystallized
around a doctrine. The Palestine question could best be handled by the
creation, if necessary, and the strengthening in any case, of regimes in
the Arab states which would move forward on the social and economic
front in a restrained, rational, and evolutionary manner. Control would
necessarily be authoritarian. Satisfaction of material needs of the people
would be the source for stability. There would be no need for demagogic
appeals to nationalism, and the left ideologues could be repressed. Such
regimes would be anti-Communist, supportive of oil interests, and, although rhetorically hostile, in fact acquiescent to Israel.

By the fall of 1957 there was every reason to doubt the validity of the
happily simplistic assumptions on which American policy had been
grounded. An effort to engineer the nationalist-leftist Syrian regime out of
existence failed spectacularly. The Syrian government disclosed that an
American-sponsored coup had been uncovered and those responsible had
been jailed, expelled, or were in hiding. Documentary evidence for these
assertions presented at the trials of the accused Syrians is good enough
to make the charge credible.[32] The follow-up to this case was what was
perceived to be an implicit Turkish-American threat to intervene. Confronted with this, even Nuri al-Said's Iraq had to promise full support
for Syria. What was demonstrated was the limited American capability to
engineer Middle East politics. Both Arab nationalism and anti-Israeli
sentiment were too strong to be circumvented by replacing one elite
with another.

31. For evidence of this see the documents presented at the trial of General Ghazi
Daghestani in Baghdad in August, 1958. Brief summaries of the proceedings can
be found in the *New York Times,* August 17, 18, 19, 1958.
32. A very brief account of this is to be found in Bradford Westerfield, *The Instruments of American Foreign Policy* (New Haven, 1963), pp. 481–84.

American realization of this did not come until after U.S. policy had suffered further disaster. Civil war developed in Lebanon in the spring of 1958. The conflict was grounded in the peculiar complexity of Lebanon's sectarian balance, identity confusion, and ideological diversity. But American support for President Chamoun, who had endorsed the Eisenhower Doctrine, seemed to reduce this complexity for both Arabs and Americans. For Arabs, the conflict was cast in terms of Arab nationalism and socio-economic goals versus Lebanese particularism and conservatism. For Americans it was understood as a conflict between pro-Western and pro-Eastern elements. But Lebanon was peripheral to the real disaster. That came with the sudden overthrow and murder of Nuri al-Said in Iraq and consequently the total collapse of the political structure which had given the surface appearance of rocklike stability. American military intervention in Lebanon and British intervention in Jordan quickly followed. There is little reason to question the conclusion that in intervening in Lebanon, the Eisenhower administration believed it was acting pre-emptively—to prevent success for a Soviet-dominated rebel movement.

Thomas Schelling wrote in *Arms and Influence,* published in 1966, that this intervention successfully deprived the Soviets of a golden opportunity to expand their influence.[33] Since Schelling had very close relations with American strategists throughout the early 1960s, the assumption that the obvious conclusion flowing from the American intervention did not penetrate the general bureaucracy is a good one. That conclusion, bluntly, was that American policy had been based on a fantasy of Soviet control of the Lebanese rebels and beyond them of the United Arab Republic. This is not simply an ex cathedra assertion. American involvement in the creation of a new Lebanese governing coalition was not concealed. The coalition that resulted had as its premier none other than Rashid Karami, one of the leading figures in the rebellion. Far from being a Soviet dupe, as he had previously been characterized, Karami was essentially conservative and devoted to the preservation of Lebanon's sovereignty.

The collapse of the doctrine had immediate and obviously serious implications for American objectives in the area. With regard to the Palestine question, the inescapable conclusion was that regimes in the Arab East which were acquiescent to the existence of a Jewish state would be placed under extreme pressure and their stability hence impaired. But this conclusion was not yet drawn in Washington. Since the Suez war was part of the fairly recent past in 1958 and the memory of the Arab defeat and revealed impotence was fresh, agitation for a third round was not yet strong. Without the constant reminder of agitation and border incidents,

33. (New Haven, 1966), pp. 49, 52.

the perception of threat to Israel was not immediate in Washington. In fact, not until 1966 did the momentum of incidents reach the point at which consciousness of the probability of a new round began to penetrate the decisional community. Therefore, between 1958 and 1966 American policy toward the Palestine question was to treat the issue as settled in its main form. Activity was focused on efforts to bring about some kind of solution to the refugee problem through the United Nations. Even here, the low intensity of concern was the most important characteristic. Little creativity or commitment in working for a solution to the problem was in evidence. Likewise there was only rhetorical concern for disarmament of the area. The really relevant policy concerning the Palestine question developed around relations with the Arab states, and by 1958 these were at a very low ebb.

POLICY DEVELOPMENT: 1959–1964

A new thrust did appear in American policy regarding the Arabs even before the presidency of John F. Kennedy, but it moved much more rapidly after January, 1961. For those regimes such as Saudi Arabia, Jordan, and Tunisia which were out of sympathy with a socialist-oriented Arab nationalism, policy amounted to assistance and encouragement in the area of socioeconomic development. Viewed with particular favor was the formula of an elite transformation at a reasonably rapid rate by which a technically competent elite would move into subcabinet positions. The assumption was that change must occur to meet the basic material and power demands of a rapidly enlarging middle class. The further assumptions were that such regimes, besides being stable, would provide a favorable setting for the oil industries and would be reasonable about the existence of Israel.

With regard to the more radical Arab regimes, the Kennedy approach was clearly to improve relations, to reestablish meaningful communications, and to exert influence in directions away from close ties with the Communist world and toward tolerance of Israel. Kennedy established a personal correspondence with Nasser and gained a good deal of respect from the more progressive element by his decision to recognize the revolutionary Yemini government. Clearly there was early success in these efforts, but the Kennedy assassination occurred before policy really crystallized in the area. The Kennedy policy quite likely would have reinforced Nasser's position in Arab leadership and, if the conclusion is correct that Nasser was the least interested of the revolutionary Arab leaders in renewed warfare, the effect would have been to make less likely a third round with Israel.

POLICY DEVELOPMENT AFTER 1964

The policy of the Johnson adminstration regarding the Arab-Israeli conflict was certain to be contradictory. Johnson's own view of the Cold War conflict and the threat of world Communism was close to that of John Foster Dulles. That his Middle East policy should begin to parallel that of Dulles is therefore hardly surprising. The Kennedy effort toward *rapprochement* with the more revolutionary Arab regimes was dropped, and relations with that section of the Arab world were permitted to worsen. This is not to suggest that there was conscious policy in the direction of isolating the revolutionary regimes as had appeared with the Eisenhower Doctrine, but the same compulsions were operative. Though there is little evidence to suggest serious interest in political engineering, American relations remained good only with conservative regimes; the policy of encouraging social and economic change in these regimes continued.

Indications of change in American policy as fundamental as that following World War II appeared in this period. The central proposition of this essay has been that American policy relating to the Palestine question has varied in intensity directly with the perception of threat to American security. Economic and ethnic pressure groups have exerted powerful influence, but they have played a secondary determining role. Possibly the most important characteristic of the Johnson years was a remarkably rapid decline in the perception of threat from the Soviet Union. Thus, while Johnson himself appears to have seen the threat persisting, his policy in Vietnam and elsewhere began to come under increasingly serious attack. His administration reacted defensively to the public clamor for de-escalation in Vietnam, but elsewhere in the Cold War area there was a sharp decline in intensity of conflict. This was true of the Middle East where relations between the Soviet Union and Iran and Turkey, in particular, improved considerably. With regard to the Arab-Israeli conflict, the utility of an appeal to American anti-Communism in attracting support against the revolutionary Arab regimes was diminished. This applied both to Israel and to the conservative Arab regimes. Indeed, prior to the sharp increase in Arab resistance to Israel in 1965 and 1966, American policy was restricted to fairly modest sales of arms to Israel and the conservative Arab states.

As the Arab-Israeli conflict intensified, especially in late 1966 and early 1967, the focus of American policy was on the United Nations as a mediating force. Involved as it was in an unpopular war in Vietnam, the United States evinced little interest either in active participation in the dispute or in seeking some solution to the dispute. Virtually nothing was done by American diplomacy until the crisis became really severe in April, 1967. By the time the probability of a third round appeared great, American ability to influence either side was slight. Communications with Cairo or Damascus were very difficult, and Israel showed little indication of following American advice to moderate the dispute, especially since such advice was in no sense part of a formula for a resolution of the overall conflict. To Israel it was always apparent that its security must rest on its own efforts.

Despite Arab perceptions of American-Israeli collusion in the June war, supporting evidence is slight. The perception is based more on long-held assumptions than on observed behavior during the conflict. The best case for collusion was made by Nasser in several speeches. He noted that the United States had made strong representations to Egypt and to Israel not to launch an attack and had asked urgently that Nasser send a representative to Washington to discuss the conflict, especially the announced blockade of the Gulf of Aqaba. Nasser agreed to send Vice-President Zakariyya Mohyeddin to arrive in Washington on June 6. Israel attacked on June 5, and Washington failed to make the kind of strong representation to Israel that could be expected, given what would otherwise appear to be a diplomatic feint.

An alternative explanation for Washington's silence is more in line with the picture presented here, however. The American public in general and American Jews in particular were so pro-Israeli in the conflict that the administration would have risked serious domestic consequences by protesting to Israel. For many days after the attack, Israel refused to admit its initiation of the attack; An American protest, therefore, would have indicated American rejection of the Israeli contention. The mild response to the attack on the American intelligence ship Liberty can be explained similarly.

Given American behavior during and immediately after the 1967 hostilities, the conclusion is strong that the overriding American interest was in halting the conflict and reducing the potential for an East-West confrontation. But by the time of the Glassboro Soviet-American conference, American policy lines were beginning to crystallize. They were to give general diplomatic support to Israel but to play little active role beyond that. Some minor initiatives were taken by the American delegation in the United Nations, but overall policy was passive. Early indications in the Nixon administration suggest a somewhat greater willingness to explore the possibility of a solution through the Big Four, but there is nothing to suggest serious innovation.

The passivity of American policy and the willingness to accommodate the diplomatic interests of Israel in the last two years of the Johnson administration is a natural consequence of the decline in perception of threat from the Soviet Union. As sensitivity to American security interests in the Middle East declines, the concern with the goal of stable, non-Communist regimes in the Arab states should show a parallel decline. This appears to be the case. No really serious effort has been made to restore American influence in those Arab states which broke relations with the United States. As this goal falls in priority, the relative influence on American policy of the American Zionist interest group increases. But because of a decline in security concern, the intensity of American interest in the dispute can be expected to continue to decline. Really active support for Israel in future crises is therefore less likely. Because of the growth of Palestinian resistance to Israel and the significant Arab public support for that activity, the situation of the American oil industry is becoming more tenuous. Whereas it has often been assumed that oil interests and Zionist interests have exercised conflicting pressures on American policy, the above analysis suggests that through most of the Cold War period the two groups were relatively satisfied with American policy, focused as it was on support for conservative Arab regimes which were little threat to Israel. But with the sharpening of the conflict, this is no longer the case. The continued strife is a persistent threat to the internal stability of the conservative states, and the conservative regimes would only be following the dictates of their vested interests to seek to pressure the United States through the oil industry to take a more active and innovative role in pursuing a settlement acceptable to Arab moderates. The attack on the oil pipeline in Israel by the Arab Popular Front in June, 1969, suggests a considerably tougher pressure policy against the oil companies. It may well be that the shift in American policy in this direction under the Nixon administration is in part due to this influence. Hard evidence for such a conclusion, however, is lacking.

The decision to sell 50 phantom jets to Israel against the strong opposition of Arabs coupled with the passive role followed on the diplomatic front reflect Zionist pressure in the determination of American policy in the late 1960s. But as the decade of the 1960s draws to a close, the most important change that is taking place in American policy toward the Palestine question is a decline in interest. Indications are that the era of intense American involvement in the area is coming to a close. As it does, the voice of the bureaucracy in the determination of initial policy is certain to be muted. Instead policy determination is likely to be increasingly reflective of a clash between two powerful and highly assertive interest groups.

14. The Soviet Union and the Palestine Conflict

Ivar Spector

No matter what happens . . . peace or new concessions on the part of Russia . . . sooner or later, Constantinople will be ours.

F. M. Dostoyevsky

By the rivers of Babylon, there we sat down, yea, we wept when we remembered Zion. . . .
If I forget thee, O Jerusalem, let my right hand forget her cunning.

Hebrew Refugees, sixth century B.C.
Psalm 137

How can I forget, I who have been nurtured
On Palestine's most sacred soil?
Soil that sings of heroism
Echoing through the centuries.

Arab Refugees, twentieth century, A.D.
Middle East Journal, Autumn, 1963

To the average Russian Orthodox Christian prior to the Russian Revolution of 1917, the possession of Constantinople (Istanbul), the cradle of Russian orthodoxy, was merely a stepping-stone to the Holy Land of Palestine. Before World War I, when the Russians spoke of Muslims, they meant the non-Arab Muslim world, especially the Turks and Tatars. It was the Bolshevik regime that made Russians cognizant of the Arab world.

413

Dᴉsᴍᴇᴍʙᴇʀᴍᴇɴᴛ ᴏғ
ᴛʜᴇ Oᴛᴛᴏᴍᴀɴ Eᴍᴘɪʀᴇ

In a complete reversal of traditional Anglo-French policy on the Near East, England and France by the secret agreement of March 4–April 10, 1915, promised tsarist Russia at the end of World War I the possession of Constantinople and the Straits. By the subsequent Sykes-Picot Agreement, signed in Petrograd in May, 1916, Turkish territory allocated to Russia included the provinces of Erzerum, Trebizond, Van, and Bitlis, as well as southern Kurdistan. France was to obtain the coastal strip of Syria, Adana, and other territory as far as the Russian frontier. To England went southern Mesopotamia, including Baghdad, and the Syrian ports of Haifa and Acre. The Entente powers took advantage of this opportunity to detach Palestine, with the Holy Places, from the Ottoman Empire, leaving the nature of the regime to be determined by future agreement.

These secret agreements were tantamount to the dismemberment of the Ottoman Empire, the last Asian colonial power in modern times. They were strongly reminiscent of a plan conceived by Nicholas I (1825–55) for the dismemberment of Turkey, which was motivated by both strategic and religious considerations. Had it not been for the Bolshevik (October) Revolution of 1917, the tsarist government would have emerged from World War I with enormous territorial acquisitions in the Near East as well as in the Far East. As early as May, 1917, Lenin's propaganda among Russian soldiers against continuation of that war boldly asked if they wished to fight to enable England to seize Mesopotamia and Palestine.[1]

One of the early steps taken by the victorious Bolshevik regime in 1917, when its leaders became aware of their unpopularity in Europe, was its "Appeal to the Muslims of Russia and the East" (December 5, 1917), urging them to join forces with the Soviet revolution. This Appeal, signed by Lenin and Stalin, repudiated in no uncertain terms the secret agreements entered into by the tsarist regime in 1915–16:

> We declare that the secret treaties of the dethroned Tsar regarding the seizure of Constantinople, which was confirmed by the deposed Kerensky, now are null and void. The Russian Republic and its government, the Council of People's Commissars, are against the seizure of foreign territories. Constantinople must remain in the hands of the Muslims.[2]

---

1. "Tainy vneshnei politiki" [The secrets of foreign policy], *Pravda,* May 10, 1917. See V. I. Lenin, *Sochineniia* [Works] (4th ed.), XXIV, 344.

2. For the complete text of this Appeal, see Ivar Spector, *The Soviet Union and the Muslim World, 1917–1958* (Seattle, 1959), pp. 33–35.

Among the Muslims of the East, to whom the Bolsheviks addressed this Appeal were not only the Turks, Persians, Tatars, and Kirghiz but also the Arabs, the "victims of rapacious European plunderers."

One factor, which may have motivated the Bolsheviks to include the Arabs, especially those of Palestine, in their purview at this time was the Balfour Declaration of November 2, 1917,[3] issued just a few days prior to the Bolshevik seizure of power on November 7. The new Soviet regime was largely dependent on the support of minorities formerly persecuted under the tsars, including the Jews, and especially on the participation of their intelligentsia. The Russian intelligentsia, for the most part, strongly opposed the Communist regime and boycotted it. In the beginning, Soviet leaders rarely trusted the articulate Russian elements of the population, most of whom belonged to the middle and upper classes which later joined the White Armies in an unsuccessful attempt to overthrow the Bolsheviks.

The Balfour Declaration, albeit unintentionally, served to divert a large part of the articulate Jewish population of Soviet Russia from Communism to Zionism. The Jewish Bund, the Jewish counterpart of the Mensheviki (the right wing of the Russian Social Democrats), soon discovered that it constituted a minority in a sea of Zionists. The Bund joined its Soviet comrades in a bitter and sustained anti-Zionist movement. This campaign was accentuated by the fact that Great Britain, author of the Balfour Declaration, was the chief instigator of Allied intervention in Russia in the period 1918–20.[4] To the Bolsheviks, therefore, Zionism became synonymous with treason. When the Jewish Bund, together with other moderate Socialists, fell into disgrace and was disbanded, the small group of Jewish Communists remained the focal point of opposition to Zionism.

Lenin's teachings provide the key to Soviet hostility toward Zionism. This Zionist idea, he once said, "is utterly false and reactionary in its very essence."[5] Lenin equated Zionism with bourgeois nationalism as opposed to proletarian internationalism preached by the Bolsheviks. The idea of a "Jewish nation," in his opinion, introduced alienation and "apartheid" into the workers' movement. It represented an exclusive "ghetto" concept inherited from the tsarist past. When Israel became a

3. The Balfour Declaration stated that "His Majesty's Government view with favour the establishment in Palestine of a National Home for the Jewish people, and will use their best endeavours to facilitate the achievement of this object."

4. "Pis'mo k amerikanskim rabochim" [A letter to American workers] (*Pravda*, August 22, 1918) in which Lenin associated England at one and the same time with seizing Palestine and beginning to seize Russia (Lenin, *Sochineniia* [Works], VII).

5. "Polozhenie bunda v partii" [The position of the bund in the party], *ibid.* p. 83; see also XV, 220–21. For a recent Soviet interpretation of Zionism, see an article by V. Rabinovitch in *Sovetskaia Rossiia* [Soviet Russia], January 24, 1969, pp. 2–3.

state in 1948 its ideology was that of Zionism. Soviet writers since that time have continued to denounce Israel, especially its ruling class, for "aggressive bourgeois nationalism."

With Zionism in disrepute in Soviet Russia, no Zionist was permitted to leave Soviet-occupied territory, especially for Palestine. Many well-known Zionists were "liquidated," or relegated to jails or concentration camps. Toward the end of 1919, however, under the Denikin regime in South Russia, hundreds of Russian Zionists, in the guise of Palestinian refugees, did leave Russia, via Odessa, for Palestine.[6] When the Soviet government learned about this emigration, it permitted the departure of limited numbers of Zionists whose ranks were infiltrated with Communists posing as Zionists. They formed the nucleus of the Communist Party of Palestine, founded in 1919 and admitted to the Comintern in 1924.

SOVIET POLICY IN
THE INTERWAR PERIOD

On July 24, 1922, Palestine became a Class A British mandate under the League of Nations, pending such time as the country was ready for complete independence. The terms of the mandate included the pledge of the Balfour Declaration, obligating Great Britain to create a Jewish national home in Palestine.[7] Under the mandate, England controlled the domestic and foreign relations of Palestine, acquired the right to maintain its own occupation forces there, and controlled communications, the judiciary, and the Holy Places. The Soviet regime, which in 1920 was still boasting of its surrender of all tsarist concessions in Turkey, Persia, and other Muslim states, attacked the mandate system as a mask for the seizure of Turkish and German possessions by the Entente powers.[8] It refused to recognize the Palestine mandate from its inception until its termination on May 15, 1948. The "bankruptcy of British policy in Palestine," according to Soviet interpretation, was revealed by a succession of Arab uprisings in 1920, 1921, 1929, 1933, and 1936–39. From the Soviet

6. The first chartered ship, which sailed for Palestine at the end of 1919 carrying several hundred Zionists, was the *Ruslan*.

7. Helen Miller Davis, *Constitutions, Electoral Laws, Treaties of States in the Near and Middle East* (Durham, N.C., 1953), pp. 328–36.

8. See *Izvestia,* June 22, 1923. The Soviet Union alleged that the mandate system was one reason for its refusal to participate in the League of Nations. In 1934, when the U.S.S.R. did join the League, it specifically restated its negative position on the mandate system (*Izvestia,* September 20, 1934).

standpoint, England established in Palestine "an imperialist regime, a military-police dictatorship, and transformed the country actually into a British colony."[9]

The Soviet government emerged from the civil war (1918–20) with an intervention complex. To prevent a recurrence of this threat to its survival, it delegated to the newly created Third International (Comintern) in 1919 the conduct of an offensive, or counterattack, against the colonial possessions or spheres of influence of England and France, with special emphasis on those in the Middle East adjacent to Soviet Russia. The first Soviet "Appeal to the Muslims of Russia and the East" was issued by the Bolshevik government in 1917. Fearing reprisals from the colonial powers, however, it caused the second Appeal to be issued by the Comintern. On July 3, 1920, the Second Congress of the Third International invited the "enslaved peoples of the Middle East" to meet in Baku, the oil center on the Caspian Sea. This same Congress passed a resolution condemning Zionists activities in Palestine.[10]

The Baku assembly demonstrated that the Arabs were by no means the focus of Soviet concern in 1920. Of the 1,891 delegates who attended, only three were Arabs. There were as yet no independent Arab states in the Near East. The Arabs received occasional, cursory mention in Soviet publications, as the victims of British and French imperialism. To Moscow, however, it was Turkey, Persia, and Afghanistan athwart the Soviet borders—all confronted by English or Anglo-French territorial encroachment —that constituted "the East" awaiting Soviet liberation. It was these three Muslim states, with some support from the West, which stemmed the tide of Soviet expansion into the Arab world and forced the Soviet government to settle for nonaggression pacts with them early in 1921.

For several years thereafter Soviet foreign policy was diverted from the Muslim world of the Near East to other areas. The Soviet government sought to normalize its relations with its European neighbors and to spread revolution in the Far East, especially in China. After Soviet agents were expelled from China in 1927 by the Kuomintang, under Chiang Kai-shek, the U.S.S.R. turned once again to the Arab world. Taking advantage of existing unrest among the Arab peoples against the English and French mandatory powers and of Arab resentment against Zionist immigration into Palestine, it played, at least indirectly, a role in fomenting and aug-

---

9. *Diplomatitcheskii slovar'* [Diplomatic dictionary] (Moscow, 1950), II, 98–99.

10. *Protokoll des zweiten weltkongresses der kommunistischen internationale* [Minutes of the Second World Congress of the Communist International] (Hamburg, 1921), pp. 198, 204.

menting the disturbances in 1929 which spread rapidly throughout Palestine and to other Arab lands.[11]

In 1929 the Stalin regime was engrossed in the First Five-Year Plan. Soviet leaders had little interest in events abroad, including what was brewing in Palestine. The outbreak of riots in Jerusalem in August and their impact throughout the Arab world reawakened Soviet interest in "the progressive revolutionary movement" taking place in the Near East.

At the Sixth Congress of the Comintern (July 19–September 1, 1928), a certain Haydar, a Palestinian delegate, criticized the Third International for its neglect of the Arab question. The Arab world, he insisted, was of great significance to the Comintern because of the confrontation in this small area of "a large number of important problems and questions, with different types of imperialist policy and all forms of colonial bondage."[12] When the riots occurred in Palestine, the Comintern attributed them to the "dismemberment of Arabistan into numerous small countries," "disfranchisement of the basic mass of the population" (the Arabs), "violent Zionist colonization," and the "growing pressure of British and French imperialism" in the Arab countries.[13] In this struggle, the Comintern accused the "Zionist bourgeois colonizers and their lackeys" of playing the role of direct agents of British imperialism, in contrast to the *fallahin* and Bedouins who provided the main driving force of the revolutionary movement.

The Communist Party of Palestine, comprised predominantly of Jews, was caught by surprise by the 1929 revolt. It was severely criticized by the Comintern for misunderstanding the revolutionary character of the Arab uprising as a "general national anti-imperialist peasant revolt," for its failure to make of the Palestinian Communist Party a Jewish-Arab movement, and for its lethargy in neglecting to support the movement. Its number-one task for the future, as outlined by the Comintern, was the "Arabization of the party from top to bottom," including the creation of Arab or joint Arab-Jewish trade-union organizations, the drafting of an agrarian program reflecting the demands of the *fallahin* and Bedouins,

11. For an account of, and comment on, these riots, see A. Shami, "Palestinskoe vosstanie i Arabskii vostok" [The Palestine insurrection and the Arab East], *Revoliutsionnyi vostok* [The Revolutionary East], no. 8, 1930, pp. 25–52.

12. *Stenografitcheskii otchet VI kongressa kominterna* [Stenographic account of the VI Comintern Congress], IV, pp. 144–47.

13. See "The Resolution of the Political Secretariat of the Executive Committee of the Communist International on 'The Insurgent Movement in Arabistan,' " October 16, 1929, in Xenia Joukoff Eudin and Robert M. Slusser, *Soviet Foreign Policy, 1928–1934: Documents and Materials* (University Park, Pa., 1966), I, 210–19, Document 33.

and the exposure of Zionism and Mejlis Islam as agents of imperialist reaction.[14]

Perhaps because of the inadequacy of the Palestinian Communists in time of crisis, a recommendation was made shortly thereafter for the restoration of the successful Imperial Orthodox Palestine Association (established in 1882), which had engaged in extensive charitable and educational activity prior to World War I and which emphasized not only scholarly research but also the cause of Arab betterment at the expense of the Greek Orthodox clergy.[15] This recommendation was not implemented at the time, possibly because of the course of international events during the next decade. After World War II, however, the Soviet government recovered from Israel some of the property of the Palestine Association and conducted a program of Soviet cultural propaganda in the Near East.

The record of Soviet participation in the Palestinian revolutionary movement of 1929 and their plans for the future of Palestine and the Arab lands are to be found in the secret documents on the programs of the Communist Party for the Arab countries, published in 1928. These were followed by another secret program on "The Tasks of the Communist Party of Palestine in the Countryside," published in 1931 in Arabic and Hebrew.[16] This anti-Zionist document, intended for the Arabs, is still of major significance. Although it was written in a different time and against a different background, it represents, almost *in toto,* the arguments used today in the Soviet press. These, and other documents pertaining to the Middle East and Palestine, were published in 1934 by the Marx-Engels-Lenin Institute of the Central Committee of the All-Russian Communist Party (Bolshevik) under the title *Documents of the Programs of the Communist Parties of the East.* Except for a brief summation of one and one-half pages, this publication remained largely unknown in the West until 1956, when an English translation became available.[17]

The purpose of these documents was to provide a guide for the Communist Parties of the Middle East as to how, with the aid of the Soviet Union, they could take over Palestine and the other Arab lands. This was to be accomplished in three stages: (1) The colonizing power must be expelled by means of an intensive national liberation movement — a

14. Mejlis Islam was an organization of Arab nobility and clergy.

15. The recommendation was made by D. Semenov in *Novyi Vostok* [New East], nos. 8–9, 1929, p. 210 ff. On the Imperial Orthodox Palestine Association, see T. G. Stavrou, *Russian Interests in Palestine, 1882–1914: A Study of Religious and Educational Enterprise* (Thessaloniki, Greece: Institute for Balkan Studies, 1963), p. 69 ff.

16. This document also appeared in Russian in *Revoliutsionnyi vostok* [The Revolutionary East], nos. 1–2, 1932, pp. 297–302.

17. See Spector, *The Soviet Union and the Muslim World,* pp. 110–80.

campaign against colonialism which, in their opinion, would create a united front of all classes except the direct agents of imperialism. (2) Once national independence had been achieved, the local Communists must conduct a campaign among the workers and peasant masses to the effect that political sovereignty was not enough — that complete liberation involved a social, as well as a political, revolution; the liberated state, therefore, must pass to the control of the workers and peasants. (3) The final stage was the seizure of power by the Communist Party. This guide became and has remained the basis of Soviet policy in the Middle East.

In general, during the decade of the thirties, there was no significant Soviet action in Palestine and the Near East. Soviet activity, for the most part, was restricted to the blueprint for Communism, outlined above, and to instructions and guidance to local Communist groups, which were weak and inarticulate, and which, in most instances, had been driven underground. The main reason for the comparative lull in Soviet-Arab relations was the rise of Fascism and Nazism in Europe and their impact on the Near and Middle East. The Arab rebellion of 1936–39, unlike that of 1929, occasioned little Soviet response. This was due to tension abroad and the Stalin purges at home, which removed from the scene or frightened into silence the remaining Soviet experts on the Middle East.[18]

During these years, the anti-Semitism of the Hitler regime evoked a sympathetic response among some Arab nationalists, especially in Palestine.[19] English officials in Palestine were inclined to tolerate the Nazis because they were anti-Communist. Although, as a result, the Soviet government may well have become disillusioned with the Arabs in the late thirties, it was in no position to assume an aggressive role in the Near East until the end of World War II. By 1945, due to the impressive victories of the Red Army, the Soviet Union enjoyed unprecedented prestige throughout Asia.

COLD WAR DIPLOMACY

At the end of World War II, the U.S.S.R. confidently anticipated the expansion of Soviet territory into the Near and Middle East by the acquisition of northern Iran and military bases from Turkey at the Dardanelles. Largely due to American leadership in the United Nations — a

18. See Walter Z. Laqueur, *The Soviet Union and the Middle East* (New York, 1959), pp. 115–18.
19. See A. M. Nekritch, *Vneshniaia politika Anglii, 1939–1941* [The foreign policy of England, 1939–1941] (Moscow, 1963), pp. 436–37.

new factor in the Mediterranean and Middle East — the Soviet government reluctantly and belatedly observed wartime treaty commitments (January 29, 1942) and withdrew Red Army occupation forces from Iran in May, 1946. The Stalin government then confronted the Turks with a five-point program, tantamount to an ultimatum, demanding that Turkey share with the U.S.S.R. responsibility for the defense of the Straits. Alarmed by Communist efforts in Greece and the prospect of an early English withdrawal from that beleaguered country as well as by Soviet designs on the Straits, the United States government on March 12, 1947, officially announced the extension of American aid to Greece and Turkey—the so-called Truman Doctrine.

The Truman Doctrine established the position of the United States in the eastern Mediterranean as the successor to traditional Anglo-French leadership. As the Cold War replaced wartime Allied collaboration, the prime objective of Anglo-American policy was to "contain" Soviet expansion. In the Near East, the only remaining opportunity open to the Soviet government to outflank its opponents was in the Arab world—in particular, in Palestine. By 1947 the British mandate there had produced widespread discontent among both Jews and Arabs. Signaling a shift in Soviet policy, the Stalin regime in 1947 began to use the term *Jews* instead of *Zionists* with reference to the Jewish population of Palestine. By posing as the friend of both Jews and Arabs, it apparently hoped to accelerate the British withdrawal from Palestine, as the Soviets themselves had been forced to retreat from Iran and Turkey, and the French from Syria and Lebanon. The departure of the Western "imperialists" from the Near and Middle East was the first and most important plank in the Soviet program for that area.

When the disposition of the British mandate in Palestine was referred to the United Nations (April–May, 1947), the Soviet delegation at once insisted that British policy was bankrupt, that the mandate be terminated, that British troops be withdrawn immediately from the country, and that the peoples of Palestine be granted complete independence, thereby "liquidating" colonialism. The U.S.S.R. opposed the creation in Palestine of a "purely Arab" or a "purely Jewish" state. It would have preferred the establishment of a binational, independent Arab-Jewish state, much in line with current Arab demands.[20] When deteriorating relations between Arabs and Jews appeared to render this solution impracticable, the Soviets openly supported the partition of Palestine into two independent states—one Arab and one Jewish.

20. See A. G. Mileikovskii, *Mezhdunarodnye otnosheniia posle mirovoi voiny* [International relations after the world war], AN, SSSR (Moscow, 1962), p. 265.

The United Nations resolution of November 29, 1947, adopted by the second session of the General Assembly, called for the termination of the mandate, the withdrawal of British troops, and the partition of the country into Arab and Jewish states, leaving Jerusalem under a United Nations trusteeship. This crucial decision was in substantial agreement with Soviet policy. According to S. K. Tsarapkin, representative of the U.S.S.R. at the United Nations First Committee on the Palestine Question (November 22, 1948), "this was the only right and just decision of the question, corresponding to the fundamental national interests of both the Jewish and Arab peoples of Palestine, each of whom has the right to self-determination and the right to establish its own independent state."[21]

Although the United States, unlike Great Britain, voted in favor of the resolution of November 29, 1947, in the months that followed, the American government opposed the plan as impracticable. The American alternative was to place Palestine under a United Nations trusteeship. At the special assembly of the United Nations (April–May, 1948) called to reconsider the Palestine question, the Soviet delegation vigorously opposed any change in the resolution of November 29 and attacked the "imperialist essence of the American trusteeship plan." Both the American plan and an English proposal for the establishment of a "provisional" or "neutral" regime failed to pass. On May 15, 1948, immediately following the termination of the Palestine mandate, the Provisional Jewish National Council of Palestine proclaimed the formation in the Jewish part of the country of the state of Israel.

There is reason to believe that the Soviet government would have preferred to be the first of the great powers to recognize Israel. During the Cold War, however, such action on the part of the U.S.S.R. might have led the Western powers to withhold recognition. The United States was the first major power to extend *de facto* recognition to Israel. On May 17, the U.S.S.R. followed suit, with *de jure* recognition. The Soviets boasted that their action constituted a more decisive and a more sincere step, which served to prevent the return of the occupying forces of Great Britain to an independent country.

Immediately following the establishment of the state of Israel, a coalition of Arab states invaded Palestine and confronted the Jewish state. The Soviet government indignantly branded Arab action as "an act of aggression." The Arabs were accused of serving as "pawns" in England's imperialist game, the object of which was to restore English colonial

21. *Vneshniaia politika Sovetskogo Soyuza: dokumenty i materialy, 1948 god, Chast' vtoraia* [Foreign policy of the Soviet Union: Documents and materials, 1948, second part] (Moscow, 1951), p. 422.

domination in Palestine and the Near East.[22] According to *Pravda* (August 28, 1948),

> As early as May of this year, when the rulers of the Arab states, in order to please the foreign imperialists, unleashed an aggressive war against the legally constituted state of Israel, the representative of the Soviet Union proposed that the Security Council immediately issue an order demanding a halt to military operations in Palestine, in accordance with Article 39 of the Charter.[23]

According to Soviet interpretation, England was primarily responsible for the Arab invasion of Israel in 1948.

Prior to the outbreak of the Arab-Israeli conflict in 1948, the Soviet government had become highly critical of the Arab League which, it alleged, was sacrificing the interests of the Arab peoples to those of Great Britain and which had become "a handy instrument of British policy in the Near East."[24] When the Arab League was established in 1945, the Soviet response was by no means entirely negative. The League was believed to include some "progressive" elements, too weak, as yet, to offset the designs of British and American "imperialists."[25] Undoubtedly, Soviet leaders had not yet forgotten the collaboration of some Arab leaders with the Nazis. It was their understanding that the League had not been created by the Arabs themselves for the promotion of Arab interests, and that England hoped to use it to establish a "greater" Arab state out of Syria, Lebanon, Transjordan, and Palestine, under British tutelage.

During the Arab-Israeli crisis of 1948, the Soviets became highly suspicious of the "feverish activity" of the Arab League in opposition to the United Nations resolution of November 29, 1947, and in favor of the creation of armed Arab Volunteer Units. They subsequently blamed the Arab League for playing an "ignominious role" in aggravating the Arab-Jewish conflict and in kindling the Palestinian war, thereby weaken-

---

22. V. B. Lutskii, *Angliiskii i Amerikanskii imperializm na Blizhnem Vostoke* [English and American imperialism in the Near East] (Moscow, 1948), p. 27.

23. A. Belokon, "The Plot Against the Peoples of Palestine," *Soviet Press Translations* (hereafter, *SPT*), Vol. III, No. 20, November 15, 1948, p. 618.

24. See M. Melekhov, "The Arab League and the Independence of the Arab States" (*Pravda*, March 24, 1948) *SPT*, Vol. III, No. 11, June 1, 1948, 324–26.

25. See V. B. Lutskii, *Liga Arabskikh Gosudarstv* [The League of Arab States] (Moscow, 1946); and P. V. Milogradov, *Arabski Vostok v mezhdunarodnikh otnosheniakh* [The Arab East in international relations] (Moscow, 1946), pp. 10–11.

ing the Arab national liberation movement.[26] A report reached Soviet authorities that the commander of the Arab Volunteer Units in Palestine, raising the Russian bogey, had falsely claimed that three Russian battalions were engaged in fighting the Volunteers, and that one colonel-general had been killed fighting the Arabs and a second hanged by them.[27]

If, as the Soviets alleged, Great Britain hoped for the defeat of Israel by the Arab forces to which the British had extended military aid, this failed to materialize, much to Soviet satisfaction. The Soviet labor organ *Trud* (January 11, 1949) stated:

> As we know, the hopes entertained by British ruling circles for the defeat of the Jewish troops and for the liquidation of the state of Israel with the assistance of a coalition of Arab countries, have not been realized. This forced England and the USA to change their tactics.[28]

The Soviet government vigorously opposed the plan advanced by the United Nations mediator, Count Folke Bernadotte, and backed by England and the United States as the "solution" to the Palestine question. It would have wrecked the earlier U.N. decision for the creation of two independent states, one Arab and one Jewish. The Bernadotte plan provided for the transfer of the Negev, which constituted two-thirds of the Jewish state, together with the Arab part of Palestine to Transjordan, ruled by the English "puppet" Abdullah. S. K. Tsarapkin, on November 22, 1948, angrily protested that the aim of the British was to prevent the creation of a Palestinian Arab state and "to permit . . . Abdullah to annex not only the areas of Palestine which were to be part of the Arab state of Palestine, but also to annex the Negev, which was to be part of the Jewish state."[29] Andrei Vyshinsky, Soviet foreign minister, spoke in the same vein before the Plenary Session of the U.N. General Assembly on the Palestine question, on December 11, 1948.[30] The implication of Soviet comments was that barring outside intervention the Arabs and Jews would have settled their own problems peacefully, in line with the U.N. resolution of November 29, 1947.

26. Lutskii, *Angliiskii i Amerikanskii imperializm na Blizhnem Vostoke* [English and American imperialism in the Near East], pp. 8–9.

27. M. Melekhov, "The Arab League," p. 324.

28. V. Mayev, "Behind the Scenes in Palestine," *SPT*, Vol. IV, No. 7, April 1, 1949, p. 214.

29. *Vneshniaia politika Sovetskogo Soyuza: dokumenty i materialy, 1948* [Foreign policy of the Soviet Union: Documents and materials, 1948], Part II, p. 427.

30. *Ibid.*, pp. 513–24.

During the Palestine crisis, 1947–48, the U.S.S.R. consistently upheld the U.N. resolution of November 29 in the expectation of gaining a foothold in Jewish Palestine. This it could accomplish only by driving out the British, the mandatory power. The Soviets supported Israel because the Jews opposed the perpetuation of the British mandate. The British, on the other hand, dubious as to the ability of an independent Palestinian Arab state to defend itself, were successful in attaching the Palestinian Arabs to Transjordan, from which there emerged the new state of Jordan. The real losers in the Palestinian crisis of 1948 were the Palestinian Arabs, who failed to secure their own independent state in Palestine.

Although the Arabs have blamed the British and Americans for the establishment of the state of Israel, in 1948 the U.S.S.R. openly took the credit for this development. Without Soviet support and Czech arms, it is doubtful that infant Israel could have survived as an independent state. Had England not lent its support to the Arabs, there might have remained a Transjordan but it is doubtful that there would have emerged a state of Jordan.

During the Palestine crisis, the Soviet government made much of the vacillation (the *volte-faces*) in British and especially in American policy in contrast to the "principled consistency" of the foreign policy of the U.S.S.R. In reality, what the U.S.S.R. stigmatized in its opponents in 1949 is precisely what has characterized Soviet policy toward Palestine over the years. Throughout the 1929 revolt, the Soviet position was pro-Arab and anti-Zionist. Although Soviet enthusiasm for the Arab cause waned during the 1930s with the impact of Fascism and Nazism in the Near East, following World War II there was renewed interest in "progressive" Arab leadership. In an abrupt *volte-face* in 1947, however, the U.S.S.R. just as staunchly supported the formation of the state of Israel and denounced Arab "aggression" against it. Before the end of 1948, another Soviet cooling-off period toward Israel had already begun.

DETERIORATION OF
SOVIET-ISRAELI RELATIONS

Ilya Ehrenburg, the well-known Soviet Jewish novelist and journalist, heralded the approaching deterioration in Soviet-Israeli relations. Replying in *Pravda* (September 21, 1948) to a German Jewish refugee who asked for an explanation of "the attitude of the Soviet Union toward the state of Israel," he pointed out that Israel was already "experiencing another invasion, less noisy, but no less dangerous—the invasion of Anglo-American capitalists." Israel, he claimed, was not ruled by the working masses, but by the Israeli bourgeoisie, who might be expected to betray the national interests of Israel "in the name of the dollar." According to Ehrenburg, the Soviet people sympathized with the struggle of "the toilers of Israel," but national independence had not brought into being a new social system:

> The citizen of a socialist society looks upon the people of any bourgeois country, including likewise the people of the state of Israel, as upon wayfarers who have not yet made their way out of a dark forest. The destiny of a people dragging the yoke of capitalist exploitation can never allure the citizens of a socialist society.[31]

Speaking ex cathedra in *Pravda,* Ehrenburg no doubt voiced some of the real reasons for the subsequent estrangement between Israel and the U.S.S.R. As long as Israel starred as the opponent of Anglo-American policy in the Near East, the U.S.S.R., in line with its own interests, championed the cause of Israel. Once conditions were normalized and Israel, as an independent state, demonstrated its intent to do business with the capitalist regimes of Great Britain and the United States, the Soviet-Israeli honeymoon came to an end. In 1951 Israel signed with the United States a "Treaty of Friendship, Trade and Navigation."[32] As "the tool of Wall Street" and the American monopolists, the Soviet image of Israel ceased to be that of the democratic, independent state, which the U.S.S.R. had helped bring into being. On the tenth anniversary of the declaration of the state of Israel, the scholarly Soviet periodical *Sovetskoe Vostokovedenie,* [Soviet Eastern studies] declared:

> The history of the past decade has indicated that the government of Israel has actually been transformed into the faithful servant of American colonizers in the Near and Middle East.[33]

The resurgence of Zionism following the establishment of Israel, with its unwelcome impact inside the U.S.S.R., contributed to the worsening of Soviet-Israeli relations. A new Anglo-American threat to the "independ-

31. "Apropos of a Certain Letter," SPT, Vol. III, No. 20, November 15, 1948, p. 625.
32. This treaty was not ratified by Israel until 1954. See also G. S. Nikitina, "Israil' i Amerikanskii imperializm" [Israel and American imperialism], *Sovetskoe Vostokovedenie* [Soviet Eastern studies], No. 5 (1958), p. 73.
33. *Ibid.,* p. 72.

ence" of the Arab countries soon resulted in a marked improvement in Soviet-Arab relations, especially those with Egypt.

Soviet policy on the Palestine question, like Anglo-American policy, was subject to change as circumstances altered. The guideline to Soviet policy was the Soviet government's concept of its own interests rather than those of Palestine. After 1950 Soviet interpretation of the Palestine conflict of 1948 underwent basic changes. In assessing the war guilt, the U.S.S.R. began to blame the "reactionary" governments of both Israel and the Arab states which were said to have acted under pressure from Great Britain and the United States.[34] Once the Khrushchev regime made its deal with Nasser, Israel was stigmatized as the sole aggressor in 1948.[35]

After World War II, the governments of Great Britain, France and the United States explored ways and means of establishing a multilateral Middle East Command for the defense of that area against the U.S.S.R. A British proposal to multilateralize Middle East defense by inviting Australia, New Zealand, France, and Turkey to form an Allied Defense Command proved unpalatable to the Wafd regime in Egypt. The four powers —Great Britain, France, the United States, and Turkey—then explored the possibility of building a Middle East Defense Command with the collaboration and participation of the Arab states and Israel.

The Soviet government reacted with alacrity to the prospect of such a hostile bloc on the southern periphery of the Soviet Union. On November 21, 1951, the U.S.S.R. warned the governments of Egypt, Syria, Lebanon, Iraq, Saudi Arabia, Yemen, and Israel to reject the invitation of the four powers (issued October 14, 1951) on the ground that it would infringe upon their independence, that foreign troops would once again be stationed on their soil, that their resources would be placed at the disposition of foreign powers, and that their relations with the U.S.S.R. would suffer.[36] Three days later the Soviet government likewise notified the United States, Great Britain, France, and Turkey—the initiators of this bloc—that the U.S.S.R. "cannot stand idly by while these new aggressive plans for the creation of a Middle East Command are being formulated in an area adjacent to the boundaries of the Soviet Union" and threatened to hold the above-mentioned powers responsible for the consequences of such a move.[37]

---

34. See, for example, the article on "Palestine" in *Bol'shaia Sovetskaia entsiklopedia* [The great Soviet encyclopedia] (Moscow, 1955), XXXI, 602.

35. See V. P. Nikhamin, ed., *Mezhdunarodnye otnosheniia i vneshniaia Politika Sovetskogo Soyuza, 1950–1959* [International relations and the foreign policy of the Soviet Union, 1950–1959] (Moscow, 1960), p. 94.

36. V. Ya. Sipols, *et al.*, eds., *SSSR i Arabski strany, 1917–1961: dokumenty i materialy* [The U.S.S.R. and the Arab countries, 1917–1961: Documents and materials] (Moscow, 1961), pp. 103–6.

37. *Ibid.*, p. 108.

Even without Soviet intervention, there is reason to doubt that in 1951 the Arab states would have joined a Middle East Command against the U.S.S.R. The Arab states were still suffering from the humiliation of their defeat in the Palestine conflict of 1948 and were divided among themselves over the leadership of the Arab world. Most of them were still unaware of a Soviet "menace." They were more concerned about threats to their newly won independence from Great Britain and France, with which they had had direct and recent experience.

About Israel's position the Soviet government had reason to be doubtful. In 1950 Israel had welcomed the Tripartite Declaration of the United States, Great Britain, and France, guaranteeing the frontiers established by the armistice agreements at the end of the Palestine conflict of 1948. Its government had affirmed its adherence to the basic purposes of NATO, of which the Middle East Command might be considered a Mediterranean counterpart. It also came out in support of American policy in the Korean war, still being waged in the Far East. Israel's foreign policy, in other words, had veered appreciably toward the West. Surrounded by hostile Arab states, the government of Israel was largely dependent on the support of the Western powers. It was hardly likely, however, to enter a military bloc opposed by its Arab neighbors.

The U.S.S.R. took the credit for "exposing" the machinations back of the project for a Middle East Command and for the failure of the Arab states and Israel to join the anti-Soviet bloc.[38] The Anglo-American purpose was subsequently achieved with the conclusion of the Turkish-Pakistani pact of 1954, followed in February, 1955, by an agreement between Turkey and Iraq. The series of agreements (1954–55) that constituted the Baghdad Pact aroused the Soviet government to the danger of conflict in the Near and Middle East.[39]

The involvement of the Arab state of Iraq in the Baghdad Pact encouraged the Soviet Union to associate itself with the widespread protests evoked by this pact in other parts of the Arab world. The Soviet government reminded all concerned that it had warmly supported the independence of Egypt, Saudi Arabia, Syria, Lebanon, Yemen, Jordan, Libya,

---

38. See M. E. Airapetian and G. A. Deborin, *Etapy vneshnei politiki SSSR* [Stages of the foreign policy of the U.S.S.R.] (Moscow, 1961), pp. 392–93; and Nikhamin, *Mezhdunarodnye otnosheniia* [International relations], pp. 82–83.

39. "Zayavlenie Ministerstva Inostrannykh del SSSR o bezopasnosti na Blizhnem i Srednem Vostoke" [A statement by the Ministry of Foreign Affairs of the U.S.S.R. on the security in the Near and Middle East], April 16, 1955, Sipols, *SSSR i Arabskie strany* [The U.S.S.R. and the Arab countries], p. 118.

Sudan, Iraq, Israel, and other states.[40] The Baghdad Pact, according to the Soviet Ministry of Foreign Affairs, was contributing to increased tension in the Middle East. Since Israel, as was to be expected, did not join the Arabs in opposition to the pact, the Soviets forecast a worsening of relations between the Arab states and Israel.

Arab hostility to the Baghdad Pact led to a series of defense agreements among the Arab states, directed primarily against Israel.[41] By May, 1956, all the Arab states, with the exception of Iraq, to the satisfaction of the U.S.S.R. "were bound together by mutual obligations against Israel, and likewise by the obligation to extend aid to one another, in the event of aggression."[42]

CONSOLIDATION OF
SOVIET-ARAB RELATIONS

In April, 1956, the Soviet Ministry of Foreign Affairs voiced its special concern about the danger of conflict between the Arab states and Israel.[43] It accused the Western powers of using the Arab-Israeli dispute over Palestine as an excuse for intervention in the internal affairs of independent Arab states and deployment of foreign troops in the Near East. The somewhat conciliatory Soviet proposal with regard to Palestine, clearly a result of the Baghdad Pact, was prepared by the Foreign Ministry:

1. The Soviet Union will lend the necessary support to measures undertaken by the United Nations, directed toward a search for ways and means of strengthening peace in the Palestine area and toward the implementation of the corresponding decisions of the Security Council.

2. The Soviet Union considers that there must be accepted in the near future measures for easing existing tensions in the Palestine area without

---

40. "Zayavlenie Ministerstva Inostrannykh del SSSR o polozhenii na Blizhnem Vostoke" [A statement by the Ministry of Foreign Affairs of the U.S.S.R. on the Near East situation], April 17, 1956, *ibid.*, p. 133.

41. These pacts included October 25, 1955, Egypt and Syria; October 27, 1955, Egypt and Saudi Arabia, followed shortly thereafter by Syria and Saudi Arabia; January 13, 1956, Syria and Lebanon; April 11, 1956, Syria and Jordan; April 21, 1956, Saudi Arabia, Egypt and Yemen; May, 1956, Egypt and Jordan.

42. Nikhamin, *Mezhdunarodnye otnosheniia* [International relations], p. 95.

43. "Zayavlenie Ministerstva Inostrannykh del SSSR o polozhenii na Blizhnem Vostoke" [A statement by the Ministry of Foreign Affairs of the U.S.S.R. on the Near East situation], April 17, 1956, Sipols, *SSSR i arabskie strany* [The U.S.S.R. and the Arab countries], pp. 133–35.

outside intervention, which is contrary to the will of the Near Eastern states and the principles of the United Nations.

The Soviet Union calls upon the interested parties to refrain from any action which might lead to the aggravation of the situation on the existing line of demarcation established by the armistice between the Arab countries and Israel, and likewise to make the necessary efforts to improve the distressing position of hundreds of thousands of Arab refugees, deprived of shelter and the means of subsistence.

3. The Soviet Union considers, that in the interests of strengthening international peace and security it is indispensable to conclude a solid peace and the settlement of the Palestine question, based on mutual agreement, and taking into consideration the legitimate national interests of the parties concerned.

On its part, the Soviet government expresses its readiness, along with the other states, to help to bring about a peaceful solution of the unsettled questions.[44]

The Western powers ignored this Soviet gesture, no doubt convinced that any agreement about Palestine would involve the scrapping of the Baghdad Pact. This Soviet proposal appears to be one of the few instances in which the U.S.S.R. in its official communications after 1948 made reference to the plight of the Palestinian refugees.

By 1956 the U.S.S.R. had become a creditor nation—a factor which enhanced its prestige in the Middle East.[45] An Israeli attack on Gaza in February, 1955, forced President Nasser to look for arms abroad. Having opposed the Baghdad Pact, which split the Arab states, and having encountered difficulty in securing arms from the West, he veered toward the Soviet bloc. In September, 1955, Egypt and Czechoslovakia entered into negotiations for Egyptian purchase of Czech arms. The resulting arms deal, which permitted the U.S.S.R. to pose as the only true friend of the Arab peoples, precipitated an armament race in the Middle East. France, which had provided Israel with small quantities of arms prior to this time, substantially increased its shipments thereafter. Thus the Soviet Union, which in 1948 had provided Israel with the weapons needed to fight its war of liberation, in 1955 began to equip the armed forces of Egypt, Israel's sworn enemy.

44. *Ibid.,* p. 135.
45. As early as February, 1955, the Soviet government offered economic and technical assistance, "with no strings attached," to Middle East states.

During the Suez crisis of July–October, 1956, which stemmed from the withdrawal of Anglo-American offers to help Egypt with the building of the Aswan High Dam and Egypt's retaliatory action in nationalizing the Suez Canal (July 26, 1956), the U.S.S.R. sided unequivocally with Egypt. The Soviet government lauded Egyptian policy as one more legitimate step toward the liberation of that country from the vestiges of its colonial past.[46] Tsarist Russia having been one of the signatories of the Constantinople Convention of 1888 on Suez, the U.S.S.R. was now directly and legitimately involved in the affairs of the Arab world—a situation the Western powers had long sought to avoid.

In spite of the prolonged crisis, during which no settlement was reached at the United Nations, Soviet leaders revealed no undue alarm about an imminent outbreak of hostilities in the Near East.[47] Marshal Bulganin, chairman of the Soviet Council of Ministers, directed several messages to Great Britain and France, urging a peaceful solution of the Suez issue. He denied that the U.S.S.R. had incited Egypt to action and claimed that the Soviet government had "learned about the nationalization of the Canal only from the radio."[48] On October 5, 1956, the U.S.S.R. vetoed a proposal before the U.N. Security Council for a Suez Canal Users' Association, which would have deprived Egypt of control of the Canal. Israel's abrupt invasion of Egypt on October 29, while negotiations were still under way, appears to have taken both Egypt and the U.S.S.R. by surprise. When, two days later, Great Britain and France, in what proved to be a predetermined intervention, joined Israel in military operations against Egypt, the U.S.S.R. openly sided with Egypt.

The swift reverses suffered by Egypt in the Suez conflict led the U.S.S.R. to seek, through the United Nations and by means of correspondence with the heads of all governments involved, an early end to hostilities and the withdrawal of all foreign forces from Egypt. The Soviet Union severed diplomatic relations with Israel and terminated a Soviet-Israeli commercial agreement for the supply of fuel. On November 1, the Soviet government declared null and void the Anglo-French-American *(Troika)* Tripartite Declaration of 1950 which guaranteed the borders of the Near Eastern states. Marshal Bulganin brushed aside the explanation of Prime Minister Ben-Gurion of Israel about Egyptian provocations—the *fedayeen* raids

---

46. See *Izvestia,* July 28, 1956, and *Pravda,* July 29, 1956.

47. See, for example, *Izvestia,* October 10, 1956, and *Pravda,* October 16, 1956.

48. Bulganin's letters of September 11, September 28, and October 23, 1956, were published in *Izvestia,* April 23, 1957. On Soviet policy during the crisis, see also D. T. Shepilov, *Suetskii vopros* [The Suez question] (Moscow, 1956), which includes the Soviet foreign minister's statements and declarations.

into Israel, the economic boycott, the indoctrination of Egyptian military leaders and troops about the destruction of Israel, violation of the Security Council resolution permitting free passage for Israeli ships through the Suez Canal, and the recently concluded military pact by Egypt, Jordan, and Syria—all of which required Israel to act in self-defense.[49] Bulganin proposed to President Eisenhower the joint use of the American and Soviet fleets in the Mediterranean to impose the United Nations decision for an immediate end to hostilities.[50] In a direct warning to Israel, he accused that country of acting "as the tool of foreign imperialist forces" and of challenging all the peoples of the East:

> Fulfilling a foreign will and acting in accordance with orders from the outside, the government of Israel criminally and irresponsibly toys with the fate of the world and the fate of its own people. It sows hatred of the state of Israel among the peoples of the East, such as cannot fail to affect the future of Israel and may pose the question of the very existence of Israel as a state.[51]

On November 10, the official Soviet news agency TASS hinted that the U.S.S.R. was prepared to send to Egypt as "volunteers" Soviet fliers, tank operators, artillerymen and officers, veterans of World War II. Soviet threats to use force to crush the "aggressors" and prevent a third world war were made only when it became clear that the United States would not join the invaders. Although the U.S.S.R. was never called upon to implement its threats, the threats produced a favorable response throughout the Arab world.

From the beginning of the Suez conflict, the Soviet government adopted a consistently hostile tone toward Israel. In Soviet assessments of responsibility for the war, not a shadow of war guilt rested upon Egypt and the other Arab states. Soviet leaders demanded that Israel (as well as Great Britain and France) compensate Egypt for the destruction of Egyptian cities and populated areas and for the closing of the Suez Canal and the destruction of its facilities; they further demanded that Israel return all Egyptian (much of it Soviet) property confiscated and removed by its

49. Ben-Gurion to Bulganin, November 8, 1956, published in *Pravda* and *Izvestia*, November 16, 1956; this was a reply to Bulganin's letter of November 5, published in *Izvestia*, November 6, 1956.

50. Bulganin to Eisenhower, November 5, 1956, published in *Pravda* and *Izvestia*, November 6, 1956.

51. Bulganin to Ben-Gurion, November 5, 1956, published in *Pravda* and *Izvestia*, November 6, 1956; a second letter followed, November 15, 1956.

invading armies.[52] The hostile propaganda of the U.S.S.R. accentuated the hatred of Israel in the Arab world, which the Soviet Union was arming against its enemy.

The primary concern of the U.S.S.R. was to secure the early withdrawal from "every inch" of Egyptian territory of all foreign troops, including those of Israel. Israel's procrastination in this respect, in spite of United Nations demands for immediate withdrawal, aroused Soviet fears that the Western powers were once again using Israel to advance their own interests in the Middle East. Without the collusion of Great Britain, France, and the United States, according to A. A. Sobolev, Soviet representative at the United Nations General Assembly, Israel would never have dared to attack Egypt or to sabotage the decision of the General Assembly in regard to the immediate and unconditional withdrawal of Israeli troops from Egypt.[53]

The Suez conflict of 1956 produced a settlement which lasted for a decade. This settlement afforded some positive advantages to those involved in the war, with the exception of Great Britain and France. Egypt retained possession of the Suez Canal. The Anglo-French-Israeli invading armies were withdrawn from Egyptian soil. Israel won access to the Gulf of Aqaba and the Straits of Tiran. Because Israel complied with demands for the withdrawal of its forces from Egyptian territory, it secured from the Eisenhower government a guarantee of Israeli sovereignty and the integrity of Israeli territory. A United Nations Emergency Force was stationed in the Sinai and at the entrance to the Gulf of Aqaba (Sharm al-Sheikh) to insure border peace between Egypt and Israel. United States prestige was greatly enhanced as a result of its opposition to an invasion which involved its NATO allies. It was the U.S.S.R., however, that emerged as the real champion of the Arab world and as an important factor, henceforth, in eastern Mediterranean affairs. The only real losers were Great Britain and France, whose aggression brought them nothing but discredit and for whose defeat the United States received the blame.

The Eisenhower Doctrine of 1957, another outgrowth of the Suez conflict, provided the U.S.S.R. with a new propaganda weapon by which to influence the Arab world. This doctrine, which authorized the president

---

52. Bulganin to Ben-Gurion, November 15, 1956, published in *Pravda* and *Izvestia*, November 16, 1956.

53. "Vystuplenie predstavitelia SSSR A. A. Soboleva na plenarnom zasedanii XI sessii general'noi assamblei OON po voprosu o vyvode Israil'skikh voisk iz Egipta" [The speech of the Soviet representative A. A. Sobolev to the plenary meeting of the 11th session of the U.N. General Assembly on the question of the withdrawal of Israeli troops from Egypt], February 26, 1957, Sipols, *SSSR i Arabskie strany* [The U.S.S.R. and the Arab countries], p. 309.

to undertake military-assistance programs in the Middle East and to use United States military forces to repel armed aggression "from any country controlled by international Communism," was promptly attacked by the Soviet Union as "a new form of colonialism" which would make the United States the policeman of the Middle East and transform that area into an American colony: "The Soviet Union decisively opposes any manifestation of colonialism, any 'doctrine' that protects and shields colonialism."[54] The Soviet News Agency TASS pointed out that this manifestation of intervention by the United States in the internal affairs of the Arab countries (American assistance was to be given only if requested) would encourage the "aggressive" and "expansionist" plans of Israeli ruling circles vis-à-vis the Arab states.[55] The recent threat to peace in the Middle East, as the Soviets were quick to point out, had come not from international Communism, but from Israel, Great Britain, and France, the invaders of Egypt. In the months to follow, support for the Eisenhower Doctrine by members of the Baghdad Pact, NATO, and Israel, increased Soviet suspicions of American intentions. From the Soviet standpoint, the Eisenhower Doctrine offered no protection against a repetition of the Anglo-French-Israeli invasion of Egypt that was not already afforded by the presence of the United Nations Emergency Force in the Middle East.

The Eisenhower Doctrine was implemented in the Near East crisis of 1958 when, at the invitation of the Lebanese and Jordanian governments, the United States landed five thousand troops in Lebanon (July 15) and the British, two thousand in Jordan (July 17). On this occasion, Israel once again ran the gauntlet of Soviet displeasure. According to TASS:

> Israel, although not formally a member of the Baghdad Pact, openly supports the aggressive measures of the Western powers, by permitting the movement across her territory of English and American troops and military equipment, and likewise by conducting mobilization measures.[56]

The use of Israeli air space for this purpose, according to TASS, made

54. "Zayavlenie TASS v sviazi s tak nazyvaemoi 'doktrinoi Eizenkhauera' [A TASS statement in connection with the so-called Eisenhower Doctrine], January 13, 1957, ibid., p. 293.

55. Ibid., p. 292; see also A. Kunina, Doktrina Eizenkhauera [The Eisenhower Doctrine] (Moscow, 1957); and Pravda, January 9 and 13, 1957.

56. "Zayavlenie TASS po povodu sessii soveta Baghdadskogo pakta" [A TASS statement on the meeting of the Baghdad Pact Council], July 30, 1958, Siplos, SSSR i arabskie strany [The U.S.S.R. and the Arab countries], p. 589; and "Nota sovetskogo pravitel'stva pravitel'stvu Izrailia" [A note of the Soviet government to the government of Israel], August 1, 1958, ibid., p. 591.

Israel an outright "accomplice" of England and the United States. As such, Israel was said to bear no small responsibility for the crisis in the Near and Middle East, which could redound to Israel's disadvantage. Aside from this veiled threat, it was clear, however, that from the Soviet standpoint the real guilt lay with the Western powers. As in previous instances, the U.S.S.R. was primarily concerned about the speedy withdrawal of British and American armed forces from Arab territory. In his address before the U.N. General Assembly (August 20, 1958), Soviet Foreign Minister Gromyko disparaged the British argument that withdrawal of British troops would result in an Israeli attack on Jordan. With Israeli delegates listening to the debate, he accused the British of seeking to incite Israeli aggression.[57]

The Soviet government also used for propaganda purposes against Israel a brochure published in October, 1957, by the editor of the Bombay weekly journal, *Blitz,* under the title "The Dagger of Israel."[58] This brochure divulged allegedly secret plans prepared by the Israeli general staff, prior to the Suez crisis of 1956, for the creation of a vastly enlarged Israeli state, stretching from the Euphrates to the Nile. This plan, which envisaged a "preventive war" against the Arab states, was predicated on the interest of the Western powers in securing military bases and establishing a regional defense system near the boundaries of the Soviet Union. Israel denied the existence of such a plan.

This document was strongly reminiscent of the "Protocols of the Learned Elders of Zion," first published in book form in tsarist Russia in 1905 and soon translated into several foreign languages, more recently into Arabic.[59] Throughout 1957 and later, the Soviet press continued periodically to voice its suspicions that Israeli leaders were planning a new attack on Egypt, based on the earlier plan of the Israeli general staff to expand at the expense of the Arab countries.[60]

---

57. *Ibid.,* pp. 737–38; see also pp. 671–72.

58. See K. Ivanov and Z. Sheinis, *Gosudarstvo Izrail': Ego polozhenie i politika* [The state of Israel: Its position and policy] (2d ed.; Moscow, 1959), pp. 48–53. This book on Israel, one of two published in the U.S.S.R. since World War II, first appeared in 1958, the tenth anniversary of the state of Israel. It is very hostile in tone.

59. The "Protocols" were based on meetings, allegedly held in Basle, Switzerland in 1897, coinciding with the first Zionist Congress. According to these spurious documents, the Jews and Freemasons were plotting to disrupt the entire Christian civilization. The tsarist government used this material to distract popular attention from the revolution of 1905.

60. See Sipols, *SSSR i arabskie strany* [The U.S.S.R. and the Arab countries], pp. 315–16, and 395–96.

From 1959 to the spring of 1967, the official Soviet press was less venomous in its comments about Israel and less concerned about the Palestine conflict than before and after these dates. Khrushchev delivered a long speech against anti-Semitism on March 8, 1963, before party and government leaders. The impression was given that he tried to apply the principles of coexistence even to Soviet-Israeli relations. When in May, 1964, he visited the Aswan High Dam to commemorate the completion of the first phase of the work there, he made no official derogatory references to Israel.[61] After Khrushchev was replaced in October, 1964, by the Brezhnev-Kosygin regime, the attitude of the U.S.S.R. toward Israel began to change, again for the worse, for at least two reasons: (1) the growing contacts between West Germany, number-one enemy of the Soviet Union, and Israel; (2) the denunciations of the U.S.S.R. made in the American press and before the United Nations by American Jewry because of discrimination against Jews in the Soviet Union, especially in regard to religious freedom.

In the post-Khrushchev era, successful Israeli economic, military, and ideological competition with the Soviet Union in many of the developing states of Africa has proved to be another factor in the existing "cold war" between the U.S.S.R. and Israel.[62] As a small country, Israel has been able to claim, with some plausibility, that it has no "colonialist" ambitions in Africa. In Africa, as well as in the Middle East, however, the Soviets depict Israel as "the bulwark of the West." Only as the "vehicle" of Western imperialism in Africa, according to Soviet writers, is Israel in a position to pose as a model for the developing countries; to furnish them with loans, technical and military assistance; and to train substantial numbers of African trade unionists and military leaders in Tel Aviv, as well as in Africa. The training of foreigners in Israel, "is closely bound up with their ideological conditioning in the Zionist spirit, with a clear-cut anti-Communist bias."[63] The Arab trade blockade against Israel has led that country to seek raw materials and markets in African states, including Ivory Coast, Dahomey, Central African Republic, Togo, Cameroon, Malawi, Congo, Kenya, Tanzania, Uganda, and others. From the Soviet

61. See *Asuan—Simbol Sovetsko-Arabskoi druzhby* [Aswan—Symbol of Soviet-Arab friendship] (Moscow, 1964).

62. See V. Vladimirov, "Israel's Policy in Africa," *International Affairs* (Moscow), No. 8 (1965), pp. 68–72; and P. Pilyatskin, "Israel's African Game," *Izvestia*, February 6, 1969. From the Israeli point of view, see Foreign Ministry of Israel, *Programme of Cooperation with the Developing Countries* (Jerusalem, 1961).

63. Vladimirov, "Israel's Policy in Africa," p. 70. Pilyatskin states that from 1957 to 1965, more than 11,600 specialists from developing countries (60 per cent of them African) received instruction and indoctrination in Israel and that over 2,500 Israeli experts were sent to Africa ("Israel's African Game").

standpoint, Israel also seeks agreements with the new African states for political purposes, namely, to secure their votes in the United Nations and other international organizations on matters of interest to Israel, including the Palestine conflict.

THE 1967 JUNE WAR

Soviet involvement in the Palestine question increased in February, 1966, with the seizure of power in Syria by the left-wing Ba'ath Party under Dr. Nureddin Attasi. Raids into Israel in the fall of 1966, led by al-Fatah from Syrian-based camps, resulted in the calling of the U.N. Security Council. Only a Soviet veto prevented the Council from passing a resolution condemning Syria and requiring it to take the necessary measures to stop such raids. In December, the Attasi regime signed an agreement with the U.S.S.R. for technical and financial aid in the construction of a dam and hydroelectric plant on the Euphrates River. Soviet strategy now became clear. With one foot in Egypt, due to the construction of the Aswan High Dam, and the other in Syria, through the building of the Euphrates Dam, the Soviet government expected to outflank the West and Israel in the Middle East. In November, 1966, it put pressure on Egypt and Syria, which had been at loggerheads since the dissolution of their union in 1961, to forget their differences, to restore diplomatic relations, and to conclude a treaty of defense, in which each was pledged to go to the aid of the other in the event of an attack.

An unsuccessful effort in the spring of 1967 to overthrow from within the none-too-popular Syrian government aroused the concern of Soviet leaders. The Attasi regime, on this occasion, weathered the storm. The Soviet government had reason to suspect, however, that it would not survive an Israeli army raid into Syria, comparable to the November, 1966, raid into Jordan, with the loss of prestige entailed by such an encounter.[64] Through its ambassador in Tel Aviv, the Soviet government in May, 1967, charged Israel with mobilizing its armed forces on the northeast border for a showdown with Syria. Although this was flatly denied, the Soviet ambassador passed up an opportunity for an on-the-spot inspection. Soviet charges were reiterated, however, before the United Nations and in the press. These warnings of an imminent Israeli invasion of Syria appear to have furthered Soviet objectives. Egypt, because of its commitments to Syria, called upon U Thant, secretary-general of the United Nations, for

64. For an expression of Soviet interest in the Attasi government, see *Pravda* and *Izvestia,* May 30, 1967.

the withdrawal of the United Nations troops that had been charged with overseeing peace on the Israeli-Egyptian border since the Suez conflict of 1956. This removed the major obstacle to a renewal of hostilities in the Palestine area.

It seems unlikely that the Soviet government either expected or wished for a war in the Near East in 1967. As late as May 24, it envisaged no emergency that required the calling of the Security Council.[65] Soviet attention appears to have been focused on the threat to Syria rather than on a possible invasion of Egypt. Soviet leaders may have discounted the prospect of a war on the ground that the United States, deeply involved in Vietnam, would pressure Israel into preserving peace. If so, it miscalculated. Following the withdrawal of the UNEF, President Nasser declared the blockade to Israeli shipping in the Gulf of Aqaba and sent Egyptian forces into the Sinai. This action culminated in the Israeli invasion of Egypt on June 5, 1967. The underlying cause of the conflict, from the Soviet point of view, was the desire of the United States and Great Britain to strike a telling blow at the national liberation movement in the Near East.

Once the June war had begun, the Soviet government exerted every effort to secure the condemnation by the Security Council of Israel as the aggressor. As Israel's remarkable military prowess quickly became apparent, Ambassador Fedorenko supported the Council's resolution (233) calling for an immediate cease fire and cessation of all military activities. He would have preferred a U.N. decision for the immediate withdrawal of "aggressor" forces behind the 1956 armistice lines. Confronted by the urgent need to save the defeated Arab governments, especially those of Egypt and Syria, from collapse, he settled for another resolution (234) demanding a cease fire by a specific deadline on June 7. He continued to fight for the condemnation of Israel and the withdrawal of Israeli forces from occupied Arab territory.[66] The shrill tone of his speeches and the fire-and-brimstone presentation of the Middle East crisis in the Soviet press revealed how deeply involved the U.S.S.R. was in the outcome. *Pravda* reported that by July 1 it had received 20,569 letters from Soviet citizens, some of them from Jews, condemning Israeli aggression.

At the United Nations, the U.S.S.R. emerged as the chief supporter of the Arab cause. Not once did Soviet delegates, including Premier Kosygin and Foreign Minister Gromyko, even suggest that the Arabs were guilty

65. See Arthur Lall, *The UN and the Middle East Crisis, 1967* (New York, 1968), pp. 29–31; see also *New York Times,* May 25, 1967, p. 16.

66. The various draft resolutions submitted by the U.S.S.R., June 13, June 19, and October 24, 1967, are available in Lall, *Middle East Crisis,* appendixes.

of a single mistake, provocation, or bad judgment. Nor did they admit that Soviet policy in any way contributed to the conflagration. Had they and the Arabs conceded, for example, the inadvisability of the closure of the Straits of Tiran or the massing of Egyptian troops in the Sinai Peninsula on the heels of the UNEF withdrawal, they could have established better communications with the West. Had they presented fewer, but better, speakers, the endless repetition of the same arguments could have been avoided and an earlier end to the crisis might have been facilitated. On June 10, the U.S.S.R. and the Soviet bloc nations threatened that if the Security Council failed to take proper action they would render assistance to the Arab states "to repel aggression" and defend their national independence and territorial integrity.

The U.S.S.R. was unable to secure the unilateral condemnation of Israel, either by the Security Council or the General Assembly. It had to drop its demands for the restitution of material damage inflicted on the U.A.R., most of which involved the capture or destruction of large quantities of Soviet equipment. In one significant respect, the U.S.S.R. position differed from that of the Arab states. On November 20, Kuznetzov clearly indicated that the Soviet Union does not accept the nonrecognition policy of the Arab states toward Israel.

> The Soviet Government . . . is in favor of recognition of the inalienable right of all the States of the Middle East, including Israel, to an independent national existence.[67]

This was a position the U.S.S.R. had taken in 1947 and had consistently followed thereafter.

The Soviet Union supported the compromise Security Council resolution (242) of November 22, 1967, as a feasible course for the settlement of the Arab-Israeli conflict. Without condemning Israel as an aggressor, it called for the "withdrawal of Israeli armed forces from territories occupied during the conflict," and recognized the "territorial integrity and political independence of every state in the area."[68] It likewise affirmed the necessity for guarantees of freedom of navigation through international waters in the area, for a "just settlement of the refugee problem," the establishment of demilitarized zones, and the designation of a special

---

67. Cited in Lall, *Middle East Crisis*, p. 256. This position was reinforced in the "Communiqué of the foreign ministers of the European Socialist Countries," *Pravda* and *Izvestia*, December 23, 1967.
68. See Lall, *Middle East Crisis*, appendix 20, pp. 303–4.

U.N. representative to work in the Near East for an acceptable settlement of the Palestine conflict.

From the beginning, the resolution of November 22, 1967, has been subject to varied interpretations. To the Arab states and the U.S.S.R. it meant that Israel must withdraw immediately from all occupied Arab territory. To the Israelis, it did not specify withdrawal from *all* territories occupied during the June war. They insisted that any Israeli withdrawal was predicated on the establishment of recognized boundaries, the beginning of direct treaty negotiations between Israel and the Arab states, and recognition of Israel's right to freedom of navigation of the Suez Canal and the Gulf of Aqaba. Thus, the Arab states made withdrawal the prerequisite to any treaty agreement. The Israelis made it depend on a treaty settlement involving the other issues outlined in the resolution of November 22.

The cease fire, therefore, resulted in no settlement of the Palestine issue and the Arab-Israeli border. The Soviet Union continued to insist that such a settlement could be reached only on the basis of the unanimously adopted Security Council resolution. The Soviet periodical, *International Affairs,* carried an unqualified justification of President Nasser's closure of the Straits of Tiran and of the massing of U.A.R. troops in the Sinai Peninsula on the eve of the 1967 war; it stresses the wholly peaceful intentions of the Egyptian President.[69] This article justifies the acts of the Palestine guerrillas in Israeli-occupied territory on the ground that they are "belligerents," whose status may be compared with that of members of the resistance movement in Nazi-occupied territories during World War II. The Soviet press has demonstrated unprecedented concern for the plight of the Arab refugees and has harped on Israeli evacuation of occupied territory as a prerequisite for peace.[70]

At least temporarily, the June war left Israel in possession of substantial segments of Arab territory, including the Sinai Peninsula (Egyptian), the Gaza Strip (Egyptian-administered), the Golan Heights (Syrian), all of Jordan west of the Jordan River, and all of the city of Jerusalem. Israel has retained possession of Sharm al-Sheikh and the control of the Straits of Tiran. In 1956, in line with U.N. requirements, Israel withdrew from conquered Egyptian territory on the assumption that it would obtain freedom of navigation in the Suez Canal, that U.N. forces would occupy Gaza

69. I. Blishchenko, "International Law and the Middle East Crisis," *International Affairs,* No. 1 (January, 1969), pp. 29–35; this article presents a defense of the Arab case, citing precedents in international law.

70. For an article by Yevgeny Primakov, "The Way to Peace in the Near East," see *Pravda,* January 11, 1969.

and Sharm al-Sheikh, and that the United States would guarantee Israel free use of the Gulf of Aqaba. The first provision was never implemented, and the other two proved ineffective in 1967. After the June war, therefore, Israel refused to rely on external guarantees without first securing a firm peace settlement with the Arab states.

The June war undoubtedly strengthened the Soviet position in the Near and Middle East, in spite of the defeat of the Arab states by Israel. The U.S.S.R., still the champion of the Arab side in the Palestine conflict, quickly replaced the bulk of Egypt's lost equipment and undertook the task of assisting in reorganization of the Egyptian armed forces. The presence of a substantial Soviet fleet in the eastern Mediterranean with access to Egyptian and Syrian ports seems to have affected the balance of power in the Middle East. The West, which held the initiative in "containing" the U.S.S.R. in the Middle East after World War II, has been forced, at least for the time being, to face now a Soviet containment policy in this area.

In some respects, the positions of the Western powers and the U.S.S.R. have been reversed. The U.S.S.R. is now pursuing the kind of "colonialism" in the Middle East that it accused Great Britain and the United States of pursuing in Palestine after World War II. Khrushchev once said,

> We think that if the Great Powers would not interfere, then the Arab countries and Israel could much sooner reach a mutual understanding and this would be instrumental in bringing about peace in this area and in finding opportunities for the liquidation of the tense situation that exists there now.[71]

The impression is given that there would be more peace in the Middle East today, if the U.S.S.R. refrained from interference in the internal affairs of the Arab states, even when it does this under the guise of protecting the Arabs against Israel and Western "imperialism."

There is reason to conclude, however, that the key to a stable peace between the Arab states and Israel lies not in Cairo, Damascus, or Amman, but in Moscow and Washington, especially in Moscow. In the light of the Soviet presence in the eastern Mediterranean, it is questionable whether a solution of the Palestine conflict would in reality serve Soviet interests. The U.S.S.R. is there because of the Arab-Israeli dispute over Palestine. Once a settlement is reached, there would be no reason for the U.S.S.R. to remain.

71. *Pravda*, February 16, 1958.

The basis of Soviet hostility toward Israel is still, in part at least, ideological.[72] The state of Israel began, according to Soviet interpretation, with a proclamation of "socialist doctrines." The leading role in the government of this country was then played by the Workers' Party of Israel — Mapai. In these early years, there emigrated to Israel many Jews who believed in the creation of a Jewish socialist state. In spite of these (from the Soviet standpoint) promising beginnings, Israel has become a stronghold of capitalism, where private initiative is greatly encouraged. Whereas today Israel is becoming more and more capitalistic, the Arab states, according to the Soviets, are veering toward socialism. This remains, therefore, an important factor in the tension between Israel and the Arab states, as well as between Israel and the U.S.S.R. Academician E. Zhukov, in a recent article, "The National Liberation Movement of the Peoples of Asia and Africa," claims that the Arabs are now convinced that the socialist states give them unequivocal support, whereas the Western capitalist states back Israel in the Arab-Israeli conflict.[73]

72. See O. E. Tuganova, *Mezhdunarodnye otnosheniia na blizhnem i srednem vostoke* [International relations in the Near and Middle East], AN, SSSR (Moscow, 1967), pp. 273–74.

73. *Kommunist,* No. 4 (March, 1969), p. 35.

15. The Palestine Conflict in Asian Perspective

M. S. Agwani

══════ The reluctance of the Asians to recognize the Zionist claim to Palestine is sometimes ascribed to the Asian intellectuals' unawareness of the Judeo-Christian heritage that underlies the emotional ties of Jewry to the Holy Land. According to this view, the Zionist claim finds ready support in the Christian West where "the Bible and the spiritual kinship of Jews and Christians maintain a continuous knowledge of the Jewish connection with Zion."[1] This thesis would not bear scrutiny in the light of empirical evidence. Europe's Judeo-Christian heritage did not prevent the sustained persecution of Jews, a circumstance to which Asian history affords no parallel. On the contrary, the Islamic tradition which incorporates and endorses much of the Judaic religion has consistently regarded the Jews as a fraternal People of the Book. Nor is the Western-educated Asian elite, which provides political leadership in the modern states of Asia, so unfamiliar with the Judeo-Christian heritage as not to comprehend Jewry's religious connection with Palestine. And yet, modern Asia has viewed the Zionist claim with suspicion and disapprobation. An explanation for this must be sought in the incompatibility between the anti-colonial upsurge in Asia and the methods and goals of the Zionist movement.

The expansion of Europe in the lands of Asia and Africa during the nineteenth and early twentieth centuries crystallized into two forms of relationship: outright *colonial* empires governed from the metropolitan centers and the *colonizing* empires involving "permanent" settlement of Europeans into the conquered lands. The former explicitly recognized the ethno-cultural personality of the colonies, the latter rejected it totally.

1. Michael Brecher, *The New States of Asia* (Oxford, 1963), pp. 125–27.

444 International Perspectives

Classic examples of the first were India and Egypt; of the second, Algeria and the Union of South Africa.

Toward the end of the First World War the Allied Powers recognized in principle, if not in practice, the right of the colonial peoples to national self-determination. This marked an appreciable advance in the freedom struggle of the Asian and African peoples. It obligated the metropolitan powers to introduce constitutional reforms in their respective colonies admittedly designed to promote self-rule. But there was no corresponding change of outlook in the colonized regions. The result was an anomalous situation fraught with tragic consequences. For whereas most of the colonial countries now strove for *national self-determination,* the colonized ones faced the prospect of *national self-obliteration.* The Balfour Declaration forced the people of Palestine into the latter category.

ZIONISM AND BRITISH IMPERIALISM

The Zionists' *quid pro quo* with imperial Britain resulting in the Balfour Declaration made them suspect in the Asian eyes from the very outset. The idea of a Jewish homeland in Palestine endorsed by the World Zionist Congress in 1897 did not reflect the aspirations of the Jewish minority in Palestine. On the contrary, the religious Jews of Jerusalem and Hebron were strongly opposed to political Zionism, holding that God will bring Israel back to Zion in His own time, and that it was impious to anticipate His decree. It was also opposed by a large section of the British Jewry which preferred to remain "hundred per cent Englishmen."[2] Nor did it appeal to the West European Jew who had assimilated himself to his surroundings. Political Zionism, then, mainly attracted the persecuted Jews of Central and Eastern Europe who had eschewed assimilation. Their cause was upheld by a small number of West European Jews headed by Chaim Weizmann, who equated assimilation with "drift" leading to "gradual decay and disruption under emancipation."[3]

The circumstances governing the issuance of the Balfour Declaration, the British efforts to secure the Palestine mandate against the expressed wishes of its people (hence, its contravention of article 22, paragraph 4 of the Covenant of the League of Nations), and subsequent Jewish immigration into Palestine under British protection are well known and have been analyzed elsewhere in this volume. We must, however, underscore

---

2. Sir Ronald Storrs, *Lawrence of Arabia, Zionism and Palestine* (London, 1940), p. 46.

3. Chaim Weizmann, *Zionism and the Jewish Future* (London, 1916), pp. 6–9.

two factors which deeply ruffled Asian susceptibilities and shaped the Asian outlook on what came to be known as the Palestine question. The first was the conscious and transparent dovetailing of Zionist aspirations and Britain's imperial interests in the Middle East and Asia. That the Zionists entered Palestine as an auxiliary of the British expeditionary force is recorded by Ronald Storrs, military governor of Jerusalem during 1917–20:

> When . . . early in March [1918] Brigadier General Clayton showed me the telegram informing us of the impending arrival of a Zionist Commission, composed of eminent Jews and the Military Administration and to "control" the Jewish population, we could hardly believe our eyes, and even wondered whether it might not be possible for the mission to be postponed until the status of the administration should be more clearly defined.[4]

In a far more forthright manner, Chaim Weizmann spoke of the criticism he encountered from fellow Zionists who said, "the alliance with Great Britain on which you lean is piercing your hand. Great Britain used Zionism to confirm the position won in Palestine by its arms." Weizmann proceeded to plead with Winston Churchill, then British colonial secretary:

> Nor need I dwell on the proposition that this alliance with Zionism is a waxing asset or on the fact well known that those greatest soldiers of history, Julius Caesar, Alexander and Napoleon, all recognised the immense importance of Palestine in their Eastern schemes and were markedly pro-Jewish in their foreign policy. Napoleon may even be claimed as the first of the modern non-Jewish Zionists. . . . *if there were no Palestine, it would, I believe, be necessary to create one in the Imperial interest.* It is a bastion to Egypt. On the one side, the existence of a Jewish Palestine leaves you absolutely free to follow whatever policy may be most convenient to you, and enables you, if you wished, to evacuate Egypt altogether and to concentrate on the Canal Zone with your army based on Palestine. . . . It is an asset on which you can draw almost indefinitely in case of danger. . . . It is difficult to understand how one can build on Arab loyalty so near the vital communications across the Isthmus of Suez. All one has seen and heard of the Arab movements leads one to believe that it is anti-European. *The Palestine Zionist policy, far from being waste, becomes a necessary*

4. *Lawrence of Arabia*, p. 44.

insurance that we quote to you at a lower rate than onyone else could dream of.[5]

Later, Ronald Storrs expressed the hope that the enterprise launched by the Balfour Declaration would yield "for England 'a little, loyal Jewish Ulster' in a sea of potentially hostile Arabism."[6] A British study published toward the close of the mandatory administration stressed the wider significance of Palestine for the British Empire:

> Whatever be the regime in Palestine, from the point of view of the British imperial lines of communication, it is as important as Egypt. From the strategic standpoint this is an advanced position in the East against any potential threat to the Suez Canal. It is the terminus of the oil pipeline from Kirkuk; it is a landing on the international air route to India and farther on, and the starting point of the high road through the desert of Iraq.[7]

The second reason why Zionism evoked disapprobation in Asia was its relentless opposition to self-government by the Palestinians. The Balfour Declaration was designed to bestow a privileged status upon the hypothetical Jewish immigrants far above the indigenous people of Palestine who had inhabited the land since time immemorial and who were now arbitrarily lumped together under the negative label of "non-Jewish communities." The Jewish immigrants and the Zionist agencies that supported them were firmly committed to frustrating any advance toward self-government in Palestine on the indefensible plea that it would give the Palestinians an upper hand in the administration of their country. They argued that constitutional reforms toward that end should be held in abeyance until large-scale immigration afforded them a clear majority over the Arabs.

In sum, the whole tenor of Zionist theory and practice was antithetical to the spirit of resurgent Asia seething with anticolonial struggles and inexorably advancing toward the goal of national self-determination.

5. The text of this "Letter Written, But Never Sent, by Weizmann to Churchill" (July, 1921) is in Richard H. S. Crossman, *A Nation Reborn* (New York, 1960), pp. 153–63; the excerpt cited here is reproduced by permission of the director, the Weizmann Archives, Rehovot, Israel (italics added).

6. *Lawrence of Arabia,* p. 53.

7. Royal Institute of International Affairs, *Great Britain and Palestine 1915–1945* (rev. ed.; New York, 1946), p. 1.

INDIA AND PALESTINE

The driving force behind Britain's Middle Eastern policy was its imperial interest in India. It is significant, therefore, that the Indian national movement played a leading role in the Asian nations' opposition to both Zionism and British policies in Palestine. The Indian concern for Palestine was voiced by the Indian National Congress and its most eminent mentors, Mahatma Gandhi and Jawaharlal Nehru.

Gandhi's credentials to speak on Zionism and Palestine were beyond reproach. He believed in the right of every people to live in freedom. He was firmly wedded to nonviolence. In the early phase of his career in South Africa, he had won the friendship and cooperation of many Jews and was an admirer of the Jewish philosopher, Martin Buber. He deeply resented the sufferings and hardships of the Jews in Central and Eastern Europe and in sorrow described them as "the untouchables of Christianity."

In response to several letters asking him about the Arab-Jewish question in Palestine and about the persecution of the Jews in Germany, Gandhi expressed his views in an article published in the *Harijan* of November 26, 1938.[8] He observed that the German persecution of the Jews had "no parallel in history." "If there ever could be a justifiable war in the name of and for humanity, a war against Germany, to prevent the wanton persecution of a whole race, would be completely justified." ("But I do not believe in any war," he added. "A discussion of the pros and cons of such a war is therefore outside my horizon or province.")

Gandhi's sympathies were "all with the Jews." But "my sympathy does not blind me to the requirements of justice." He then went on to examine the rationale of the Zionist movement. "The cry for a national home for the Jews does not make much appeal to me. The sanction for it is sought in the Bible and the tenacity with which the Jews have hankered after return to Palestine." This plea, he believed, could not be sustained on moral or political grounds.

The Palestine of the Biblical conception is not a geographical tract. It is in their hearts. But if they must look to the Palestine of geography as their national home, it is wrong to enter it under the shadow of the British gun.

The argument then turned on the legitimacy of the *means* employed to achieve the national home. "A religious act," observed Gandhi, "cannot

8. Reproduced in *The Bond* (Jerusalem), April, 1939, pp. 39–44.

be performed with the aid of the bayonet or the bomb. They can settle in Palestine only by the goodwill of the Arabs. . . . As it is, they are co-sharers with the British in despoiling a people who have done no wrong to them." In later years, he reiterated the point and asked: "Why should they depend on American money or the British arms for forcing themselves on an unwelcome land? Why should they resort to terrorism to make good their forcible landing in Palestine?"[9]

Finally, as to the Palestinians' right to self-determination, Gandhi observed:

> Palestine belongs to the Arabs in the same sense that England belongs to the English, or France to the French. It is wrong and inhuman to impose the Jews on the Arabs. What is going on in Palestine today cannot be justified by any moral code of conduct. The mandates have no sanction but that of the last war. Surely, it would be a crime against humanity to reduce the proud Arabs, so that Palestine could be restored to the Jews, partly or wholly as their national home.[10]

Gandhi's article evoked a rejoinder from Martin Buber in the form of an open letter. Buber argued that the Jews are "a people like no other, for it is the only people in the world which, from its earliest beginnings, has been both a nation and a religious community"; that "three thousand years ago our entry into this land took place with the consciousness of a mission from above to set up a just way of life through the generations of our people"; and that the demand for a Jewish state springs from the demand made on Jewry by the Holy Scripture—a demand "whose fulfilment is bound up with the land." He, however, agreed that the Arabs, too, had a rightful claim to Palestine:

> We consider it a fundamental point that in this case two vital claims are opposed to each other, two claims of a different nature and a different origin which cannot be objectively fitted against one another and between which no objective decision can be made as to which is just, which unjust. We considered and still consider it our duty to understand and to honour the claim which is opposed to ours and to endeavour to reconcile both claims.

Nonetheless, Buber realized that reconciliation would mean "internal

9. Cited in D. G. Tendulkar, *Mahatma,* 8 vols. (Bombay, 1953), VII, 189.
10. *The Bond* (Jerusalem), April, 1939, pp. 39–44.

resistance on the Jewish side" for it would compromise the Zionist character of the state.[11]

Public opinion in India was stirred by the tragic events in Palestine following the large immigration of Jews in the 1930s, but the feeling was widely shared that the persecution of Jewry by Hitler gave them a moral right to the active support of the entire civilized world. Jawaharlal Nehru moved a resolution in the All-India Congress Committee (A.-I.C.C.) urging the British to facilitate Jewish immigration into *India*. At the same time, the Congress rejected the Jewish demand to enter Palestine against the expressed wishes of its people. In October, 1937, the Congress protested against the "reign of terror" as well as the partition proposals in regard to Palestine and pledged solidarity with the Arab struggle for national freedom. The following year, it resolved that "Britain would be well-advised in revoking its present policy and leave the Jews and the Arabs to amicably settle the issues between them" and appealed to the Jews "not to take shelter behind British imperialism."[12]

Earlier, addressing the fiftieth session of the Indian National Congress (1936), Nehru observed that "the Arab struggle against British imperialism in Palestine is as much part of the great world conflict as India's struggle for freedom." As he saw it, England was putting up "Jewish religious nationalism against Arab nationalism" so as to

> make it appear that her presence was necessary to act as an arbitrator and to keep the peace between the two. It is the same old game we have seen in other countries under imperialist domination; it is curious how often it is repeated.

He was perturbed that the Jews "preferred to take sides with the foreign ruling power" and thus "helped it to keep back freedom from the majority of the people." It did not surprise him, therefore, that the "majority, comprising the Arabs chiefly and also Christians, bitterly resent this attitude of the Jews." On the British atrocities in Palestine Nehru said,

> the whole Arab world is aflame with indignation, and the East, Muslim and non-Muslim alike, has been deeply affected by this brutal attempt to crush a people struggling for their freedom.[13]

11. Martin Buber, *Israel and the World* (2d ed; New York, 1963), pp. 227–33.
12. Tendulkar, *Mahatma*, IV, 252, 336.
13. *Toward Freedom: The Autobiography of Jawaharlal Nehru* (New York, 1941), p. 247.

About this time, the developments in Palestine and Europe led Nehru to the conclusion that the future of Palestine could "only be built upon stable foundations of Arab-Jew cooperation and elimination of imperialism." This required that the Jews abandon their exaggerated claims and seek peaceful accommodation with the Palestinians.[14]

That this approach was in accord with opinion in other Asian countries was put on record by the Asian Relations Conference, the first unofficial gathering of the Asian nations, held at Delhi in 1947. Alongside the Arab nations, a Jewish delegation from Palestine participated in its deliberations. Dr. Hugo Bergmann, chief of the Jewish delegation, declared that he was impressed by the "Asian system of multi-racial, multi-religious and multi-cultural political organizations" and reminisced:

> This lesson Europe was unable to teach us. We do not want to be ungrateful to Europe. We have learned many important lessons there. We learned to appreciate logical reasoning and methodical thinking. . . . But one thing we could not learn in Europe: the mutual cooperation of groups of men belonging to different races and creeds.[15]

Bergmann pledged that his people "will not go the European way of solving, so to speak, problems by dispossessing populations."[16] As it happened, even as the Jewish spokesman made the solemn declaration before the conference, the Zionist movement irrevocably committed itself to an exclusivist Jewish state, snuffing out all hopes of genuine "multi-racial, multi-religious and multi-cultural" coexistence and cooperation in Palestine. The Zionists were excluded from all subsequent Asian conferences; of this more will be said.

PALESTINE AND THE U.N.

On April 2, 1947, the British government referred the Palestine question to the United Nations. By the time the resolution concerning the creation of the United Nations Special Committee on Palestine (UNSCOP) came up for discussion at the first plenary session of the General Assembly, it crystallized along two lines: one was represented by China, then passing

14. *Glimpses of World History* (Bombay, 1962), pp. 789, 791–92, 794.
15. Asian Relations Organization, *Asian Relations: Being Report of the Proceedings and Documentations of the First Asian Relations Conference, March–April, 1947* (New Delhi, 1948), p. 57.
16. Cited in G. H. Jansen, *Afro-Asia and Non-Alignment* (London, 1966), p. 55.

through the convulsions of a grim civil war; the other by India, standing at the threshold of freedom. Quo Tai-chi, the Chinese delegate scored the Arab and Jewish claims in general terms and argued that it was no use trying "to turn the clock of history by twenty years" or "twenty centuries," and that the "disquieting and agonizing" problem of Palestine could not be solved "unless and until Islam and Jewry and Christendom return to the teachings of the prophets and the saints of the Holy Land."[17]

Asaf Ali, a veteran leader of the Indian National Congress, speaking on behalf of India and "eighty million people of Indonesia, and many more millions of Malaysia and Burma who are not represented here," urged that justice be done to Palestine and that considerations of "power politics" and "economic interests" not be permitted to vitiate the issues.[18] Earlier, in the course of the subcommittee debate, the Indian delegation had submitted a draft resolution stipulating that the proposed UNSCOP "shall bear in mind the principle that independence for the population of Palestine should be the primary purpose of any plan for the future of the country." The Indian spokesman raised the point that "a Jewish national home is easily counterdistinguishable from a Jewish State, that a Jewish national home, as mentioned in the Mandate, is not inconsistent with a completely independent and sovereign Arab Palestine State." If the mandate had any meaning whatsoever, he argued,

> it must go right back to Article 22 of the Covenant of the League of Nations from which it derives power. . . . Naturally, if these terms of reference are laid down for the Committee, its report will contain, among other recommendations, a proposal on the question of establishing, without delay, the independent State of Palestine.[19]

As it happened, the final draft adopted by the subcommittee diluted the Indian suggestions and merely called upon the Special Committee to give "most careful consideration to the religious interests in Palestine of Islam, Judaism and Christianity."[20]

The eleven members of the Special Committee — among them only two Asian nations, India and Iran — took up their assignment against a grim background of violence. Organized attacks by the terrorists of the Irgun

17. United Nations, General Assembly, *Official Records,* first special session, plenary meetings, April 28–May 15, 1947, I, 152–54.

18. *Ibid.,* p. 163.

19. United Nations, General Assembly, *Official Records,* first special session, main committees, April 28–May 15, 1947, III, 199, 206.

20. *Ibid.,* pp. 309, 368–69.

Zvai Leumi on the Arabs as well as the British forces were aimed to shatter the latter's morale and were part of the stratagem to gain political mastery of Palestine by force.[21] The committee's report, completed by August 31, 1947, put forth two alternative plans for the solution of the Palestine problem. The first recommended partition of Palestine into two sovereign states, Jewish and Arab; the second favored an independent federal state of Palestine. It is important to note the Asian members of the UNSCOP opposed partition and commended a federal solution.

The rationale of the partition plan was that "the claims to Palestine of the Arabs and Jews, both possessing validity, are irreconcilable," and that "partition will provide the most realistic and practical settlement, and is the most likely to afford a workable basis for meeting in part the claims and national aspirations of both parties." The case for a federal state, on the other hand, rested on the premise that "any solution for Palestine cannot be considered as a solution of the Jewish problem in general." Hence, a realistic and equitable solution should take into account two basic questions, namely, (1) whether Jewish nationalism and the demand for a separate and sovereign Jewish state must be recognized at all costs, and (2) whether a will to cooperate in a federal state could be fostered among the Arabs and Jews. The signatories to the federal plan — India, Iran, and Yugoslavia — believed that the answer to the first was in the negative, since "the well-being of the country and its peoples as a whole is accepted as out-weighing the aspirations of the Jews in this regard." As to the second, the answer was in the affirmative "as there is a reasonable chance, given proper conditions, to achieve such cooperation." It was further observed that "partition, both in principle and in substance, can only be regarded as an anti-Arab solution. The federal plan, however, cannot be described as an anti-Jewish solution. To the contrary, it will best serve the interests of both Arabs and Jews."[22]

Subsequent debate in the plenary meeting of the General Assembly revealed that the reasoning underlying the federal plan accorded with the judgment of almost all the Asian nations that participated in the deliberations. Romulo, the leader of the Philippines delegation, declared on November 26 that it was clear to his government that

---

21. The Irgun Zvai Leumi (National Military Organization) was established in 1936 by the Jewish "Revisionists" (who demanded revision of the mandate in order to meet the Zionist claim).

22. United Nations, General Assembly, *United Nations Special Committee on Palestine: Report to the General Assembly,* second session, suppl. 11, September 16–November 29, 1947, I, 47, 59.

the rights conferred by mandatory power, even if subsequently confirmed
by an international agreement, do not reiterate the primordial right of a
people to determine the political future and to preserve the territorial
integrity of its native land. . . . The issue is whether the United Nations
should accept responsibility for the enforcement of a policy which, not
being mandatory under the specific provisions of the Charter, nor in
accordance with its fundamental principles, is clearly repugnant to the
valid nationalist aspirations of the peoples of Palestine. The Philippines
Government believes that the United Nations ought not to accept any
such responsibility.

To him, the partition plan was analogous to the "infamous proposal" by
the metropolitan power (U.S.) to partition the Philippines on grounds of
religious diversity. Sanctioning of partition by the world body, he argued,
would "turn us back on the road to the dangerous principles of racial
exclusiveness and to the archaic doctrines of theocratic governments."[23]

In a somewhat milder vein, Liu Chieh of the Chinese delegation commended that in attempting a solution of the Palestine problem "the welfare
of the inhabitants of Palestine must be considered of paramount importance." The yardstick in the measurement of any proposal, he pleaded,
"must be the extent to which peace and tranquility in that part of the world
may be assured by its adoption." He declared that the partition plan "being
not satisfactory on these counts," his government instructed him to abstain
from voting.[24]

Muhammed Zafrullah Khan of Pakistan assailed the partition plan on
moral, legal, and practical grounds. By endorsing the partition plan the
U.N. would be launching upon a course which commits it to carrying
through a scheme which "lacks moral justification, is beyond the legal and
juridical authority of the United Nations, and is impossible of achievement." He said,

in making this futile, this fatal attempt, you set at nought the wishes of
the sixty-six per cent of the people of Palestine. You destroy the faith
and trust of all the surrounding and neighboring states in the fairness
and impartiality of the United Nations. . . . You sow doubt and mistrust
of the designs and motives of the Western Powers. You take the gravest
risk of impairing, beyond the possibility of repair, any chance of real

23. United Nations, General Assembly, *Official Records,* second session, plenary
meetings, September 16–November 29, 1947, II, 1314–15.
24. *Ibid.,* pp. 1379–80.

cooperation between East and West, by thus forcibly driving what in effect amounts to a Western wedge into the heart of the Middle East. . . . Having cut Palestine up in that manner, we shall then put its bleeding body upon a cross forever.[25]

The representative of Iran joined other Asian delegations in underscoring the incompatibility of the draft resolution concerning partition with the principles of the U.N. Charter. It openly violated article 1, paragraph 2 of the charter which "gives all Members the right to govern themselves freely. . . . and the right to choose the form of government which best suits them." "We cannot support this draft resolution," he declared, "and violate our most sacred obligations. . . . We ought not to take here a decision which would result in exposing not only the Near and Middle East, but perhaps the whole world, to fire and slaughter. This is why, in loyalty to the principles of the Charter and conscious of the respect which is due to them, the delegation of Iran will vote against the partition of Palestine."[26]

The Indian viewpoint was set forth in a special note submitted by its representative on the UNSCOP. This document is of singular significance because it offers a penetrating analysis of the Palestine problem in the perspective of history and evolves a solution that is both workable and consistent with the requirements of justice and peace. The Balfour Declaration, it said, had no legal validity because the British government had no legitimate right to make it at the time when it was made. The mandate which incorporated the Balfour Declaration contravened the Covenant of the League of Nations in that the Palestinians were not consulted in regard to the choice of the mandatory, and the stipulation requiring the mandatory to ensure the well-being and development of the indigenous people of the mandated territory was totally disregarded. Another grievous mistake was made when the mandatory permitted the Jewish Agency not merely to collaborate with the administration of the country but "to run its own educational, industrial and economic system for a portion of the population" amounting to "a parallel government." This encouraged the Jewish immigrants to magnify their original demand for a "national home" into the clamor for a full-fledged Jewish state reinforced by the ceaseless terrorist and other military activities of the Haganah, the Irgun, and the Stern Gang. The document also questioned the rationale of Zionism. The ancient association of a people with a land

25. *Ibid.*, pp. 1370–77.
26. *Ibid.*, pp. 1328–29.

did not create political or legal rights in the present times. Nor is the plea tenable that profession of a faith by a person clothes him with any special rights in a country. Besides, the Jews had no more religious interest in Palestine than the Muslims and the Christians. Equally indefensible was the argument that Jewish political rights derived from their efforts to develop a part of Palestine since 1920, for all these efforts had been directed not at helping the people of Palestine but at converting it into a Jewish state. As to the contention that the Jews need a state because they are homeless, it would not bear close examination:

> Can they for the same reason ask for the New York State which has well over three million Jews already, or for England? But the United States of America and England are strong enough to resist a demand by force of arms if necessary. Or is it Palestine, where immigration has been carried out to a large extent with the help of the mandatory Power's forces, because it is considered unable to defend itself against the forces which the Jews have organized?

Furthermore, it was wrong to confuse the issues in Palestine with the problem of European Jewry. The responsibility for rehabilitating the victims of Hitler's tyranny devolved upon the entire civilized world and should be discharged through liberalization of immigration policies by various governments.[27]

All this pointed to the conclusion that the destiny of Palestine should be decided on the basis of self-determination, a principle that forms the keystone of the U.N. Charter. "In 1947, it is too late to look at the matter from any other angle." Self-determination could take either of the two forms: partition, or a federal state of Palestine. Partition would be unworkable because neither of the two states could be viable and Arab-Jewish relations would thus be further embittered. Hence, the only solution that would be just and workable would be a democratic solution with constitutional guarantees of the rights — religious, linguistic, educational, and cultural — of the Jewish minority already settled in Palestine. It was also suggested that immigration for political ends must be discontinued "although not altogether for any community whether Christian, Jewish or Muslim."[28]

Evidently, the Asian opinion endorsed the basic Palestinian demand that the mandate be ended and self-government granted to the people of

27. *United Nations Special Committee on Palestine: Report to the General Assembly,* II, 24–27.

28. *Ibid.*

Palestine as a whole. This was also the view of the Arab states represented in the United Nations. The latter, however, made a serious error in initially rejecting the federal plan proposed by India, Iran, and Yugoslavia. When the final vote was taken in the General Assembly on November 29, 1947, the Asian states, with two exceptions, China and the Philippines, voted against partition. China disapproved of partition but opted to abstain; the Philippines completely reversed its previous stand, reportedly under extrinsic persuasion or pressure.[29]

Asia and the Arab-Israeli Conflict

The unilateral declaration of the establishment of the state of Israel in May, 1948, and Israel's subsequent admission to the United Nations marked the beginning of yet another phase in the evolution of the Asian outlook on the Palestine question. The forebodings of the Asian nations that partition would aggravate rather than resolve the basic conflict under-lying the Palestine problem were more than confirmed by the grim events that followed it. Almost one million Palestinian Arabs were evicted from their ancestral homeland, just as Hitler's tyranny had uprooted Jews from theirs. Israel forcibly occupied large areas that had been originally assigned to the Palestinians by the U.N. resolution of November 29, 1947, and resolved to retain them on the plea of security. Israel's existence as a sovereign nation introduced a new ingredient in the situation — its admitted anxiety to cultivate political and economic relations with the nations of Asia.

Israel's diplomatic overtures to win friends in Asia gave top priority to India. But India stuck to its original stand. When the issue of Israel's admission to the U.N. came to a head in May, 1949, India voted against its admission. M. C. Setalvad, India's chief delegate, pleaded that his government "could not recognize a state which had been achieved through the use of force and not through negotiations."[30] After prolonged hesitation, India eventually recognized Israel on September 17, 1950. An official statement, however, hastened to add that the recognition of Israel did not mean an endorsement of the Israeli position regarding its bound-

---

29. For evidence suggesting that the U.S. caused both official and unofficial pressure to be exerted on some countries, including the Philippines, in order to help secure the required two-thirds majority for the partition plan, see Forrestal, *Forrestal Diaries* (New York, 1951), pp. 309, 322, 344–49, 357–58; and *Foreign Policy Reports*, XXIII, February 15, 1948, 290.

30. Cited in the *The Hindu* (Madras), May 13, 1949.

aries and the rights of the Palestinians to return to their homeland.[31] During this period India also entertained the hope of persuading Israel to fulfill the necessary requirements of an Arab-Israeli *rapprochement;* these hopes had melted away by 1952, and India firmly expressed its unwillingness to establish diplomatic ties with Tel Aviv.

The chances of Israel's acceptance by other Asian nations were scarcely better. Tel Aviv was practically ignored by Afghanistan, Indonesia, and Pakistan. Communist China received an Israeli goodwill mission in 1955 but hurriedly gave up the idea of going any further. Nationalist China recognized the Jewish state but showed no interest in exchange of diplomatic missions. This was also the case with the Philippines, Ceylon, Burma, Thailand, and Iran. Of the Asian nations that recognized Israel in the early -years, only Turkey established a diplomatic mission in Tel Aviv. Burma, Thailand, and the Philippines established missions during the 1950s. Ceylon established diplomatic ties with Israel in January, 1960, but in August the newly elected government of Cirimava Bandaranayake speedily reversed the decision of the previous regime. The prime minister observed in a press statement that the earlier move was "incompatible" with the policy pursued by the late Mr. Bandaranayake and added, "my Government now proposes to take certain urgent remedial measures with a view to strengthening and fostering our relations with the Arab countries."[32] Ceylon withdrew its nonresident minister from Tel Aviv. The result of this prolonged battle in the diplomatic field was a curious pattern encompassing relationship, semirelationship, and nonrelationship. It is an indication of the fact that Israel's credentials for admission to the Asian community are seriously questioned by many of its members and only gingerly endorsed by some.

Having realized in the early years that it stood little chance of being accepted as an Asian state, Israel attempted to project itself as a pioneering state possessing an abundant reservoir of technical and organizational skills suited to Asian needs. Israeli publicity underscored the achievements of its cooperative agriculture, its *nahal* units (which combined army service with agricultural training), and its new methods of solving social and economic problems. Ben-Gurion spoke of the "historic mission" of Israel to assist in the progress and development of Asia.[33] This arduous exercise in image-manship met with limited success in some smaller

31. See Government of India, External Publicity Division, *India and Palestine: Evolution of a Policy* (New Delhi, n.d.), p. 31.

32. *Middle East Record* (Tel Aviv), I (1960), 180.

33. *Ibid.,* p. 276.

and remote Asian countries but made no dent in the greater part of the continent.

On the other hand, the issue of Palestine continued to concern not only individual Asian nations but the new forums of Asian and Afro-Asian deliberation and coordination. The unresolved conflict between the Jewish state and Palestinians barred the admission of Israel to these conferences. The consensus that emerged at the Asian Relations Conference in Delhi was reaffirmed at subsequent gatherings. While consistently supporting the rights of the Palestinians, the resolutions adopted at these conferences also reflect the shifting shades of emphasis corresponding to the evolving mood of Asia. The communiqué issued at the end of the Colombo Conference of the prime ministers of Burma, Ceylon, India, Indonesia, and Pakistan, held in April–May, 1951, expressed "grave concern over the sufferings of Arab refugees in Palestine," "urged the United Nations to bring about and expedite the rehabilitation of these refugees in their original houses," and "affirmed their desire to see a just and early settlement of the Palestine problem."[34]

Palestine was again discussed at Bandung in April, 1955. The distinctive features of the Bandung Conference were (1) the enlargement of the Asian forum to include the sovereign nations of Africa and (2) the uneasy awareness of the global impact of the Cold War. In reference to Palestine, Nasser told the conference that "never before in history has there been such a brutal and immoral violation of human principles," and asked, "is there any guarantee for the small nations that the big powers who took part in this tragedy would not allow themselves to repeat it again, against another innocent and helpless people?"[35] The Bandung communiqué also pointed to the ominous potentialities of the Palestine conflict:

> In view of the existing tension in the Middle East caused by the situation in Palestine and the danger of that tension to world peace, the Asian-African Conference declared its support of the rights of the Arab people of Palestine and called for the implementation of the United Nations resolutions on Palestine and of the peaceful settlement of the Palestine question.[36]

Israel's invasion of Egypt in October, 1956, confirmed the apprehen-

---

34. Text of the communiqué in Jansen, *Afro-Asia,* pp. 412–14.

35. Cited in Richard Wright, *The Color Curtain: A Report on the Bandung Conference* (New York, 1956), p. 145.

36. Text of the communiqué in Institute of Pacific Relations, *Selected Documents of the Bandung Conference* (New York, 1955), p. 33.

sions of the Bandung nations. It also revealed Israel's continuing collusion with colonial powers. Nehru promptly declared that the Israeli action and the subsequent Anglo-French ultimatum constituted "a flagrant violation of the United Nations Charter. . . . This aggression is bound to have far-reaching consequences in Asia and Africa."[37] "We are going back," he observed soon after the Anglo-French invasion of Egypt, "in the twentieth century to the predatory methods of the eighteenth and nineteenth centuries. The difference today is that there are self-respecting independent nations in Asia who are not going to tolerate this kind of incursion."[38] At the U.N. General Assembly, Krishna Menon observed: "We desire to state without any superlatives that we regard the action of Israel as an invasion of Egyptian territory, and the introduction of the forces of the U.K. and France as an aggression without any qualification."[39] Reactions in other Asian capitals were equally spontaneous and strong and were reminiscent of the anticolonial statements of the past decades. Turkey, the only Middle Eastern nation that maintained a diplomatic mission in Tel Aviv, brusquely withdrew it.

Following a decade of rampant Cold War, and the resultant extension of rival military alliances to the Asian continent, the political outlook in the majority of Asian nations crystallized in a positive aversion to international power blocs — an aversion symbolized by the concept of non-alignment. The "Afro-Asian spirit" blossomed into the "Belgrade spirit," desirous of reaching out to establish rapport with the nations of other continents. But to most of the participating nations of the Belgrade Conference of 1961 Israel did not appear to fit into this broader, nongeographical framework. Palestine once again figured in the deliberations, and the final resolution at Belgrade made a caustic reference to "the imperialist policies pursued in the Middle East." Three years later, the Cairo Conference of Non-Aligned Nations specifically endorsed the struggle of the Palestinian people "for liberation from colonialism and racism."[40]

Over the two decades following the creation of Israel, the question of almost one million homeless Palestinians remained unresolved. As the principal beneficiary of the U.N. resolution of November 29, 1947, it was

---

37. Cited in Brecher, *New States,* p. 138.

38. Cited in United Nations, General Assembly, *Official Records,* first emergency special session, plenary meetings. November 1–10, 1956, p. 31.

39. *Ibid.*

40. Texts of the Belgrade and Cairo resolutions are in Indian Society of International Law, *Asian-African States: Texts of International Declarations* (New Delhi, 1965), pp. 26, 45.

expected of Israel to honor the claims of the Palestinians which were also endorsed by the world body. To have done so would have created the necessary climate for normal relations with Israel's Arab neighbors, and it would have secured for Israel the friendship and cooperation of the Asian nations. Instead, Israel chose the course of treating the rightful demands of the Palestinians as a denial of its own existence and holding the neighboring Arab states responsible for keeping the restive Palestinians under leash on pain of dire reprisals. Israel abandoned the Palestine Conciliation Commission, repudiated the Egyptian-Israeli armistice agreement in 1956, and made it clear that the primary condition of peace was Arab acquiescence to the Jewish state as a *fait accompli* and liquidation of the Palestinian claims.

The widely publicized theme that Israel's existence was imperiled by the Arab states was contravened by Israeli foreign minister Abba Eban who wrote in 1965, "it is not absurd to imagine Arab leaders ardently urging 'a return to the frontier of 1966 or 1967,' just as they now urge a return to the frontier of 1947 which they once set aside by force."[41] It is curious that repeatedly the Arabs are blamed for setting aside the frontier "by force," and repeatedly the beneficiary is Israel. Abba Eban's prediction was translated into reality in June, 1967. It is not the purpose of this essay to assess the ramifications of this conflict. Suffice it to say that the Israeli conquest of 26,000 square miles of Arab territory, the formal annexation of the old city of Jerusalem, and the eviction of more Palestinians from their homes has once and for all exploded the myth of Israel's peaceful disposition. This time even Iran and Turkey, who had lent a sympathetic ear to Tel Aviv in the past, came forward with unequivocal censures. "The days of occupation and retention of one country's territory by another are over," said Iran's Ardeshir Zahedi. "The longer the occupation of Arab territories continues, the more rancorous the feeling will be. If it is peace we seek, one of the first steps towards it is to remove the justified grievances."[42] Ihsan Caglayangil, the Turkish foreign minister, told the U.N. General Assembly that "a grave responsibility rests on the government of Israel. In its own obvious interest, it must give proof of its attachment to the principles of the U.N."[43] The prime minister of India observed that "there can be no doubt that Israel has escalated the situa-

---

41. "Reality and Vision in the Middle East," *Foreign Affairs,* XLIII (July, 1965), 631.

42. United Nations, General Assembly, *Official Records,* fifth emergency special session (A/PV 1530) June 21, 1967.

43. *Ibid.* (A/PV 1532) June 22, 1967.

tion into an armed conflict."[44] At the United Nations, the Afro-Asian nations joined other states to secure evacuation of the occupied territories in the face of continued Israeli defiance of the world body.

THE ASIAN PERSPECTIVE

The Zionist case for national self-determination evoked no favorable response in Asia. The Asian nationalists of an early generation regarded Palestine as the home of the Palestinians in the sense that other countries belonged to their respective peoples. On the other hand, the Zionist movement's close links with the imperialist interests of Britain in Asia roused considerable hostility against both. This coupled with the Jewish opposition to self-government by the people of Palestine placed Zionism outside the mainstream of Asian nationalism.

Sympathy for the Jewish victims of Nazism was not lacking among the Asian nations. But the idea of visiting the sins of Nazi Germany upon the Palestinians did not appeal to them. However, in view of the Jewish tragedy in Europe, there were many in Asia who began to favor the creation of a binational state in Palestine. This obviously required that the Arab-Jewish issue in Palestine be separated from the wider question of world Jewry. But the Jews were inflexibly committed to an exclusivist Jewish state and mustered the support of the great powers to achieve it.

The circumstances attending the partition and its consequences raised another barrier between Israel and Asia. For in the Asian view the tragic aspect of the Palestine problem is not that the Palestinians have refused to be liquidated as a people, it is rather that Israel turned a blind eye to the sufferings of Palestinians.

Nor did Israel identify itself with the anticolonial causes in Asia. It rarely took a clear stand on such questions. On the contrary, its voting record in the United Nations and other international bodies placed it in the opposite camp. The fact that the vast majority of the Jewish people live on the continents of Europe and America creates an emotional bond between Israel and the Western world which has no counterpart in its relationship with Asia. The Israelis believe that their scientific skills and technical know-how would galvanize the developing nations of Asia, but the picture of Israel as a reservoir of unique skills and practical wisdom is somewhat overdrawn. In fact, the Zionist belief in the uniqueness of the Jewish race and its "historic mission"; the ideological amalgam of

44. Cited in *Times of India* (New Delhi), June 7, 1967.

race, religion, and politics; and, above all, the Israeli model of a garrison state, subsisting on permanent tension with its neighbors and permanent unsettlement of Jewish life abroad, have little practical relevance to the pressing needs of the Asian nations for development and peace.

16. Zionism and Race in Afro-Semitic Relations

Ali A. Mazrui

═══════ It is impossible to comprehend fully the intellectual attitudes of black peoples to the current Middle East crisis without understanding their attitudes to the two Semitic peoples involved in the crisis. Our interest here is partly in the black peoples of the African continent and partly in the black peoples of the Western diaspora. This essay therefore addresses itself back to the fundamentals of intergroup relations in order to provide the foundation for comprehending black responses to clashes between the Arabs and the Jews.

At the center of much of the political thought of black people is the fear or resentment of *domination*. The concept of domination has important roles to play in Afro-Jewish relations. And in those roles the concept takes three major forms: there is first racial domination; second, economic domination; and third, intellectual domination.

By racial domination is here meant the kind of exercise of power that reduces the dignity of one race in its relations with another. The race whose dignity is compromised does not necessarily have to be poor or exploited. It need not, in other words, be economically as well as racially dominated. In the economic sphere it could be prosperous and influential. But if there are important social clubs a man cannot enter, or certain residential areas he cannot live in, or political positions he cannot hold because of his race, then the dignity of the group as a whole is compromised, even if the group does not suffer economic indigence or exploitation.

The second form of domination does indeed presuppose exploitative relationships. It signifies that one group has exerted a degree of economic control over another which is fundamentally disadvantageous to the weaker party. In this case the indignity need not be manifested in racial gradations at all. There may be no areas of residence that are taboo to the exploited

463

group, nor positions that are shut, nor clubs that are inaccessible. It is even conceivable that there are no special racial differences between the exploited and those who exploit. In this case the differences could be basically class differences, favoring those who have already arrived at economic power and perpetuating some of the economic handicaps under which the other group labors. There may be additional differences, like regional variations or the accents with which the different groups speak, but just as racial humiliation need not be accompanied by economic domination so too is economic domination often unrelated to issues of race. There are of course occasions when the two forms of domination — economic and racial — reinforce one another. But what needs to be noted is that they can in fact be separate.

A third pertinent form of domination is intellectual domination. This can at times be connected with racial issues. But the essential nature of intellectual domination is an assertion of intellectual superiority by one group and an imposition of some of its ideas and values on others. The others may accept these ideas and values after a while and may even internalize them completely and make them their own. The element of intellectual domination might remain if there persists an edge of superiority enjoyed by the intellectual donors over the intellectual recipients.

BLACKS AND JEWS IN THE UNIVERSE OF RACE CONFLICT

Now let us look more closely at the place of these three forms of domination in Afro-Jewish relations. I use Afro-Jewish relations here to mean relations not just between people in the African continent and the Jews, but between black peoples and Jewish peoples everywhere. The area of maximum shared experience between black peoples and Jewish peoples lies in the universe of race conflict. Clearly there can be no doubt that both groups have been among the most oppressed in the history of civilization.

Moses as a symbol of nationalism has been important both to Africans in southern Africa and to black Americans in the United States. Garvey, the great Jamaican leader of a back-to-Africa movement in the United States early in this century, has been designated a *black Moses*. The whole concept of "black Zionism" as a desire by black peoples in the Western Hemisphere to find their way back to the ancestral soil has borrowed considerably from the liberation imagery of Jewish history. Albert Luthuli, the first winner from Africa of the Nobel Prize for Peace, entitled his book *Let My People Go,* echoing the Mosaic imperative. The fact that South African Jews have been in the forefront of white liberalism and white demands for reform in southern Africa has on occasion also made it easy for black nationalists in southern Africa to share a language of historical discourse with the Jews.

But there have been important differences between the racial predicament of the black man and the racial predicament of the Jew in the white world as a whole. One difference lies in what we might call *racial mobility*. We know that *social mobility* is the capacity permitted by a given society for an individual to move from one class to another. Where people born in slums, for example, get fair educational opportunities and stand a good chance of being successful in business, it becomes possible for a child born of working-class parents to find his way to the commanding heights of the economy or of the professions.

Racial mobility — the capacity of an individual to change his racial affinity — is possible in societies with a high rate of intermarriage or in societies where racial differences are allowed to persist in spite of cultural homogenization. Pre-revolutionary Zanzibar, for example, was a society with a high rate of intermarriage. It was therefore conceivable for a family to be African in one generation and become Arab in the next. In the years since independence a reverse trend is of course discernible — families which previously designated themselves as Arab are now becoming African.

Racial mobility creates a credibility gap in that the single-generation transfer may be regarded as racial pretension rather than a genuine change of racial affinity. But even in the case of social mobility a credibility gap sometimes exists in that the newly successful may be accused of giving themselves airs. It takes more than one generation in the case of a change of social class to stabilize the social switch. But it sometimes takes even longer to stabilize a racial switch.

The degree of racial mobility enjoyed by the American Jew is much greater than that commanded by American blacks. As the American black scholar C. Eric Lincoln once put it,

> Some Jews can and do pass into the dominant white group, often through the simple expedient of changing their names. Like Negroes, some may pass temporarily in order to enjoy advantages or avoid discrimination in business or social life. In a New York suburb, for example, there is a Jew whose legal name is John Smith; and as Dr. John Smith he has a good dental practice. How he would fare if he practiced as Jacob Goldstein is problematic. Dr. Smith himself has no doubt but that, in the community where he lives, there is a considerably larger practice available to Dr. Smith than there would be, say, to Dr. Goldstein.[1]

1. C. Eric Lincoln, *The Black Muslims in America* (Boston, 1961), pp. 231–32.

There is school of thought among black people that regards all Semitic peoples as having been originally part of the colored world. A branch of these broke off, gradually won their way into the bosom of whitehood, and became white men. These were the Jews. The other wing of the Semitic peoples remained in the fold of Afro-Asianism, militantly opposed to white domination and politically aligned to the other colored races of the globe. These were the Arabs.

The theory that the Semites and the Negroes have a history that is intermingled has, in fact, affected much of scholarship. The Semites, the Hamites, and the black peoples have, it is known, interacted in a variety of ways.. What has been historically in dispute is what the nature of that interaction has been. The attachment of the Somalis to a Semitic civilization, the points of similarity between Amharic and the written language of pre-Islamic southern Arabia, the impact of the Arabs on the racial mixture of northern Africa, the penetration and infiltration of Islamic values and cultural mores among diverse peoples in West and East Africa, the role of the Hamites in African civilizations and their relationship to Semitic groups — all these questions are part of the total picture of a massive interaction between Semites, Hamites, and black peoples. (Many eighteenth- and nineteenth-century Western historians had such a low opinion of Negro capabilities that they tended to attribute any great achievement in Africa to the influence of the Fula or, later, the Hamites. But one does not have to share these racialistic prejudices to recognize the racial intermixture and cultural interaction between these different groups.)

Historical evidence, however, is not entirely hostile to the view that the Semites split into two groups, one that intermingled with the whites and became part of the white world and another that identified with Afro-Asian forces and became part of the colonized group. Among the colonized groups are indeed some colored Jews, but the most important Jewry became semiassimilated into the Northern Hemisphere of the world, made an impact on the history of the globe partly through their participation in the European evolution, and sometimes suffered hardships as a minority group in white lands. Where they were not suffering these hardships, the white Jews of the Northern Hemisphere have sometimes been seen by black militants in the Western Hemisphere as renegades from the cause of black peoples. As Eric Lincoln observed in relation to the attitudes of Black Muslims, especially in the United States,

> There is a feeling in some quarters that the Jews, as Semites, are "not quite white" and should be grouped with the Arabs as members of the Black Nation. "How can we be accused of being anti-Semitic," one

Muslim Minister asked "when our Arab brothers are Semitic?" For those who accept this implication, the Jews are traitors; black men who reject their true identity, scorn their black brothers and pass themselves off as white."[2]

The other aspect of the Jewish racial predicament which differentiates the Jews from the black people is, quite simply, the concept of the *chosen people*. The concept of the chosen people has been both the strength of the Jews and their weakness. It has enabled the Jews to survive as a culturally distinct entity in spite of generations of intermingling with other groups in different parts of the world. Yet the fact remains that the cultural exclusiveness of the Jews and their conception of themselves as a group endowed by God with a peculiar destiny have made their racial predicament very different from that of the black people. What the black people are fighting against is precisely racial exclusiveness. They are asserting a need for areas of maximum intermingling, including permissive intermarriage. It is true that in black America today there is an ethic of antimiscegenation, a distrust of black people who marry white people. But black antimiscegenation in the United States is basically a *protest;* it is not inherent in the cultural values of the group but arises substantially out of a posture of militancy in a given period of time. Jewish antimiscegenation, on the other hand, is culturally sanctioned and is at the core of Jewish values of identity.

This is another great difference between the Jews and that other wing of the Semites, the Arabs. While the Jews owe their survival in part to their endogamy, the Arabs happen to be among the most mongrel peoples on earth. In skin color the range is from the white Arabs of Syria and Lebanon to the brown Arabs of the Hadhramaut and the Yemen to the black Arabs of parts of Saudi Arabia, Oman, and, of course, the Sudan. We see those Arabs scattered across both sides of the Red Sea, neither completely African nor completely Asian — and certainly impossible to classify neatly in pigmentation.[3]

In the kind of religion they bequeathed to the world, there is also an important difference between Jews and Arabs, as between Jews and the black races. Judaism is an exclusive religion in a way in which Islam and the traditional religions of Africa are not. In other words the religious heritage of the Jews is again monopolistic and exclusive, whereas

2. *Ibid.,* p. 165.

3. For a further discussion of the implications of Arab tolerance of intermarriage, see the chapter on "Political Sex," in Mazrui, *Violence and Thought: Essays on Social Tensions in Africa* (London, 1969), pp. 312–18.

the religion which came with the Arabs aspires to universal validity and to accommodating diverse groups within it.

Bildad Kaggia, who later became a symbol of the Kikuyu wing of radical thought in Kenya, was in the colonial period a preacher who became involved in the Mau Mau insurrection. He stood trial with Jomo Kenyatta and spent some years in detention. In the course of a cross-examination in the courtroom at Kapenguria a letter was produced which Kaggia had written to Kenyatta in 1950. The following is the exchange which took place between Somerhough for the prosecution and Kaggia in the witness box:

Prosecution: I am suggesting that in paragraph four of that letter [to Kenyatta] you are saying three things: that when you went to Europe you abandoned the CMS religion and all those other religions which have beeen brought here; I understand you to say that you only meant denomination?

Kaggia: Yes.

Prosecution: Then you say that when you returned to this country in 1946 you refused to have anything to do with any of the religions of the Europeans and you were left simply standing on the Bible?

Kaggia: Yes.

Prosecution: And in the last paragraph, did you say that the third stage of your spiritual development was to abandon the whole of the Bible?

Kaggia: If you read the last paragraph properly you will see it says that I came to find that the Bible contained the customs and laws of the Jews and that I abandoned those.

Prosecution: But that is not what the letter says. I will read it again. "I realise it contained the laws of the Jews and so I abandoned the teaching of the Bible."

Kaggia: Yes, as far as the laws and customs were concerned which are in the Bible. That is my meaning. I would like to explain the parts of the Bible. The Bible contains one part prophecy, one part Moses' law; another part is of Jewish customs; and the fourth is the teaching of Jesus Christ. And when I talk of laws and customs which I abandoned, those are the things which were meant solely for the Jewish people; but when we come to prophecies and the teaching of Jesus Christ, they are meant for the whole of mankind, which I, too, believe and practise.[4]

4. This rendering of the exchange occurs in Montagu Slater's *The Trial of Jomo Kenyatta* (London, 1965), pp. 195–96. The exclusiveness of "being Jewish" was

Kaggia later became a leading radical in Kenya and the deputy leader of the Kenya Peoples' Union before the party ran into the political troubles of 1969 which led to its being finally banned. Kaggia's rejection, at this early point in his thinking, of the Judaic part of the Bible on grounds that it was an ethnocentric code of laws, intended only for the Jews and therefore irrelevant for the African, is of interest.

The Paradox of the Privileged Oppressed

But although racially the Jews have been among the oppressed peoples of the world, economically there is no doubt that on balance the Jews have been among the more privileged groups of the world. When we divide the world between the haves and the have-nots, it is quite clear where world Jewry belongs. In the Middle Ages an old European contempt of usury was extended to the whole enterprise of making profit. Aristocrats of Europe rated commercial activity sufficiently low to permit its energetic infiltration by Jews. Jews as moneylenders gradually led to Jews as bankers. European literature is full of examples of Jews as great financiers. In Walter Scott's *Ivanhoe* we have the portrayal of Isaac redeeming Richard the Lion-Hearted through his participation in raising the ransom. In Shakespeare's *Merchant of Venice* we have Shylock in possession of the "right" to exact a pound of flesh — a Jew dangerously greedy unless he was controlled by the laws of the society.

Discrimination against Jews in certain areas of endeavor in European societies forced the Jews to specialize in other areas. They became preeminent in some professions and in business. Their role in business gave them a share in the commanding heights of the economy. Indeed, while black people in North America have had a share unfavorably disproportionate to their numbers, the Jews have had a share most favorably disproportionate to their numbers. The same conspicuous affluence has sometimes marked the Jews in Europe.

---

tested in a new way in Israel early in 1970 when the Israeli Supreme Court decided to allow two children of a Jewish father and a non-Jewish mother—both parents were atheists—to be registered as of Jewish nationality. The Israeli government decided to change the law which had made such a court ruling possible. The orthodox rabbinic law which said that only converts and children born of Jewish mothers were Jewish was to be reaffirmed after all (see Ivan Yates, "Who shall define a Jew?" *Observer* [London], February 1, 1970).

Within Africa, Jewish prosperity in the south is marked and was resented by Afrikaaners before it began to be noticed by Africans. Jews are among the richest people in southern Africa.

Both the Jewish fate as an oppressed racial group and the Jewish good fortune as an economically privileged group played their parts in the creation of Israel. As I have had occasion to say before, Hitler was at once the greatest enemy of Jews in history and the greatest benefactor of Israel.[5] The brutalities of Hitler's anti-Semitism gave Zionism a great boost. Hitler destroyed Jews in Germany — and in the macabre and cruel process helped to create the state of Israel. But it was not simply the role of Jews as victims of oppression which helped to create Israel. It was also in part the role of Jews as a financially powerful group in world affairs. There can be no doubt that Zionism, as a movement to create a national home for the Jews, would not have gone far had it lacked access to immense financial resources for its implementation. Even the establishment of a political party in a single country needs enormous financial support. A movement to create a home for Jews — with the necessity of securing resources for their transportation, producing propaganda to create an international climate favorable to such a move, and the capital to sustain the new settlements — was something which only a group happily privileged in financial influence could have undertaken.

We might therefore say that discrimination against Jews in Europe helped the creation of Israel in two ways: One was in arousing the conscience of Europe in the twentieth century to the need for some form of protection for this racial minority, but another, with a longer history, was the role of medieval European anti-Semitism in forcing Jewish minorities to specialize in business techniques and financial enterprises, with the result that they acquired an impressive base for economic and political initiative. The Armenians may have been oppressed in Turkey and Russia over the ages; the Kurds have been oppressed in the Arab world. But no national home for them has emerged. As minorities they differed from the Jews in one fundamental respect: they had not specialized in wealth.

Jewish immigration into Palestine began in 1882, and by 1917 the number of Jews who had found their way there from central and eastern Europe and their offspring amounted to 75,000. Massive support for the actual migration itself and for the policy of purchasing as much land as possible within Palestine could only have been undertaken by a community with great international resources. A financial giant interested in the problem at that time was Lord Rothschild. It was in fact to Lord Rothschild that

5. See Mazrui, *Violence and Thought,* p. 248, for comments on Israel's appeal to an outraged Western conscience.

Lord Balfour addressed on November 2, 1917, the famous Balfour Declaration, which the Zionist movement adopted as its own legal basis. There can be little doubt that the influence of the Rothschilds and other Jewish millionaires in the Western world was an important part of the success of Zionism. The birth of Israel had wealth behind it. But the role of Jewish affluence did not end with the birth of Israel. Jewish affluence in the Diaspora has also been an important part of the maintenance of Israel. Many Jews in the United States and elsewhere regard contributions to Israel as being a kind of voluntary tax on their own earnings.

In the United States the phenomenon of Jewish wealth has become intermingled with long-standing black resentment of Jewish commercial power in black areas. Many of the larger shops and enterprises in the black areas of the United States are owned by Jews and sometimes are run exclusively by them. As some black Americans have complained,

> The Jew comes in and brings his family. He opens a business and hires his wife, his mother-in-law, all his brothers-in-law, and then he sends to the old country to get his father and mother, sisters and brothers— even his uncles — and he hires all of them. Meanwhile, the so-called Negroes are footing the bill, but there isn't a black face behind a single counter in the store."

The stereotype continues to say that soon the Jew opens another business —a laundromat perhaps. Some of his relatives are transferred there. A liquor store follows, "because by now he has got enough money to buy off the crooks downtown." The stereotype goes on to assert that the Jew soon follows the Negro customer home and buys the flat he lives in. But by that time, the Jew is providing the Negro with his food, his clothes, his services, his home, and the whiskey he has to get to keep from hating himself. "But the Jew doesn't live above the business any more. He has moved out to the suburbs and is living in the best house black money can buy."[6]

During the Depression in the early 1930s, black hostilities against the Jews reached new heights, particularly when a campaign started with the slogan "Don't buy where you can't work!" The fact that Jewish enterprises employed, so far as was possible, fellow-Jews, instead of the black people in whose areas the enterprises were operated, heightened the tensions. There were riots as Jewish businessmen became targets of indignant and hungry black mobs.[7] At this stage black anti-Semitism had little to do with

---

6. Cited by Lincoln, *Black Muslims,* p. 167.

7. See St. Clair Drake and Horace R. Cayton, *Black Metropolis* (New York, 1945), pp. 430–32.

the Zionist movement. Its causes were basic to the structure of Jewish business in big cities, with special reference to the Jewish economic presence in black ghettos. But in a later period, when Afro-Asian nationalism made its impact on black opinion in the United States, black anti-Semitism and black anti-Zionism interacted and reinforced one another to some extent. Malcolm X, the assassinated black militant, was perhaps the most forthright spokesman of this school of thought. In an interview with C. Eric Lincoln, he once said that he made no distinction between white Jews and white Gentiles. They were all white. To concede such a distinction would be to imply that he liked some whites better than others. "This would be discrimination and we do not believe in discrimination."

What Malcolm did believe in was in a conspiracy between the white Jews and the white Gentiles to drive the Arabs out of their Palestinian homeland. Why had the Gentiles supported the Jews in the fight for the creation of Israel? Malcolm's theory went thus:

> The European and American Christians helped to establish Israel in order to get rid of the Jews so that they could take over their businesses as they did the American Japanese during the war. The scheme failed, and the joke is on the white man. The American Jews aren't going anywhere.[8]

Malcolm felt particularly strongly about American Jewish contributions to the maintenance of Israel. The voluntary tax which many American Jews imposed on themselves as a contribution to Israel appeared to Malcolm X as a case of Jewish exploitation of black people in the United States in order to finance Jewish aggression against the Arabs in the Middle East. In his words,

> In America, the Jews sap the very life-blood of the so-called Negroes to maintain the state of Israel, its armies and its continued aggression against our brothers in the East. This every Black Man resents. . . . Israel is just an international poorhouse which is maintained by money sucked from the poor suckers in America.[9]

Jewish contributions from southern Africa to the maintenance of Israel are also significant, and became a little more conspicuous than usual in the June war of 1967 when South African Jewry rallied in support of Israel

---

8. Cited in Lincoln, *Black Muslims*, p. 166.
9. *Ibid.*

and even offered volunteers to fight in the Middle East. To African radicals from South Africa, Israel became a symbol of white conspiracy linked to the imperial forces of the Western world. At the beginning of the 1967 crisis the African National Congress cabled President Nasser from Dar-es-Salaam expressing its support for Nasser in his conflict with Israel and describing the war threat in the Middle East as "being directly engineered as an act of provocation and aggression by Anglo-American powers."[10]

Yet there can be little doubt that the Jews have been among the most radical reformers in South Africa as well as in the United States. They have been in the forefront of civil-rights movements and have tried to give direction and sense of purpose to black discontent where black leadership has sometimes been lacking. But Jewish liberalism has suffered the same fate that Gandhism has suffered in the history of black protests. While both liberal movements and Gandhism have been effective in increasing political and social equality, they have both been found inadequate to the task of achieving economic equality. And so even the motivation behind Jewish liberalism has come under the shadow of black suspicion in some cases. The NAACP in the United States has sometimes been regarded by black militants as a "tiger" under Jewish command, unleashed every so often to harass white Gentiles. The Jew in turn is supposed to be constantly trying to keep the black man agitated about

such nonsense as sitting beside a white man on a bus, thus keeping them too busy to think about building supermarkets and department stores. Meanwhile, the white man is so busy trying to segregate the Negroes in the back of the bus that *he* has no time for business. The Jew then steps in and provides the food, clothes and services for both contestants. He may even provide the bus! And he is certain to provide the Negro with enough money to keep the fight going.[11]

Conspiratorial versions of anti-Semitism are of course not peculiar to black people, but black economic subjugation and black radicalism have indeed interacted to arouse a profound distrust of Jewish affluence and to attribute to that affluence a capacity to manipulate important factors in the modern world to serve Jewish purposes.

The great paradox then about the Jews is that of a race humiliated and victimized and yet at the same time belonging to the class of the privileged in the world distribution of wealth. Abba Eban, Israel's foreign

10. *Nationalist* (Dar es Salaam), June 1, 1967.
11. Cited by Lincoln, *Black Muslims,* pp. 166–67.

minister, said to one visiting African delegation, as he has no doubt said to others: "We have all traveled a long path of discrimination, sorrow, and pain—some for color, some for religion." An African statesman, President Dacko of the Central African Republic, replied: "Henceforth neither you nor we will know what it is to be lonely again."[12] It may be that the black man and the Jew have indeed shared the same burden of loneliness—but they have never shared the same level of affluence.

BLACK POWER AND BRAIN POWER

We now come to the concept of domination in the intellectual sphere. It would not of course be correct to say that the Jews have directly imposed their ideas on black men or that they have sought to manipulate them ethically or ideologically. But Jews in fact have made an intellectual impact on black people—an impact that consists in nothing less than the amazing impact of the Jews on the history of ideas at large. The great Jewish figures who have influenced the evolution of Western ideas and morals range from Jesus Christ to Karl Marx. The ethical component of modern civilization includes a disproportionate contribution from the ideas of Jewish thinkers and Jewish prophets. And in the present day a disproportionate number of the towering figures in the academic world in the United States are Jews. This Jewish propensity to intellect is, in fact, one of the most remarkable things about Jewish history.

But does this capacity for scholarship give the Jews the power of intellectual manipulation of other peoples? Has such a power featured in Afro-Jewish relations? Among sections of black Americans there is a view that "the Jews are the brains of the white race." They have been recognized as being among the leading thinkers and writers, and they are suspected in black-militant circles of being "shrewd enough to manipulate the rest of the whites—to say nothing of the so-called Negroes."[13] It would also seem that the Jews are suspected by blacks of having a stranglehold on public opinion in the United States through their control of mass media. Either through outright ownership of radio and television stations or through their massive advertising capability and the power to withdraw advertisements, the Jews, it is thought, are able to "dictate" the editorial policies of certain radio and television stations as well as

12. Cited by Mordechai E. Kreinin, *Israel and Africa: A Study in Technical Cooperation* (New York, 1964).
13. Cited by Lincoln, *Black Muslims*, pp. 165–66.

magazines and newspapers: "they hire Gentiles to 'front' for them so as not to antagonize the public; but on crucial issues, such as the Suez Canal, they control the thinking of the people."[14]

In 1968 and early 1969 the issue of the control of schools in New York City exploded into another area of Afro-Jewish antagonism. The black communities of New York City were agitating for the adoption of a system of education which would permit more local control of schools. They wanted a greater voice in determining who taught in black schools and what was taught within them. Ultimately local control of hiring and firing became the issue. This resulted in a head-on collision between black educational reformers and the teachers' union in New York City. The teachers' union in New York City happened to be dominated by the Jews, and many of the teachers in black schools were indeed Jewish. The idea of entrusting hiring and firing to local black communities was therefore perceived as a direct challenge to the security of tenure of Jewish teachers. The teachers' union won the first round, denying the local communities the power to control hiring and firing as well as curriculum. But the issue brought to the fore once again the profound distrust of Jewish control of the educational system in some parts of the country held by certain sections of black opinion. Openly anti-Jewish speeches were heard more often from black militants.[15] The so-called "Jewish stranglehold" on neighborhood schools was sometimes linked to the disproportionate Jewish presence in the American university system. The two levels of Jewish participation in education created an impression of a disproportionate intellectual influence upon the minds of others.

Jewish synagogues were included among the institutions from which black militants were demanding "reparations" because of their part in the historical "exploitation of blacks." The idea of reparation emerged in Detroit in April, 1969, at a black economic-development conference. Mr. James Forman, director of international affairs for the Student Non-Violent Coordinating Committee, was addressing the all-black audience when he suddenly read an unscheduled "black manifesto" demanding five hundred million dollars in reparations from white churches and synagogues. The manifesto called for a southern land bank; four major publishing and printing industries to be located in Detroit, Atlanta, Los Angeles, and New York; an audio-visual network to be based in Detroit,

14. *Ibid.*, p. 166.

15. For a discussion of open anti-Semitism and "black racism" among militants at American universities, see Matthew Hodgart's report and the correspondence following in the *Times* (London), May 23, 26, 29, 1969.

Chicago, Cleveland, and Washington D.C.; a research-skills center on the problems of black people; a labor strike and defense fund; a black university, and an international black fund-raising effort.[16]

The Christian churches have been at least as involved as the synagogues in the reparations issue. But the picture is part of increasing black pressure on certain aspects of Jewish life in the United States. By early 1969 it was already being suggested that while in Eastern Europe Jewish migrations to Israel, when permitted, were due to official pressure, in the United States Jewish migration to Israel was in part a response to black militancy and black pressures on the Jews. Speaking in New York in March, 1969, at a special conference on emigration to Israel attended by seven hundred people, Jacques Torczyner, president of the Zionist Organization of America, said he knew of "several instances in which Jewish merchants relinquished their businesses because of black extremists' pressure." Uzi Narkis, director-general of the Department of Immigration and Absorption of the Jewish Agency, reported at that meeting that 4,300 Jews from North America, including 500 Canadians, had settled in Israel the previous year, the highest number since the establishment of Israel as a nation in 1948. He added that 25,000 American Jews had settled in Israel since 1948 and predicted another 7,000 would emigrate to Israel by the end of 1969. There was a clear feeling that one factor behind the renewed attraction of Israel for American Jews was the racial situation in the United States, with special reference to black anti-Semitism.[17]

Jews in New York sensed this more immediately perhaps than Jews in many other centers, but then there were more Jews in New York than in the entire state of Israel. In April, 1969, an entire page of the *New York Times* was taken over by a photograph of Hitler. The advertisement was from the Committee to Stop Hate, an interdenominational organization. The caption under the massive picture read "April 20th is his birthday. Don't make it a happy one. Adolf Hitler would love New York City's latest crisis. Black against Jew. Jew against black. Neighbor against neighbor." Whether the crisis over New York schools was an aspect of Jewish intellectual dominance or something simpler, the fact remains that it became an important contributory factor to the rise of Afro-Jewish tensions in the United States.

16. See *Christian Science Monitor,* May 10, 1969.
17. *New York Times,* March 31, 1962.

ENTERPRISE AND AID
IN AFRICAN DEVELOPMENT

If we look at the influence of the Jews on internal events within Africa, it will be quite clear that their role in matters of African development has been positive and that their role in matters of African unity has, on balance, been negative.

The developmental contribution is connected in part with the controversial prosperity of southern Africa. There is no doubt that the Jews have played an important role in the development of that region, and have managed this while at the same time holding relatively liberal racial attitudes.

It is also quite clear that the Jews have had a much greater share of the economic wealth of southern Africa than have the Afrikaaners. Jewish South Africans have long been part of the English-speaking South African community and have been among the most influential members of that community. But, as Colin and Margaret Legum once argued, if the Marxists were right in their assertion that power lies among those who control the means of production, Afrikaanerdom would not today be ruling the Republic of South Africa. The Legums pointed out that the key "means of production, distribution and exchange," and the most important section of the press, were in the hands of the English-speaking South Africans:

> The disparity between capitalist power and political power in South Africa is clear. English-speaking South Africans control 99 per cent of mining capital, 94 per cent of industrial capital, and 75 per cent of commercial capital. But the political interests they support have no chance of achieving power as things stand today. Nor can this disparity be explained in terms of the diffusion of capitalist power: the bulk of it is controlled by seven financial houses. Between them they control over a thousand of the largest companies, with combined financial resources exceeding £ 1,000 million."[18]

Not all this wealth, of course, was Jewish, but the Jewish component seemed to have been particularly conspicuous. The Legums pointed out that in its early struggles to achieve power, Afrikaanerdom caricatured

18. Colin Legum and Margaret Legum, *South Africa: Crisis for the West* (London, 1964), pp. 107–8.

this powerful financial complex as "Hoggenheimer"—the "foreign, imperialist and capitalist octopus." The Legums continue, "[Afrikaanerdom] looked upon this fat, cigar-smoking, diamond-studded, hook-nosed, oligarch as the heir of Cecil John Rhodes, still regarded as Afrikaanerdom's greatest enemy."[19]

The biggest Jewish name in the industrial complex of Southern Africa is Oppenheimer. When Sir Ernest Oppenheimer died in 1957, Harry Oppenheimer inherited three major business empires—De Beers, Rhodesian Anglo-American, and the Anglo-American Corporation of South Africa. Through this business empire he has exercised some control over the world diamond market, the world's largest gold-producing group, and much of the copper output of southern Africa. His interests include uranium, coal, lead, zinc, real estate, railways, ranching, fertilizers, chemicals, explosives, and munitions. "His ninety-odd companies have a market value of more than £ 500 million; they produce between £ 15 and £ 20 million in profit a year."[20]

Kwame Nkrumah was staggered by Oppenheimer's economic omnipresence in such a large part of the African continent, and he wrote about it. Lenin had described imperialism as the highest and most elaborate stage of capitalism, but Lenin had not addressed himself to neo-colonialism—a form of economic control which falls short of territorial annexation. It is this phenomenon that Nkrumah discusses in his book *Neo-Colonialism, The Last Stage of Imperialism*. In this book Nkrumah has a good deal to say about what he calls "The Oppenheimer Empire":

> The king of mining in South Africa, indeed in Africa, is Harry Frederick Oppenheimer. One might almost call him the king of South Africa, even the emperor, with an ever-extending empire. There is probably hardly a corner of southern Africa's industrial and financial structure in which he has not got a very extended finger of his own or the hook of some affiliate or associate. These fingers and hooks attach the Oppenheimer empire firmly to other empires as great or greater.

Nkrumah goes on to say that Mr. Oppenheimer is director, chairman, or president of some seventy companies. "These directorships as well as those held by important colleagues and nominees, whose names recur

19. *Ibid.*, p. 121–22. Pierre van den Berghe, curiously, plays down these aspects of the race situation in South Africa in his otherwise stimulating book *South Africa: A Study in Conflict* (Berkeley and Los Angeles, 1967).

20. Legum and Legum, *South Africa*, pp. 117–18.

monotonously on the boards of an ever-extending complex of company boards, give the lie to the fiction of respectable separateness, even where there is no obvious financial link." In the following few chapters Nkrumah provides facts and figures about what he also calls the Oppenheimer "octopus"—asserting that, through associate companies, the economic tentacles of this octopus had extended and touched far-flung parts of Africa, including "Tanganyika, Uganda, the Congo, Angola, Mozambique, West Africa, and even into the Sahara and North Africa."[21]

Harry Oppenheimer is in fact a good example of the Jewish tycoon with liberal tendencies. But in race relations his vast empire is precisely what comes into conflict with that liberalism. He does believe in some degree of racial equality, but he is also concerned to protect his economic interests in southern Africa and beyond. His behavior as an investor sometimes clashes with the broader vision of justice. In 1963 he decided to spend £ 10 million to build a munitions factory in order to enable South Africa's armies to become independent of external imports. The company, African Explosives, seemed to many African nationalists as a military consolidation of white power.

Three years before, the Sharpeville shootings of defenseless Africans had led to world indignation and to domestic fear of an uprising in South Africa. Morale fell and capital started leaving South Africa. The economy was in danger of a serious slump. It took Oppenheimer's personal intervention in the financial world to help restore confidence and reattract investment into South Africa. Oppenheimer went to the United States to arrange a £ 10 million loan for one of his companies. The successful negotiations for a massive loan to support business interests in South Africa helped clear the economic cloud and restore some confidence in the security of investment in South Africa. "Oppenheimer needs to maintain international confidence for the interests and policies which he is committed to supporting—even if the result assists Verwoerd. This is Oppenheimer's real dilemma: the more successful he is as a financier, the less successful he is as a radical politician."[22]

It was mentioned above that the famous Balfour Declaration was addressed to Lord Rothschild. The Rothschilds have also been important in the business world of southern Africa, with special reference perhaps

21. (London, 1965), pp. 110–19. That Nkrumah's estimate of the number of Oppenheimer's companies is twenty fewer than that of Legum and Legum does not lower the impact.

22. *Ibid.*, For some specimens of Oppenheimer's liberal thinking, consult his T. B. Davie Memorial Lecture at the University of Cape Town, *The Conditions for Progress in Africa* (Cape Town, 1962) and his *Towards Racial Harmony* (Johannesburg, 1956).

to the Rhodesian Selection Trust. These business interests are all part of the impressive Jewish participation in the industrial development and financial growth of southern Africa.

Another area of Jewish participation in African development lies in African relations with Israel. In Israel itself one of the most startling aspects of the composition of the population is the disproportionate availability of skilled manpower. That surplus of brain power among Israelis has often been put at the disposal of African countries. Doctors, engineers, road builders, veterinary officers, military advisers, and other kinds of skilled manpower have often been offered on generous terms for utilization by African countries. Many more projects could have been aided had there been greater readiness on the part of African governments to utilize this particular external resource. (In 1962, shortly after Israel began her drive to win friends among the newly independent African states, an American newsmagazine depicted "the bond between tiny Israel and the vast reaches of Africa" as "one of the strangest unofficial alliances in the world.") [23]

A third area of Jewish participation in the development of Africa lies in the field of American technical assistance to Africa. An impressionistic judgment, based on encounters in East Africa, suggests that there is probably a disproportionate Jewish participation in the American Peace Corps. Many young Jews, recently graduated from American colleges and universities, have been ready to offer their services to countries short of skilled manpower. Among American professors to African universities, there is again a Jewish component which is disproportionate to the numbers of Jews in the United States. This is particularly marked in the social sciences, where up to 50 per cent of American visiting staff in East Africa have been Jewish. The phenomenon arises partly because of the large Jewish presence in many American universities, but it may also be possible that American Jews, in their history as part of a Semitic nation scattered round the world, have been among the more internationalist of Americans in their perspectives.

SECESSIONIST MOVEMENTS
AND THE EXODUS COMPLEX

Although the Israeli role in African development has been impressive, the Israeli role in matters concerned with African unity has, on balance, been a negative factor. Where African unity has been envisaged in develop-

23. *Newsweek,* August 20, 1962.

mental terms, and appears to be immediately functional, Israel has fulfilled her role as a developmental friend of Africa. But in broader issues of territorial integration, and even with regard to the liberation of southern Africa, Israel's impact has tended to militate against Pan-African goals. The three most important threats to national unity in the history of independent Africa have been, first, the problem of Southern Sudan; second, the problem of Katanga; and third, the problem of Biafra. In each of these secessionist movements, the sympathies of Israel have been with the separatists. In the case of the Sudan the reasons are obvious and quite understandable. Northern Sudan is predominantly Arab in identification and sympathy and is committed to a policy of opposition to Israel. It is not, therefore, surprising that the Israelis should regard the bid by Southern Sudan to separate itself from the North as something hopeful and worthy of support. The Israelis have not been too blatant in this sympathy, fearing a reaction from black Africa should they presume to be greater champions of Southern Sudan than black Africans themselves are. Refugees in Uganda, assuming that the Israelis would be ready supporters and sympathizers, have been known to make approaches for help, financial and technical, in their quarrels with Khartoum. But the Israeli embassy in Kampala has been cautious. There has been a risk of adverse reaction from the Uganda government should the Israeli embassy be busy organizing dissidents from a neighboring African country, while the government of Uganda itself assured that country of a good-neighbor policy and neutrality in the quarrel between the North and the South. Nevertheless, to the extent that diplomatic propriety permits, the Israelis have extended sympathy to the Southern rebels and have drawn attention to their plight where the atmosphere in African capitals has permitted it. They have also given advice to dissident Sudanese about how best to make their contacts with African governments and seek moral and financial support.

Israel's policies on Biafra and the Katanga secession were less understandable. Perhaps at the heart of it was what might be described as the *Exodus complex*. The Exodus complex consists in one facet, in a highly protective concern for minorities, which involves a concept—and its modern surrogates—that I have had occasion elsewhere to call *nomadic self-determination*.[24] It consists, in another facet, in a generalization of ritual separation as a means of gaining freedom and identity.

24. See Mazrui, *Towards a Pax Africana* (Chicago, 1967), pp. 10–14; of interest in this conection is Erskine Childers, "The Other Exodus," *Spectator* (London), May 12, 1961, and the correspondence that followed.

The Exodus complex should have some behavorial relevance if we accept the proposition that there is such a thing as a "Jewish frame of reference" on matters connected with identity and tolerance. Such a frame of reference may have inspired Israeli sympathies on the side of the Ibo in the Nigerian civil war. This bond of sympathy for the Biafran cause continued to be admitted even after the federal side had won. Abba Eban commented soon after the federal victory that Israel had been unashamedly on the side of the Ibo in that tragic confrontation and that Biafra would have won had there been more Israels in the international system with the courage of their convictions.

Assertions of genocide against the Ibo may have played a part in activating the Exodus complex in Jewish observers. The horrors of the events that preceded the second Jewish Exodus, that repeat of history in which Hitler took the part of the Pharaoh, included the terrifying attempt to exterminate the Jewish people. The Ibo, fighting a state whose history had included appalling popular massacres of the Ibo in the north, symbolized to many Jews something very similar to the horrifying plight of the Jews in Nazi Germany. It is true that the Jews have sometimes been self-righteous about their martyrdom, but at its most sincere, Jewish recollection of what they suffered has been an important contributory factor to Jewish liberalism and humanitarianism. On the issue of Biafra, the Exodus complex had been activated in a humane, if perhaps mistaken, direction.

Israeli attitudes toward Katanga's bid to secede from the Congo were more explicitly political.[25] Moise Tshombe's most prominent, influential, and unequivocal support in Africa on the issue of Katanga's secession came from Sir Roy Welensky, then prime minister of the Federation of Rhodesia and Nyasaland. The Jewish origins of Tshombe's comrade-in-arms afforded the Arabs at that time an extra area of political innuendo in their less public propaganda activities. Harry Oppenheimer, himself a strong supporter of Sir Roy Welensky, was gravely concerned about the security of mining interests in southern Africa, and he seems to have been drawn toward the Katanga lobby in a bid to protect the wealth of Katanga against the unpredictable tendencies of Patrice Lumumba, then prime minister of the Congo. As for the diplomatic behavior of the Israelis themselves, there seemed to be important factors propelling them toward a sympathetic relationship with the Katanga lobby. Attitudes toward Katanga's secession did not neatly divide the West from the East. Had

25. For a further discussion of Israel's role in the Katanga secession see the chapter "Moise Tshombe and the Arabs," in Mazrui, *Violence and Thought*, pp. 231–67.

there been a Cold War division on the issue Israel would probably have been inclined toward the Western side, since there lay much of Israel's support and security. But in fact the United States favored the territorial integrity of the Congo on principle and therefore opposed the Katanga secession. Britain and France were against U.N. interference in the Congo and in favor of letting Katanga break loose if the central government were unable to stop it. Israel, for reasons partly concerned with diplomatic considerations in relation to France and perhaps partly related to the sensibilities of the Exodus complex in the face of upheaval in the rest of the Congo, was favorably inclined toward the Katangese desire for autonomy. Israel's position at that time was either distinctly anti-Lumumbist or ambivalent enough to be interpreted as such. In other words, there was enough ambiguity in Israeli policy toward the African nationalist movement at that stage to make African radicals suspicious of Israel and to give Israel's opponents political ammunition.

The African states that had supported Lumumba's position on the Congo had been feeling the need for greater coordination. In January, 1961, they met in Casablanca. The heads of Ghana, Guinea, Mali, the United Arab Republic, Morocco, and the Algerian government in exile met in that old North African city—and the radical Casablanca faction of African states came into being. It was on the side of Lumumba in the Congo. It was also explicitly against Israel in the communiqué it issued. Surprise was expressed in parts of the world that Nkrumah, who seemed to be availing himself of the offers of assistance provided by Israel, should nevertheless have signed his name to the Casablanca communiqué denouncing Israel. Speculations were that Nkrumah had been forced into it by his Arab colleagues. This might well have been one factor, but Nkrumah's position was rendered easier in that the evidence indicated Israeli ambivalence on the most important nationalist issue in Africa at that moment in time.

It is arguable that the preservation of the present territorial boundaries of African states and the liberation of southern Africa are the two most immediate goals of Pan-African sentiment. There is more consensus on those issues—in spite of the four countries that recognized Biafra—than on any other issue affecting Africa. And yet on both the issue of secessionism and the issue of liberation of southern Africa, the part that Israel has played has been less than compatible with Pan-African goals. The Organization of African Unity has consisted of states both north and south of the Sahara. Among the more radical members of the organization are those from north of the Sahara. Their bid to recruit support against Israel has again been facilitated by those Israeli sympathies which were not fully compatible with Pan-African goals.

At the OAU summit conference held at Algiers, in September, 1968, a special resolution on the Middle East was passed alongside another resolution on the unity of Nigeria.

It was considerably milder in tone than the one passed by the OAU Council of Ministers in Addis Ababa in February, 1968. The earlier resolution had spoken about "Zionist aggression." A number of African states objected to this language. The summit resolution in September demanded the withdrawal of all foreign troops from Arab soil and urged the strict application of the United Nations Security Council resolution of November, 1967. Voting on the Middle East resolution at Algiers was thirty-six for, none against, with three abstentions (Lesotho, Swaziland, and Botswana).

Yet another area in which Israel symbolizes the negation of Pan-African goals consists in the image of Israel as a courageous and industrious immigrant community which has managed to defy a hostile environment and survive with honor. This Israeli model of heroic isolation has been important both for white South Africans and more recently for white Rhodesians. A minister of defense in South Africa once extolled Israel in the following terms: "They stand alone in the world, but they are full of courage." *Die Burger* draws similar inspiration from Israel's example of victorious loneliness:

> We in South Africa would be foolish if we did not at least take account of the possibility that we are destined to become a sort of Israel in a preponderantly hostile Africa, and that fact might become part of our national way of life.[26]

But while the white communities of southern Africa have evidenced an empathetic identification with Israel, especially during the 1967 June war, black Africans, especially the more radical groups, have, on the whole, been supportive of Arab interests. To some extent, as I have argued elsewhere, it is curious that the radical nationalists south of the Sahara should more readily accept Arabs as fellow Africans than do conservative black Africans. It is curious because, in its essence, African nationalism is a *race-conscious* nationalism but it is also true that within the African continent itself African nationalism becomes less

26. See *Die Transvaler,* December 17, 1960, and *Die Burger,* March 13, 1962, cited by Legum and Legum, *South Africa.* On the other hand, Afrikaaner nationalism has often suspected sections of the local Jewry of having leanings toward Communism; see, for example, Muriel Horrell, comp., *A Survey of Race Relations in South Africa* (Johannesburg, 1965), pp. 22–24.

racially exclusive as it assumes greater militancy. On the whole, it is perhaps the mystique of the African *continent* rather than that of the Negro *race* which has tended to inspire Pan-African radicalism.[27] A refusal to recognize the Sahara as a dividing line between black and Arab Africa has therefore been characteristic more of radical African nationalists than of conservative ones.

While Israel has been caught on the side of secessionist movements in Africa, the Arabs have consistently been on the side of forces seeking to preserve the territorial integrity of African countries. The Arab role in supporting Lumumba against Tshombe's separatism, Egyptian participation on the federal side in the Nigerian civil war, and the more predictable Arab support for Khartoum against Southern secessionists, have all combined to give the Arabs the image of being African integrationists, and not forces of fragmentation.

BLACK GENTILES AND WHITE JEWS

I have attempted to demonstrate in this paper that an adequate understanding of black attitudes to the Palestine question depends in part on an understanding of black attitudes to the Semites. I have in fact concentrated on the attitudes of black radicals, both in Africa and in the diaspora. On balance, black radicals tend to be drawn toward the Arabs. What should be remembered is that they would probably have been inclined that way even if Israel had never been created. In addition, black radicals have also tended to be somewhat uneasy about Israel and its links with the Western world. It should also be remembered that the radicals would probably have been uneasy about Israel even if there had been no Arab-Israeli animosity on the world scene.

With regard to black radical attitudes to the Jews, these have been in part conditioned by the concept of *domination* in relation to the historic role of the Jews. I have tried to indicate a distinction between racial domination, economic domination, and intellectual domination. In the field of racial domination there has been an important area of shared experience between black people and the Jews. Both groups have known the agonies of humiliation. In the case of the Jews, this took its worst form as outright genocide in Nazi Germany. In the case of black people, this took its worst form as outright slavery—death by overcrowding and lynching and a life of enslaved misery and indignity have constituted the depths of black humiliation.

---

27. See Mazrui, *Violence and Thought,* pp. 245–46.

But here ends the commonly experienced domination of blacks and Jews. In terms of economic domination, there is little doubt that the Jews of the world have been among the privileged. They have been among the richest groups in different societies, and the success of Zionism has owed much to the affluence of world Jewry. The blacks have been among the poorest sections of the world. Southern Africa remains a classic example both of black racial humiliation and of Jewish economic affluence.

The third area of relations of domination is the intellectual one. Here I have indicated the disproportionate Jewish contribution to the intellectual heritage of mankind, as contrasted with the much more modest role of the blacks. This in itself does not imply Jewish domination over blacks, but it does predict areas of tension between blacks and Jews. In the United States, for instance, there is the intellectual tension arising out of Jewish control of black schools in places like New York, and Jewish preponderance in academic circles generally is contrasted to the under-representation of the blacks.

Meanwhile, even in terms of racial humiliation, the Jews are being upgraded. Israel looks now to be less like a heroic David poised against an Arab Goliath and more like an aggressive little boy who has found that he has some kind of power over a weak but proud old man. Israel appears to have become the mini-bully of the Near East. Jewish organizational and technological superiority has suddenly given Israel the power to experiment in the domination of others. The words of James Baldwin thus acquire an additional depth of meaning: "The Jew is singled out by Negroes not because he acts differently from other white men, but because he doesn't."[28]

---

28. "Negroes are Anti-Semitic because They're Anti-White," *New York Times Magazine,* April, 1967, p. 137; see also the reply to Baldwin's article written by Robert Gordis, "Negroes are Anti-Semitic because They Want a Scapegoat," in *ibid.*

Selected
Bibliography

Arabs, Arab Nationalism, and the
Fragmentation of the Arab World

Antonius, George. *The Arab Awakening: The Story of the Arab National Movement.* 1938. New York: G. P. Putnam, 1946.

Atiyah, Edward S. *An Arab Tells His Story: A Study in Loyalties.* London: J. Murray, 1946.

————. *The Arabs.* London: Penguin, 1955.

Berque, Jacques. *The Arabs: Their History and Their Future.* Trans. Jean Stewart. New York: Praeger, 1964.

Childers, Erskine B. *Common Sense About the Arab World.* New York: Macmillan, 1960.

Haim, Sylvia G., ed. *Arab Nationalism: An Anthology.* Berkeley and Los Angeles: University of California Press, 1962.

Hottinger, Arnold. *The Arabs: Their History, Culture and Place in the Modern World.* Berkeley and Los Angeles: University of California Press, 1963.

Hourani, Albert H. *Arabic Thought in the Liberal Age: 1798–1939.* London: Oxford University Press, 1962.

Ionides, Michael G. *Divide and Lose: The Arab Revolt of 1955–1958.* London: Geoffrey Bles, 1960.

Kerr, Malcolm H. *The Arab Cold War, 1958–1964: A Study of Ideology in Politics.* 1965. 2d ed. New York: Oxford University Press, 1967.

Laqueur, Walter Z. *Communism and Nationalism in the Middle East.* New York: Praeger, 1956.

Nuseibeh, Hazem Zaki. *The Ideas of Arab Nationalism.* Ithaca, N. Y.: Cornell University Press, 1956.

Sharabi, Hisham B. *Governments and Politics of the Middle East in the Twentieth Century.* Princeton: Van Nostrand, 1962.

Thompson, Jack H., and Reischauer, Robert D., eds. *Modernization of the Arab World.* Princeton: Van Nostrand, 1966.

Tibawi, Abdul Latif. *A Modern History of Syria Including Lebanon and Palestine.* New York: St. Martins, 1969.

PALESTINE PRIOR TO 1917

Burckhardt, J. L. *Travels in Syria and the Holy Land.* London: John Murray, 1822.

Dane, Edmund. *British Campaigns in the Nearer East, 1914–1918.* 2 vols. London: Hodder & Stoughton, 1917–1919.

De Haas, Jacob. *History of Palestine: The Last Two Thousand Years.* New York: Macmillan, 1934.

Graves, Philip. *Palestine: The Land of Three Faiths.* [1923]. New York: G. H. Doran, [1924].

Great Britain. Foreign Office. Historical Section. Handbooks. *Syria and Palestine* [Handbook no. 60]. London: H.M.S.O., 1920.

Hyamson, Albert M., ed. *The British Consulate in Jerusalem in Relation to the Jews of Palestine, 1838–1914.* 2 vols. London: E. Goldston for the Jewish Historical Society, 1939–41.

Oliphant, Laurence. *Haifa, or Life in Modern Palestine.* New York: Harper & Bros., 1887.

Parkes, James W. *A History of Palestine from 135 A.D. to Modern Times.* New York: Oxford University Press, 1949.

Rogers, Mary Eliza. *Domestic Life in Palestine.* 1862. Cincinnati: Poe and Hitchcock, 1867.

Tibawi, Abdul Latif. *British Interests in Palestine, 1800–1901: A Study of Religious and Educational Enterprise.* London: Oxford University Press, 1961.

Wavell, Archibald P. *The Palestine Campaigns.* London: Constable, 1928.

Zeine, Zeine N. *The Struggle for Arab Independence: Western Diplomacy and the Rise and Fall of Faisal's Kingdom in Syria.* Beirut: Khayats, 1960.

THE BALFOUR DECLARATION AND THE BRITISH MANDATE

Bentwich, Norman. *England in Palestine*. London: K. Paul, Trench, Trubner, 1932.

Boustani, Wedi' Faris. *The Palestine Mandate: Invalid and Impractical: A Contribution of Arguments and Documents Towards the Solution of the Palestine Problem Today*. Beirut: American Press, 1936.

Gardner, Brian. *Allenby of Arabia: Lawrence's General*. New York: Coward-McCann, 1966.

Geneva Research Center. *The Palestine Mandate*. Geneva: League of Nations Association of the U. S., 1930.

Howard, Harry N. *The King-Crane Commission: An American Inquiry in the Middle East*. Beirut: Khayats, 1963.

―――. *The Partition of Turkey: A Diplomatic History, 1913–1923*. 1931. New York: H. Fertig, 1966.

Jastrow, Morris, Jr. *Zionism and the Future of Palestine: The Fallacies and Dangers of Political Zionism*. New York: Macmillan, 1919.

Jeffries, J. M. N. *Palestine: The Reality*. London: Longmans, Green, 1939.

Keddourie, Elie. *England and the Middle East: The Destruction of the Ottoman Empire, 1914–1921*. London: Bowes & Bowes, 1956.

Kimche, Jon. *The Unromantics: The Great Powers and the Balfour Declaration*. London: Weidenfeld & Nicolson, 1968.

Lawrence, Thomas E. *Seven Pillars of Wisdom: A Triumph*. Garden City: Doubleday, Doran & Co., 1935.

Lloyd George, David. *The Truth about the Peace Treaties*. 2 vols. London: Victor Gollancz, 1938.

Loder, John DeVere. *The Truth about Mesopotamia, Palestine and Syria*. London: George Allen & Unwin, 1923.

Meinertzhagen, Richard. *Middle East Diary, 1917–1956*. New York: Yoseloff, 1960.

Miller, David Hunter. *My Diary at the Conference of Paris, With Documents*. 21 vols. New York: Appeal Printing Co., 1924.

Stein, Leonard J. *The Balfour Declaration*. New York: Simon & Schuster, 1961.

Storrs, Sir Ronald. *Orientations*. London: Nicholson & Watson, 1937. American edition entitled *The Memoirs of Sir Ronald Storrs*. New York: G. P. Putnam, 1937.

Stoyanovsky, J. *The Mandate for Palestine: A Contribution to the Theory and Practice of International Mandates.* London: Longmans, Green, 1928.

Temperley, Harold W. V., ed. *A History of the Peace Conference of Paris.* 6 vols. London: H. Frowde, Hodder & Stoughton, 1920–1924.

Wright, Quincy. *Mandates Under the League of Nations.* Chicago: University of Chicago Press, 1930.

ZIONISM AND ZIONIST ASPIRATIONS

Avnery, Uri. *Israel Without Zionists: A Plea for Peace in the Middle East.* New York: Macmillan, 1968.

Bar-Zohar, Michel. *The Armed Prophet: A Biography of Ben-Gurion.* Trans. Len Ortzen. London: Barker, 1967.

Basheer, Tahseen, ed. *Edwin Montagu and the Balfour Declaration.* New York: Arab League Office, 1966.

Batal, James. *Zionist Influence on the American Press.* Beirut: Nasser Press, 1956.

Ben-Gurion, David. *Israel: Years of Challenge.* New York: Holt, Rinehart & Winston, 1963.

——— *Rebirth and Destiny of Israel.* Trans. Mordekhai Nurock. New York: Philosophical Library, 1954.

Berger, Elmer. *Judaism or Jewish Nationalism: The Alternative to Zionism.* New York: Bookman Associates, 1957.

———.*The Jewish Dilemma.* New York: Devin-Adair, 1945.

———. . . . *Who Knows Better Must Say So!* New York: American Council for Judaism, 1955.

Buber, Martin. *Israel and the World: Essays in a Time of Crisis.* 2d ed. New York: Schocken Books, 1963.

Cohen, Israel. *A Short History of Zionism.* London: Frederick Muller, 1951.

———. *The Zionist Movement.* London: Frederick Muller, 1945.

Cooke, Hedley V. *Israel: A Blessing and a Curse.* London: Stevens, 1960.

Eban, Abba. *Voice of Israel.* New York: Horizon Press, 1957.

Ernst, Morris L. *So Far So Good.* New York: Harper & Bros., 1948.

Goldmann, Nahum. *The Genius of Herzl and Zionism Today.* Jerusalem: Zionist Executive, 1955.

Gruszow, Avner [Avner]. *Memoirs of an Assassin.* Trans. by Brugo Partridge. New York: Yoseloff, 1959.

Ha'Am, Ahad [Ginzberg, Asher]. *Al parashat deraklum* [At the Crossroads]. 3 vols. Jerusalem: 1894–1904.

———. *Nationalism and the Jewish Ethic: Basic Writings of Ahad Ha'Am.* Ed. Hans Kohn. New York: Schocken Books, 1962.

———. *Selected Essays of Ahad Ha'am.* Trans. Leon Simon. 1912. Cleveland: World Publishing Co., 1962.

———. *Essays, Letters and Memoirs.* Trans. Leon Simon. Oxford: East and West Library, 1946.

Halperin, Samuel. *The Political World of American Zionism.* Detroit: Wayne State University Press, 1961.

Halpern, Ben. *The Idea of the Jewish State.* Cambridge: Harvard University Press, 1961.

Hecht, Ben. *Perfidy.* New York: Julian Messner, 1962.

Hertzberg, Arthur, ed. *The Zionist Idea: A Historical Analysis and Reader.* 1959. New York: Atheneum, 1969.

Herzl, Theodor. *Complete Diaries.* Ed. Raphael Patai. Trans. Harry Zohn. 5 vols. New York: Herzl Press, 1960.

——— *Diaries.* Ed. and trans. Marvin Lowenthal. New York: Dial Press, 1956.

———. *The Jewish State: An Attempt at a Modern Solution of the Jewish Question.* Trans. Sylvie D'Avigdor and Israel Cohen. New York: Scopus Publishing Co., 1943.

Hirsch, David E. *A Record of American Zionism.* New York: Zionist Organization of America, 1956.

Jabotinsky, Vladimir [Zhabotinskii, Vladimir]. *The Jewish War Front.* London: Allen & Unwin, 1940.

Janowsky, Oscar I. *Foundations of Israel: Emergence of a Welfare State.* Princeton: Van Nostrand, 1959.

Korn, Itzhak, Lurie, Zvi, and Tsur, Jacob. *The Future of the Zionist Organization: Proposals.* Jerusalem: World Zionist Organization, 1967.

Lilienthal, Alfred M. *What Price Israel.* Chicago: Henry Regnery 1953.

Litvinoff, Barnet. *The Road to Jerusalem: Zionism's Imprint on History.* London: Weidenfeld & Nicolson, 1966. First published as *To the House of their Fathers: A History of Zionism.* New York: Praeger, 1965.

Magnes, Judah L. *In the Perplexity of the Times.* Jerusalem: Hebrew University, 1946.

Mardor, Meir. *Haganah.* Trans. H. A. G. Schmuckler. New York: New American Library, 1966. British edition entitled *Strictly Illegal.* London: R. Hale, 1964.

Menuhin, Moshe. *The Decadence of Judaism in Our Time.* New York: Exposition Press, 1965.

Petuchowski, Jakob Josef. *Zion Reconsidered.* New York: Twayne, 1966.

Rabinowicz, Oscar K. *Fifty Years of Zionism: A Historical Analysis of Dr. Weizmann's "Trial and Error."* London: Anscombe, 1950.

Rosenblatt, Bernard A. *Two Generations of Zionism: Historical Recollections of an American Zionist.* New York: Shengold, 1967.

Ruppin, Arthur. *The Jews in the Modern World.* London: Macmillan, 1934.

Sachar, Howard M. *The Course of Modern Jewish History.* 1958. New York: Dell, 1963.

Sacher, Harry. *Israel: The Establishment of a State.* London: Weidenfeld & Nicolson, 1952.

Selzer, Michael. *The Aryanization of the Jewish State.* New York: Black Star Publishing Co., 1967.

Sokolow, Nahum. *History of Zionism, 1600–1918.* 2 vols. London: Longmans, Green, 1919.

Stein, Leonard J. *Zionism.* London: Ernest Benn, 1925.

Sykes, Christopher. *Two Studies in Virtue.* New York: Knopf, 1953.

Taylor, Alan R. *Prelude to Israel: An Analysis of Zionist Diplomacy, 1897–1947.* New York: Philosophical Library, 1959.

Weizmann, Chaim. *Trial and Error: The Autobiography of Chaim Weizmann.* Philadelphia: Jewish Publication Society, 1949.

———. *Zionism and the Jewish Future.* London, 1916.

DOCUMENTS AND ANTHOLOGIES

Arab Higher Committee. *A Collection of Official Documents Relating to the Palestine Question, 1917–1947, Submitted to the General Assembly of the United Nations.* New York, 1947.

———. *The Palestine Arab Case: A Statement by the Arab Higher Committee.* Cairo: Costa Tsoumas, 1947.

Arab Office, London. *The Future of Palestine.* London, 1947.

Arab Office, Washington, D. C. *The Problem of Palestine: Evidence Submitted by the Arab Office, Jerusalem, to the Anglo-American Committee of Inquiry, March, 1946.* Washington, D. C.: The Arab Office, 1946.

Documents on International Affairs, 1928–. Ed. J. H. Wheeler-Bennett, et al. London: Oxford University Press, 1929–.

Great Britain. Colonial Office. *Report by His Majesty's Government in the United Kingdom of Great Britain and Northern Ireland to the Council of the League of Nations on the Administration of Palestine and Trans-Jordan, 1922–38* [Palestine Report]. Colonial Numbers 5, 9, 12, 20, 26, 31, 40, 47, 59, 75, 82, 94, 104, 112, 129, 146, 166. London: H.M.S.O. 1923–39.

————. *Report of the High Commissioner on the Administration of Palestine, 1920–25.* Colonial Number 15. London: H.M.S.O. 1925.

————. High Commissioner for Palestine. *An Interim Report on the Civil Administration of Palestine During the Period 1st July, 1920–30th June, 1921.* Parliamentary Papers, Cmd. 1499. London: H.M.S.O., 1921.

————. Palestine. *Correspondence with the Palestine Arab Delegation and the Zionist Organisation* [Churchill White Paper]. Parliamentary Papers, Cmd. 1700. London: H.M.S.O., 1922.

————. *Report on Immigration, Land Settlement and Development by John Hope Simpson . . .* [Hope Simpson Report]. Parliamentary Papers, Cmd. 3686–3687. London: H.M.S.O., 1930.

————. *Statement of Information Relating to Acts of Violence.* Parliamentary Papers, Cmd. 6873. London: H.M.S.O., 1946.

————. *Statement of Policy by His Majesty's Government in the United Kingdom Presented by the Secretary of State for the Colonies to Parliament by Command of His Majesty* [Passfield White Paper]. Parliamentary Papers, Cmd. 3692. London: H.M.S.O., 1930.

————. *Statement of Policy Presented by the Secretary of State for the Colonies . . .* [Accompanying Peel Commission Report]. Parliamentary Papers, Cmd. 5513. London: H.M.S.O., 1937.

————. *Statement of Policy Presented by the Secretary of State for the Colonies . . .* [Accompanying Woodhead (Partition) Commission Report]. Parliamentary Papers, Cmd. 5893. London: H.M.S.O., 1938.

————. *Statement of Policy Presented by the Secretary of State for the Colonies . . .* [MacDonald White Paper]. Parliamentary Papers, Cmd. 6019. London: H.M.S.O., 1939.

————. Palestine Partition Commission. *Report of the Palestine Partition Commission* [Woodhead Commission Report]. Parliamentary Papers, Cmd. 5854. London: H.M.S.O., 1938.

————. Palestine Royal Commission. *Minutes of Evidence Heard at Public Sessions* [Peel Commission Evidence]. Colonial Number 134. London: H.M.S.O., 1937.

————. Commission on Palestine Disturbances of August, 1929. *Report of the Commission* [Shaw Commission Report]. Parliamentary Papers, Cmd. 3530. London: H.M.S.O., 1930.

————. Foreign Office. *Correspondence between Sir Henry McMahon and the Sharif of Mecca, July, 1915–March, 1916.* Parliamentary Papers, Cmd. 5957. London: H.M.S.O., 1939.

————. *Documents on British Foreign Policy, 1919–19–.* Ed. E. L. Woodward and R. Butler, 1946–58; R. Butler and J. P. T. Bury, 1959–. London: H.M.S.O., 1946–.

————. *Report of a Committee Set up to Consider Certain Correspondences between Sir Henry McMahon and the Sharif of Mecca in 1915 and 1916.* Parliamentary Papers, Cmd. 5974. London: H.M.S.O., 1939.

————. *Statements Made on Behalf of His Majesty's Government During the Year 1918 in Regard to Certain Parts of the Ottoman Empire.* Parliamentary Papers, Cmd. 5964. London: H.M.S.O., 1939.

————. Anglo-American Committee of Enquiry. *Report of the Committee of Enquiry Regarding the Problems of European Jewry and Palestine.* Parliamentary Papers, Cmd. 6808. London: H.M.S.O., 1946.

————. Palestine. *Land Transfers Regulations.* Parliamentary Papers, Cmd. 6180. London: H.M.S.O., 1940.

————. Palestine Commission on the Jaffa Riots, 1921. *Palestine Disturbances of May, 1921: Reports of the Commissioners of Inquiry with Correspondence Relating Thereto* [Haycraft Commission Report]. Parliamentary Papers, Cmd. 1540. London: H.M.S.O., 1921.

————. Palestine Royal Commission. *Report of the Palestine Royal Commission . . .* [Peel Commission Report]. Parliamentary Papers, Cmd. 5479. London: H.M.S.O., 1937.

Hadawi, Sami, ed. *United Nations Resolutions on Palestine: 1947–1966.* Rev. ed. Beirut: Institute for Palestine Studies, 1967.

Hurewitz, Jacob C., ed. *Diplomacy in the Near and Middle East: A Documentary Record, 1535–1914.* 2 vols. Princeton: Van Nostrand, 1956.

Jewish Agency for Israel. *Book of Documents Submitted to the General Assembly of the United Nations Relating to the Establishment of the Jewish National Home.* Comp. Abraham Tulin. New York: 1947.

————. *The Jewish Case before the Anglo-American Committee of Inquiry in Palestine: Statements and Memoranda.* Jerusalem, 1946.

————. *Memorandum Submitted to the Palestine Royal Commission.* London, 1936.

Joint Foreign Committee of the Board of Deputies of British Jews and the Anglo-Jewish Association. *Correspondence with His Majesty's Government Respecting the Eventual Peace Negotiations.* London, 1917.

Joint Palestine Survey Commission. *Report of the Joint Palestine Survey Commission.* New York, 1928.

————. *Reports of the Experts Submitted to the Joint Palestine Survey Commission.* Boston: Daniels Press, 1928.

Khalil, Muhammad, ed. *The Arab States and the Arab League: A Documentary Record.* 2 vols. Beirut: Khayats, 1962.

Al-Marayati, Abid A. *Middle Eastern Constitutions and Electoral Laws.* New York: Praeger, 1968.

Palestine. *Supplementary Memorandum by the Government of Palestine Including Notes on Evidence Given to the United Nations' Special Committee on Palestine up to 12th July, 1947.* Jerusalem: Government Printer, 1947.

————. Survey Department. *A Survey of Palestine: Prepared in December, Committee of Inquiry.* 2 vols. Jerusalem: Government Printer, 1946.

Palestine Arab Refugee Office. *Official Documents, Pledges, and Resolutions on Palestine.* New York: Palestine Arab Refugee Office, 1959.

The Palestine Year Book and Israeli Annual. Vols. I–IV, 1944/1945–1948/1949. Ed. Sophie Udin. New York: Zionist Organization of America and Palestine Foundation Fund, 1945–49.

Paris Peace Conference. Inter-Allied Commission on Mandates in Turkey. "Report of the American Section of the Inter-Allied Commission on Mandates in Turkey" [King-Crane Commission Report]. *Editor and Publisher,* December 2, 1922, Section Two, pp. iv–xxvi.

The Suez Canal: A Selection of Documents Relating to the International Status of the Suez Canal and the Position of the Suez Canal Company, November 30, 1854–July 26, 1956. New York: Praeger, 1956.

The Suez Canal: Facts and Documents. Ed. Muhammad Abu Nusair, *et al.* Cairo: Selected Studies Committee, 1956.

A Survey of International Affairs, 1920/23–. Ed. Arnold J. Toynbee, *et al.* London: Oxford University Press, 1927–.

Comprehensive Works on Palestine: 1917-1948

Abcarius, Michael F. *Palestine Through the Fog of Propaganda.* London: Hutchinson, 1946.

Andrews, Fannie Fern [Phillips]. *The Holy Land Under Mandate.* 2 vols. Boston: Houghton Mifflin, 1931.

Atiyah, Edward S. *The Palestine Question.* London: Diplomatic Press, 1948.

Azcárate y Florez, Pablo de. *Mission in Palestine, 1948–1952.* Washington, D. C.: Middle East Institute, 1966.

Barbour, Nevill N. *Nisi Dominus: A Survey of the Palestine Controversy.* London: G. G. Harrap, 1946. American edition entitled *Palestine: Star or Crescent?* New York: Odyssey Press, 1947.

Beatty, Ilene. *Arab and Jew in the Land of Canaan.* Chicago: Henry Regnery, 1957.

Begin, Menahem W. *The Revolt: Story of the Irgun.* Trans. Samuel Katz. New York: Schuman, 1951.

Bernadotte af Wisborg, Folke. *To Jerusalem.* Trans. Joan Bulman. London: Hodder & Stoughton, 1951.

Bethmann, Erich W. *Decisive Years in Palestine, 1918–1948.* New York: American Friends of the Middle East, 1957.

Burrows, Millar. *Palestine Is Our Business.* Philadelphia: Westminster Press, 1949.

Cattan, Henry. *Palestine, The Arabs and Israel: The Search for Justice.* London: Longmans, 1969.

Crossman, Richard H. S. *Palestine Mission: A Personal Record.* New York: Harper & Bros., 1947.

Edwardes, O. S. *Palestine: Land of Broken Promise: A Statement of the Facts Concerning Palestine and an Examination of the Anglo-American Commission.* London: Dorothy Crisp, 1946.

Esco Foundation for Palestine, Inc. *Palestine: A Study of Jewish, Arab and British Policies.* 2 vols. New Haven: Yale University Press, 1947.

Gabbay, Rony E. *A Political Study of the Arab-Jewish Conflict: The Arab Refugee Problem; A Case Study.* Geneva: Librarie Droz, 1959.

Glubb, Sir John Bagot. *A Soldier with the Arabs.* New York: Harper, 1957.

Hurewitz, Jacob C. *The Struggle for Palestine.* New York: W. W. Norton, 1950.

Hyamson, Albert M. *Palestine Under the Mandate, 1920–1948.* London: Methuen, 1950.

Jeffries, J. M. N. *The Palestine Deception.* London: Daily Mail, 1923.

Joseph, Bernard. *The Faithful City: The Siege of Jerusalem, 1948.* New York: Simon & Schuster, 1960.

Khouri, Fred J. *The Arab-Israeli Dilemma*. Syracuse, N. Y.: Syracuse University Press, 1968.

Kimche, Jon, and Kimche, David. *A Clash of Destinies: The Arab-Jewish War and the Founding of the State of Israel*. New York: Praeger, 1960.

―――. *Both Sides of the Hill: Britain and the Palestine War*. London: Secker & Warburg, 1960.

Kirk, George. *The Middle East, 1945–1950*. Survey of International Affairs, 1939–1946. Ed. Arnold J. Toynbee. London: Oxford University Press, 1954.

Kisch, Frederick H. *Palestine Diary*. London: Victor Gollancz, 1938.

Koestler, Arthur. *Promise and Fulfillment: Palestine, 1917–1949*. New York: Macmillan, 1949.

Lorch, Netanel. *The Edge of the Sword: Israel's War of Independence, 1947–1949*. New York: G. P. Putnam, 1961.

Lowdermilk, Walter C., *Palestine: Land of Promise*. New York: Harper & Bros., 1944.

Marlowe, John. *Rebellion in Palestine*. London: Cresset Press, 1946.

―――. *The Seat of Pilate: An Account of the Palestine Mandate*. London: Cresset Press, 1959.

Nardi, Noach. *Education in Palestine, 1920–1945*. Washington, D. C.: Zionist Organization of America, 1945.

O'Ballance, Edgar. *The Arab-Israeli War, 1948*. 1956. New York: Praeger, 1957.

Polk, William R., Stamler, David H., and Asfour, Edmund. *Backdrop to Tragedy: The Struggle for Palestine*. Boston: Beacon Press, 1957.

Robinson, Jacob. *Palestine and the United Nations: Prelude to Solution*. Washington, D. C.: Public Affairs Press, 1947.

Royal Institute of International Affairs. Information Department. *Great Britain and Palestine, 1915–1945*. 1937. Rev. ed. New York: Oxford University Press, 1946.

Sakran, Frank Charles. *Palestine Dilemma: Arab Rights Versus Zionist Aspirations*. Washington, D. C.: Public Affairs Press, 1948.

Sayegh, Fayez A. *Zionist Colonialism in Palestine*. Beirut: Research Center, Palestine Liberation Organization, 1965.

Sykes, Christopher. *Crossroads to Israel*. Cleveland; World Publishing Co., 1965. British ed, *Cross Roads to Israel*. London: Collins, 1965.

Tibawi, Abdul Latif. *Arab Education in Mandatory Palestine: A Study of Three Decades of British Administration*. London: Luzac, 1956.

Trevor, Daphne. *Under the White Paper: Some Aspects of British Administration in Palestine from 1939–1947.* Jerusalem, 1948.

Wilson, R. D., *Cordon and Search, With the 6th Airborne Division in Palestine.* Aldershot, England: Gale & Polden, 1949.

Worsfold, William Basil. *Palestine of the Mandate.* London: T. F. Unwin, 1925.

SOCIAL, ECONOMIC, AND DEMOGRAPHIC FACTORS

Erskine, Beatrice. *Palestine of the Arabs.* London: George Harrap, 1935.

Fitch, Colrence Mary. *The Daughter of Abd Salam: The Story of a Peasant Woman of Palestine.* Boston: Bruce Humphries, 1934.

Granovsky, Abraham [Granorsk, A.]. *The Fiscal System of Palestine.* Jerusalem: "Palestine and Near East" Publications, 1935.

―――. [Granott, Abraham]. *The Land System in Palestine: History and Structure.* Trans. M. Simon. London: Eyre & Spottiswoode, 1952.

Granqvist, Hilma N. *Birth and Childhood Among the Arabs: Studies in a Muhammadan Village in Palestine.* Helsinki: Soderstrom, 1947.

―――. *Child Problems Among the Arabs: Studies in a Muhammadan Village in Palestine.* Helsinki: Soderstrom, 1950.

―――. *Marriage Conditions in a Palestine Village.* 2 vols. Helsinki: Akademische buchhandlung, 1931–35.

Grant, Elihu. *Palestine Today.* Baltimore: J. H. Furst, 1938.

―――. *The People of Palestine.* Philadelphia: J. B. Lippincott Co., 1921.

Hadawi, Sami. *Palestine: Loss of a Heritage.* San Antonio, Texas: The Naylor Co., 1963.

Himadah, Sa'id, ed. *Economic Organization of Palestine.* Beirut: American Press, 1938.

Learsi, Rufus [Goldberg, Israel]. *Fulfillment: The Epic Story of Zionism.* Cleveland: World Publishing Co., 1951.

Loftus, P. J. *The National Income of Palestine, 1945.* Jerusalem, 1948.

Luke, Harry Charles Joseph, ed. *The Handbook of Palestine and Transjordan.* 1922. 2d ed. London: Macmillan, 1930.

Mogannam, Matiel E. T. *The Arab Woman and the Palestine Problem.* London: Herbert Joseph, 1937.

Nathan, Robert R., Glass, Oscar, and Creamer, Daniel. *Palestine: Problem and Promise: An Economic Study.* Washington, D. C.: Public Affairs Press, 1946.

Palestine. Census Office. *Census of Palestine, 1931.* 2 vols. Alexandria, 1933.

―――. *Report and General Abstracts of the Census of 1922* (taken 23rd October, 1922). Comp. J. B. Barton. Jerusalem: Greek Convent Press, 1923.

―――. Department of Migration. *The Statistics of Migration and Naturalization* [1934–]. Jerusalem, 1935–.

―――. Office of Statistics. *Statistical Abstract for Palestine,* 1936–37– [1945–46]. Jerusalem: Government Printers Office, 1937–47.

―――. *Vital Statistics Bulletin* (quarterly). Jerusalem: Office of Statistics, 1936–47.

Robnet, George W. *Conquest Through Immigration: How Zionism Turned Palestine into a Jewish State.* Pasadena, Calif.: Institute for Special Research, 1968.

Ruppin, Arthur. *Three Decades of Palestine: Speeches and Papers on the Upbuilding of the Jewish National Home.* Jerusalem: Schocken Books, 1936.

Weulersse, Jacques. *Paysans de Syrie et du Proche-Orient.* Paris: Gallimard, 1946.

ARAB-ISRAELI CONFLICT: 1948-1967

Abu-Lughod, Ibrahim, ed. *The Arab-Israeli Confrontation of June 1967: An Arab Perspective.* Evanston, Ill.: Northwestern University Press, 1970.

Adams, Michael. *Chaos—Or Rebirth: The Arab Outlook.* London: British Broadcasting Co., 1968.

Aruri, Naseer, ed. *The Palestinian Resistance to Israeli Occupation.* Wilmette, Ill.: Medina University Press International, 1970.

―――, and Ghareeb, Edmund, eds. *Enemy of the Sun: Poems of the Palestine Resistance.* Washington, D. C.: Drum and Spear Press, 1970.

Association of Arab-American University Graduates. *Arab Areas Occupied by Israel in June, 1967.* Chicago, Ill., 1970.

―――. *Israel's Occupation of Palestine and other Arab Territories.* Chicago, Ill., 1970.

Bar-Yaacov, Nassim. *The Israel–Syrian Armistice: Problems of Implementation, 1949–1966.* Jerusalem: Magnes Press, 1967.

Bar-Zohar, Michel. *Suez Ultra-Secret*. Paris: Fayard, 1964.

Bloomfield, Louis M. *Egypt, Israel and the Gulf of Aqaba in International Law*. Toronto: Carswell, 1957.

Bromberger, Merry, and Bromberger, Serge. *Secrets of Suez*. Trans. James Cameron. London: Pan Books, 1957.

Brook, David. *Preface to Peace: The United Nations and the Arab-Israel Armistice System*. Washington, D.C.: Public Affairs Press, 1964.

Burns, E. L. M. *Between Arab and Israeli*. 1962. New York: I. Obolensky, 1963.

Childers, Erskine B. *The Road to Suez: A Study of Western-Arab Relations*. London: MacGibbon & Kee, 1962.

Clark, D. M. J. *Suez Touchdown: A Soldier's Tale*. London: Peter Davies, 1964.

Cohen, Abner. *Arab Border Villages in Israel: A Study in Continuity and Change in Social Organization*. Manchester: Manchester University Press, 1965.

Davis, John H. *The Evasive Peace: A Study of the Zionist-Arab Problem*. London: John Murray, 1968.

Dayan, Moshe. *Diary of the Sinai Campaign*. New York: Harper & Row, 1966.

Dodd, Peter, and Barakat, Halem. *River without Bridges: A Study of the Exodus of 1967 Palestinian Arab Refugees*. Beirut: Institute for Palestine Studies, 1968.

Doherty, Kathryn B. *Jordan Waters Conflict*. New York: Carnegie Endowment for International Peace, 1965.

Draper, Theodore. *Israel and World Politics: Roots of the Third Arab-Israeli War*. New York: Viking Press, 1967.

Elath, Eliahu. *Israel and Her Neighbors: Lectures Delivered at Brandeis University*. Cleveland: World Publishing Co., 1957.

Ellis, Harry B. *Israel and the Middle East*. New York: Ronald Press, 1957.

Eytan, Walter. *The First Ten Years: A Diplomatic History of Israel*. New York: Simon & Schuster, 1958.

Feinberg, Nathan. *The Legality of a "State of War" After the Cessation of Hostilities Under the Charter of the United Nations and the Covenant of the League of Nations*. Jerusalem: Magnes Press, 1961.

Francos, Ania. *Les Palestiniens*. Paris: Julliard, 1968.

Frischwasser-Ra'anan, Heinz Felix. *The Frontiers of a Nation: A Re-Examination of the Forces which Created the Palestine Mandate and Determined Its Territorial Shape*. London: Batchworth Press, 1955.

Hadawi, Sami. *Bitter Harvest: Palestine Between 1914–1967*. New York: New World Press, 1967.

Henriques, Robert. *A Hundred Hours to Suez: An Account of Israel's Campaign in the Sinai Peninsula*. New York: Viking Press, 1957.

Howard, Michael, and Hunter, Robert. *Israel and the Arab World: The Crisis of 1967*. London: Institute for Strategic Studies, 1967.

Hutchison, Elmo H. *Violent Truce: A Military Observer Looks at the Arab-Israeli Conflict, 1951–1955*. New York: Devin-Adair, 1956.

Jiryis, Sabri. *The Arabs in Israel, 1948–1966*. Trans. Meric Dobson. Beirut: Institute for Palestine Studies, 1968.

Johnson, Paul. *The Suez War*. New York: Greenberg, 1957.

Kerr, Malcolm H. *The Middle East Conflict*. New York: Foreign Policy Association, 1968.

Khadduri, Majdia D., ed. *The Arab-Israeli Impasse: Expressions of Moderate Viewpoints on the Arab-Israeli Conflict*. Washington, D. C.: R. B. Luce, 1969.

Khuri, Musa. *Tension, Terror and Blood in the Holy Land: The True Facts of the Palestine Question*. Damascus: Palestine Arab Refugees Institution, 1955.

Kimche, Jon. *Seven Fallen Pillars: The Middle East, 1915–1950*. 1950. New York: Praeger, 1953.

Laqueur, Walter Z., ed. *The Israel-Arab Reader: A Documentary History of the Middle East Conflict*. New York: Citadel, 1969.

————. *The Road to War, 1967: The Origins of the Arab-Israeli Conflict*. London: Weidenfeld & Nicolson, 1968. American edition, *The Road to Jerusalem: Origins of the Arab-Israeli Conflict, 1967*. New York: Macmillan, 1968.

Love, Kennett. *Suez: The Twice-Fought War: A History*. New York: McGraw-Hill, 1969.

Al-Messiri, Abdul Wahab. *A Lover from Palestine and Other Poems*. Illus. Kamal Boullata. Washington, D.C.: Free Palestine Press, 1970.

Mirshid, Walid Abi. *Israeli Withdrawal from Sinai*. Beirut: Institute for Palestine Studies, 1966.

Nutting, Anthony. *No End of a Lesson: The Story of Suez*. London: Constable, 1967.

O'Ballance, Edgar. *The Sinai Campaign of 1956*. 1959. New York: Praeger, 1960.

Parkes, James W. *Arabs and Jews in the Middle East: A Tragedy of Errors*. London: Victor Gollancz, 1967.

Peretz, Don. *Israel and the Palestine Arabs.* Washington, D. C.: Middle East Institute, 1958.

Perowne, Stewart. *The One Remains.* 1954. New York: E. P. Dutton, 1955.

Pfaff, Richard H. *Jerusalem: Keystone of an Arab-Israeli Settlement.* Washington, D. C.: American Enterprise Institute for Public Policy Research, 1969.

Robertson, John Henry [Connell, John]. *The Most Important Country: The True Story of the Suez Crisis and the Events Leading to It.* London: Cassell, 1957.

Robertson, Terence. *Crisis: The Inside Story of the Suez Conspiracy.* New York: Atheneum, 1965.

Rodinson, Maxime. *Israel and the Arabs.* Trans. Michael Perl. London: Penguin, 1968.

Rosenne, Shabtai. *Israel's Armistice Agreements with the Arab States: A Juridical Interpretation.* Tel Aviv: Blumstein's Bookstore for the International Law Association, Israeli Branch, 1951.

Safran, Nadav. *From War to War: The Arab-Israeli Confrontation, 1948–1967: A Study of the Conflict from the Perspective of Coercion in the Context of Inter-Arab and Big Power Relations.* New York: Pegasus, 1969.

Sartre, Jean-Paul, ed. *Le conflit Israélo-Arabe.* Special Number of *Les Temps Modernes.* Paris, 1967.

Sayegh, Fayez A. *Arab Property in Israeli-Controlled Territories: Israeli Measures for the Disposal of Arab Property.* New York: Arab Information Office, 1956.

―――. *The Arab-Israeli Conflict.* 1956. 2d ed. New York: Arab Information Office, 1964.

―――. *Discrimination in Education Against the Arabs in Israel.* Beirut: Research Center, Palestine Liberation Organization, 1966.

Seminar of Arab Jurists on Palestine (Algiers, 1967). *The Palestine Question.* Trans. Edward Rizk. Beirut: Institute for Palestine Studies, 1968.

Sharabi, Hisham B. *Palestine and Israel: The Lethal Dilemma.* New York: Pegasus, 1969.

Stevens, Georgiana G. *Jordan River Partition.* Stanford, Calif.: Hoover Institution on War, Revolution and Peace, 1965.

Stock, Ernest. *Israel on the Road to Sinai, 1949–1956: With a Sequel on the Six-Day War, 1967.* Ithaca, N. Y.: Cornell University Press, 1967.

Suez Ten Years After: Broadcasts from the B.B.C., Third Programme. By Peter Calvocoressi *et al.* Ed. Anthony Moncrieff. London: British Broadcasting Co., 1967.

Thomas, Hugh. *Suez.* New York: Harper & Row, 1967. British edition entitled *The Suez Affair.* London: Weidenfield & Nicolson, 1967.

Vester, Bertha Hedges [Spafford]. *Our Jerusalem: An American Family in the Holy City, 1881–1949.* Garden City, N. Y.: Doubleday, 1950.

Wilson, Evan M. *Jerusalem: Key to Peace.* Washington, D. C.: Middle East Institute, 1970.

Wint, Guy, and Calvocoressi, Peter. *Middle East Crisis.* Baltimore: Penguin, 1957.

Zahri, S., and Hiezra, A. *The Economic Conditions of the Arab Minority in Israel.* Givat Haviva, Israel: Centre for Arab and Afro-Asian Studies, 1966.

THE GREAT POWERS, PALESTINE,
AND THE ARAB-ISRAELI CONFLICT

American Assembly. *The United States and the Middle East.* Ed. Georgiana G. Stevens. Englewood Cliffs, N.J.: Prentice-Hall, 1964.

Association of Arab-American University Graduates. *The United States, Israel and the Arab States.* Chicago, 1970.

Badeau, John S. *The American Approach to the Arab World.* New York: Harper & Row, 1968.

Campbell, John C. *Defense of the Middle East: Problems of American Policy.* New York: Harper & Bros., 1958.

Cremeans, Charles D. *The Arabs and the World: Nasser's Arab Nationalist Policy.* New York: Praeger, 1963.

Crum, Bartley C. *Behind the Silken Curtain: A Personal Account of Anglo-American Diplomacy in Palestine and the Middle East.* New York: Simon & Schuster, 1947.

Cumming, Henry H. *Franco-British Rivalry in the Post-War Near East: The Decline of French Influence.* London: Oxford University Press, 1938.

Eden, Sir Anthony. *Full Circle: The Memoirs of Anthony Eden.* Boston: Houghton Mifflin, 1960.

Ellis, Harry B. *Challenge in the Middle East: Communist Influence and American Policy.* New York: Ronald Press, 1960.

Eudin, Xenia J., and Slusser, Robert M. *Soviet Foreign Policy, 1928–1934: Documents and Materials*. 2 vols. University Park, Pa.: Pennsylvania State University Press, 1967.

Finer, Herman. *Dulles Over Suez: The Theory and Practice of His Diplomacy*. Chicago: Quadrangle Books, 1964.

Fitzsimmons, Matthew A. *Empire by Treaty: Britain and the Middle East in the Twentieth Century*. London: Ernest Benn, 1965.

Forrestal, James. *The Forrestal Diaries*. Ed. Walter Millis with E. S. Duffield. New York: Viking, 1951.

Hanna, Paul L. *British Policy in Palestine*. Washington, D. C.: American Council on Public Affairs, 1942.

Hopwood, Derek. *The Russian Presence in Palestine and Syria, 1843–1914*. New York: Oxford University Press, 1969.

Hourani, Albert H. *Great Britain and the Arab World*. London: John Murray, 1945.

Hurewitz, Jacob C., ed. *Soviet-American Rivalry in the Middle East*. New York: Praeger, 1969.

Jansen, Godfrey H. *Nonalignment and the Afro-Asian States*. New York: Praeger, 1966.

Joseph, Bernard. *British Rule in Palestine*. Washington, D. C.: Public Affairs Press, 1948.

Kirk, George. *The Middle East in the War*. Survey of International Affairs, 1939–1946. Ed. Arnold J. Toynbee. London: Oxford University Press, 1952.

Kohn, Hans. *Nationalism and Imperialism in the Hither East*. New York; Harcourt, Brace, 1932.

Laqueur, Walter Z. *Struggle for the Middle East: The Soviet Union in the Mediterranean, 1958–1968*. New York: Macmillan, 1969.

Lenczowski, George, ed. *United States Interests in the Middle East*. Washington, D. C.: American Enterprise Institute, 1968.

———. *Oil and State in the Middle East*. Ithaca, N. Y.: Cornell University Press, 1960.

Manuel, Frank E. *The Realities of American-Palestine Relations*. Washington, D. C.: Public Affairs Press, 1949.

Monroe, Elizabeth. *Britain's Moment in the Middle East, 1914–1956*. Baltimore: Johns Hopkins Press, 1963.

Safran, Nadav. *The United States and Israel*. Cambridge: Harvard University Press, 1963.

Schectman, Joseph B. *The United States and the Jewish State Movement: The Crucial Decade, 1939–1949.* New York: Herzl Press, Yoseloff, 1966.

Sayegh, Fayez A. *The Dynamics of Neutralism in the Arab World.* San Francisco: Chandler, 1964.

Seton-Williams, M. V. *Britain and the Arab States: A Survey of Anglo-Arab Relations, 1920–1948.* London: Luzac, 1948.

Shwadran, Benjamin. *The Middle East, Oil and the Great Powers.* 1955. 2d ed. rev. New York: Council for Middle Eastern Affairs Press, 1959.

Spector, Ivar. *The Soviet Union and the Muslim World, 1917–1958.* Seattle: University of Washington Press, 1959.

Stevens, Georgiana G., ed. *The United States and the Middle East.* Englewood Cliffs, N. J.: Prentice-Hall, 1964.

Stevens, Richard P. *American Zionism and U. S. Foreign Policy, 1942–1947.* New York: Pageant Press, 1962.

Truman, Harry S. *Memoirs.* 2 vols. Garden City, N. Y.: Doubleday, 1955–56.

Index